Mouton Grammar Library

A Grammar of Dolakha Newar

Mouton Grammar Library 40

Editors
Georg Bossong
Bernard Comrie
Matthew Dryer

Mouton de Gruyter
Berlin · New York

A Grammar
of Dolakha Newar

by

Carol Genetti

Mouton de Gruyter
Berlin · New York

Mouton de Gruyter (formerly Mouton, The Hague)
is a Division of Walter de Gruyter GmbH & Co. KG, Berlin.

⊚ Printed on acid-free paper which falls within the guidelines of the
ANSI to ensure permanence and durability.

Library of Congress Cataloging-in-Publication Data

Genetti, Carol, 1961−
   A grammar of Dolakha Newar / by Carol Genetti.
      p. cm. − (Mouton grammar library ; 40)
   Includes bibliographical references and index.
   ISBN 978-3-11-019303-9 (cloth : alk. paper)
   1. Dolakha dialect − Grammar.   2. Newari language −
Dialects − Nepal − Dolakha − Grammar.   I. Title.
   PL3801.N595D656   2007
   495'.49−dc22
                                                    2007007835

Bibliographic information published by the Deutsche Nationalbibliothek

The Deutsche Nationalbibliothek lists this publication in the Deutsche Nationalbibliografie;
detailed bibliographic data are available in the Internet at http://dnb.d-nb.de.

ISBN 978-3-11-162931-5
ISSN 0933-7636

© Copyright 2024 by Walter de Gruyter GmbH & Co. KG, D-10785 Berlin.
This volume is text− and page−identical with the hardback published in 2007.
All rights reserved, including those of translation into foreign languages. No part of this book
may be reproduced or transmitted in any form or by any means, electronic or mechanical,
including photocopy, recording or any information storage and retrieval system, without permission
in writing from the publisher.
Printed in Germany.

Acknowledgements

This book represents almost twenty of years of work, undertaken in rare moments as I established an academic career, married, raised children, and chaired a department. The support, encouragement, and direct assistance of others have been invaluable in giving me the focus and ability to complete this manuscript. It is my pleasure here to acknowledge and thank these many contributors. I also gratefully acknowledge the financial support provided by the U.S. National Science Foundation (grant BNS-8811773), and by the Universitiy of California at Santa Barbara.

First and foremost, I will always be grateful to the people of Dolakha for their participation in this project as well as for their wonderful hospitality and friendship. I am especially grateful to my primary consultants, Kalpana Shrestha and Rama Shrestha, who spent countless hours patiently teaching, translating, answering questions, and gradually revealing to me the complexities of this beautiful language. Nawa Raj Shrestha of Kopindol, Nawa Raj Shrestha of San Francisco, California, and Miss Indu Pradhan were also invaluable consultants. In addition, many Dolakhae people participated in this research by telling stories, recording conversations, answering questions, teaching me vocabulary, correcting my pronunciation, and helping me in countless other ways. I gratefully acknowledge the following: Sanu Laxmi Joshi, Kali Laxmi Shrestha, Ami Maskey, Muluk Maya Shrestha, Padam Kumari Shrestha, Shyama Shrestha, Kalam Maskey, Purna Bahadur Shrestha, Krisna Murari Maskey, Laxmi Narayan Shrestha, Tirtha Narayan Joshi, Bhagawan Das Shrestha, Prathi Ma Joshi, Babita Pradhan, Shasi Kala Shrestha, Bisnu Laxmi Shrestha, Bhuban Shrestha, Tulasi Joshi, Dip Naren Shrestha, Surendra Shrestha, and Bisnu Shrestha.

In addition to the direct linguistic support, I was also aided tremendously by the encouragement, support, and pure friendship of the families of Kalpana Shrestha, Rama Shrestha, and Amar Kumar Pradhan. I would also like to thank the family of the late Nil Ratna Kansakar for their care and assistance during my first trip to Nepal, as well as Todd and Joy Lewis. The friendship and support of Min Bahadur Bista and Rajeswari Bista encouraged me to continue with this project, even when other factors in my life were sweeping me away. Thanks also to Steven and Jean Watters, for providing me with a loving family home from which to work.

I also received encouragement and support from members of the academic community in Nepal, especially Tej Ratna Kansakar, Nirmal Man Tuladhar. Sunder Krisna Joshi, Rudra Laxmi Shrestha, Daya Ratna Shakya, Kashinath

Tamot, and Kamal Prakash Malla. Thanks to the faculties of the departments of Newari and Linguistics at Tribhuvan University.

It is also my pleasure to thank a number of people who have helped me to understand Kathmandu Newar and its structures, especially Manoj Kansakar, Rajendra Shrestha, David Hargreaves, Tej Ratna Kansakar, Rajeswari Bista, and Austin Hale. Understanding Nepali was also critical, and to this end I am grateful to Min Bahadur Bista; I have profited much from his work, translations, and insights into the Nepalese language, culture, and people.

This book would never have been completed without the priceless opportunity to be in residence at the Research Centre for Linguistic Typology in Melbourne, Australia, where the majority of the manuscript was written and revised. In the entire world, there is not a better place to write a grammar than in that centre, surrounded by others with the same pursuit. Special thanks to R.M.W. Dixon and Alexandra Aikhenvald for inviting me to partake in the vibrant intellectual atmosphere of RCLT and for all their ideas, comments, advice, and encouragement. Thanks also to Randy LaPolla, Alec Coupe, and David Bradley for many profitable discussions on Tibeto-Burman languages in general and on Dolakha Newar in particular. Thanks to all the RCLT scholars for their many comments, ideas, and suggestions, and to Siew-Peng Condon, for taking care of the details.

My work has also profited greatly from the input of my colleagues in the Department of Linguistics at the University of California, Santa Barbara, who have contributed to my view of language and grammatical structure, especially Marianne Mithun and Sandra Thompson. Graduate students at UCSB have also contributed to this work. I'd especially like to thank Keith Slater and Kristine Hildebrandt, who taught me much as I taught them. Huge thanks to Ellen Bartee, Monica Turk, and Mara Henderson for their countless hours of work on formatting and preparing the copy. I'd also like to thank the excellent staff of the department, especially Mary Gervase, Mary Rae Staton, and Dana Spoonerow, for their competence, wisdom, and humor.

To my parents, who taught me to follow my dreams, to Paul, who makes living my dream possible, and to Olivia and Marcus, who will carry their own dreams forward, I can only say that love is like a language; not even a book full of words can express its true nature, or my joy in the everlasting exploration of its depths.

Contents

Acknowledgements v
List of figures xvi
List of tables xvii
Abbreviations xviii

Chapter 1
Context 1
1.   Introduction 1
2.   Linguistic relationship 2
2.1.   The Sino-Tibetan and Tibeto-Burman families 2
2.2.   The position of Newar within Tibeto-Burman 3
3.   The Newars 5
3.1.   Proposed origins 5
3.2.   Newar culture 8
4.   The Newar language and Newar dialects 10
4.1.   A rose by any other name: Newari, Newar, Nepal Bhasa, Newa
        Bhae; Dolakhali, Dolakha, and Dolakhae 10
4.2.   Newar as a national language of Nepal 11
4.3.   The distribution of Newars throughout Nepal 12
4.4.   Newar dialects 13
4.5.   Classical Newar 15
5.   The village of Dolakha and the Dolakhae language 17
5.1.   Location, size, population 17
5.2.   Synopsis of Dolakha history 19
5.3.   Language contact: A link between social history and language ... 21
5.4.   Previous work on Dolakha Newar 22
5.5.   Typological characterization 23
5.6.   The primary differences between the Dolakhae and Kathmandu
        dialects 24
6.   Linguistic theory and description 25
6.1.   The functionalist framework and language description 25
6.2.   The "problem" of variation 28
7.   Data for the study 29
7.1.   Primary linguistic consultants 29
7.2.   Discourse data 30

Chapter 2
Segmental phonetics and phonology 32
1. Introduction 32
2. Consonants 32
2.1. Stops and affricates 33
2.2. Fricatives 39
2.3. Nasals 40
2.4. Approximants 41
2.5. Phonological processes affecting consonants 42
3. Vowels 44
3.1. High vowels 47
3.2. Mid vowels 47
3.3. Low vowels 51
3.4. Vowels in sequence 53
3.5. Vowel harmony 58
4. Phonotactics 61
4.1. Syllable structure 61
4.2. Word structure 63
5. Stress 64

Chapter 3
Prosody 69
1. Introduction 69
2. Intonation units 69
3. Phrasal accent 70
4. Terminal pitch contours 75
4.1. Falling terminal contours 75
4.2. Level terminal contours 79
4.3. Rising terminal contours 80
4.4. Rise-fall terminal contour 85
5. Transitional continuity 87
6. Summary 89

Chapter 4
Nouns and noun morphology 90
1. Introduction 90
2. Phonotactic properties of nouns 90
3. Incorporating new nouns into the language 91
3.1. Compounding 92
3.2. Derivational suffixation 93
3.3. Lexicalization of headless relative clauses 94
3.4. Borrowing 95
4. Morphological categories relevant to nouns 96
4.1. Number 97

4.2.	Case	100
4.3.	Individuation and extension	127

Chapter 5
Personal pronouns, interrogatives, indefinites, and demonstratives 129

1.	Introduction	129
2.	Personal pronouns	129
2.1.	Forms of the personal pronouns	132
3.	Interrogatives	133
4.	Indefinites	138
5.	Demonstratives	141
5.1.	The unmarked demonstratives ām, and u	142
5.2.	Demonstratives of immediate location	145
5.3.	Demonstratives of manner	146
5.4.	Demonstratives of type and characteristic	148
5.5.	Demonstratives of quantity	149
5.6.	Demonstratives of size	151
5.7.	Demonstratives of location	151

Chapter 6
Verbs and verb morphology 154

1.	Introduction	154
2.	Phonotactic structure of verbs	155
3.	Borrowed verbs	156
4.	Inflectional morphology of the Dolakhae verb	157
4.1.	Verb paradigms	157
4.2.	The forms of verbal stems	167
4.3.	Morphological structure of the affirmative finite paradigms	168
4.4.	Negation	175
5.	Imperative, prohibitive, and optative paradigms	178
5.1.	The imperative	179
5.2.	The prohibitive	182
5.3.	The optative	185
6.	Non-finite verb forms	186
6.1.	Primary non-finite verb forms	186
6.2.	Other non-finite suffixes	189
7.	The causative derivational suffix	190
8.	Irregular verbs	190
8.1.	The copula khyaŋ	190
8.2.	The existential verb dar-	191

8.3.	Other irregular verbs	193
9.	Summary	193

Chapter 7
Adjectivals 195

1.	Introduction	195
2.	Adjectival verbs	195
2.1.	Attributive uses of adjectival verbs	197
2.2.	Referential uses of adjectival verbs	198
2.3.	Predicative uses of adjectival verbs	199
2.4.	Other inflectional morphology and adjectival verbs	202
2.5.	Irregular adjectival verbs	204
2.6.	Borrowed adjectival verbs	206
2.7.	Summary	206
3.	Simple adjectives	207
3.1.	Native simple adjectives	207
3.2.	Borrowed simple adjectives	208
3.3.	Simple adjectives in attributive and referential functions	209
3.4.	Simple adjectives in predicative function	210
4.	On the status of the category "adjective"	212

Chapter 8
Quantifiers 214

1.	Introduction	214
2.	Lexical quantifiers	214
3.	Numerals and classifiers	217
3.1.	The decimal-based system of numerals	217
3.2.	The vigesimal-based system of numerals	219
3.3.	Numeral classifiers	220

Chapter 9
Adverbials 228

1.	Introduction	228
2.	Temporal adverbs	228
3.	Locational adverbs	230
4.	Manner adverbs	232
5.	Intensifiers	235

Chapter 10
Particles and clitics of individuation and extension 237

1.	Introduction	237
2.	Clitics of individuation and extension	237
2.1.	The individuating clitic =(u)ri	239
2.2.	The extensive clitic =(u)ŋ	242

3.	Three particles with discourse function	245
3.1.	The particle of restriction *jukun*	246
3.2.	The topic particle *wā*	246
3.3.	The focus particle *tuŋ*	248
4.	Other particles	252
4.1.	Clause-initial particles	252
4.2.	Sentence-final particles	254

Chapter 11
Noun-phrase structure 261

1.	Introduction	261
2.	Elements of the noun phrase and their order	261
3.	Coordination	268
4.	Apposition	270
5.	Lists	272
6.	Noun-phrase embedding	272
7.	Summary of noun-phrase structures	274

Chapter 12
Clause types 275

1.	Introduction	275
2.	Copular clauses	275
2.1.	The copula *khyaŋ*	276
2.2.	The copula *jur-*	279
3.	Verbless clauses	283
4.	Intransitive clauses	284
4.1.	Existence, location, and possession	286
4.2.	Intransitive clauses with motion verbs	292
5.	Dative-experiencer clauses	294
5.1.	Nepali pattern 1: Emotional and cognitive states	295
5.2.	Nepali pattern 2: Emotional and cognitive states with stimulus noun	296
5.3.	Nepali pattern 3: Forgetting and remembering	297
5.4.	Dolakhae pattern 1: Experience of uncontrollable events	297
5.5.	Dolakhae pattern 2: 'like to', 'want to' using *yer-* 'come'	298
5.6.	Dolakhae pattern 3: *mal(dan)-* 'need'	298
5.7.	Other Dolakhae predicates with dative experiencers	299
6.	Transitive clauses	300
7.	Ditransitive clauses	304
7.1.	Ditransitive clauses with transfer verbs	304
7.2.	Ditransitive clauses with speaking verbs	305

Chapter 13
Grammatical relations 307
1. Introduction 307
2. Subject: A, S, and CS 308
2.1. Verb agreement 308
2.2. Complementation structures 311
2.3. Relative clauses 312
2.4. Reflexives 313
3. Objects: O and R 315
3.1. Object casemarking 316
3.2. Relative clauses 317
3.3. The emphatic possessive *āme tuŋ* 317
4. Dative-experiencer constructions 318
4.1. Subject behavior and dative experiencers 318

Chapter 14
Constituent order 320
1. Introduction 320
2. Transitive verbs: AOV and OAV orders 322
3. Ditransitive verbs: AROV and other permutations 326
4. Post-verbal arguments 327

Chapter 15
Clause-level syntactic constructions 330
1. Introduction 330
2. Causative constructions 330
3. The verb *bir-* 'give' and the marking of affected participants 333
4. Non-declarative constructions 336
4.1. Imperative and prohibitive constructions 337
4.2. Optative construction 339
4.3. The hortative construction 341
4.4. Interrogative constructions 341
5. Reflexives and reciprocals 344
6. Negation 347
7. Comparative and superlative constructions 350

Chapter 16
Tense and aspect 354
1. Introduction 354
2. Tense 354
2.1. The future tense 355
2.2. The present tense 357
2.3. Past tense 361
2.4. Past-anterior tense 363

2.5.	A system of four tenses	366
2.6.	The interplay of tenses in a narrative text	368
3.	Aspect	373
3.1.	The auxiliary *con-* 'stay': continuous aspect	373
3.2.	The auxiliary *tar-:* extended state and perfect aspect	381
3.3.	The auxiliary *d(h)on(-ker)-* 'finish': completive aspect and sequential ordering	383
3.4.	The auxiliary *ṭen-* and the suffix *-raiː* 'be about to'	385
3.5.	The auxiliaries *suru yet-* and *twārtar-*; inception and cessation	386

Chapter 17
Nominalization and related structures 387

1.	Introduction	387
2.	The syntax of nominalization	388
2.1.	Modification of nouns within a noun phrase	388
2.2.	Verbal complements	395
2.3.	Non-embedded nominalizations	400
3.	The distribution of the nominalizers	403

Chapter 18
Complementation 408

1.	Introduction	408
2.	Complementation structures	408
2.1.	Simple nominalized complements	409
2.2.	Direct quote followed by *haŋ-a khā*	415
2.3.	Quotative complements	417
2.4.	Infinitive complements	418
3.	Complementation strategies	421
3.1.	Infinitive verb plus grammatical auxiliary	421
3.2.	Embedded quotation with *haŋ-an*	422
4.	Complement-taking predicates and their complements	424

Chapter 19
The participial construction 428

1.	Introduction	428
2.	Morphology of the participial construction	428
3.	Defining characteristics of the construction	429
3.1.	Point (i)	430
3.2.	Point (ii)	431
3.3.	Point (iii)	432
3.4.	Point (iv)	432
4.	Structures and functions of the participial construction	432
4.1.	Incorporating a grammaticalized auxiliary into a clause	433
4.2.	Lexicalized expressions	435

4.3.	With direct-quote complements	436
4.4.	Recapitulations	438
4.5.	Joining clauses which denote actions, events, and states	439
5.	Issues in syntactic analysis	446
5.1.	Anaphora and control	446
5.2.	Scope of illocutionary force and negation	447
5.3.	Case prolepsis	450
5.4.	A syntactic analysis of the participial construction	452
6.	The participle followed by -*li* and -*i*	455

Chapter 20
Adverbial Clauses 460

1.	Introduction	460
2.	Types of adverbial clauses	461
2.1.	Conditional adverbial clauses	463
2.2.	Concessive adverbial clauses	465
2.3.	Temporal adverbial clauses	467
2.4.	Purposive adverbial clauses	473
2.5.	Causal adverbial clauses	475
2.6.	Simulative adverbial clauses	476
3.	Syntax of adverbial clauses	477
3.1.	Dependency and subordination	477
3.2.	Adverbial and participial clauses and the notion of converb	483

Chapter 21
The sentence: Prosodic and syntactic structuring 485

1.	Introduction	485
2.	Defining the syntactic sentence	486
2.1.	The correlative construction: Two finite clauses in one syntactic sentence	487
3.	Quoted speech	489
3.1.	Quoted speech and syntactic complexity	493
4.	Other types of syntactic complexity	498
5.	Defining the prosodic sentence	503
6.	Syntax-prosody interactions	506
6.1.	Parallels in syntactic and prosodic structure	506
6.2.	Syntax/prosody mismatches	509
6.3.	Narrative sentences	511
7.	Closing words	515

Appendix A List of verbal affixes 516
Appendix B Phonological and grammatical words 519
Appendix C Dolakha Newar word list 522
Appendix D Text: A boy makes his fortune 539

Notes 557
References 566
Index 578

List of figures

Figure 1. Pitch and intensity over the noun *muru* 'needle' 65
Figure 2. Pitch and intensity over negated verb *mwā-mwāl* 'did not search' 65
Figure 3. Pitch and intensity over *gulpanuŋ* 'never' 66
Figure 4. Pitch and intensity over *cula* 'finger' pronounced in isolation 67
Figure 5. Pitch and intensity over the word *cula* 'finger' uttered in a frame................67
Figure 6. Pitch trace for *jim nām ^he māji=e mica* 'My name is the boatman's daughter'..72
Figure 7. Pitch trace for *^chi=ya ^hātta kho-e* 'Why do you cry?' 72
Figure 8. Pitch trace for *ināgu khā=ri chin ˈgunta=ŋ da-hat* 'You don't say this to anybody' 74
Figure 9. Pitch trace for *^āmun nibār chor-ju* 'He wrote "sun"'....................74
Figure 10. Pitch trace for *^utsuk lāg-ai jur-a rā* \\ 'He became impatient'.....................77
Figure 11. Pitch trace for *^chana nimtiŋ jā ^chu-e ma-kheu* \ 'This rice was not cooked for your benefit'..77
Figure 12. Pitch trace for *ji ^bālaka* 'I am a child' 80
Figure 13. Pitch trace for *janta ^pyāṭāwāt-a/* 'I am hungry' 82
Figure 14. Pitch trace for *^chẽ=ku na-i mo-khoŋ-a-lāgin/* 'Because I am not able to eat'..82
Figure 15. Pitch trace for *thi-gur ^mula then-nasin //* 'When (he) arrived on a road' 83
Figure 16. Pitch trace of *āme ^santān ma-da-u-ju* 'Then he had no heirs'......................85
Figure 17. Pitch trace of *je=^-ku on-a* 'He went to work' 87
Figure 18. Two systems of grammatical organization................................308
Figure 19. Categories of indirect and direct objects 315
Figure 20. Categories of primary and secondary objects.........................315
Figure 21. The category of object in Dolakha Newar...................................316
Figure 22. Past-anterior tense for prior situations...............................366
Figure 23. Past tense for past events and present states..........................367
Figure 24. Present tense for present events.....................................368
Figure 25. Bistructural analysis 438
Figure 26. Structural representation of two clauses in sequence, the first of which contains an embedded clause..................................499
Figure 27. The participial construction within an embedded clause.......................500
Figure 28. A participial clause within an embedded clause which is itself embedded 500
Figure 29. An embedded clause within an embedded clause within the first clause of a participial chain..501
Figure 30. A three-clause participial chain embedded into a finite clause preceded by two adverbial clauses 502

List of tables

Table 1.	Newar speakers by zone	13
Table 2.	Consonant phonemes	33
Table 3.	Vowel phonemes	44
Table 4.	Summary of phonological processes affecting vowels in sequence	58
Table 5.	Terminal contour type and syntactic finality/continuity	88
Table 6.	Clitic casemarkers	101
Table 7.	Dolakha Newar postpositions	105
Table 8.	First-person pronouns	130
Table 9.	Second-person pronouns	130
Table 10.	Third-person pronouns	131
Table 11.	Interrogative words	133
Table 12.	Inflection of *yau* 'some; any'	140
Table 13.	Demonstratives	142
Table 14.	Verb roots in four conjugation classes	156
Table 15.	Finite inflection: N-stem verbs	159
Table 16.	Imperative, prohibitive, and optative inflections: N-stem verbs	160
Table 17.	Non-finite inflection: N-stem verbs	160
Table 18.	Finite inflection: T-stem verbs	161
Table 19.	Imperative, prohibitive, and optative inflection: T-stem verbs	162
Table 20.	Non-finite inflections: T-stem verbs	162
Table 21.	Finite inflection: R-stem verbs	163
Table 22.	Imperative, prohibitive, and optative inflections: R-stem verbs	164
Table 23.	Non-finite inflections: R-stem verbs	164
Table 24.	Finite inflections: L-stem verbs	165
Table 25.	Imperative, prohibitve, and optative inflections: L-stem verbs	166
Table 26.	Non-finite inflections: L-stem verbs	166
Table 27.	Tense morphemes and stem alternations across inflectional verb classes	169
Table 28.	Person/number suffixes (affirmative finite paradigm)	170
Table 29.	Imperative verb forms	179
Table 30.	Non-finite verb forms	187
Table 31.	The Dolakha Newar numerals from 1 to 40	217
Table 32.	Numerals and their corresponding multiples of 10 and 100	218
Table 33.	Multiples of 10 in vigesimal system	219
Table 34.	Lexical elements of the noun phrase	261
Table 35.	Grammatical elements of the noun phrase	262
Table 36.	Some noun-verb compounds with *yet-* 'do'	303
Table 37.	Distribution of NR1 and NR2 nominalizers	405
Table 38.	Complement-taking predicates, complement types and complement strategies	426
Table 39.	Intonation boundaries across modifying and sequential participial clauses	444
Table 40.	Adverbial suffixes	461
Table 41.	Prosodic transcription conventions	492

Abbreviations

1, 2, 3	person markers	INC	inclusive
ABL	ablative	IND	individuation particle
AGR	agreement particle	INF	infinitive
ALL	allative	INST	instrumental
ASS	assertion particle	INTR	intransitive
ASSOC	associative	IRR	irrealis
BV	borrowed verb	LOC	locative
CAUS	causative	MARK	mark of comparison
CL	classifier	NEG	negative
COMP	complementizer	NR1	nominalizer/relativizer 1
COND	conditional	NR2	nominalizer/relativizer 2
COP	copula	NR3	nominalizer/relativizer 3
DAT	dative	ONOM	onomatopoeia
DEM	demonstrative	OPT	optative
DIM	diminutive	p	plural
ERG	ergative	PART	participle
EMPH	emphatic particle	PA	past anterior
EVID	evidential (hearsay) particle	PL	plural
EXC	exclusive	PR	present
EXCL	exclamation	PRT	particle
EXIST	existential	PROH	prohibitive
EXPR	expressive vocabulary	PST	past
EXT	extension particle	PURP	purpose
FOC	focus particle	Q	question particle
FS	false start	REDUP	reduplication
FUT	future	REFL	reflexive
GEN	genitive	s	singular
h	honorific (verb form)	SPEC	specific identity particle
HON	honorific	TEMP	temporal
HORT	hortative	TOP	topic particle
IMP	imperative	TR	transitive

Chapter 1
Context

1. Introduction

Newar is a Tibeto-Burman language spoken by approximately 825,000 people (Yadava 2003: 141). Most speakers are located in the Kathmandu Valley of Nepal, although there are other Newar communities scattered throughout the country. The village of Dolakha is one such community. It is clear from historical records that Dolakha was well-established as a Newar settlement by the 14th century and it is likely that it originated centuries earlier. The variety of Newar which is spoken in Dolakha is referred to by the speakers as *Dolakhae*, a term which I will use interchangeably with the longer *Dolakha Newar*. Dolakhae is mutually unintelligible with the dialects of the Kathmandu Valley.

This book is a comprehensive description of the phonology and grammar of the Dolakha Newar language. It is a detailed study of the essential elements of the language, how they interact, and how they are used by speakers of the language in the process of communication. It covers in detail the phonetics, phonology, morphology, and syntax of the language. Semantics, pragmatics, and discourse are referred to in conjunction with these other areas.

The primary purpose of this initial chapter is to provide context, both broad and narrow. This chapter will begin by acquainting the reader with the linguistic, historical, and social background of the Newars in general and with the Dolakha Newars in particular. It will be seen that in many ways the current state of our knowledge in these areas is incomplete, and on more than one occasion it will be necessary to resort to speculation on matters of history and linguistic affiliation.

For those who have little familiarity with Newar linguistics, a linguistic overview is provided in §1.5.5.5, which highlights the primary typological characteristics of Dolakhae grammar. This discussion includes a summary of the major grammatical distinctions between the Dolakhae and Kathmandu dialects.

The chapter concludes with a discussion of the theoretical and methodological context in which this grammar is written.

2. Linguistic relationship

2.1. The Sino-Tibetan and Tibeto-Burman families

The Newar language is a member of the Sino-Tibetan (ST) family of languages. Sino-Tibetan is one of the largest linguistic families on the globe, comprising at least 400 languages and covering a massive geographic area, ranging from China in the east, through Laos, Vietnam, Thailand, Burma, Bhutan, Nepal, Bangladesh, India, and Pakistan. The genetic groupings among these languages are many and complex, prompting comparisons between this family and Indo-European, in terms of both complexity and time depth (Matisoff 1994: 36). The ST family is traditionally divided into two major branches: Sinitic, representing the various Chinese languages, and Tibeto-Burman (TB), comprising the rest of the family (but cf. van Driem 1997 for an altogether different view of the basic family structure).

There is general agreement that Tibeto-Burman languages comprise the bulk of the Sino-Tibetan family and also have the widest geographic distribution. However for practical reasons, it is difficult to identify the precise number of languages in the family. To begin with, there are still some geographic areas which remain relatively inaccessible to scholars, and which may contain as yet undocumented languages. Western Nepal, northern Burma, northeastern India, and south-eastern Tibet can be noted as particularly unexplored areas (De-Lancey 1987: 799). Additionally, many of the Tibeto-Burman languages are known by more than one name, and sometimes one name applies to more than one language.[1] Finally, the age-old problem of classifying linguistic systems as "languages" and "dialects" hinders our ability to arrive at an accurate count of languages in the family. Many languages are very closely related and exact degrees of divergence are impossible to determine. Even in cases of mutual unintelligibility, it is not always possible to make a dividing line and use the term "language" as opposed to "dialect". The Dolakhae dialect is a case in point. While the Dolakhae and Kathmandu dialects are not mutually intelligible, Dolakhae speakers are ethnographically Newars in every sense and consider their language to be Newar. While acknowledging these problems with counting languages, a number of scholars have produced general estimates of the number of languages in TB. One "very approximate" estimate is 351 (Matisoff 1994: 36). This estimate still may be low, however, when one considers the density of languages in some relatively small geographic areas. For example Hansson (1991) lists 88 distinct languages in the Rai (Kiranti or Bahing-Vayu) language family, which is located solely in eastern Nepal.

The Tibeto-Burman family, as well as being a large family, also shows surprising diversity in terms of typological characteristics. Interestingly, the primary typological divisions tend to be regional. The Tibeto-Burman languages to the east of the Himalayas and the Tibetan Plateau generally share typological characteristics with other languages of South-east Asia. This large linguistic area has been referred to as the "Sinosphere" (Matisoff 1990: 113). Phonologically, ST languages in the Sinoshpere tend to have simplified syllable structures as well as tone systems. Morphologically, they tend toward the isolating type. They exhibit predominantly monosyllabic words, a greater use of grammatical particles than inflectional affixes, and compounding as opposed to derivational morphology. Syntactically, the languages of the Sinosphere are more likely to have verb serialization and simple juxtaposition as opposed to developing complex systems of clause linkage.

Many languages in the western side of the Sino-Tibetan family, by contrast, show significant typological resemblances with the other languages of the South Asian subcontinent. They thus are in the "Indosphere" (Matisoff 1990: 113). In these languages, words tend to be polysyllabic, often with heavier syllables than those found in the east, and tone systems, while attested, are not as frequent. Those tone systems which do occur also tend to make fewer tonal contrasts than is commonly found in the Sinosphere (Maddieson 2005: 58–61). In these languages there is often considerable inflectional morphology, from fully developed casemarking systems to extensive pronominal morphology found on the verb. These languages generally mark a number of types of inter-clausal relationships and have distinct constructions involving verbal auxiliaries.[2] The Newar dialects are clearly representative of the latter type.

2.2. The position of Newar within Tibeto-Burman

While many of the TB languages show relatively clear genetic affiliation with particular subgroups, Newar is one of a number of languages whose precise positioning within TB remains a mystery. This is undoubtedly due in part to centuries of contact with Indo-Aryan languages, which has resulted in numerous morphological and phonological changes, as well as the loss of a large amount of vocabulary in favor of Indo-Aryan loans.

Despite these language-contact effects, it is clear that Newar is indeed a TB language. Shafer (1952) argues for this point by comparing numerous cognate sets with reconstructed Old Bodish, Burmese, and reconstructed Kukish. Since that time, many other cognate sets with various TB languages have been noted. For example, Glover (1970) states that Newar shares 28% of its core vocabulary with Chepang. In addition to cognate sets and basic sound correspondences, traces of old morphological distinctions also give evidence of Proto-Tibeto-Burman (PTB) provenience. One particularly clear example is the lexical distinction between causative and non-causative verbs, which is realized in Newar by a distinction between plain versus aspirated initial stops, e.g. Dolakhae *gyāt-*

'fear', *khyāt-* 'scare'. This distinction is a reflex of the PTB causative prefix *s-; the realization of this as a distinction in aspiration is found in numerous languages of the family (Benedict 1972: 97).

While it is currently considered to be beyond debate that Newar is a TB language, the genetic positioning of this language within the family remains an open question. Shafer (1952: 93) makes the following conclusion:

> From the limited number of comparisons brought together here one may tentatively say that Newarish (Newari and Pahari) is probably neither Baric nor Karenic, but somewhat intermediate between Bodic and Burmic; that is, its ties are with the languages to the north (Tibet) and the east (Burma and the Indo-Burmese frontier), rather than with the Tibeto-Burmic languages of Assam.

This passage implies that Newar defies positioning within a standard tree diagram, but functions as an intermediate language between two large genetic divisions, sharing characteristics of both.

Glover (1970) groups Newar with Chepang in West Central Himalayish. His study is lexicostatistical in nature, based on the percentages of shared basic vocabulary over time. According to his data, Newar and Chepang share 28% of their core vocabulary. Bradley (1997) also suggests there is a link between Newar and Chepang, as he places them both in his "Central Himalayan" subgroup of TB, along with Magar and Kham. However, he provides no concrete evidence in support of this grouping. A similar view is shared by Kansakar, based on a typological study of Tamang and Newar. He states that language systems of the Tamangs and Newars can be traced back "to common origin, a proto nucleus that is shared by the Gurung-Thakali-Tamang-Magar-Manangbe group of western Himalayan languages under the Bodish section" (1999a: 34).

Voegelin and Voegelin (1977) group Newar in the Gyarong-Mishmi family, which basically incorporates the non-pronominalized Bodic languages, excluding Tibetan. Interestingly, this hypothesis expressly excludes the possibility of a relationship between Newar and the pronominalized Kiranti languages spoken in eastern Nepal.

Benedict (1972: 5) suggests that Newar is perhaps part of the Kiranti family, which he labeled "Bahing-Vayu". However, he later states "Newari, the old state language of Nepal, shows many points of divergence and cannot be directly grouped with Bahing and Vayu" (1972: 5). Thus he sees it at best as lying somewhat outside the primary Kiranti nucleus.

The possibility of a link between Newar and Kiranti has also been explored briefly in Genetti (1994: 130–137) and more substantially in several works of George van Driem (1992, 1993, 2001: 759–766). Van Driem argues that conjugational endings in the conservative Dolakha Newar verb are cognate with affixes in the Kiranti languages. He writes, "Both in overall structure as well as in several particulars the Dolakha conjugation is demonstrably cognate with the verbal agreement systems of Kiranti languages" (2001: 764). Based on this and other evidence, including comparative work on some Thangmi and Newar vocabulary carried out by Turin (1999), van Driem suggests that Newar, Thangmi, and Baram together form a subgroup within a higher-level family he calls "Mahakiranti". He labels the subgroup "Para-Kiranti", indicating, like Benedict, that this branch lies outside the primary Kiranti nucleus. It should be noted that majority of evidence suggestive of a genetic affiliation between Newar and Kiranti is the conjugational data and van Driem (2004) pulls back from the Mahakiranti hypothesis, noting that further evidence from languages in other branches of Tibeto-Burman significantly weaken the argument for shared morphological innovation between Newar and Kiranti. However, he continues to maintain the likelihood of a genetic relationship between Newar, Baram, and Thangmi, which he now refers to as "Newaric" or "Mahanevari".

Van Driem's change in opinion is illustrative of the drawbacks of making statements of genetic relationship based solely on limited conjugational similarities. While such similarities may be suggestive of a relationship, they cannot be used to confirm it; corroborating work on lexical and phonological correspondences is needed before any hypothesis can be substantiated. Essentially, the state of our knowledge is at this point insufficient to be certain about a genetic relationship in any direction; historical work which confidently reconstructs low levels of genetic relationship needs to be completed before the higher level groupings can be finalized. In the meantime, the development of hypotheses is a crucial step in the process, suggesting avenues for future work. In my view, there is sufficient evidence to encourage further work into a possible genetic affiliation with Thangmi and Baram. There also appears to be sufficient evidence to warrant further comparison with the Central Himalayan languages. Until such careful comparative work is undertaken, we can only form hypotheses.

3. The Newars

3.1. Proposed origins

Although the Newar have developed over the centuries into a single homogeneous ethnic group, historians agree that the modern Newars are the result of centuries of intermarriage between the original inhabitants of the Kathmandu Valley and numerous other groups who became assimilated into Newar culture. This view is expressed in the following comment by Nepali:

> The term Newar is applied to designate a number of former ethnic groups who have, through centuries of interbreeding, been welded into a homogeneous

community with common traditions of language and other social heritage. It is, therefore, a gross over-simplification to regard them as belonging to one single racial origin. (1965: 18)

At issue, then, is not only the identity of the early indigenous people of the Kathmandu Valley, but also that of the various groups who became assimilated into the single ethnic group now referred to by the name "Newar". There are several theories in the literature regarding these issues.

Beginning with the identity of the early TB predecessors, the most widely cited view is that these were the Kirata, who are referred to as early as the Rig-vedic literature (Nepali 1965: 30) and are generally associated with Nepal and more particularly the Himalayas (Slusser 1982: 9). According to Nepali (1965: 11), the Kirata displaced the very early inhabitants of the Kathmandu Valley, (the so-called "pastoral dynasties" of cow and buffalo herders) and ruled there for an entire millennium prior to their defeat by the Licchavis in approximately the 3rd century A.D. The most intriguing aspect of this proposal is that this group is assumed to be related to the modern Kiranti of eastern Nepal (Benedict's Bahing-Vayu group). Suggestive evidence is provided by Slusser:

> The early chronicles identify the Kiranti with the Kirata when they affirm that the Valley Kirata, vanquished by the Licchavis, settled in the region between the Tamur and Arun rivers, a region embraced by the Kirant Pradesh [the current location of some of the modern Kiranti groups–cg]. Traditional ties of these eastern hill people with the Kathmandu Valley are apparent from customs that ordain the annual return to the Valley of some Kirantis for the observance of religious ceremonies. (1982: 10)

Nepali (1965: 30) suggests that further evidence for this historical relationship is the traditional claim of some Rai groups that their ancestors came from a place with a lake which dried up, a description that fits the Kathmandu Valley both in legend and in geological fact.

Van Driem (2001: 737–741) outlines a debate about whether the Tibeto-Burman ancestors of the modern Newars were the aboriginal inhabitants of the Kathmandu Valley, or whether they are descended from a group who migrated into the valley around the end of the Licchavi period (approximately the 9th century A.D.). He concludes that both are viable hypotheses, and that both are consistent with an ultimately Kiranti genetic and linguistic link.

Doherty (1978) provides a different view. Struck by the lexico-statistical evidence of Glover (1970), and assessing the linguistic evidence available at the time, he suggests that "a major ancestral portion of the Newari people seems to derive from the south-eastern Tibetan sphere, at an early but uncertain date, and their entry into the valley was from the north and not from the south as an Indo-Mongolian group of less clearly northern origin". LaPolla takes a similar view, stating that "Tibetan-Burman migration into Nepal, Sikkim, and Bhutan was originally almost entirely from directly north, that is, Tibet (Poffenberger 1980), and so the earlier languages generally show a close relation to Tibetan" (2001: 239). He goes on to say "the Kiranti languages and what Bradley (1997) calls the Central Himalayan languages (Magar, Kham, Chepang, Newari) came into Nepal relatively early" (LaPolla 2001: 239). The latter quote seems to allow the possibility that the Kirantis and the Newars have a direct shared ancestor.

Another suggestion which has been made in the literature (e.g. Grierson 1927; Nepali 1965) is that Munda or Austronesian peoples may have contributed very early on to both the Newar and the Kiranti groups. This suggestion of a Munda substratum is originally attributed to Konow by Grierson (1927: 55), who bases it on several traits in these languages that are also found in the Munda family, but reportedly not in other TB languages. These traits include categories of dual number, inclusive and exclusive distinctions for the first person, and pronominal suffixation on the verb. This hypothesis has never been substantiated, and it may be noted that all of these features may be found in TB languages outside of the eastern Himalayan region which is said to be the locus of the substratum. The strongest evidence in favor of this hypothesis is the presence of highly complex systems of verb agreement found in Kiranti; however, DeLancey (1989) argues that elements of these agreement systems are reconstructible for Proto-Tibeto-Burman (although this position remains controversial, cf. LaPolla 1992). Nevertheless, without more substantive evidence than a small number of shared typological features (which are in fact shared by a wide number of languages and language families), the hypothesis of a Munda substratum appears untenable.

Turning to the identities of other ethnic groups who, through intermarriage and acculturation, have contributed to the current Newar identity, most are considered to be immigrants from India. Nepali (1965) discusses the Abhiras, supposedly of Gujarat, who settled in the Tarai and ruled there prior to the Licchavi dynasty.[3] He writes of the Abhiras and the Kiratas that "the assimilation of these two peoples...possibly provided the foundation of Newar culture in the Valley" (1965: 12). This suggests that non-TB people may have contributed to the Newar ethnic identity from a very early time.

The next major wave of immigration appears to have been the Licchavis, a tribe from Northern India, and part of the Vrjjis federation. The Licchavi dynasty in Nepal is dated roughly from A.D. 300 to 879 (Slusser 1982). The original ethnic identity of this group is controversial. Basham (1963: 41) states that the Licchavis of northern India "may have been Mongols from the hills, but were more probably a second wave of Aryan immigrants". Slusser, while noting the possibility of an ultimate TB origin of the Licchavis, still asserts that Sanskrit/Prakrit was spoken by these people. It is clear that over time the original inhabitants of the Valley and the Licchavi immigrants became integrated and that the immigrants adopted the TB language spoken in the Valley. Evidence for this comes from the presence of a single Newar ethnic group that dominated the Kathmandu Valley politically and culturally until the establishment of the Shah dynasty in the mid-18th century.

Another wave of immigration from the south occurred during the early portions of the Malla period (A.D. 1200–1768). This was caused by Muslim raids of many areas in northern India and southern Nepal, causing displacement and subsequent immigration into the Kathmandu Valley (Slusser 1982: 8). The Maithili people from southern Nepal figure heavily as immigrants during this period and they clearly played a significant role in the Newar royal court, which saw the widespread use of the Maithili language as a literary medium during this time (K. Pradhan 1991: 14). In addition, several of the kings of the Malla era were Maithilis married to the daughters of Newar nobles (Slusser 1982: 65). While Maithili was prevalent in the court, however, "Newari continued to be the common language of the Kathmandu Valley" (Slusser 1982: 65), again suggesting that many of the new Indo-Aryan speaking immigrants became integrated into the Newar ethnic group.

This scenario of integration of newcomers is also reflected in a comment by Nepali (1965: 17), who notes that, prior to the establishment of the Shah dynasty in the mid-18th century, early conquerors of the Valley were assimilated into Newar culture. The non-assimilation of the Gorkha conquerors under Prithvi Narayan Shah thus marked a significant shift in the history of the Newars, and set up for the first time a clear social division between the Newars and the ruling Brahmin-Chetri caste. Subsequent waves of immigration have not been incorporated into the Newars, who are now seen as a homogeneous ethnic group.

3.2. Newar culture

Throughout the centuries during which they held primary political control of the Kathmandu Valley and other regions of modern Nepal, the Newars prospered notably and developed a highly complex material culture, the characteristics of which have been the subject of numerous books and studies. Interested readers are referred to the major works of Nepali (1965), Slusser (1982) Lewis (1984), Levy (1984), and Gellner (1992), and to the studies cited therein. Here I will give a very brief and necessarily oversimplified account of the primary cultural characteristics of the Newar people, in the interest of providing non-specialists with a brief glimpse of the cultural context of the community.

The social organization of the Newars includes a division between mutually tolerant Buddhist and Hindu groups. Indeed these religions have become quite intertwined in the Newar community, and even share a common body of deities (Gellner 1992: 73–104; Nepali 1965: 415). The division between religions constitutes one of the primary divisions in the complex Newar caste system, which is also based on traditional occupational groupings. The caste system proscribes many aspects of life, including participation in festivals and ceremonies, marriage alliances, membership in guthis (civic-religious organizations; Gellner 1992: 231–250), and possible occupations. The complex Newar caste system is in turn embedded into the larger caste system of modern Nepal.

Newars traditionally live in extended families. Sons are expected to remain in their father's house, to which they bring their wives and into which children are born. There are strict social hierarchies observed within the family, depending primarily on the position of the son with respect to his brothers. The incidence of extended families living under a single roof seems to be decreasing in the modern era, as people pursue educational and employment opportunities throughout the country and as many modern couples prefer to live independently.

The Newar year is marked by parallel but interacting cycles of festivals. In addition, the life of the individual is marked by a number of ceremonies which serve as milestones and to circumscribe the position of the individual within the society. Festivals and ceremonies are highly symbolic in nature, and are generally presided over by either Hindu or Buddhist priests, depending on the festival and/or the caste of the family.[4]

Newars generally live in urban environments. Houses are traditionally built close together, often sharing common walls. Newar settlements tend to be built on hills or by streams, and are surrounded by arable lands. Newar architecture is beautiful and renowned. Traditional buildings are built of brick, and are often three or four stories in height. The bottom story is often taken up by small shops, or, in smaller villages, is used to house livestock. It is common to find several houses built around a single courtyard, providing a community area whose upkeep is either shared or rotated between families. Newar homes usually include verandas, balconies and rooftop patios.

As Newars are highly devout people, temples, sculptures of deities, and shrines abound in Newar communities. Most temples are built in pagoda style, and are filled with carvings and statues of deities, holy animals, and ritual objects. Like other traditional Newar architecture, temples are usually embellished by beautiful and intricate woodcarving. The same style of carving is found in door and window frames, pillars, and other support posts of traditional houses.

The Newars are widely renowned for their skills as traders and as artisans. As traders, they are dispersed in cities and villages throughout Nepal. They also maintain traditional trading practices with Tibet, and extensive trading practices with India. As artisans, Newars are renowned for their woodwork, metalwork, sculpture, and paintings.

The Newars have a centuries-long literary tradition, which began with the translation into Newar of functional works in Sanskrit. The earliest attested

Newar manuscripts date from the early 12th century (Malla 1990); the earliest Newar epigraphy is also dated at that time (B. G. Shrestha 1999). The language of these old manuscripts is referred to as "Classical Newar"; see §1.4.4.5 for further discussion. Newar literature began to flourish in the 17th century (Malla 1982: 40) and continues unabated to this day. Modern Newar society boasts many excellent Newar poets and novelists, as well as contemporary Newar literary journals, magazines, newspapers, and societies.

4. The Newar language and Newar dialects

4.1. A rose by any other name: Newari, Newar, Nepal Bhasa, Newa Bhae; Dolakhali, Dolakha, and Dolakhae

The Newar language has had many appellations over the years and continues to be referred to by a variety of names. The English term "Newari" was apparently coined by Hodgson (1847) and was the standard name used by Western scholars for about 150 years. Thus the majority of the linguistic literature on this language refers to it as Newari. However, some people in the Newar community, including some prominent Newar linguists, consider the derivational suffix -i found in the term Newari to constitute an "Indianization" of the language name. These people thus hold the opinion that the term Newari is non-respectful of Newar culture. For this reason, a number of scholars, including myself, have chosen to refer to the language as "Newar", leaving off the suffix.

In 1995, the government of Nepal officially changed the name of the language from Newari to another common appellation, "Nepal Bhasa", "Nepal" being the original name for the Kathmandu Valley, and "bhasa" being the Sanskrit word meaning 'language'. "Nepal Bhasa" has been used in Nepalese academic circles for some time.[5]

The speakers of the Kathmandu dialect refer to their language as "Newa: bhae", this being the modern reflex of "Nepal Bhasa" after the application of regular sound changes. This term, while perhaps being appropriate for the Kathmandu dialect, is not the ideal choice to refer to the family of dialects as a whole, especially those like Dolakhae, which did not undergo the same sound changes as the Kathmandu dialect.

Currently there is no consensus among the Newars themselves or among the scholars working on Newar as to which language name is best. I have chosen to use the term Newar as the term which seems the least objectionable to people both within and outside the Newar community. It also has the advantage of being very similar to "Newari", so scholars first encountering the language are likely to correctly assume that the two terms refer to the same language.

Fortunately, the situation regarding the name of the Dolakha dialect is not quite so difficult. The term "Dolakha Newar" transparently refers to the variety of Newar spoken in Dolakha. Another alternative is "Dolakhali", which follows standard Indological tradition, adding the same derivational suffix as is found in "Newari". I have heard native speakers of the language use the term Dolakhali many times and there appears to be no stigma attached to it. The term "Dolakhae", built from "Dolakha" plus the genitive clitic, is the term used by the members of this community when they are speaking in the language itself, and some also use it when speaking English or Nepali. I have chosen to use this as a shorter alternative to Dolakha Newar. I use the two interchangeably and mean nothing different by them.

4.2. Newar as a national language of Nepal

Prior to the implementation of the Nepalese Constitution of 1990, Nepali, the official language of Nepal, was the only language allowed in certain social settings. Broadcasting and journalism in languages other than Nepali was restricted, and only Nepali could be used as a medium of instruction in schools. These restrictions were perhaps particularly difficult for the Newar community, as the policies interfered with their long literary tradition and restricted their relatively strong political base.

In part due to demands for the increased recognition and empowerment of the multiple ethnic groups in Nepal, a political revolution took place in the spring of 1990, resulting in a new constitution that took affect in November of that year. The dramatic innovations of the constitution included a change to a system of multiparty democracy. There were also considerable changes in the policies toward ethnic minorities, including changes in language policy. The 1990 constitution states under Article 6 "Language of the Nation":[6]

(1) The Nepali language in the Devanagari script is the language of the nation of Nepal. The Nepali language shall be the official language.
(2) All the languages spoken as the mother tongue in the various parts of Nepal are the national languages of Nepal.

In addition, Article 18 of the Constitution reads:[7]

(1) Each community residing within the Kingdom of Nepal shall have the right to preserve and promote its language, script, and culture.
(2) Each community shall have the right to operate schools up to the primary level in its own mother tongue for imparting education to its children.

These constitute significant changes from earlier government policies.

The Newars moved quickly to take advantage of the new policies. There are now many newspapers in Newar as well as television and radio broadcasts. The last decade has also seen the establishment of an entirely Newar-medium school in Kathmandu. There is also some instruction in Newar at a number of primary schools in the Kathmandu Valley. In addition, several organizations have been established which are expressly designed for the purpose of retention and promotion of the Newar language.

Despite these efforts and the relatively large population of speakers, there are still strong concerns in the Newar community about the long-term prospects for the language. According to Yadava (2003: 153), about two-thirds of the Newar population claim to speak the language. Since this is based upon self-reports, there is no information on fluency or contexts of use. Unfortunately, there is a clear trend among children of many Newars not to learn the language. Most of these children are educated at excellent English-medium schools, where they may have some Nepali instruction but no instruction in Newar. Many of these are boarding schools, with students from a diverse array of backgrounds who communicate in Nepali or English. Newar children at these schools thus experience a significant disruption in the transmission of Newar. Thus it is clear that a much smaller percentage of Newars under the age of 25 speak the language than those over the age of 25. The challenge for the Newar population will be to find contexts of use for the Newar language amidst the rapidly changing society of the 21st century, and to find ways to make the acquisition and use of the Newar language vital to children who fully participate in the global society made possible by the Internet, satellite television, and the dominance of English as the language of education and commerce. The Newars are a prime example of one of the great challenges of our time: how to prize and maintain the priceless languages and cultures of the many ethnic minorities across the globe while still allowing them to be full participants in the increasingly global and technologically sophisticated society that is uniting our world.

4.3. The distribution of Newars throughout Nepal

While the Newar population is concentrated in the Kathmandu Valley, Newars can be found throughout Nepal, some in clearly Newar settlements, and others widely scattered. Table 1 shows the 1990 census figures for numbers of people who report speaking Newar as their mother tongue, by administrative zone (based on His Majesty's Government 1993):

Table 1. Newar speakers by zone

Zone	Number
Mechi	7,288
Koshi	25,890
Sagarmatha	7,506
Janakpur	28,760
Bagmati	521,854
Narayan	36,108
Dhaulagiri	3,792
Lumbini	2,048
Bheri	1,524
Karnali	90
Seti	595
Mankali	245
TOTAL	657,751

The largest number of speakers is concentrated in the Bagmati Zone, which includes the districts of the Kathmandu Valley, notably the Kathmandu, Lalitpur, and Bhaktapur districts. In 1990 these districts were home to 449,604 people claiming Newari as their mother tongue, roughly 68% of the total. Otherwise, Newars are found in relatively large numbers in the eastern zones, and relatively small numbers in the western zones, excluding the Narayan and Lumbini zones, which are in the lowland Tarai region along the Indian border, a prime area for trade.

4.4. Newar dialects

The Kathmandu dialect has been the subject of the majority of the linguistic studies on Newar, and unless modified by a place name, the term "Newari" refers to this dialect when it is applied to a single linguistic variety. To the extent that any Newar dialect can be said to represent a "standard", the Kathmandu dialect would clearly be the most amenable to this appellation.[8] Anyone wishing to begin study of the literature in English on contemporary Kathmandu Newar will want to particularly note the following works. There are two excellent Newar-English dictionaries: Hale and Manandhar (1980), and Kölver and Shresthacarya (1994). Shresthacarya (1981) is another excellent lexical resource, though it focuses only on verbs. A full grammar of Kathmandu Newar just appeared in English (Hale 2006 and Shrestha; Joshi (1992), is a grammar written in Newar. Malla (1985) and Hargreaves (2003) provide more limited sketches. One can also glean a fair amount from doctoral dissertations by Tuladhar (1985), U. Shrestha (1990) Hargreaves (1991, revised and published in

2005) and Genetti (1990, revised and published 1994). There are numerous linguistic articles on various aspects of contemporary Kathmandu Newar. Readers are referred especially to work by the following authors, all of whom have produced at least several articles on the language: DeLancey, Genetti, Hale, Hargreaves, Joshi, Kansakar, Kiryu, B. Kölver, U. Kölver, Malla, Shakya, U. Shrestha, and Shresthacarya. Readers interested in literature in German should take note of the work by Conrady and B. and U. Kölver. Works in Japanese are avaialable by Hashimoto and Kiryu. Most commendable, however, are the many works by native Kathmandu Newar scholars who produce linguistic studies in the language itself. Although these works are accessible to only a small handful of international scholars, the value of these studies in developing an independent linguistic tradition and in bringing academic issues about the language directly to the Newar speech community is immense. Readers are especially referred to the works of the following scholars: S. K. Joshi; T. R. Kansakar; T. B. Maharjan; I. Mali; K. P. Malla; Newa.; D. Newami; P. Sayami; S. R. Sharma; D. R. Shakya; R. R. Sharma; B. G. Shrestha; I. Shresthacarya; K. Tamot; S. R. Tamrakar; and D. Vajrācārya.

The dialect of Bhaktapur, located some distance to the east of Kathmandu, is conservative in some respects. There is much less literature on the Bhaktapur dialect than on the Kathmandu dialect. Hashimoto (1977) is an extensive lexical study. Joshi (1984) contains a grammatical description. Tamot (1985) is a study in Newar on this dialect.

Putting aside the Dolakha dialect for the moment (see below), linguistic work on other Newar dialects is quite limited. Mali (1982) produced a study of the Pahari dialect. The morphology of the Tansen dialect was the subject of a thesis (in English) and a publication written (in Newar) by O. Shrestha 2000, 2001 respectively). The verb morphology of the Badikhel Pahari dialect has been described by R. L. Shrestha (2003). Newami (1984, 1993) produced studies of the Bandipur dialect in Newar. Shakya (1992) is a study of morphology in six dialects of Newar (Kathmandu/Patan, Pyangāõ, Bhaktapur, Bandipur, Dolakha, and Badikhel), while Shakya (2000) presented data on ten Newar dialects (Kathmandu/Patan, Payngāõ, Bhaktapur, Bandipur, Dhulikhel, Dolakha, Balami, Gopali, Gamal, Pahari).

As of this writing, there has yet to be any systematic survey of Newar dialects in Nepal generally, or even in the Kathmandu Valley. I have compiled the following list of possible localities with independent Newar communities, based on my own discussions with a number of Newars and on the work of Shakya (1992, 2000). My understanding is that these localities have long-established Newar communities, probably arising from old outposts for trade. The extent to which these cities and villages have distinct dialects is likely to depend on the age of the communities and on the amount of contact maintained with other Newars throughout their histories.

Eastern	Central	Western
Chainpur	Tansen	Bandipur
Bhojpur	Gorkha	Old Pokhara
Terathum	Arughat	Dumre
Ilam	Rumjatar	Narayangad
Taplejung	Phalpa	Ridi (Gulmi)
Dhankuta	Hetauda	Baglung
Dharan	Butwal	Butwal
Biratnagar		Chitlang
Tauthali		
Listi		
Duti		
Lek		

The final four villages listed in the eastern column are of particular interest to this study as they have been mentioned to me by Dolakha Newars as relatively nearby Newar communities where the people speak something similar to Dolakha Newar. I undertook preliminary fieldwork on the Tauthali dialect in 2004; I found it to be very similar to the Dolakha dialect although with sufficient differences to establish that it is a distinct variety. Thus the Tauthali and Dolakha dialects establish a sub-branch we may call "Eastern Newar" (possibly with other varieties, such as Listi, Duti, and Lek). As these varieties are mutually unintelligible with those of the Kathmandu Valley, on purely linguistic terms, we could classify Eastern Newar as a distinct language and Newar as a language family rather than as a single language. Alternatively, we can represent these varieties as families of dialects. Regardless of the nomenclature, further work on the varieties of Newar outside of the three major cities of the Kathmandu Valley is needed before a full appreciation of the extent of Newar is discovered.

4.5. Classical Newar

In addition to work on synchronic dialects, linguists can benefit greatly from the long literary tradition of the Newar people. Written attestations of the language date back to the 12th century A.D. and continue unabated to the present day. The language used in these manuscripts is not uniform; the documents were produced over a considerable period of time and in several distinct Newar varieties. The name "Classical Newar(i)" is used as a cover term for the language used in manuscripts dating from the 12th through the 19th centuries, but it must be kept in mind that the language varieties found in these manuscripts are heterogenous. In the words of the Nepal Bhasa Dictionary Committee (2000: vii), "All we know at this stage is that Classical Newari is not a single homogenous monolithic stage nor a variety, dialect or stylistic label". Despite the heterogeneity, the existence of the extensive set of written manuscripts has been an invaluable resource to linguists interested in Newar, allowing for a considerable number of historical studies that provide insight into the development of the modern dialects, particularly that of Kathmandu.

The most extensive work on Classical Newar is *A Dictionary of Classical Newari* compiled by the Nepal Bhasa Dictionary Committee, and published in Kathmandu in the year 2000. The committee was composed of the very top Newar historical linguists, headed by Kamal P. Malla. The dictionary, 20 years in the making, is a tremendous achievement. Data for this work were compiled from 96 manuscript sources, many of them originally produced on palm leaves, and also including inscriptions in stone and copper. The dictionary comprises 530 pages, two columns per page, in small type. Each entry is labeled for part of speech and translated into English. This basic information is wonderfully supplemented by the dates and names of the manuscripts in which the word was attested, together with translated example sentences taken directly from the manuscripts. This volume comprises an invaluable resource for Newar and Tibeto-Burman studies and a stupendous achievement by the Newar linguistic community.

Prior to the appearance of this work, the primary materials available on Classical Newar were those produced by Hans Jørgensen in the 1930s. These included his 1936 work, *A Dictionary of the Classical Newari Compiled from Manuscript Sources*, his 1941 work, *A Grammar of the Classical Newari*, and two extensive transliterated and translated texts (1931, 1939). Jørgensen's work was primarily based on some of the more recent Classical Newari texts, mostly dating from the 17th through the 19th centuries. One of the earliest works ever written in Newari is also available in transliterated and translated form, thanks to the efforts of Dhanavajra Vajrācārya and Kamal P. Malla. This is the *Gopalarajavamsavali*, a historical chronicle from the 14th century. The beginning of this work is written in "corrupt Sanskrit" (Vajrācārya and Malla 1985: iii, quoting Bendall 1903), but the language changes to an older form of Newar, although with numerous Indo-Aryan loan words.

The early Classical Newar manuscripts were written on palm or birch leaves; later manuscripts appeared on paper (Malla 1982: 29). The scripts vary somewhat, but all are derived from the early Brahmi. The Devanagari came into widespread in the Shah dynasty beginning in the mid-18th century (Malla 1982: 29). Full study of these materials thus requires years of careful and devoted scholarship. The primary contributors to this field include Jørgensen, Kansakar, B. and U. Kölver, Malla, and Tamot.

5. The village of Dolakha and the Dolakhae language

5.1. Location, size, population

The village of Dolakha is located approximately 145 kilometers to the east of Kathmandu, in the Dolakha district of the Janakpur zone. The village is composed of a series of *tols* 'neighborhoods' which are set on a steep, south facing hillside, high above the Tama Kosi river. The altitude is given as varying between 1700–1830 meters, or approximately 5500–6000 feet (Kalinchowk Youth Club 1988: 7). From Dolakha, one can see a spectacular view of the high peaks of the Himalayas, particularly the peak Gauri Shankar which towers above the village at 7,154 meters (23,471 feet). Dolakha is only about three kilometers from the Dolakha District government center of Carikot, which is directly on the road between Kathmandu and Jiri.

The most recent statistics on the population of Dolakha are the results of a baseline survey conducted and published in 1988 by the Kalinchowk Youth Club with the assistance of the United Nations Volunteer Participatory Development Program. The door-to-door survey lists the total population of Dolakha as 5,645 (Kalinchowk Youth Club 1988: 19).[9] While no explicit statistics on the ethnic breakdown of the village exist to my knowledge, generally it is assumed that the majority of these residents are Newar, although Thangmis, Tamangs and members of other groups are represented in smaller numbers. The Dolakha Newars are overwhelmingly Hindu, and tend to be from the Shrestha castes, including the Chatharia Shresthas (Mallas, Joshis, Pradhans, Amatyas, Rajbhandaris, etc.) and the Panctharia Shresthas (Shresthas proper and other groups) (Nepali 1965).

The number of speakers of the Dolakhae language is certain to be much larger than suggested by the door-to-door survey. This is because there is a strong trend in the village for young people to move to other parts of Nepal to follow business and educational pursuits, thus there is a large community of Dolakhae speakers in the Kathmandu Valley, and there are many others scattered throughout Nepal. Most teenagers move out of Dolakha for at least several years; many people remain permanently outside the village, although they may visit often, or leave their young children there to be raised by grandparents or other members of their extended family. There is a strong trend for Dolakhae people to marry Newars from the Kathmandu Valley or other areas outside of Dolakha. This provides further incentive to reside permanently outside the village. Children raised in these households tend to speak Nepali or other Newar dialects, although some may learn to speak Dolakhae if there are sufficient numbers of Dolakhae speakers living in or visiting the household. In general, though, there is a current trend for children not to learn the Dolakhae dialect. If this trend continues, the vitality of the language may be greatly diminished within one or two generations. One may thus consider the Dolakha dialect to be endangered.

While the lack of transmission of Dolakhae to the children of many Dolakha Newars is alarming, it should be noted that many in the community are making a conscious effort to preserve and promote the Dolakhae language. There have been three recent MA theses produced by Dolakha Newars on their language and culture (I. Pradhan 2001; U. Pradhan 2003; Y. K. Shrestha 2002). The last ten years has also seen the production of two newspapers in the language. In addition, Dolakha Nepal Bhasa Khalak is an active society expressly founded for the promotion of the Dolakhae language. Community gatherings, such as meetings of the Kalingchowk Youth Club, are multilingual, with speeches being made in Dolakhae, Kathmandu Newar, Nepali, and/or English. Thus the Dolakhae people are aware of the decline in the transmission of the language to the younger generation and are actively working to reverse this trend. Whether these efforts will be ultimately successful remains to be seen, but they are a clear attestation to the strength of the Dolakhae community, a clear prerequisite for language retention.

The vast majority of the residents of Dolakha are farmers who work their fields surrounding the village. They also raise chickens and livestock, mainly goats, cows, and water buffalo. Barter is common. Most people provide for their own sustenance, and may trade their goods with friends and relatives in the Kathmandu Valley as a way of obtaining goods not available in Dolakha. The second most common occupation is government service; the number of people reporting to be government employees in 1988 was 195 (Kalingchowk Youth Club 1988: 20); it is likely that most of these work in the government offices at Carikot. There are reported to be 21 small shops, 13 tea shops, and several other modest businesses. Dolakha also contains a hospital, an eye hospital, and a number of schools. Dolakha Newars who reside outside of the village have a wide range of professions, especially commerce.

Dolakha is known for its antiquity and in particular its ancient temples. The most famous of these is the Bhimsen temple, which is important not only to the Newars but also to the Eastern Tamangs (Bickel 2000: 695; Tautscher 1998: 176–178). The legend which I was told by a Dolakha elder was that a group of porters were traveling over the hill and one traveler, discouraged that his rice was not cooked when his pot came into contact with a certain rock, struck the rock with a spoon, and that the rock began to bleed a mixture of blood and milk. People then realized that this rock was an incarnation of the god Bhimsen, asked his forgiveness, and built a temple surrounding it. A more elaborated, but slightly different, version of this story may be found in Tautscher (1998: 177). The Bhimsen temple continues to be influential in Nepal to this day. Many people from Kathmandu make pilgrimages to worship at this temple, as the god

Bhimsen is particularly well known for granting success in business. The stone itself is still claimed to be miraculous. Tautscher (1998: 177) provides the following account:

> Bhimesvar is known to 'sweat' (liquid oozes from the stone) indicating a crisis in the kingdom of Nepal or even a threat to the royal family of Nepal. Bhimesvar is said to have 'sweated' in 1949, before the Rana prime ministers lost their ruling power, and in 1990 when heavy demonstrations occurred against the Panchayat government. The chief district officer of Dolakha himself had to worship the statue of Bhimewvar and the sweat of Bhimsen was carried in a cotton pad to the royal court in Kathmnadu for sacrifical *puja* to appease the god.

While the Newars of Dolakha celebrate many of the same ceremonies as those of the Kathmandu Valley, the customs and rituals observed in the ceremonies are often unique. Mahani (Dasain) is the most important annual festival in Dolakha and the manner of celebration is unique to this community. Many Dolakhae people return to the village from other parts of Nepal to participate in Mahani annually.

5.2. Synopsis of Dolakha history

The municipality of Dolakha has a long history. Unfortunately, the details of this history are at times sketchy, although a number of stone inscriptions and old documents do provide us with a rough outline. The most in-depth work on Dolakha history is *Dolakhako Aitihasik Ruprekha* [Collection of Dolakha History] by the eminent historians Dhanavajra Vajrācārya and Tek Bahadur Shrestha (1974). The brief synopsis given here is primarily based on this work.

Concerning the prehistory of Dolakha, there has been some speculation that the area was originally ruled by Kiratas. Vajrācārya and T. B. Shrestha (1974: 16–17) cite three pieces of evidence in favor of this hypothesis. The first is the location of Dolakha which is in close proximity to modern Kiranti groups.[10] The second is that some cultural traditions appear to be similar to those of modern Kirantis. And the third is that the majority of Dolakha Newars fall into the Shrestha caste category, a category which traditionally applied to administrators and tradesman, as opposed to priests, farmers, or artisans. This suggests that when Newars originally established the settlement in Dolakha, they went as administrators to an area where the population was largely non-Newar. However, while Dolakha is located in the eastern region of the country, the current non-Newar inhabitants in the area immediately surrounding Dolakha are not Kirantis, but speakers of either West Himalayish languages (Thami and Tamang) or Sherpa (Bodish).

Regarding the dating of the Newar settlement of Dolakha, it is clear that it was well-established by the time of the Malla period (A.D. 1200–1768). It is possible that the initial establishment was significantly earlier. Vajrācārya and T. B. Shrestha (1974: 16) note an assertion made by the historian Babu Ram Acharya that the development of Dolakha occurred after the establishment of trade links between India and China, during the reign of Amsuvarma, who ruled during the Licchavi period in the early 7th century.[11] Desiring to provide secure shelters for travelers on this route, Amsuvarma created "security posts" along the passage. Dolakha is said to have been one of these posts, serving as well as a trade link between the Kathmandu Valley and eastern Nepal. Whether or not the establishment of a security post marked the original settlement of Newars in Dolakha is unknown, however it is very clear that Dolakha was well-established as a walled Newar settlement and fort by the early 14th century. Therefore the split of the Dolakha Newars from the Newars of the Valley occurred between 700 and 1600 years ago. Given this fact, it is not surprising to find the high degree of linguistic diversity which is found dividing the Kathmandu Valley and Dolakha "dialects".

Beginning in the Malla period, the history of Dolakha becomes clearer. At that point, it was considered to be a city, having the required attributes of a wall surrounding the settlement for security, a surrounding forest, and evidence of cultural development in the form of temples and courtrooms (Vajrācārya and T. B. Shrestha 1974: 3). In the early portion of the Malla era, Dolakha was considered to be a feudal state, under the ultimate rule of the kingdoms of the Kathmandu Valley.[12] However during the later Malla era, as the Malla kings began to lose power, the rulers of Dolakha broke away from their feudal lords and attained independence. This appears to have happened primarily in the 16th century A.D., during which time the leaders of Dolakha took titles indicating increased independence and power, until the title *rājadhirāj* 'king' was taken by Indra Singh Dev, who assumed the rule of Dolakha in A.D. 1534 (BS 1591). This independence was officially recognized in the treaty of Pashupati (in Kathmandu) in A.D. 1548 (BS 1605). Under the reign of Indra Singh Dev, Dolakha prospered economically and advanced culturally, and trade relations with Tibet were at their height. After about a century of independence (the exact date is unknown), Dolakha was again annexed to the kingdom of Kathmandu (Vajrācārya and T. B. Shrestha 1974: 39). Although Dolakha was considered to be a state of Kathmandu, there was very little interference from Kathmandu in internal matters.

Around the same time that Dolakha lost its independence, at least in name, to Kathmandu, Prithvi Narayan Shah, the king of a small principality called Gorkha west of the Kathmandu Valley, began his campaign for territorial, and subsequent economic, expansion. His primary aim was to wrest control of the Kathmandu Valley from the three Newar kingdoms. He managed this in part by using force or diplomacy to take control of surrounding communities, hence isolating and eventually blockading the Kathmandu Valley. He successfully defeated the three Newar kingdoms in the late 1760s and shifted his capital to Kathmandu in March of 1770 (K. Pradhan 1991: 105). This campaign took more than 20 years to complete. The surrender of Dolakha to Prithvi Naryan Shah occurred in the middle of this campaign, in 1754. K. Pradhan writes that at the time Dolakha had a predominantly Newar population, but also that "a large settlement of Khasa [Nepali–cg] speaking people was found there" (1991: 95). Dolakha was important to Shah for several reasons: the fertile farmland that surrounded the city, its position in trade with Tibet, and its iron deposit (K. Pradhan 1991: 95). Prithvi Naryan Shah wrote a letter to the main citizens of Dolakha, offering them protection for their lives and property in exchange for their surrender. Dolakha surrendered without resistance, extending Shah's territories to the east of the Kathmandu Valley (K. Pradhan 1991: 95). The relations between the new Shah government and Dolakha were strong. However, during the Rana regime (A.D. 1846–1951), Dolakha lost much of its influence. At the same time, a new trade route was established between Kalimpong and Tibet, which caused Dolakha to lose some of its economic vitality. While Dolakha has never regained the economic and political influence it held in previous centuries, it has become a small modern city of Nepal. Its historical significance is still held in respect, and the beautiful temples and monuments which are found throughout the village are reminders of its rich historical past.

5.3. Language contact: A link between social history and language

One fact that the synopsis of Dolakha history makes clear is that the Dolakhae people have not been isolated from other linguistic groups. Instead, the history of Dolakha is in large part a history of the social and political relationships that the Dolakhae people have held with members of other political and ethnic groups, all speakers of other languages. Possible links with the Kiranti peoples are suggested by early historical records. There were undoubtedly centuries of trade with Tibet as well as interaction with the Newars of the Kathmandu Valley. There were strong political alliances between Dolakha and Prithvi Naryan Shah (who established Nepali as the national language as he unified Nepal). And the village has been and is currently surrounded by Tamang and Thami settlements.

When speakers of two languages interact intensively, one or both languages often undergo lexical or structural changes of varying degrees. Scholars working on such language-contact phenomena have identified two primary types of effects, although other types also exist. The term "borrowing" refers to "the incorporation of foreign features into a group's language by speakers of that language" (Thomason and Kaufman 1988: 37). Borrowing may occur with casual or intensive contact, and is more likely to affect the morphology and syntax when there is extensive bilingualism occurring over a period of time. "Substratum interference" occurs when a population shifting to a target language does not learn the language properly, but speaks it in a slightly changed form consistent with their native language. When speakers of the target language adopt the change, substratum interference has occurred.

If the Dolakhae language was affected by substratum interference, it would necessarily have entailed Kiranti or other Tibeto-Burman peoples learning Dolakhae and becoming integrated into the Dolakhae community. If such an event occurred, it would have happened during the earliest periods of Dolakha history, and clear evidence of it would be obscured at the current time. Evidence of borrowing, by contrast, is plentiful. Lexical borrowings from Indo-Aryan languages (especially Nepali, Sanskrit, and Hindi, but possibly Maithilli and other languages) are plentiful in the language. There are also clearly words of English origin, but it is likely that they were borrowed through the medium of Nepali.[13] Structural borrowings are also in evidence, and for these the source language appears to be consistently Nepali.

Almost all Dolakha Newars are bilingual in Nepali and Dolakhae. Nepali is the lingua franca of the local area, as it is throughout Nepal; people use Nepali to speak with others whose mother tongue is different. Nepali is also the primary medium of instruction in schools, although in Dolakha, some of the classes for younger children are currently conducted in Dolakhae. The result of this sustained bilingualism is in evidence throughout the Dolakhae language. The large number of Nepali loan words in natural Dolakhae discourse is frequently commented on by monolingual Nepali speakers, Kathmandu Newars, and the Dolakhae people themselves. Since the phonology and morphology of Dolakhae and Nepali are different, however, there are particular strategies that Dolakhae people use to allow for the smooth incorporation of the foreign words. In addition, there are a number of parallel grammatical structures between the two languages which may indicate calquing (the realization of a structure of the source language through exact morphemic translation in the target language). Instances of influence of Nepali on Dolakha Newar structures will be noted throughout the grammar.

5.4. Previous work on Dolakha Newar

The first studies of the Dolakha Newar dialect were conducted by the Newar scholars Indra Mali (1979), Prem Sayami (1986), and Kashinath Tamot (1987, 1989). By far the most extensive work has been conducted by Dr. Rudra Laxmi Shrestha, whose work includes an early study of Dolakha verb inflection (1989, in English), a Ph.D. dissertation with a descriptive study of the language (1993), an extensive analysis of the Dolakhae verb (2000a), and a Dolakhae-Kathmandu Newar wordlist (2000b).

Other than R. L. Shrestha (1989), the primary studies available in English are my own works. Genetti (1988) was my first report on the language, to be superseded by Genetti (1990, published as 1994). I have also written articles on a number of aspects of the phonology and grammar of the language; rather than enumerate them here, I refer the reader to the references.

5.5. Typological characterization

This section is designed to give a very brief summary of the primary typological characteristics of the language, to inform those who have little exposure to languages of this area (which are quite similar typologically), and to indicate the primary areas that may be of interest to non-specialists.

Dolakhae has a relatively simple phonemic inventory, with three series of stops (and one series of affricates) in five places of articulation. Breathy voice, found in Kathmandu Newar and Nepali, is mostly lost in Dolakhae, although occasional breathy pronunciations of some words may be heard. There are six vowels which may be nasalized phonemically, but no distinctive vowel length. There are a few morphophonemic processes, including a limited vowel harmony process that affects vowels of prefixes. The phonology of the language is the topic of Chapter 2; prosodic patterns are discussed in Chapter 3.

Dolakhae is a verb-final language with many of the typological features that are commonly found with languages of this type. For example, the language has postpositions as opposed to prepositions, is predominantly suffixing, and most modifiers precede the noun within the noun phrase. The subject of a transitive verb precedes the object in unmarked contexts; however, pragmatic factors frequently lead to other constituent orders being attested. Word order is more broadly discussed in §11.2 and Chapter 14.

In Dolakhae, case is marked by a paradigmatic set of enclitics that appear on noun phrases. The three core cases are ergative, absolutive, and dative. Ergative is found marking subjects of transitive verbs. Absolutive case is unmarked. It is found with subjects of intransitive verbs and some objects (specifically, those which are semantically patients and whose referents are either inanimate, or animate and new to the discourse). The dative case enclitic is found marking objects which are semantic recipients, or objects which are semantic patients with animate and given referents. Some subjects are also occasionally marked with the dative case, although "dative-experiencer" constructions do not seem to be as extensive in Dolakhae as has been described for some other South Asian languages (see the papers in Verma and Mohanan 1990). A full discussion of casemarking may be found in §4.4.4.2.

There is clear evidence for a subject category in Dolakhae. The language does not distinguish between direct and indirect object, instead there is a single category of object that incorporates both patients and recipients. Grammatical relations are discussed in Chapter 13.

There is a clear distinction between finite and non-finite verb morphology. The finite verb reflects the person and number of the subject, and inflects in four distinct tenses. Separate inflectional paradigms are found in the negative, imperative, and optative moods (§6.5). Non-finite morphology includes three morphemes in paradigmatic alternation which both nominalize and relativize clauses. Their distribution is quite complex, as discussed in Chapter 17. Other non-finite morphology includes the infinitive and the participle (a converb). Both are used extensively in clause combining.

The participial construction (Chapter 19) is one of the most intriguing parts of Dolakha syntax. The participle can be classified as a converb, which equally allows one clause to modify another in an adverbial relationship and the chaining of clauses to indicate events in sequence. It is also used to incorporate auxiliaries into a clause and for other purposes. There is no switch reference system.

Complement clauses and adverbial clauses are also common and are often interwoven with clause chains and embedded direct quotation to create long and intricate sentences. Every language has its genius and, in my opinion, the genius of Dolakhae lies here. The relationships in these structures are highly complex and fascinating. Each type of non-finite clause and its properties are discussed in Chapters 17 through 20. Chapter 21, on the sentence, addresses the interaction of these types of clause combining, and the important role of prosody in the structuring and comprehension of these structures.

5.6. The primary differences between the Dolakhae and Kathmandu dialects

As mentioned above, the Dolakhae and Kathmandu dialects, while clearly both Newar and closely related, are mutually unintelligible. There are several particular areas of divergence which contribute to this. A more in-depth discussion of these differences may be found in Genetti (1994).

Probably the strongest factor contributing to the unintelligibility between Dolakhae and Kathmandu Newar is a major phonological change that radically affected the Kathmandu dialect but not Dolakhae. This change entailed the loss of all syllable-final consonants, with compensatory lengthening of the nuclear vowel.[14] A concomitant change was the development of phonemic vowel length. Although the lost consonants still appear in some environments (especially before vowel-initial case suffixes, in which case the consonants are syllable-initial, as opposed to syllable-final), the basic sound and rhythm of the language was altered dramatically, making communication with Dolakhae speakers more difficult. Additional phonological changes which further obscured the similarities include the substantial loss of breathy voice in Dolakhae (Kathmandu has an extensive breathy voiced series which extends to the sonorants), and the loss of the /l/ ~ /r/ distinction in Kathmandu (retained in Dolakhae).

The most surprising morphological distinction between the Dolakhae and Kathmandu dialects is found in the system of finite verb morphology. All three dialects of the Kathmandu Valley have a system of finite verb inflection which has been called the "conjunct/disjunct" system. (Hale (1980) originally described the system. Hargreaves (1991, 2005) is a more thorough examination of the semantic parameters upon which the conjunct/disjunct system, and other aspects of Kathmandu grammar, are based.) The conjunct verb forms are found in finite clauses with a volitional verb if: (i) the clause is declarative with a first-person actor, (ii) the clause is interrogative and has a second-person actor, (iii) the clause is reported speech and the actor of the utterance verb and the actor of the volitional verb in the reported clause are coreferential (based on Hargreaves 2005: 6). Disjunct verb forms are used in all other finite environments.

The parameters on which the Kathmandu system are based are volitionality (or control, Hargreaves 2005) and evidentiality (more specifically epistemic source, Hargreaves 2005). This area is one of the most intriguing of Kathmandu Newar grammar, perhaps a large part of its own genius. By contrast, the Dolakhae system of finite verb inflection seems quite mundane; the finite verb marks four tense distinctions and agrees with its subject in person and number (although some intimations of conjunct/disjunct parameters may be found, see §6.4.3.4).

Further differences between the two languages exist in almost every area of the grammar. The most significant ones are probably the differences in nominalizing and relativizing morphology, the fact that Kathmandu Newar has two participial constructions where Dolakhae has only one, and the fact that Dolakhae has a strong subject category, in contrast to Kathmandu Newar, where the subject category is controversial (Genetti 1986; Hale and Watters 1973). Once again, the reader is referred to Genetti (1994) for a fuller comparison and discussion of these and other differences.

6. Linguistic theory and description

6.1. The functionalist framework and language description

The primary goal of this volume is to provide a description of Dolakhae that will be useful and accessible to people with a wide range of interests. First and foremost, this book is for the Dolakhae people and their descendants, especially since the number of native speakers of the language appears to be currently on the decline. Secondly, it is written for specialists in Newar and Himalayan linguistics, who may be searching for particular details of the language to inform or illuminate comparative studies or descriptive studies in other languages. Thirdly, it is written for anyone who may be interested in learning to speak the Dolakhae language; there are no pedagogical materials in existence, so at least this description could be a starting point and assist in such a task. And finally, it is written for the larger community of linguists, who are trying to understand the nature of language by studying individual languages in depth, by performing comparative cross-linguistic studies on a wide range of phenomena, and by revising and developing theories of language and linguistic structure.

Given the diverse audience for this book, it is crucial that it be as free from the trappings of specific linguistic theories as possible. Linguistic theories are constantly being advanced, revised, argued against, and discarded, so a grammatical description that is too theory-specific has two major disadvantages. First, it is more or less unintelligible to those who lack explicit training in the particular theory being used, and second, after the theory is replaced by a new or better version, the grammar ceases to be of general interest. On the other hand, a true understanding of the structures and intricacies of the language will certainly be furthered by the use of linguistic terminology that is ultimately theory-based. Thus terms like "noun", "verb", "relative clause", "suffix" and "phoneme" convey important concepts basic to understanding the structures of languages, and the exclusion of such terms would result in a grammar that was overly simplistic, redundant, and frustrating to anyone with linguistic training. I will therefore do my best to write this book at a level such that any reader with a background in basic linguistics will be able to understand it.

Even though I choose to limit the amount of theory-particular terminology used in this book, there is still a clear theoretical framework in which this study is placed. The framework has been roughly termed "functionalist" or "functional-typological". The basic premise behind this theory is that the nature of language is most profoundly understood by an examination not only of linguistic structures, but also by how those structures are used by speakers in communication, in other words, how structures function in language. Functional factors are quite diverse. For example, they may be semantic (the signaling of basic lexical or propositional meaning), discourse-related (the structuring of information in the larger communicative context), sociolinguistic (dependent on the establishment and negotiation of societal roles), or cognitive (related to how the mind categorizes and processes information about the world). Thus the explanatory parameters are diverse. This allows for a very rich view of language and the many forces that shape it.

Functionalist theory is also enriched by taking a "panchronic" view of language; that is, it does not make a strong division between structures in the modern language and the history of those structures. Instead, functionalists see linguistic structures as being constantly shaped by the speakers who use them to meet the many demands of human communication. Linguistic structure is in a constant state of flux. A purely synchronic description of language, like a photographic snapshot, produces a static representation of a dynamic element. While no grammar can be a complete description of something as complex, varied and ever-changing as a language, incorporation of historical observation at least provides some insight as to where some structures came from and why.

In order to understand the relationship between function and structure, it is important to look at linguistic structures as they occur in natural, spoken discourse. The data in this book are thus of two primary types: elicited materials (the translations of words and sentences by native speakers of the language in a relatively context-free environment) and tape-recorded narrative and conversational texts. The two data types are complementary. Elicited data is most conducive to understanding the structure of the phonological system, collecting lexical materials, filling out paradigms, and the testing of speaker's subjective judgments about the grammaticality of linguistic structures. Textual data is most conducive to seeing the full array of linguistic structures possible in language, how they are actually used, and what they are used for. Sometimes the two types of evidence are contradictory; a consultant may say in elicitation that a certain structure is ungrammatical, then use that structure in a conversation the next day. Usually consultants, if confronted by such inconsistency, will acknowledge that given the context of the conversation, the construction is grammatical. Experiences of this type serve to emphasize the importance of the relationship between context and structure.

Finally, an advantage of the functionalist framework in the writing of descriptive grammars is that it is sufficiently flexible to allow the language to be seen in its own terms. There are no theoretical requirements that certain types of categories be present in every language – even lexical categories as common as noun and verb may not be found in all languages. One needs to look at the details of the language to see if the presence of such categories is justified. In the functionalist framework, many categories are seen as being non-absolute, but best represented as continua. For example, a given language may have forms that are "more noun-like" or "more verb-like", if clear definitional criteria for these categories are impossible to find. Similarly the category of "subject" may be problematic. Some languages may have a strong subject category, with many independent types of evidence indicating that the language uses the subject principle extensively in the organization of its grammar, while other languages may have no subject at all, or only have weak evidence for subject. Since the functionalist framework does not require that every language have, for example, a subject, each language is examined in its own terms, as opposed to being pushed into a "universal" mold which does not do justice to its structure.

6.2. The "problem" of variation

One dimension of field research in linguistics which, I suspect, many people confront and few people discuss (but cf. Dorian 1994, 2001; Genetti 2003a), is that of inter-speaker variation. Classes in field methodology and many field research projects generally use only one consultant, and the result is data which has considerable internal consistency. It is well known that variation may be found which correlates with social or geographic distinctions in the language community, but what is often not acknowledged is that people of the same social background and neighborhood, even members of the same family, may have different linguistic systems. Bradley (1979: 41) writes about this phenomenon in a discussion of sound change in the Tibeto-Burman language Akha, and notes that "full brothers, raised in the same house, have different phonological systems, or different realizations of the same phonological units" (1979: 41).

In my work on Dolakhae, I have found that different speakers, though of similar age and closely related (raised in the same household), have different systems of vowel harmony, different pronunciations of some common vocabulary items, different inflections of the copula, different distributions of nominalizing morphology, etc. Since this type of variation is not commonly cited in the literature, and I was therefore not expecting it, I initially attributed these differences to the artificiality of the elicitation context where I first noticed them. As I examined the textual materials in detail, however, I found that the variation was attested in natural discourse as well.

The phonology and grammar of a language are constructed of multiple elements and structures which interact to form subsystems which in turn interact. The type of variation which I have encountered suggests that while many of these elements, structures, and subsystems are quite stable and consistent, others are not. A child learning the language does not have a consistent pattern to adopt, and may develop an independent (though obviously not entirely novel or unrelated) pattern. While variation may indicate that a particular subsystem is undergoing linguistic change, there is no reason to suppose that all variation is change-oriented. Instead, variation may persist in a language, and need not be "resolved" into a consistent pattern. (See Genetti (1999, 2003a) for more discussion of this point.)

The presence of variation, however, adds another degree of complexity to the writing of a reference grammar. For example, there is not a single vowel harmony system that is "the system" of the language. The only way to adequately represent the language is to discuss the variation openly. At times this may be frustrating to the reader who is searching for a single answer to a question, but the end result is a more accurate portrayal of the language.

7. Data for the study

7.1. Primary linguistic consultants

The Dolakha data presented here was gathered during four field trips to Nepal, taken between 1987 and 2004, and in several meetings with a native speaker in California in 1998. My primary consultants have been Mrs. Kalpana Shrestha, Mrs. Rama Shrestha, Mr. Nawa Raj Shrestha (of Kopindol), Mr. Nawa Raj Shretha (of San Francisco), and Miss Indu Shrestha. All five are trilingual in Dolakhae, Nepali, and English. As I worked most extensively with the first three of these consultants, I will discuss them in some detail.

Kalpana and Rama Shrestha are first cousins, related through their fathers who are brothers. Therefore they were raised in the same household in Dolakha for a number of years. Rama is the older of the two female cousins. She lived in Dolakha in the early years of her life until her father joined the government service, and then she lived and traveled with her parents and two older brothers in other areas of Nepal, primarily the southern Tarai. Rama was about eight years old when she left Dolakha and her period of travel with her family lasted seven years. During this time she always spoke Dolakhae with her family and Nepali with others. She made one trip back to Dolakha in the seventh grade and stayed for some time. At 15 she moved with her family to Kathmandu. She has since made only rare trips back to Dolakha, always for ritual occasions. She always speaks Dolakha with her family members and other people from the village now residing in Kathmandu. She is married to a man from Bhaktapur, and so now lives in that city. She can understand the Bhaktapur and Kathmandu Newar dialects, but does not speak either one, and replies in Nepali when addressed by her in-laws.

Kalpana is two years younger than Rama. Therefore Rama's departure at eight years of age occurred when Kalpana was six. Kalpana remained in Dolakha until she was 12, at which point she moved with her father and brother to Kathmandu. When she was 16 her father moved back to Dolakha and her grandmother, who was basically monolingual in Dolakhae, came to Kathmandu. Kalpana always speaks Dolakhae with her family and other people from the village, but speaks Nepali and Kathmandu Newar as well. In early 1990 she was married to a Newar from Pokhara, where she now resides. As her husband speaks the Pokhara dialect of Newar, the two use Nepali as the language of the household.

Nawa Raj is about nine years younger than Kalpana. He lived in Dolakha until the fifth grade, then moved with his parents, two sisters, and his uncle to Janakpur. At the age of 15, he moved to Kathmandu where he completed high school and started college. In Kathmandu, he lived either with family or friends from Dolakha, and always speaks Dolakhae with anyone from the village. Nawa Raj understands a little Kathmandu Newar, but doesn't speak it himself. He speaks Nepali with Nepalese outside the Dolakhae community, and speaks Hindi and English as well.

As mentioned above, there is variation in details of the phonological and grammatical structures of these three speakers. This may be partially due to their slightly different backgrounds, and to the different periods of time that they lived in the village. However, none of the speakers were conscious that the others spoke differently, and all were surprised when I pointed the differences out.

In addition to the consultants mentioned here who patiently answered my numerous questions, helped me to record and transcribe narrative and conversational texts, recorded phonological forms and wordlists, and corrected my many errors, I was also assisted at numerous points by many others in the Dolakha Newar community. Indeed, I have been extremely impressed by the interest of the Dolakhae community in this project and by their unfailing support and generosity. Never did I come across a single person who did not want to assist me and to share with me their knowledge and insights of the language. Although this book bears my name as author, the credit for it really goes to the entire Dolakhae community. Without their insights, constant support, and willingness to help, this project would never have been possible.

7.2. Discourse data

During my first trip to Nepal in 1987, all of my discourse data were gathererd from the extensive Dolakha Newar community in Kathmandu. Oral narratives were either collected in a one-on-one setting between myself and the speaker or were taped by Kalpana Shrestha. In addition, I collected several written narratives, which Kalpana Shrestha then helped me to fully transcribe and gloss. During my second trip to Nepal, I spent most of my time in Kathmandu. However, I made one trip out to Dolakha in January 1989 during which I recorded as much data as possible. Most of this occurred at Kalpana's ancestral home where she invited people to come for the evening to tell stories. While some of the stories were told by a single speaker in isolation, most of the data collected at this time occurred in a setting with a number of Dolakhae speakers, including a handful of children, so that the stories were addressed more to the others than to the tape recorder. The narratives recorded at this time were either folk stories or personal narratives. One session was dominated by the telling of ghost stories and stories about encounters with tigers in the woods. These stories are in many ways the most interesting since the tape recorders were all but forgotten and the discourse was characterized by the rapid transfer of speakers eager to tell of their own experiences and expressing disbelief at the increasingly tall tales of others. Some conversational data was also collected at this time. Two narratives were collected at the Dolakha primary school. The storytellers were male teachers and the stories were addressed to a large group of children who had gathered for the event. More conversational data was collected during my trip in 1993. These conversations were recorded by Nawa Raj Shrestha; I was not present. In total, I have oral narratives told by 17 different speakers, and conversational data from ten different speakers. Six of the convesational speakers also produced narratives. I also have written narratives produced by four speakers, three of whom also produced oral narratives.

I also have in my corpus a collection of Dolakha songs, collected in part to please myself as well the consultants who enjoyed both the rendition of the songs and the opportunity to hear themselves singing on the tape recorder. The songs are characterized by frequent repetition and relatively simple grammatical structure. They do not exhibit any unique use of grammatical constructions so will not be referred to.

The discussion of Dolakhae grammar will thus draw on both the elicited data and the discourse materials. The discourse materials form the basis for the majority of the analysis. This is preferable since these data illustrate speech from a larger number of speakers and it does not suffer from artificiality that can arise in the elicitation setting. Speakers are also producing the speech naturally and are not becoming confused by the task of translating constructed sentences for a linguist.

Elicited data is very useful, however, especially for investigation of paradigmatic relationships among forms and exploration of less common structures. If an example is not specifically marked as being elicited, it has been taken from connected discourse.

Chapter 2
Segmental phonetics and phonology

1. Introduction

The building blocks of language begin with the sounds. How sounds are produced, how they are perceived, and the physical properties of the sound waves themselves constitute the field of phonetics. The systematic manner in which sounds combine and interact so that they may differentiate meaning is the field of phonology. These two fields, while in principle differentiated by the distinction between the physical and the systematic, are highly interactive. The phonetic properties of sounds significantly determine their phonological behavior. At the same time, phonological patterns produce particular phonetic configurations. This chapter is thus not organized with a strong delineation between phonetics and phonology. Instead, the primary division is between consonants and vowels, and then subtypes within each category. Each section contains phonetic description, phonological distribution, discussion of phonemic status, and phonological behavior. These primary sections are followed by discussions of phonotactics and stress.

2. Consonants

Table 2 lists the consonant phonemes of Dolakha Newar. The phonemes are presented in the orthography used throughout this book. Digraphs formed with *h* indicate aspiration if the preceding letter represents a voiceless sound; they indicate breathy voice if the preceding letter represents a voiced sound. The choice of the subscript dot to indicate the retroflex series of stops follows common practice in South Asia.

There are 28 consonant phones in total. Of these, the three breathy-voice stops exhibit considerable variation and have a questionable status as full phonemes in the language; this is fully discussed in §2.1.1. In addition, [ḍ] and [r] are in fact in complementary distribution; however, there is reason to believe that speakers consider them to be distinct (§2.1.2.3). The remaining consonant phonemes are robust. Evidence of their phonemic status together with phonetic description will be given in the following sections.

Table 2. Consonant phonemes

Bilabial	Dental	Alveolar	Retroflex	Palato-alveolar	Palatal	Velar	Glottal
p	t		ṭ	c		k	
ph	th		ṭh	ch		kh	
b	d		ḍ	j		g	
(bh)	(dh)		(ḍh)	(jh)			
m		n				ŋ	
		s					h
		l	r				
w					y		

2.1. Stops and affricates

The production of stops and affricates entails the complete obstruction of the oral cavity by full contact of the articulators involved. While stops are released to a vowel or glide directly, affricates are released to the position of a fricative before transitioning into the following vowel. In Dolakha Newar, the three palato-alveolar consonants are all affricates. Note that, like the stops, they occur in three primary series, including one voiced element and two voiceless elements. While the two voiceless series of stops are differentiated by aspiration created by a lengthened voice onset time, the two voiceless affricates are differentiated by the length of the fricative phase of the sound. Although the affricates are thus phonetically distinct from the stops, they still follow the same overall phonological patterning.

2.1.1. Aspiration, voice, and breathy voice

Stop consonants occur in three primary series: voiceless unaspirated, voiceless aspirated, and voiced. In addition, a small number of words are variably pronounced with breathy voice.

Voiceless unaspirated stops are characterized by a very brief interval between the time the stop is released by the articulators and the onset of voicing caused by vibration of the vocal cords. This is referred to as "voice onset time." A brief acoustic study of voice onset time in a wordlist produced by two female speakers revealed that the average voice onset time for voiceless unaspirated stops for these Dolakhae speakers is about 17 milliseconds. Voiceless aspirated stops exhibit increased voice onset times. The average voice onset time for aspirated stops in the same acoustic study showed that the average voice onset time for these speakers is approximately 91 milliseconds.

Parallel to the plain and aspirated voiceless stops are the two plain and aspirated voiceless affricates, pronounced in the palato-alveolar region. As affricates, they begin with a stop closure, which is released to the position of a fricative, creating turbulent airflow in the second half of the sound. The distinction between the two voiceless affricates is phonetically realized as a short versus extended period of the fricative phase of the sound. In the same acoustic studies, the two produced an average fricative length of 32 milliseconds for the "unaspirated" fricative and 157 milliseconds for the "aspirated" sound.

The voiced stops and the single voiced affricate are characterized by vibration of the vocal cords during the closure of the stop, prior to the stop's release. The fricative phase of the voiced affricates produced by the same two speakers averaged around 70 milliseconds.

The term "breathy voice" – also called "murmur" by Ladefoged (1993: 144–145) and "whispery voice" by Laver (1994: 198–200) – is used in the phonetics literature to refer to sounds produced with a distinctive shape of the larynx. During regular (or "modal") voicing, the vocal cords are held together with sufficient tension to cause them to vibrate as air is pushed through them from the lungs. Breathy voice is produced by holding together only part of vocal cords, creating partial vibration. Air is allowed to pass unimpeded through the other part. The resulting combination of vibrating and non-vibrating airflow produces the breathy sound that is characteristic of consonants and vowels in many South Asian languages. The Kathmandu dialect of Newar is phonetically remarkable for the presence of extensive breathy voice, which co-occurs not only with stop consonants, but also with nasals and approximants. In Dolakha Newar, breathy voice has been largely lost. There is no evidence of breathy voice occurring with nasals or approximants. I am aware of only a handful of words which have breathy voice occurring with stops. Even these words are not consistently pronounced with breathy phonation, but occur with modal voicing in connected discourse. Native speakers also differ in their identification of words with breathy-voiced consonants. For example, while some speakers claim that the verb *dhon-* 'finish' has a breathy-voiced initial stop, other speakers say *don-*, with a plain voiced stop, is correct. For those speakers that have breathy voice, it appears to be distinctive, but only for a handful of words. In addition, the distinction is neutralized in rapid speech.

In line with the variation in production of breathy-voice articulation across speakers and across speech events is evidence that the lack of breathy voice may be transferred to Dolakhae speakers' production of Nepali. One native speaker of Dolakhae, Miss Indu Pradhan, pointed out to me that older speakers of Dolakha Newar pronounce Nepali breathy-voiced stops with modal voicing. For examples, some Dolakhae speakers pronounce the Nepali word *ghar* 'house' as *gar*. Similar observations have been made by Ms. Uma Pradhan in her 2003 MA thesis on the pronunciation of Nepali by Dolakha Newar school children. It is possible that the degree of bilingualism and literacy in Nepali attained by the younger generations of Dolakha Newars is serving to bolster the category of breathy voice in Dolakhae, as Nepali also has a breathy-voiced category of stop phonemes. This may explain the age-graded differences in the production of breathy voice: fully educated speakers literate in the Devanagari alphabet appear to have greater awareness of the phonemic distinction but still produce it variably. Some older speakers and preliterate children have not been sensitized to the distinction through the writing system and so do not produce it. A fuller study of the phenomenon of breathy voice in Dolakhae, including its acoustic correlates and variation across speakers, speech events, and genres, is clearly warranted.

2.1.2. Place of articulation

Having discussed the stops and affricates in relation to aspiration and voicing, we now turn to place of articulation. Stops are pronounced at four distinct places of articulation: bilabial, dental, retroflex and velar. Affricates are pronounced only at the palato-alveolar place of articulation.

2.1.2.1. Bilabial stops

There are three robust bilabial stop phonemes in this language: /p, ph, b/. Their phonemic status is established by the following minimal set:

(1) *pir-ju*   'wait'-3sPST
     phir-ju   'put on clothes'-3sPST
     bir-ju   'give'-3sPST

In addition to these three phonemes, there are also a few words which are pronounced by some speakers with breathy-voiced bilabial stops, e.g. *bhõr* 'paper', *bhū̃ī* 'ground', and *bho* 'plate'. As the number of words with this sound is limited and younger speakers tend not to pronounce it at all, the status of the phoneme /bh/ is marginal.

The aspirated bilabial stop /ph/ is pronounced as a labio-dental fricative [f] between vowels. Examples include *tuphi* 'broom', phonetically ['tufi], and *ma-pha-u* 'ill' [NEG-able-NR1], phonetically [mʌ'fʌu]. The aspirated stop and the labio-dental fricative [f] are in free variation word-initially, e.g. *phon-ju* [ask-3sPST] may be pronounced ['phwɔn-dʒwu] or ['fɔn-dʒu].

2.1.2.2. Dental stops

There are three robust dental stop phonemes. All are produced with the tip of the tongue pressed against the juncture of the upper teeth and the alveolar ridge. The phonemic status of the three stops is established by the following minimal pairs:

(2) tār-ju   'hear'-3sPST
    thār-ju   'weave'-3sPST

(3) ta-en   'put'-PART
    da-en   'exist'-PART

(4) thari   'variety'
    dari   'yogurt'

In addition, there are a few words with breathy-voiced dental stops, e.g. *dhū* 'tiger' and the verb *dhon-* 'finish'. The breathy voice, especially in the common word *dhon-,* is observed only in careful pronunciation.

2.1.2.3. Retroflex stops

Retroflex stops are pronounced with the tip of tongue making contact with the post-alveolar region of the vocal tract. Unlike some languages, retroflex consonants in Dolakhae generally do not produce a strong "r-coloring" on surrounding sounds.

The phonemic status of the retroflex stops is established by the following minimal set:

(5) ṭin-gi   'discard'-1sPST
    ṭhin-gi   'cause to sleep'-1sPST
    ḍin-gi   'sleep'-1sPST

The voiced retroflex stop is in near complementary distribution with the central approximant /r/. The voiced stop only occurs in word-initial position. By contrast, in native Newar vocabulary, the approximant only occurs following a vowel. The examples in (6) and (7) illustrate this pattern.

(6) ḍen- 'cut'
    ḍin- 'sleep'
    ḍon- 'stand'
    ḍār- 'beat'
    ḍwāku 'big'
    ḍusi 'millet'
    ḍur- 'drag'

(7) sara 'horse'
    bur-gi 'give birth'-1sPST
    turi 'mustard'
    cher 'head'
    nibār 'sun'
    dari 'yogurt'
    gār 'wound'
    gōgar 'rooster'

Despite the prevalence of this basic pattern of complementary distribution, there is evidence to suggest that /ḍ/ and /r/ are distinct phonemes. First, /ḍ/ does not change to /r/ when it is put in post-vocalic position by prefixation. Thus when the verb ḍin-gi 'I slept' is negated, it produces ma-ḍin-gi with a clearly pronounced stop rather than *ma-rin-gi with /r/. Second, the Nepali language does make a clear phonemic distinction between /r/ and /ḍ/ (e.g. rālo 'clapper (of bell)' vs. ḍālo 'basket for storing rice'; rām (proper name) vs. ḍām 'scar, mark'), so when Nepali words are borrowed into Dolakhae, the original pattern of complementary distribution is obscured. Words like rājā 'king' and rānī 'queen' are common Dolakhae vocabulary items. Third, the Devanagari alphabet, which is used to write both Nepali and Newar, has different letters for /r/ (र) and /ḍ/ (ड). As Dolakhae children are educated, they are taught to differentiate these two sounds. For these reasons, it appears that most speakers of Dolakhae are conscious of a distinction between /ḍ/ and /r/. They will thus be treated as separate phonemes in this grammar.[15]

It should be noted, however, that the phonemicization of /r/ and /ḍ/ appears to be a relatively recent phenomenon, and that older speakers may not differentiate between them. This assertion is based on an observation made to me by Miss Indu Pradhan of Dolakha. She has noticed that older speakers in Dolakha pronounce Nepali words beginning with /r/ with voiced retroflex stops, e.g. /ḍāni/ and /ḍājā/ in place of /rāni/ 'queen' and /rājā/ 'king'. This behavior is in line with a phonological system that treats [ḍ] and [r] as allophones of a single phoneme, the stop being found in word-initial position. It is clear that this behavior is not found with younger speakers of the language. The influence of

Nepali has effectively established a phonemic distinction between sounds which were previously allophones.

The breathy-voiced retroflex stop is attested in careful pronunciation of the word *ḍhōr* 'jackal'.

2.1.2.4. Palato-alveolar affricates

The palato-alveolar affricates are produced by the blade of the tongue producing an alveolar stop, and then release of the stop to the position of a fricative in the post-alveolar region. There are three robust palato-alveolar affricates: /c/, /ch/, and /j/, which would be represented as [tʃ], [tʃ:], and [dʒ] respectively in the International Phonetic Alphabet. As mentioned above, the voice onset time difference evident in the voiceless affricates is realized as shorter versus greater length of the fricative phase of the sound. The phonemic status of these three affricates can be found in the following minimal set:

(8)   ci   [tʃi]   'salt'
        chi   [tʃ:i]   'you'
        ji   [dʒi]   'I'

The only example of a breathy-voiced /jh/ in my lexical data set is *jhyālā* 'window'. This is clearly derived from the Nepali form *jhyāl*.

The affricates may be phonetically realized as simple fricatives in connected speech. This is especially likely to happen directly after liquids, e.g. /tār-ju/ [listen 3sPST] '(s/he) listened' may be pronounced ['tar-ʒu].

2.1.2.5. Velar stops

The velar stops are produced with the back of the tongue making contact with the velum. The phonemic status of these stops is established in the following minimal pairs:

(9)   kīja   'younger brother'
        gīja   'gums'

(10)   kār-gi   'take'-1sPST
        khār-gi   'pick'-1sPST

(11)   goi   'nut'
        kho-i   'see'-1FUT

When velar stops are pronounced before a front vowel or the glide /y/, the tongue is fronted, resulting in a palatal articulation. Examples are given in standard orthography and International Phonetic Alphabet in (12):

(12) khi   [chi]   'feces'
     kē   [cẽ]   'lentils'
     gyāt-ki   ['ɟjat-ci]   'frighten'-1sPST

2.1.2.6. Phonemic contrasts across places of articulation

The minimal pairs presented so far have established the phonemic contrasts across the stops pronounced at each place of articulation. The following minimal sets establish the phonemic contrasts across places of articulation:

(13) Bilabial, dental, and velar
     phār-gi   'cover'-1sPST
     thār-gi   'weave'-1sPST
     khār-gi   'pick'-1sPST

(14) Dental and retroflex
     tār-gi   'hear'-1sPST
     ṭār-gi   'fix'-1sPST
     thon-gi   'drink'-1sPST
     ṭhon-gi   'wake someone up'-1sPST
     da-en   'exist'-PART
     ḍa-en   'fall over'-PART

(15) Dental, palato-alveolar, and velar
     thi   'one'
     chi   'you'
     khi   'feces'

(16) Retroflex and palato-alveolar
     ṭhor-gi   'take apart'-1sPST
     chor-gi   'send'-1sPST

2.2. Fricatives

There are only two fricative phonemes in Dolakhae: /s/ and /h/. Their phonemic independence is established by the following minimal pairs:

(17)   si   'louse'
       hi   'blood'
       sor-   'watch'
       hor-   'bloom'

The phoneme /s/ is a voiceless apico-alveolar fricative, produced by the tip of the tongue coming close enough to the alveolar ridge to produce strident turbulent airflow.

The phoneme /h/ is phonetically a breathy-voiced glottal fricative, produced by a configuration of the glottis that allows for some voicing and some unimpeded airflow. In the International Phonetic Alphabet, this sound is represented by the symbol [ɦ]. Speakers vary in the degree of audible breathiness of this fricative. There is no phonemic contrast with a voiceless glottal fricative [h] in Dolakhae.

2.3. Nasals

There are three nasal consonants, pronounced at the bilabial, alveolar, and velar places of articulation. Their phonemic status may be established by the following minimal set:

(18)   mā   'mother'
       nā   'odor'
       ŋā   'fish'

The phoneme /ŋ/ has slightly restricted distribution. In syllable-initial position, it does not appear to precede the vowels /o/ or /u/, or the glide /w/. It may occur with all other vowels and the glide /y/, as exemplified by the verb stems in (19):

(19)   ŋil-gi   'smile; laugh'-1sPST
       ŋen-gi   'listen'-1sPST
       ŋār-gi   'bite'-1sPST
       ŋat-ki   'discard'-1sPST
       ŋyāt-ki   'buy'-1sPST

The phoneme is not restricted in syllable-final position; it can follow vowels of any type, as shown in (20):

(20) biŋkeŋ 'very; many; much'
 pāŋ 'fruit'
 luŋmā 'mortar, flat'
 toŋ 'drink(IMP)'
 naŋsir 'cuticle'

As with the velar stops, there is palatalization of the velar nasal before front vowels and the glide /y/. The nasal in this position is still produced with the back of the tongue, but the position is considerably fronted and there is a palatal off-glide:

(21) ŋil-gi ['ŋʲɪl-gi] 'smile'-1sPST
 ŋen-gi ['ŋʲɛn-gi] 'listen'-1sPST
 ŋyāt-ki ['ŋʲat-ki] 'buy'-1sPST

2.4. Approximants

There are four approximants in Dolakhae; two are liquids, /r/ and /l/, and two are glides, /y/ and /w/.

The liquid /l/ is a voiced alveolar lateral, with little if any allophonic variation. The phonemic distinctions between /l/ and /r/, /l/ and /n/, and /l/ and /ḍ/ can be established by the following minimal pairs:

(22) hir-gi 'wash'-1sPST
 hil-gi 'trade'-1sPST

(23) lā 'month'
 nā 'odor'

(24) lār-gi 'tell'-1sPST
 ḍār-gi 'beat'-1sPST

Note that /l/ will not contrast with /r/ word-initially in native Dolakhae vocabulary, as /r/ does not occur in this position; see §2.1.2.3.

The liquid /r/ has two significantly different allophones. In syllable-initial position, /r/ is phonetically realized as a voiced tap. This sound is produced by a ballistic movement which raises the tip of the tongue to briefly make contact with the post-alveolar region. This results in a tapped "r-like" sound being produced.

There is some variation in the phonetic realization of the phoneme /r/ in syllable-final position. Some speakers produce a light post-alveolar trill. Others produce a central approximant. Some pronunciations appear to be a combination of the two, beginning as a weak trill or single tap and ending with an approximant. All of these pronunciations differ from the simple tap found in syllable-initial position in having an increased duration and a regular wave form.

The glides /w/ and /y/ are bilabial and palatal central approximants respectively. As glides they are transitional sounds, characterized by movement of the articulators. The palatal glide begins with the tongue high and fronted as for the vowel /i/. The bilabial glide begins with tongue high and back and with lips rounded, as for the vowel /u/. Both glides involve transition to the articulation of the following vowel.

The distributions of both glides are intimately related to the allophonic realizations of the mid vowels (see §2.3.2) so will not be fully discussed here. The phonemic contrast between /w/ and /y/ can be established by the following minimal pairs:

(25)   wā   'rain'
         yā   'rice, unhusked'
         gwār   'shelter for animals'
         gyār   'fear'

2.5. Phonological processes affecting consonants

There are only a handful of phonological processes that affect the pronunciation of consonant segments. Processes that affect consonants at only a single place of articulation were discussed above (e.g. spirantization of /ph/ to [f]). Three other phonological processes which affect a variety of consonants are labialization, gemination, and deletion leading to syllable reduction.

2.5.1. Labialization

Consonants preceding the round vowels, /u/ and /o/, and the glide /w/ are pronounced with co-articulated lip rounding. The most dramatic effect of this process is on the bilabial stops and nasal, as the lip rounding on these segments is especially pronounced and the precise position of the bilabial closure is altered. Thus bon-gi [read-1sPST] is pronounced [ˈbʷɔn-gi] with closure being made with the slightly inner portion of the lips. Similarly, bū 'field' is pronounced [bʷū], again with an inner biliablial closure. Labialization, while not strongly audible, can be noticed visually with any of the other consonants, e.g. duku 'goat' [dʷukʷu].

2.5.2. Gemination

Gemination (consonant lengthening) is lexical, phonological, and morphological in this language. Lexical gemination, where all instrances of a word are consistently pronounced with a geminate consonant, is relatively rare. Examples of words with lexical geminate consonants are given in (26):

(26) halli   'turmeric'
     bittā   'wall'
     chākkal   'noon'
     dyāmma   'thick' (of clouds)
     sojjā   'porridge'
     hātta   'why'
     tākku   'time'

It is possible that some of these words came by their gemination through phonological or morphological processes followed by lexicalization.

Phonological gemination results from the full regressive assimilation of one consonant to the preceding consonant. The process is not obligatory; pronunciations both with and without the regressive gemination may be observed. Some speakers strongly prefer the non-geminate forms:

(27) butni   bunni   'sack'
     gatke   gakke   'extremely'
     bwāt-ker-ju   bwāk-ker-ju   'run'-CAUS-3sPST

Morphological gemination is a productive derivational process that results in an intensification of the meaning of a word:

(28) nulu   'new'   nullu   'brand new'
     yeku   'many'   yekku   'so many'
     guli   'how many'   gulli   'so many'
     ḍwāku   'big'   ḍwākku: 'very big'
     dāti   'middle'   dātti   'right in the middle'

In some cases this process has given rise to lexicalization of a particular extension of the meaning of the original word. Some common examples are *littaŋ* 'again', which derives from *litaŋ* 'next', *nicchi* 'all day' from *nichi* 'one day', *cacchi* 'all night' from *cachi* 'one night', and *nakka* 'just now' from *naka* 'new'. Thus morphological gemination results in new examples of lexical gemination.

2.5.3. Deletion leading to syllable reduction

In rapid speech, there is extensive phonetic accommodation resulting in the reduction and deletion of syllables. There are a number of processes which are involved in this accomodation. One of the most striking is the deletion of intervocalic consonants. This process is most commonly found with velar consonants, but other consonants may be deleted if the speech is very rapid.

Deletion of the consonant results in two vowels coming together. These vowels may then form diphthongs, be in hiatus, shorten, or one may become a glide; they follow the regular phonological processes for vowels discussed in §2.3.4. Note that syllable reduction does not interact with the assignment of lexical stress, which will be on the phonetically initial syllable.

Examples of deletion leading to syllable reduction are presented in (29). Note that when a nasal consonant deletes, the nasalization is realized on the preceding vowel.

(29) sāŋat   sā̃at   'friend'
      gunān   gwān   'who(ERG)'
      ināgu   ināu   'this type'
      ju-e-lāgin   ju-e-lāin   'become'-NR2-'because'
      haŋ-an   hā(n)   'say'-PART
      chuŋ-a   chūwa   'cook'-NR2

3. Vowels

There are six basic vowel phonemes in Dolakha Newar. All six may occur contrastively nasalized. These phonemes are given in Table 3. The phonetic values of each vowel are described below.

Table 3. Vowel phonemes

	Plain		Nasalized	
	Front	Back	Front	Back
High	i	u	ĩ	ū̃
Mid	e	o	ẽ	õ
Low	ā	a	ā̃	ã

The following minimal sets establish the phonemic independence of the oral vowels:

(30) /i/ versus /u/
      ti   'broth'
      tu   'dandruff'

(31) /i/ versus /e/, /ā/, and /o/
      mi   'man'
      me   'tongue'
      mā   'mother'
      mo   'chaff'

(32) /i/ versus /a/
      bini   'niece'
      bina   'nephew'

(33) /e/ versus /u/
      depān   'on; top'
      dupān   'inside'

(34) /e/ versus /a/
      ler-gi   'choose'-1sPST
      lar-gi   'cut grass'-1sPST

(35) /ā/ versus /u/
      āpen   'those'
      upen   'these'

(36) /ā/ versus /a/
      nās   'nose'
      nas   'seven'

(37) /a/ versus /o/
      ṭhar-gi   'sow'-1sPST
      ṭhor-gi   'break down'-1sPST

(38) /a/ versus /u/
      gan   'hammer'
      gun   'who'

(39) /o/ versus /u/
      kho   'river'
      khu   'thief'; 'six'

The following minimal pairs establish the phonemic independence of each pair of oral and nasal vowels:

(40) /i/ versus /ĩ/
      si   'louse'
      sĩ   'wood'

(41) /e/ versus /ẽ/
      pe   'four'
      pẽ   'leech'

(42) /a/ versus /ã/
      phasi   'sheep'
      phãsi   'jackfruit'

(43) /ā/ versus /ā̃/
      sā   'cow'
      sā̃   'hair'

(44) /o/ versus /õ/
      bo   'plate'
      b(h)õ   'ground; floor'

(45) /u/ versus /ū/
      chu   'cook'
      chū   'mouse'

It should be noted that nasalized vowels cannot be analyzed as derivative of oral vowels followed by nasal stops, which occur independently in the language. The following pairs illustrate this distinction:

(46) kū   'smoke'   jukun   'only'
      khã   'talk; conversation'   likhan   'behind'
      kōsa   'bone'   onsā-mi   'man'
      sā̃   'hair'   sā=n   'cow'=ERG
      thẽ   'like'   then-ju   'arrive'-3sPST
      chẽ   'house'   chen-ju   'comb'-3sPST

3.1. High vowels

The two high vowels, /i/ and /ɯ/, represent the high front unrounded and high back rounded vowels that are found in most languages. The vowel /i/ may be pronounced with a slightly lower, centralized pronunciation in closed syllables, as illustrated in (47). This lax pronunciation is less likely before the nasal /n/.

(47) jimŋā   [ˈdʒɪmŋā]   'fifteen'
      kitke tar-ju [ˈkɪtke ˈtɑr-ʒu]   'put against'-3sPST
      chipsin   [ˈtʃɪpsɪn] ~ [ˈtʃɪpsin] 2pERG
      ninmā   [ˈnɪnma] ~ [ˈninma]   'mother-in-law'
      ānthiŋ   [ˈantʰɪŋ]   'in that manner'

In open syllables, /i/ is pronounced in the periphery of the vowel space, producing an articulation commonly described as "tense".

The vowel /ɯ/ is also a peripheral "tense" vowel. It also may occur with a lower and more centralized pronunciation. The environments where this occurs are more restricted than with /i/, comprising syllables closed with an oral stop or /r/, e.g. /butni/ [ˈbʊtni] 'sack', /tapuk/ [ˈtʌpʊk] 'gun', /kalgur/ [kɑlgʊr] 'pea'.

3.2. Mid vowels

The mid front unrounded vowel /e/ is pronounced as a more centralized "lax" vowel when in a closed syllable or followed by /ɯ/. It has a more peripheral pronunciation in syllable-final position, or when followed by /i/. This distribution is illustrated in (48):

(48) me   [me]   'other'
      thē   [tʰē]   'like'
      āpen   [ˈapɛn]   'they'
      cher   [tʃɛr]   'head'

Before the vowel /i/, the phoneme /e/ is pronounced as [e]. However, before the vowel /ɯ/, the phoneme /e/ is pronounced as [ɛ] or [ə]:

(49) ye-i   [jei]   'come'-INF
      ye-u   [jɛu] ~[jəu]   'come'-NR1

The phoneme /e/ may be alternately pronounced as [jʌ] before syllable-final /ŋ/. This is very commonly found in the copula, which may be pronounced either as [khɛŋ] or [khjʌŋ] (or [khjə̄ū]). Another example comes from a recorded narrative. There is an emphatic construction which involves reduplicating the verb stem, suffixing it with /ŋ/, and placing it before the regularly inflected verb. When verb *yer-* 'come' reduplicates by this strategy, the stem is realized as [jʌŋ]:

(50)   ani   yā   bu-en   ya-ŋ   yer-gi
       then unhusked.rice   carry-PART   come-REDUP   come-1sPST

   'Then picking up the rice I came.'

There is a complex relationship between the glide /y/ and the vowel /e/. There is no phonemic distinction made between the sequence [je], which commences with the glide, and the simple vowel [e], which occurs without it. In word-initial position, [je] and [e] are in free variation, although particular speakers seem to favor one pronunciation or the other, and some speakers consistently pronounce the glide:

(51)   yer-gi   ['jɛr-gi] ~ ['ɛr-gi]   'come'-1sPST
       yelpanuŋ   ['jɛlpanuŋ] ~ ['ɛlpanuŋ]   'always'
       yeku   ['jɛkku] ~ ['ɛkku]   'many'
       yẽsa   ['jẽsa] ~ [ẽsa]   'sickle'

When a verb stem beginning with *ye-* is prefixed by one of the language's three prefixes, the glide is necessarily present, e.g. [məˈjɛtku] *ma-yet-ku* [NEG-do-1pPST] 'we didn't do (something)'.

When the syllable is closed by a high vowel, the glide is necessarily present:

(52)   ye-i   ['je-i]   'come'-1FUT
       ye-u   [jɛu] ~ [jəu]   'come'-NR1

The allophones [je] and [e] are also not distinguished following consonants. Instead, the presence of the off-glide is predictable. It occurs only after velar consonants, triggering palatalization (as discussed in §2.1.2.5). We find [je] after velars and [e] after all other consonants:

(53)   ŋen-ju   ['ŋʲɛn-dʒu]   'ask'-3sPST
       ken-ju   ['cʲɛn-dʒu]   'show'-3sPST
       ger   [ɟʲɛr]   'ghee'
       khẽja   ['cʰʲẽʒa]   'egg'
       belcā   ['bɛltʃa]   'rolling pin'

chẽ	[tʃʰē]	'house'
depān	[ˈdepan]	'top; above'
sel	[sɛl]	'marrow'

Thus we find that the glide-vowel sequence [je] and the simple vowel [e] are partially in complementary distribution and partially in free variation. These are clearly allophones of a single phoneme. The question remains as to how to represent this phoneme orthographically. Choosing to use either allophone exclusively results in a phonetically opaque transcription. If /ye/ is chosen, it entails the writing of a glide in many words where none is ever found, especially in the post-consonantal environment. On the other hand, choosing to represent the phoneme as /e/ ignores the phonetic presence of the glide in many pronunciations of the phoneme word-initially. I have therefore decided to represent this single phoneme in two ways orthographically: as /e/ in post-consonantal environments and as /ye/ word-initially.

The mid back rounded vowel /o/ also has complex allophonic realizations involving a glide. Once again, we find inter-speaker variation in this regard. For some speakers, the distribution of allophones is quite straightforward, with [wɔ] occurring in word-initial position and after prefixes and [o] elsewhere, as illustrated in (54):

(54)	*on-a*	[ˈwɔn-ə]	'go'-3sPST
	mo-õ	[moˈwo]	NEG-'go'
	oho	[ˈwɔho]	'silver'
	b(h)õ	[bõ]	'ground; floor'
	ḍon-a	[ˈḍon-ə]	'stand'-3sPST

For other speakers, a labial glide is audible following bilabial consonants. The vowel varies from [o] to [ɔ]:

(55)	*phon-ju*	[ˈpʰwon-dʒu] ~ [ˈpʰwɔn-dʒu]	'beg'-3sPST
	bho	[bwo̦] ~ [bwɔ̦]	'plate'
	b(h)õ	[bwõ] ~ [bwɔ̃]	'ground; floor'
	bon-ju	[ˈbwon-dʒu] ~ [ˈbwɔn-dʒu]	'read'-3sPST

The labial glide is also sometimes present after velars, especially if the /o/ is followed by a consonant. This appears to be free variation:

(56) gōgar   ['gōgər] ~ ['gʷōgər] ~ ['gʷɔ̄gər]   'rooster'
      khosu   ['khosu] ~ ['khwosu] ~ ['khwɔsu]   'cloud; fog'
      khon-gi   ['kʰon-gi] ~ ['kʰwon-gi] ~ ['kʰwɔn-gi] 'see'-1sPST
      kho-eu   ['kho-yɛu] ~ ['khwo-yɛu] ~ ['khwɔ-yɛu] 'cry'-3sFUT

The realization of /o/ in word-initial position depends on what precedes it. If it is pronounced in isolation, /o/ is preceded by a glottal stop. If it is preceded by a consonant, /o/ is realized as [wɔ]. If it is preceded by a vowel, /o/ is realized as [o] and the juncture is one of hiatus:

(57) oho   ['ʔoho]   'silver'
      ām oho   [am 'wɔho]   'that silver'
      āme oho   ['ame 'oho]   'his silver'

As with the vowel /e/, we find that /o/ has a number of allophones, some of which are predictable and some of which are not. It is clear that we find no evidence of contrast between any of the allophones, and hence that the phonetic realizations [o], [wɔ], [wo] are subsumed under a single phoneme.

It should also be noted that the phonemic sequence /wa/ never occurs in this language. Thus it is reasonable to ask whether /o/ should be considered to be derivative of /wa/. There are two reasons why this analysis is problematic. First, when we examine the structure of non-initial syllables, we see that, while rare, it is possible for the second syllable of a polysyllabic word to begin with a cluster. The second member of the cluster may only be /r/:

(58) tiŋgriŋga   'tall, skinny'
      tupri   'topi' (type of Nepalese hat)
      thuprā   'many'

If the phoneme /o/ were to be represented as /wa/, then the simple description of non-initial clusters would no longer be possible. Instead, one would have to allow for three-member onsets, but only when the third member was /w/ and the vowel was /a/, e.g. thwathrwa 'old'. The representation thothro allows for the simpler generalization as well as a phonetic transparency.

Regarding the orthographic representation of this phoneme, the allophone /o/ is phonetically the most common. It occurs most frequently in post-consonantal environments. While some speakers consistently pronounce /o/ with a glide in word-initial contexts, others leave the glide off entirely, and strikingly have a glottal stop. As glottal stop does not function as a consonant in this language, its presence seems to emphasize the vocalic and "glideless" nature of the initial segment. For this reason, the phoneme /o/ in word-initial environments is represented as /o/ and not /wo/.

3.3. Low vowels

There are two low vowel phonemes in Dolakha Newar: /a/ and /ā/. The orthographic representation follows standard practice of transliteration of the Devanagari alphabet. The Devanagari symbol अ, used for the low, back vowel, is commonly transliterated a, while the symbol आ, used for the low, central vowel, is commonly transliterated ā. These two Devanagari characters are employed to represent the two low vowels when writing Newar. Using the standard transliteration equivalents here gives the advantage of allowing comparability when forms are compared across dialects of Newar or with other languages of Nepal and South Asia.

The phoneme /ā/ is a low central vowel equivalent to that transcribed by [a] in the International Phonetic Alphabet. It is quite robust and tends to be a bit longer in duration than the other vowels in the inventory. This vowel is often fronted before syllable-final coronal consonants:

(59) sanyāl ['sənyæl] 'evening'
 hātta ['hætta] 'why'
 ānthiŋ ['ænthɪŋ] 'in that manner'
 ma-ŋyāt ['maɲʲat] NEG-'buy'
 lyās-misā ['lyæsmisa] 'young woman'

The phoneme /a/ is much more variable, with phonetic allophones. The following observations are made on the basis of recordings of a wordlist by two female native speakers. For both speakers, the basic allophone is slightly higher and more centralized than [ɑ]; to my ear it sounds about halfway between that vowel and [ə]. This sound occurs consistently in word-final environments:

(60) duta ['dutɑ] 'into'
 gunta ['guntɑ] 3s-DAT
 thoṭa ['tʰoṭɑ] 'stairway'
 sona ['sonɑ] 'flower'
 ḍon-a ['ḍon-ɑ] 'stand'-3sPST
 tinmut-a ['tɪnmut-ɑ] 'jump'-3sPST

The basic allophone also occurs before /r/ for both speakers, regardless of whether the following /r/ follows a syllable boundary or is syllable-final:

(61) tar-ju   ['tar-ʒu]   'put'-3sPST
    nugar   ['nugɑr]   'heart'
    gōgar   ['gōgɑr]   'rooster'
    sarchi   ['sartʃʰi]   'one hundred'
    dari   ['dɑri]   'yogurt'

Both speakers pronounce the vowel as rounded after labial consonants. This sounds like a more centralized version of the vowel [ɒ] as represented in the International Phonetic Alphabet.

(62) pamṭu   ['pɒmṭu]   'wing'
    suba   ['subɒ]   'mortar'
    baji   ['bɒdʒi]   'beaten rice'
    paksin   ['pɒksin]   'witch'

Both speakers pronounce the phoneme as [ə] before syllable-final dental and alveolar consonants, as in the following words:

(63) sijal   ['sidʒəl]   'copper'
    turkan   ['turkən]   'mustard'
    sanyāl   ['sənyæl]   'evening'
    jāŋal   ['dʒaŋəl]   'bird'
    bākhan   ['bakʰən]   'story'
    sāŋat   ['saŋət]   'friend'
    bã̄laske   [bāləske]   'beautifully; well'
    gatke   ['gətke]   'very'
    chanta   ['tʃəntɑ]   2sDAT

One speaker had some exceptions to this pattern, e.g. *mukan* 'mushroom' is [mukan], which contrasts with the [ə] in the final syllable of *turkan* 'mustard'.

One speaker has a more general environment for [ə], producing it before other syllable-final consonants (but never before /r/):

(64) nakka   ['nəkka]   'just now'
    khapṭu   ['khəpṭu]   'back' (body part)

She also produces the allophone [ə] in most non-initial open syllables of polysyllabic words:

(65) yelpanuŋ   ['jɛlpənuŋ]   'always'
    caṭan   ['tʃəṭən]   'spoon'
    sakhi   ['səkʰi]   'dung'
    chana   ['tʃəna]   2sGEN
    ma-ŋyāt   ['mə-ŋyat]   NEG-'buy'
    na-eu   ['nəyəu]   'eat'-3sFUT

The other speaker generally has [ɑ] in word-internal open syllables, although one exceptional word is *chana* ['tʃəna], the second-person-genitive pronoun, a highly frequent lexical item.

3.4. Vowels in sequence

There are six possible sequences of vowels which can occur within a single syllable in monomorphemic words. However, the number of monomorphemic words containing these sequences is quite small, especially those with initial mid vowels. These sequences are exemplified in (66):

(66) Sequences within a single syllable in monomorphemic words
      /eu/   jeu   'maybe'
      /oi/   kōisa   'knife held with foot'
      /āi/   ṭhā̃ī   'place'
              nāi   'butcher caste'
      /āu/   āu   'now'
              chāuri   'animal young'
      /ai/   kaimu   'husband'
              upāī   'this size'
      /au/   thau   REFL
              caukos   'door frame'

It is also possible for the sequences /āe/ and /ae/ to occur within a single morpheme. However, these vowels are pronounced in hiatus; they each comprise a separate syllable without an intervening glide:

(67) Sequences across syllables in monomorphemic words
      /ae/   kae   'son'
              chae   'grandchild'
              thae   2HON

/āe/ ṭāen 'far'
twāer-a 'become white'-3sPST

We can summarize the pattern by saying that low and mid vowels may be followed by a high vowel within a syllable. Low vowels may also be followed by /e/, but the sequence is then disyllabic, with the vowels pronounced in hiatus.

While the number of monomorphemic words containing vowel sequences is quite small, the number of polymorphemic words containing vowel sequences is very large. Virtually all n-stem and r-stem verb paradigms involve multiple instances of vowel-final stems taking vowel-initial suffixes. In particular, the infinitive suffix -i and the two nominalizers -u and -e may suffix to stems ending with any of the six vowel phonemes. Similarly, the genitive casemarker =e freely cliticizes to words ending with all six vowel phonemes. These are the only three affixes which are vowel initial. There are no vocalic sequences where the second element is /o/, /a/, or /ā/.

When suffixes beginning with /i/, /u/, and /e/ combine with the six vowel phonemes, the result is a set of interesting phonological processes which create a range of phonetic realizations.

3.4.1. Shortening of identical high vowels

When two identical high vowels are brought together across a morpheme boundary, a single vowel of normal length is produced. As Dolakhae does not have phonemic vowel length, this behavior is in line with the phonotactic patterns of the language:

(68) Shortening of identical high vowels in sequence
    bi-i   [bi]   'give' (INF)
    ṭhī-i   [ṭʰi]   'put to sleep' (INF)
    si-i   [si]   'die' (INF)
    bu-u   [bu]   'carry' (NR1)
    chu-u   [tʃʰu]   'cook' (NR1)

3.4.2. Vowels in hiatus before /e/

When a morpheme of the form -e is bound to a stem ending in the vowel /e/, the two vowels are syllabified into two separate syllables with two distinct beats. There is a clear drop in pitch on the second syllable. In the following examples, periods are used to represent syllable boundaries:

(69) Sequences of /e/ in hiatus; open final syllable
  ye-e   [ˈje.e]   'come'-NR2
  twāle=e   [ˈtwa.le.e]   'neighbor'=GEN
  me-e   [ˈme.e]   'tongue'=GEN
  dake=e   [ˈdɑ.ke.e]   'make'-NR2

An interesting form is *chae=e* 'of the grandchild', which is pronounced as trisyllabic with three distinct beats in careful speech: [ˈtʃa.e.e].

A slightly different pattern emerges when the third-person-singular future suffix *-eu* or the participial suffix *-en* are suffixed to a verb stem ending in /e/. Here the result is again a disyllabic sequence of two distinct beats, but this time the second vowel, being in a closed syllable, has a distinctly centralized "lax" pronunciation. Some gliding of the tongue from one vowel position to the other is audible, but it falls short of constituting a full glide /y/:

(70) Sequences of /e/ in hiatus; closed final syllable
  ye-en   [ˈje.ɛn]   'come'-PART
  ye-eu   [ˈje.ɛu]   'come'-3sFUT
  dake-en   [ˈdɑke.ɛn]   'make'-PART
  dake-eu   [ˈdɑ.ke.ɛu]   'make'-3sFUT

When a suffix beginning with /e/ is bound to a stem ending in a low vowel, the resulting sequence is either two vowels in hiatus, or the insertion of a transient palatal glide, not as strong as a full instance of the phoneme /y/:

(71) Sequences of low vowels plus /e/
  khēja-e   [ˈcʰʲẽ.ʒa.e] ~[ˈcʰʲẽ.ʒa.ʲe]   'egg'-GEN
  na-eu   [ˈnɑ.ɛu] ~[ˈnɑ.ʲɛu]   'eat'-3sFUT
  khicā-e   [cʰʲi.tʃa.e] ~[cʰʲi.tʃa.ʲe]   'dog'-GEN
  tā-eu   [ta.ɛu] ~ [ta.ʲɛu]   'hear'-3sFUT

3.4.3. *Glide insertion before /e/*

When a suffix beginning with the phoneme /e/ is bound to to a high vowel, the result is a disyllabic sequence with an inserted glide:

(72)   Palatal glide insertion between high vowels and /e/
       bi-eu   ['bi.jɛu]   'give'-3sFUT
       khu-eu   ['kʰu.jɛu]   'steal'-3sFUT
       kisi-e   ['cʲi.si.je]   'elephant'-GEN
       cakku-e   [tʃak.ku.je]   'knife'-GEN

When the preceding vowel is /o/, a labial glide [w] is inserted before the suffixes *-e, -eŋ* and *-en*. In rapid speech, the /o/ deletes and the form reduces to a single syllable:

(73)   Labial glide insertion between /o/ and most suffixes with /e/
       kho-e   ['kʰo.we]~[kʰwe]   'river'-GEN
       khõ-eŋ   ['kʰõ.wɛŋ] ~[kʰwɛ̃ŋ]   'see'-3sFUT
       so-en   ['so.wɛn] ~ [swɛn]   'watch'-PART

In the r-stem conjugation class, the 3s future suffix is *-eu* as opposed to *-eŋ*. When this suffix is added to a verb stem ending in /o/, /w/ is not inserted, and we find instead a transient palatal glide /y/, e.g. *kho-eu* 'cry-3sFUT' ['kho.jɛu]. Also unlike the previous examples is the fact that forms with this shape never reduce to a single syllable. I believe this different behavior is due to the rounded nature of the final /u/ in the suffix. The sequence /weu/ is not attested in the language to my knowledge.

3.4.4. Glide formation before high vowels

When a high vowel is suffixed to a non-identical high vowel, the first vowel is realized as a glide and the sequence is monosyllabic. If the stem vowel is nasalized, the nasalization is transferred to the suffix vowel, which functions as the syllable nucleus:

(74)   Glide formation of high vowels
       bi-u   [bju]   'give'-NR1
       dĩ-u   [djũ]   'sleep'-NR1
       khu-i   [kʰwi]   'steal'-INF
       khũ-i   [kʰwĩ]   'cook meat'-INF

3.4.5. Diphthongization

When a high vowel is suffixed to a stem ending with a non-high vowel, the two vowels are syllabified into a single rhyme, creating diphthongs. A few adjustments in vowel quality occur: mid vowels are lax if the glide has the opposite value for backness, and the low back vowel centralizes to schwa:

(75) Diphthongization
      ye-u   [jɛu]   'come'-NR1
      kho-u   [kʰou]   'cry'-NR1
      tā-u   [tau]   'hear'-NR1
      na-u   [nəu]   'eat'-NR1
      ye-i   [jei]   'come'-INF
      kho-i   [kʰɔi]   'cry'-INF
      tā-i   [tai]   'hear'-INF
      na-i   [nəi]   'eat'-INF

An alternative analysis is to view the high vowels as syllable-final glides (§2.4.4.1).

3.4.6. Summary of processes affecting vowels in sequence

The preceding sections have described and exemplified a variety of phonological processes affecting vowels in sequence across a morpheme boundary. These processes are summarized in Table 4.

As there are no suffixes in the language beginning with any non-high vowel other than /e/, the processes are only attested in limited environments (i.e. before /i/, /u/, or /e/). The changes are rather idiosyncratic so it is difficult to make simple generalizations. For example, one cannot generalize that mid vowels become lax when followed by another vowel, as laxing is not attested if /e/ is followed by /i/, or /o/ by /u/. Table 4 thus appears to be clearest way of presenting these complex processes, at least without invoking the more complex descriptive mechanisms of formal theories of phonology.

Table 4. Summary of phonological processes affecting vowels in sequence

V1	V2	Process	Effects	
High	Same High	Shortening	/i-i/	→ [i]
			/u-u/	→ [u]
High	Different High	Glide formation of V1	/i-u /	→ [yu]
			/u-i/	→ [wi]
Non-High	High	Diphthongization	/e-u/	→ [ɛu]
			/e-i/	→ [ei]
			/o-u/	→ [ou]
			/o-i/	→ [ɔi]
			/a-u/	→ [əu]
			/ā-u/	→ [ai]
High	/e/	Palatal glide insertion	/i-e/	→ [ije]
			/u-e/	→ [uje]
/e/	/e/	Hiatus	/e-e/	→ [e.e]
/e/	/eu/	Hiatus with laxing of V2	/e-eu/	→ [e.ɛu]
	/eŋ/		/e-eŋ/	→ [e.ɛŋ]
/o/	/e/	Labial glide insertion	/o-e/	→ [owe]
				→ [we]
Low	/e/	Hiatus (w/ transient glide)	/ā-e/	→ [a.e]
				→ [a.je]
			/a-e/	→ [ɑ.e]
				→ [ɑ.je]

3.5. Vowel harmony

There are three prefixes in Dolakha Newar, the negative *ma-*, the prohibitive *da-*, and the optative *tha-*. All three prefixes have the same phonotactic structure and the same /a/ phoneme. All three undergo indentical patterns of harmony with the vowel of the verbal stem. As with other aspects of the phonetics and phonology of Dolakhae, there is considerable inter-speaker variation in the patterns of vowel harmony. I have worked in detail on vowel harmony with three native speakers, no two of whom produce the same patterns. Since I have no sense that any of these three patterns is dominant or represents a standard, I will describe each system independently. This has the advantage of presenting the language as it actually is: rich with variation.

The most limited system of vowel harmony is one where only one vowel harmonizes. The prefix vowel /a/ surfaces as /ā/ before /ā/ in the stem; it surfaces as /a/ elsewhere:

(76) kār-   mā-kā-u   NEG-'take'-3s
      wāl-   mā-wāl   NEG-'mix'
      nar-   ma-na-u   NEG-'eat'-3s
      hat-   da-hat   PROH-'say'
      bir-   ma-bi-u   NEG-'give'-3s
      ḍin-   ma-ḍī   NEG-'sleep'
      thur-   ma-thu   NEG-'understand'
      pul-   ma-pul   NEG-'pay'
      yet-   ma-yet   NEG-'do'
      then-   ma-theŋ   NEG-'arrive'
      bon-   ma-boŋ   NEG-'read'
      khor-   da-kho   NEG-'cry'

However, even this simple system is not as simple as it first appears, as the harmonization of /ā/ is blocked by an intervening glide, regardless of whether the glide is in the C1 or C2 position of the syllable onset:

(77) syāt-   ma-syāt   NEG-'kill'
      mwāt   ma-mwāt   NEG-'survive'
      yāl-   ma-yāl   NEG-'chew'
      wāl   ma-wāl   NEG-'mix'

The other two speakers have more extensive systems of harmony, with the primary difference being in the harmonization of round vowels. As with the speaker already discussed, both other speakers show harmony with the stem vowel /ā/:

(78) nār-   mā-nā-u   NEG-'knead'-IMP
      ḍār-   dā-ḍā-u   PROH-'beat'-IMP
      gān-   mā-gā̃   NEG-'dry'
      tār-   mā-ta̅-u   NEG-'hear'-3s

As with the first speaker, the presence of the glide /y/ blocks the harmony, but only if it is in C2 position within the syllable:

(79) syāt-   da-syāt   PROH-'kill'
      gyāt-   da-gyāt   PROH-'fear'
      ŋyāt-   ma-ŋyāt   NEG-'buy'
      yāl-   mā-yāl   NEG-'chew'
      yer-   mā-yā   NEG-'come'[16]

The glide /w/ also does not block harmony in C1 position, e.g. mā-wāl [NEG-mix]. Interestingly, if the verb begins with the sequence C + /wā/, the entire /wā/ is copied in the prefix. Thus from the verb mwāl- 'search' one derives the negative mwā-mwāl.

Both speakers also extend the harmony to the vowel /o/:

(80) khor-   do-kho   PROH-'cry'
     or-   mo-or-gi[17]   NEG-'bring in clothes'-1sPST
     on-   mo-ō   NEG-'go'
     ton-   do-toŋ   PROH-'drink'

One of the two speakers also has harmony with /u/. However, the prefix vowel surfaces as /o/, not as /u/. The other speaker does not have harmony induced by /u/, and the prefix vowel remains /a/:

(81) pul-   do-pul   da-pul   PROH-'pay'
     bur-   mo-bu   ma-bu   NEG-'carry'
     ṭun-   mo-ṭū   ma-ṭū   NEG-'ripe'
     chut-   do-chut   da-chut   PROH-'cook bread'

We can analyze these three distinct systems of vowel harmony as follows. The speaker with the most limited system has a simple rule of full-vowel copying triggered only by the vowel /ā/. The speaker who harmonize from /ā/ and from /o/ appears to have a system of full-vowel copying triggered by two of the six vowels. The third speaker appears to have full-vowel copying only of /ā/. Otherwise, he harmonizes only the feature [round], which, when applied to the non-high vowel /a/, produces the vowel /o/.

The role of glides in vowel harmony is quite complex. For one speaker, all glides block the harmony process. This can perhaps be analyzed as the result of the feature [+high] effectively blocking the spread of a non-high vowel.

For the other two speakers, only non-initial /y/ blocks harmony, while /w/ is copied together with /ā/. One way to approach this conundrum would be to analyze the sequences /yā/ and /wā/ not as sequences of glide plus vowel, but as single unit phonemes (most conveniently thought of as monophonematic diphthongs, /iā/ and /uā/). Under this analysis, the sequence /uā/ would copy due to its round component, whereas /iā/ would be blocked from copying as it contains no round elements. It is important to note that this reanalysis of the phonotactic and phonemic structure is only attributable to some speakers of the language. For more discussion of these points, see §2.4.1.

It should be noted that although there is variation in the patterns of vowel harmony across speakers, the presence of the different harmony patterns will never obscure the meaning of the word, even though different phonemes may surface in the prefixes. This is because there are only three prefixes in the language and they are sufficiently differentiated by the initial consonant. Thus the vowels carry no functional load in this position and are free to vary.

4. Phonotactics

4.1. Syllable structure

There are two ways to analyze the syllable structure of Dolakha Newar. If one bases the analysis of syllable structure on the transcription of words in the orthographic traditions of the area (and used throughout this book), the syllable structure would be represented as follows:

(82)   Syllable structure based on standard orthographic practice
       (C) (G) V $\left\{ \begin{array}{c} C \\ \text{high V} \end{array} \right\}$

The template of (82) formalizes the statement that syllable onsets, when present, may consist of a single consonant or a consonant followed by a glide. Syllable rhymes consist obligatorily of a vowel and optionally of either a consonantal coda or a high vowel.

However, when one analyzes the phonotactic patterns of the language in detail, several facts come to light which suggest a quite different analysis of the Dolakhae syllable. Central to the discussion is the behavior of the glides. As discussed in §2.3.2, the mid vowels /e/ and /o/ have allophones [je] and [wɔ] respectively. This reveals two important facts: first, that the phonemes /y/ and /w/ have restricted distribution with respect to vowels, and second, that single phonemic segments, in this case /e/ and /o/, may have a complex structure. Just as affricates are single phonemes that have first a stop and then a fricative phase, so the mid vowels are single phonemes that have first a glide and then a stable vowel, under certain circumstances.

The restrictions on the co-occurrence of glides and vowels are quite extreme. If we analyze all sequences of [je] and [wɔ] as allophonic variants of /e/ and /o/, then, with two exceptions that I know of, all instances of /y/ or /w/ are followed by the vowel /ā/. This is true whether the glide is the single element of an onset, e.g. *yā* 'rice, unhusked', or whether it is in the second onset position, following another consonant, e.g. *gyāt-a* [fear-3sPST].[18] This raises the possibility that /yā/ and /wā/ should be treated as unit phonemes of complex internal structure, rather than as sequences of glide plus vowel. One piece of evidence in favor of this position is found in vowel harmony. For some speakers, the entire sequence /wā/ harmonizes, e.g. *mwā-mwāl* 'did not search'. This suggests a strong unity between the vowel and the glide. (On the other hand, the sequence /yā/ does not exhibit the same behavior (§2.3.5).) If one were to analyze /yā/ and /wā/ as single vowel phonemes, then the statement of syllable structure could be simplifed to disallow onset clusters.

Turning to the rhyme, the fact that the vowel nucleus may be followed either by a consonant or by a high vowel raises the possibility that what are orthographically high vowels are actually consonantal glides. If we analyze words like /goi/ 'nut' as /goy/, we can simplify our statement of the structure of the rhyme, stating that the rhyme consists of an obligatory vowel optionally followed by a consonant.

If we were to combine these two alternative views of the syllable structure, the syllable template would simplify considerably to (C)V(C). While this analysis is intriguing in its implications for segment structure and phonological theory, representing the language this way orthographically would be problematic. The Devanagari alphabet in which speakers are educated promotes an awareness of glides in the onset as independent elements of the phonology. Also, Nepali has onset glides which co-occur with a range of vowels. As there are many words borrowed from Nepali into Dolakha Newar, these borrowings dilute the strength of the pattern which argues for a monophonematic analysis of the sequences /yā/ and /wā/. Representing these orthographically as unit phonemes would thus strike the native speakers as odd and arbitrary.

Turning to the rhyme, many of the syllables ending in high vowels in the language are bimorphemic, with the high vowel representing a separate morpheme, such as the infinitive -i. This morpheme surfaces as a vowel in many of its allomorphs, so it is likely that speakers think of this morpheme as a vowel. Thus words like kho-i, the infinitive of 'cry', are more likely to be conceptualized as /khoi/ than as /khoy/. And again the orthography represents the final segment as vocalic, i.e. खोइ khoi, a factor which reinforces the interpretation of the final segment as a vowel.

These alternative views of the syllable structure have different descriptive goals. One describes the syllable structure as it is likely to be understood by the speakers of the language. The second describes the syllable structure as revealed through patterns of distribution of occurrence of segments over native vocabulary items. Given the high degree of borrowing from Nepali and the high degree of literacy using the Devanagari alphabet, it is not surprising that the two should produce different results.

Regardless of which view of syllable structure one adopts, a full description of the syllable structure requires some additional observations. First, glides in C2 position do not follow /r/ or /h/. The glide /y/ does not follow /m/ or /w/, while /w/ does not follow /y/.

Second, the possible consonants that may serve in the coda are /p, t, k, m, n, ŋ, r, l, s/, i.e. voiceless unaspirated stops and nasals from the bilabial, dental, and velar places of articulation, as well as the liquids and /s/. Systematically excluded from this position are the retroflex stops, aspirated stops, voiced stops, and /h/. (Whether or not the glides are excluded depends upon your view of syllable structure, as discussed directly above.) Words with each of these codas are presented in (83):

(83) ṭap   'earrings, post'
      lwāp doṅ-   'get up from lying position'
      kālat   'wife'
      sāŋat   'friend'
      kok   'crow'
      gwārtak   'round'
      nyāmnyām   'temples' (body part)
      thām   'pillar'
      barkhuṅ   'pigeon'
      ṭāen   'far'
      bārpāŋ   'tomato'
      bujiŋ   'housefly'
      ḍhōr   'jackal'
      cher   'head'
      kāpal   'forehead'
      sel   'marrow'
      cānas   'midnight'
      ḍās   'bedbug'

4.2. Word structure

The vast majority of lexical roots in Dolakha Newar are of one or two syllables. Trisyllabic and quadrisyllabic roots are found, but these tend to be made up of compounds, e.g. twāŋ-sona 'rhodedendron' < [unknown etymon] + sona 'flower', ḍwāku-kocu 'small pox' < ḍwāku 'big' + kocu 'pox', dudu-kãkar 'fresh corn' < dudu 'milk' + kãkar 'corn'. It is also possible to have partial or full reduplication result in words of three or four syllables, e.g. hākupāku 'black raspberry', huhujāna 'owl', kampalimpa 'rainbow'. A handful of words which appear to be monomorphemic are three or four syllables in length, e.g. kuciri 'fingernails; claws', yālāguri 'gland'.

Polymorphemic words are often one or more syllables longer than monomorphemic words, although this depends on the shape of the affix, the shape of the stem, and the rate of speech. Inflected verbs can be up to five syllables in length, e.g. mo-bō-gupeju 'We did not read it'.

5. Stress

The term "stress" is used in linguistics to refer to the relative prominence of syllables in a word. In Dolakha Newar, when words are pronounced in isolation, the first syllable is the most prominent, so can be said to be stressed. The primary cue for stress is pitch, which correlates with the acoustic property of fundamental frequency. On disyllabic words pronounced in isolation, there is a slight rise in pitch in the first syllable and then a fall through the rest of the word. Intensity, another feature commonly found to mark stress, plays a relatively marginal role in this language, although it may decrease slightly over the course of the word. Length does not seem to be relevant to stress; in words with two vowels of identical quality, sometimes the initial vowel is longer, sometimes they are of similar duration, and sometimes the final vowel is elongated. Figure 1 shows the fundamental frequency and intensity changes over the word *muru* 'needle' pronounced in isolation. The figure displays both fundamental frequency and intensity over time. Fundamental frequency (to 300 hertz, represented by a heavy line) and intensity (to 100 decibels, represented by a light line) are represented on the x-axis while time is represented on the y-axis. In this fairly typical example, the fundamental frequency rises to the mid-point of the first vowel and then falls steadily over the rest of the word. The intensity rises throughout the first vowel, and then shows a slight drop over the second.

Disyllabic words formed by the addition of a verbal prefix follow the same pattern as disyllabic monomorphemic words. *Figure 2* illustrates the fundamental frequency and intensity changes over the verb *mwā-mwāl* 'did not search' pronounced in isolation (note that "aa" in the acoustic figures represents the orthographic symbol /ā/). In this example the fundamental frequency peaks around the beginning of first the steady-state vowel /aì/, and then falls steadily. Intensity is level during the first vowel and falls slightly over the second.

In words of three syllables pronounced in isolation, stress decreases with each successive syllable, such that the third syllable is lowest in fundamental frequency and intensity. Figure 3 illustrates changes in fundamental frequency and intensity over the word *gulpanuŋ* 'never'. Fundamental frequency rises over the first syllable and falls steadily over the second and third. Intensity is fairly even over the first two syllables, but is reduced on the third. This might be partially due to the presence of the two nasal consonants, which naturally have reduced intensity when compared to the vowel.

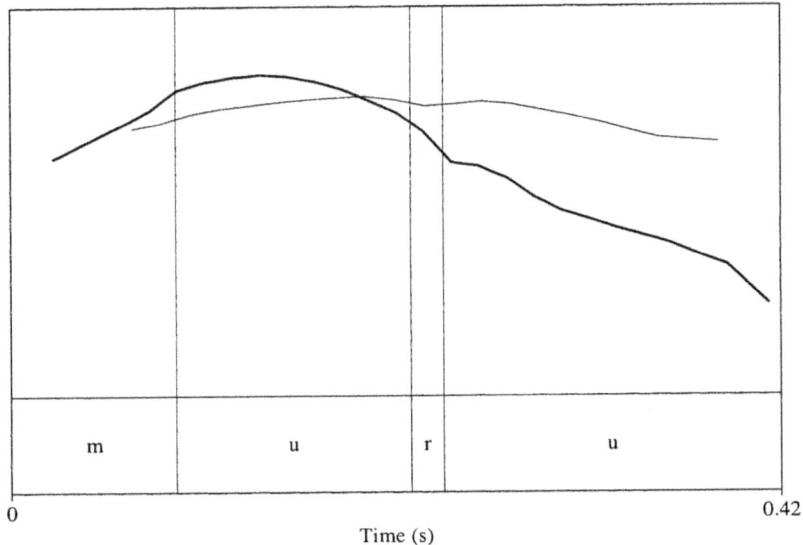

Figure 1. Pitch and intensity over the noun *muru* 'needle'[19]

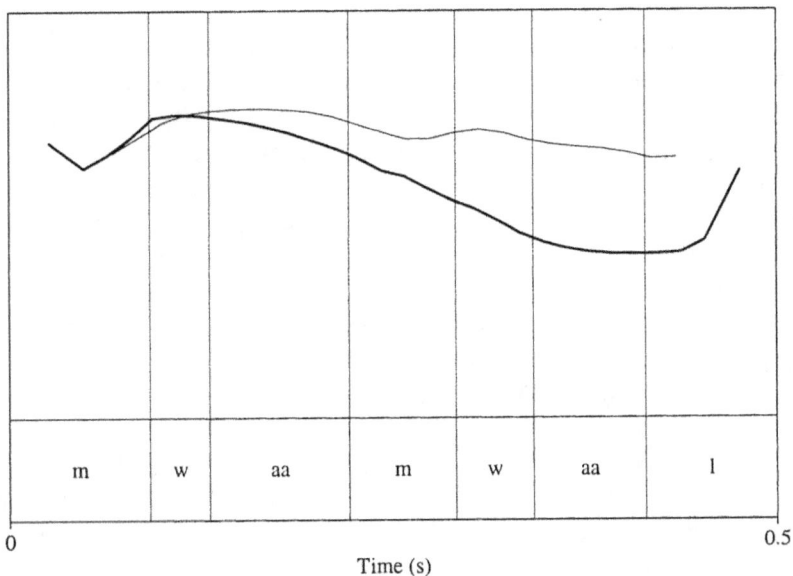

Figure 2. Pitch and intensity over negated verb mwaì-mwaìl 'did not search'

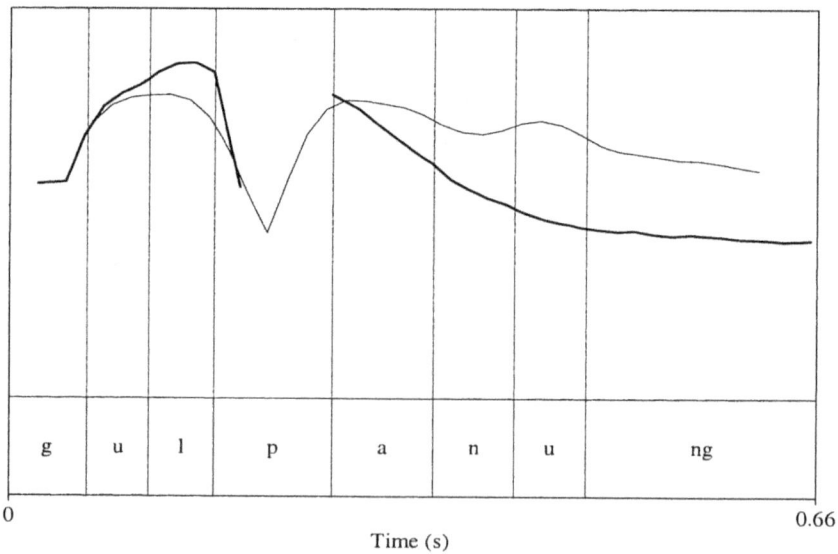

Figure 3. Pitch and intensity over *gulpanuŋ* 'never'

The preceding discussion was concerned exclusively with words pronounced in isolation. In connected speech, the word-level stress pattern is often obscured by the phrasal intonation contours. For example, when recording words put into the carrier sentence *āmun X cor-ju* [3sERG X write-3sPST] 'He wrote X', where X was replaced by the word in focus, one speaker consistently applied a distinctive intonation pattern to the carrier sentence. She produced strong rising intonation from *āmun* through the focused word, then a pause, and then falling intonation on *cor-ju*. This meant that the prosodic stress patterns found when the words in focus were pronounced in isolation were lost when the same words were pronounced in the carrier sentence. Figure 4 illustrates the word *cula* 'finger' pronounced in isolation by this speaker. One can see a clear fall in both fundamental frequency and intensity from the mid-point of the first vowel through the end of the word. This is the expected pattern, which can be attributed to lexical stress.

Figure 5 illustrates the same word as it was pronounced in the carrier sentence. The intensity contour shows a fall, though not as dramatic as that on the token pronounced in isolation. The pitch pattern is clearly distinct, with a pronounced rise on the second syllable. There is no sign of the falling pitch attributable to lexical stress; lexical stress is thus subordinated to phrasal intonation.

Section 5 Stress 67

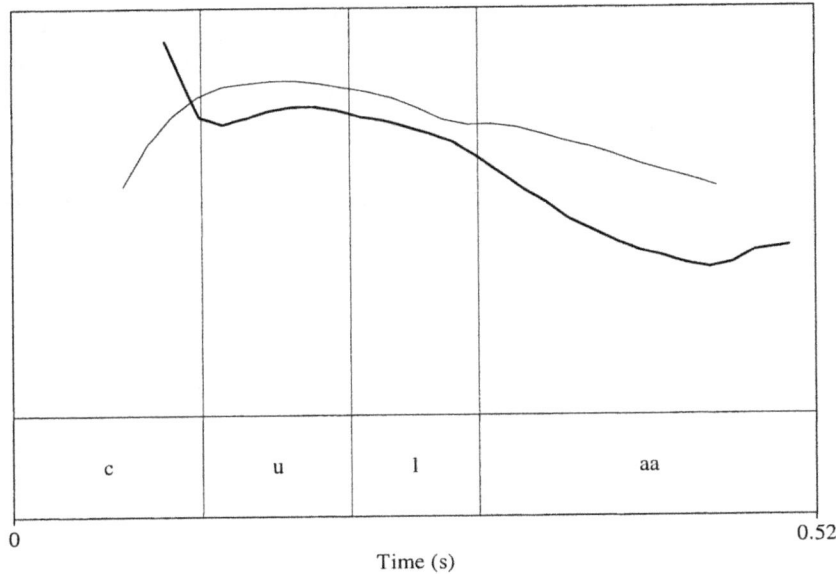

Figure 4. Pitch and intensity over *culā* 'finger' pronounced in isolation[20]

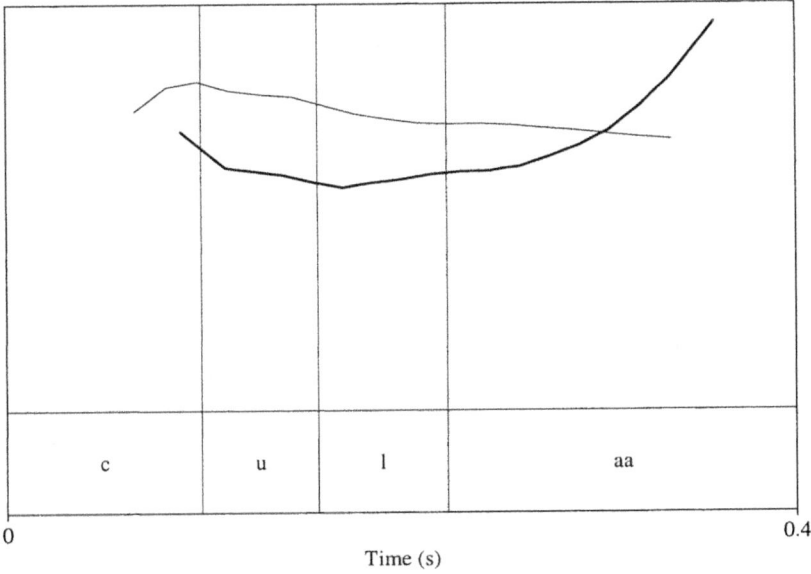

Figure 5. Pitch and intensity over the word *culā* 'finger' uttered in a frame

This raises the question of whether the apparent stress patterns found when words are pronounced in isolation could be analyzed as intonation rather than as lexcial stress. It is possible to analyze the prominence on the initial syllable as resulting from an intonation pattern specific to words in isolation. At this point, there does not appear to be strong support of either analysis. What is clear is that if one analyzes Dolakha Newar as having first-syllable stress, it clearly has a very low functional load. It is predictable, not phonemic, and is largely obscured by intonation.

Chapter 3
Prosody

1. Introduction

The term prosody refers to a combination of phonetic features that serve to convey emotion and attitude and to segment, group, and organize connected discourse. These features include intonation (pitch realized over units larger than a single word), pause, accent, intensity, voice quality, and rate of speech. The current description will only focus on two aspects of prosody: accent and intonation.

2. Intonation units

Connected speech is divided into distinct units, referred to here as "intonation units", which are delineated by a variety of prosodic features. Intonation units generally end with one of a small set of "terminal intonation contours". They are frequently followed by a pause. The pitch level is often reset from the end of one unit to the beginning of another. There also may be a change in the rate of speech across units, with slowing at the end of one unit and speeding up at the beginning of another. All of these features are gradient: intonation contours can be larger or smaller; pauses can be shorter or longer, adjustment of rate of speech can be to a greater or lesser degree. This means that some unit boundaries are difficult to determine, especially in fast speech. It appears that boundaries themselves may be of different strengths, with some clearly defined "strong" boundaries, and some "weaker" boundaries. This variability, and its implications for discourse structure, requires further study.

When explicitly discussing intonation, I will use distinct transcription conventions discussed in this chapter. To begin with, I will mark the division of speech into intonation units by placing each intonation unit on a separate line of text, as in (1):[21]

70   Chapter 3   Prosody

(1)   (1.6) ām   ^gā̃ũ=ku =ri /
              that village =LOC=IND

        (0.8) nis-mā bobu kae da-u   ju-en   con-a _
              two-CL father son have-NR1 be-PART stay-3sPST

        'In that village there were two, a father and son.'

Intonation units vary in their size. Some intonation units may consist of a single word, as in (2):

(2)   bhānche=uri
       cook=IND

       'the cook'

Other units may contain entire clauses, even entire complex sentences. The example in (3) illustrates a complex sentence in a single intonation unit. Syntactically, this unit contains a participial clause followed by a finite clause.

(3)   rājā thi -mā ye-en =uri ãku khã ŋeŋ-an   coŋ-gu   hã   āle
       king one-CL come =IND there talk listen-PART stay-3PA EVID then

       'It is said that one king came and was listening to their talk there.'

It is useful to keep track of pauses in the speech stream, as these are very common and are a key component of prosodic structuring. Pauses generally come between intonation units, but may come within them. Very short pauses, between 100 and 200 milliseconds (ms), will be transcribed with a single period placed on the line before the segmental material of the intonation unit. Medium-length pauses, with durations between 300 ms and 600 ms, will be marked by a sequence of two periods. Long pauses, over 700 ms in duration, will have the duration placed in parentheses.[22] In example (1), the first intonation unit was preceded by a pause of 1.6 seconds (1600 ms), while the second intonation unit was preceded by pause of 0.8 seconds (800 ms). These durations are represented in parentheses at the beginning of each line of text.

3. Phrasal accent

Most intonation units have one or more words that are acoustically prominent. Some of this prominence may be due to the sonority (inherent loudness) of the segments. Syllables with the vowel /ā/ are particularly sonorous and words with this vowel often sound prominent even when not accented.

Words which the speaker chooses to emphasize prosodically can be said to receive phrasal accent. There are at least two types of phrasal accent: normal and emphatic. Normal phrasal accent results in an increase of prominence on a syllable of the accented word which is noticeable but unremarkable. Emphatic phrasal accent, by contrast, results in a quite remarkable increase in acoustic prominence.

The phonetic realization of normal phrasal accent depends on the phonotactic structure of the accented word. Monosyllabic words which receive phrasal accent begin at a higher pitch than the preceding syllable. If there is no intervening obstruent consonant between the nucleus of the preceding syllable and the nucleus of the accented syllable, then the increase is realized as a rising pitch over the coda of the preceding syllable. If an obstruent does intervene between the two vocalic nuclei, then the pitch of the preceding syllable is generally level, and there is an abrupt step up in pitch after the obstruent. In both cases, the pitch on the accented syllable falls. Accented syllables also generally have increased amplitude. Figure 6 presents the pitch trace for an intonation unit with an accented monosyllabic word, the emphatic (contrastive focus) particle *he*. Since no stop intervenes between it and the preceding syllable, one can see a marked rise in fundamental frequency leading up to the peak, which corresponds to the onset of the accented vowel. Normal phrasal accent is transcribed with a circumflex (^) before the word which receives accent.

Polysyllabic words with phrasal accent may have the accent realized on any syllable of the word. In words with initial aspirated consonants or affricates, the initial syllable is likely to be the most prominent. Otherwise, the acoustic prominence delivered by phrasal accent appears most commonly to be on the final syllable of the word. Further investigation into this issue is warranted.

Syllables preceding an accented syllable in a polysyllabic root will either have level pitch or rising pitch. Again, level pitch occurs when there is an intervening obstruent at the syllable boundary; rising pitch occurs when there is not. Figure 7 illustrates the changes of pitch over the accented word *hātta* 'why' embedded into a sentence in a narrative. One can see that the pitch on the first syllable levels out, then there is a sharp step up in pitch to the beginning of the second syllable, which falls.

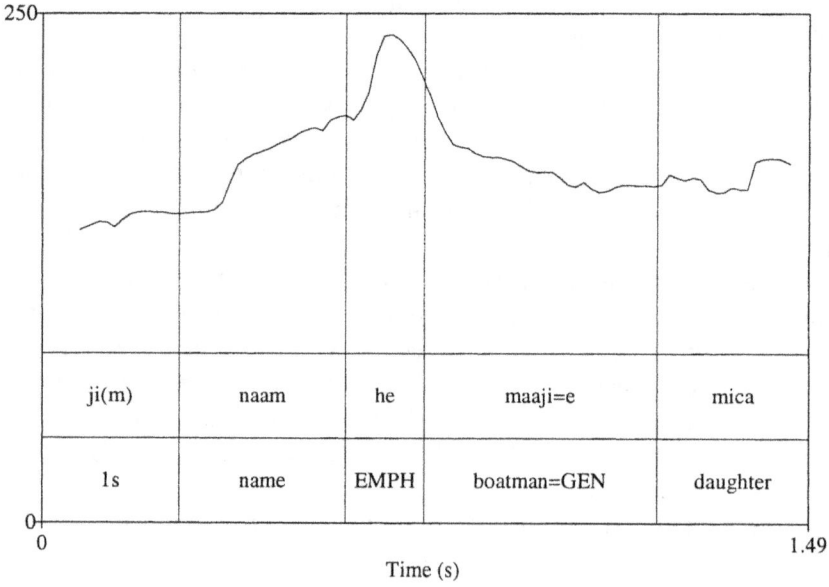

Figure 6. Pitch trace for *jim nām ^he māji=e mica* 'My name is the boatman's daughter'

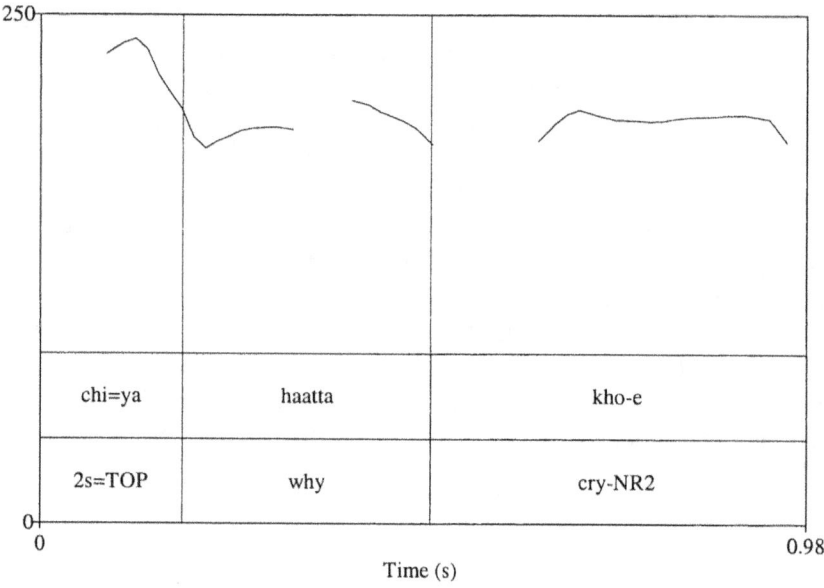

Figure 7. Pitch trace for *^chi=ya ^hātta kho-e* 'Why do you cry?'

Emphatic accent occurs when the speaker chooses to give exceptional prominence to a word in an utterance. It differs from normal phrasal accent by matter of degree. The increase in pitch from the preceding syllable is significantly greater than with normal accent and the fall in pitch is sharper, generally falling to about the pitch level of the preceding syllable. The result is an overall rise-fall. This is illustrated in Figure 8. The phrasal accent is realized on the second syllable of *gunta=ŋ*, where the fundamental frequency rises about 90 hertz, then falls about 60; the fall continues over the final word of the intonation unit. Emphatic phrasal accent will be transcribed with a superscript exclamation point (*!*) before the accented word.

In the absence of phrasal accent, most words will have a falling or level contour in connected discourse. This produces either a continuation of a preceding falling pitch or a slight word-initial rise followed by a fall. The latter case can be seen in the unaccented pronoun *chin* in Figure 8 below. The former case is illustrated in Figure 9. This sentence was elicited, targeting the word *nibār* 'sun' placed into a frame. The pitch pattern over the two syllables of this word is falling. The fall naturally blends with the fall from the accented syllable in *āmun* 's/he'.

It is also possible for words to occur in prosodically neutral contexts with level pitch and neither syllable being prominent. In some intonation units with the level terminal contour, all words are of equal prominence so no word can be said to receive phrasal accent.

This study has identified two types of phrasal accent, normal and emphatic, and described their phonetic realizations. It is likely that other types of phrasal accent exist, probably with different contour shapes. I do have some evidence from elicitation for a rising accent, although I have not seen this in my narrative data. This is likely to be a fruitful area for future studies.

74   Chapter 3   Prosody

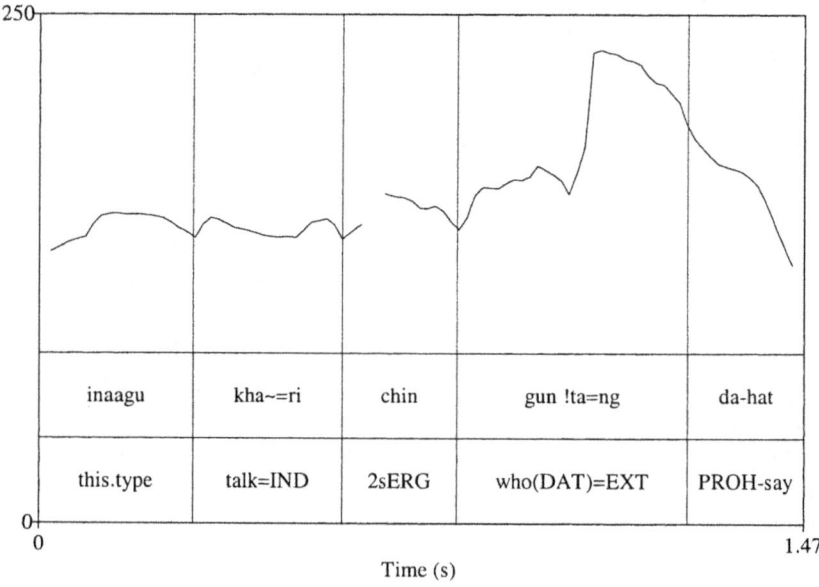

Figure 8. Pitch trace for *ināgu khã=ri chin ˈgunta=ŋ da-hat* 'You don't say this to anybody'

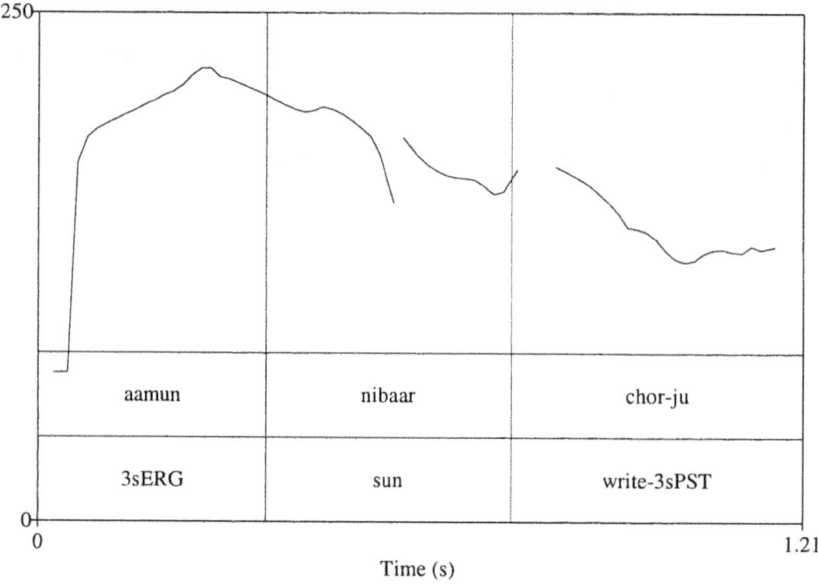

Figure 9. Pitch trace for *^āmun nibār chor-ju* 'He wrote "sun"'

4. Terminal pitch contours

Each intonation unit is characterized by a distinct intonation contour. As many of these contours exhibit the majority of pitch movement at the end of an intonation unit, they are referred to as "terminal pitch contours". There are a number of distinct terminal pitch contours that are found in the production of narrative. The majority of contours can be sorted into four phonological categories. There is some evidence for a fifth category in my narrative data (a fall-rise), but I have a very few examples and cannot comment upon it. A few contours (about 4%) are difficult to categorize and appear to have idiosyncratic characteristics. Others are abandoned or "truncated" as the speaker changes his or her mind about how to proceed. The goal of the present work is to describe the commonly found patterns in a study of narratives produced by five native speakers of Dolakhae.

4.1. Falling terminal contours

All of the intonation units with falling terminal contours have a fairly steady fall from the prosodically accented syllable to the end of the unit. The slope of the fall, and hence how dramatically it is perceived to fall, depends on the position of the prosodically accented syllable and the pitch of that syllable. In cases where the prosodic accent falls on one of the last three syllables, the slope is steeper and more marked than in cases where the prosodic accent is positioned early in the prosodic unit. In addition, if the pitch of the accented syllable is high, the fall will be more dramatic. We can thus see that falling contours crucially interact with phrasal accent to produce the phonetic pitch fall in an intonation unit. The actual pitch curve is the result of the interaction between these phonological units.

Falling (and level) contours differ from rise and rise-fall terminal contours in that the pitch change is realized globally over the intonation unit, as opposed to being produced only over the last syllable or two. This clearly shows that speakers are planning their terminal intonation from the beginning of the unit or shortly thereafter.

We can distinguish phonetically between two types of falling contours: high falls and mid falls. Contours classified as high falls show a marked decline in fundamental frequency from the last accented syllable in the word to the end of the unit. They start at a high pitch relative to a speaker's natural pitch range, with a fundamental frequency over 190 hertz for female speakers and over 170 hertz for male speakers. High falls show a drop in fundamental frequency of at least 35 hertz, but often the fall is much greater, even 100 hertz or more.

Figure 10 gives the pitch trace for a high-falling contour produced by a male speaker. The first word *utsuk* has prosodic accent, reaching a pitch of just over 200 hertz, especially high for this male speaker. After this there is a steady fall through the rest of the intonation unit, ending at around 130 hertz. The high fall will be transcribed with a double backslash after the intonation unit.

Contours classified as "mid fall" have a smaller decline in fundamental frequency over the course of the unit, less than 35 hertz, and generally between 15 hertz and 25 hertz. They also start at a lower pitch. This can vary from a "mid-range" pitch for the speaker, with a fundamental frequency between 140 and 170 hertz depending on the individual, to a fundamental frequency as low as 120 hertz. As with high falls, the falling contour is realized between the final accented syllable and the end of the unit, and the slope will vary depending on the positioning and height of that accent.

Figure 11 illustrates the change in fundamental frequency on a mid-fall contour produced by a female speaker. There are two phrasal accents in this unit, one on the first syllable of *chana* 'your', and one on the syllable *chu-e* 'cook'-NR2. The pitch falls after the first accented word then jumps up again for the second accent. The fundamental frequency at this point is 143 hertz, in the lower-mid pitch range for this speaker. The fundamental frequency drops 18 hertz to end at 125 hertz. Mid fall will be transcribed with a single backslash after the intonation unit.

Although these two types of falling terminal contours may be distinguished phonetically, it appears that they represent a single phonological category "fall". Evidence of this comes from the fact they occur in the same functional environments (discussed below), so cannot be said to be contrastive. In addition, individual speakers seem to prefer one category over the other. Three of the five speakers of this study used mid falls regularly. For these speakers, high falls only occurred in intonation units containing emphatic phrasal accents. Thus for these speakers the high fall occurs in a phonetically predictable environment. The fourth speaker regularly produced high falls, with mid falls only occurring in units with minimal importance and low amplitude. These units can be thought of as being prosodically reduced over all, an effect which limits both the pitch range and the amplitude of the unit. Again, the variation between high-fall and mid fall is predictable. The fifth speaker produced very few falls during the portion of the narrative studied, so no patterns could be established.

Turning to the use of falling terminal contours, they primarily occur in two environments in narrative: on intonation units occurring at the ends of sentences, and on intonation units containing only contrastive noun phrases. Although these contours occasionally occur with non-finite verbs or adverbials, such examples are sporadic in the data examined.

Section 4   Terminal pitch contours   77

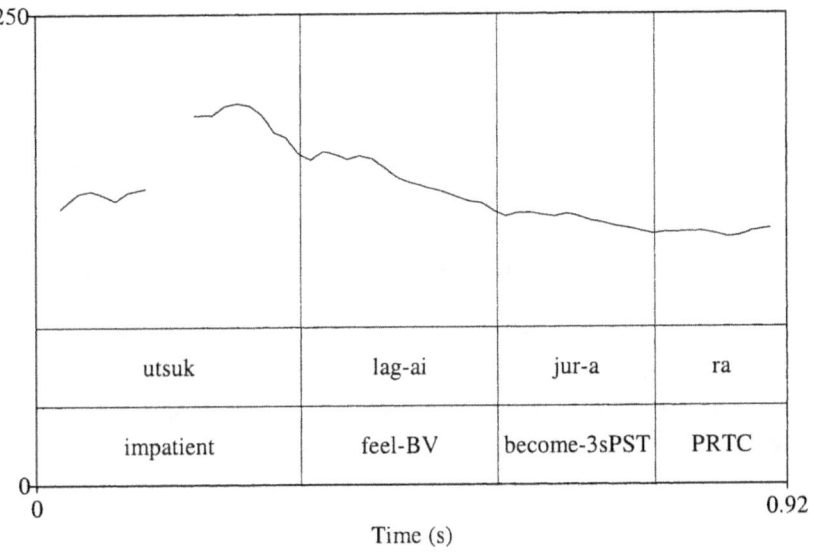

Figure 10. Pitch trace for ^utsuk lāg-ai jur-a rā \\ 'He became impatient'

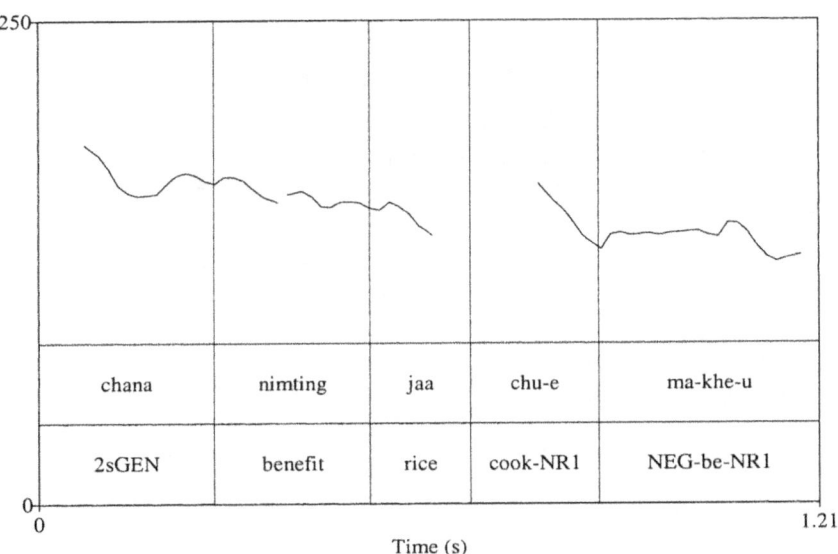

Figure 11. Pitch trace for ^chana nimtiŋ jā ^chu-e ma-kheu \ 'This rice was not cooked for your benefit'

About two-thirds of the examples of falling contours occurred on intonation units which are syntactically sentence-final. Most of these are cases which contain non-embedded finite verbs, but a few include copula complements where copulas have been elided. It is clear that speakers are using falling contours as a prosodic marker of finality produced simultaneously with morphosyntactic markers of finality (finite morphology, copular clause structure).

Falls are also regularly found in narrative on intonation units that only contain a noun phrase.[23] This is particularly true where there are several active characters in a story and the narrative switches between them, i.e. in contrastive contexts. An example is given in (4). Here the speaker is recounting a story of three sisters. She has finished relating that two sisters had difficult marriages and not enough to eat. The introduction of the third and happy sister in the first intonation unit is marked by a high fall:

(4)   .. āle   rāja=ke   oŋ-gu   thi-mā=n=ri   \\
         then king=ALL go-NR1 one-CL=ERG=IND

     (0.7) sukhā=n   ānthi   yeŋ-an   coŋ-an   libi /
            happiness=INST that.manner do-PART stay-PART later

     'Then the one who went with the king was later living that way
     in happiness...'

A third, minor pattern is that falling intonation occurs on noun phrases following periods of speaker disfluency. The falling contour appears to establish the identity of an important referent as the narrative gets back on track. In example (5), the speaker experienced a period of disfluency during which she produced two truncated intonation units. When she then produced the utterance with the correct noun phrase, she did so with a high-falling terminal contour. She then continued fluently with the remainder of the sentence.

(5)   ... āmta   ekdam   ām   --
         3sDAT   very   3s

     .. mebu   āme   āme   --
        other 3sGEN 3sGEN

     ... cijmā=n   \\
        stepmother=ERG

```
...  ekdam  dukha    bir-ai         \\
     very   trouble  give-3sPR
```

'She very-- another her, her -- stepmother gave her very much trouble.'

4.2. Level terminal contours

Contours classified as level exhibit very limited pitch variation over the duration of the intonation unit. Although accented syllables early in the unit may have falling fundamental frequencies of up to 25 hertz, the rest of the material in the prosodic unit is pronounced at a sustained level pitch; the fundamental frequency does not vary over the unit by more than 10 or 12 hertz. The two final syllables, in particular, are usually quite level and often have elongated vowels. In some units with level contours, accented syllables are realized only by an increase in amplitude and do not have falling pitch. Other units appear to have no accented syllable at all, as all syllables are pronounced with similar pitch and amplitude. Level contours will be transcribed with a low line following the unit (__).

Figure 12 illustrates the pitch trace for a level contour produced by a female speaker. The portions of the intonation unit that correspond to the stops have been marked so that one can see that the drops in pitch are attributable to these and are not part of the intonation pattern of the unit. The first syllable *ji* 'I' is pronounced with a fundamental frequency of 203 hertz. The first two syllables of the second word start with the fundamental frequency around 201 hertz and drop to about 190. The final vowel is again around 201 hertz. Thus we can see that this unit does not vary by more than 13 hertz over the four syllables. Neither is there a clear direction of movement; the unit is not consistently falling or rising.

All speakers used level contours on at least some intonation units which constituted embedded quotation, and three of the five speakers used level contours frequently in this environment, especially at the ends of embedded sentences. Genetti and Slater (2004) refer to this as "narrative final" intonation, since the use of embedded quotation is a narrative device. The production of a distinctive intonation pattern for embedded quotation constitutes a means for the speaker to signal to the hearer that he or she is making a shift from producing the voice of the narrator to producing the voice of the character. Other prosodic cues to signal embedded speech include changes in amplitude, global changes in pitch, and changes in voice quality.

Level contours also occurred in other environments, especially when speakers produced intonation units with low amplitude. The reduction in variation in both pitch and loudness is a way of producing prosodically backgrounded material, which is generally of low importance.

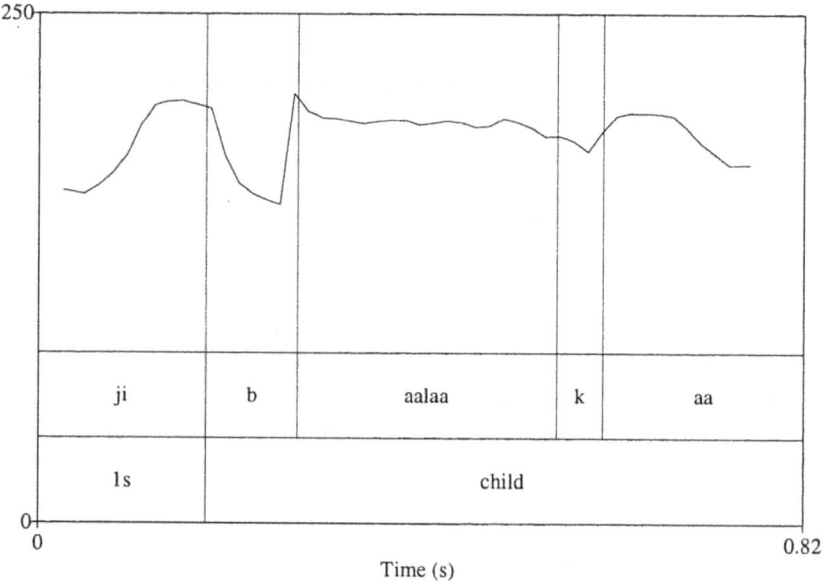

Figure 12. Pitch trace for *ji ^bālaka* 'I am a child'

4.3. Rising terminal contours

Rising contours differ from level and falling contours in that the primary pitch movement is not realized over the entire intonation unit but is located on the final syllable. The intonation over the unit prior to the final syllable is determined by the position and height of phrasal accents, together with a general fall (attributable to declination), usually ending on the penultimate syllable (but occasionally on the antepenult). There is then generally a step up in fundamental frequency of at least ten hertz from the end of the penult to the beginning of the ultima. The fundamental frequency then rises steadily over the rhyme of the syllable. The rise is sustained past the mid-point of the final segment (vowel or nasal coda). This is frequently followed by a slight decrease in fundamental frequency at the very end of the unit, usually about 25% of the total amount of the rise. As this decrease in fundamental frequency is often accompanied by a decrease in amplitude, the final slight drop in pitch is not strongly audible and the overall perceptual effect is of a rising pitch contour. Rising terminal contours will be transcribed with a single slash.

Rising contours produce a significant pitch movement on the final syllable. The final syllable can thus be said to carry a phrasal accent assigned to it by the rising contour. This phrasal accent will not be transcribed.

Section 4   Terminal pitch contours   81

Figure 13 illustrates the changes in fundamental frequency for an intonation unit with a rising contour. The first word *janta* [1SDAT] is unaccented and pronounced at a low pitch. The first syllable in *pyāṭāwāt-a* [hungry-3sPST] receives phrasal accent. The fundamental frequency starts at 209 hertz then falls to 182 by the end of the penultimate vowel. The fundamental frequency at the beginning of the ultimate vowel is ten hertz higher, followed by a rise on the vowel back to 209. The total increase in fundamental frequency, including the initial step up, is 28 hertz.

Many intonation units end in a final nasal consonant. This is especially true as a number of verbal suffixes used in clause linkage end in /n/, as does the ergative casemarker. These morphemes often occur at the ends of intonation units. When an intonation unit with a rising contour ends in a nasal consonant, the vowel is usually quite short and the nasal elongated. A significant portion of the final rise is realized on the nasal itself.

Figure 14 illustrates the fundamental frequency over a rising intonation unit with a final nasal consonant. The first word receives a phrasal accent. The fundamental frequency drops sharply across the first two syllables, then declines gradually through the penult. The final syllable has a total increase in fundamental frequency of 19 hertz, evenly divided over the vowel and the nasal.

A subtype of rising contours is the marked rise. The difference between rise and marked rise is purely a matter of degree. I transcribe as marked rises those with an increase of over 35 hertz in the last two syllables of the unit. Often the increase is substantially greater than this, above 40 hertz, and sometimes as much as 80 or 90 hertz. Unlike the two falling contours, which are differentiated by both total pitch change and initial fundamental frequency, there is no noticeable difference in the ending pitches of rise and marked rise contours. Two speakers, one male and one female, do produce a few high rising contours with impressively high end points (260–280 hertz for the female speaker, 180–200 hertz for the male speaker), however, they also produce marked rises with lower end points under similar functional conditions. Thus final pitch does not seem to be significant. Marked rise will be transcribed by two slashes.

The decision to take 35 hertz as a cut-off point between rise and marked rise contours is arbitrary, in that one could as easily choose a higher or lower cut-off point. Examination of all rising contours shows that they occur in a steady continuum and no clear dividing line establishes two distinct groups. The decision to divide the contours into two groups is based on auditory perception, as strongly rising contours are quite salient, or "marked".

82   Chapter 3   Prosody

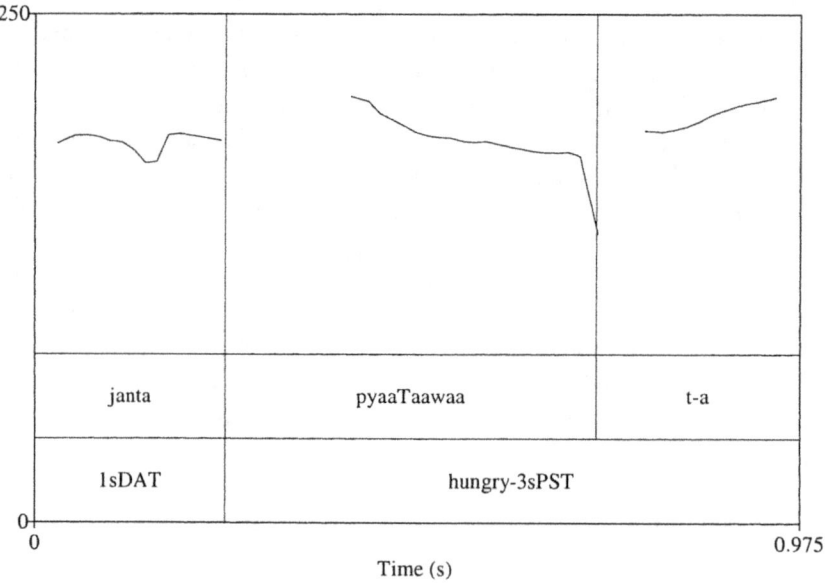

Figure 13. Pitch trace for *janta ^pyāṭāwāt-a/* 'I am hungry'

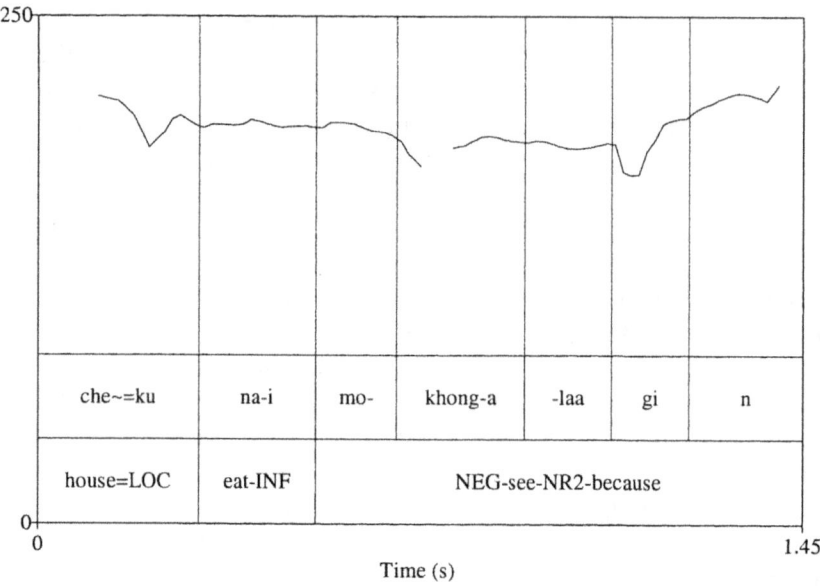

Figure 14. Pitch trace for *^chẽ=ku na-i mo-khoŋ-a-lāgin/* 'Because I am not able to eat'

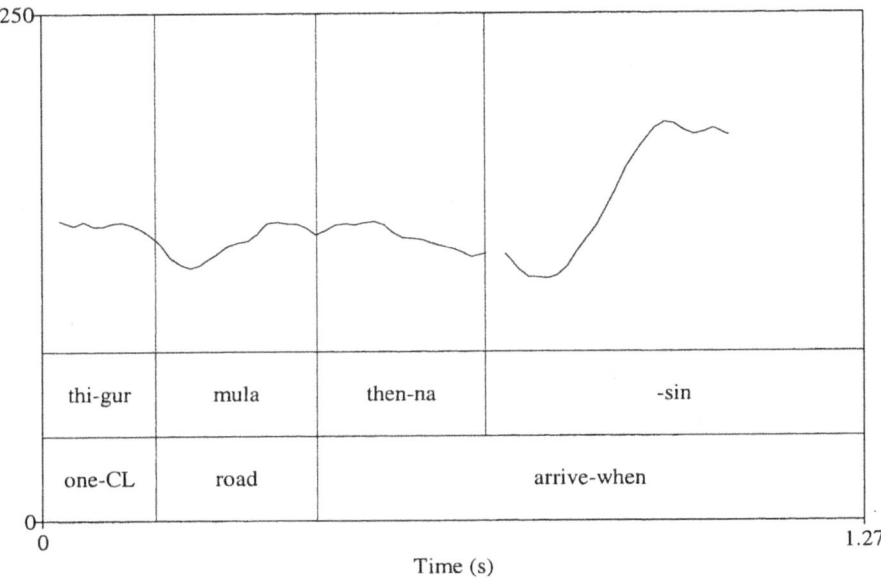

Figure 15. Pitch trace for *thi-gur ^mula then-nasin* // 'When (he) arrived on a road'

Figure 15 illustrates the changes in fundamental frequency over an intonation unit classified as marked rise. The phrasal accent results in a pitch rise on *mula* 'road', after which the pitch falls more than 20 hertz to the beginning of the ultimate vowel. The vowel shows a rise of 70 hertz, followed by a rise-fall on the nasal coda. Although we can distinguish phonetically between two types of rising terminal contours, the two constitute distinct phonetic realizations of a single phonological category. The rise and marked rise are not contrastive; we do not find one in one particular set of lexico-syntactic and discourse environments in comparison with the other. Also, as mentioned earlier, the rise contours form a continuum and do not cluster into two distinct classes. In my data there are differences between speakers in the degree to which marked rising contours are used. While some speakers produced them frequently in the recorded speech, others did so only rarely or not at all. This can probably be attributed to differences in the degree of modulation used by different speakers.

The majority of rising contours are used on intonation units which do not constitute the ends of syntactic sentences. Rising intonation units tend to contain noun phrases, adverbials, or dependent clauses, all elements which are syntactically dependent on a following head. Hence rising contours are overwhelmingly anticipatory; they mark that more is to come. As one would expect then, rising contours are generally not found on intonation units containing a non-embedded finite verb that completes a syntactic sentence. When they do, the intonation units are usually analyzable as anticipatory within the broader discourse structure, despite the fact that at the syntactic level the speaker has completed a sentence. For example, sequences of finite clauses can be used to relate events that occur in a tight series. When this happens, these finite clauses can occur with rising intonation. An example is given in (6). Here the speaker is telling of the hardships that two sisters experience, which she contrasts with the happy life of the third sister. There are two nearly identical episodes relating how each sister is refused food by her husband. The end of each episode is marked by the production of a finite verb, but their larger structure as a series of related events is marked by rising intonation:

(6)   a. ... āmta   nai   ma-bi-u ,   /
               3sDAT   food   NEG-give-3PA

               'He didn't give her (the first sister) any food.'

five lines later

            b. āle   bhānche=n   āmta   jā   na-i   ma-bir-ju ,   /
               then   cook=ERG   3sDAT   rice   eat-INF   NEG-give-3sPST

               'Then the cook did not give her (the second sister) rice to eat.'

three lines later

            c. sukhā=n   ānthi   yeŋ-an   coŋ-an   libi ,   /,
               happiness =INST   that.manner   do-PART   stay-PART   later

               '(The third sister) was living in happiness later...'

Thus the speaker is using syntax and intonation to structure the discourse at two independent levels. Syntax is used to convey the episodic structure and intonation is used to convey the inter-episodic relation and higher-level structuring. Further discussion of the interaction of syntax and prosody can be found in Chapter 21.

My data set contains one narrative where the speaker used rising intonation with considerable frequency: almost 70% of the intonation units in the first 100 seconds of her narrative had a rising terminal contour. In addition, almost 90% of the intonation units with rising contours occurred at the ends of sentences. This pattern would appear to run counter to the normal pattern in the narratives, whereby sentence-finality is marked with falling intonation. After some reflection, I believe that the reason the speaker used rising intonation so frequently was not to repeatedly mark continuation, as one might think given the overall patterns in the language, but to mark appeal, specifically to check whether the listener was comprehending the story. My impression is based on the fact that I was the sole listener to the rendition of the story, which I recorded just a few weeks after I began studying the language. Obviously, my knowledge of the language was limited, and my consultant, as she related the story, kept watching me expectantly and with some concern. I remember feeling awkward about nodding repeatedly as if I really were understanding the story, but it seemed to satisfy her as she related the quite complex story to the end. Further study of intonational contours preceding backchannel responses is warranted to test this hypothesis.

4.4. Rise-fall terminal contour

The rise-fall terminal intonation contour has similar properties to the rising contour. Like the rise, it is predominantly realized over the last syllable of the intonation unit (although, as with the rise, the increase in fundamental frequency occasionally begins on the antepenult). Like the rise, the rise-fall terminal contour can be said to assign a phrasal accent to the final syllable of the unit. As mentioned above, rising contours often show a slight drop in fundamental frequency at the end of the final segment in the unit. This is always less than half the distance of the total rise of the contour and the decrease tends to co-occur with a drop in amplitude, rendering the falling portion of the sequence less salient. Contours classified as rise-fall have a different profile. The final fall begins earlier in the unit, typically around the mid-point of the vowel or toward the beginning of a nasal consonant. In addition, the decrease in fundamental frequency is roughly equivalent to the preceding increase, so that the starting and ending pitches of the contour are at about the same level. Finally, the amplitude over the portion of the pitch fall remains relatively strong. The result is a contour with an audibly falling portion. The rise-fall contour is transcribed with a slash followed by a backslash (/\).

The amount of change in fundamental frequency found with rise-fall contours varies by speaker, as does the frequency with which this contour is used. Most speakers in my sample use this contour sparingly, and these generally show an increase and decrease of 25 hertz or greater. One speaker used this contour frequently in his narrative, but with reduced size: the rises and falls in his speech are between 10 and 20 hertz.

Figure 16 represents the change in fundamental frequency across an intonation unit with a rise-fall terminal contour. With the exception of a slight rise-fall on *santān* 'heirs' due to phrasal accent, the fundamental frequency is held quite steady at close to 140 hertz prior to the final syllable. The fundamental frequency then rises 40 hertz in the first half of the vowel and falls 40 hertz in the second half of the vowel.

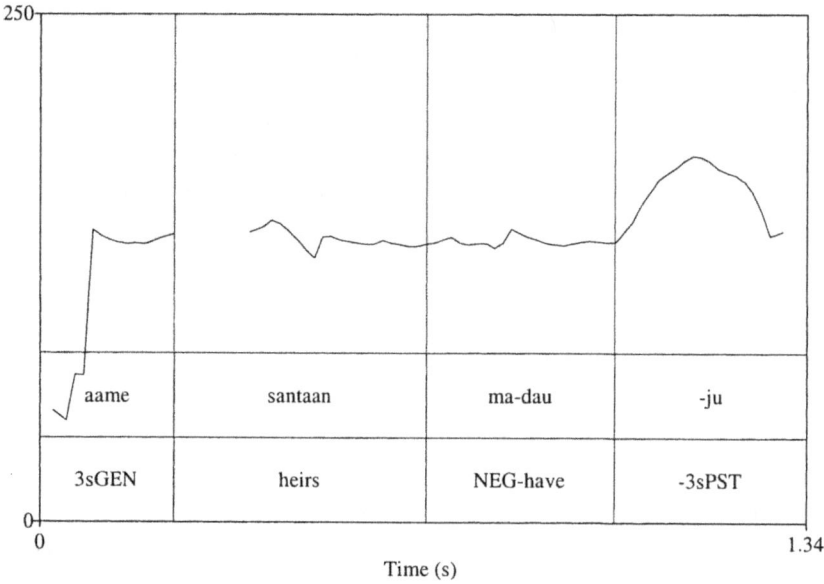

Figure 16. Pitch trace of *āme ^santān ma-da-u-ju* 'Then he had no heirs'

Rise-fall terminal contours are most often used for exclamatory utterances, such as vocatives, imperatives, and clauses where the speaker is communicating a strong belief in the truth value of the proposition. The use of a rise-fall pitch shape in this context mirrors its use as the marker of emphatic phrasal accent.

A different type of rise-fall contour is found on intonation units that have an overall falling trajectory. The rise-fall portion is again realized over the last vowel, which is typically lengthened. The rise-fall portion is smaller in amplitude than in examples such as that illustrated in Figure 16. The overall fall combined with the small rise-fall and vowel lengthening give a strong sense of finality. Genetti and Slater (2004: 7) call this a "subtype of prototypical final intonation". An example is given in Figure 17:

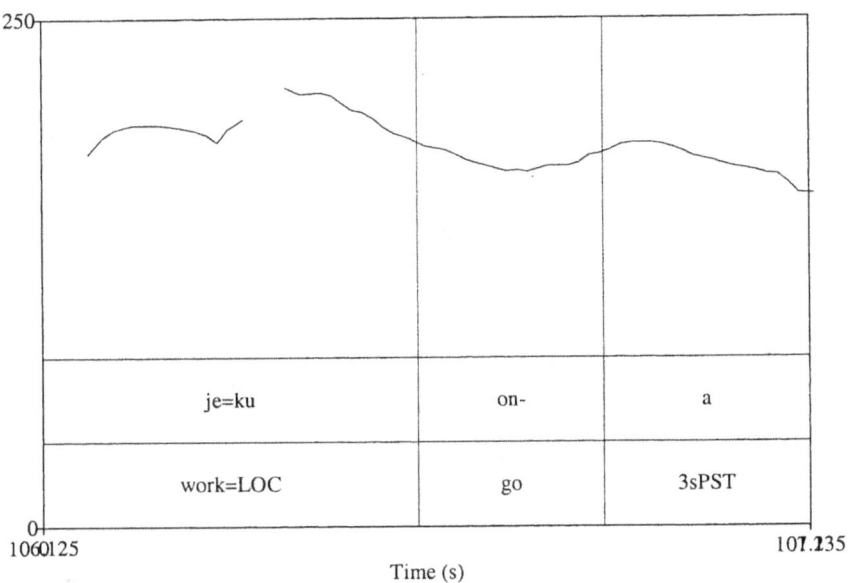

Figure 17. Pitch trace of *je=^-ku on-a* 'He went to work'

5. Transitional continuity

The preceding section provided description of four types of terminal contours: falls, levels, rises, and rise-falls. While the function of intonation contours is quite complex, we can still identify the primary uses of each contour type. Falling terminal contours are generally used to mark syntactic finality and contrastive noun phrases. Level terminal contours are primarily used in embedded quotations, most of which are also syntactically final within the quote. Rising terminal contours are most commonly used to signal anticipation of more to come or to solicit appeal. Rise-fall contours are used on exclamatory units, which are most likely to be final, not anticipating further material.

From these primary functions, we can see that Dolakha Newar speakers are using intonation to mark "transitional continuity"; in other words, speakers are signaling intonationally whether they intend to continue with the "discourse business at hand," or whether they have reached the end of a significant unit (Du Bois et al. 1993). Transitional continuity is one of the "signpost" functions of intonation (Chafe 1987: 386), ways for the speaker to signal to the hearer his or her intentions for the immediate speech. Of the four types of terminal contours, the falling, level, and exclamatory contours are overwhelmingly "final" in this sense. Rises, on the other hand, are overwhelmingly "continuing." These correlations can be found when we examine the distribution of these contours *vis-à-vis* units that are syntactically final (contain a non-embedded finite verb or other material which marks a lack of syntactic continuation) and syntactically continuing (ending in arguments, adverbials, or dependent clauses which hold a syntactic relation with material yet to come). In a study of the interaction of prosody and syntax in four narratives, I found the following correlations between final intonation contours and syntactic content of the intonation unit:

Table 5. Terminal contour type and syntactic finality/continuity

Contour Type	Syntactically Final #	%	Syntactically Continuing #	%
Falling, level, rise-fall	70	67.3	27	25.7
Rising contours	34	32.7	78	74.3

One can easily see that while there are very strong patterns, the correlations between contour type and syntactic content are not absolute. This shows that speakers are manipulating the syntactic and prosodic levels independently, and may produce the expected correlations or deviate from them for functional reasons. Many of the counter-examples to the expected correlations represent significant sub-patterns. For example, cases where falling contours occur on contrastive noun phrases or rising contours indicate appeal. Other times, the deviation from expected pattern may occur when the speaker is marking distinct levels of structure (as in example (6) above). Each case of deviation is unique and can only be understood through a qualitative investigation of the discourse. Further examples and discussion of "syntax/prosody mismatches" are given in §21.6.2.

The presence of exceptions to the expected syntax/prosody correlations illustrates that the identification of transitional continuity cannot automatically be read from the terminal intonational contour, but must additionally be sensitive to independent syntactic or functional elements in the surrounding discourse context. There is not an absolute correlation between the phonological level of terminal contour and the functional level of transitional continuity. Thus these two dimensions need to be transcribed independently. Following Du Bois et al. (1993), final transitional continuity will be marked with a period, while continuing transitional continuity will be marked with a comma. Example (6) above has both dimensions transcribed.

6. Summary

As this discussion has indicated, prosody is one of the central systems by which speakers parse and organize connected speech. It is used both to break the speech into manageable chunks (intonation units) which are easily processed cognitively (Chafe 1994: 53–70). It is also used to highlight and background particular units, and particular words within those units. And, crucially, it is used as a "signpost" which provides cues to the hearer about the relationships between units, as well as whether or not the material constitutes embedded direct quotation. However, the signpost function does more than simply provide cues to the hearer. It also allows for higher level prosodic structuring, as speakers use transitional continuity to combine single intonation units into structured groups which I label "prosodic sentences" (Genetti and Slater 2004). A full discussion of prosodic sentence is deferred until Chapter 21 (§21.5).

There is one other important function of prosody which I am not able to address, that of conveying affect, or the emotional state or attitude of the speaker. It is clear that prosody in Dolakha Newar has this function; however, I will leave this topic for future study, ideally by a native speaker of the language.

Chapter 4
Nouns and noun morphology

1. Introduction

The traditional definition of a noun is based on semantics: a word that refers to a person, place, or thing. However, semantic definitions for word classes are notoriously insufficient when describing languages in detail. It is much better to identify the word classes of a language based on shared morphological and syntactic behavior and that will be the approach taken in this book.

In Dolakha Newar, there are two clear criteria which uniquely identify nouns as an independent lexical class. First, only nouns and pronouns may function as arguments of a verb without any morphological modification (excluding case-marking). This criterion allows us to differentiate nouns from verbs and adjectives; these may only function as arguments if they are first modified by derivational morphology. Second, nouns can be differentiated from pronouns in that nouns form an open lexical class. New nouns may be added to the class by the mechanisms of compounding, suffixation, the lexicalization of headless relative clauses, and borrowing. In addition, nouns do not have the idiosyncratic patterns of inflection for number and case that are found with pronouns. Instead, number and case are realized by clitics.

2. Phonotactic properties of nouns

In Dolakhae, nouns may have a number of phonotactic shapes. Most nouns are disyllabic, although monosyllabic nouns are also common. Trisyllabics occur infrequently, while quadrisyllabic nouns are rare, but attested. It seems likely that many of the trisyllabic and quadrisyllabic nouns may have arisen historically from compounding or derivational processes, e.g. *ḍusili* 'millet stalk' is clearly based on *ḍusi* 'millet'. Examples of nouns of various sizes and shapes are given in (1). It may be noted that syllable types are unrestricted, that is, syllables of any type may occur in any position within the word. In this way nouns differ from verbs, which have very limited phonotactic possibilities:

(1) Nouns of varying shapes and sizes

Monosyllabic nouns
bo	'plate'	d(h)ū	'tiger'
khā	'talk; language'	ne	'iron'
si	'louse'	phā	'pig'
cher	'head'	khwāl	'face'
lon	'womb'	pāŋ	'fruit'
mes	'female water buffalo'	tir	'riverbank'

Disyllabic Nouns
jyālā	'cost'	lyuri	'bronze'
pwākal	'hole'	pyākhan	'dance'
ṭuṭi	'foot; leg'	baji	'beaten rice'
ciku	'ant'	dari	'yogurt'
duku	'goat'	kōsa	'bone'
kehẽ	'younger sister'	lokhu	'water'
luŋā	'stone'	sāŋat	'friend'
wāsar	'medicine'	calti	'sweat'
kumlo	'bundle'	nemlā	'moon'
jāŋal	'bird'	turkan	'mustard'

Trisyllabic Nouns
kuciri	'claws; fingernails'	mogara	'upper back'
ṭēburi	'navel'	swā̃hārā	'field, non-irrigated'
nasputi	'ear'		

Quadrisyllabic Nouns
kurāmuni	'condensed milk'	yālāguri	'gland'

3. Incorporating new nouns into the language

Nouns in Dolakhae may be derived through the processes of compounding and suffixation. In addition, some nouns are created through the lexicalization of headless relative clauses. Finally, nouns are freely borrowed from other languages, most notably Nepali, Sanskrit, and other Indo-Aryan languages.

3.1. Compounding

Compounding is the creation of a noun via the juxtaposition of two other words, generally both nouns, without any intervening morphology. The compounds I have found in the language are well-established vocabulary; compounding is not a highly productive process and new compounds appear to be rare.

In some nominal compounds, the two elements that combine are both transparently elements of the current lexicon. In other cases, only one element is recognizable. When two nouns form a compound in Dolakhae, the first noun is generally the modifier of the second:

(2)
Compound	Formatives	Gloss
onsa̅-mi	man-person	'man'
misā-mi	woman-person	'woman'
khicā-wā	dog-tooth	'canine tooth'
cyas-pyāṭā	?-belly	'lower belly'
deu-culā	god-finger	'index finger'
dāti-culā	middle-finger	'middle finger'
paksin-culā	witch-finger	'ring (4th) finger'
cirkan-culā	sparrow-finger	'little finger'
lokhu-bati	water-cat	'otter'
dudu-kãkar	milk-corn	'fresh corn'
kãkar-sã	corn-hair	'corn silk'
mikhā-sã	eye-hair	'eyebrow; eyelash'
mā-cilā	mother-goat	'goat, female'
phāŋā-kocu	blanket-pox	'measles'
kwākar-beŋ	?-frog	'frog'
pāhā-beŋ	?-frog	'toad'
ban-phā	forest-pig	'wild pig'
ban-bati	forest-cat	'lynx'
ban-khā	forest-fowl	'pheasant'
twās-mica	?-daughter	'daughter's blood friend'
kā-sukā	?-thread	'sacred thread'
bār-pāŋ	?-fruit	'tomato'
ṭwāŋ-sona	?-flower	'rhododendron'

Compounds may also be created by combining two nouns which denote elements that occur as natural sets. In such cases, neither noun modifies the other:

(3)	Compound	Formatives	Gloss
	mā-bā	mother-father	'parents'
	kae-mica	son-daughter	'children'
	sut-pānt	suit-pants	'suit' (western-style)
	tisā-wāsti	jewelry-clothes	'attire'
	bō-khosu	cloud-fog	'clouds and fog'
	luŋmā-tuphi	mortar-pestle	'mortar and pestle'

Compounds are also found when the first noun denotes a specific type and the second noun denotes a general entity, e.g. *bulbul ciḍiyā* 'bulbul bird', *pāŋ simā* 'fruit tree', *phāpar mari* 'phapar bread', *duku pujā* 'goat ritual'.

It is also common to form compounds when the first element is either *ḍwāku* 'big' (from the verb *ḍwākar-* 'be big; become big') or *cicā* 'small' (from *cicār-* 'be small; become small'). Forms with *ḍwāku* are treated here as compounds as opposed to nonce concatenations of adjective plus noun simply because these sequences regularly denote a particular object and are clearly lexicalized. In the case of *cicā* there is a clear argument in favor of analyzing these as compounds; the adjectival form of the verb is not *cicā* but *cicā-u* with the final nominalizing suffix NR1, which is absent from the compounds. Examples of compounds formed with *ḍwāku* and *cicā* are given below:

(4)	Compound	Formatives	Gloss
	ḍwāku-kocu	large-pox	'smallpox'
	cicā-kocu	small-pox	'chickenpox'
	cic-bā (cij-bā)	small-father	'step-father'
	cic-mā (cij-mā)	small-mother	'step-mother'
	ḍwāku-mulā	large-finger	'thumb'
	ci-chŭ	small-rat	'house shrew'

3.2. Derivational suffixation

I know of only one productive derivational suffix which derives nouns from other nouns. It is the diminutive *-cā* which is used to denote the young of animals:

(5)	Derived Noun	Formatives	Gloss
	cil-cā	goat-DIM	'kid'
	sā-cā	cow-DIM	'calf'
	phasi-cā	sheep-DIM	'lamb'
	khā-cā	chicken-DIM	'chick'

The form can also be used on kin terms, especially when referring to children:

(6) binā   'niece'   binā-cā   'little niece'
     sāilā   'third child'   sāilā-cā   'little sāila'

I have also seen this suffix with two quantifiers: *uli* 'this much' ~ *uli-cā* 'this little', and *bāti* 'a little' *bāti-cā* 'just a little'.

3.3. Lexicalization of headless relative clauses

It is also possible to create new nominal terms via the lexicalization of headless relative clauses. A relative clause is defined as a clause which modifies a noun and in which the referent of that noun plays a syntactic role, such as subject or object. Relative clauses are discussed in detail in §17.2.1.1. In the following example, the head noun *mi* 'man' is being modified by the relative clause *mes syāk-u*.

(7) [[mes   syāk-u]$_{REL}$ mi]$_{NP}$
     w.buffalo kill-NR1   man

   'The man who kills water buffalos'; 'butcher'

Note that the noun *mi* 'man' can never appear within the relative clause. Thus the phrase *mi=n mes syāk-u* [man=ERG w.buffalo kill-NR1] will never be used as a relative clause modifying a head noun with the meaning in (7) (although it may be used as a nominalized clause; see §17.2.3).

In Dolakhae, it is common to leave the head noun unspecified, creating a headless relative clause. Certain headless relative clauses are used repeatedly in Dolakhae and may be said to have lexicalized. This is especially common with relative clauses created from verbs with adjectival meaning. The resultant structure has the meaning 'one who is X', or more simply 'the X one', where X stands for the adjectival meaning coded by the verb. In this use, these forms commonly co-occur with the individuating clitic =*(u)ri* which is used to specify one out of a group (§10.2.1):

(8) cicā-u=ri   'the small one'   <cicār- 'to be small'
     ḍwāk-u=ri   'the big one'   <ḍwākar- 'to be big'
     hāka-u=ri   'the black one'   <hākar- 'to be black'
     hẽga-u=ri   'the red one'   <hẽgar- 'to be red'

Section 3 Incorporating new nouns   95

This process is also common with occupational terms:

(9)   *hāluwā chuk-u*   'haluwa cook'   <*hāluwā* 'haluwa' *chut-* 'cook'
       wāsti hi-u   'laundress'   <*wāsti* 'clothes' + *hir-*'wash'
       tisā dake-u   'jeweler'   <*tisā* 'jewelry' + *daker-* 'make'
       jā chu   'cook'   <*jā* 'rice' + *chur-* 'cook'
       ḍoli bu   'litter carrier'   <*ḍoli* 'litter' + *bur-* 'carry'

As these terms usually include the object of the verb, it is clear that these are lexicalizations of relative clauses as opposed to being the derivation of simple nouns. In addition, one always has the option of following these lexicalizations with a head noun, such as *mi* 'person', which again gives the process a syntactic, as opposed to a derivational, flavor. Thus the extent to which these items are truly lexicalized, in the sense of comprising distinct lexical items, is unclear.[24]

3.4. Borrowing

The other way of incorporating new nouns into Dolakhae is the process of borrowing. Not surprisingly, the most common source language for borrowed nouns are Indo-Aryan, most notably Nepali. English nouns may also be found, however these may have been borrowed through Nepali. The extent of borrowing from Indo-Aryan may be attested by the large number of Indo-Aryan nouns found in my lexical database, composed primarily of words found in narrative, but also additionally containing elicited words. Of these, about 39% were Indo-Aryan loans and about 59% were either native Dolakhae lexemes or nativized Indo-Aryan borrowings (i.e. nouns originally borrowed from Nepali or other Indo-Aryan languages, but with unique phonological adaptations). The remaining 2% were from English. The large number of Nepali loans may clearly be attributed to extensive bilingualism; virtually all Dolakhae speakers are bilingual in Nepali. As a result of this large percent of lexical borrowings, Newars from other regions of the country have often commented to me that Dolakhae is "mixed Newari/Nepali". While this may be true at the lexical level, especially so with nouns, it is clear that the grammatical system of Dolakhae is quite original and that the language differs from Nepali in many ways.

Nouns may be borrowed into Dolakhae without any morphological modification. Borrowed nouns are treated just like native nouns morphologically, and thus undergo the same suffixation and cliticization processes, as the following examples illustrate. For clarification, I will indicate the source language of the borrowed nouns with either (IA) for Indo-Aryan or (E) for English following the gloss:

(10) **pharsi=n**   suntali=ta   bihā   yeŋ-an
      pumpkin(IA)=ERG Suntali=DAT marriage do-PART

      'After the pumpkin married Suntali...'

(11) ānāgu   **rādi=n**   phār-gi
      that.type rug(IA)=INST wrap-1sPST

      'I wrapped her in a rug of that type.'

(12) **gilās=ku**   mahi hā-en   tar-ai
      glass(E)=LOC lassi bring-PART put-3sPR

      'He brings out lassi (beverage made with yogurt) in a glass.'

(13) **dāi=pen**   sõ-mā=n=ri   ām ciḍiyā jāŋal
      e.brother(IA)=PL three-CL=ERG=IND that bulbul bird

      hā-en   yer-hin
      bring-PART come-3pPST

      'The three elder brothers came, bringing that bulbul bird.'

(14) ām **sugā=ta**   thi-mā sāuji=n   ŋyāt-ai
      that parrot(IA)=DAT one-CL shopkeeper(IA)=ERG buy-3sPR

      'Then one shopkeeper bought that parrot.'

Although I do have a large number of borrowed nouns in my lexical database, the frequency of borrowed nouns in running discourse varies considerably depending on what is being discussed. They occur rarely in casual conversation, and more frequently in narratives, with the highest frequency in my data being found in the traditional Hindu epics.

4. Morphological categories relevant to nouns

The three morphological categories relevant to nouns are number, case and individuation/extension. All three of these categories are marked by morphological clitics. They occur in the following order:

STEM=PLURAL=CASE=INDIVIDUATION/EXTENSION

It should be noted that there is no grammatical gender in Dolakhae.

4.1. Number

There is a single nominal clitic used to indicate number; it is =*pen*, the plural marker. This clitic has idiosyncratic case inflection, as the stem changes to /=pis/ before casemarkers:

(15) Inflection of the plural marker =*pen*
      Absolutive   =*pen*
      Ergative   =*pisin* ~ =*pisna*
      Dative   =*pista*
      Allative   =*piske*
      Genitive   =*pe*

    The evidence for the plural being a clitic is not as strong as it is with the casemarkers, or clitics of individuation and extension (see below). In many ways the plural seems to be intermediate between an affix and a clitic. The plural morpheme is clearly phonologically bound to its host; it cannot occur independently of a host, and when a word with the plural morpheme is pronounced in isolation, the plural has the characteristic prosodic weakness found with final syllables of monomorphemic words.
    The primary reason to consider the plural morpheme to be a clitic rather than a suffix is that in the absence of a head noun the morpheme is bound to the either a genitive phrase, as in (16), or a headless relative clause, as in (17). This appears to be evidence of a weaking of the boundedness between the plural morpheme and the category of noun.

(16)   **jātra=e=pisin**   *mān-ai*   *yet-ai*
        festival=GEN=PL celebrate-BV do-3sPR

        'The (people) of the festival celebrate.'

(17)   *kār-a*   **oŋ-gu=pen**
        take-PURP go-NR1=PL

        'The (people) who go to take it.'

    On the other hand, unlike the case clitics, the plural is not always bound to the final lexical element in the noun phrase. The one case where the plural is non-final in the NP is when the noun is followed by a numeral plus classifier. In this case the plural morpheme is on the noun, not on the numeral phrase:

(18) **didā=pen**   nis-mā=ŋ   yer-a
       e.brother=PL two-CL=EXT   come-3sPST

'The two elder brothers came.'

Note that the plural is not required when a numeral is present in a noun phrase. The following example is taken from the same text as the preceding, just a few sentences earlier:

(19) **didā**   nis-mā=ŋ   jaŋgal   ū-i   doŋ-guju
      e.brother   two-CL=EXT   jungle   go-INF finish-3PA

'The two elder brothers had gone to the jungle.'

The plural morpheme appears to be more like a suffix and less like a clitic when we examine its distribution in conjoined noun phrases. In such cases the plural marked occurs independently on both elements, e.g. *dānābi=pen ho debgan=pen* 'the giants and the gods'.

Turning to semantics, the plural category marked by =*pen* is referred to as an associative plural. As such, one of its uses is that of signaling basic plurality, i.e. the presence of more than one object of the same type. Examples (20)–(22) illustrate this meaning of the plural clitic:

(20) **mucā=pen=ri**   din prati din   dwākar-hin
      child=PL=IND   day by day   grow-3pPST

'Day by day the children grew.'

(21) ām   pipāna ye-u   **mi=pen**   gun   jeu?
      that outside come-NR1   person=PL   who   maybe

'Who are the people who came to the veranda?'

(22) **kīja=pen=uŋ**   sit-a
      y.brother=PL=EXT die-3sPST

'The (two) younger brothers died.'

However, =*pen* may also be used more generally to indicate a group of related, as opposed to identical, objects. In the following example, there is only one dowry, thus the plural form *theki=pen* refers to the many objects that the dowry consists of:

(23) ām   jammai   mica=uri=e   **thekhi=pen**   āu
     that together daughter=IND=GEN   dowry=PL   now

   mica=e   palaŋ =na   samet   yeŋ-an
   daughter=GEN bed=INST   accompanying   bring-PART

   'Bringing all the daughter's dowry things together with the daughter's bed...'

Similarly, in the following example *cijmā=pen* does not refer to multiple stepmothers, but instead to the stepmother and others associated with her, in this case, her husband and daughter:

(24) āme   **cijmā=pen**   mā-yer-a   haŋ-an
     3sGEN   stepmother=PL   NEG-come-3sPST   say-PART

   khusi   ju-en   con-gu
   happy   become-PART   stay-3sPA

   'Her stepmother and all, saying: "She didn't come", were very happy.'

In example (25), *lū cə̃di=pen* is not restricted in reference to multiple pieces of gold and silver, but indicates riches more generally:

(25) āmun   lū   cə̃di=pen   guli   bu-i   phar-ai
     3sERG   gold silver=PL   how.much   carry-INF   able-3sPR

   'She is able to carry so much gold, silver, etc.'

Whether a given example of =*pen* should be interpreted as a simple plural, as in examples (20)–(22), or as an associative plural, as in examples (23)–(25), depends upon the context in which it used. Both real-world knowledge (as in the knowledge that one generally does not have more than one stepmother) and text-based knowledge (as in the knowledge that there was only one wedding being discussed, thus one dowry) contribute to the interpretation of these forms.

It should be noted that the plural marker is optional. It is common to find nouns appearing without =*pen* even though the context clearly establishes them as semantically plural. The following sentence is from a story in Hindu mythology which relates the battle of gods and demons during the creation of the world:

(26) **debgan-na** kā-i doŋ-an-li
      god-ERG take-INF finish-PART-after

'After the gods had taken (the airak) ...'

In the context of the story, it is clearly a group of gods which take the *airak* 'liquor', as opposed to being a single god; however, the noun is not formally marked as plural. Another clear example of a semantically plural noun appearing without the plural clitic is given in (27):

(27) ŋā-mā **dū** wā gwār=ku thi-gur=uri ur-ai
      five-CL tiger TOP shelter=LOC one-CL=IND circle-3sPR

'Five tigers circled the one shelter.'

The omission of the plural marker in the presence of a numeral is common (see also (19) above).

A final point to make is that no other number categories are marked on the noun. There are no dual, paucal, or other number categories relevant to Dolakhae grammar.

4.2. Case

4.2.1. *NP-Internal and NP-level clitic casemarkers*

The marking of case, the indexing of syntactic and semantic roles of noun phrases, is a central part of Dolakha Newar grammar. Case is used to indicate the essential relationships which hold between animate participants, inanimate objects, and the verb. The set of Dolakhae casemarkers is given in Table 6, which lists the conventional gloss for each morpheme, the phonological forms by which each morpheme is realized, and whether each casemarker is found NP-internally or at the NP-level only.

This section of the grammar will first consider the syntactic positioning and morphological status of the casemarkers, then will move on to a discussion of the range of casemarking found on the core arguments (subjects and objects), with particular attention to the nature of ergativity in Dolakhae. Following this will be a discussion of casemarkers which are found on "oblique arguments", namely the various local cases.

Table 6. Clitic casemarkers

Gloss	Form(s)	Positioning
Ergative	=na, =n	NP-level
Dative	=ta	NP-level
Instrumental	=na, =n	NP-level
Locative	=ku	NP-level
Ablative 1	=lān	NP-level
Ablative 2	=na, nasi	NP-level
Allative	=ke	NP-internal or NP-level
Genitive	=e	NP-internal only

4.2.2. *Syntactic positioning of casemarkers*

The Dolakhae casemarkers fall into two sets with regard to their syntactic positioning. NP-external casemarkers, which are in a paradigmatic relationship (i.e. they occupy the same position with respect to the noun and do not co-occur), are consistently positioned after the plural clitic (if there is one) and before any discourse clitics and particles. These casemarkers indicate the grammatical and/or syntactic relationship between the noun phrase and the verb.

The two NP-internal casemarkers (the genitive and, in some uses, the allative) are also in a paradigmatic relationship. They differ from the NP-level casemarkers in that they occur noun-phrase internally and indicate the relationship between a dependent noun and its head. Consider the following sentence:

(28)   [*mucā=e*   *muthu=ku*]$_{NP}$ *dudu*   *on-a*
        child=GEN   mouth=LOC   milk   go-3sPST

       'The milk went into the child's mouth.'

Here we see the genitive morpheme =*e* occurring within the noun phrase, marking a dependency relationship between the modifying noun *mucā* 'child' and the head noun *muthu* 'mouth'. The NP-level locative morpheme =*ku* is found at the end of the noun phrase *mucā=e muthu* and indicates its relationship with the other elements of the clause.

The genitive =*e* may function as an internal casemarker even in cases where the head noun on which it is dependent is not present, as in the following:

(29)   [*megu=ri*   *mi=e*]$_{NP}$ *ŋen-ju*
        other=IND   man=GEN   ask-3sPST

       '(He) asked the other man's (question).'

The allative =*ke* may occur in either position, but with a meaning difference. When it occurs at the NP-level, the allative indicates a human goal:

(30)   ji   wā   **rājā=ke**   tuŋ   ū-i
        1s   TOP   king=ALL   FOC   go-1FUT

        'I will go to the king.'

When it occurs internally, the allative indicates a genitive relationship between the head and the dependent noun, with an additional implicature of a locative relationship along with the possessive. Thus, the allative signals that the possessor is in physical possession of the item. This is most clearly illustrated with the following pair of elicited examples:

(31)   Elicited
        [**āme**   sarchi   dyābā]$_{NP}$ dam
        3sGEN   100   rupee   exist

        'He has 100 rupees (maybe with him now, maybe not).'

(32)   Elicited
        [**āmke**   sarchi   dyābā]$_{NP}$ dam
        3sALL   100   rupee   exist

        'He has 100 rupees on him (i.e. with him right now).'

In the following sentence, the genitive =*e* co-occurs with the locative =*ku*. The former is NP-internal and the latter is noun-phrase final. However, since the head noun is not present in this noun phrase, the two casemarkers are contiguous:

(33)   [[***jogi=e*]=ku**]$_{NP}$ then-ju
        yogi=GEN=LOC   arrive-3sPST

        'He arrived at the yogi's (place).'

It is clear that although the two casemarkers are contiguous, they are performing different functions. The first is indicating the place or abode of the yogi, even though a head noun such as *thāī* 'place' is not present. The second is indicating the relationship of the yogi's place as the locative goal of the motion verb. Examples such as these, where an internal casemarker occurs contiguous to an NP-level casemarker, are the only examples where casemarkers may combine.

4.2.3. Morphological status of casemarkers

The Dolakhae casemarkers fall into two classes morphologically: clitics and postpositions. All of the core casemarkers and the more general of the locational casemarkers are clitics. The arguments for considering them to be clitics are discussed in detail below. As a preview to these arguments, the four primary arguments for clitic status are as follows: (1) they have unique phonological properties that show they are bound morphemes as opposed to independent words; (2) they do not occur in the absence of a host; (3) they do not select a particular lexical class (e.g. noun) as their host but are bound to the final element of the noun phrase, regardless of its lexical class; and (4) they have scope over the entire noun phrase, as opposed to having scope over only the word to which they are bound. Clitics differ from affixes in that they exhibit unique phonological processes not shared by affixes and in the fact that they do not select a particular lexical class as their host. Clitics differ from independent words in that they are phonologically bound. More detailed argumentation and exemplification is given below.

I will use the term "postposition" to refer to casemarkers that are independent phonological words.[25] They are larger than a single syllable, are not phonologically bound, do not cause reduction in the preceding word, and may occur in the absence of a host. Postpositions have quite specific locational meanings.

4.2.3.1. Clitics

Clitic casemarkers in Dolakhae have a number of properties which show they are phonologically bound morphemes as opposed to independent words. The ergative/instrumental morpheme has two allomorphs, =na, which occurs after consonants, and =n, which occurs after vowels. This pattern is shown by the following inflected words:

(34) mucā=n   'child'=ERG   mes=na   water buffalo=ERG
      tuṭi=n   'foot'=INST   caṭan=na   spoon=INST

Since phonological alternations of this type do not occur across word boundaries, but commonly occur across internal morpheme boundaries, this is excellent evidence that the ergative/instrumental morpheme is phonologically bound. This pattern of alternation is unique to this clitic and is not a general process that is found across affix boundaries or with other clitics. In addition, words with clitics often show patterns of reduction characteristic of phonological words. For examples, vowels can devoice or be deleted before the dative casemarker =ta, e.g. micata > micta [daughter-DAT]. This is evidence that the clitics and the host together form a single phonological word. Moving to prosody, when words with these clitics are pronounced in isolation, the clitics are prosodically weak as expected in the final syllable of a word. Finally, clitics do not take independent stress.

While the casemarkers are phonologically bound, it is clear that they are not suffixes, as they take the entire noun phrase into their scope. One argument in favor of this analysis is that noun phrases consisting of conjoined nouns may be casemarked only once, following the second conjunct:

(35)   ām   **bobu=ri**   o   **mā=uri=n=ri**   salāhā   yet-ai
       that father=IND and mother=IND=ERG=IND confer do-3sPR

'That father and mother conferred.'

The casemarker is clearly an NP-level, as opposed to a word-level, morpheme.

A second argument in favor of analyzing the casemarkers as bound clitics is that they are morphologically bound: they must have a host and never occur independently without a preceding noun phrase. This is not a necessary property of postpositions, and indeed postpositions may occur "stranded" without a preceding noun phrase (see below).

Another argument in favor of treating casemarkers as clitics as opposed to suffixes is that suffixes (and prefixes) are restricted in their distribution in being morphologically bound to members of a single lexical class. In Dolakhae the casemarkers are not restricted to nouns but occur following whatever element is final in the noun phrase. In the following example, the ergative clitic =n is phonologically bound to a numeral suffixed with a classifier:

(36)   titā   kehẽ   **sõ-mā=n**   khā   lā-en   con-hin
       e.sister   y.sister three-CL=ERG   talk   talk-PART   stay-3pPST

'The three sisters were talking.'

Due to these factors, the casemarkers are analyzed as clitics as opposed to suffixes or independent words.

4.2.3.2. Postpositions

There is another class of case elements which are clearly not clitics, but which have independent status as separate words. These words function as postpositions following nouns or pronouns and all but two also occur as independent adverbs. The postpositions are listed in Table 7:

Table 7. Dolakha Newar postpositions

Gloss	Form(s)
'behind'	likhan(a)
'in front'	hākhen(a)
'inside'	dupān(a)
'on'	depān(a)
'with'	nāpa
'like'	thẽ(nāgu)
'up to; until'	ṭul, ṭulle, ṭulke, ṭuleŋ

All of these forms have considerable phonological bulk, most being disyllabic. Unlike the clitics, there are no phonological rules that are invoked by juxtaposition with a preceding element, and the word preceding a postposition does not undergo phonological reduction. Postpositions receive independent lexical stress.

Three of these postpositions differ from clitics in that they require a preceding pronoun to be in genitive case, as illustrated in the examples (32)–(34).[26] This property is never found with clitics.

(37) āme **nāpa**
 3sGEN with
 'with him'

(38) jana **likhana**
 1sGEN behind
 'behind me'

(39) jana **hākhena**
 1sGEN front
 'in front of me'

Evidence that postpositions are not morphologically bound is that postpositions may appear independently in a relative clause, when the referent of the noun with which it is associated is coreferential with that of the head:

(40) **nāpa** oŋ-gu sāŋat
 ASSOC go-NR1 friend
 'the friend he went with'

Clitics may not be "stranded" in this manner. Thus the set of cliticts and the set of postpositions clearly have distinct phonological and morphological beahavior. Clitics are phonologically and morphologically bound to the NP, whereas postpositions are not.

4.2.4. The casemarking of subjects: Ergative, absolutive and the notion of transitivity

Dolakha Newar, like most languages of Nepal, has an ergative system of casemarking. It has a casemarker which is obligatorily present on "A" arguments, that is, the gramamtical subjects of transitive or ditransitive verbs, as in (41)–(44), but which is obligatorily absent on "S" arguments, that is, the grammatical subjects of intransitive verbs, as in examples (45)–(47):[27]

(41)   *dolakhā mi=n   jukun puja   yet-ai*
Dolakha person=ERG only worship do-3sPR

'Only Dolakhae people do that ceremony.'

(42)   *kwākarbeŋ=na sā   na-e*
frog=ERG   cow eat-NR2

'A frog ate a cow.'

(43)   *chin   janta   da-syāt!*
2sERG 1sDAT PROH-kill

'Don't you kill me!'

(44)   *jin=uri   chanta   sāk-u   sāk-u   bi*
1sERG=IND 2sDAT tasty-NR1 tasty-NR1 give(1FUT)

'I will give you tasty tasty (things).'

(45)   *ãku   biruwā   bur-a*
there plant   sprout-3sPST

'A plant sprouted there.'

(46)   *āmu besna khor-a*
3s   very   cry-3sPST

'She cried very much.'

(47) **āme mā** ekdam ma-pha-ene sit-a
 3sGEN mother very NEG-able-PART die-3sPST

 'Her mother became very ill and died.'

Subjects of intransitive verbs carry no casemarker. These subjects may be considered to be in absolutive case, which in this language is unmarked. (Some objects of transitive verbs are also unmarked, hence in absolutive case; see §13.3.1.)

The ergative and absolutive distinction has been characterized here in terms of transitivity, as subjects of transitive and ditransitive verbs are in ergative case and subjects of intransitive verbs are in absolutive case. This of course brings up the very important question of what constitutes a transitive (or ditranstitive) verb in Dolakhae, and what constitutes an intransitive verb.

Transitive verbs are those with two notional participants, one of which tends to be agentive and an instigator of the action (I will refer to this as the "A"), and the other tending to be patientive, or affected by the action (referred to as "O"). Examples of transtive verbs are: *thun-* 'braid', *bon-* 'read', *cir-* 'tie', *jon-* 'catch', *khur-* 'steal' and *ŋār-* 'bite'. Note that one cannot simply braid, but one must braid something. Thus *thun-* 'braid' is a two-argument, or transitive, verb. Ditransitive verbs, which also take an ergative subject, are those with three arguments, one being a recipient ("R"), such as *bir-* 'give' and *hat-* 'say'. In both cases, the verb implies three participants, e.g. A gives O to R, or A says O to R.

Intransitive verbs are those with only one notional participant (referred to as "S"), which may be agentive, instigating an action, may simply undergo an action or change of state, or may be in a particular state. Examples of intranstive verbs are: *bor-* 'fly', *cikār-* 'be cold', *dār-* 'boil (of liquid in a pot)', *gar-* 'ascend', *hār-* 'fall (of ripe fruit falling from a tree)', *khor-* 'weep', *lār-* 'heal'; recover from illness', *sir-* 'die', and *sut-* 'shrink'.

In some languages, such as English, the distinction between transitive and intransitive verbs is not strongly made, and many verbs may be used with either valence, e.g. the verb *grow* may be used intransitively in *The tomatos will grow in the sun*, or it may be used transitively, as in *I will grow tomatos*. Such verbs are referred to as "ambitransitive". In Dolakhae, however, with only a few exceptions (discussed below), the distinction between transitive and intransitive verbs is quite consistent. The transitivity of a verb can be determined not only from the inherent semantics of the verb and the casemarking of the subject, but also from the verb morphology.

The clearest marker of grammatical transitivity in verbs is the third-person-past form of the verb. The suffix is *-a* when the verb is intransitive and *-ju* when the verb is transitive. Other differences are found in negative, imperative, prohibitive, and optative forms (see §6.5). Speakers are quite consistent in treating verbs as belonging to one class or the other, and it is rare to find cases where the subject casemarking does not follow the predicted pattern.

Some verbs in Dolakhae come in transitive/intransitive pairs. In these pairs, the transitive verb has a voiceless aspirated initial consonant and the intransitive verb has a voiced initial consonant:[28]

(48) gyāt- 'fear' khyāt- 'scare'
ḍin- 'sleep' ṭhin- 'put to sleep'
ḍon- 'wake up; get up' ṭhon- 'wake someone up'
yārgar- 'be hanging' yārkhār- 'hang'

It is also common to transitivize verbs through the addition of the regular causative suffix -ker, as in dār- 'boil (INTR)', dāker- 'boil (TR)', gut- 'to be damaged (INTR)', gutker- 'to damage (TR)'. For more on the causative construction, see §15.2. Note that there is no syntactic or morphological strategy for detransitivizing a verb.

There are a very small number of verbs which do not fall into the patterns described above, and which may appear as either transitive or intransitive. One of these verbs is then- 'arrive; reach', which may appear with the intransitive third-person-singular-past ending -a, or with the transitive third-person-singular-past ending -ju, as the following alternatives illustrate.

(49) āmu chē **then-a**
āmu chē **then-ju**
3s house arrive-3sPST

'He arrived at/reached the house.'

In narrative text, the transitive forms with -ju are more common. Interestingly, speakers seem to prefer that subjects be in the absolutive case with this verb, even when the transitive ending is found (as in the example above). I have one example of this verb occurring with an ergative subject. It is taken from a written folk story:

(50) **maila** rājkumār=na=ŋ lita khunu ye-u tuŋ
second.eldest prince=ERG=EXT next day come-NR1 FOC

ṭhāĩ=ku **then-ju**
place=LOC arrive-3sPST

'The next day, the second-eldest prince reached the very place (the eldest) had come to.'

Thus the transitivity status of the verb is indeterminate.

Another verb which appears in both transitive and intransitive form is *hur-* 'peel off'. Unlike the previous two verbs discussed, this verb has clear semantic distinctions which accord with the two classifications. When treated as intransitive, the verb takes an absolutive subject and is interpreted as a single-argument predicate:

(51)   [āme   masti=e   tika]$_{NP-S}$ **hur-a**
       3sGEN   forehead=GEN   tika   peel-3sPST

'The tika on his/her forehead peeled off (of its own accord).'

When treated as transitive, the verb takes an ergative subject and is interpreted as a two-argument predicate:

(52)   [āmun]$_{NP-A}$ [tika]$_{NP-O}$ **hur-ju**
       3sERG   tika   peel-3sPST

'She/he peeled off the tika (purposely).'

This is the only verb I know of that has clearly transitive and intransitive variants with a correlation in semantic interpretation, and yet which lacks a causative suffix.[29]

In some ergative languages, other considerations besides the number of arguments inherent in the semantics of the verb may influence the ergative case-marking of subjects. For example, in Nepali, subjects of transitive verbs are ergative only in perfective contexts.[30] Other semantic and discourse factors which have been found to be relevant to the perceived transitivity of verbs include affectedness of the patient, degree to which the patient is individuated, volitionality of the agent, person of the agent, whether the verb involves an action or a non-action, and whether the clause is negative or affirmative.[31] None of these factors seem to play a role in the treatment of verbs as transitive or intransitive in Dolakhae. Example (55) illustrates ergativity in a sentence with a negated verb and a non-volitional agent. Example (56) shows a cognate-object verb 'to talk a talk', where the syntactic object *khā* is not individuated and is difficult to differentiate from the action of the verb itself. This example also shows a highly unaffected object, as does example (57). Example (58) has continuous, hence imperfective aspect. Finally, example (59) shows ergative morphology in a sentence with a non-active verb, an unindividuated object, a non-agentive agent and imperfective aspect. The subject noun phrases in these examples all take the ergative case:

(53) āle **āmun** hātiŋ sabda mā-tār-ju
     then 3sERG nothing word NEG-hear-3sPST

   'Then she didn't hear a word.'

(54) ām **kehẽ=n** khā lār-ju
     that y.sister=ERG talk talk-3sPST

   'The younger sister talked.'

(55) **āmun** hirā=e mālā khoŋ-an
     3sERG diamond=GEN necklace see-PART

   'He saw the diamond necklace...'

(56) **un** ... dwārā cul-en con-a
     3sERG fangs sharpen-PART stay-3sPST

   'She is sharpening her fangs...'

(57) **un** tuŋ si-eu
     3sERG TOP know-3FUT

   'He will know.'

Thus, the primary factor which determines the transitivity of verbs in Dolakhae is whether an event is construed as involving one or two participants. There are only a few transitive verbs which do not seem easily classifiable by this criterion. The verb *hut-* 'bark' is consistently treated as transitive, both when it is used in narrative texts, and in elicitation. This seems odd since *hal-* 'to cry out' is an intransitive verb. The verb *lor-* 'vomit' is also transitive; it is possible that the vomitus has been construed as an object of sorts. Finally, *birāt-* 'to err' is transitive. This verb is borrowed from the transitive Nepali verb *birāunu* which Turner ([1931] 1980) translates as 'forget; miss (mark); do wrongly; make a mistake over something'. Apparently this was borrowed into the language as a transitive verb, and thus retains its classification.

4.2.5. The casemarking of experiencers: Dative-experiencer constructions

Certain verbs in Dolakha Newar have an argument structure which requires one argument to be a semantic experiencer who undergoes a physical or emotional state. Some verbs additionally allow for an additional argument which semantically is the stimulus for the experience. Dative-marked experiencers exhibit only some of the behavioral properties that establish A and S arguments as grammatical subjects. They will therefore not be considered subjects, but simply experiencers.

Dative-experiencer constructions are extremely common throughout South Asia and are taken as a criterion for establishing the South Asian subcontinent as a linguistic area.[32] In Dolakhae, dative experiencers are not as widely attested, either in overall frequency, or in range of use, as in some other South Asian languages, especially Nepali. In my entire text database, there are only 50 examples with dative experiencers. Of these, 36 are clear calques on Nepali structures and involve Nepali vocabulary, most commonly Nepali verbs which require dative case on the experiencer. In the following examples, both the dative experiencers and the borrowed Nepali vocabulary are represented in bold:

(58) chana khā **ista** **man par-ai** ma-ju
2sGEN talk 1pEXC.DAT like feel-BV NEG-happen

'We don't like your talk.' (cp. Nepali: *timro kurā hāmilāi man pardaina.*)

(59) **janta** ekdam **saram lāg-ai** jur-a
1sDAT very modest touch-BV happen-3sPST

'I feel very modest.' (cp. Nepali: *malāi ekdam saram lagyo.*)

(60) **chanta birs-ai** ju-eu
2sDAT forget-BV happen-3FUT

'You will forget.' (cp. Nepali: *timilāi birsnechau.*)

(61) **thijita dukha** jur-a
1pINC.DAT trouble happen-3sPST

'We experienced trouble.' (cp. Nepali: *hāmilāi dukha bhayo.*)

(62) **thaeta** hāti **wāsta** le?
2HON.DAT what care PRT

'What do you care?' (cp. Nepali: *tapāīlāi ke wāsta?*)

(63) u **janta ṭhāhā** ma-da
this 1sDAT knowledge NEG-have

'I don't know this.' (cp. Nepali: *yo malāi ṭhāhā chaina.*)

Even sentences containing dative experiencers that do not involve borrowed Nepali vocabulary often reflect parallel structures in Nepali, and thus also appear to be calques:

(64) **thaeta**   hāti   jur-a?
      2HON.DAT what happen-3sPST

      'What happened to you?' (cp. Nepali: *tapāĩlāi ke bhayo?*)

(65) **thijita**   bāmalak-u   ju-en
      1pINC.DAT   bad-NR1   happen-PART

      'Bad things have happened to us...' (cp. Nepali: *hāmilāi narāmro bhayo.*)

There are only two native Dolakhae verbs which regularly take dative experiencers. One is the auxiliary verb *yer-*. When occurring independently, this is the intransitive verb 'come' which takes an absolutive subject. However, this verb may also function as a complement-taking predicate, with an infinitive complement (§18.2.4). In this construction, the meaning changes to 'want to; like to; be skilled at' and requires the experiencer to be in dative case:

(66) **āmta**   lokhu   tõ-i   yer-a
      3sDAT   water drink-INF come-3sPST

      'He wanted to drink some water.'

Although Nepali does not use the verb *āunu* 'to come' in this way, the verb *cahinu* 'want' used in this manner does take a dative experiencer.

The other Dolakhae verb which regularly takes a dative experiencer is *mal(dan)-* 'need' when it occurs with a nominal object:

(67) āu   chana   kehē   **mātri=ta=ŋ**   mal-a
      now 2sGEN y.sister Matri=DAT=EXT   need-3sPST

      'Now your sister Matri also needs some (children).'

(68) **ista**   nichi   u   maldan-a
      1pEXC.DAT one.day this need-3sPST

      'We will need this one day.'

Again, this pattern follows Nepali closely. In that language the verb *cahinu* 'to want; need' would be used, which requires a dative experiencer.

To conclude, the Dolakha Newar dative-experiencer construction appears to be primarily borrowed from Nepali. The majority of predicates with dative-experiencer argument structure involve Nepali vocabulary. The remaining predicates appear to be either direct calques on Nepali strucutres or to represent similar patterns of agreement for verbs with similar semantic content.

4.2.6. *The casemarking of objects: Absolutive and dative*[33]

In many languages, the class of objects is divided into two separate subclasses: direct objects of transitive and ditransitive verbs (e.g. *I brushed **her hair**; I donated **my savings** to the charity*) and indirect objects of ditransitive verbs (e.g. *I donated my savings to **the charity***). In Dolakhae, however, there is no syntactic evidence to show that these two classes of objects are distinct (Genetti 1997), so the two categories will be collapsed in the following discussion. A full discussion of the sytactic category of object may be found in §13.3.

Objects in Dolakhae may be either unmarked (hence in absolutive case) or marked by the dative =*ta*. Whether an object is casemarked or not depends on several factors. The basic patterns are summarized in (69):

(69)   Recipient objects (R) of ditransitive verbs are always casemarked.
       Patientive objects (O) of transitive and ditransitive verbs will be casemarked if:
              (a) the referent of the object is human and "given" in the discourse;
              (b) the referent of the object is non-human but animate, and it occurs in a clause crucial to the resolution of a narrative plot

Recipient objects always receive the dative casemarker =*ta*. The recipients are always human, and are almost always "given", which means that at the time of mention, the speaker assumes that the hearer will be able to successfully identify the referent. Examples of recipient objects are given in (72)–(76):

(70)   **janta**   hātiŋ   na-i   ma-bi-u
       1sDAT   nothing   eat-INF   NEG-give-3sPST

       'They give me nothing to eat.'

(71)   **pāṇḍuk=ta**   rāje   bir-ju
       Panduk=DAT   kingdom   give-3sPST

       'They gave the kingdom to Panduk.'

(72) āu   **sugā**=**pista**   na-ker-ai   yā
      now parrot=PL.DAT   eat-CAUS-3sPR   unhusked.rice

      'Now he fed the rice to the parrots.'

(73) ināgu   khā=ri   **guntaŋ**   da-hat
      this.type   matter=IND   nobody.DAT   PROH-say

      'Don't tell anyone about this type of matter.'

(74) jin   **chanta**=**ri**   thi-gur   khā   syẽ-i
      1sERG   2sDAT=IND   one-CL   matter   teach-1FUT

      'I will teach you one thing.'

When patientive objects of transitive and ditransitive verbs are casemarked by the dative, they are almost always human. Only two examples of non-human patients are found co-occurring with =*ta*. In both cases, the referent of the object is an animal, and the object is used at the climax of a narrative, when manipulation of the animal is crucial for resolution of the plot. Consider the following example:

(75) kae=uri=n   tapakka   **sācā**=**ta**   phen-ju
      son=IND=ERG   all.at.once   calf=DAT   release-3sPST

      'Then the son suddenly released the calf.'

At the point in the story when this sentence is used, the hearer has heard about the son's desire to win a bet with his friends, and his careful preparation of the trick he will use. The release of the calf described in this sentence is the beginning of the trick and the culmination of his plan.

It is much more common for human objects to be casemarked with =*ta*. Such objects are casemarked if the referent is "given" at the time of mention, which roughly means that the speaker assumes that the hearer should be able to identify the referent (Chafe 1994: 71–81). First- and second-person referents are always treated as given, hence are always casemarked when they appear in object position:

(76) **thijita**   mepsin   helā   yer-eu
      1pINC.DAT   other.ERG   insult   do-3FUT

      'Others will insult us.'

(77) **janta** pulis=ke da-yeŋ!
    1sDAT police=ALL PROH-take
    'Don't take me to the police!'

(78) mwāt-ke-i mal-a **chanta**
    live-CAUS-INF must-3sPST 2sDAT
    'I must bring you back to life.'

For third-person referents, the given status is most commonly achieved through previous mention, i.e. the referent has been referred to in the previous discourse. This can be seen in example (81). In the first line, the noun phrase *thi-mā kae=uri* serves to introduce a son as a referent in the narrative. In (81b), the same referent is treated as given due to its previous mention; hence it is marked with dative case in the object role:

(79) a. **thi-mā kae=uri** optecā ju ām tākku
    one-CL son=IND small be(3PA) that time
    'Then (they had) one small son at that time.'

   b. ām **mucā=ta** bābu=ri=n mucā ju-e-lāgin
    that child=DAT father=IND=ERG child be-NR2-because

    muryā=ku ta-ene
    lap=LOC put-PART
    'Because he was a child, the father put the child on his lap...'

4.2.7. The oblique cases: Dative

The dative case is also found on some oblique (or adjunct) noun phrases, that is, noun phrases which are not arguments of the verb. First, the dative is used to mark objects of exchange:

(80) **yā=ta** dyābā bi-en ta-uĩ
    unhusked.rice=DAT rupee give-PART put-1PA
    'I had given rupees for the rice.'

Second, it is rarely used to mark locative goals, especially with human locations:

(81) **āmta**   deu   yer-ŋasin
      3sDAT god   come-when

      'When the god came to her (i.e. possessed her)...'

4.2.8. The oblique cases: =na and =nasi

The clitic =*na*, described above as an ergative casemarker on subjects, is also used to mark oblique noun phrases. Most commonly it is used to indicate instrumental case:

(82) dolakhā=e   **bhāsā=n**   har-sin   ka
      Dolakha=GEN   language=INST   say-IMP   ASS

      'Tell (the story) using the language of Dolakha.'

(83) ām   **jal=na**   dokseta   chir   yeŋ-an   bi-u
      that   liquid=INST   all.DAT   sprinkle   do-PART   give-IMP

      'Sprinkle them all with that liquid.'

(84) ānāgu   **rādi=n**   phar-gi
      that.type   rug=INST   cover-1sPST

      'I covered her with that type of rug.'

(85) **ṭuṭi=n**   khi=ku   nur-saŋ
      foot=INST   feces=LOC   step-although

      'Although he stepped in feces with his foot...'

(86) **bikh=na**   wāl-en
      poison=INST   paint-PART

      'Painting them with poison...'

(87) **tarawāra=na**   pwāl-en   bi-sāt
      sword=INST   strike-PART   give-as.soon.as

      'As soon as he struck him with the sword...'

The clitic =*na* is also used with nouns or expressive vocabulary (ideophones) to indicate the manner in which an action is performed. These appear to be metaphorical extensions of the instrumental use of this clitic. Such noun phrases often have an adverbial flavor:

(88) **dukha=n** tuŋ coŋ-an con-hin
trouble=INST FOC stay-PART stay-3pPST

'(They) lived with trouble (i.e. unhappily, with difficulty).'

(89) mucā=n **cākalcukul=na** metha-en
child=ERG EXPR=INST play-PART

'The child with a "cākul cukul sound" (i.e. babbling) was playing.'

(90) **laglaglag=na** tuŋ-an
EXPR=INST shiver-PART

'I shivered with a "laglaglag" feeling...'

(91) **camcamcamcam=na** yer-ŋasin
EXPR=INST come-when

'When (she) came with a "cam-cam-cam-cam" (pounding of dancing feet)...'

(92) **gargar=na** mi cho-ke-sin
EXPR=INST fire burn-CAUS-IMP

'Build a fire that roars.'

Related to this use is the expression *ām kāran=na* 'for that reason', a clear calque on the Nepali equivalent *tyo kāran-le*:

(93) **ām kāran=na** ināgu khā=ri guntaŋ da-hat
that reason=INST this.type talk=IND nobody.DAT PROH-say

'For that reason, tell no one of this type of matter.'

The clitic =na is also used as a temporal locative. Most commonly it is found with months or names of festivals, as in the conversational exchange given in (94):

(94) Speaker A: **pus=na** phoŋ-a rā?
Pus=TEMP ask-NR2 Q

'Was it during Pus that he asked?'

Speaker B: *sithinakhat=na*
Sithinakhat=TEMP

'During the festival of Sithinakhat.'

My consultants have told me that the locative =*ku* could be used in the above examples as well with no meaning difference.

Related to =*na* in form and function is the clitic =*nasi*, which transparently contains =*na* as one of its etymons. The form =*nasi* may be used as a temporal ablative, thus translates as 'since'. It most commonly follows the pronoun *āmu* 'that', thus gives the meaning 'since then':

(95) *āmu=nasi jaŋgal=e janābar=pen khusi ju-en*
that=since jungle=GEN animal=PL happy become-PART

'Since then, the animals of the jungle became happy...'

Although I have no textual examples of =*nasi* being used in non-temporal contexts, according to my consultants, it can also be used spatially, where it contrasts with the ablative clitic =*lān*, as illustrated in the following elicited examples:

(96) Elicited
iskul=nasi uta yer-a
school=ABL here come-3sPST

'She came here from school.'

(97) Elicited
iskul=lān uta yer-a
school=ABL here come-3sPST

'She came here from school.'

The use of =*lān* is said to be appropriate when the school is a short distance away, while =*nasi* would be used when the school is farther away, such as in another town.

4.2.9. *The oblique cases: Locative clitics and postpositions*

4.2.9.1. *The general locative* =*ku*

The clitic =*ku* is the most frequent of the locative casemarkers. It has a very general meaning, as it marks inanimate spatial locations and goals. Thus it may be variously translated into English as 'in', 'on', 'to', 'through', or 'at'. The appropriate meaning is determined by context:

(98) ām chẽ=ku on-a
 3s house=LOC go-3sPST

 'He/she went to the house.'

(99) ām chẽ=ku con-a
 3s house=LOC stay-3sPST

 'He/she stayed at the house.'

(100) āmta kho=ku ŋat-a on-a
 3sDAT river=LOC throw-PURP go-3sPST

 '(She) went to throw him into the river.'

(101) jāki nasputi=ku ta-en bir-ju
 uncooked.rice ear=LOC put-PART give-3sPST

 'He put the rice into his ear.'

(102) cher=ku ḍār-ju
 head=LOC beat-3sPST

 'She beat him on the head.'

(103) luŋā kā-en jhyālā=ku kak-e bir-gi
 rock take-PART window=LOC throw(PART) give-1sPST

 'I picked up a rock, and threw it through the window.'

The noun which hosts the locative clitic may be abstract or temporal, as in the following examples:

(104) kabul=ku hār-ai jur-a
 bet=LOC lose-BV happen-3sPST

 'He lost the bet.'

(105) mahani=e mokā=ku
 Dasain=GEN occasion=LOC

 'On the occasion of Dasain...'

(106) **antim=ku=ri**
 end=LOC=IND

 'In the end...'

(107) u **khā=ku** sihā khusi tuŋ jur-a
 this talk=LOC lion happy FOC become-3sPST

 'The lion became happy with this talk.'

(108) basanta **ritu=ku** twā̃ŋsona bãlaske hor-a
 spring season=LOC rhodedendron beautifully bloom-3sPST

 'In the spring season, the rhododendron bloomed beautifully.'

(109) **man=ku** kalpanā yet-cu
 mind=LOC imagination do-3sPST

 'He imagined it in his mind.'

4.2.9.2. The ablative =lān

The ablative casemarker is =lān. It is used primarily to indicate a spatial source, thus it may be easily translated as 'from':

(110) libi **gā̃ū=lān** phark-ai jur-a
 later village=ABL return-BV happen-3sPST

 'Later he returned from the village.'

(111) chi cā̃ḍa ō **uku=lān=ri!**
 you quickly go(IMP) here=ABL=IND

 'You quickly go from here!'

(112) **gibilān** hār-mun chin?
 where.ABL bring-2sPST 2sERG

 'From where did you bring this?'

(113) nis-mā misā=e **lon=lān=uŋ** santān ma-da
 two-CL woman=GEN womb=ABL=EXT offspring NEG-have

 'From the wombs of the two women there were no offspring.'

(114)   pharsi=e   chē   suntali=e   chē=lān   ṭāen ju
        pumpkin=GEN   house Suntali=GEN house=ABL   far   be(3PA)

   'The pumpkin's house was far from Suntali's house.'

(115)   uku=lān   moti   jhar-ai   ju-ju   sã̄=lān
        here=ABL   pearl fall-BV   be-3PA   hair=ABL

   'From here pearls used to fall, from her hair.'

The ablative is found in the lexicalized expression ā̃ku=lān li, which means 'after that' or 'following that'. The form li means 'back', 'backwards', or 'after', depending on the environment:

(116)   ā̃ku=lān   li   dāl   ānthi   tuŋ   yen-ju
        there=ABL   after   dal   that.manner   FOC   bring-3sPST

   'After that, he brought dal in exactly the same manner.'

Otherwise, the ablative is generally not found in temporal expressions.

The ablative case can also be used to express path of motion, thus can translate as 'via', e.g. dwālnga mula=lan thā̃ta yer-gi [Dwalnga road=ABL up come-1sPST] 'I came up via the Dwalnga road.'

This constellation of meanings is similar to that marked by the "meditative case" in Kiranti languages (see, e.g. van Driem 1987: 51). However, in those languages the same form is also used for abstract media such as languages (e.g. 'in Nepali'). In Dolakhae this function is signaled by the instrumental case (see (84) above) not the ablative, so the category is not identical to the Kiranti meditative.

4.2.9.3. The allative =ke

The allative marker is =ke. This is the only casemarker which can be used in either the NP-internal or the NP-level position (see §4.4.2.2). When in the NP-level position, the allative functions as a locational genitive, to indicate that someone is in physical or metaphorical possession of an item:

(117)   āmke   dyābā   dam
        3sALL   rupee   EXIST

   'He/she has money on him.'

(118) **āmke** santān ma-da
 3sALL offspring NEG-EXIST

 'He had no children (at that time).'

(119) jin chemā phō-i **thaeke**
 1sERG forgiveness beg-1FUT 2HON.ALL

 'I beg your forgiveness.'

When the allative is found NP-internally, it may be followed directly by another casemarker. The second casemarker is the NP-level casemarker, indicating the case of the entire noun phrase, and the head noun of the phrase is unexpressed:

(120) **māji=ke=lān** sampati kār-ju
 boatman=ALL=ABL wealth take-3sPST

 'He took the valuables from that which the boatman had with him.'

It is much more common to use the allative at the end of a noun phrase. In this position it indicates an animate goal:

(121) **sihā=ke** on-hin
 lion=ALL go-3pPST

 'They went to the lion.'

(122) lita=ŋ **jogi=ke** tuŋ on-a
 next=EXT yogi=ALL FOC go-3sPST

 'The next one went to the same yogi.'

(123) āle āpen **twāŋsona=ke** oŋ-an
 then 3p rhodedendron=ALL go-PART

 'Then they went to Rhodedendron...'

(124) āle **rājā=ke** ye-u=ri dosari jur-a
 then king=ALL come-NR1=IND pregnant become-3sPST

 'Then the one who went to the king became pregnant.'

4.2.9.4. The locational postpositions dupān(a), depān(a), likhan(a), and hākhen(a)

There are four locational postpositions. They are postpositions, not clitics, because they are not bound to the noun phonologically, as attested by the fact that they are stressed independently. In addition, all but *dupān* also occur in my data as lexical adverbs (the adverbial counterpart of *dupān* is *duta*; see §9.3). Furthermore, at least *likhana* and *hākhena* require a preceding pronoun to be in genitive case. Nouns preceding these postpositions, however, are in absolutive case.[34]

All four postpositions may be pronounced as trisyllabic, with a final vowel /a/, or as disyllabic, with the /a/ dropped. My consultants report that there is no significant meaning difference between them. The longer forms are characteristic of slower, and possibly more polite, speech. The meanings of the four locational postpositions are given in (125):

(125) *dupān(a)* 'inside'
 depān(a) 'on, on top'
 likhan(a) 'behind'
 hākhen(a) 'in front'

In each case, the semantics are much more specific than the meaning of the general locative clitic. Examples (126)–(129) illustrate the use of these postpositions. Note that both *likhana* and *hākhena* may also be used temporally:

(126) inār **dupān** thau khwāl khon-ai
 well inside REFL face see-3sPR

 'He sees his face inside the well.'

(127) pukhur **dupān** oŋ-an
 lake inside go-PART

 'Going into the lake...'

(128) suntali=n pharsi=ta sona simā **depān**
 Suntali=ERG pumpkin=DAT flower tree on

 ta-en bir-ai
 put-PART give-3sPR

 'Suntali puts the pumpkin on the flower tree.'

(129) pali **depān** coŋ-gu kok
roof on stay-NR1 crow

'The crow staying on the roof.'

(130) cilā **likhana** jin ithi chit-agi
goat behind 1sERG like.this pull-1sPR

'I am pulling the back of the goat like this.'

(131) Elicited
chana **likhana** gun?
2sGEN behind who

'Who is behind you?'

(132) mahani **likhana**
Dasain after

'After Dasain...'

(133) jana **hākhen** tuŋ dū=n ithi yeŋ-an
1sGEN front FOC tiger=ERG like.this do-PART

'A tiger was doing this right in front of me...'

(134) gatkeŋ barsa **hākhena**
many year before

'Many years ago...'

4.2.10. The oblique cases: Associative postposition nāpa

The associative postposition is *nāpa*. It has the same syntactic distribution as the other postpositions, similarly requires dative case on a preceding pronoun, and may also occur independently as an adverb (with the meaning 'together'). As an associative postposition, it refers to someone who will perform the action of the verb together with the subject:

(135) āle ām mi āme **nāpa** on-a
then that man 3sGEN ASSOC go-3sPST

'Then that man went with him.'

(136) ji=ŋ   chana   **nāpa** tuŋ sir-i
      1s=EXT   2sGEN   ASSOC   FOC die-1FUT

   'I also will die with you.'

(137) kharāyo **nāpa** inār   da-u   ṭhā̃ī=ku   on-hin
      rabbit   ASSOC   well   have-NR1   place=LOC   go-3pPST

   'They went with the rabbit to the place where the well was.'

In my narrative texts, I have two examples of the postposition *nāpa* being used with a locative sense. When used in this manner it indicates an immediate proximity:

(138) kho=e   tir   **nāpa** ḍwā-ku   jaga   da-u
      river=GEN   bank   ASSOC   big-NR1   field   have-3PA

   'There was a large field right on the bank of the river.'

(139) kulsi   **nāpa** tuŋ   yā   jāudi-en
      stairway   ASSOC   FOC   unhusked.rice   rest.load-PART

   'I put the rice down right next to the stairway...'

Both of these functions of *nāpa* are clearly related to the lexical meaning of the adverb. In the associative sense, it indicates two animate beings undertaking joint action; in the locational sense, it indicates two inanimate elements which are physically adjacent.

4.2.11. The oblique cases: thẽ(nāgu) *'like'*

The postposition meaning 'like' has two forms, *thenāgu* and *thẽ*. There appears to be no significant difference in meaning between them when they occur as postpositions. However, only the form *thẽ* is also found as a marker of adverbial clauses; see §20.2.6 for discussion.

In most of my examples, the postposition *thẽ(nāgu)* follows nouns and pronouns in absolutive case:

(140) ām   **thẽ**   tuŋ   boŋ-gu   sāŋat=pen
      3s   like   FOC   read-NR1   friend=PL

   'Friends who were educated just like him.'

(141) dolakhā mi   **thenāgu** bã̄la-ku
      Dolakha person like   beautiful-NR1

      'Beautiful like a person from Dolakha.'

(142) nāpa   oŋ-gu   sā̄ɲat upen **thenāgu** upādre
      ASSOC go-NR1   friend 3p   like   tyrannical

      'The friend who went with him was tyrannical like them.'

I do have one example, however, where *thē* follows a noun in ergative case. It is given in (143):

(143) jin   **thē**   ṭhākkar wā   gunān   nar-ju?
      1sERG   like   trouble TOP who.ERG eat-3sPST

      'Who has eaten (experienced) trouble like me?'

This example is particularly interesting as there are two ergative arguments, but only one transitive verb. More research on this structure is needed.

4.2.12. The oblique cases: ṭul(ke) 'during; up to; until'

This postposition has various phonological shapes, namely *ṭul*, *ṭule*, *ṭulle*, and *ṭulke*. I know of no semantic difference between these forms. It is possible that the lengthening in *ṭulle* is due to morphological gemination resulting in intensification of meaning (§2.2.5.2); I do not have a sufficient number of examples to either prove or disprove this analysis.

When this postposition is used with a noun phrase indicating a finite period of time, the postposition indicates that the action of the verb took place over the entire period. Hence it translates into English as "for" or "during":

(144) sō-lā   **ṭulle** pita tuŋ mā-yā-en
      three-month during   out FOC NEG-come-PART

      'Not coming out for three months...'

The postposition *ṭul(ke)* may also be used to indicate a temporal end-point, e.g. *thanu ṭule=ŋ* [today until=EXT] 'until today'. Related to this is its use with a spatial noun. I only have a few examples of this. In all of them, the postposition indicates that the spatial noun was the specific end-point of motion denoted by a verb, in other words, that the motion occurred up until that point.

(145) gyānbāhādur=e   swā̃hārā ṭulke li   liṇā-en   yer-gi
       Gyanbahadur=GEN garden   until back walk-PART come-1sPST

'(I) came back walking backwards until Gyanbahadur's garden.'

4.3. Individuation and extension

The final morphological categories relevant to nouns are individuation and extension. These are marked by two clitics which are in paradigmatic relation. These clitics are actually not limited to nouns, but also occur bound to members of other lexical classes. A full discussion of their behavior, including the phonological evidence for their status as clitics, their distributional properties, and their semantics, can be found in §10.2.

There is, however, one point to make with regards to nouns specifically. This concerns the individuating clitic =*uri*. This clitic is commonly found on kin terms where it appears to have lexicalized (although it is not obligatory). The clitic of individuation is normally positioned in the noun after the casemarker; however, when the clitic co-occurs with kin terms, it commonly *precedes* the clitic casemarker. Thus one can compare the relative ordering of the casemarker and =*uri* with kin terms in (146) and non-kin terms in (147):

(146)   kae=uri=ta   'son'=IND=DAT
        bobu=ri=n   'father'=IND=ERG
        mica=uri=ta   'daughter'=IND=DAT
        mā=uri=n   'mother'=IND=ERG
        kehẽ=uri=n   'sister'=IND=ERG

(147)   chẽ=ku=ri   'house'=LOC=IND
        rājā=n=ri   'king'=ERG=IND
        mucā=ta=uri   'child'=DAT=IND
        kwākarbeŋ=na=uri   'frog'=ERG=IND

It is interesting that the clitic =*uri* may actually occur with kin terms twice in a single noun phrase, once preceding the casemarker and once following, as in the ergative form for 'mother': *mā=uri=n=uri*. These cases make sense if the kin term being used is the (transparent) lexicalized noun of kin term plus clitic (in this case *mā=uri*), and the second use of the clitic is the "true clitic", specifically marking individuation.

A final piece of evidence in favor of analyzing these combinations as lexicalizations is their ordering with respect to the plural clitic. With most nouns the plural clitic precedes both the clitic casemarkers, and the clitics of individuation and extention, as in *mi=pen=ri* [person=PL=IND]. However, the plural clitic is positioned after *=uri* when the host noun is a kin term, as in *kae=uri=pisin* [son=IND=PL.ERG]. Again this ordering paradox is understandable if we analyze *kaeuri* as a lexicalized noun.

Chapter 5
Personal pronouns, interrogatives, indefinites, and demonstratives

1. Introduction

In this chapter I will describe a range of words which are etymologically and functionally related: personal pronouns, interrogatives, indefinites, and demonstratives. These forms are often all referred to as "pronouns" in the linguistic literature. Strictly speaking, however, the term "pronoun" is limited to those proforms which function as noun phrases. Many of the forms under discussion in this chapter are not pronouns in the strict sense; for example, some are noun-phrase internal, such as the interrogative quantifier *guli* 'how much/how many', and others are adverbial in function, such as the deictic *ānthi* 'in that manner'. However, it is clear that many of these forms are constructed from the same etyma, and they all function within the broader domain of deixis and anphoric reference. Therefore they will all be discussed as a group in this chapter.

2. Personal pronouns

Personal pronouns, unlike nouns, form a closed lexical class. They also differ from nouns in that they do not appear as heads of relative clauses. Personal pronouns are similar to nouns in that they have a strong referential function, most commonly referring to entities with established reference in the discourse. The first-person pronouns, inflected for the relevant cases, are given in Table 8.

We can see that the language makes a primary distinction between singular and plural, with a secondary inclusive/exclusive distinction within the plurals. Semantically, these two classes differ in that inclusive forms include the speaker and addresee (and possibly others) together, while the exclusive forms indicate the speaker and others but exclude the addressee. The inclusive forms are transparently derived from a concatenation of the first- and second-person-singular pronouns. As for the alternation between *chiji* and *thiji*, I have heard both variants commonly used. Speakers seem to use one or the other form regularly in their own idiolect. Interestingly, when I pointed out the two variant pronunciations to several speakers, they all expressed surprise and said they had never noticed this variation. Further comments on the forms are provided in the following section.

130 Chapter 5 *Pronouns and related forms*

Table 8. First-person pronouns

First-Person Pronouns			
	Singular	Plural	
		Inclusive	Exclusive
ABS	*ji*	*chiji/thiji*	*isi*
ERG	*jin*	*chijin/thijin*	*isin*
DAT	*janta*	*chijita/thijita*	*ista*
ALL	*janke*	*chijike/thijike*	*iske*
GEN	*jana*	*chiji/thiji*	*isi*

The second-person pronouns are divided by honorific status and number, yielding the four paradigms presented in Table 9:

Table 9. Second-person pronouns

Second-Person Pronouns				
	Non-Honorific		Honorific	
	Singular	Plural	Singular	Plural
ABS	*chi*	*chipen*	*thamu*	*thapen*
ERG	*chin*	*chipsin*	*thamun*	*thapsin*
DAT	*chanta*	*chipista*	*thaeta*	*thapista*
ALL	*chanke*	*chipiske*	*thaeke*	*thapiske*
GEN	*chana*	*chipe*	*thae*	*thape*

In my body of narrative discourse, the honorific and non-honorific pronouns occur in a ratio of about 1:10. Recall that second-person forms, indicating the addressee, are always used in interactional contexts. Examples with the honorific forms in my data are consistently found in contexts where the speaker is considerably younger than the addressee, generally by a generation or more. In addition, honorifics are used to address deities, or others held in reverence, such as a man who has saved one's life, regardless of age. It should be noted, however, that honorifics are not obligatory in these contexts. There are numerous cases in my discourse data of elders being addressed with non-honorific pronouns as well.

The third-person pronouns also have a four-way split. The relevant parameter that accompanies number in this paradigm is proximity. The forms of the third-person pronouns are given in Table 10:

Table 10. Third-person pronouns

Third-Person Pronouns	Proximal Singular	Plural	Distal Singular	Plural
ABS	u	upen	ām(u)	āpen
ERG	un	upsin	āmun	āpsin
DAT	uta	upista	āmta	āpista
ALL	uke	upiske	āmke	āpiske
GEN	ue	upe	āme	āpe

It is important to note at the outset that the forms *u* and *ām* function as both pronouns and demonstratives. It would be possible to say that Dolakha Newar lacks third-person pronouns altogether and that demonstratives may function anaphorically as heads of noun phrases. I do not have any strong objections to this analysis; however, I prefer to think of some uses of these forms as being pronominal since of the various demonstratives in the language, one only finds *ām* and *u* functioning pronominally, that is, as the head of a noun phrase. The other two nominal demonstratives *osa* and *āsa* are not attested in my data as heads of noun phrases. My practice has been to analyze *ām* and *u* as pronouns if they constitute heads of noun phrases and if they carry inflection for number or case when appropriate. In certain contexts, however, contextual factors suggest a different interpretation, particularly if the referent is inanimate and the context is strongly deictic, in which case, these factors appear to indicate that the forms are functioning as demonstratives. The boundary is clearly fuzzy, as with many grammatical categories.

In my discourse data, the distal pronoun occurs much more frequently than the proximal pronoun and so appears to be unmarked. The distal is always the form chosen when speakers are translating the English pronoun 's/he' in elicitation. When the proximal *u* is used, it tends to have a stronger deictic sense than the pronoun *ām*; it refers to something or someone visible in the speech situation, as in the following example:

(1) u   joŋ-an?
     this   hold-PART

   'Shall I hold this (microphone)?'

When *u* is used anaphorically, it is generally found in contexts where two similar referents are being distinguished, so it still has deictic function.

(2)   **u=ri**   bātho   ju-e-lāgin
       this=IND clever be-NR2-because

'Because he was clever (in contrast to his brother, who was not)...'

2.1. Forms of the personal pronouns

While the elements representing casemarkers (ergative /n/, dative /ta/, allative /ke/, genitive /e/) can easily be identified in most pronominal forms, the presence of idiosyncratic morphophonological changes in the pronominal stems suggests that these forms have lexicalized and should be analyzed as independent pronominal declensions, not as concatenations of stems and casemarkers. (For functions of the cases, see §4.4.2.)

The paradigms are not complex, but a few comments are in order. It is clear that the first singular pronoun *ji* and the second singular pronoun *chi* have parallel stem alternations, thus the first-person forms, *ji/janta/janke/jana*, are identical to the second-person forms, *chi/chanta/chanke/chana*, in every respect but the initial consonant. However, when the two pronouns are concatenated in the inclusive form, the stems do not undergo these alternations. Thus we find *chijita*, not **chanjanta* or any similar form. This suggests that the alternations may have been established after the compounding of the inclusive form, and/or that the alternations are restricted to disyllabic contexts.

Turning to the first plural exclusive forms, the absolutive and genitive declensions fall together, being *isi* in both cases. This is probably due to an old sound change, whereby the vowel of the genitive element was lost, i.e. **isi-e>isi.*

The second- and third-person-plural forms are clearly formed with the regular plural clitic *=pen*, as the patterns of case inflections are identical to those found with plural nouns. The kernel element of the second-person honorific is *tha-*, while that of the third singular is *ā-*. Both pronouns also show an element *-mu* in the absolutive and ergative forms. While the third person retains the /m/ throughout the paradigm, the honorific form loses the /m/ in the dative and genitive declensions.

The singular honorific forms *thaeta* (2sHON.DAT) and *thaeke* (2sHON.ALL) are formed off the genitive *thae*. This strategy, of composing complex dative and allative forms by concatenation of genitive with dative or allative elements, is productively found in the modern Kathmandu dialect. There the dative and allative nominal casemarkers are *(yā)ta* and *(yā)ke* respectively, with the optional syllable being the genitive (see Kölver 1977 for an interesting discussion of the semantic difference between these forms). This tendency to create complex cases out of a concatenation of genitive with dative or allative is also likely to be responsible for the stem alternations in the first- and second-person paradigms discussed earlier. Thus compare the first-person pronominal forms *jana* (genitive), *janta* (dative), and *janke* (allative); if we assume that the genitive form first induced the vocalic change in the stem, then the presence of the vowel change in the dative and allative forms can be attributed to an earlier concatenation of genitive plus dative or allative. These forms are now lexicalized. It is not possible to form the dative or allative off the absolutive pronominal forms *ji* or *chi*.

3. Interrogatives

The Dolakhae interrogatives (question words) are given in Table 11:

Table 11. Interrogative words

Interrogative Words	
gu(ri)	'which' (non-human)
gun	'who; which' (human)
gunān	'who' (ERG)
gunta	'whom' (DAT)
gune	'whose' (GEN)
guli	'how much; how many'
gulpa	'when'
gibi	'where'
gibilān	'from where' (ABL)
githi	'how; in what manner'
gināgu	'how; what type'
hāti	'what'
hātta	'where'

Most of the interrogative forms are transparently formed off a base *gun*, and some are easily analyzable into base plus casemarker, e.g. the dative *gunta*. The ergative *gunān*, however, is unusual in the presence of the vowel /ā/, not a normal element of the ergative clitic. The etymon /li/ found in *guli* 'how many; how much' also occurs within demonstratives; the same is true of the /thi/ of *githi* and the /nāgu/ of *gināgu* (see §5.5.4). The words *hāti* and *hātta* clearly form a separate etymological set.

Both *gu(ri)* and *gun* may occur within a noun phrase, in which case they request the identification of one out of a set, hence translate into English as 'which'. The two are used in distinct contexts. I have only one example of *gu* in my discourse data; unfortunately it occurred in the first utterance on the tape and there is not sufficient context to determine its reference. However, in elicitation, the two forms are very clearly divided such that *gu(ri)* co-occurs with non-human nouns and *gun* co-occurs with human nouns, as in examples (3) and (4):

(3)   Elicited
      gu   chẽ=ku   con-a?
      which   house=LOC   stay-3sPST

      'Which house does he live in?'

(4)   **gun**   mucā   **gun**   mucā?
      which   child which   child

      'Which child, which child (was it)?'

The form *gun* may also occur as a pronoun, in which case it constitutes an absolutive noun phrase. It is used to request the identity of the referent who is involved in the action of the verb, so I have translated it into English as 'who'. The ergative interrogative pronoun *gunān* and the dative interrogative pronoun *gunta* are clearly based on *gun* morphologically. These forms are clearly pronouns; they replace an entire noun phrase and cannot co-occur with a nominal head or any nominal modifiers:

(5)   chi **gun**?
      2s who

      'Who are you?'

(6)   **gun** jana   chẽ   con-a?
      who   1sGEN   house   stay-3sPST

      'Who is at my house?'

(7)   chanta   **gunān**   tel   lāŋ-an   bir-ai?
      2sDAT   who.ERG   oil   massage-PART   give-3sPR

      'Who is massaging you with oil?'

(8)   luŋmā   ho   tuphi   mucā   **gunān**   bu-eu?
      mortar   and   broom   child who.ERG   give.birth-3FUT

      'Who will give birth to a mortar and broom child?'

(9) bā=n   **gunta**   bir-agu?
     father=ERG who.DAT give-2hPR

    'Father, whom will you give me to?'

The pronoun *gun* may also be followed by the associative postposition *nāpa*, rendering the meaning 'with whom':

(10) āu   jin   **gun nāpa** khā lā-i?
     now 1sERG who   ASSOC   talk talk-1FUT

    'Now with whom will I speak?'

The interrogative form *gune* is transparently formed from *gun* 'who' plus the genitive clitic. An example of this form is given in (11):

(11) gune=ŋ   mā   gune=ŋ   bā
     whose=IND   mother whose=IND   father

     gune=ŋ   pyāṭāmāri mirga syāŋ-an   na-uju?
     whose=IND   pregnant   deer   kill-PART eat-3sPA

    'Whose mother, whose father, whose pregnant deer did (the lion) kill and eat?'

The pronoun *guli* is used to ask the quantity of concrete items, abstract entities (such as emotions), and actions. Thus it translates into English both as 'how many' and 'how much'. In (12), the question word functions as the complement of the verbless clause:

(12) chana   mol   **guli?**
     2sGEN   price how.much

    'How much is your price?'

In addition to occuring as the head of a noun phrase, *guli* may occur within a noun phrase, where it questions the quantity of the referent of the nominal head. The position of *guli vis-a-vis* the noun in such cases is variable; compare examples (13) and (14).

(13) dhū   nāpa   **guli**   laḍanta yet-ki?
     tiger ASSOC how.many   fight   do-1sPST

    'How many (times) did I fight with a tiger?'

(14) **guli** dhū nāpa?
how.many tiger ASSOC

'With how many tigers?'

This variability in positioning is commonly found with quantifiers, see §11.2.

In addition to its interrogative functions, the pronoun *guli* 'how much; how many' may also be used as an intensifier. When it is used in this manner, it translates into English as 'so; so much; so many':

(15) **guli** onsā-mi=pen hār-ju
how.many man-person=PL bring-3sPST

'He brought so many men.'

(16) mā dar-sa **guli** khusi ju
mother exist-if how.much happy become.3PA

'If her mother were alive, how happy she would be.'

(17) āmun lū cãdi=pen **guli** bu-i phar-ai
3sERG gold silver=PL how.much carry-INF able-3sPR

'She was able to carry so much gold and silver.'

It is interesting to note that the Nepali pronoun *kati* 'how much' may be used in the same way. Also, I have often heard native Dolakhae and native Nepali speakers use "how much" with the same intensifying function when speaking English.

The forms *gulpa* 'when', *gibi* 'where', *gibilān* 'from where', and *hātta* 'why' all have adverbial function, as they question either the time, the location, or the reason of the action expressed in the predicate:

(18) ām khā **gulpa** har-i?
that matter when say-1FUT

'When shall I speak of that matter?'

(19) āu **gibi** ū-ita?
now where go-2hFUT

'Now where will you go?'

(20) **gibilān** hār-mun chin?
where.ABL bring-2sPST 2sERG

'From where did you bring this?'

(21) chi **hātta** gyāt-an?
2s why feat-2sPR

'Why are you afraid?'

The question words *githi* and *ginãgu* both translate into English as 'how', but they have quite different meanings. While *githi* questions the manner in which an action is done, *ginãgu* questions the type of thing being discussed. (The same distinction is made in Nepali; *githi* is the equivalent of Nepali *kasari*, while *ginãgu* is the equivalent of *kasto*.)

(22) āpsin hirā=e jā **githi** na-eu?
3pERG diamond=GEN rice how eat-3FUT

'How will they eat rice made of diamonds?'

(23) chi **ginãgu**?
2s what.type

'What type (of person) are you?'

The form *hāti* 'what' is used to question the identity of an object (24), the content of a direct quote (25), or the appropriate action to be taken (26):

(24) dāi=e janchi=lān **hāti** hār-a?
e.brother=GEN sash=ABL what fall-3sPST

'What fell from my brother's sash?'

(25) **hāti** hat-ai?
what say-3sPR

'What does he say?'

(26) āu **hāti** yer-i mal-a?
now what do-INF must-3sPST

'Now what must I do?'

One also finds *hāti* in pre-nominal position, when it is used to question the specific identity of the following (general) noun:

(27) **hāti** āpat par-ai jur-a?
what trouble befall-BV become-3sPST

'What trouble has befallen you?'

(28) **hāti** khã har-sin
what talk say-IMP

'Tell me what thing.'

4. Indefinites

There is a set of indefinite proforms in Dolakha Newar that are transparently composed of interrogative proforms and the extensive clitic =(u)ŋ (§10.2.2). The non-specific indefinite meaning is only found when the verb is negated. Examples are given in (29)–(34):

(29) āpista **gunān=uŋ** phon-da mā-yā
3pDAT who.ERG=EXT beg-PURP NEG-come

'No one came to ask them (to marry).'

(30) u situgā̃s **hāti=ŋ** ma-jur-sā
this situ.grass what=EXT NEG-happen-if

'If nothing happens to this situ grass.'

(31) **gulpa=nuŋ** mica mā-yār-a
when=EXT daugher NEG-come-3sPST

'Her daughter never came (home).'

(32) u khã=ri **gunta=ŋ** da-hat
this matter=IND who.DAT=EXT PROH-say

'Speak of this matter to no one.' OR 'Don't speak of this matter to anyone.'

(33) thau=ta **gibi=ŋ** ma-gyāt-ki
REFL=DAT where=EXT NEG-fear-1sPST

'I wasn't afraid anywhere.'

(34) **gunān   gunta=ŋ**   helā   yer-i   ma-ṭe
     who.ERG   who.DAT=EXT   insult   do-INF   NEG-PROH

   'No one should insult anyone.'

The form *hātiŋ* may also be used to modify a noun; again this is only found in clauses with a negated verb. In such cases the proform means "not a single X" or "any X at all", where X stands for the noun:

(35) āle   āmun   **hāti=ŋ**   sabda   mā-tār-ju
     then   3sERG   what=EXT   word   NEG-hear-3sPST

   'Then he didn't hear a single word.'

(36) āmun   wā   **hāti=ŋ**   jawāph   bi   ma-pha-ene
     3sERG   TOP   what=EXT   answer   give.INF   NEG-able-PART

   'He was unable to give any answer at all...'

The only example in the texts of another indefinite proform being used to modify a noun is the following:

(37) ām   mele   **gibi=ŋ**   chē=ku   mo-õ
     3s   other.LOC   where=EXT   house=LOC   NEG-go

   'He never went to any other house at all.'

I have one other interesting indefinite example with *gibi*. Interestingly, it does not carry the extensive clitic, but instead is repeated or reduplicated:

(38) libi   **gibi**   **gibi**   khā   kukhurikā   haŋ-an   hal-a
     later   where   where   chicken   EXPR   say-PART   call.out-3sPST

   'Later a rooster crowed somewhere.'

There is one other indefinite proform which has unusual case inflection as shown in Table 12. The inflection is almost identical to that found for *dokhu* 'all' (§8.2), with a clear formative *-se*. The absolutive form can be used either attributively, modifying a nominal head, or as a fully referential nominal. The

Table 12. Inflection of *yau* 'some; any'

'Some; any'	
ABS	*yau*
ERG	*yausenuŋ*
DAT	*yauseta*
ALL	*yausekeŋ*
ABL	*yauseku*
GEN	*yause*

inflected case forms are always referential. (The obvious exception is the genitive, which is necessarily modifying.) Elicited examples of *yau* are given below:

(39) Elicited
    yau keṭi bihā yer-saŋ chanta bãla-ku
    any girl marriage do-although 2sDAT good-NR1

    'Any girl you marry will be good for you.' (lit. 'Even if you marry some girl, she will be good for you.')

(40) Elicited
    yauseku jana kitāb twārtar-ai
    somebody.LOC 1sGEN book leave-1sPR

    'I left my book at somebody's (house).'

(41) Elicited
    yause dyābā khur-saŋ chana hāti matlab?
    somebody.GEN money steal-although 2sGEN what care

    'Even if somebody's money is stolen, what business is it of yours?'

The precise semantic distinction between the indefinite forms with *yau* and those formed from the interrogative pronoun plus clitic is difficult to determine. Consider the next three examples:

(42) Elicited
    *ām mi=n **gune=ŋ** dyābā khu-eu*
    that man=ERG whose=EXT money steal-3FUT

    'That man will steal anybody's money.'

(43) Elicited
yause dyābā khur-ju
somebody.GEN money steal-3sPST

'(S/he) stole somebody's money.'

(44) Elicited
dokse dyābā khur-ju
all.GEN money steal-3sPST

'(S/he) stole everyone's money.'

The semantic distinction is subtle. In (42), the indefinite proform denotes an indefinite set consisting of all money owners; the thief will choose among them indiscriminately, thus each member is equally likely to be robbed. The reference is thus both non-specific and indefinite. In (43), there is one specific person who has been robbed, however it is not known who this person is, hence the reference is specific indefinite. One can contrast this to (44) where *dokse* conveys the fact that every member of a set of money owners has been robbed.

While this appears to be a subtle yet clear three-way distinction, I have a number of discourse examples of interrogative-proforms-plus-clitic being used in specific indefinite noun phrases. It is worth noting that I have no examples of *yau* in my discourse data.

5. Demonstratives

In this section, I will be discussing the demonstratives, a set of words with similar morphological and etymological makeup, and which share the property of referring either to referents or events previously mentioned in the discourse ("anaphoric reference"), or to places, locations, or objects in the speech setting ("deictic reference").

The Dolakhae demonstratives are listed in Table 13. They are given with their standard glosses, although the meaning of a particular form may change considerably depending on the context. The demonstratives fall into two sets, which can be characterized roughly as proximal (close to the speaker) and distal (farther from the speaker).

It is clear that these forms share many etyma found in the interrogative pronouns. There are a number of three-way sets, composed of interorgative, proximal, and distal members differing in shape only in the initial (C)V and expressing the same type of semantic categories, e.g. *githi*, *ithi*, and *ānthi* are the interrogative, proximal, and distal markers of manner, while *guli*, *uli*, and *āmli* are the interrogative, proximal, and distal markers of quantity. These parallel semantic and phonological patterns are clearly reflections of processes of word formation.

Table 13. Demonstratives

Proximal		Distal		Semantic Type
u	'this'	*ām(u)*	'that'	unmarked
osa(i)	'this here'	*āsa*	'that there'	immediate location
ithi	'this manner'	*ānthi*	'like that'	manner
ināgu	'this type'	*ānāgu*	'like that'	type
uli	'this much'	*āmli*	'that much'	quantity, unmarked
ustule	'this much'	*āmstule*	'that much'	quantity, emphatic
ulistule	'this much'	*āmlistule*	'that much'	quantity, extreme
ithi	'here'	*hati*	'there'	location, unmarked
uku	'here'	*ãku*	'there'	location, unmarked
osaku	'right here'	*āsaku*	'right there'	location, in sight
ukuna	'over here'	*hukuna*	'over there'	location, distance
upaĩ	'this size'	*āpaĩ*	'that size'	size, unmarked
opaĩ	'this size'			size, emphatic
upāle	'this time'			time

As mentioned above, the base forms of the deictic elements, *u* and *ām(u)*, function both as third-person pronouns and as demonstratives. In general, I interpret the form as pronominal when occurring as the head of a noun phrase, and when inflected for number and case if appropriate. I consider these forms to be unambiguously demonstratives when they co-occur with a noun. However, sometimes particular contexts suggest a strongly deictic interpretation even in the absence of a noun, in which case the form may be better analyzed as a demonstrative than as a pronoun. This is particularly true when the noun refers to an abstract entity, as in the following:

(45)　ām　tuŋ　lā-en　bi-sin!
　　　that　FOC　tell-PART　give-IMP

　　　'Tell that particular one (i.e. story)!'

5.1. The unmarked demonstratives *ām*, and *u*

The two most common demonstratives are also the most semantically neutral. These are *u* and *ām(u)*, the unmarked proxminal and distal demonstratives respectively. They are usually noun-phrase internal, co-occuring with a noun and frequently other nominal modifiers. In my narrative discourse data, *ām* is considerably more frequent than *u*, and functions to indicate that the referent of the accompanying noun has the same identity as a referent mentioned earlier in the discourse. However, this demonstrative does not occur obligatorily with all previously mentioned nouns, so it has not grammaticalized into a full-fledged definite article. Some typical examples of the distal demonstrative are given in (46)–(49):

(46) **ām** cilā phutta on-a!
that goat EXPR go-3sPST

'That goat jumped away *phutta!*'

(47) āle **ām** buḍyā=ta=uri dyābā pāch cha hajār
then that old.woman=DAT=IND money five six thousand

bi cho-en chor-ju.
give.INF send-PART send-3sPST

'Then she gave that old woman five or six thousand rupees and sent her away.'

(48) **āmu** pujā yer-i don-ke tuni
that ceremony do-INF finish-PART until

'Until that ceremony is finished...'

(49) **ām** thi-mnā jāki jin **ām** jogi=ta bir-gi
that one-CL rice 1sERG that yogi=DAT give-1sPST

'I gave that measure of uncooked rice to that yogi.'

Often the noun modified is abstract. Some commonly used phrases include *ām tākku* 'that time' and *ām karan=na* 'for that reason'.

In conversational contexts, *ām* may be strongly deictic, referring to an entity in the immediate environment of the interlocutors, as exemplified in (50)–(52):

(50) **ām** jal=na dokseta chir yeŋ-an bi-u
that liquid=INST all.DAT sprinkle do-PART give-IMP

'Sprinkle all that elixir on them.'

(51) **ām** bhut hātta hākar-an?
that ghost why call-2PR

'Why do you call that ghost?'

(52) **āmu** pāŋ janta=ŋ hā-u
 that fruit 1sDAT=EXT bring-IMP

 'Bring me that fruit.'

The proximal form *u* is found less commonly in narrative discourse in my data, occurring primarily in quotative contexts which invoke an interactional schema. It is used for deictic reference, as in examples (53–55), but may also be used anaphorically to refer to something that has just been discussed, as in (56)–(58):

(53) u sugā=n tuŋ har-eu sugā=e mol
 this parrot=ERG FOC say-3FUT parrot=GEN price

 'This parrot will himself say the parrot's price.'

(54) u rāje janta mā=ŋ māl
 this kingdom 1sDAT need-EXT NEG.need

 'I don't need this kingdom.'

(55) u bā jeu, u mā jeu, u kae-mica jeu
 this father maybe this mother maybe this son-daughter maybe

 'Maybe this is the father, maybe this is the mother, maybe these are the children.'

(56) ji u bācā=ku hār-ai jur-sa...
 1s this bet=LOC lose-BV happen-if

 'If I lose this bet...'

(57) u khā khyaŋ rā ma-khe rā?
 this talk be Q NEG-be Q

 'Is this talk true or not?'

(58) u janta ṭhāhā ma-da
 this 1sDAT knowledge NEG-have

 'I don't know this.'

Note that, unlike the pronominal forms, there are no plural demonstratives. The same demonstratives found with singular number also occur in noun phrases that are semantically plural:

(59) āle **ām** nis-mā mwāt-a
then that two-CL survive-3sPST

'Then those two survived.'

(60) u nis-mā thape iri tuŋ kʰyaŋ
this two-CL 2HON.GEN daughter.in.law FOC be

'These two are your daughters-in-law.'

The absolutive plural pronoun *āpen* can never be used in this environment. This fact provides further evidence that the third-person pronouns and demonstratives are distinct.

5.2. Demonstratives of immediate location

The demonstratives of immediate location are *osa(i)* and *aasa*. The proximal form *osai* occurs only a handful of times in my discourse data, whereas *aasa* does not appear at all. They appear to be strongly deictic, indicating an object in the immediate physical environment of the interlocutors. Some discourse examples follow:

(61) osai jana dyābā hā-sin
this.here 1sGEN money bring-IMP

'Bring out this here money (which I just gave to you).'

(62) osai ci kʰursāni chanta na-i-ta tuŋ kʰyaŋ
this.here salt chili 2sDAT eat-INF-DAT TOP be

'This here salt and chili is to eat you with.'

During elicitation, a speaker volunteererd the phrase *osa=e bāje* 'this here person's grandfather'. In discussing these forms, speakers acknoweldge the existence of *āsa* which they translate as 'that one there'. However I have no examples of the form being used in this manner. Also, some speakers appear to use this form as a hesitation particle, so one must listen to the prosody of a sentence to determine its function.

5.3. Demonstratives of manner

There are two demonstratives of manner in Dolakhae: *ithi* and *ānthi*. They translate into English as 'like this' and as 'like that' respectively. However, the two are used in quite different ways. To begin with, as with other proximals, *ithi* is used much more commonly in interactional contexts: conversation, first-person narratives, and reported speech. The distal form, by contrast, is used extensively in third-person narrative and has strong narrative functions. This distribution is nicely exemplified in one text, where a speaker is relating stories about seeing tigers in the jungle. She uses *ithi* extensively when relating the manner of her own experiences, then changes to *ānthi* when she reports her brother's experiences.

The demonstrative *ānthi* is common in third-person narrative to refer to a preceding action, a preceding series of actions, or a direct quote. When *ānthi* is used in this function, it directly precedes the verb. In these contexts, it translates either as 'that', or as 'like that':

(63) **ānthi** yeŋ-an ninpatti nar-ai
 that do-PART everyday eat-3sPR

 'Doing that (i.e. acting in that manner), she ate daily.'

(64) "luŋmā tuphi bur-ju" haŋ-an hat-cu
 mortar broom give.birth-3sPST say-PART say-3sPST

 ānthi har-i ho sumake=ŋ con-a rājā
 that say-INF when silent=EXT stay-3sPST king

 'They said: "(She) gave birth to a mortar and broom." When they said that (i.e. spoke like that), the king remained silent.'

(65) **ānthi** da-hat!
 like.that PROH-say

 'Don't say that (i.e. speak in that manner)!'

It is not entirely clear whether in such cases *ānthi* should be analyzed as a pronoun instantiating a noun phrase or as an adverbial. The adverbial analysis has the advantage of creating synatctic consistency with the other uses of *ānthi* (discussed below), as well as the related interrogative and proximal forms *githi* and *ithi*. However, adverbials exhibit freedom of positioning not found when *ānthi* is used anaphorically to an event, series of events, or direct quote. Its limited positioning when it has these functions suggests that it may indeed be acting pronominally.

The second most common function of *ānthi* is to refer to the manner in which an action was performed. This use may be anaphoric, referring to a manner of performing an action already established in the preceding discourse. In interactional contexts it may also be deictic, if the manner of the action is something observable to the speech-act participants. When *ānthi* has a manner reading, it may be placed in any position within the clause, and does not necessarily precede the verb directly.

(66)   **ānthi**   sugā=pista   jon-ke-i-ta
         like.that   parrot=PL.DAT   catch-CAUS-INF-DAT

'In order to catch parrots in that fashion (as described before)...'

(67)   āle   **ānthi**   chū   yer-nasin   wā
         then   like.that   mouse   come-when   TOP

'Then when the mouse came like that (as he did in the previous episode)...'

(68)   kok   **ānthi**   hal-a   ka
         crow   like.that   call.out-3sPST   ASS

'The crow calls out like that.'

Finally, when the focus particle *tuŋ* directly follows *ānthi*, it means 'in exactly that manner':

(69)   āmu   **ānthi**   **tuŋ**   sit-a
         3s   like.that   FOC   die-3sPST

'He died in exactly the same way.'

(70)   **ānthi**   **tuŋ**   yet!
         like.that   FOC   do.IMP

'Do exactly that!'

The pronoun *ithi*, the proximal complement of *ānthi*, seems to be used only rarely to refer to a series of actions or to reported speech. One example of this use of *ithi* is (71):

(71) **ithi** haŋ-a ta-en
    this say-PART put-PART

    '(Rhodedendron) having said this...'

In my data, it is common to find *ithi* being used to indicate the manner of action. Since this form is used commonly in interactional contexts, the function tends to be deictic, referring to manners of actions evident to both the speaker and the addressee (including gestures made by the speaker which indicate manner). As when *ānthi* is used in this way, *ithi* exhibits flexibility of positioning:

(72) ām jāŋal **ithi** hal-a subi subi subi
    that bird like.this call.out-3sPST EXPR EXPR EXPR

    'That bird calls out like this: "Subi subi subi".'

(73) **ithi** **ithi** **ithi** **ithi** li tuŋ yer-gu
    like.this like.this like.this like.this back FOC come-1sPST

    'Like this, like this, like this, like this, I came backwards.'

5.4. Demonstratives of type and characteristic

In contrast to *ithi* and *ānthi*, the demonstratives *ināgu* and *ānāgu* refer not to manners of actions, but to types of things or personal characteristics. Both *ināgu* and *ānāgu* may modify nouns, in which case they mean 'of this/that type', as in examples (74)–(76):

(74) ra ām tākku **ānāgu** calan cal-ai ju-en
    and that time that.type custom be.in.use-BV happen-PART

    'And at that time, there was a custom of that type in use...'

(75) **ināgu** khā hati ithi da-hat
    this.type matter there here PROH-say

    'Don't say this kind of thing here and there.'

(76) **ināgu** mucā nis-lā da-u mucā yeŋ-an
    this.type child two-month have-NR1 child bring-PART

    'Bringing a child like this (indicating a child in the room), a child of two months...'

The forms *ināgu* and *ānāgu* may also be used to refer to states or to personal characteristics. In these cases, the forms are best translated as 'like this/that'. The following example is illustrative:

(77)   ji   **ināgu**   bãla-ku
       1s   like.this   beauty-NR1

       'I am beautiful like this.'

(78)   chi   **ānāgu**   bāmala-ku
       you   like.that   ugly-NR1

       'You are ugly like that.'

The forms *ānāgu* and *ināgu* may also refer more generally to a class of things, in other words, things of a general type:

(79)   kurāmuni   ger   baji   cāku   cāklat=pen
       condensed.milk   ghee   beaten.rice   sweets   chocolate=PL

       ekdam   sā-ku   sā-ku   phalphul=pen   **ānāgu**   jukun
       very   tasty-NR1   tasty-NR1   fruit=PL   like.that   only

       pita   kā-en   bir-ai
       out   take-PART   give-3sPR

       'Condensed milk, ghee, beaten rice, sweet chocolates, extremely tasty fruits, only things like that does (he) take out and give (her).'

(80)   āle   **ināgu**   tuŋ   na-en   tātā   moṭo   ju-ju
       then   this.type   FOC   eat-PART   e.sister   fat   become-3PA

       'Then by this type of thing, elder sister has become fat.'

5.5. Demonstratives of quantity

There are six distinct demonstratives which can be used to indicate quantity. The six-way distinction is produced by combining the two-way proximal/distal distinction and a three-way distinction in degree.

The forms *uli* and *āmli* are the unmarked set, indicating 'this much' and 'that much' respectively, without any particular emphasis on degree. Examples are given in (80)–(82):

(81) jana   nasputi=ku   guli   nyen-a   **āmli**   bi-sin
     1sGEN ear=LOC   how.much   fit-3sPST   that.much   give-IMP

   'However much will fit into my ear; give me that much.'

(82) ām   thākkar   **āmli=ŋ**   nar-gi
     that trouble   that.much=EXT   eat-1sPST

   'I experienced that much trouble.'

(83) janta   jā   **uli**   **uli**   khene   na-i   bi-eu
     1sDAT   rice   this.much   this.much   if   eat-INF   give-3FUT

   'He will give me about this little amount of rice to eat.'

To increase the degree of the amount indicated, one may use *ustule* and *ām-stule*:

(84) Elicited
     oho!   **ustule**   jāl   yeŋ-an
     oho   this.much   net   do-PART

   'Oho! They have caught me in this big of a net...'

The form *gustule*, which fits into this set, functions as an intensifier. Although the intial /g/ morphologically links to this interrogative series of forms, I have never seen it used in a true interrogative context.

(85) u=ri   **gustule**   moto   jur-a
     this=IND   how.much   fat   become-3sPST

   'This one became so fat.'

Finally, to indicate an even greater quantity, speakers can draw on the longest forms, *ulistule, āmlistule,* and, as an intensifier, *gulistule*. I have seen these forms accompanied with gestures indicating great size. The following text example shows the form being used in a narrative by Parbati, the beautiful consort of the god Vishnu:

(86) ji   **ulistule**   bãla-ku   pārbati
     1s   this.much   beautiful-NR1   Parbati

   'I am Parbati of this incredible beauty...'

5.6. Demonstratives of size

Similar to the demonstratives of quantity are the demonstratives of size: *upaĩ*, *āpaĩ*, and *wāpaĩ*. These mean 'this size' and 'that size' and 'this incredible size', the latter translation indicating a greater degree of size and a correspsonding amazement at it. All three forms may be accompanied by gestures; I have seen *opaĩ* pronounced with both hands over the head and then stretching out to the sides:

(87)   kwākarbeŋ=na   **āpaĩ**   sā   nar-ŋasin
       frog=ERG   that.size   cow   eat-when

       'When the frog ate a cow that big...'

(88)   baeŋkar   **upaĩ**   bhut
       huge   this.size   ghost

       'A ghost this huge...'

(89)   Elicited
       opaĩ   moṭo   mi
       that.big   fat   man

       'Incredibly fat man.'

5.7. Demonstratives of location

There are eight locational deictics: *uku*, *ãku*, *osaku*, *āsaku*, *ukuna*, *hukuna*, *ithi*, and *hati*. The *-ku* etymon in the first two pairs is transparently the locative casemarker. The form *ithi* is homophonous with the proximal manner deictic; context must disambiguate these.

The forms *uku* and *āku* are the unmarked locative demonstratives corresponding to 'here' and 'there'. As with the other demonstratives, the proximal forms are more likely to be deictic, indicating something in the proximity of the interlocutors, while the distal forms are more likely to be anaphoric, referring to locations previously established in the discourse:

(90)   āle   **ãku**   nitheŋ   sor-a   on-na   on-na
       then   there   daily   watch-PURP   go-when   go-when

       'Then going there to watch every day....'

(91) ãku   biruwā   bur-a
      there plant   sprout-3sPST

      'A plant sprouted there.'

(92) hātta yer-ahin   uku thiji   chẽ=ku
      why   come-3pPR here 1pINC.GEN   house=LOC

      'Why do they come here to our house?'

(93) uku   tuŋ ta-en   tar-ai
      here FOC put-PART   put-3sPR

      'She puts and keeps it right here.'

As in (92), these forms are commonly followed by the focus particle *tuŋ*. The combination specifies an exact location, i.e. *uku tuŋ* 'right here', *ãku tuŋ* 'right there'. Both forms may also be followed by the ablative clitic =*lān*, deriving *uku=lān* 'from here', and *ãku=lān* 'from there'.

I have no examples of the forms *osaku* and *āsaku* from natural discourse, probably because my conversational data is limited. In elicitation, my consultant produced *jana sāŋat āsaku con-a* as 'My friend is right there' which she accompanied by a pointing gesture. This thus appears to be more strongly deictic to an entity in the proximity of the speaker and hearer than is *ãku*. My consultants judged the proximal form *osaku* to be deictic and to indicate a point closer to the speaker and hearer than *uku*.

By contrast, the forms *ukuna* and *hukuna* are used as locational deictics when the location is a bit of a distance away, although it may still be within the sight of the interlocutors. Narrative examples are given in (93)–(94):

(94) hukuna   chẽ=ku
      over.there   house=LOC

      'At the house over there.'

(95) bācā   hukuna   yeŋ-ane
      a.little   over.there   take-PART

      'Taking it a little ways away...'

All of my discourse examples of *ukuna* occur in conjunction with *paṭi* 'side', as in example (96):

(96) āle ittaŋ **ukuna** paṭi ḍen-ai
then again over.here side cut-3sPR

'Then again she cuts from this side.'

The final pair of locational deictics is *ithi* and *hati*. It is not clear to me how they differ from *uku* and *ãku*. They are quite rare in my data. The form *hati* is used by some people as a hesitation particle, so one must listen closely to the intonation to determine when the form has a deictic function. Some examples of these locationals are given in (97)–(98):

(97) āle mebu deu=pen=ri **hati**=ŋ on-a
then other god=PL=IND there=EXT go-3sPST

'Then the other gods went there.'

(98) āle isi **ithi** yer-gu
then 1pEXC here come-1pPST

'Then we came here.'

I also have a few examples where these two forms are used together:

(99) ināgu khã **hati ithi** da-hat
this.type talk there here PROH-say

'Don't talk about this kind of thing here and there.'

(100) **hati** dukha **ithi** dukha yeŋ-an con-agi
there trouble here trouble do-PART stay-1sPR

'I am experiencing troubles here, troubles there.'

Chapter 6
Verbs and verb morphology

1. Introduction

This chapter will examine the phonological and morphological properties of Dolakhae verbs, with particular attention paid to the verbal paradigm, its morphological divisions, and the functional roles of the various inflections.

There are a number of criteria which may be used to identify verbs as constituting an independent lexical class in Dolakhae. To begin with, native Dolakhae verb stems have a characteristic phonological shape: roots are either monosyllabic or disyllabic and must end in one of four consonants: /n/, /t/, /r/, or /l/. The four consonants define four inflectional classes, and, with the exception of a few irregular verbs (see §6.7), the form of any verb with any inflection may be determined by which of the four classes the verb belongs to.[35]

There are extensive morphological criteria which indicate that verbs are a distinct lexical class, as only verbs may inflect for the following verbal categories: negative, imperative, prohibitive, optative, causative, person, tense, infinitive, participle, NR1 and NR2. In addition to these purely formal criteria, there are of course notional and distributional criteria which also apply uniquely to verbs (e.g. only verbs may denote events in the main line of a narrative; verbs are the only obligatory element in a relative clause); however, as the formal criteria are quite strong and are certainly sufficient to identify any verb in Dolakhae, these other criteria will not be further discussed.

In addition to the classification of verbs by stem class, verbs may also be classified by two other morphological dimensions. First, with a handful of exceptions, verbs may be classified as being either transitive or intransitive. While most of the verbal paradigm does not vary with this classification, a few inflections, such as the third-person past, do. A discussion of the semantic aspects of transitivity, and its relation to ergativity, is given in §4.4.2.4.

The second major morphological dimension relevant to verbs is that of finiteness. This dimension differs from those of stem class and transitivity, since it does not categorize verb stems, but instead categorizes verbal inflections. Finite verb forms reflect tense, and the person and number of the subject of the verb. There are two full and distinct finite paradigms, the affirmative-declarative paradigm and the negative paradigm. In addition, the imperative, prohibitive, and optative moods all have distinct paradigms, although these are abbreviated as they do not have distinct inflections for the full range of persons and numbers. By contrast, non-finite verb forms do not inflect for tense, person, or number, and neither do they have separate suffixal inflection for negation or mood. Whereas finite verb forms almost always occur in sentence-final position, non-finite verb forms are found in a variety of sentence-medial clauses, thus function as complements, participles, and in other roles. Chapters 17 through 21 discuss these structures in more detail.

2. Phonotactic structure of verbs

Most verb roots in Dolakhae are monosyllabic, although some disyllabic roots are also found. In some cases, the disyllabic verbs are transparent compounds. However, in many cases independent meanings cannot be found for the two syllables of the root and any previous internal structure has been lost. Disyllabic roots differ from monosyllabic roots in the placement of the negative morpheme. While the negative morpheme *ma-* always prefixes to monosyllabic verbs (e.g. **ma**-*bi-u* [NEG-give-3PA] 'did not give'), it infixes between the first and second syllables in disyllabic roots (*me-**ma**-tha* 'didn't play' from root *methar-*). This difference is reflective of the original bimorphemic etymology of disyllabic verbs. See §6.4.4.1 for more details and exemplification.

Verb stems vary in their shape depending on the morphological environment in which they occur. The verb stem found in the past-tense form of the third-person singular will always end in one of the following four consonants: /n, t, r, l/. These four consonants are taken to be representative of verb class. Examples of verb roots of varying shapes in the four classes are given in Table 14.

It should be noted that the r-stem verbs are the most common, easily numbering two to three times as many members as the other verb classes in my data. L-stem verbs appear to be the rarest (and I have no examples of disyllabic l-stem verbs), with n-stems and t-stems intermediate in number between the two.

There are some interesting gaps in the co-occurrence of vocalic nuclei across the four verb classes. N-stem verbs favor mid- and high-vowel nuclei; I only have one example of an n-stem verb with /ā/ (*gān-* 'be dry'), and none at all with /a/. T-stem verbs, by contrast, favor low and high vowels, the very notable exception being *yet-* 'do', which is the most common t-stem verb in terms of overall text frequency. R-stem verbs freely co-occur with all vowels, although I have only two examples with /e/, one being the very common *yer-* 'come'. The causative suffix also creates an r-stem verb and has /e/ as a nucleus: *-ker*. L-stem verbs occur with low and high vowels only; I have no examples of the sequences /ol/ or /el/.

Table 14. Verb roots in four conjugation classes

N-Stems		T-Stems		R-Stems		L-Stems	
on-	'go'	hat-	'say'	sir-	'die'	bul-	'rub'
phen-	'release'	cyāt-	'burn'	sor-	'look'	gal-	'be thin'
khon-	'open'	jut-	'fall'	sur-	'sew'	hal-	'cry out'
syen-	'teach'	gyāt-	'fear'	tar-	'put'	pwāl-	'till'
ṭhun-	'bury'	libāt-	'be late'	tār-	'hear'	jwāl-	'swim'
bon-	'read'	mut-	'squirt'	hakar-	'call'	cul-	'sharpen'
con-	'stay'	mwāt-	'survive'	hẽgar-	'be red'	tul-	'fall'
khon-	'see'	yet-	'do'	kār-	'take'	ŋil-	'smile'
ḍin-	'sleep'	sat-	'call'	khur-	'steal'	mal-	'need'
ḍen-	'cut'	sit-	'die'	hir-	'wash'	mwāl-	'try'
ḍon-	'stand'	tinmut-	'jump'	gar-	'climb'	wāl-	'mix'
ton-	'drink'	ṭit-	'dip'	chor-	'send'	pwāl-	'peel'
gān-	'dry'	pyāt-	'get wet'	botār-	'divide'	il-	'spread'
mon-	'swell'	syāt-	'kill'	peŋker-	'kick'	sul-	'hide'
ŋen-	'ask'	hut-	'bark'	dāer-	'boil'	pul-	'return'

3. Borrowed verbs

It is very common for speakers of Dolakhae to incorporate Nepali verbs into their speech. However, since the Dolakhae verb must end in one of four consonants which determines the verb's inflectional pattern, borrowed verbs are combined with Dolakhae verb roots in order to fit the language morphologically. There are two patterns of incorporation, based upon the transitivity of the borrowed verbs.

When a transitive verb is borrowed from Nepali, the Nepali infinitive suffix -*nu* (and a preceding short /a/ if there is one) is dropped from the infinitive form of the verb and the resulting stem is combined with the Dolakhae verb *yet-* 'do'. This derives a transitive t-stem verb. If the Nepali verb is morphologically causative, the vowel in *yet-* 'do' changes to /ā/. Examples are given in (1); Nepali forms are in the first column and Dolakhae forms in the second:

(1) tāknu   tākyet-   'stare'
    chirnu   chiryet-   'sprinkle'
    gāḍnu   gāḍyet-   'bury'
    jitnu   jityet-   'win'
    mānu   mānyet-   'obey'
    māsnu   māsyet-   'spend'
    nikālnu   nikālyet-   'draw out'
    ṭikranu   ṭikret-   'stand'

tarkāunu	tarkyāt-	'flirt'
haṭyāunu	haṭyāt-	'push aside; expel'
jalāunu	jalyāt-	'burn'
patyāunu	patyāt-	'believe'
salkāunu	salkyāt-	'kindle'

I analyze these as single words due to their phonotactic structure. The root-initial /y/ of the Dolakhae verb *yet-* 'do' syllabifies as the second element of the consonant cluster which begins the second syllable. In the form *ṭikret-* from Nepali *ṭikranu*, the /y/ does not surface, as the combination of /kry/ would be an illicit cluster. Thus phonotactic patterns argue that these forms are single words.

I have one example of an English verb borrowed in this manner. It is 'check', and the Dolakhae form is *chekyet-*.

When an intransitive Nepali verb is borrowed into Dolakhae, the Nepali *-nu* infinitive is again dropped (together with a final short /a/, if there is one), and the verb is suffixed with *-ai*, which I gloss "BV" for "borrowed verb". The Nepali verb is then followed directly by the Dolakhae intransitive verb *jur-*, which means 'be', 'become', or 'happen', depending on the context. The resulting biverbal complex is then treated as an r-stem verb. I consider these forms to be biverbal complexes rather than single words because the borrowed-verb suffix marks the relationship between the two verbs, because there is no phonological evidence that the two syllabify as a single word, and because each word is independently stressed. Examples are given in (2); again, Nepali forms are in the first column:

(2)	lāgnu	lāg-ai jur-	'be touched by; feel'
	phuṭnu	phuṭ-ai jur-	'burst'
	phulnu	phul-ai jur-	'swell'
	pharkanu	phark-ai jur-	'return'
	pākanu	pāk-ai jur-	'ripen'
	khasnu	khas-ai jur-	'fall'
	janmanu	janm-ai jur-	'be born'
	halnu	hal-ai jur-	'swing (of rope)'
	galnu	gal-ai jur-	'be thin'

4. Inflectional morphology of the Dolakhae verb

4.1. Verb paradigms

As mentioned above, all Dolakhae verbs may be neatly separated into four complementary stem classes (the exceptions which prove the rule are the existential verb and the copula, see §6.8). All four classes may be readily identified by the presence of a distinct stem-final consonant which is always present in the third-person-singular-past form of the verb. The four consonants which occur in this position are /n/ (e.g. *ton-ju* 'drink-3sPST'), /r/ (e.g. *bir-ju* 'give-3sPST'), /t/ (e.g. *khyāt-cu* 'frighten-3sPST'), and /l/ (e.g. *pul-ju* 'pay-3sPST'). In accordance with this regularity, the four classes will be referred to as n-stems, r-stems, t-stems, and l-stems. In addition, the citation form of the verb used throughout this grammar will consist of the stem with its characteristic final consonant, but lacking any inflectional morphology, e.g. *ton-* 'drink'.

While the characteristic stem-final consonant is always present in the third-singular-past forms of the verb, it is often absent or changed via morphophonological process in a number of other forms. These changes are absolutely regular and consistent within the paradigm for any given stem class.

The complete verbal paradigms are given on pages 159–166. For ease of reference, the paradigms reflect all the inflected verb forms for each stem class. The finite affirmative and negative paradigms are presented first, followed by the imperative, prohibitive, and optative forms, followed by the non-finite forms. All forms for both transitive and intransitive verbs are given. Cases where the intransitive form differs in inflection or stem from the transitive will be given in bold. Thus differences between the transitive and intransitive paradigms may be easily discerned.

There is some variation in the inflection of particular forms. Details of the variation will be given in the discussion that follows the paradigms. In addition Appendix A lists every allomorph of every verbal affix together with the relevant morphological environments.

For the purpose of clarifying the morphological structure of the forms, allophonic variation, such as the nasalization of adjacent vowels in the syllable rhyme, is not represented. However, morphophonemic variation, such as the vowel harmony found in the prefixes, is represented. In cases where a vowel deletes when adjacent to an identical vowel, the deleted vowel is shown in parentheses to indicate its presence morphologically.

The future forms have the particle *jeu* 'maybe' in parentheses. Some speakers, when checking the accuracy of the verb paradigms, insisted that the *jeu* be present, to indicate the speaker's lack of certainty that the event will take place. However, many future forms in connected discourse lack *jeu*, thus it is not a true suffix. Also regarding the future forms, some speakers dislike producing future honorific forms in statements, as it is socially inappropriate to tell a respected person what he or she will do in the future.

Table 15. Finite inflection: N-stem verbs

Transitive Verb: bon- 'read'

Affirmative					Negative		
	Past Anterior	Past	Present	Future	Past Anterior	Past/Present	Future
1s	bō-gu-ī	boŋ-gi	bon-a-gi	bō-i	**mo-bō-u-ī(-ju)**	mo-boŋ-gi	mo-bō-i (jeu)
1p	bō-gu-pe	bon-gu	bon-a-gu	bō-i	**mo-bō-gu-pe(-ju)**	mo-boŋ-gu	mo-bō-i (jeu)
2s	bō-u-n	bon-mun	bon-a-n	bō-i-na	**mo-bō-gu-n(-ju)**	mo-bo-n	mo-bō-i-na (jeu)
2p	bō-gu-min	bon-min	bon-a-min	bō-i-nan	**mo-bō-gu-min(-ju)**	mo-bo-min	mo-bō-i-nan (jeu)
2HON	bō-gu-pe	boŋ-gu	bon-a-gu	bō-i-ta	**mo-bō-gu-pe(-ju)**	mo-boŋ-gu	mo-bō-gu (jeu)
3s	bō-gu(-ju)	**bon-ju**	bon-a-i	bō-e-ŋ	**mo-bō-gu(-ju)**	**mo-bo-ŋ**	mo-bō-e-ŋ (jeu)
3p	bō-gu-tan	bon-hin	bon-a-hin	bō-i-tan	**mo-bō-gu-tan(-ju)**	mo-bo-hin	mo-bō-i-tan (jeu)

Intransitive Verb: ḍin- 'sleep'

	Past Anterior	Past	Present	Future	Past Anterior	Past/Present	Future
1s	ḍin-gu-ī	ḍiŋ-gi	ḍin-a-gi	ḍī(-i)	**ma-ḍiŋ-gu-ī(-ju)**	ma-ḍiŋ-gi	ma-ḍī(-i) (jeu)
1p	ḍin-gu-pe	ḍiŋ-gu	ḍin-a-gu	ḍī(-i)	**ma-ḍiŋ-gu-pe(-ju)**	ma-ḍiŋ-gu	ma-ḍī(-i) (jeu)
2s	ḍī-u-n	ḍin-mun	ḍin-a-n	ḍī(-i)-na	**ma-ḍiŋ-gu-n(-ju)**	ma-ḍi-n	ma-ḍī(-i)-na (jeu)
2p	ḍin-gu-min	ḍin-min	ḍin-a-min	ḍī(-i)-nan	**ma-ḍiŋ-gu-min(-ju)**	ma-ḍi-min	ma-ḍī(-i)-nan (jeu)
2HON	ḍin-gu-pe	ḍiŋ-gu	ḍin-a-gu	ḍī(-i)-ta	**ma-ḍiŋ-gu-pe(-ju)**	ma-ḍiŋ-gu	ma-ḍīŋ-gu (jeu)
3s	ḍin-gu(-ju)	**ḍin-a**	ḍin-a-i	ḍī-e-ŋ	**ma-ḍiŋ-gu(-ju)**	**ma-ḍī**	ma-ḍī-e-ŋ (jeu)
3p	ḍin-gu-tan	ḍin-hin	ḍin-a-hin	ḍī(-i)-tan	**ma-ḍiŋ-gu-tan(-ju)**	ma-ḍi-hin	ma-ḍī(-i)-tan (jeu)

*Bold font indicates forms which differ in the transitive and intransitive paradigms

Table 16. Imperative, prohibitive, and optative inflections: N-stem verbs

Transitive Verb: *bon-* 'read'

	Imperative	Prohibitive	Optative
Singular	bo-ŋ/bō-sin (HON)	**do-bo-ŋ, do-bō-gu** (HON)	**tho-bo-ŋ**
Plural	bo-n/bō-sin (HON)	do-bo-min, do-bo-n do-boŋ-gu (HON)	tho-bo-hin

Intransitive Verb: *ḍin-* 'sleep'

	Imperative	Prohibitive	Optative
Singular	ḍī/ḍī-sin (HON)	**da-ḍī, da-ḍiŋ-gu** (HON)	**tha-ḍī**
Plural	ḍi-n/ḍī-sin (HON)	da-ḍi-min, da-ḍi-n da-ḍī-gu (HON)	**tha-ḍi-hin**

Table 17. Non-finite inflection: N-stem verbs

	Transitive Verb: *bon-* 'read'	**Intransitive Verb:** *ḍin-* 'sleep'
Infinitive	bō-i	ḍī-(i)
Participle	boŋ-an	ḍiŋ-an
NR1	boŋ-gu	ḍiŋ-gu
NR2	boŋ-a	ḍiŋ-a
Conditional	bon-sa	ḍin-sa
Temporal	bon-na(sin), bon-ɲa(sin)	ḍin-na(sin), ḍin-ɲa(sin)
Concessive	bon-saŋ	ḍin-saŋ
Purposive	bon-da	ḍin-da

Table 18. Finite inflection: T-stem verbs

Transitive Verb: hat- 'say'

Affirmative

	Past Anterior	Past	Present	Future
1s	ha-ku-ī	hat-ki	hat-a-gi	har-i
1p	ha-ku-pe	hat-ku	hat-a-gu	har-i
2s	ha-ku-n	hat-mun	hat-a-n	har-i-na
2p	ha-ku-min	hat-min	hat-a-min	har-i-nan
2HON	ha-ku-pe	hat-ku	hat-a-gu	har-i-ta
3s	ha-ku(-ju)	hat-cu	hat-a-i	har-e-u
3p	ha-ku-tan	hat-hin	hat-a-hin	har-e-u

Negative

	Past Anterior	Past/Present	Future
1s	ma-ha-ku-ī(-ju)	ma-hat-ki	ma-har-i (jeu)
1p	ma-ha-ku-pe(-ju)	ma-hat-ku	ma-har-i (jeu)
2s	ma-ha-ku-n(-ju)	ma-hat-mun	ma-har-i-na (jeu)
2p	ma-ha-ku-min(-ju)	ma-hat-min	ma-har-i-nan (jeu)
2HON	ma-ha-ku-pe(-ju)	ma-hat-ku	ma-har-i-ta (jeu)
3s	ma-ha-ku(-ju)	ma-hat	ma-har-e-u (jeu)
3p	ma-ha-ku-tan(-ju)	ma-hat-hin	ma-har-e-u (jeu)

Intransitive Verb: gyāt- 'fear'

Affirmative

	Past Anterior	Past	Present	Future
1s	gyā-ku-ī	gyāt-ki	gyāt-a-gi	gyār-i
1p	gyā-ku-pe	gyāt-ku	gyāt-a-gu	gyār-i
2s	gyā-ku-n	gyāt-mun	gyāt-a-n	gyār-i-na
2p	gyā-ku-min	gyāt-min	gyāt-a-min	gyār-i-nan
2HON	gyā-ku-pe	gyāt-ku	gyāt-a-gu	gyār-i-ta
3s	gyā-ku(-ju)	gyāt-a	gyāt-a-i	gyār-e-u
3p	gyā-ku-tan	gyāt-hin	gyāt-a-hin	gyār-e-u

Negative

	Past Anterior	Past/Present	Future
1s	ma-gyā-ku-ī(-ju)	ma-gyāt-ki	ma-gyār-i (jeu)
1p	ma-gyā-ku-pe(-ju)	ma-gyāt-ku	ma-gyār-i (jeu)
2s	ma-gyā-ku-n(-ju)	ma-gyāt-mun	ma-gyār-i-na (jeu)
2p	ma-gyā-ku-min(-ju)	ma-gyāt-min	ma-gyār-i-nan (jeu)
2HON	ma-gyā-ku-pe(-ju)	ma-gyāt-ku	ma-gyār-i-ta (jeu)
3s	ma-gyā-ku(-ju)	ma-gyāt	ma-gyār-e-u (jeu)
3p	ma-gyā-ku-tan(-ju)	ma-gyāt(-hin)	ma-gyār-e-u (jeu)

Table 19. Imperative, prohibitive, and optative inflection: T-stem verbs

Transitive Verb: *hat-* 'say'

	Imperative	Prohibitive	Optative
Singular	hat/har-siŋ (HON)	da-hat, da-hat-ku (HON)	tha-hat
Plural	hat-un/har-sin (HON)	da-hat-un, da-hat-min da-hat-ku (HON)	tha-hat-hin

Intransitive Verb: *sit-* 'die'

	Imperative	Prohibitive	Optative
Singular	sit/sir-siŋ (HON)	da-sit, da-sit-ku (HON)	tha-si
Plural	sit-un/sir-sin (HON)	da-sit-un, da-sit-min da-sit-ku (HON)	tha-sit-hin

Table 20. Non-finite inflections: T-stem verbs

	Transitive Verb: *hat-* 'say'	**Intransitive Verb:** *gyār-* 'fear'
Infinitive	har-i	gyār-i
Participle	haŋ-an	gyāŋ-an
NR1	ha-ku	gyā-ku
NR2	haŋ-a	gyāŋ-a
Conditional	har-sa	gyār-sa
Temporal	hat-na(sin), hat-ŋa(sin)	gyāt-na(sin), gyāt-ŋa(sin)
Concessive	har-saŋ	gyār-saŋ
Purposive	hat-a	gyāt-a

Table 21. Finite inflection: R-stem verbs

Transitive Verb: kār- 'take'

Affirmative

	Past Anterior	Past	Present	Future
1s	kā-u-ī	kār-gi	kār-a-gi	kā-i
1p	kā-u-pe	kār-gu	kār-a-gu	kā-i
2s	kā-u-n	kār-mun	kār-a-n	kā-i-na
2p	kā-u-min	kār-min	kār-a-min	kā-i-nan
2HON	kā-u-pe	kār-gu	kār-a-gu	kā-i-ta
3s	kā-u(-ju)	kār-ju	kār-a-i	kā-e-u
3p	kā-u-tan	kār-hin	kār-a-hin	kā-e-u

Negative

	Past Anterior	Past	Present	Future
1s	mā-kā-u-ī(-ju)	mā-kār-gi	mā-kā-gi	mā-kā-i (jeu)
1p	mā-kā-u-pe(-ju)	mā-kār-gu	mā-kā-gu	mā-kā-i (jeu)
2s	mā-kā-u-n(-ju)	mā-kār-mun	mā-kā-n	mā-kā-i-na (jeu)
2p	mā-kā-u-min(-ju)	mā-kār-min	mā-kā-min	mā-kā-i-nan (jeu)
2HON	mā-kā-u-pe(-ju)	mā-kār-gu	mā-kā-gu	mā-kā-i (jeu)
3s	mā-kā-u(-ju)	**mā-kār-ju**	**mā-kā-u**	mā-kā-e-u (jeu)
3p	mā-kā-u-tan(-ju)	mā-kār-hin	mā-kā-hin	mā-kā-e-u (jeu)

Intransitive Verb: khor- 'cry, weep'

Affirmative

	Past Anterior	Past	Present	Future
1s	kho-u-ī	khor-gi	khor-a-gi	kho-i
1p	kho-u-pe	khor-gu	khor-a-gu	kho-i
2s	kho-u-n	khor-mun	khor-a-n	kho-i-na
2p	kho-u-min	khor-min	khor-a-min	kho-i-nan
2HON	kho-u-pe	khor-gu	khor-a-gu	kho-i-ta
3s	kho-u(-ju)	**khor-a**	khor-a-i	kho-e-u
3p	kho-u-tan	khor-hin	khor-a-hin	kho-e-u

Negative

	Past Anterior	Past	Present	Future
1s	mo-kho-u-ī(-ju)	mo-khor-gi	mo-kho-gi	mo-kho-i (jeu)
1p	mo-kho-u-pe(-ju)	mo-khor-gu	mo-kho-gu	mo-kho-i (jeu)
2s	mo-kho-u-n(-ju)	mo-khor-mun	mo-kho-n	mo-kho-i-na (jeu)
2p	mo-kho-u-min(-ju)	mo-khor-min	mo-kho-min	mo-kho-i-nan (jeu)
2HON	mo-kho-u-pe(-ju)	mo-khor-gu	mo-kho-gu	mo-kho-gu (jeu)
3s	mo-kho-u(-ju)	**mo-khor-a**	**mo-kho**	mo-kho-e-u (jeu)
3p	mo-kho-u-tan(-ju)	mo-khor-hin	mo-kho-hin	mo-kho-e-u (jeu)

Table 22. Imperative, prohibitive, and optative inflections: R-stem verbs

Transitive Verb: kār- 'take'

	Imperative	Prohibitive	Optative
Singular	**kā-u**/kā-sin (HON)	**dā-kā-u**, dā-kā-gu (HON)	**thā-kā-u**
Plural	kā-n/kā-sin (HON)	dā-kā-min, da-kā-n dā-kā-gu (HON)	thā-kā-hin

Intransitive Verb: khor- 'cry; weep'

	Imperative	Prohibitive	Optative
Singular	**kho**/kho-sin (HON)	**do-kho**, do-kho-gu (HON)	**tho-kho**
Plural	kho-n/kho-sin (HON)	do-kho-min, do-kho-n do-kho-gu (HON)	tho-kho-hin

Table 23. Non-finite inflections: R-stem verbs

	Transitive Verb: kār- 'take'	Intransitive Verb: khor- 'cry'
Infinitive	kā-i	kho-i
Participle	kā-en	kho-en
NR1	kā-u	kho-u
NR2	kā-e	kho-e
Conditional	kār-sa	khor-sa
Temporal	kār-na(sin), kār-ŋa(sin)	khor-na(sin), khor-ŋa(sin)
Concessive	kār-saŋ	khor-saŋ
Purposive	kār-a	khor-a

Section 4 Inflectional morphology   165

Table 24. Finite inflections: L-stem verbs

Transitive Verb: wāl- 'mix'

Affirmative

	Past Anterior	Past	Present	Future
1s	wāl-gu-ī	wāl-gi	wāl-a-gi	wāl-i
1p	wāl-gu-pe	wāl-gu	wāl-a-gu	wāl-i
2s	wāl-gu-n	wāl-mun	wāl-a-n	wāl-i-na
2p	wāl-gu-min	wāl-min	wāl-a-min	wāl-i-nan
2HON	wāl-gu-pe	wāl-gu	wāl-a-gu	wāl-i-ta
3s	wāl-gu(-ju)	wāl-ju	wāl-a-i	wāl-e-u
3p	wāl-gu-tan	wāl-hin	wāl-a-hin	wāl-e-u

Negative

	Past Anterior	Past/Present	Future
1s	mā-wāl-gu-ī (-ju)	mā-wāl-gi	mā-wāl-i
1p	mā-wāl-gu-pe (-ju)	mā-wāl-gu	mā-wāl-i
2s	mā-wāl-gu-n (-ju)	mā-wāl-mun	mā-wāl-i-na
2p	mā-wāl-gu-min (-ju)	mā-wāl-min	mā-wāl-i-nan
2HON	mā-wāl-gu-pe (-ju)	mā-wāl-gu	mā-wāl-i-ta
3s	mā-wāl-gu(-ju)	mā-wāl	mā-wāl-e-u
3p	mā-wāl-gu-tan (-ju)	mā-wāl-hin	mā-wāl-e-u

Intransitive Verb: ŋil- 'smile; laugh'

Affirmative

	Past Anterior	Past	Present	Future
1s	ŋil-gu-ī	ŋil-gi	ŋil-a-gi	ŋil-i
1p	ŋil-gu-pe	ŋil-gu	ŋil-a-gu	ŋil-i
2s	ŋil-gu-n	ŋil-mun	ŋil-a-n	ŋil-i-na
2p	ŋil-gu-min	ŋil-min	ŋil-a-min	ŋil-i-nan
2HON	ŋil-gu-pe	ŋil-gu	ŋil-a-gu	ŋil-i-ta
3s	ŋil-gu(-ju)	**ŋil-a**	ŋil-a-i	ŋil-e-u
3p	ŋil-gu-tan	ŋil-hin	ŋil-a-hin	ŋil-e-u

Negative

	Past Anterior	Past/Present	Future
1s	ma-ŋil-gu-ī (-ju)	ma-ŋil-gi	ma-ŋil-i
1p	ma-ŋil-gu-pe (-ju)	ma-ŋil-gu	ma-ŋil-i
2s	ma-ŋil-gu-n (-ju)	ma-ŋil-mun	ma-ŋil-i-na
2p	ma-ŋil-gu-min (-ju)	ma-ŋil-min	ma-ŋil-i-nan
2HON	ma-ŋil-gu-pe (-ju)	ma-ŋil-gu	ma-ŋil-i-ta
3s	ma-ŋil-gu(-ju)	ma-ŋil	ma-ŋil-e-u
3p	ma-ŋil-gu-tan (-ju)	ma-ŋil-hin	ma-ŋil-e-u

Table 25. Imperative, prohibitve, and optative inflections: L-stem verbs

Transitive Verb: wāl- 'mix'

	Imperative	Prohibitive	Optative
Singular	wāl/wāl-sin (HON)	dā-wāl, dā-wāl-gu (HON)	thā-wāl
Plural	wāl-dun/wāl-sin (HON)	dā-wāl-min, dā-wāl-dun dā-wāl-gu (HON)	thā-wāl-hin

Intransitive Verb: ŋil- 'smile; laugh'

	Imperative	Prohibitive	Optative
Singular	ŋil/ŋil-sin (HON)	da-ŋil, da-ŋil-gu (HON)	tha-ŋil
Plural	ŋil-dun/ŋil-sin (HON)	da-ŋil-min da-ŋil-dun da-ŋil-gu (HON)	tha-ŋil-hin

Table 26. Non-finite inflections: L-stem verbs

	Transitive Verb: wāl- 'mix'	Intransitive Verb: ŋil- 'smile; laugh'
Infinitive	wāl-i	ŋil-i
Participle	wāl-en	ŋil-en
NR1	wāl-gu	ŋil-gu
NR2	wāle	ŋil-e
Conditional	wāl-sa	ŋil-sa
Temporal	wāl-na(sin), wāl-ŋa(sin)	ŋil-na(sin), ŋil-ŋa(sin)
Concessive	wāl-saŋ	ŋil-saŋ
Purposive	wāl-da	ŋil-da

4.2. The forms of verbal stems

As mentioned above, Dolakhae verb stems fall into four inflectional stem classes, according to whether the final consonant of the stem is /n/, /t/, /r/ or /l/. The form of the stem that occurs will vary with the inflection, and the patterns of stem variation are unique for each class. The form of the inflectional suffixes found may also vary by class, but the number of cases where such variation is idiosyncratic, as opposed to being the result of a regular phonological alternation, are very few in number.

There are four forms of n-stem verbs which occur in the n-stem verbal paradigms: C(C)Vn-, C(C)Vŋ-, C(C)Ṽ- and C(C)V. It should be noted that three of these stems, C(C)Vn-, C(C)Vŋ-, and C(C)Ṽ - occur before the phoneme /g/, e.g. *bon-gu-min* [read-2pPA], *mo-boŋ-gi* [NEG-read-1sPST], *mo-bõ-gu-ī* [NEG-1sPA]. These forms are clearly differentiated in very careful speech. In rapid or casual speech, the sequences C(C)Vŋ-g and C(C)Ṽ-g are difficult to differentiate, as the latter form generally results in the production of an /ŋ/ phonetically. Similarly, the sequence /ng/, while clearly containing a phonetic alveolar nasal in some examples, is often heard as [ŋg] in others, exhibiting the common process of place assimilation. Interestingly, I have had more than one consultant insist on differentiating these forms as indicated in the paradigms, saying for example, that the past-anterior negative forms of intransitive verbs "have /ŋ/", while their transitive counterparts "have no /ŋ/". These judgements appear to illustrate awareness of morphophonemic alternation, despite the facts of phonetic accommodation which regularly produce /ŋ/ before /g/.

In the affirmative paradigm, the stem-final /n/ is present in all but the future inflection. It deletes, leaving its trace as nasalization of the stem vowel. In the negative paradigm, there is considerably more alternation of the stem-final consonant. While speakers insist on the absence of the stem-final consonant and a nasalized stem vowel in the negative past-anterior forms of transitive verbs, the /ŋ/ is consistently present in the negative past-anterior forms of intransitive verbs. In the future, the nasal consonant is lost, leaving its trace as nasalization of the stem vowel; this is the same pattern as found in the affirmative paradigm. The most surprising stem alternation in this class is found in the negative past/present, where the stem-final /n/ is deleted before any suffix not beginning with /g/. The loss of the nasal is especially clear in the third-person-plural forms *mo-bo-hin* and *mo-ḍi-hin* where there is no adajcent nasal and the oral quality of the vowel is undeniable.

The stem-final consonant in t-stem verbs surfaces as /t/ in all past- and present-tense inflections, is deleted in the past anterior, and is replaced by /r/ in the future. In the participle and nominalized forms, the /t/ changes to /ŋ/, so that the t-stem and n-stem forms are indistinguishable with these suffixes. It should also be noted that the voicelessness of the /t/ final has historically caused devoicing of the initial consonant of the suffixes. Thus only with t-stem verbs do we find the allomorph /cu/ of the third-singular-past morpheme and the allomorph /ku/ of the past anterior, NR1, and the second-person-honorific morphemes. This is true even in cases where the /t/ has been deleted, indicating a historical process of first devoicing, and then deletion of the final /t/.

The stem-final consonant in r-stem verbs surfaces only in the past and affirmative present inflections. In all other inflections it deletes, leaving a vowel-final stem. This numeric preference for stems which lack the final /r/ has led R. L. Shrestha (1989, 1993, 2000b) to analyze this class as a class of vowel-final stems. I prefer to recognize the /r/ as stem-final because of the symmetry with the other verb classes, the lack of motivation for the insertion of /r/, and because it is likely that this class had a final consonant historically. Both analyses equally describe the relevant facts.

The l-stem class is the simplest of the four classes of verb stems, as there is no morphophonemic variation in the stem at all; the stem-final /l/ is present in every inflection.

4.3. Morphological structure of the affirmative finite paradigms

The overall morphological structure of the Dolakhae affirmative finite verb may be schematized as in (3):

(3)   STEM-TENSE-PERSON/NUMBER

4.3.1. Tense

The Dolakhae verb inflects for four tenses: the past anterior, the simple past, the present, and the future. Of the four, the past anterior, present, and future are realized by the presence of an overt morpheme, while the simple past is unmarked.[36] It appears that of the tenses, the simple past and future should be reconstructed for Proto-Newar, while the past anterior and the present are Dolakhae innovations. For discussion, see Genetti 1994. In the current chapter, only the formal properties of the four tenses will be discussed. A complete description of how the tenses are used is given in §16.2.

The past-anterior tense has three allomorphs: /gu/, /ku/, and /u/. The form /gu/ is the most common, and should be taken as the base form of the morpheme. The devoicing of /g/ to /k/ in the t-stem paradigms reflects a regular process of assimilation to the preceding voiceless consonant. In r-stem forms, both the stem-final /r/ and the initial /g/ of the suffix are absent in the past anterior.[37, 38]

As mentioned above, the simple past is unmarked. The only morphophonological process that applies in the past tense is the devoicing of suffixes with voiced initials following a stem-final /t/.

The present tense morpheme is /a/. It always follows the stem-final consonant. The suffixal paradigm found in the present tense is identical to that found in the past tense, with the exception of the second-person-singular and third-person-singular forms.

The future morpheme is /i/, and it is realized as [e] before /u/, suggesting a dissimilation process of lowering of one high vowel before another high vowel. The same process is found in the third-person-future form of n-stem verbs, where the suffixal complex is -e-ŋ. In this case the lowering process occurs before a velar nasal, a consonant which also involves a high position of the tongue body. There are a considerable number of stem changes which occur before the future tense marker, which suggests that this form is considerably older than either the past anterior or the present. The final nasal of the n-stem verb deletes before the future suffix, leaving its trace as nasalization on the diphthong that arises when the vowel of the stem directly precedes /i/. Stem-final /t/ changes to /r/ in the future, while stem-final /r/ is deleted.[39]

The forms of the tense morphemes and the co-occurring stem alternations are summarized in Table 27:

Table 27. Tense morphemes and stem alternations across inflectional verb classes

	N-Stem		T-Stem		R-Stem		L-stem	
	Stem	Suffix	Stem	Suffix	Stem	Suffix	Stem	Suffix
Anterior	Ṽ-/ŋ-	-gu-	V-	-ku-	V-	-u-	l-	-gu-
Present	n-	-a-	r-	-a-	r-	-a-	l-	-a-
Future	Ṽ-	-i-	V-	-i-	V-	-i-	l-	-i-

4.3.2. Person and number

One of the most unusual features of Dolakhae as a Newar dialect is the presence of verbal morphology which reflects the person and number of the subject of the verb. The dialects of the Kathmandu Valley do not show an agreement pattern; instead the verb in those dialects inflects in accordance with a complex "conjunct/disjunct" system, which is largely evidential in nature.[40] Since the initial discovery of agreement in Dolakhae, some agreement systems have been attested in other Newar dialects from outside the Kathmandu Valley (Shakya 1992; R. L. Shrestha 2003). The system most closely related to Dolakhae was found in Tauthali, a dialect also spoken in the hills to the northeast of the Kathmandu Valley. The presence of the clearly cognate pattern of extensive verbal morphology strongly suggests shared history, hence that there is an eastern branch to the Newar family containing at least these two dialects.[41]

4.3.3. *The morphological forms in synchronic and diachronic perspective*

Table 28 presents the person/number suffixes of the finite verb. Readers are referred to the paradigms given in §6.3.1 for details of inflection across the four stem classes:

Table 28. Person/number suffixes (affirmative finite paradigm)

	Past Anterior	Past ~ Present	Future
1s	-ĩ	-gi	Ø
1p	-pe	-gu	Ø
2s	-n	-mun/-n	-na
2p	-min	-min	-nan
2HON	-pe	-gu	-ta
3s	-ju	-ju, -a/-i	-u,- ŋ
3p	-tan	-hin	-tan

    The person/number suffixes follow the tense morpheme of the verb. These suffixes reflect the person and the number of the grammatical subject;[42] the person and number of the object are never represented in the verb morphology. Person and number are not separately marked; instead each person/number combination has a unique set of suffixes which are distributed across the four tenses.

    The Dolakhae verb inflects for three persons (first, second, and third), and for singular and plural number. While the pronominal paradigm distinguishes inclusive and exclusive first person, that distinction is not marked in the verb.

    The second-person paradigm distinguishes not only singular and plural number, but also honorific status. There is only one honorific verb form which is used for both singular and plural honorific subjects. The conditions under which honorific verb forms are used are the same as hold for the use of honorific pronouns, discussed in §5.2. Interestingly, the honorific verb forms are identical to those of the first-person plural in all tenses except the future.

    Each person/number combination is distinguished in all four tenses with the exception of the first-person future, which has no suffix, either in the singular or plural. Since the other first-person-singular forms have the vowel *-i*, one may speculate that an old *-i* may have been applied to the future as well, but that it was deleted by the regular phonological rule which elides one of two adjacent identical vowels.

The suffixes found in the past and present are identical except for the second-person singular, which has -*mun* in the present and -*n* in the past, and the third-person singular, which has -*i* in the present and -*ju* or -*a* in the past (depending on transitivity). It is the similarity of these paradigms, together with the lack of morphophonemic alternations in the present tense, which suggest that the present is a relatively new innovation in the tense system. (Historical-comparative evidence also favors this conclusion; see Genetti 1994: 129–130.)

Synchronically, the person/number suffixes are not further analyzable into distinct subparts. However, there are some regularities in the paradigm which may reflect the historical structure of these forms and it is also possible to make some hypotheses as to possible cognate morphemes which may be instructive for those interested in historical issues. While some of these hypotheses are suggestive that the Dolakhae morphology may be cognate to that found in other Tibeto-Burman languages inside and outside Nepal, without more detailed historical evidence – ideally regular sound correspondences in cognate vocabulary – we cannot confidently draw a conclusion of any but the broadest historical relationship. Nevertheless, the presence of possibly cognate verb morphology may point to likely avenues for further detailed historical research, which could in turn prove or disprove some of the hypotheses given here.

To begin with the first-person forms, the nasalization on the first-person-singular -*ĩ* is suggestive of an old nasal consonant, probably *ŋ. The hypothesis is bolstered by the presence of an irregular first-person-singular form of the verb *on*- 'go'. It is *u-e-ŋ* in the future tense, with a clear velar nasal marking first-person singular. A number of Tibeto-Burman languages in Nepal and elsewhere have the phoneme /ŋ/ in the first-person verbal morphology (DeLancey 1989), so if the Dolakhae paradigm is conservative, then this may be a reflex of this older Tibeto-Burman form.

The first-person-plural suffix -*pe* is transparently related to the nominal plural clitic =*pen* (with cognate -*pĩ* in the Kathmandu dialect). The suffix -*ta* found marking the second-person honorific in the future is appears likely to be cognate with the suffix -*ta* found in the Kathmandu dialect marking animate plural nouns.

The second-person forms all share a common /n/. This is the most robust correlation between a particular form and meaning in the paradigm. DeLancey (1989) finds a common second-person ending /na/ in a number of Tibeto-Burman languages, so again the Dolakhae morpheme may be a reflex of older Tibeto-Burman morphology.

The second- and third-person-plural forms also share an /n/ element, which could be from an old plural. Plurals with /n/ are found throughout the Kiranti languages, so once more we see that there may be a historical connection outside the Newar family.

The third-person form *-ju,* which is found in both the past tense (with transitive verbs) and the past anterior (with transitive and intransitive verbs) might be a reflex of the verb *jur-* 'be; become; happen') in nominalized form (NR1-*ju*). The fact that the negative past-anterior forms may be followed by *ju* even when fully inflected, points to this as a likely concatenation with an otherwise finite form.

The third-person-plural form *-tan* may be divided into *ta* plus *n*, the former being the same plural found in the honorific (and cognate to a plural in the Kathmandu dialect), and the latter being the same /n/ plural found throughout the second- and third-person paradigms.

4.3.4. "Disagreement" between subjects and verbs

As stated above, the Dolakhae verb agrees with its subject in person and number. This generalization is true for the vast majority of examples which occur in natural speech. There are a small number of cases where the verb fails to agree with the subject, and these can be divided into two classes. In the first class, first-person or second-person subjects occur with verbs inflected with third-person morphology, thus there is "disagreement" in person. In the second class, third-person-plural subjects occur with third-person-singular morphology; in these cases the "disagreement" is one of number.

In my data, I have six naturally-occurring examples of the first type of "disagreement". In all six examples, a clause with a first-person subject also contains a verb with third-person morphology.[43] This disagreement is clearly not accidental, as it only occurs with verbs where the subjects are non-volitonal. The six examples are given here; the phenomenon occurs twice in (8):

(4) *ji=ŋ*   tharthar **tut-a**
     1s=EXT   EXPR   shiver-3sPST

   'I also shivered, going "tharthar".'

(5) *isi*   sõ-mā   pe-mā   jammai   lāṭa   **jur-a**
     1pEXC   three-CL   four-CL   together   dumb   become-3sPST

   'We three or four become dumbfounded.'

(6) *ji=ŋ*   **sir-eu.**   ji   chana   nāpa   tuŋ   **sir-i**
     1s=EXT   die-3sFUT   1s   2sGEN together FOC   die-1FUT

   'I will also die. I will die with you.'

(7) **ji gyāt-a** haŋ-an sir-ai jeu
    1s fear-3sPST say-PART know-3PR maybe
    'Maybe he knows I'm afraid.'

(8) ām situgãs tãs yeŋ-an ta-ene
    that situ.grass stick do-PART put-PART

    sir-sa ji didā **sit-a** haŋ-an si-u
    die-if 1s e.brother die-3sPST say-PART know-IMP

    u situgãs hātiŋ ma-jur-sa
    this situ.grass nothing NEG-happen-if

    ji mwāt-a haŋ-an si-u
    1s survive-3sPST say-PART know-IMP

    'He stuck the situ grass to the door and said "If it dies, know that I, your elder brother, died. If nothing happens to this situ grass, know that I survived".'

In these examples, the use of the third-person form explicitly indicates lack of volition or control on the part of the subject.[44] This is especially clear in example (8), taken from a story where a young girl has just found out that her benefactor is to be put to death. In this example, the statement 'I will die' is repeated twice, the first time with third-person morphology on the verb (*ji=ŋ sir-eu*), and the second time with first-person morphology (*ji...sir-i*). The first clause also contains the extensive clitic =ŋ, which in this case translates clearly as 'also', meaning that she also will die as a natural result of her benefactor's death (as no one will remain to help and feed her). The second clause, with the first-person morphology, indicates her conscious decision to die alongside her benefactor, rather than to await a slow and inevitable death in his absence. By using the first-person morphology in this case, the subject of the sentence is expressing that she will have control over the normally non-volitional, non-controlled event. Thus speakers have the ability to subtly manipulate the agreement to suggest differences of volitionality. This analysis is confirmed by the following minimal pairs, which were elicited from Mrs. Rama Shrestha:

(9) *ji buḍā ju-eu*
    1s old become-3sFUT
    'I will become old.'

(10) *ji   buḍā   ju-i*
      1s   old   become-1FUT

      'I am determined to become old.'

(11) *chi   tul-eu*
      2s   fall-3sFUT

      'You will fall.'

(12) *chi   tul-ina*
      2s   fall-2sFUT

      'You will fall intentionally (e.g. as we have planned).'

While it is possible to manipulate the agreement system in this way, it is not at all common, and it has certainly not grammaticalized in the sense of becoming a regular or required feature of the grammar of the language. One can certainly use first-person morphology with non-control verbs without any added implication of heightened volition (e.g. *ji gyāt-ki* 'I was afraid', used in a story about an encounter with a ghost). It is the use of the third-person morphology with first-person subjects which is marked, and which emphasizes the lack of volition. This use of the morphology is similar to the use of the conjunct/disjunct system in the Kathmandu Valley dialects (Hargreaves 1991, 2005), although there the system has become an integral part of the core grammar of the language, and is much more extensive than the optional manipulation of agreement morphology in Dolakhae.

The other type of disagreement between subject and verb involves number, namely the use of third-person-singular morphology where plural morphology is expected. This is also relatively rare, although it is certainly more widely attested than disagreement in person. Some examples follow:

(13) **āpsin   bãlaku   keṭi   ṭwāŋsona=ta   khon-ju**
      3pERG   beautiful   girl   Twaŋsona=DAT   see-3sPST

      'They saw the beautiful girl Twaŋsona.'

(14) *āpen   thau   thau   ṭhā̃i=ku   on-a*
      3p   REFL   REFL   place=LOC   go-3sPST

      'They each went to their own homes.'

(15)   **upsin**   kā-i   **mwāl-ai**
       3pERG   take-INF   try-3sPR

       'They try to take it.'

(16)   **āpen**   lita   wā   **ye-uju**
       3p   later   TOP   come-3sPA

       'They came later.'

Disagreement in number never occurs with first- or second-person verb forms. As far as I am able to determine, it has no obvious pragmatic effects.

It is interesting to note that lack of agreement in number with third-person subjects is also common in spoken Nepali (Genetti 1999); its use in Dolakhae may be the result of extensive Nepali-Dolakhae bilingualism.

4.4. Negation

This section will discuss the forms of negated verbs. Negation is further discussed in §15.6.

4.4.1. *Form and positioning of the negative affix*

The Dolakhae verb is negated with the affix *ma-*, which is subject to vowel harmony as described in §2.3.5, thus deriving the allomorphs *mā-* and *mo-*.[45] This morpheme is bound to the final syllable of the root. Since verb roots can be either one or two syllables in length, this affix is sometimes prefixed and sometimes infixed. Before monosyllabic verbs, *ma-* appears as a prefix; this comprises the vast majority of cases. With disyllabic verbs, the negative affix is positioned between the two syllables of the verb stem. It can then be thought of as an an infix with all disyllabic verb stems, as each part consitutes a separate phonological syllable, and so the position of the negative morpheme can be phonologically determined. The positioning of the negative morpheme in disyllabic stems is exemplified below (in third-person-singular forms of the present negative paradigm):

(17)   *yārkhār-*   *yār-mā-khā-u*   'hang'
       bothar-   *bo-ma-tha-u*   'divide'
       bohar-   *bo-ma-ha*   'bloom'
       chasar-   *cha-ma-sa*   'itch'

chusār-	chu-mā-sā-u	'send (someone)'
cicār-	ci-mā-cā	'shrink'
cikar-	ci-ma-ka	'become cold'
hākar-	hā-ma-ka	'become black'
jāudir-	jāu-ma-di-u	'put down a load'
liŋār-	li-mā-ŋā	'walk'
lipul-	li-mo-pul	'return'
methar-	me-ma-tha	'play'
morlur-	mor-mo-lu	'bathe'
tapjyāt-	tap-ma-jyā	'break (INTR)'
onsir-	on-ma-si-u	'be acquainted with; know (someone)'

In a few cases, one can identify a lexical source of the first element, suggesting a historical process of compounding to derive these verbs, e.g. the first syllable of *lipul-* 'return' is undoubtedly related to the adverb *li* 'back; behind', and the first syllable of *morlur-* 'bathe' is clearly *mor* 'body'. In most cases, however, the lexical source of the first syllable is not obvious, and these words have clearly lexicalized into unanalyzable single units. The result is synchronic infixation of the negative morpheme into disyllabic stems.

4.4.2. Primary differences between the affirmative and negative paradigms

The most important distinction between the affirmative and negative paradigms is the number of tenses distinguished. While four tenses are consistently distinguished in the affirmative paradigm, only the r-stem class of verbs distinguishes four tenses in the negative paradigm. In the remaining three classes, the past and present tenses are conflated under negation. Examples (18) and (19) illustrate the distinct present and past negative inflections of r-stem verbs, while examples (20) and (21) illustrate the same t-stem verb form being used in both past and present contexts:

(18) chana   nasputi=ku   wā   ajaŋ   **mā-khā**
      2sGEN   ear=LOC   TOP   still   NEG-fill

   'Your ear is still not full.'

(19) gulpanuŋ   mica   **mā-yār-a**
      never   daughter   NEG-come-3sPST

   'The daughter never came back.'

(20)　thanu　kesi　　　　bā=n=uŋ　　　　　māyā　ma-yet
　　　today　tomorrow　father=ERG=EXT　love　NEG-do

'These days father also doesn't love (me).'

(21)　chū=n　　　　hāti　khā̃=ŋ　　ma-hat
　　　mouse =ERG　what　talk=EXT　NEG-say

'The mouse didn't say any of that talk.'

It does seem strange that the past and present tenses are only distinguished in negative contexts in one of the four conjugation classes. My impression is that this situation is unstable, and that some speakers are creating a distinction in the other classes by the process of simple affixation of the negative prefix to verb stems with regular past tense inflection. In my discourse corpus, I have one example of a t-stem verb inflected in this way:

(22)　āme　　bā=n=uŋ　　　　　　māyā　ma-yet-cu　　　āmta
　　　3sGEN　father=ERG=also　love　NEG-do-3sPST　3sDAT

'Her father also didn't love her.'

I have also had consultants volunteer *mo-on-a* 'did not go' during elicitation, suggesting that the process is extending to verbs in other classes. Further exploration is warranted.

4.4.3. The past-anterior negative paradigm

The negative paradigm of the past anterior differs from the affirmative paradigm in several respects. To begin with, the stem-final consonant in n-stem forms differs in the affirmative and negative paradigms. While the stem of the the affirmative past anterior regularly ends in /n/, the negative paradigm of the transitive verb has lost the /n/, leaving instead a nasalized vowel, while the negative paradigm of the intransitive verb has /ŋ/. In the first-person-singular forms there is an alternation involving the presence of the /g/-initial of the past anterior; thus I have recorded both *mo-bõ-guĩ* and *mo-bõ-uĩ* for the verb *bon-* 'read', and *ma-ḍiŋ-guĩ* and *ma-ḍĩ-uĩ* for the verb *ḍin-* 'sleep'.

There is more than one form possible for the inflection of the second-person plural in the n-stem past-anterior paradigm. The following forms are both produced by consultants, who say there is no difference between them:

(23) n-stem, transitive   *mo-bō-min-ju/mo-bō-gu-min*   'read'
       n-stem, intransitive *mo-cō-min-ju/mo-coŋ-gu-min* 'stay'

4.4.4. The past and present negative paradigm

As in the past-anterior paradigm, verb stems undergo some changes when negated in the past and present. N-stem verbs have the stem-final /ŋ/ in the first-person forms (in both cases preceding /g/), while the stem-final has been lost elsewhere in the paradigm. R-stem verbs similarly lose their stem-final consonant in this paradigm.[46]

The third-person-singular forms of the past and present paradigm inflect differently depending on the transitivity of the verb, although the class of l-stems is an exception to this generalization. The transitive forms have either *-u* or *-ŋ* (an alternation found elsewhere in the verb paradigm), while the intransitive forms, and the l-stem transitives, have no suffix at all. Thus we find the following:

(24) n-stem   *mo-bo-ŋ/ma-ḍī*   'read'/'sleep'
       t-stem   *ma-ha-u/ma-gyā* 'say'/'fear'
       r-stem   *mā-kā-u/mo-kho* 'take'/'cry' (present)
       l-stem   *mā-wāl/ma-ŋil*   'mix'/'laugh'

All other persons in the past and present paradigm have the same inflectional suffixes as are found in the affirmative.

4.4.5. The future negative paradigm

The future negative paradigm is the most regular in its inflection; it is transparently formed by simple affixation of *ma-* to the affirmative future form. It thus does not differ from the future affirmative in either stem form or suffixal inflection.

5. Imperative, prohibitive, and optative paradigms

In addition to the regular finite affirmative and negative paradigms, separate verbal inflections are also found in the imperative, prohibitive and optative moods. Most of these forms contain morphology which is clearly related to that found in the affirmative and negative paradigms; however, the patterns of stem alternation differ somewhat.[47]

5.1. The imperative

There are several different strategies by which a verb may be put in the imperative mood. Recall that the subject of an imperative construction is always second person. It may additionally be singular or plural, honorific or non-honorific. The non-honorific imperatives are the most common in narrative and in the conversational dialogue which I have recorded.

Verb inflections for non-honorific imperatives are given in Table 29:

Table 29. Imperative verb forms

		Singular	Plural	Gloss
N-Stems	Transitive	*jo-ŋ*	*jo-n*	'catch'
	Intransitive	*õ*	*o-n*	'go'
T-Stems	Transitive	*hat*	*hat-un*	'say'
	Intransitive	*sit*	*sit-un*	'die'
R-Stems	Transitive	*so-u*	*so-n*	'look'
	Intransitive	*yā*[48]	*yā-n*	'come'
L-Stems	Transitive	*pul*	*pul-dun*	'pay'
	Intransitive	*tul*	*tul-dun*	'fall'

Interestingly, the patterns of stem alternation and suffixation that one finds in the non-honorific imperative are identical to those of the third-person-singular-negative forms in the past/present. In both paradigms the following patterns hold:[49]

(25)   N-stem Transitive   CV-ŋ
       N-stem Intransitive   CṼ
       T-stem Transitive   CVt
       T-stem Intransitive   CVt
       R-stem Transitive (present)   CV-u
       R-stem Intransitive (present) CV
       L-stem Transitive   CVl
       L-stem Intransitive   CVl

The plural is formed by inflecting the verb with a suffix which surfaces as *-n*, *-un*, or *-dun*. Verb stem alternations found with this suffix are given in (26):

(26) N-stem Transitive   CV-n
      N-stem Intransitive   CV-n
      T-stem Transitive   CVt-un
      T-stem Intransitive   Cvt-un
      R-stem Transitive   CV-n
      R-stem Intransitive   CV-n
      L-stem Transitive   CVl-dun
      L-stem Intransitive   Cvl-dun

The /n/ found in the suffix is likely to have the same historical source as the plural /n/ found in the affirmative paradigms. Since the t-stem and l-stem verbs retain their final consonants, the suffix must contain a vowel to allow proper syllabification of the resulting word. This suggests that the /u/ found in these forms may have originally been epenthetic. However, this analysis does not account for the presence of the suffix-initial /d/ found with the l-stem forms. This historical puzzle will be left for future (preferably compartive) work.

Some textual examples illustrating a variety of imperative verb forms are given in (27)–(32):

(27) jana   mica   **ya-ŋ**
      1sGEN   daughter   take-IMP

  'Take my daughter.'

(28) chi **cõ!**
      2s   stay(IMP)

  'You stay!'

(29) chipe   thau   thau   chē   **o-n**
      2pGEN   REFL   REFL   house   go-IMP.PL

  'Go each to your own house.'

(30) thi-pul   **hat**
      one-time   say(IMP)

  'Say it one time.'

(31) jā   na-en   yā
      rice   eat-PART   come.IMP

  'Eat your dinner then come.'

(32) bihā   yeŋ-an   bi-e   khā lā-u   āle
     marriage do-PART give-NR2 talk talk-IMP then

'Talk about when you were given in marriage then.'

In addition to these forms are a set of imperative forms using the suffix -si. I was able to elicit this suffix only with intransitive verbs, and only with t-stem, r-stem and l-stem forms:

(33) tinumr-si 'jump'
     gar-si   'climb'
     ŋil-si   'smile'

The only discourse example of this form occurs several times in one narrative. It is actually a prohibitive form, with the prohibitive prefix da- (here do- due to vowel harmony):

(34) chi do-khor-si
     2s   PROH-cry-IMP

     'Don't cry.'

This appears to be a gentler imperative, i.e. a recommendation or advice more than a strict command. The example above was used in comforting someone. To order a child to stop crying one would say do-kho! [PROH-cry], using the regular prohibitive form.

Honorific imperatives do not differentiate between singular and plural addressees. Neither are there separate forms for transitive and intransitive verbs. The suffix -sin is used throughout. This -sin may well be etymologically made up of the -si suffix just exemplified plus the second-person-plural -n seen in a number of inflections. It inflects across verb classes as follows (the stem form doesn't vary with transitivity of the verb):

(35) N-stems CV-sin   cō-sin   'stay'
     T-stems CVr-sin har-sin   'say'
     R-stems CV-sin   bi-sin   'give'
     L-stems CVl-sin hāl-sin   'sing'

Honorific imperatives are used under the same social conditions as honorific pronouns (see §5.2). Some examples from narrative discourse follow:

(36) janta   lukhā khoŋ-an   **bi-sin**
      1sDAT   door open-PART give-IMP

'Open the door for me.'

(37) cā̃ḍa   **jā-sin!**
      quickly come-IMP

'Come quickly!'

(38) thamun boṭhā-en   **bi-sin**
      2hERG   distribute-PART give-IMP

'You distribute it for us.'

(39) thaeta dhū=n   khyāŋ-a   thamun har-sin nā
      2hDAT   tiger=ERG   scare-NR1 2hERG   say-IMP AGR

'You tell (a story of) a tiger scaring you.'

5.2. The prohibitive

The prohibitive prefix is *da-*. It has the same morphological distribution and undergoes the same vowel harmony patterns as the negative, thus we find *dā-kāu* 'don't take' and *do-kho* 'don't cry'. The prohibitive functions as a negative command; it is used to tell someone not to do something. As such it is essentially a second-person form. The singular form of the verb has a single addressee who is told not to undertake the action, while the plural form has a plural addressee. As with the imperative, the prohibitive has separate honorific forms.

The stem alternations found in the non-honorific prohibitive singular are the same as those found in the imperative singular. Clearly the strategy for forming the prohibitive is just to add the prefix to the simple imperative form. The examples in (40) contrast the imperative forms of the first column with the prohibitive forms in the second column; note that the prohibitive forms carry the prohibitive affix.

Section 5 Imperative, prohibitive, and optative

(40) N-stem Transitive   bo-ŋ   do-bo-ŋ   'read'
      N-stem Intransitive   ḍī   da-ḍī   'sleep'
      T-stem Transitive   hat   da-hat   'say'
      T-stem Intransitive   sit   da-sit   'die'
      R-stem Transitive   kā-u   dā-kā-u   'take'
      R-stem Intransitive   kho   do-kho   'cry'
      L-stem Transitive   wāl   dā-wāl   'mix'
      L-stem Intransitive   ŋil   da-ŋil   'smile'

Some examples of singular prohibitive forms from connected discourse are given below:

(41) u   khā=ri   gunta=ŋ   **da-hat**
      this   talk=IND who.DAT=EXT   PROH-say

      'Don't say this thing to anybody.'

(42) uku   **dā-yā**   nā!
      here   PROH-come   AGR

      'Don't come here!'

(43) chin   janta   **da-syāt!**
      2sERG   1sDAT   PROH-kill

      'Don't you kill me!'

(44) suntali   **do-kho!**
      Suntali   PROH-cry

      'Suntali, don't cry!'

There are two distinct strategies for forming plural prohibitives. One is to follow the same principle by which singular prohibitives are constructed, simply adding the prohibitive affix to the plural imperative form. This is illustrated below, with the plural imperatives in the first column, followed by the plural prohibitives:

(45) N-stem Transitive   bo-n   do-bo-n   'read'
      N-stem Intransitive   ḍi-n   da-ḍi-n   'sleep'
      T-stem Transitive   hat-un   da-hat-un   'say'
      T-stem Intransitive   sit-un   da-sit-un   'die'

R-stem Transitive	kā-n	dā-kā-n	'take'
R-stem Intransitive	kho-n	do-kho-n	'cry'
L-stem Transitive	wāl-dun	dā-wāl-dun	'mix'
L-stem Intransitive	ŋil-dun	da-ŋil-dun	'smile'

The second strategy to form plural prohibitives is to take the stem of the plural imperative and add the second-person-plural suffix -*min*. The prohibitive affix is also used. Thus from the imperative plural forms in (45) the examples in (46) are derived:

(46) N-stem Transitive   do-bo-min   'read'
      N-stem Intransitive   da-ḍī-min   'sleep'
      T-stem Transitive   da-hat-min   'say'
      T-stem Intransitive   da-sit-min   'die'
      R-stem Transitive   dā-kā-min   'take'
      R-stem Intransitive   da-kho-min   'cry'
      L-stem Transitive   dā-wāl-min   'mix'
      L-stem Intransitive   da-ŋil-min   'smile'

In addition to the non-honorific prohibitive forms just discussed, there are also honorific prohibitives. These are formed with the suffix -*gu* found in other second-person-honorific inflections:

(47) N-stem Transitive   do-boŋ-gu   'don't read'
      N-stem Intransitive   da-ḍiŋ-gu   'don't sleep'
      T-stem Transitive   da-hat-ku   'don't say'
      T-stem Intransitive   da-sit-ku   'don't die'
      R-stem Transitive   dā-kā-gu   'don't take'
      R-stem Intransitive   do-kho-gu   'don't try'
      L-stem Transitive   dā-wāl-gu   'don't mix'
      L-stem Intransitive   da-ŋil-gu   'don't smile'

I have no examples of plural prohibitives or honorific prohibitives in my discourse data. Speakers tell me that the -*gu* form may be used with both singular and plural subjects. Examples of the honorific prohibitives with singular subjects are given below:

(48) mā   thamun dukha bwār **dā-pā-gu**
      mother 2sERG trouble worry PROH-worry-2h

      'Mother, don't be troubled or worried.'

(49)   piri   **da-gyāt-ku**
       son.in.law PROH-fear-2h
       'Don't be afraid, sister-in-law.'

Finally, there is one other strategy for forming a prohibitive verb. This strategy is paratactic, involving the first verb in the infinitive form, followed by the auxiliary verb *ma-ṭe*. The auxiliary is clearly derived from a verb meaning 'to be proper', which, while to my knowledge not present in Dolakhae (where *jir-* is used with this meaning), is found in Kathmandu Newār (*teye*, Kölver and Shresthacarya 1994: 141). An example of this prohibitive form being used in conversational speech is the following:

(50)   hāḍbāḍ   **yer-i** **ma-ṭe**   ka
       quickly   do-INF   NEG-PROH   ASS
       'You shouldn't do it too quickly/haphazardly.'

5.3. The optative

The optative verb is prefixed by the optative morpheme *tha-*. This prefix undergoes the same vowel harmony processes as the other two prefixes in the language. Thus we find forms such as *thā-yā* from *yer-* 'come', and *tho-cō* from *con-* 'stay'. Functionally, this form is used to mean "let it be thus", so is used for cursing, blessing, and wishing.

The optative has both singular and plural forms. The singular forms are formed simply by prefixing the optative morpheme to the imperative verb. Thus we have:

(51)   N-stem Transitive   *tho-boŋ*   'may he read'
       N-stem Intransitive   *tha-ḍī*   'may he sleep'
       T-stem Transitive   *tha-hat*   'may he speak'
       T-stem Intransitive   *tha-si*   'may he die'
       R-stem Transitive   *thā-kāu*   'may he take'
       R-stem Intransitive   *tho-kho*   'may he cry'
       L-stem Transitive   *thā-wāl*   'may he mix'
       L-stem Tntransitive   *tha-ŋil*   'may he smile'

The plural optative is formed by putting the optative prefix in place of the negative prefix in the negative third-person-plural form of the verb (present/past). Thus the following forms are derived:

(52) N-stem Transitive   tho-bo-hin   'may they read'
      N-stem Intransitive   tha-ḍi-hin   'may they sleep'
      T-stem Transitive   tha-hat-hin   'may they talk'
      T-stem Intransitive   tha-sit-hin   'may they die'
      R-stem Transitive   thā-kā-hin   'may they take'
      R-stem Intransitive   tho-kho-hin   'may they cry'
      L-stem Transitive   thā-wāl-hin   'may they mix'
      L-stem Intransitive   thā-ŋil-hin   'may they smile'

Some examples of the optative from connected discourse are given in (53)–(55):

(53) he   bimesor he   bāgabān mucā=pen   nis-mā   nāplaŋ-ane
      EXCL Bimsen   hey god   child=PL   two-CL   meet-PART

      jukun **tha-si**
      only   OPT-die

      'Hey God Bimsen, may I die only after meeting my two children again.'

(54) mahani=ta   uku   **tho-cõ**
      Dasain=DAT   here OPT-stay

      'May you stay through (the festival of) Dasain.'

(55) chana=uri   gwāri gulpanuŋ bā̃la-ku   ju-en   **tho-cõ**
      2sGEN=IND   heel   never   good-NR1 be-PART OPT-stay

      yelpanuŋ tapjyāŋ-an   **tho-cõ**
      always   break-PART   OPT-stay

      'May your heels never stay good. May they always be cracking.'

6. Non-finite verb forms

6.1. Primary non-finite verb forms

Non-finite verb forms differ from finite forms in that they do not convey information about tense, person, or number, and in that they do not have separate suffixal paradigms which indicate negation or mood. The non-finite verb forms are the key to complex sentence construction in this language, as the type of non-finite form used will determine the syntactic and semantic relations between clauses.

There are four primary non-finite inflections which are used in a variety of environments. These are the infinitive, the participle, and the two nominalizers, glossed NR1 and NR2. The inflection of these four non-finite forms across stem classes is given in Table 30. As there are no differences in pattern of stem alternation depending on the transitivity of the verb, only transitive forms are illustrated:

Table 30. Non-finite verb forms

	Infinitive	Participle	NR1	NR2
N-stem 'read'	bō-i	boŋ-an(i)	boŋ-gu	boŋ-a
T-stem 'say'	har-i	haŋ-an(i)	ha-ku	haŋ-a
R-stem 'take'	kā-i	kā-en(i)	kā-u	ka-e
L-stem 'mix'	wāl-i	wāl-en(i)	wal-gu	wal-e

The infinitive suffix is *-i.* The stem alternations preceding it are the same as those found in the future inflection of the finite verbs. The infinitive is used in the formation of both adverbial clauses (Chapter 20) and complement clauses (Chapter 18).

The participle is *-an(i)* or *-en(i)*. The alternation of the final /i/ vowel is discussed in §19.6. The t-stem and n-stem classes fall together in this inflection, as both have stem-final /ŋ/ preceding the suffix. The participle is a very common verb form in Dolakha Newar. A full description of this construction is given in Chapter 19.

The two suffixes glossed NR1 and NR2 are used to nominalize clauses and to form relative clauses. Thus the gloss "NR" stands for "nominalizer/relativizer", and the two are simply numbered NR1 and NR2, as their distribution vis-a-vis one another is complicated. For more information on how these suffixes are used, see Chapter 17.

The NR1 suffix is *-gu*. The /g/ devoices to /k/ in the t-stem class; this follows the regular morphophonological principles of the t-stem paradigm. The final /g/ is deleted in the r-stem forms.

The NR2 suffix is /a/ or /e/. Note the similarity between the allomorphs of both stem and suffix here and in the participial form.

In addition to these four non-finite verb forms whose functions vary with the morphosyntactic environment, there are four additional non-finite forms based directly on the verb stem. All four are used as markers of adverbial clauses. A full description of the syntax and semantics of adverbial clauses is given in Chapter 20; only the morphological details are discussed here.

The conditional and concessive suffixes are related, the concessive *-saŋ* appears to be formed from the condtional plus the clitic of extension *=ŋ*. Both suffixes are bound to a verb stem ending in a final consonant. The only irregularity is that stem-final /t/ changes to /r/ in this inflection:

(56) N-stem   *on-sa*   'go-if'
      T-stem   *har-sa*   'say-if'
      R-stem   *bir-sa*   'give-if'
      L-stem   *pul-sa*   'pay-if'

The suffix marking temporal adverbial clauses has two pronunciations: *-na* and *-ŋa*. Particular speakers appear to use one or the other consistently. Of my two primary consultants, one used [na] and the other [ŋa]. When I pointed this difference out to them both were surprised, never having noticed that their pronunciations were different. A longer form of the suffix *-nasin*, *-ŋasin* is also found and this also seems to vary by speaker. Only the short form, however, is used in repetitions of sequential verbs in order to indicate ongoing action, e.g. *on-na on-na* 'going on and on'. For more information on the semantics of temporal adverbial clauses, see §20.2.3. This morpheme is bound to the stem-final consonant of the verb with no irregularities.

The purposive suffix is *-da* or *-a*, the /d/ being present with n-stem and l-stem verbs and absent with t-stem and r-stem verbs. Thus we have the following paradigm:

(57) N-stem   *con-da*   'stay-PURP'
      T-stem   *ŋat-a*   'discard-PURP'
      R-stem   *nar-a*   'eat-PURP'
      L-stem   *pul-da*   'pay-PURP'

Again we find the pattern of the adverbial suffix attaching to the simple stem which carries the characteristic final consonant of the verb class.

There are five other adverbial suffixes which may be mentioned here. They do not attach directly to the verb stem, but follow either the NR1 nominalizer (the causal suffix only) or the infinitive (the remaining forms). These forms are exemplified in (58). The syntactic and semantic dimensions of these forms are discussed in §20.2.

(58) *lāgin*   cause (NR2)   *bihā yeŋ-a-lāgin*   'because she married'
      ho   temporal (INF)   *khō-i-ho*   'when he saw'
      ta   purposive (INF)   *na-i-ta*   'in order to eat'
      sāt   temporal (INF)   *janmai ju-i-sāt*   'as soon as was born'
      thẽ   simulative (INF)   *jō-i-thẽ*   'as if to catch'

6.2. Other non-finite suffixes

There are three other verbal suffixes which affix to the infinitive form of the verb, so which do not inflect for the person and number of the subject. The first is the immediate future *-rai*. This is a rare verb form, at least in my data, and seems to be used only in monoclausal examples, when the speaker is making the hearer aware of an imminent event:

(59) sāŋat=pen ū-i-rai
      friend=PL go-INF-about.to

      'My friends are about to go.'

(60) janta   dū=n   na-i-rai!
      1sDAT   tiger=ERG eat-INF- about.to

      'A tiger is about to eat me!'

When I first began eliciting future verb forms from my consultant, she often produced this form of the verb. Another way of indicating imminent future is to use the auxilary verb *ten-* 'about to', discussed in §16.3.4.

Another verbal suffix is the irrealis *-iuri*. This is almost certainly derived from the infinitive followed by the clitic of individuation *=uri* (see §10.2.1).

(61) āu   hāti   yer-iuri?
      now what   do-NR3

      'Now what should I do?'

(62) bihā   yer-iuri khã
      marriage   do-NR3   talk

      'The talk that she might marry.'

The final morpheme to be discussed in this section is the hortative *-lau*, which follows the infinitive form of the verb:

(63) u=ri   thijin   kā-i-lau
      this=IND 1pINC.ERG   take-INF-HORT

      'Let's take this.'

(64) isi   chē=ku   ū-i-lau
      1pEXC(GEN)   house=LOC   go-INF-HORT

'Let's go to our house.'

7. The causative derivational suffix

The causative suffix -ker- is the only derivational verbal suffix that I know of.⁵⁰ It suffixes to the stem-final consonant, except in r-stem verbs where the final /r/ is dropped. Thus we derive:

(65) ton-ker-   'nurse (young)'   < ton- 'drink' + CAUS
      yet-ker-   'make do'   < yet- 'do' + CAUS
      na-ker-   'feed'   < nar- 'eat' + CAUS
      pul-ker-   'make pay'   < pul- 'pay' + CAUS

The resulting causative verb is then morphologically an r-stem verb, with all the characteristic inflectional patterns. The only exceptional morphological behavior of causative verbs is the participial suffix. There are two participial forms of the causative verb, and I have not been able to discern any difference between them in function. The predicted form is -en(i), thus we find forms such as bon-ke-eni 'teach', from the causativized simplex bon- 'read'. However, it is more common to find the participial form lacking the participial suffix, e.g. bon-ke. For information on the syntactic aspects of the causative construction, see §15.2.

8. Irregular verbs

Most verbs in Dolakhā Newar are entirely regular, and follow the inflectional patterns described above without any discrepancies. Two verbs, however, stand out as being quite irregular and paradigmatically defective. These are the copula khyaŋ and the existential dar-. In addition, several other frequent verbs have some idiosyncratic inflections.

8.1. The copula khyaŋ

The equational copula is khyaŋ. I have recorded only the following forms of this verb:

(66) khyaŋ ~ kheŋ ~ khyã͂ũ ~ khũ   Present Affirmative
     ma-khe[51]   Present Negative
     khya-u ~ khe-u   NR1

As can be seen, there are a number of possible pronunciations of the copula. These result from two phonological alternations which produce four possible forms: the sequence /ya/ alternates with /e/, and final /ŋ/ alternates with /ũ/. The distribution of these forms appears to be idiolectal, and speakers seem fairly consistent in using only one in their speech. My impression is that *khyaŋ* is the most common, and it is also favored by the consultants that I have worked the most extensively with, so I have chosen it to represent the morpheme.

I know of only three morphological forms of this verb. The forms *khyaŋ* and *ma-khe* are the most common:

(67) ji   chana   kaimu   **khyaŋ**
     1s   2sGEN   husband   be

     'I am your husband.'

(68) chana   nimtiŋ   chuŋ-a   **ma-khe**
     2sGEN   benefit   cook-NR2   NEG-be

     'This is not cooked for your benefit.'

The NR1 form *khya-u* is attested in my data only before the collocation *ju-en con-a* 'it turns out that', as shown in the following example:

(69) inãgu   paksin   **ma-khya-u**   ju-en   con-a
     this.type   witch   NEG-be-NR1   be-PART   stay-3sPST

     'It turns out (she) is not a witch of this type.'

Copular function in the past or future tenses are conveyed with the copular verb *jur-* 'be, become, happen', a regular r-stem verb. For further discussion of copula constructions, see 12.2.

8.2. The existential verb *dar-*

The verb *dar-* functions primarily as an intransitive verb with a single argument. It is used to predicate existence, location, possession, and attribution.

I have recorded the following forms of *dar-*.

(70) dam/damu   present
      dat-a   past
      da-u(ju)   past anterior
      da-eu   future
      ma-da   negative past/present
      ma-da-u(ju)   negative past anterior
      ma-da-eu   negative future
      dar-sa   conditional
      da-i   infinitive
      da-en   participle
      da-e   NR2
      da-u   NR1
      da-ker-   CAUS ('make')

Most of the forms of *dar-* suggest an original r-stem source for this verb; all forms except the present and the past follow the regular r-stem pattern of stem alternation.

The present form of *dar-* is generally *dam*, less commonly *damu*. I have not been able to ascertain any functional distinction between *dam* and *damu*, and I suspect that the difference may be idiolectal. Interestingly, there are no other inflected verbs in Dolakhae which end in /m/, thus its presence in this very common verb is somewhat mysterious. The past form, *dat-a*, suggests a t-stem verb, but this is the only form of *dar-* characteristic of t-stems that I have recorded.

It is interesting that all the forms of the verb I know of are morphologically third-person-singular forms. However, with this verb there is no variation in form corresponding to variation in person and number of the subject, as the following examples with first-person subjects illustrate:

(71) ji   **damu**
      1s   have

      'I exist; I am here (to help you in your difficulties).'

(72) isi   **da**   he   **dam**   le[52]
      1pEXC   have   SPEC   have   PRT

      'We are here; you have us.'

The syntax and semantics of this verb are discussed in §12.4.1.

8.3. Other irregular verbs

There are several other verbs which, while following the primary patterns of inflection, have a few irregular forms.

The verb *on-* 'go' has a phonological alternation in the stem vowel, which surfaces as /u/ before both the future suffix *-i/-e* and the infinitive suffix *-i*. Thus we find *ū-i* for the first-person-future form of the verb, *ū-eŋ* for the third-person future, and *ū-i* for the infinitive. This appears to be height assimilation to a following high vowel. It should be noted, however, that this is not a general process, as other n-stem verbs with /o/ do not undergo raising, e.g. *cō-i*, the first-person-future form of 'stay'.

The verb *on-* 'go' also has a suppletive hortative form *ŋā* 'Let's go!'. This is non-honorific, used when the speaker is suggesting a joint action with someone of the same or lower rank. For example, the phrase *lo ŋā!* 'Ok, let's go!' is used by a boy addressing his friends. The regular hortative form of 'go', *ū-i-lau*, is used when the speaker is addressing a person of higher rank.

The verb *yer-* 'come' has several idiosyncratic forms. The negative is *mā-yā*, with the suffix vowel changed from /e/ to /ā/, and then the vowel of the negative prefix harmonizing with it. The form *yā* is also found in the simple imperative, as in *jā na-en yā* [rice eat-PART come.IMP] 'Eat (rice) and come!'. The honorific imperative is suppletive. While one would expect either *yer-sin* or *yār-sin*, the actual form is *jā-sin*. This form reflects an old layer of honorific vocabulary found in Newar. While some of this vocabulary is still accessible and used in certain segments of the Kathmandu Newar population, to my knowledge, this is the only remnant of it to be found in Dolakhae.

The final irregular verb to note is *mal-* 'must'. It has a suppletive negative form *māl-* and does not take the negative prefix:

(73) u   rāje   janta   mā-ŋ **māl**[53]
      this kingdom 1sDAT   need need(NEG)

'I don't need this kingdom.'

9. Summary

This chapter has presented the rather complex picture of verbal morphology in Dolakha Newar. We have seen that verbal inflectional morphology is quite extensive, with many paradigms, most of which have idiosyncratic properties. This feature of the language is especially interesting when compared with the comparatively simple morphological profile of the verb in the Kathmandu Newar dialect. The focus of this chapter has been on the forms of the verb rather than on their uses. Discussions of how the verbs function occur throughout the book, but especially in Chapter 12 on clause types, Chapter 15 on clause-level syntactic constructions, Chapter 16 on tense and aspect, and Chapters 17–21, which outline clause combining strategies in the language.

Chapter 7
Adjectivals

1. Introduction

Lexical items which are used for the specification of property concepts may be referred to as "adjectivals". In Dolakha Newar, as in many languages, adjectivals belong to two distinct lexical classes. The majority of such lexical items are grammatically verbs; however they differ from verbs in interesting ways. There is also a class of terms which can be called "simple adjectives". The two groups are morphologically quite distinct and so do not form a single lexical class. However, there is an extent to which they share syntactic behavior. These points are discussed in §7.4.

2. Adjectival verbs

The majority of Dolakhae adjectivals are morphological verbs with verbal inflections. They include members of all four conjugation classes, although the overwhelming majority of adjectival verbs belong to the r-stem verb class. A representative sample of adjectival verbs is given in (1). Since adjectival verbs almost always occur suffixed by the nominalizer NR1 (§17.2.1), they are given in this form, together with the stem:

(1) gāŋ-gu   gān-   'dry'
     ṭuŋ-gu   ṭun-   'ripe'
     bãla-ku   bãlat-   'good; beautiful'
     bā-ma-la-ku   bā-ma-lat-   'bad; ugly'
     kwā-ku   kwāt-   'hot (of liquids)'
     ḍwā-ku   ḍwākar-   'big'
     sā-ku   sār-   'tasty'
     wõga-u   wõgar-   'green'
     hẽga-u   hẽgar-   'red'
     twāya-u   twāyar-   'white'
     hāka-u   hākar-   'black'
     siya-u   sier-   'grey'
     phuta-u   phutar-   'brown'
     mwāsa-u   mwāsar-   'yellow'
     cāka-u   cākar-   'sweet'

khwāga-u	khwāgar-	'cold (of liquids)'
jyāta-u	jyātar-	'heavy'
pẽga-u	pẽgar-	'sour'
thika-u	thikar-	'full'
khāya-u	khāyar-	'bitter'
thāka-u	thākar-	'difficult'
ṭāhāga-u	ṭāhāgar-	'long'
cumba-u	cumbar-	'sharp; pointed'
kwāta-u	kwātar-	'thick'
khiŋa-u	khiŋar-	'dark'
lo-u	lor-	'well-suited'
ja-u	jar-	'sharp'
nāl-gu	nāl-	'tired'
luba-u	lubar-	'warm'
sāla-u	sālar-	'thin'

We can make two interesting observations about this list. First, as mentioned above, the vast majority of these forms are in the r-stem conjugation class. There are only two adjectival verbs which are n-stem, four which are clearly t-stem, and one which is l-stem. The remaining examples are r-stem. Second, the vast majority of r-stem verbs are disyllabic, the only exceptions being *ja-u/jar-* 'sharp' and *lo-u/lor-* 'well-suited'.

The reason for the predominance of disyllabics is historical. Comparison of modern Kathmandu and Classical Newar forms reveals that we can reconstruct monosyllabic lexical items for the proto-language, for example **kwāt* 'thick', **pāŋ* 'sour', **jhyāt* 'heavy', etc. Whether these proto-forms were true adjectives or adjectival verbs is unknown at this time. However, the comparative evidence suggests that they must have been independent monosyllabic lexical items after the division of the rest of the verbs into distinct lexical classes, and after the split between the Dolakha and Kathmandu Valley dialects. The Dolakha Newars then incorporated these lexical items into its verbal system by systematically making them r-stems. This was accomplished through the suffixation of the formative *-ar-*, which can be seen as a derivational suffix used to create verbs.

Regarding forms with nasalized vowels and /g/, e.g. *pẽgar-* 'sour', the evidence suggests that these reconstruct with an earlier velar nasal (e.g. **pāŋ*), which was reinterpreted as nasalized vowel plus /g/.

2.1. Attributive uses of adjectival verbs

When adjectival verbs are used in attributive contexts, they are suffixed with NR1 and put into a noun phrase preceding a head noun:

(2) āle kuciri=lān **sā-ku**   **sā-ku**   cij   piṭa
    then nail=ABL   tasty-NR1 tasty-NR1 thing out

   kā-en   bir-ai
   take-PART give-3sPR

   'Then from his nails he took out many tasty things and gave them (to her).'

(3) ji wā **ma-pha-u**   mi   rā
    1s TOP NEG-able-NR1 person Q

   'I was a sick person?'

(4) **ḍwā-ku** cār guṭhi yār   dam
    big-NR1 four guṭhi member exist

   'There are the four big guṭhi members.'

(5) **ṭāhāga-u** nis-gur simā then-ju
    tall-NR1 two-CL tree arrive-3sPST

   'S/he arrived at two tall trees.'

(6) āle **hẽga-u** wāsti ināgu   phi-en   liŋā-i
    then red-NR1 clothes like.this put.on-PART walk-INF

   ma-ji-uju
   NEG-appropriate-3PA

   'It was not appropriate to put on red clothes and go out like this.'

(7) thi-mā **bãla-ku**   onsā-mi   pharsi=lān ye-en
    one-CL beautiful-NR1 man-person pumpkin=ABL come-PART

   coŋ-gu   khon-ai
   stay-NR1 see-3sPR

   'She sees a beautiful man coming out of the pumpkin.'

(8) ṭwā̃ŋsona   thi-gur **bā̃la-ku**   **hēga-u**   sona   khyaŋ
     rhododendron one-CL   beautiful-NR1   red-NR1 flower   be

   'Rhododendron is a beautiful red flower.'

In (2), the repetition of the adjective has a distributive function; it indicates many different types of tasty food were given.

In (3), the form *ma-pha-u* is used. This is commonly used to indicate illness. It is etymologically the negated verb *phar-* 'to be able', but it has lexicalized to mean 'sick' or 'ill'. Some other attributive adjectival verbs may be negated, most notably *mā-sā-ku* 'not tasty'; this appears to be lexically restricted.

There are some interesting variations in word order in these examples. In (4) and (5) we can see the adjectival verb preceding the numeral, while in (7) and (8) it follows the numeral. Adjectival verbs almost always precede the noun they modify, although there are exceptions, such as *u misāmi thi-mā bā̃la-ku* [this woman-person one-CL beautiful-NR1] 'this one beautiful woman'. For more on word order in the noun phrase, see §11.2.

Attributive adjectival verbs may be modified by intensifiers, such as the native Dolakhae adverb *biŋkeŋ*, e.g. *biŋkeŋ bā̃la-ku thi-gur simā* [very beautiful-NR1 one-CL tree] 'one very beautiful tree', and the borrowed Nepali intensifier *ekdam*, e.g. *ekdam sā-ku sā-ku phalphul=pen* [very tasty-NR1 tasty-NR1 fruit=PL] 'very tasty fruits'.

Attributive adjectives may occur with the individuating clitic =*u(ri)*. The only examples I have found in discourse involve kin terms. In one example, there are two elder brothers. In order to differentiate between them, the speaker uses the attributive adjectives *ḍwā-ku* 'big' and *cicā* 'small'. The individuating clitic also is found, hence *cicā=uri dāi* refers to the younger of the elder brothers. A similar example is *ḍwā-ku=ri iri* 'eldest daughter-in-law'. This clitic is frequently found in lexicalized kin terms, and this appears to be a related use. It is fully in keeping with the function of this clitic, which is to delimit an individual out of a group (§10.2.1).

2.2. Referential uses of adjectival verbs

It is also possible to use nominalized adjectival verbs as heads of noun phrases. They then become referential. If the referent is specific, then the adjectival verb is cliticized with the individuating clitic =*(u)ri*. The examples in (9) and (10) were adjacent utterances in a conversation. The line in (9) contains a question, and the line in (10) contains the interlocutor's reply. Both use the same strategy for creating a referential noun phrase from an adjectival verb:

(9)   *gu=ri   le?   cicā=uri?*
      which=IND   PRT   small=IND

   'Which one? The small one?'

(10) *ḍwā-ku=ri*
      big-NR1=IND

   'The big one.'

Some adjectival verbs may occur as noun phrases without *=(u)ri*, but in these cases the reference is either general, as in *sā-ku sā-ku bi* [tasty-NR1 tasty-NR1 give-IMP] 'Give (me) tasty things', or refers to an event, as in (11):

(11) *thijita   bāmala-ku   ju-en*
      1pINC.DAT   bad-NR1   happen-PART

   'A bad thing happening to us...'

2.3. Predicative uses of adjectival verbs

Adjectival verbs may be incorporated into the predicate in one of two ways. Most commonly they are used as copula complements. In this syntactic position they may occur either in a verbless clause, or with one of the copulas *khyaŋ* or *jur-*, or with the verb *yer-* 'come'. More rarely, they inflect directly as finite verbs. Adjectival verbs in the copula complement slot are always nominalized with NR1, the same nominalizer that is used in attributive contexts. Thus the nominalized forms of adjectival verbs are highly frequent, at least in my data set, while the finite forms are rare. This suggests that the nominalized forms may be lexicalized as distinct adjectives, although the connection between the nominalized and the verbal forms is still acknowledged by speakers. Evidence that the nominalized adjectival verbs have lexicalized includes the great frequency with which nominalized adjectival verbs are used and the fact that consultants supply nominalized forms as the ready translations of adjectives in English or Nepali. Also, when consultants are asked for clauses with predicative adjectives, nominalized forms in copula complements are always given first. While it is possible to elicit the inflected forms, they are not readily volunteered.

Adjectival verbs may be used in copula complement position in the absence of any verb. This predicates an ongoing state:

(12) u   bāmala-ku
      this   ugly-NR1

      'This one is ugly.'

(13) ji   ināgu   bãla-ku
      1s   like.this   beautiful-NR1

      'I am beautiful like this.'

It is also possible to predicate ongoing states with the copula *khyaŋ*; this is often interpreted as emphatic:

(14) āmu   mandir   bãla-ku   khyaŋ!
      that temple   beautiful-NR1   be

      'That temple is beautiful!'

To predicate past states, the copula *jur-* 'become; happen' is used in the past-anterior tense. Since the copula *khyaŋ* has no tense forms other than the present, any other tense must be marked with *jur-*.

(15) opteca   ju   ām   tākku
      small   be(3PA)   that   time

      'He was small, at that time.'

The copula *jur-* is also used to predicate entrance into a state:

(16) kae   dwā-ku   jur-a
      son   big-NR1   become-3sPST

      'The son grew up.' (lit. 'became big')

(17) do-tāŋ   bãla-ku   jur-a
      all.type   good-NR1   become-3sPST

      'Everything became good.'

If the entrance into the state was a gradual process, the verb *yer-* 'come' is used instead of *jur-*:

(18) khwāl=uŋ   hēga-u   yer-a
      face=EXT   red-NR1   come-3sPST

      'Her face also became rosy.'

In elicitation, the adjectival verb preceding *yer-a* is given in the participial, as opposed to the nominalized, form:

(19)   Elicited
       bārpāŋ=e   acār   **sā-en**   yer-a
       tomato=GEN   acar   tasty-PART   come-3sPST

       'The tomato acar gradually became tasty.'

(20)   Elicited
       simā   **wōga-en**   yer-a
       tree   green-PART   come-3sPST

       'The tree became green.' (i.e. 'leafed out')

Finally, adjectival verbs may inflect with finite verb morphology to indicate entrance into a state. This occurs only twice in my discourse corpus:

(21)   **hākar-a**   jammai   sarir
       black-3sPST   together body

       'All our bodies became black.'

(22)   uku   thi-tāŋ   cij=na   gustule   **bāmalat-a**
       here one-type   thing=ABL   how.much   bad-3sPST

       'Here one thing is so bad.'

In elicitation, consultants allow the inflection of adjectival verbs for different persons, e.g. *ji ḍwākar-gi* [1s big-1sPST] 'I grew', from *ḍwākar-* 'big'. Also, their use may be more common with dative-marked experiencers, which overwhelmingly co-occur with verbs in the third-person-singular past, e.g. *janta cikar-a* [1sDAT cold-3sPST] 'I am cold'.

It is worth noting that while both adjectival verbs and non-adjectival verbs may occur as copula complements, the interpretation of the construction differs. Thus compare examples (23) and (24):

(23)   [sona]$_{cs}$ [hēga-u]$_{cc}$ (khyaŋ)
       flower   red-NR1   be

       'The flower is red.'

(24)   [ām mi]_{CS} [pujā ye-ku]_{cc} (khyaŋ)
       that man   worship do-NR1 be

       'That man is the one who worshiped.'

When an adjectival verb occurs in the copula complement position, as in (23), it refers to a property, in this case 'red'. When a verb occurs in the copula complement position, as in (24), it refers to an individual who performed the action of the verb or is in a verbal state. Essentially, (24) results in a referential copula complement whereas (23) does not. This constitutes further evidence that the adjectivals are an independent subclass of verbs.

2.4. Other inflectional morphology and adjectival verbs

Negation of adjectival predicates is most commonly produced by negating the copula:

(25)   Elicited
       u   sona   hēga-u   ma-khe
       this flower red-NR1   NEG-be

       'This flower isn't red.'

(26)   khīga-u   ma-ju
       dark-NR1   NEG-become

       'It isn't dark.'

It is also possible to negate adjectival verbs directly. There are several patterns to this negation. If the verb has a simple monosyllabic structure, the negative morpheme *ma-* prefixes to the adjective. Thus we can find pairs such as *ja-u/ma-ja-u* 'sharp/dull' and *sā-ku/mā-sā-ku* 'tasty/not tasty'. However if the adjectival verb is disyllabic, then the negation is infixed after the first syllable. This follows the regular negation pattern of disyllabic stems (see §6.4.4.1):[54]

(27)   ci-mā-cā   'didn't shrink'   < cicār- 'small'
       ci-ma-ka   'didn't get cold'   < cikar- 'cold'
       khō̃-ma-ga   'didn't become cold (of liquids)'   < khōgar- 'cold'
       hā-ma-kā   'didn't become black'   < hākar- 'black'
       twā-mā-yā   'didn't become white'   < twāyar- 'white'

Note that the negative infix undergoes vowel harmony (see §2.3.5). In *twā-mā-yā* the final syllable has the phoneme /ā/, not /a/ as in the non-negated form *twāya-u*. This is the same suppletive negative pattern that one finds with the verb 'come': *yer-a* 'came'/*mā-yā* 'didn't come'. This could indicate that 'come' is an old etymon in this, and possibly other, disyllabic adjectives.

Another adjectival verb with infixal negation is *bā-ma-lat-* 'bad; ugly'. In this case the disyllabicity of the non-negated *bãlat-* is due to its etymology, as it is an old compound formed with *bāna* 'mark; shape' (Nepal Bhasa Dictionary Committee 2000: 325).

In addition to negative morphology, it is also possible to put the causative suffix on adjectival verbs. This introduces a second participant into the clause, whose role is to bring about the state coded by the adjectival verb:

(28)   *jammai*   **hāka-ke**
       all   black-CAUS.PART

       'Making us all black...'

(29)   Elicited
       āmun   *inār*   **gã̄-ker-ju**
       3sERG   well   dry-CAUS-3sPST

       'She caused the well to dry up.'

(30)   Elicited
       āmun   *cyā*   **kwā-ker-ju**
       3sERG   tea   hot-CAUS-3sPST

       'She heated the tea.'

There are no morphophonemic irregularities when causativizing adjectival verbs; they follow the same pattern as other verbs in this regard.

I have no examples of adjectival verbs inflecting with the imperative. This may be due to a culturally based way of speaking. Having an attribute is not something one has control over, and in my data, Dolakhae speakers only order others to do something over which they have control. I do have one example of an adjectival verb co-occurring with the optative, however it does not prefix to the adjectival verb directly. Instead the adjectival verb is nominalized and acts as the copula complement, and the optative prefix is found on the auxiliary which indicates continuous aspect:

(31)   **bãla-ku**   ju-en   **tho-cõ**
good-NR1   become-PART   OPT-stay

'May they (become and) remain beautiful.'

The only other verbal morphology which occurs on adjectival verbs in my discourse data is the participle (see Chapter 19). The use of this form with *yer-* 'come' was illustrated in (19) and (20) above. Another example, where the participle indicates an event in a sequence is given in (32):

(32)   jammai   **hāka-ke**   bikh=na   wāl-en
all   black-CAUS.PART   poison=INST   paint-PART

thijita   dukha   jur-a.
1pINC.DAT   trouble   happen-3sPST

'Making us all black and painting us with poison, we have experienced trouble.'

2.5. Irregular adjectival verbs

There are a few adjectival verbs which exhibit exceptional behavior. The most obvious of these are *cicā-u/cicār-* 'small' and *optecā-u/optecār-* 'very small; tiny'. While consultants accept these forms with the NR1 nominalizer, these two adjectival verbs also commonly occur without it. This is true in both attributive and predicative contexts, as the following forms with *optecā* show:

(33)   **opte   opte**   tākku
tiny   tiny   time

'The time when he was very little (young).'

(34)   **optecā**   ju   ām   tākku
tiny   be(3PA)   that   time

'He was very little (young) at that time.'

The following examples with *cicā* were elicited:

(35) Elicited
cicā misāmi
small woman

'a small woman'

(36) Elicited
ji cicā
1s small

'I am small.'

The syllable -*cā* (probably related to the diminutive suffix; see §4.3.2) which is found in both of these forms is clearly a later addition to old adjectival stems *ci*- and *opte*-. The latter can be still be found occurring without it, as in (33) above. In addition, *ci*- commonly occurs as an adjectival stem in Kathmandu Newar, suffixed by numeral classifiers. Thus we can see that these forms are etymologically bimorphemic. It is also clear, however, that the two may also occur as verbs, as the following elicited examples indicate:

(37) Elicited
sābun cicār-a
soap small-3sPST

'The soap became small.'

(38) Elicited
sābun optecār-a
soap tiny-3sPST

'The soap became tiny.'

Thus we can see these forms have both non-inflecting adjectival forms, and inflecting verbal forms. They are intermediate between adjectives and verbs.

The other adjectival verb which is irregular in its inflection is *sā-ku* 'tasty'. The presence of the -*ku* NR1 suffix indicates that this is a t-stem verb. Note that the cognate form in the Kathmandu dialect is also t-stem (Class II). However, on more than one occasion, my consultant provided me with the third-singular-past form *sār-a* 'It became tasty', which indicates an r-stem inflection. Thus this adjectival verb is intermediate between two conjugation classes.

2.6. Borrowed adjectival verbs

In addition to the native Dolakha Newar verbs discussed so far, speakers may also use borrowed Nepali verbs to form new adjectival compounds. Examples are given in (39):

(39) but lāg-ai jur- [ghost touch-BV become-] 'possessed'
 pāk-ai jur- [ripe-BV become] 'ripe'
 thābi thābi bag-ai jur- [top top flow-BV become-] 'shallow'

Following the usual pattern for borrowing intransitive verbs from Nepali (see §6.3), the borrowed verb is suffixed with -ai (glossed "BV" for "borrowed verb"), then followed by the copula jur-.

The compound adjectival verb can be suffixed with NR1 to form an attributive modifier of a following noun. Thus we find thābi thābi bag-ai ju kho 'shallow river' with the NR1 form of the verb. However, the behavior of these compound adjectival verbs is different in predicative contexts. While a native adjective will fill the copula complement position before the copula jur- to indicate entrance into a state, these do not. Instead, the borrowed adjectival forms a compound with jur- which together function as an intransitive verb, as in example (40):

(40) [kerā]$_{NP-S}$ [pāk-ai jur-a]$_{V-INTR}$
 banana ripen-BV become-3sPST

 'The banana ripened.'

To use the NR1 form in the complement clause slot would sound redundant, e.g. *pāk-ai ju jur-a.

2.7. Summary

We can see that the set of adjectival verbs share morphological properties with other verbs: they occur nominalized, they take negative and causative inflectional suffixes, and they may inflect with at least some finite morphology. On the other hand, the majority of the forms occurring in natural discourse are nominalized, so the nominalized form is unmarked. In addition, speakers recognize the nominalized forms as translations of English and Nepali adjectives, indicating properties as opposed to things or individuals who have those properties. They are thus semantically distinct from verbs as well. As we shall see, they are quite distinct from simple adjectives as well, although the two classes do share some syntactic behavior.

3. Simple adjectives

The second class of adjectivals to be discussed is that of simple adjectives. Simple adjectives come from two sources: the native Dolakha Newar lexicon and Nepali. Although they come from different sources, they have similar behavioral properties. With a couple of important exceptions, they share the same morphological behavior (absence of inflection). In addition (although again with one exception), they share the same syntactic behavior.

3.1. Native simple adjectives

A list of Dolakha Newar simple adjectives is given in (41); I doubt that it is exhaustive:

(41) *dosari*   'pregnant'
      pyāṭāmāri   'pregnant'
      lāŋtā(ŋ)   'naked'
      bicara   'late (passed on)'
      gāntāŋ   'thin; emaciated'
      gwārtāk   'round'
      kwāitāk   'curved; bent; hunchbacked'
      gara   'deep'
      bahar   'young, fertile (of female animals)'
      paṭhyauri   'young, virile (of male animals)'
      batthar   'dilapidated'
      ṭaen   'far'
      nulu   'new'
      wẽ   'crazy (of male)'
      wini   'crazy (of female)'
      lyās-mā   'attractive; youthful (of male human)'
      lyās(i)-misā   'attractive; youthful (of female human)'
      rāk-mura   'angry'

These simple adjectives clearly have different phonotactic properties than the adjectival verbs. They take a wide variety of phonotactic shapes: all but one are disyllabic or trisyllabic; light and heavy syllables are found in any combination; and they end either in a vowel, a velar consonant, or /r/.

Almost all of these native simple adjectives convey physical properties; thus they are semantically unified. The only exception is *rāk-mura* 'angry', which has idiosyncratic morphological behavior discussed below, and which describes an emotional state. It is interesting to note that there are no antonymic pairs or opposites. For some of these adjectives, the antonym is conveyed with a lexeme borrowed from Nepali, e.g. *buḍe* from Nepali *buḍo* 'old', or *nisantān* 'infertile'. For others, the antonymic meaning is formed by using a negated predicate, e.g. *ṭāen ma-khe* 'It is not far'. There are three pairs of adjectives which have distinct forms for males and females. This is rather unusual in this language where the marking of gender in the grammar and the lexicon is rare. The pair *lyāsi/lyās-misa* has irregular behavior (as do its cognate forms in other Newar dialects), as discussed below.

3.2. Borrowed simple adjectives

Nepali has a very large number of lexical adjectives, any of which can be borrowed into Dolakhae. In some cases, the Nepali adjectives alternate with native simple adjectives or adjectival verbs of the same meaning, e.g. *golo* 'round', *jawāni* 'attractive; youthful', and *ṭhulo* 'big'. In other cases, the borrowed Nepali adjective appears to be the only way to express the concept, e.g. *moṭo* 'fat'. Example (42) lists some of the most common Nepali adjectives for which native Dolakhae lexical items either do not exist or which are rare enough not to be known by my consultants:

(42) *dhani*   'wealthy'
      garib   'poor'
      buḍe < *buḍo* 'old (of animate)'
      purāno   'old (of inanimate)'
      moṭo   'fat'
      khusi   'happy'
      dukhi   'sad'
      kā̃ci   'raw'
      kāno   'blind'
      gose   'stupid'
      dyāmba   'thick (of blankets, clouds)'
      thāḍo   'still'

Another interesting adjective is *bahirā*, which in Nepali means 'outside', but when used as an adjective in Dolakha Newar means 'deaf', an interesting metaphorical extension.

3.3. Simple adjectives in attributive and referential functions

Simple adjectives may directly modify a noun within a noun phrase, as shown in examples (43) through (47). Although it is simple to elicit such examples, they are actually quite rare in my narrative data.

(43) ām bwārā=ku=ri thi-mā **pyāṭāmāri** gisā coŋ-gu
that barn=LOC=IND one-CL pregnant cow stay-3PA

'A pregnant cow used to stay in that barn.'

(44) **khusi** din bityāŋ-an con-ahin
happy day spend-PART stay-3pPR

'They are spending many happy days.'

(45) Elicited
āmun sindar gwārtāk luŋā=ku tar-ju
3sERG red.powder round rock=LOC put-3sPST

'He put the powder on the round rock.'

(46) Elicited
luŋā **gara** kho=ku dub-ai jur-a
rock deep river=LOC sink-BV be-3sPST

'The rock sank in the deep river.'

(47) Elicited
mandir ū-ita **nulu** wāsti phi mal-a
temple go-PURP new clothes wear(INF) must-3sPST

'To go to the temple, (one) must wear new clothes.'

As with adjectival verbs, simple adjectives may be made referential by the addition of the individuating clitic =uri. Thus, from gāntāŋ 'thin' we derive gāntāŋ=ri 'the thin one', from kwāitāk 'hunchback' we derive kwāitāk=ri 'the hunchbacked one', etc. Another way to create a referential noun phrase is simply to use a semantically empty head noun, such as mi 'person', e.g. gāntāŋ mi 'the thin person; the thin one'. This structure functions as a strategy for creating a referential adjective, even though syntactically it still consists of an adjective modifying a head noun.

The adjectives lyās-mā and lyās(i)-misā are the masculine and feminine forms, respectively, for an adjective meaning 'attractive' or 'youthful'. They are also used to mean 'boyfriend/girlfriend' or 'lover'. In these forms we can obviously identify an etymon *lyās* 'young'. The masculine form takes the suffix *-mā* which is probably related to the numeral classifier for animates of the same form (§8.3.3). The feminine form takes *misā*, transparently related to the first half of the compound in the noun *misā-mi* 'woman'. These two forms can function as nouns independently, as in (48):

(48)   *lyāsimisā=pista   thamun madirā ho amrit*
      young.woman=PL.DAT 2hERG liquor and elixir

      bohtha-en   bir-gu
      distribute-PART give-2hPST

      'You distributed the liquor and elixir to the young women.'

However, it is also possible to elicit attributive forms within a noun phrase: *lyāsmā mi, lyāsmisā misāmi* 'attractive man, woman', *lyāsmā/lyāsmisa khicā* 'young male/female dog'. These particular adjectives thus have idiosyncratic behavior including some nominal properties.

3.4. Simple adjectives in predicative function

To predicate that a referent is in an ongoing state, a simple adjective may be used in copula complement position. It may occur with or without the copula *khyaŋ*. I have no examples of this structure in my discourse data, but they were easily elicited:

(49)   Elicited
      ām mi wē khyaŋ
      that man crazy be

      'That man is crazy.'

(50)   Elicited
      āme   parsi nulu khyaŋ
      3sGEN sari   new be

      'Her sari is new.'

Predicative adjectives are more commonly found with the copula *jur-*, which predicates entrance into a state:

(51) āle rājā=ke ye-u=ri dosari jur-a
 then king=ALL come-NR1=IND pregnant become-3sPST

 'Then the one that went to the king became pregnant.'

(52) u=ri guṣṭule moṭo jur-a
 this=IND how.much fat become-3sPST

 'This one has become so fat.'

(53) āle ām tākku bobu=ri kānā ju-i don-guju
 than that time father=IND blind become-INF finish-3PA

 'Then at that time, the father had become blind.'

When *jur-* is in its past-anterior form *ju-*, it indicates a past state, as opposed to past entrance into a state:

(54) pharsi=e chẽ suntali=e chẽ=lān ṭāen ju
 pumpkin=GEN house suntali=GEN house=ABL far be(3PA)

 'The pumpkin's house was far from Suntali's house.'

Simple adjectives may also be modified by an intensifier, as in (55) and (56):

(55) janābar=pen biŋkeŋ dukhi ju-en
 animal=PL very sad become-PART

 'The animals became very sad...'

(56) āmu wā ekdam moṭo ju-ene
 3s TOP very fat become-PART

 'She became very fat...'

Since simple adjectives are not verbs, they differ from adjectival verbs in not being able to inflect directly for verbal categories. This includes the finite suffixal complex, the negative prefix, and the causative. Instead, these categories are marked on the copula:

(57) Elicited
 khusi ma-khe
 happy NEG-be

 '(Someone) is not happy.'

(58) Elicited
āmu kānā ma-jur-a
3s blind NEG-become-3sPST

'S/he did not become blind.'

In addition, while adjectival verbs can co-occur with *yer-* 'come' to indicate a gradual entrance into a state, this does not appear to be the case with simple adjectives.

4. On the status of the category "adjective"

In this chapter, I have described two classes of "adjectivals", which I have called adjectival verbs and simple adjectives. As noted above, in many respects the NR1 forms of adjectival verbs appear to have lexicalized and the vast majority of verbal "work" is done by the copula. However, adjectival verbs still can inflect, if they only do so occasionally. The class of simple adjectives, by contrast, has no inflection. This is a major difference in morphological behavior and argues that two adjectival categories are lexically distinct.

Although the two classes of adjectivals differ in their morphological behavior, they have similar syntactic behavior: they both may modify nouns within the noun phrase; they both may be modified by intensifiers; they both may be used referentially with the addition of the clitic =*uri*; and they both occur in the copula complement position. In addition, both adjectival verbs and simple adjectives may be found in comparative constructions, where once again they occur in copula complement position (for more information on comparatives, see §15.7):

(59) Elicited
priyesh soen inku ḍwā-ku khyaŋ
Priyesh MARK Inku big-NR1 be

'Compared to Priyesh, Inku is big.' OR 'Inku is bigger than Priyesh.'

(60) Elicited
oho soen lū mahā̃go
silver MARK gold expensive

'Gold is more expensive than silver.'

Although this shared syntactic behavior might appear to argue for treating these two disparate morphological categories as a single lexical class, it turns out that most of this behavior is not exclusively restricted to these classes. Nouns may also be modified by intensifiers, may be used referentially with =*uri*, and may occur in the copula complement position in simple clauses and in comparative constructions. These points are illustrated with examples (61)–(64):

(61) ekdam lū   oho=pen   besna khoŋ-ane wā
     very gold silver=PL very see-PART TOP

'Seeing much gold and silver.'

(62) u   khā̃=ri   guntaŋ   da-hat
     this talk=IND nobody.DAT   PROH-say

'Don't say this thing to anybody.'

(63) muca ḍāktar jur-a
     child doctor become-3sPST

'The child became a doctor.'

(64) ām   mi soen   chana bā   **bāla-ku** mi khyaŋ
     that man MARK 2sGEN father good-NR1 man be

'Compared to that man, your father is a good man.'

Adjectival verbs and simple adjectives both may modify nouns within a noun phrase without any intervening derivational morphology or genitive case-marking. This is not true of nouns, and from this we can see that nouns are lexically distinct from adjectivals. However, there is another small lexical class which can modify a noun within a noun phrase: the class of intensifiers, as illustrated in (61) above. Thus, in this language, there is no morphological or syntactic behavior which is shared by adjctial verbs and simple adjectives to the exclusion of all other lexical classes.[55] We can therefore conclude that adjectival verbs and adjectives are lexically distinct.

Chapter 8
Quantifiers

1. Introduction

Quantifiers are used to refer to the number or quantity of elements. They occur within the noun phrase, most commonly with the nouns they modify, which serve as heads of the construction. Quantifiers may also occur in headless noun phrases.

There are three primary types of quantifiers: lexical quantifiers, such as *yeku* 'many' and *dokhunuŋ* 'all' (§8.2); demonstratives of quantity (§5.5.5); and numerals with their obligatory classifiers (§8.3). Only one quantifier may occur in any given noun phrase; in my data, quantifiers never combine. The lexical class of quantifiers can thus be identified by a combination of syntactic and semantic criteria: quantifiers are lexical items which convey quantification and which belong to the closed set of terms that can fill the quantifier slot in the noun phrase.

2. Lexical quantifiers

The lexical quantifiers of Dolakha Newar are given in (1):

(1) *yeku/yekku*   'many'
     gatkeŋ/gakkeŋ   'very many'
     bācā   'a little'
     bāti(-cā)   'a few'
     dokhunuŋ   'all'
     kehi   'some'(< Nepali)
     harek   'every' (< Nepali)
     ekdam   'many' (< Nepali 'very')

The form *yeku* 'many' may be given a geminate /k/ for intensification, thus *yekku* 'very many'. The same process is found in the forms *gatkeŋ/gakkeŋ*. Intensifying gemination is further discussed in §2.2.5.2.

In elicitation, the forms *bācā* and *bāti* appear to differ in that the former is used with mass nouns and the latter with count nouns. However, some forms in text appear to go against this generalization (e.g. (3) below). Both forms are commonly reduplicated, e.g. *bācā bācā* 'just a little'. It is also possible to suffix *bāti* with the diminutive *-cā*, as in example (4) below.

The forms *kehi* and *harek* are borrowed from Nepali. These meanings are conveyed by *bācā* 'a little' and *dokhu-* 'all' in the native vocabulary. The form *ekdam* is also a Nepali borrowing. It is a very common intensifier in both Nepali and Dolakha Newar. It is the only lexical item which doubles as a quantifier and an intensifier. It is semantically equivalent to the native Dolakhae quantifier *gatkeŋ*.

Some examples of the native lexical quantifiers in connected discourse are given in (2)–(5):

(2) chiji   mica =ta   **yeku** sā-ku   na-ke-saŋ
     1pINC.GEN daughter =DAT many tasty-NR1 eat-CAUS-although

     'Although we feed our daughter many tasty (foods)...'

(3) sõ-mā   tuŋ **bācā**   gyār da-u
     three-CL FOC a.little fear   have-3PA

     'The three of them had a little bit of fear.'

(4) āu   **bāti-cā**   sukhā   ju-eu
     now a.little-DIM happiness be-3FUT

     'Now there will be a little bit of happiness.'

(5) **gakkeŋ**   barsa hākhena
     very.many year   before

     'Many years ago...'

The quantifier meaning 'all' or 'every' has the stem *dokhu-*. When it is used to modify a head noun, the forms *dokhunuŋ* and *dokhu* are both found. The latter only occurs in my data in the speech of older speakers. When 'all' occurs in the absence of a head and is the final element of the noun phrase, it bears the case assignment of the noun phrase. The case inflections are idiosyncratic; the forms are given in (6):

(6) *dokhu/dokhunuŋ*   Absolutive
     dokhusenuŋ   Ergative
     dokhusetaŋ/doksetaŋ   Dative
     dokse(=e)   Genitive
     dokhuselān   Ablative
     dokhubale   'times'
     dokhutāŋ/doktāŋ   'types'

Notably, these forms have an additional formative *-se-* which is not found with lexical nouns. This element appears to be related to the *-s-* which one finds in the irregular inflection of the plural clitic and pronominal inflectional paradigms (§5.2), and which one also finds in case inflections in Kathmandu Newar. In addition, it should be noted that the patterns of inflection for 'all' are similar to those of *yau* 'some(body); anybody' (§5.4).

The morpheme 'all' is very common in my discourse data. It occurs in a wide range of environments and with a number of inflections, as shown in (7)–(15):

(7) Attributive
     dokhunuŋ thōsi rāches=na   nar-ai
     all   meat   ogress=ERG eat-3sPR

     'The ogre eats all the meat.'

(8) Attributive
     dokhu sāŋat=e   jā   but-a
     all   friend=GEN   rice cook-3sPST

     'All the friends' rice was cooked.'

(9) Absolutive, subject
     dokhunuŋ mwāt-a
     all   survive-3sPST

     'All of them survived.'

(10) Absolutive, object
     dokhunuŋ kuciri dupān   ta-ene   yen-ai
     all   nail   inside put-PART bring-3sPR

     '(She) puts all of it inside her nails and brings it.'

(11) Ergative
     dokhusenuŋ kharāyo lipul-e   khoŋ-an
     all.ERG   rabbit   return-NR2 see-PART

     'All (the animals) seeing the rabbit return...'

(12) Dative
     ām   jal=na   **doksetaŋ** chir   yeŋ-an   bi-u
     that liquid=ERG   all.DAT   sprinkle do-PART   give-IMP

     'Sprinkle all of them with that liquid.'

(13) Genitive
dokse=e   kaparā   sil!
all.GEN=GEN chamber.pot wash.IMP

'Wash everyone's chamber pots!'

(14) Types
thanu kesi   **doktāŋ**   sampati joret-ki
today tomorrow all.types wealth earn-1sPST

'These days I earned all types of wealth.'

(15) Places
dokhubale purba paschim cār-ai   disā
all.place   east west four-EMPH directions

'In all places, the east, the west, the four directions...'

3. Numerals and classifiers

Dolakha Newar has two competing numeral systems: a decimal system, based on groups of ten; and a vigesimal system, based on groups of 20. Most numerals may not occur in in isolation, but must occur with a numeral classifier.

3.1. The decimal-based system of numerals

The numbers from 1 to 40 are given in Table 31. As speakers never pronounce numerals in isolation, they are presented with the general classifier *-gur*:

Table 31. The Dolakha Newar numerals from 1 to 40

1	thi-gur	11	j(h)im-thi-gur	21	ni-thi-gur	31	swi-thi-gur
2	nis-gur	12	j(h)im-nis-gur	22	ni-nis-gur	32	swi-nis-gur
3	sõ-gur	13	j(h)im-sõ-gur	23	ni-sõ-gur	33	swi-sõ-gur
4	pe-gur/ pẽ-gur	14	j(h)im-pe-gur	24	ni-pe-gur	34	swi-pe-gur
5	ŋā-gur	15	j(h)im-ŋā-gur	25	ni-ŋā-gur	35	swi-ŋā-gur
6	khu-gur	16	j(h)im-khu-gur	26	ni-khu-gur	36	swi-khu-gur
7	nas-gur	17	j(h)im-nas-gur	27	ni-nas-gur	37	swi-nas-gur
8	cyā-gur	18	j(h)im-cyā-gur	28	ni-cyā-gur	38	swi-cyā-gur
9	gu-gur	19	j(h)im-gu-gur	29	ni-gu-gur	39	swi-gu-gur
10	j(h)i-gur	20	ni(i)-gur	30	swi-gur	40	pi-gur

We can see that, with the exception of *j(h)i/j(h)im-*, the principles of combination are regular. The numeral referring to the tens' place is directly followed by the numeral referring to the ones' place with no added elements or phonological changes. The numeral ten is *j(h)i* when indicating ten exactly, but has an allomorph *j(h)im* when combining to form the numerals from 11 to 19. This is also found in Kathmandu Newar, so probably reconstructs for the proto-language.

The single numerals and their corresponding multiples of 10 and 100 are presented in Table 32.

Table 32. Numerals and their corresponding multiples of 10 and 100

1	thi-gur	10	j(h)i-gur	100	sar-chi
2	ni-gur	20	ni(i)-gur	200	nis-sar
3	sõ-gur	30	swi-gur	300	sõ-sar
4	pe-gur	40	pi-gur	400	pe-sar
5	ŋā-gur	50	ŋai-gur	500	ŋā-sar
6	khu-gur	60	khwi-gur	600	khu-sar
7	nas-gur	70	nai-gur	700	nas-sar
8	cyā-gur	80	cyai-gur	800	cyā-sar
9	gu-gar	90	gwi-gur	900	gu-sar

We can see that, with the exception of ten itself, the multiples of ten are constructed by the addition of an *-i* suffix to the simple numeral. The resultant vowel combinations follow the regular rules of phonological adjustment (discussed in §2.3.4), such that round vowels become glides and low vowels become diphthongs. Three changes which appear to be idiosyncratic are the loss of nasalization on *sõ*, the loss of the /s/ in *na-i-gur* 'seventy' and the simplification of *pe-i* to *pi* 'forty'. The vowel length on *ni(i)* 'twenty' is variable. Some speakers make a point of producing it, saying the vowel must be long to differentiate this form from 'two'. Other speakers produce it as short, apparently relying on its different positioning within the numeral to differentiate its function. Vowel length is not otherwise contrastive in the language.

The multiples of 100 are transparently formed by the suffixation of *-sar*. Note however, that the order of the formatives is reversed in *sar-chi* where the *sar-* precedes the numeral for one. This reversal in ordering is again found with 1000, which is *dol-chi*. Two-thousand is *nis-dol*, etc. Unusual behavior of 'one' and its base-ten multiples is common in Tibeto-Burman languages (see Matisoff 1997: 17–24).

Another interesting point is that numerals that end in either the multiple for hundreds *-sar*, or the multiple for thousands *-dol*, do not take numeral classifiers (e.g. *nis-sar mi* 'two-hundred people', not **nis-sar-mā mi*). Thus the morphemes *-sar* and *-dol* serve a dual function: they both convey specific numerals and they classify large groups. Ten-thousand is thus *j(h)i-dol*.

Forming the more specific larger numerals requires the simple juxtaposition of numerals and does not involve any idiosyncratic behavior to my knowledge, e.g. *sõ-sar-swi-sõ-gur* 'three-hundred thirty-three', etc. However, it should be noted that in daily interaction, Nepali numerals are generally used for most numbers above 20 that are not multiples of ten. Even multiples of ten above 40 are usually replaced with Nepali forms.[56]

3.2. The vigesimal-based system of numerals

In addition to the decimal-based system for forming numerals just discussed, there is a competing system based on multiples of 20. It utilizes the noun *ṭhãĩ* 'place'. The forms for 10 to 100 are given in Table 33:

Table 33. Multiples of 10 in vigesimal system

10	j(h)i-gur
20	ni(i)-gur
30	swi-gur
40	ne-ni-nis-thãĩ
50	ne-ni-nis-thãĩ-o-j(h)i-gur
60	ne-ni-sõ-thãĩ
70	ne-ni-sõ-thãĩ-o-j(h)i-gur
80	ne-ni-pi-thãĩ
90	ne-ni-pi-thãĩ-o-j(h)i-gur

We can see that the multiples of 10 through 30 are the same as in the decimal system. For multiples of 40 and above, the combination *ne-ni* is used. Consultants translate this as 'twenty-twenty'. This is then followed by the number of "places" that 20 is multiplied by, e.g. *ne-ni-nis-thãĩ* is 'twenty-twenty, two places', or 40; *ne-ni-sõ-ṭhãĩ* with three "places" is 60, and *ne-ni-pi-ṭhãĩ* is 80 (with the vowel of *pe* 'four' assimilating to the string of high vowels, producing *pi*. Note that these forms do not take numeral classifiers; this is not surprising as the numeral itself ends in a noun.

One question which naturally arises is why the core of the vigesimal system is *ne-ni* instead of *ni-ni* 'twenty-twenty'. It appears that a simple dissimilation process has occurred, lowering the first of two high vowels. However, in checking this system with another consultant, she produced a slightly different form, which was *ni-e-ni-e-nis-ṭhãĩ* for 'forty', etc. After each form of 'twenty', she added the vowel /e/. The only morpheme which has this shape in the language is the genitive. Thus one can hypothesize that the original system was based on a collocation such as "of twenty of twenty two times". However it is possible that there is some other etymological source for the /e/ that I am not currently aware of.

In order to form the other multiples of ten, one adds *o-j(h)i-gur* 'and ten'. The morpheme *-o* is a form of the conjunction *ho* normally found conjoining noun phrases or their elements. Because these numerals end with the formative *j(h)i*, they must then occur with a numeral classifier.

The existence of a vigesimal system of numerals is particularly interesting because this is the first time that this has been described for any Newar dialect.[57] Matisoff (1997: 39) states that in languages where decimal and vigesimal systems are more or less in free variation, the vigesimal system is apparently older. Interestingly, none of the vigesimal systems described by Matisoff have a reduplicated or repeated form of the numeral for 'twenty'. Nor do any of the cases he cites involve the multiplication of 20 by a counted noun/numeral classifer, such as *thāī* 'place'. Thus this system seems a quite unusual one, even within the relatively unusual category of vigesimal numeral systems.

3.3. Numeral classifiers

In Dolakha Newar, most numerals do not occur in the absence of a numeral classifier. The use of a particular classifier is determined by semantic properties of the noun being enumerated; the classifiers thus serve to classify the nouns semantically.

The only numerals which do not co-occur with classifiers are *sar* 'one-hundred' and *dol* 'one-thousand' which occur in combinations such as *nis-dol* 'two-thousand'. Although these clearly function to quantify and to form higher numerals (see above), they clearly fill the syntactic position of the numeral classifier. They thus appear to be mensural classifiers, measuring groups of 100 and 1,000 respectively.

The morphosyntactic environments in which numeral classifiers appear are quite limited. They occur after native Dolakha Newar numerals, with the exceptions of multiples of 100 and 1000, as discussed above. They do not occur with numerals borrowed from Nepali. Classifiers also occur after the morphemes *jau* 'right' and *khau* 'left', e.g. *khau-pā ṭuṭi* [left-CL leg] 'left leg'. The classifier for numbers of times that an action is performed may suffix directly to the interrogative word *gul-*, e.g. *gul-pul* 'How many times?'; however this is apparently lexicalized as one does not use other classifiers with interrogative words, for example, one finds *guli mi* 'How many people', not *gu-mā mi*, with the classifier for animates *-mā*.[58] Numeral classifiers do not occur in any other morphosyntactic environment.

There are a total of 28 numeral classifiers that I know of in this language. Of these, 16 are "sortal"; they classify the noun by its semantic qualities. Seven classifiers are "mensural"; they classify the noun by its quantity and so are used as measures of mass or abstract nouns (Aikhenvald 2003: 114–115). Four other classifiers are neither clearly sortal nor clearly mensural. Of these, one is used for classifying types of things, one is locational in classifying sides of things, and two are used to classify activities.

Beginning with the sortal classifiers, the most semantically transparent and regular is the classifier -*mā* for animate beings. Because the numeral *thi-* 'one' plus a classifier is commonly used to introduce new referents into the discourse, this is also the most frequent classifier in my narrative data. This classifier is used with all animates, including deities, humans, kin, animals, birds, fish, amphibians, reptiles, and insects. A representative sample of nouns is given in (16):

(16) Some animate nouns classified by -*mā*

bā	'father'	*iri*	'daughter-in-law'
bajai	'grandmother'	*jāŋal*	'bird'
batijā/batiji	'nephew/niece'	*kae*	'son'
bikara	'snake'	*kastimā*	'bee'
binā/bini	'nephew/niece'	*khicā*	'dog'
buḍi	'old woman'	*kisi*	'elephant'
chae	'grandchild'	*kok*	'crow'
chū	'mouse; rat'	*kusi*	'flea'
chwi	'great grandchild'	*kwākarbeŋ*	'frog'
cijbā	'stepfather'	*lokhubaṭi*	'otter'
cijmā	'stepmother'	*mābā*	'parents'
ciku	'ant'	*makar*	'monkey'
cilā	'goat'	*mi*	'person'
deor	'brother-in-law'	*pẽ*	'leech'
didā	'elder brother'	*phā*	'pig'
dobā	'uncle'	*rājā*	'king'
d(h)ū	'tiger'	*sāŋat*	'friend'
gisā	'cow'	*sipāĩ*	'soldier'
gõgar	'rooster'	*sı*	'louse'
gubāju	'priest (Buddhist)'	*sihā*	'lion'
imā	'eagle'	*ṭuhurā*	'orphan'

There are three classes which are based primarily on the shape of the object being classified, with consistency of the object being a secondary criterion for classification. Interestingly, there is no classifier for flat (primarily two-dimensional things). Instead, there is one classifier for three-dimensional roundish things and two for primarily one-dimensional long things.

The classifier -gar classifies three-dimensional objects in which all three dimensions are roughly of equal size, resulting in ball-shaped, block-shaped, or lumpy objects. The size of the item classified is unimportant, as this can refer to large, lumpy things, such as palaces, or very small round things, such as seeds. A sample of the nouns classified by -gar is given in (17):

(17) A selection of nouns that are classified by -gar (roundish objects)

ālu	'potato'	mahal	'palace'
bārpāŋ	'tomato'	mikhā	'eye'
bandagobi	'cabbage'	mogara	'upper back'
bwārā	'shed'	nagarā	'drum (round)'
cher	'head'	nugar	'heart'
chē	'house'	pālo	'ginger'
gwār	'barn'	pāŋ	'fruit'
gwāri	'ankle'	phoŋa	'pillow'
hākupāku	'raspberry, black'	pukhur	'pond'
kāwli	'cauliflower'	puyā	'seed'
kãkar	'corn kernel'	pwākal	'pit (in ground)'
karbul	'pea'	pyāṭā	'belly'
khēja	'egg'	pyāj	'onion'
kwāluŋmā	'pestle'	tusi	'cucumber'
luŋā	'stone'		

The classifier -pu classifies things which are primarily one dimensional and of flexible consistency. In the following list of nouns classified by -pu, there are two words which cannot be characterized in this way, since they are not particularly flexible. These are ciplebhēde 'eggplant', which even if not truly flexible are at least long, slightly bent, and a bit soft. The other is dwārā 'fangs', or a row of uneven teeth. Some of the nouns classified by -pu are listed in (18):

(18) A selection of nouns that are classified by -pu (long flexible objects)

ãti	'intestines'	mukan	'mushroom'
borā	'green beans'	muru	'needle'
cherā	'woolen mat'	nasputi	'ear'
ciplebhēde	'eggplant'	parsi	'sari'
cumṭu	'tail'	pomṭu	'wing'
dwārā	'fangs'	sã	'hair'
galaīcā	'carpet'	sãrpuli	'ribbons'
gukhi	'rope'	sigri	'necklace'
hā	'root'	situgãs	'Situ grass'
kãrā	'arrow'	sona	'flower'

khursāni	'chili'	sukul	'straw mat'
mālā	'garland'	sū	'straw'
me	'tongue'	tannā	'bedcover'

The classifier -kã is also used with nouns which are two-dimensional, but nouns classified in this manner are solid instead of flexible, although they are often of a curved shape. A selection of nouns classified by -kã is given in (19). Interestingly, many of the nouns on this list are tools, but certainly not all of them. This fact is probably due to the fact that many tools are of this shape and consistency. Another possibility is that this class is that of tools and things used to make them.

(19) A selection of nouns that are classified by -kã (long solid objects)

caṭan	'cooking spoon'	sī	'wood'
cuphi	'machete (khukuri)'	simā	'tree'
gan	'hammer'	siṭhu	'plough'
kaṭhi	'stick'	suba	'large mortar'
kãcā	'branch'	tār	'lock'
kaĩci	'scissors'	tārcā	'key'
kakana	'bracelet'	tarawāra	'sword'
pā	'ax'	ṭikhi	'bamboo, small'
pōṭa	'bamboo, large'	yēsa	'sickle'

The classifier -pā appears to be a classifier for body parts, especially limbs. Some of the nouns which -pā classifies are given in (20):

(20) A selection of nouns that are classified by -pā
(parts of other things, limbs, extensions)

culā	'finger; toe'	lukhā	'door'
cumṭu	'tail'	mikhā	'eye'
lāhā	'hand; arm'	naspuṭi	'ear'
lapti	'leaf'	ṭuṭi	'leg; foot'
lākmā	'shoe'		

A few of these items appear at first glance not to fit into the category. Doors of houses presumably are classified here due to a semantic metaphor which sees a house as a body and the door as one of its parts. The use of this classifier with leaves is presumably a reflection of the leaf as a part of the tree. Shoes are probably included as they are extensions of feet, or foot-shaped. In my discourse data this classifier is also used with *māri* 'bread' (e.g. chapati). In the narrative, a character gives *thi-pā māri* to a mouse; I believe this refers to piece of the bread which the character tears off, as opposed to referring to a whole bread.

The classifier -*pta* is used for items of clothing, particularly those worn by men, e.g. *ṭupri* 'topi (hat)', *ganji* 'vest', *pānt* 'pants', *sert* 'shirt', *kusā* 'raincoat'. I have noted that it is also used for *rādi*, which refers to a woolen blanket or thin rug.

The classifier -*ṭwāk* is used for the various pieces of women's clothing that are wrapped around the body, such as *parsi* 'sari', *paṭukā* 'shawl', *laŋgi* 'wrap-around skirt' (similar to an Indonesian sarong). This classifier can also be used with *rumāl* 'towels' which are similar in consisting of long pieces of fabric and are sometimes worn wrapped around the body.

There are a handful of classifiers which appear to classify only one thing, as far as I am aware. They are listed in (21):

(21) -*pānā*   *bõr*   (pieces of) paper
      -*pat*   *lapti* leaves
      -*ḍē*   *kãkar* ears of corn
      -*bācā*   oaths
      -*oti*   words
      -*nu*   days
      -*cā*   nights
      -*lā*   months
      -*da*   years

Of these, the first three co-occur with the specific nouns given in the second column. The remaining four classifiers are used to measure units of time. They do not co-occur with nouns, but constitute independent noun phrases.[59]

It is interesting to note that while one would predict *thi-da* for 'one year', the form *da-chi* is found instead, with the order reversed and the /th/ palatalized to /ch/. We similarly find *ni-chi* 'one day', *ca-chi* 'one night, all night', and *la-chi* 'one month'. This is the same irregular ordering and palatalization that one finds with '100' *sar-chi* and '1,000' *dol-chi*.

The last and most common of the sortal classifiers is -*gur*. This is the general classifier which is used to classify abstract nouns as well as anything that does not nicely fit into the categories already mentioned. It is also possible for speakers to use -*gur* even when there is a more specific classifier available. It was mentioned above that there is no shape classifier for two-dimensional or flat things; instead things of that shape are classified by -*gur*. A few of the nouns which -*gur* occurs with are given in (22):

(22) A selcection of nouns classfied by *-gur* (general classifier)

bākhan	'story'	lahar	'queue'
biruwā	'plant'	lõ	'road'
bo	'plate'	luŋmā	'flat mortar'
butni, bunni	'sack'	lusi	'pestle, for suba'
bū	'field'	māŋas	'dream'
cij	'thing'	melā	'fair'
cukā	'side; top'	muryā	'lap'
dāl	'dal'	muthu	'mouth'
des	'country'	nā	'odor'
dila	'resting spot'	nās	'nose'
din	'day'	nakti	'star'
dulā	'palm of hand'	naku	'cheek'
gala	'neck'	nemlā	'moon'
gār	'wound'	nibār	'sun'
gara	'pit (in ground)'	oli	'garden'
gā̃ū	'village'	pati	'side'
guthi	'civic organization'	pali	'roof'
hã̄sā	'winnowing basket'	phāŋā	'blanket'
himāl	'Himalaya'	pharsi	'pumpkin'
inār	'well'	phasa	'wind'
jagā	'flood'	pokā	'packet'
jhyālā	'window'	pulca	'terrace wall'
kajit	'civic group'	pyākhan	'dance'
khã	'talk; language'	sānahi	'horn (muscial)'
khāṭ	'bed'	sã̄par	'bun (hair)'
kho	'river'	simā	'tree'
khopṭu	'lower back'	swābāu	'habit'
khwāl	'face'	swālāhā	'nest'
kipā	'shade; shadow'	swã̄hārā	'field, non-irrigated'
kisim	'type'	ṭap	'earrings'
kuṭhā	'room'	ṭhota	'stairwell'
kuciri	'fingernails; claws'		
kulsi	'stair'		
kunā	'corner'		

Turning to the mensural classifiers, there are a number of classifiers which are commonly used for the measurement of mass nouns. Example (23) lists some of these, along with typical nouns that they would quantify:

(23) | Classifier | Quantity | Example noun | |
|---|---|---|---|
| -dārpa | 'bowls' | dari | 'yogurt' |
| -phā | 'pathi' | jāki | 'uncooked rice' |
| -mnā | 'mana' | jāki | 'uncooked rice' |
| -thopā | 'drop' | lokhu | 'water' |
| -muthi | 'mouthful' | turi | 'mustard' |
| -kto, -koto | 'pieces' | thõsi | 'meat' |
| -tākā | 'rupees' | dyābā | 'money' |
| -laskar | 'crowd; queue' | mi | 'person' |

The classifier -tākā is used with money to count rupees. The general classifier is used for the counting of *paysa* (hundredths of rupees). Thus we find *nis-tākā dyābā* 'two rupees' contrasting with *nis-gur dyābā* 'two paysa'.

The classifiers -phā and -mnā are used for pathis and manas, respectively. Both of these are standard units of measures in Nepal. One pathi is equivalent to eight manas.

The classifier -jo(r) is used for pairs of things, such as shoes, earrings, etc., or for other things that come in sets, such as decks of cards, lock/key sets, etc. This morpheme is clearly the result of the incorporation of the Nepali noun *jor* 'pairs' into the classifier system. This classifier is mensural as it serves to delimit a set for counting, rather than classifying something in terms of its inherent semantic characteristics. For example, the noun *lākmā* 'shoe' is normally classified with -pā because of its inherent relationship to feet. However, -jor is used instead to delimit sets (pairs) shoes for counting. Thus we can contrast *sõ-pā lākmā* 'three shoes' with *sõ-jor lākmā* 'three pairs of shoes'.

The numeral classifier -tā(ŋ) is neither sortal nor mensural, as it is not used to classify objects by their semantic properties nor to measure them. Instead it is used to group things by type. Thus we can contrast *sõ-pu sona* 'three flowers' with *sõ-tā sona* 'three types of flowers'. This morpheme is also found lexicalized in the form *doktāŋ* 'all types' (see above). No other classifier occurs with the formative *dok-* 'all'.

The classifier -kana is locational and so neither measures nor sorts nouns. Instead, it indicates the sides of objects, e.g. *thi-kana* 'on one side' or *nis-kana* 'on two sides'. Although clearly composed of a numeral plus a classifier, these function more as adverbials than as modifiers of nouns.

There are two numeral classifiers that are used to quantify activities as opposed to objects. The classifier *thāī* is used to indicate the number of places where something happens, so indirectly it indicates the number of times something happens. It is the most transparent of all the classifiers in its lexical source, as it is clearly the noun *thāī* 'place' which is being used as a classifier. It is not used with itself; that is, one does not find *thi-thāī thāī* for one place (the general classifier -gur is found instead). Rather, one uses this to classify things done at different places, e.g. *nis-ṭhā̃ĩ je* is 'two jobs; jobs at two places'. The other classifier which is used to quantify activities is *-pul* 'times', e.g. *nis-pul sõ-pul* 'two or three times'. These two activity quantifiers may be contrasted in the following elicited pair of sentences:

(24)   Elicited
        āmun **nis-ṭhā̃ĩ** *mi   tir-ju*
        3sERG two-CL fire light-3sPST

        'He lit fires in two places.' (i.e. 'He lit two fires.')

(25)   Elicited
        āmun **nis-pul** *mi   tir-ju*
        3sERG two-CL fire light-3sPST

        'He lit a fire two times.' (i.e. 'He lit two fires.')

While both of these sentences can mean 'He lit two fires', in (24) the implication is that he lit fires in two different places, whereas (25) could mean either this or that he lit a fire two times in the same place.

Chapter 9
Adverbials

1. Introduction

The term "adverbial" is a cover term for the classes of lexical adverbs and intensifiers. Although these two classes have similar properties, they still differ enough to justify keeping them in separate lexical classes.

Adverbs are an open lexical class, highly amenable to borrowing from Nepali. They differ from nouns, verbs, and pronouns in that they never inflect. They differ from adjectives in that they never occur within a noun phrase. Finally, they differ from particles in having lexical, as opposed to grammatical, meanings and have greater freedom of positioning. Adverbs are never modified, nor do they act as heads of phrases or otherwise form constituents. They do not occur with intensifiers.

The positioning of adverbs depends on their semantics. Adverbs which set the temporal settings for an event tend to be clause-initial, while those which express temporal duration, direction, location, or manner tend to occur before the verb. Unlike noun phrases, postpositional phrases, and clauses, adverbs are never post-verbal.

Intensifiers differ from adverbs in that they may occur within the noun phrase where they either function as quantifiers or they intensify an adjective. Intensifiers also combine with adjectives to form adjectival phrases, behavior not shared with adverbs.

2. Temporal adverbs

Temporal adverbs function either to indicate the time at which an event occurred or to indicate its duration. Those which set the time of an event are almost always positioned clause-initially or directly after the clause-initial subject:

(1)   āu   thanu   hā-e   jāki=e   jā   chu
        now   today   bring-NR2   uncooked.rice=GEN   rice   cook.IMP

        'Now today cook rice of the rice (I have) brought.'

(2) **nichi =uri** thi-mā buḍyā ye-ene
one.day=IND one-CL old.woman come-PART

'One day an old woman comes...'

(3) isi **kesi** tuŋ on-agu
1pEXC tomorrow FOC go-1pPR

'We go tomorrow.'

(4) **āu** nini=n har-sin
now aunt =ERG say-IMP

'Now aunt say it.'

When temporal adverbs communicate the duration of an event, they may additionally occur directly before the verb. The example given in (5) has three temporal adverbs. The clause-initial adverb sets the general time of the events relative to the preceding discourse, whereas the later two are preverbal and indicate the duration of the events:

(5) libi ām misā ānthi nicchi sit-ŋa cacchi mwāt-ŋa
later that woman like.that all.day die-when all.night survive-when

'Later when that one is dead all day, alive all night...'

The temporal adverbs which occur in my database are given in (6):

(6)
āu	'now'	thanu	'today'
libi	'later'	mega	'yesterday'
lita	'next'	miɲe	'before yesterday'
yelpanuŋ	'always'	kesi	'tomorrow'
sadāŋ	'always'	kansa	'after tomorrow'
ninpatti	'daily'	kālsi	'next year'
nienin	'day by day'	nāga	'last year'
nicchi	'all day'	suni	'in the morning'
cacchi	'all night'	khacin	'later same day'
la-chi	'one month'	balni	'evening'
da-chi	'one year'	nāscā	'late night'
hābi	'before'	lita khunu	'next day'
litaŋ	'again'		

I have one example of a temporal adverb being used as a noun. It takes the genitive clitic which allows it to modify another noun: *balni=e khã* 'evening talk' (i.e. 'the type of thing one talks about in the evening').

3. Locational adverbs

The adverbs of location are distinct from locational nouns in that they cannot occur within a noun phrase, hence cannot be modified nor inflect for number or case. The locational adverbs include the forms for 'up' and 'down' listed in (7):

(7) *kobi*   'down; below'
     kota   'down'
     thābi   'up, above'
     thāta/thã̄ta 'up'

The two forms with *-bi* are used with stative verbs to indicate static locations at a place above or below the deictic center. The two forms with *-ta* are directionals. They are used with motion verbs to indicate movement upwards or downwards away from the deictic center. Examples are given in (8)–(11):

(8) Elicited
    thābi āme   sāŋat con-a
    above   3sGEN   friend stay-3sPST

    'His friend lives above.'

(9) **kobi** con-a   ka   luŋā twāpar=ku
    below   stay-3sPST   ASS rock flat.top=LOC

    'It was below, on the flat top of rock.'

(10) **thāta** chāta   ŋat-ki
     up   umbrella   throw-1sPST

     'I threw the umbrella up.'

(11) chi **kota** tuŋ ye-en   bi-u
     2s   down   FOC come-PART   give-IMP

     'You come down and give it to me.'

These adverbs can be contrasted with the locational postpositions used with particular nouns, e.g. *gã̄u depān* 'above the village' (§4.4.2.9).

Obviously related to the above forms are the directionals *duta* 'into' and *pita* 'out', which also occurs with motion verbs. I have never seen forms *dubi or *pibi to contrast with them; speakers appear to use the postpositions *dupān* and *pipana* instead.

(12) [bāhādur bāje=e chē=ku]_NP ***duta*** on-gi
 Bahadur Baje =GEN house=LOC into go-1sPST

 'I went into Bahadur Baje's house.'

(13) ãku yelpanuŋ ***pita*** yer-a
 there always out come-3sPST

 'It always come out there.'

Example (12) clearly shows that the adverb *duta* is distinct from the preceding noun phrase, as it follows the locative clitic, which serves to mark the terminal boundary of the NP.

The forms *likhana* and *hākhena* function both as adverbs and as postpositions. The latter usage is discussed in §4.4.2.9. As adverbs the forms occur independently and mean 'after; back' and 'before; front' respectively. These meanings can be applied to both spatial and temporal contexts. The following two sentences were found in a narrative where the speaker was talking about the order in which he and some other men went in a line:

(14) ji=uri ***hākhena*** jur-gi
 1s=IND front be-1sPST

 'I was in the front (i.e. going first).'

(15) āle ***likhana***=ri ām harkha bāhādur jur-a
 then after=IND that Harkha Bahadur be-3sPST

 'Then in the back (i.e. going last) was Harkha Bahadur.'

The forms *li* and *lichilen* are also found as directional adverbs. They both mean 'backwards'. My sense is that the latter form is more explicit as the lexeme *li* is used in a number of other lexical items. In the sentence in (16), the speaker uses both forms as she repeats the verb:

(16) ***lichilen*** liŋā-en gyān bāhādur=e swãhārā
 backward walk-PART Gyan Bahadur=GEN garden

ṭulke li liŋā-en yer-gi
up.to backwards walk-PART come-1sPST

'Walking backwards, I came walking backwards as far as Gyan Bahadur's garden.'

4. Manner adverbs

The specification of the manner of an action may be conveyed by various morphosyntactic mechanisms. Probably the most common strategy is the participial construction, which has manner modification as one of its primary functions. This is fully discussed in §19.4.5.3. Here only two examples will be given:

(17) bwāŋ-an yer-a
run-PART come-3sPST

'(She) came by running.'

(18) cicā=uri dāi =na **ānthi** tuŋ yeŋ-an on-a
small=IND e.brother=ERG that.manner FOC do-PART go-3sPST

'The younger of the elder brothers went doing exactly the same thing.'

In addition, there are manner demonstratives which are used anaphorically, see §5.5.3.

There is a fair number of manner adverbs in Dolakha Newar, many of which are borrowed from Nepali, which has a particularly rich expressive vocabulary. Beginning with native Newar forms, there are several adverbs which appear to be derived with the affix -(s)ke. By far the most common of these are bãla-ske 'well', derived from the adjective bãlat- 'good'. Its negative counterpart is bāmala-ske 'badly', with the negative affix embedded in it (see §6.4.4.1). These common manner adverbs are exemplified in (19) and (20):

(19) jāri=n **bãlaske** hat-ai
b.in.law=ERG well say-3sPR

'My brother-in-law says it well.'

(20) twāŋsona=n būsi=ta **bāmalaske** ginlā yeŋ-an
Rhododendron=ERG Bunsi=DAT badly insult do-PART

'Rhododendron badly insulted Bunsi...'

There are at least two other adverbs which also end in *-ke*. These are *sumake* 'silently', and *cyāpcyāprake* 'stumblingly'. I am not certain that these were formed with the same suffix, or whether the suffix may have broader derivational possibilities.

In addition to these manner adverbs, speakers make extensive use of expressive vocabulary, some apparently native and some borrowed from Nepali. These can be thought of as ideophones, "a vivid representation of an idea in sound, a word often onomatopoeic, which describe a predicate...with respect to manner, colour, sound, smell, state, or intensity" (Doke 1935). These adverbs are generally difficult to translate, and their meanings may be slightly different depending on the verb with which they occur. For example, contrast the phonotactically and semantically related terms in (21)–(24):

(21)   kho   dupān   **swāṭṭa**   morlu-en
        river inside   EXPR   bathe-PART

        'Quickly bathing in the river.'

(22)   pukhuri=e   lokhu   **swāṭṭa**   sut-a
        lake=GEN   water   EXPR   dry-3SPST

        'The water in the lake completely dried up.'

(23)   Elicited
        gukhi   **bwāṭṭa**   charbut-a
        rope   EXPR   snap-3sPST

        'The rope suddenly/completely snapped.'

(24)   Elicited
        gilās   **pwāṭṭa**   tapjyāt-a
        glass   EXPR   broke-3sPST

        'The glass suddenly/completely broke.'

Additional examples are given in (25). Like the examples above, these forms tend to be specialized for particular verbs and difficult to translate. The translations given below should be considered approximations:

(25)   *jurukka ḍoŋ-an*   'stand right up'   < 'stand'
        musukka ŋil-en   'smile in a particular way'   < 'smile'
        phisikka ŋil-en   'smile without showing teeth' < 'smile'
        suikucca ju-en   'running at a wild pace'   < 'be; become; happen'
        thapakka ta-en   'put it just so'   < 'put'

phutta oŋ-an	'jump away'	< 'go'
dyāppa jaudi-en	'plunk it down'	< 'rest a load'
bugluŋga tu-en	'fall head over heels'	< 'fall from height'
puklukka da-en	'tumble down'	< 'fall from standing'

A number of these are borrowed from Nepali. They tend to be trisyllabic with a geminate cluster between the second and third syllables, usually -*kk*-. Other borrowed manner adverbs of a more general nature include *haḍbaḍ* 'hastily; in a hectic manner', *haṭanapaṭa* 'in a hurry', *bākhācākhā* 'partially completed; halfway', *turuntai* 'immediately', and *sarāsar* 'directly'.

Another set of ideophones appear to be roughly onomatopoeic. They may be incorporated into the clause by the verb *yet-* 'do', which implies someone is making the noise, they may be marked with the instrumental =*na*, or they may simply occur independently. They are generally reduplicated, and may be repeated more than two times. Some examples are given in (26). Note that the last three are not strictly onomatopoeic as they do not represent sounds but feelings and sights.

(26)
dwāŋdwāŋ yet-	'make a banging noise'
tāktāk yet-	'make a knocking noise'
syā̃syā̃syā̃syā̃	'sound of panting'
tyā̃tyā̃tyūtyū	'sound of child babbling'
camcamcam	'sound of dancing, jewelry-clad feet'
gargar=na	'sound of roaring fire'
hararararararaŋ	'sound of dancing'
lililililin	'twinkling'
jinininin	'shivering'
pilipili	'dim'

Some examples of these forms taken from connected discourse are given in (27)–(29):

(27) muсā **cwā̃cwā̃** kho-en   coŋ-gu   hā
      child EXPR   cry-PART stay-3PA EVID

'The child was crying "*cwā̃cwā̃*".'

(28) **bulbulbul=na**   dudu yer-a
      EXPR=INST   milk come-3sPST

'Milk came bubbling/gurgling out.'

(29) **tāŋtāŋ** yet-ke   hirā=e   jā   hā-en   bir-ju
     EXPR   do-CAUS.PART diamod=GEN   rice bring-PART   give-3sPST

'Making it go "tāŋtāŋ", (they) brought and gave him the diamond rice.'

Manner adverbs are most commonly positioned directly before the verb, although on rare occasion a noun phrase will intervene, as in (28) above.

5. Intensifiers

Intensifiers in Dolakha Newar occur most commonly before the verb. If the verb is formed by a compound structure with borrowed Nepali vocabulary, the intensifier occurs before the compound, not within it. Thus in *besna māyā yet-ai* '(They) loved (her) very much', the intensifier *besna* precedes the noun in the compound *māyā yet-*, which is composed of the Nepali noun 'love' followed by the Dolakha verb 'do' (see §12.6). It is possible for an argument to intervene between the intensifier and the verb, but this is rare. One example is given in (30):

(30) āle   lita khunu **besna** khasi=ta   ḍu-en   yen-ai
     then next day   very   goat=DAT   drag-PART   bring-3sPR

'Then the very next day (they) bring the goat, dragging very hard.'

Intensifiers may also occur directly before an adjective, either within the noun phrase or within the copula complement. The combination of the intensifier and the adjective can be said to form an adjectival phrase:

(31) [ām janābar=pen]cs [[**biŋkeŋ** dukhi]AP]CC ju-en
     that animal=PL   very   sad   become-PART

'The animals became very sad...'

The intensifiers which have occurred in my data are given in (32).

(32) besna   'very'
     biŋkeŋ   'very'
     ekdam   'very' (< Nepali)
     nikkai   'very' (< Nepali)
     guli   'so much' (< interrogative of quantity)
     ulisṭule   'to this extreme amount' (< demonstrative of quantity)

There seems to be very little difference between the first four intensifiers semantically and they appear in the same morphosyntactic environments and even with the same predicates. It could be that with more data finer distinctions in meaning may be discerned. For now, I will give them all the same gloss. The first two are native Dolakhae forms, while *ekdam* and *nikkai* are both Nepali borrowings. Of these four intensifiers, *ekdam* is the most common. It is also the only one that may occur as a quantifier (see §8.2). The intensifier *besna* is the more frequent of the two native intensifiers in my data.

The last two forms on this list both function as independent elements within the noun phrase. They do occur as intensifiers, but at least in my data are much less frequent than the other forms in the list. For discussion and exemplification; see §5.3 and §5.5.5.

Chapter 10
Particles and clitics of individuation and extension

1. Introduction

Particles are grammatical morphemes which are not phonologically bound to their host and which do not participate in affixation. They do not function as verbs or arguments, nor do they have lexical content like adverbs. Also, many particles can follow and precede words from a wide range of lexical classes. They thus tend not to be restricted to particular syntactic positions. Clitics differ from particles in being phonologically bound. They are not stressed independently and they form a single phonological word with their hosts. Technically speaking, particles and clitics cannot form a single lexical class as they differ in morphological status. However, the clitics of individuation and extension are functionally similar to three particles with discourse function. Indeed, the three particles and two clitics never co-occur, so in one sense they seem to be in a loose paradigmatic relationship despite their different morphological behavior. In addition to these clitics and particles, the language has various other particles which have a variety of semantic and syntactic properties. This chapter therefore covers a rather disparate set of elements. The only properties which they all share is that they are not lexical and do not inflect.

2. Clitics of individuation and extension

The clitics of individuation and extension are =(u)ri and =(u)ŋ respectively. As mentioned above, they form a loose paradigm with three particles: the topic marker wā, the focus particle tuŋ, and the particle of restriction jukun. The distribution of these five morphemes is quite complex, both at the level of the individual morphemes and at the level of the system as a whole. Here I will illustrate the range of environments in which each morpheme is found and present hypotheses about their underlying functions and their distributions.

There is clear phonological evidence that the clitics =(u)ri and =(u)ŋ are phonologically bound. They are unstressed and, although there is some variability, the presence or absence of the /u/ vowel is phonologically predictable based on the phonological shape of the host.

Beginning with the individuating clitic =(u)ri, when it follows a host ending in a vowel, the /u/ is present and the two conjoined vowels undergo the regular phonological rules governing vowel sequences within a single phonological word (§2.3.4). For example, a preceding /i/ vowel becomes a glide, a sequence of two /u/ vowels shortens to one, and the remaining vowels form diphthongs:

(1)
Host	Gloss	Cliticized Form	Phonetic form
misā	'woman'	misā=uri	[mi.sau.ri]
kae	'son'	ka =uri	[kɑ.ɛu.ri]
ṭhā̃ĩ	'place'	ṭhā̃ĩ=uri	[tʰã.ju.ri]
kōsa	'bone'	kōsa=uri	[kō.sau.ri]
bobu	'baby'	bobu=uri	[bo.bu.ri]

In some environments, the clitic =uri shortens to /ri/, losing its initial vowel. This occurs only rarely when the clitic follows a vowel, e.g. ota=ri [this=IND], mā=ri [mother=IND], māyā=ri [love=IND]. However, the shortening is usually found when the clitic is bound to a consonant-final stem:

(2)
Host	Gloss	Cliticized form	Alternate form
kae=n	'son (ERG)'	kae=n=ri	kae=n=uri
din	'day'	din=ri	din=uri
ām	'that'	ām=ri	ām=uri
lon	'womb'	lon=ri	
sāŋat	'friend'	sāŋat=ri	
bikās	(proper name)	bikās=uri	

Most of the variation between /uri/ and /ri/ is found after the ergative clitic =n; in this position the two forms of the clitic appear to be about equally distributed. Despite this variation in the presence of the initial vowel, it is still clear that this morpheme is phonologically bound. It is unstressed and undergoes the same rules governing vowel sequences as are found in word-internal environments.

The clitic =(u)ŋ also has two allomorphs, one with /u/ and one without. However the rules governing their distribution are different than those for =uri. This is because this clitic ends in a consonant, not a vowel, and so does not necessarily instantiate a separate syllable. The allomorph /ŋ/ is found when the clitic is bound to a vowel-final stem, while the allomorph /uŋ/ is found when the clitic is bound to a consonant-final stem. The presence of the /u/ vowel allows the final nasal to syllabify. Examples are given in (3):

(3)
Host	Gloss	Cliticized form
guli	'how much'	guli=ŋ
cachi	'one night'	cachi =ŋ
isi	'we (EXC)'	isi=ŋ

isin	'we (EXC.ERG)'	*isin=uŋ*
thi-gur	'one-CL'	*thi-gur=uŋ*
rāk	'anger'	*rāk=uŋ*

As the form of the clitic is clearly dependent on the form of the host, we can see that this morpheme is also phonologically bound.

The particles *tuŋ* and *wā* are very clearly not bound. They both constitute prominent syllables with the former having a heavy rhyme and the latter having the vowel /ā/, the longest and most sonorous in the inventory. They are also independently stressed.

Although these four morphemes fall into two different morphological categories with respect to phonological boundedness, they all occur in the same similar positions within the clause and they are mutually exclusive: they never co-occur. Thus these four morphemes still form a loose paradigmatic set and together they embody a single subsystem of the grammar.

2.1. The individuating clitic =(u)ri

The clitic =*(u)ri* probably occurs in the widest set of environments of the four clitics and is also the most semantically consistent. Its primary to function is to individuate the referent of the host to which it is bound. Thus it puts one referent in profile with respect to a group. As mentioned in §4.4.3, this clitic is found with great frequency on kin terms on which it appears to have lexicalized. Thus this morpheme puts into profile one family member out of the otherwise undifferentiated family group, e.g. *bā=uri* 'the father' (as opposed to other family members). In example (4), a daughter and a stepdaughter are being discussed. The presence of the clitic profiles each independently, which reinforces the difference in identity and thus the contrast between them:

(4)   ***u=ri***   ekdam   moṭo   jur-eu
         this=IND   very   fat   be-3sFUT

         chiji   ***mica=uri***   gal-ai   jur-a
         1pINC.GEN   daughter=IND   skinny-BV   become-3sPST

         'This one will become very fat; our daughter has become skinny.'

This example also shows how the individuating morpheme is used to mark contrastive noun phrases. By individuating two referents in succession, they are thus contrasted.

The individuating function of this morpheme is also nicely illustrated in (5)–(6). The speaker is relating a time when he and two family members were required to go out in the middle of the night to observe a religious ritual. The speaker begins by identifying the family members by name. He then proceeds with the narrative as follows:

(5) āle isi **sõ-mā=uri** thi-gur tuŋ gut ju-en oŋ-ane
    then 1pEXC three-CL=IND one-CL FOC group be-PART go-PART

'Then the three of us went in one group...'

Here the individuating clitic differentiates the three men from the rest of the family. The focus particle *tuŋ* is marking the new information, highlighting the fact that they went in a single group. Later in the narrative, the speaker relates how the three were afraid as it was very dark and quite possible that they would encounter ghosts. They decided to walk single file and debated who will go in front. The result was related as follows:

(6) **ji=uri** hākhena jur-gi
    1s=IND front be-1sPST

'I was in the front.'

dāti=ku tāto dāi jur-a
middle=LOC Tato e.brother be-3sPST

'In the middle was Tato Dai.'

āle **likhana=ri** harkha bāhādur jur-a
then back=IND Harkha Bahadur be-3sPST

'Then in the back was Harkha Bahadur.'

In the first line, the clitic individuates the speaker out of the group of three men who are the primary characters at this point in the story. In the third line, the clitic individuates the position (the back as opposed to the front and middle). The second line lacks the clitic; the use of the clitic is not obligatory. Why speakers choose to specifically mark individuation in some cases but not in others is an area for further investigation.

Because of its individuating function, this morpheme is often found co-occurring with *thi-mā*, the numeral 'one' plus a classifier (here the classifier for animates). The clitic reinforces the fact that one referent out of a group is being profiled, as in example (7):

(7) dokhunuŋ jāl=lān phutk-ai jur-a
all net=ABL escape-BV be-3sPST

'All of them escaped.'

thi-mā=uri jāl=ku tuŋ coŋ-an con-a
one-CL=IND net=LOC FOC stay-PART stay-3sPST

'One of them was staying in the net.'

In individuating a referent, this morpheme often adds a sense of specificity or particularity that is not otherwise present:

(8) ām gā̃ū=ku=ri
that village=LOC=IND

'In that particular village...'

(9) nichi =uri
one.day=IND

'One particular day...'

(10) u khā=uri guntaŋ da-hat!
this talk=IND nobody.DAT PROH-say

'Don't say this particular thing to anyone!'

(11) [thae sona pi-e thāī =uri]$_{NP}$ dhan=e pokā dam
2hGEN flower plant-NR2 place=IND wealth=GEN packet have

'In that particular place where the flowers are planted, there is a packet of wealth (i.e. treasure).'

The individuating clitic usually occurs at the end of a noun phrase, after any casemarkers. It may also be found on adjectives within a noun phrase. This is particularly found with adjectivals that modify kin terms, e.g. *cicā=uri dāi* 'the younger of the elder brothers'. In this example, the noun defines a set of possible referents and the adjective with the clitic profiles one out of that group. The clitic may also be used on adjectivals to make them referential. In this function the clitic takes on a derivational quality, e.g. *cicā=uri* 'the small one'; *lāŋtāŋ=ri* 'the naked one'. Similarly, the clitic is often found with headless relative clauses (§17.2.1.1), where it also serves to reinforce the referential interpretation, e.g. *likhana hā-e-ri* [back bring-NR2=IND] 'the one you bring behind you'.[60]

It is also possible for the clitic =(u)ri to be bound to a non-finite verb, taking the whole clause as its scope. Of the eight examples of this in my data, three are found with a preceding adverbial clause ending in *ṭulle* 'until'. The individuating function seems to fit here, as one can see it as individuating the point in time at which the events in the clause occur, as in (12):

(12) ām   dhan   ma-kā-ṭulle=uri
     that wealth NEG-take-until=IND

'Until the time when that wealth is taken...'

In the other examples, the clitic occurs either in a participial or a temporal adverbial clause. Presumably a similar analysis is possible, that the clitic functions to individuate the particular time at which the events occur. This analysis fits the available examples; however, with such a small number of examples, it must remain tentative.

2.2. The extensive clitic =(u)ŋ

The extensive clitic =(u)ŋ is almost exactly opposite in meaning to the individuating clitic, a fascinating fact given that the two are in a tight paradigmatic relationship. Whereas =(u)ri profiles one element out of a group and thus individuates it, =(u)ŋ delineates a group of which a profiled element is a part. The interpretation and translation of this morpheme varies considerably depending on the lexical class and semantic qualities of the host.

When =(u)ŋ is bound to a noun phrase with a singular referent, it translates as 'also', as in examples (13)–(16):

(13) ji=ŋ   ū-i
     1s=EXT   go-1FUT

'I also will go.' (Said after others said they were leaving)

(14) **mica=ŋ**   āmta   bi   chor-ju
     daughter=EXT   3sDAT   give(INF) send-3sPST

'(He) gave his daughter also to him (i.e. in addition to the other things).'

(15) mā   ji=ŋ   [thamun je   yeŋ-a   thãĩ   tuŋ]_NP-OBL
     mother 1s=EXT   2hERG   work   do-NR2   place   FOC

>
> *ji=ŋ*   *je*   *yet-a*   *ū-i*
> 1s =EXT work do-PURP go-1FUT
>
> 'Mother, I also will go to work at the same place where you work.'

(16)   **āme=ŋ**   *hat-cu*
       3sGEN=EXT say-3sPST

> 'He said his also (i.e. asked his question in addition to the other man's).'

In these examples we can see that the clitic serves to link the referent of the noun phrase to which it is bound with another referent which has been previously mentioned. The two referents are related in being involved in the same type of event in the same way (both leaving, both working at the same place, etc.). Speakers sometimes use this clitic in specifically predicating parallels between referents. When they do this, all the noun phrases are cliticized, as in (17).[61]

(17)   **mā=ŋ**   *jawāni*   **dai=ŋ**   *jawāni*
       mother=EXT youthful e.brother=EXT youthful

> 'Mother is youthful, and elder brother is also youthful.'

In example (18), there are three noun phrases all marked with the extensive clitic. They together form a complex object of the verb *hār-* 'bring'. The repeated clitic emphasizes that the person running has all three referents in tow:

(18)   *āle*   **mantri=ŋ**   **mucā=ŋ**   *hirā=e*   **mālā=ŋ**
       then minister=EXT child=EXT diamond=GEN garland=EXT

       bwāt-ke   *hā-en*
       run-CAUS(PART) bring-PART

> 'Then running bringing the minister, the child, and the diamond garland...'

When *=(u)ŋ* is bound to a noun phrase that has a specifically plural referent, specified for plurality either by the plural affix or by a numeral plus classifier, the clitic emphasizes that the referents form a group. It thus translates as 'both' or 'all':

(19) *isi   sõ-mā=ŋ*   on-gu
    1pEXC three-CL=EXT go-1pPST

    'We all three went.'

(20) *āle ām   nis-mā =ŋ*   mwāt-a
    then that two-CL=EXT survive-3sPST

    'Then those two both survived.'

(21) *upista=ŋ*   bo   hā-en   bi-u
    these.DAT=EXT plate bring-PART give-IMP

    'Bring plates for all these.'

When a plural noun phrase with =(u)ŋ occurs with a negated verb, it means 'not even one' or 'not one of the X', where X refers to the numeral. This often occurs with the numeral 'one', as in (22):

(22) *bā̃ḍā=ku thi-gur=uŋ*   ma-da-i   don-ju
    pot =LOC one-CL=EXT NEG-exist-INF finish-3sPST

    'In the pot there was not even one (grain of rice) left.'

In the following example, the clitic occurs on a numeral within a genitive noun phrase, but the overall function is the same:

(23) *ŋā-mā   mica=e=ŋ*   bihā   ma-ju   ni
    five-CL daughter=GEN=EXT marriage NEG-be(3PA) yet

    'Not one of the five daughter's marriage had occurred yet.'

Again the extensive function emphasizes a group where each member has the same properties, in this case the fact that they were not involved in a particular activity or state.

The extensive clitic is also found with temporal adverbials. In this environment it indicates that the activity occurred over the entire time indicated by the adverbial:

(24) *ninpatti*   'daily'   *ninpatti=ŋ*   'every single day'
    lita khunu   'next day'   *lita khunu=ŋ*   'all the next day'
    cachi   'one night'   *cachi=ŋ*   'the entire night'

Similarly, when the clitic is combined with the demonstrative of quantity *uli* 'this much', we find *uli=ŋ* 'just this much'. In all these cases, the clitic functions to delimit an amount and to specify that the entire amount as a complete unit, and any point within that amount as being relevant to the predicate. This analysis also explains the use of *āmli=ŋ ka* [that.much=EXT ASS] to mark the end of a story. The demonstrative *āmli* 'that much' is circumscribed by the clitic and shown to contain the entire story; hence one can infer that the speaker has finished. The final element is the assertive particle discussed in §10.4.2.2

The clitic is also commonly used with the demonstrative of manner *ānthi* 'like that'. The combination *ānthi=ŋ* indicates 'just like that'. In this case we see that the manner is bounded and then extended to the new context.

The extensive clitic is also used to derive indefinite pronouns from interrogative pronouns (§5.4). This again fits with the function of the clitic in delimiting a set of all possible referents; any of the referents within the set (or none of the referents, if the verb is negated) will equally apply to the predicate.

(25) āpista **gunān=uŋ** phon-da mā-yā
  3pDAT who.ERG=EXT ask.for-PURP NEG-come

  'Nobody came to ask for them (in marriage).'

(26) **hāti=ŋ** āpat par-ai jur-sa
  what=EXT trouble touch-BV be-COND

  'If any trouble befalls you...'

Finally, the extensive clitic is found as an etymon in some forms of the quantifier *dokhunuŋ* 'all' (§8.2). Again the clitic has been used in the delimitation of a set.

3. Three particles with discourse function

There are three particles in Dolakha Newar which speakers have discourse-level functions. The particle *wā* is a marker of topic, while the particle *tuŋ* marks elements which are in focus. The particle *jukun* serves to significantly restrict the reference of arguments; it is less common than the other two. These three particles do not co-occur on the same noun phrase; neither do they co-occur with either of the clitics of individuation and extension.

3.1. The particle of restriction *jukun*

The particle *jukun* means 'only'. It thus emphasizes that the set of possible referents of the *jukun*-marked constituent excludes all others; hence the set is precisely delimited. While I have well over 150 examples in my discourse database of each of the other four morphemes, I have only 17 examples of *jukun*. Its use is illustrated in (27)–(29):

(27) ji   hātta kho=e   dāti=ku   jukun cō-i   mal-a
     1s   why   river=GEN middle=LOC   only stay-INF must-3sPST

'Why must I stay only in the middle of the river?'

(28) thābi thābi=ri jā   jukun ta-en
     top   top=IND   rice only put-PART

'In the top part, she only put rice...'

(29) dāju=n   jukun kām   yeŋ-an
     e.brother=ERG   only work do-PART

'Only the elder brother worked...'

I have one example of this particle occurring after a participial clause. The use of the particle results in a strict conditional interpretation holding between the clauses:

(30) kāsi oŋ-an   jal-ai   ju-en   jukun u   pāp kaṭaun-ai jur-a
     Kasi go-PART burn-BV   be-PART   only this sin cut-BV   be-3sPST

'Only by going to Kasi and burning (i.e. committing self-immolation) will this sin be cut from you.'

3.2. The topic particle *wā*

The particle *wā* is used to mark a topic. In other words, it is used to highlight a referent as especially being the entity to which the clause pertains. The topic particle is used primarily with noun phrases, although it can also be used with temporal adverbials and with non-finite clauses. Constituents marked with *wā* tend overwhelmingly to be clause-initial, although they may appear postposed after the verb. Topics also tend strongly to be grammatical subjects, but this is not an absolute. Some examples with the topic particle are given in (31)–(36):

(31) **dolakhā khã=e**   me wā da tuŋ ma-da
Dolakha language=GEN song TOP exist FOC NEG-exist

'There aren't any songs in the Dolakha language.' (i.e. 'As for songs in the Dolakha language, they don't exist.')

(32) **janta wā** ekdam pir lāg-ai jur-a
1sDAT TOP very worry touch-BV be-3sPST

'I am very worried.' (i.e. 'As for me, I am very worried.')

(33) **āu wā** mo-oŋ-gi. libi
now TOP NEG-go-1sPST later

'Now I didn't go. Later.'

(34) **jin wā** mebu tuŋ khõ-ui
1sERG TOP other FOC see-1sPA

'As for me, it was another I used to see.'

(35) **un wā** cher=na=ŋ khā lār-ju
this.ERG TOP head =INST=EXT talk talk-3sPST

'This one also started talking with his head.'

(36) **āmta wā** hirā=e jā bir-ju
3sDAT TOP diamond=GEN rice give-3sPST

'To him they gave the diamond rice.'

It is possible to have two arguments of a single clause marked with the topic particle, although I only have a few examples of this structure. In the following example, some boys are talking to their friend's father, and relating what he told them.

(37) [thae kae=n wā]$_{NP-A}$ [ista wā]$_{NP-R}$ [mula=ku
2hGEN son=ERG TOP 1pEXC.DAT TOP road=LOC

kwākarbeŋ=na kisi na-e]$_{NP-O}$ khā lār-ju
frog=ERG elephant eat-NR2 talk talk-3SPST

'Your son told us that in the road a frog ate an elephant.'

This seems to be the equivalent of using rising intonation on two NPs in a single clause in English, i.e. <u>Your son</u> told <u>us</u> that in the road a frog ate an elephant.

The topic particle is also used following an adverbial clause with the suffix *-nasin* 'when' (§20.2.3), or, more rarely, a participial clause (Chapter 19).[62] Interestingly, in all 20 of these examples, the verb is either a motion verb or a verb of visual perception, e.g. *sor-nasin* 'when (X) saw'. In all of these examples, some characters in the story are about to witness something surprising, usually an event which either resolves a situation established in the narrative or significantly moves the story forward. An example is given in (38):

(38)   *suntali=n*   **sor-nasin**   *wā*   *thi-mā*   *bãla-ku*   *onsāmi*
       Suntali=ERG   look-when   TOP   one-CL   beautiful-NR1   man

   pharsi=lān   *pita ye-en*   *coŋ-gu*   *khon-ai*
   pumpkin=ERG   out   come-PART   stay-NR1   see-3sPR

   'When Suntali looked, she saw a handsome man come out of the pumpkin.'

Just as, within a clause, the topic marker comes right before the crucial new information about the established topic, so at the level of the narrative, the topic marker is positioned just before the climactic points of the story.

3.3. The focus particle *tuŋ*[63]

The particle *tuŋ* occurs in a variety of environments, all of which can be considered to be focused. That is, elements marked by *tuŋ* constitute new and important information which is set against the backdrop of the presupposed information in the clause. Most of the constituents focused by *tuŋ* are noun phrases, although we also find this particle following demonstratives, adverbs, and some non-finite clauses. The vast majority of focused elements occur directly before the verb (including borrowed Nepali nouns in N-V compounds). The preverbal slot is thus the primary position for focused elements (see §14.2). In a few cases, the focused element is postposed, after the verb.

I will now provide examples of the focus particle. As the focusing function is only evident from the context in which it appears, I will precede each example with a brief outline of the context.

Example (39) was produced at a point in the discourse when two of the conversational participants have independently decided to leave the current gathering and go have dinner. One says to the other:

(39) **nāpa** **tuŋ** ū-i āle
together FOC go-1FUT then

'Let's go together then.'

The presupposed information is that the two will go; the focused information is the suggestion that they leave together.

In the next example, one speaker is considering which story to tell for the linguist's tape recorder. After discussing several alternatives, another speaker says:

(40) **ām** **tuŋ** lā-en bi-sin
that FOC tell-PART give-IMP

'Tell that one!'

What is presupposed is that the other speaker will tell some story. What is in focus is the particular story referred to by the demonstrative. Note that this focusing function serves to bring a strong sense of specificity to the focused item. Perhaps a better translation of the above example would be 'Tell that particular one'.

In discussing the assassination of Indira Gandhi, a speaker of the language produced the sentence given in (41):

(41) **gāḍ** coŋ-gu **tuŋ** syāŋ-an bi-e rā?
guard stay-NR1 FOC kill-PART give-NR2 Q

'Was it the guard who killed her?'

What is known is that Indira Gandhi has been assassinated by someone. The particle *tuŋ* marks the guard as the focus of the interrogative, marked by the particle *rā* at the end of the clause.

The following example was taken from a narrative relating a story about three sisters. While the lives of two of the sisters in the story were settled by their marriages to cooks, the fate of the third sister was resolved in this manner:

(42) thi-mā rājā=n **nāpa** **tuŋ** hā-en yer-a
one-CL king=ERG together FOC bring-PART come-3sPST

'A king brought (her) together with him and (they) came (to his palace).'

The king had already been introduced into the story, so the new information is that he brought her together with him. Later in the same story, the woman becomes pregnant. At this point her sisters (who have been living in relative poverty) say:

(43) isi   tuŋ con-da   ye-i
      1pEXC FOC stay-PURP   come-1FUT

   'We will come to stay.'

The presupposed information is that someone will come to stay with the sister to help her through childbirth and the beginnings of motherhood. This is culturally expected. The focused information is the identification of the two sisters as those who will come and stay with her.

   In the next example, a young man has just returned home with two women. His mother asks him who the women are and he replies:

(44) u   nis-mā   **thape** iri   tuŋ khyaŋ
      this two-CL   2HON   daughter.in.law FOC be

   'These two are your daughter-in-laws.'

One heuristic for determining whether or not information is focused is its ability to appear as answer to an information question (e.g. Payne 1997: 267); in this example it clearly does.

   The focused information does not have to be the only new information in a clause. In one recording session in the village, speakers took turns telling of their encounters with tigers in the woods (probably tall tales, as tigers reportedly don't roam so far north). One speaker produced the following sentence:

(45) **jana**   **hākhen** tuŋ   dhū   ithi   yeŋ-an   coŋ-an
      1sGEN   front   FOC   tiger like.this   do-PART   stay-PART

      coŋ-gu   ju-en   coŋ-a
      stay-NR1   be-PART   stay-3sPST

   'It turns out there was a tiger right in front of me, doing this.'

In this sentence, both the tiger and its behavior are new information, however, the speaker chooses to focus the location of the tiger – right in front of her – rather than the tiger itself (the whole conversation was about tigers) or its behavior. I have no examples of *tuŋ* occurring more than once in a single clause; if there are multiple pieces of new information, the speaker must decide which to focus.

A nice example of a focused adverbial is taken from the same narrative a bit later. The example in (46) was accompanied by the speaker standing and pantomiming her steps backwards:

(46) *ithi   ithi   ithi   ithi   li   tuŋ*
     this.manner this.manner this.manner this.manner back FOC

   yer-gi   ka
   come-1sPST ASS

   '(Going) like this, like this, like this, like this, backwards I came.'

Since walking backwards is a relatively unusual thing, it is understandable that it is focused. It also highlights the speaker's dilemma and her unwillingness to have the tiger at her back.

The focus particle may also be used after a non-finite clause, where it plays a very similar function. Consider the example in (47):

(47) *ām   misā bihā   yeŋ-an   ma-bir-nasin   tuŋ   ām sit-a*
     that woman marriage do-PART NEG-give-when FOC 3s die-3sPST

   'That woman died without having been given in marriage.'

The important point being communicated in this sentence is not that the woman died, a fact established in the preceding discourse, but her unmarried state at the time of her death.

In the following example, the focus particle has scope over a chain of two clauses joined by the participial construction. At this point in the narrative, the speaker is producing the voice of a character that has been ordered to have sex with a man she has never met so that she will conceive an heir to the throne. This sentence was produced in a single intonation unit:

(48) *ji wā chāi   yeŋ-an   bãlaske wāsti phi-en   tuŋ   ū-i*
     1s TOP makeup do-PART nicely   clothes wear-PART FOC go-1FUT

   'I will put on make up and dress nicely and go.'

What is in focus here is not the fact that she will go, but that she will go only after having prepared herself for her new lover by applying make-up and dressing nicely.

All of these examples clearly establish *tuŋ* as a particle that marks a focused constituent. What remains unclear is why a speaker decides to mark focused elements sometimes and not others. It is not the case that every clause or even every sentence has an element focused in this way, and there are many pieces of new information which speakers choose not to focus. The same question can be asked of the topic particle wā. While one can see why arguments marked with wā are topical, one can also see other topical arguments that are not so marked. It is clear that the answer to these questions lies in part on the interaction of these particles with each other and with the individuating clitic. Speakers employ the four of these as a unified system in the structuring of discourse, but I am only now beginning to glimpse how this complex interplay works. This is clearly a topic that would prove fruitful under further study.

4. Other particles

In addition to the particles above, there are several other particles which primarily occur at the peripheries of clauses and sentences. These can be roughly divided into clause-initial particles and clause-final particles, although the particle āle interestingly occurs in both positions, depending on the genre.

4.1. Clause-initial particles

The particles which occur in clause-initial position are listed in (49). The function of these particle is to express loose interpropositional relations across sentence boundaries. All but the first are borrowed from Nepali. I have only one or two examples of each, so they will not be further discussed.

(49) āle   'then; and then'
      natra   'or else'
      ani   'then'
      balla   'finally'
      baru   'in that case'
      tyasale   'therefore'
      tara   'but'

The particle āle occurs often in my data, both in conversational and narrative discourse. It has an interesting bimodal distribution: in narrative, it is used clause-initially, most commonly also sentence-initially; in interactional conversation, it is used primarily in sentence-final position at the ends of turns.

Within narrative discourse, āle is used most commonly at the beginnings of sentences that instantiate a new episode, although it may also be found after non-finite clauses when the following clause will move the storyline forward:

(50) **āle** litaŋ dosari jur-a
then again pregnant be-3sPST

'Then she became pregnant again.'

(51) **āle** mucā=ta besna kucin ṭi-en bi-e
then child=DAT very pinch pinch-PART give-NR2

ju-en con-a
be-PART stay-3sPST

'Then it turns out (he) pinched the child very hard.'

(52) **āle** nakchẽ on-gi
then Nakche go-1sPST

'Then I went to Nakche.'

In all of these examples, the events of the clauses which contain *āle* are all sequential with respect to the preceding discourse.

The particle *āle* is also found on clauses which summarize the result of preceding events, as in (53), or indicate that the previously narrated events are continued for some time, as in (54):

(53) **āle** ānthi coŋ-an con-a
then that.manner stay-PART stay-3sPST

'Then she was living like that.'

(54) **āle** ānthi jur-ŋa jur-ŋa
then that.manner do-when do-when

'Then, acting in that manner for some time...'

In these cases the particle has more of a resultative than a sequential function.

The particle *āle* serves as a cue from the speaker to the hearer about the structuring of the narrative, thus it has a "signpost" function, similar to that discussed in relation to the transitional continuity of intonation contours in §3.5. The particle stands outside of the substance of the narrative itself, that is, it is not part of the interwoven threads of argument structure, casemarking, pragmatic status, and clause combining.

As the position for *āle* in narrative is overwhelmingly at the beginning of a clause, it is quite striking that it is found utterance-finally in interactive conversational discourse. I do not have extensive recordings of this genre, so my data are limited. However, in the recordings that I do have, *āle* is used after short utterances which are used in negotiations between speakers and hearers about what is about to happen:

(55)   *isi=ŋ   ū-i   āle*
       1pEXC=EXT   go-1FUT   then

   'We'll both go then.'

(56)   *jā   na-en   yā   āle*
       rice eat-PART   come.IMP   then

   'Eat and come back then.'

(57)   *kesi   ū-i   hat-agu   āle?*
       tomorrow go-1FUT   say-2hPR   then

   'Did you say you will go tomorrow then?' (lit. 'Did you say: "I will go tomorrow" then.')

In other similar examples, however, the particle is sentence-initial. It would be interesting to study the functions and positioning of this morpheme in more interactional data.

4.2. Sentence-final particles

There are four particles which occur primarily after a non-embedded finite verb, but before any postposed arguments (§14.4). Some of these appear to have interactional functions and their meanings are difficult to specify.

4.2.1. The question particle *rā*

The most semantically transparent particle is the question particle *rā*. The question particle is used on questions which can be answered by a simple yes or no:

(58)   *dolakhā   khā   tuŋ   lā-eu   rā?*
       Dolakha language   FOC   tell-3sFUT   Q

   'Will (she) tell it in the Dolakha language?'

(59) thamu =ri   ānthi   ŋil-agu   **rā?**
     2HON=IND that.manner   laugh-2hPR   Q

   'Are you laughing like that?'

(60) dyābā thi-gur dam   **rā?**
     money one-CL   exist Q

   'Do you have one rupee?'

The question particle is also used with tag questions (§12.2.1.1).

I have a small number of examples where *rā* is used clause-internally after a noun phrase. It is used by the speaker to express significant doubts about the identity of a referent who is purported to have a role in an event. This can be seen as a type of question, but one which combines the interrogativity of the particle with a special focus on the NP. The result is the conveyance of disbelief. This strategy is exemplified in (61)–(62):

(61) kwākarbeŋ=na **rā** apaĩ   kisi   na-eu?
     frog=ERG   Q   this.big   elephant   eat-3sFUT

   'A frog will eat an elephant this big?'

(62) hāti   **rā** pāthi=e   pwākal=lān   pita ye-eu?
     elephant   Q   measuring.cup=GEN   hole=ABL   out   come-3sFUT

   'An elephant will come out of a pathi measuring cup?'

Another question particle, transparently related to the first, is *hārā*. I only have a small number of examples of this. It appears to be used to ask whether or not the material in the preceding clause is true, thus translates as 'Is it so'. It is pronounced with marked rising intonation. An example is given in (63):

(63) āme   tuŋ   gaḍ   hā   **hārā?**
     3sGEN   FOC   guard   EVID   Q

   'They say he was her guard, right?'

4.2.2. The assertive particle *ka*

The particle *ka* is found in my data almost entirely in conversational discourse and in first-person narratives. It does occur in my narrative texts, but in all but two of these examples, the particle occurs within embedded speech. This particle is thus primarily used in interactional contexts.

Speakers appear to use the particle *ka* primarily after clauses which relate facts which the speaker is asserting as true. The material preceding the particle is almost always a single clause relating a single fact:

(64)   kesi   yer-eu   **ka**
         tomorrow come-3sFUT ASS

         'He will come tomorrow.'

(65)   āu   ye-i   **ka**
         now come-1FUT ASS

         'Now I will come.'

(66)   tātā=n   u   lār-ai   **ka**
         e.sister=ERG this tell-3sFUT ASS

         'Tata tells this.'

(67)   āmu wā kok   **ka**
         that TOP crow ASS

         'That is a crow.'

In many cases, this morpheme appears to be used in future contexts, e.g. (64), where it contrasts with the particle *jeu* 'maybe' (the particle more commonly found with predictions which expresses a degree of doubt). In the following examples, *ka* is used with verbs which are in past tense but which actually are predictions. In the context of both of these cases, the speaker believes she is in mortal danger (from a ghost in one case and from a tiger in another). This use of the past tense signals the speaker's certainty that the end is near (§16.2.3); this certainty is accentuated by the use of the assertive particle:

(68)   āu   don-a   **ka**   ma-khe rā?
         now finish-3sPST ASS NEG-be Q

         'Now I'm finished, right?'

(69)   āu   syāt-cu   **ka**
         now kill-3sPST ASS

         'Now I'm dead.' (lit. 'Now it killed (me).')

Example (70) is the only biclausal example I have with this particle in my database. In the context, a child has just cried and someone has asked why. The material of the final clause (khor-a) is presupposed; what is asserted is the material of the first clause, the reason for the tears. In this example, the function of the construction appears to be the marking of focus:

(70) āmun hirā=e mālā khoŋ-an khor-a **ka**
 3sERG diamond=GEN garland see-PART cry-3sPST ASS

 'He saw the garland of diamonds and cried.'

Most of my examples where the particle *ka* occurs with past tense verbs are taken from first-person narratives which relate encounters with ghosts or tigers. It seems possible that the particle is being used to assert that the events really did occur (even though they may seem to some a bit far-fetched) or to lend a sense of immediacy to the narration:

(71) a bajai a bajai hat-agi **ka** jin=uri but=ta
 hey g.mother hey g.mother say-1sPR ASS 1sERG=IND ghost=DAT

 'I say to the ghost: "Hey grandmother, hey grandmother".'

(72) wā::: yet-cu **ka**!
 ONOM do-3sPST ASS

 He screamed: "Waaaaaaaa!".'

4.2.3. *The dubitative particle* jeu

Whereas the particle *ka* expresses the speaker's belief that assertion of the clause is true, the particle *jeu* does the opposite; it expresses the speaker's doubt. Speakers translate this particle as 'maybe' in English:

(73) ji gyāt-a haŋ-an sir-ai **jeu**
 1s fear-3sPST say-PART know-3sPR maybe

 'Maybe he knows I am afraid.'

(74) āle āmu chanta chanta=ŋ thõsi na-i bi-eu **jeu**
 then that 2sDAT 2sDAT=EXT meat eat-INF give-3sFUT maybe

 'Now maybe they will give you meat to eat.'

(75)   āu   nis-mā   didā =ŋ   sit-a   ***jeu***
       now   two-CL   e.brother=EXT   die-3sPST   maybe

'Now maybe (my) two elder brothers both died.'

4.2.4. The hearsay particle hā

The particle *hā* is evidential. It indicates that the source of the speaker's knowledge of the event is based on hearsay rather than on direct participation or observation. This function is nicely exemplified in the following example, taken from conversation:

(76)   āme   tuŋ   gāḍ   ***hā***   hārā?
       3sGEN   FOC   guard   EVID   Q

'I heard it was her own guard, is it so?'

The particle *hā* is used at the beginning of folk stories to indicate that the story is something that is commonly related but about which the speaker does not claim direct knowledge. The following phrase is formulaic for the first line of such narratives:

(77)   thi-gur   gāũ   da-u   ***hā***
       one-CL   village   exist-3PA   EVID

'There existed a village.'

Speakers vary in the degree to which they use this particle in narrative. Some speakers don't use it at all. Others use it only on the first few sentences which establish the setting and the characters. Some speakers also use it for the introduction of new significant characters or on events that are surprising. Others use it more liberally, presumably to allow maximum specification of the evidential source, and remove the speaker from being responsible for its truth. It is interesting to note that this morpheme is never found in first-person narratives, a fact which is easily explained, as the evidential source for those narratives is the speaker's experience.

4.2.5. The agreement particle nā

The particle *nā* has an interactional function. It is used primarily after imperatives, where it is produced with marked rising intonation. The function appears to be to elicit the addressee's agreement that he or she will follow the command. Because the addressee is given the opportunity to agree (or not), this particle softens the sense of command conveyed by the imperative. This function of the particle is illustrated in (78) and (79):

(78)   *thamun   har-sin   **nā**?*
       2hERG   say-IMP   AGR

       'You say it, okay?'

(79)   *ji   samj-ai   jur-sin   **nā**   mā?*
       1s   remember-BV   be-IMP   AGR   mother

       'Remember me mother, okay?'

I also have a few examples of this particle occurring after questions. In the following, the speaker is proposing that she and the addressee leave together, and so *nā* is appropriate for eliciting agreement:

(80)   *isi   nāpa   ū-i   **nā**?*
       1pEXC   together   go-1FUT   AGR

       'We'll go together, okay?'

Another example has this particle following *sir-amin* 'you know'. Although not after an imperative, the speaker seems to be using the particle to elicit from his friends agreement that he can tell them his story:

(81)   *chipista   thi-gur   khā   har-i   sir-amin   **nā**?*
       2pDAT   one-CL   talk   say-1FUT   know-2pPR   AGR

       'I'll tell you one thing, you know?'

A more detailed study of this particle and its interactive functions is warranted.

4.2.6.   The particle le

The particle *le* is another interactional particle which is used in many of the same environments as *ka*, *rā*, and *nā*: questions, imperatives and assertions. In questions, *le* may be used in information questions utilizing interrogative words (§5.3). This particle thus clearly contrasts with *rā*, which is used in yes/no questions (as discussed above). Both particles are found in the following utterance taken from a conversation. The first question requires an answer with specific information, but the second only a yes or no reply.

(82)   gu=ri   **le**?   cicā-u=ri   rā?
        which=IND   PRT   small-NR1=IND   Q

'Which one? The small one?'

Although *le* is sometimes used with information questions it does not always occur in this environment and I do not understand when a speaker chooses to use it and when not. The particles *rā* and *le* may also combine, producing *rā le*. I only have this in two examples and both entail yes/no questions. An example is given below:

(83)   har-i   sā-i   rā   **le**?
        say-INF   know-1FUT   Q   PRT

'Will I know what to say?'

I regret to say that the function of *le* when it is used in other environments remains opaque to me. It would be useful to work with a native speaker to contrast imperatives with *le* with imperatives with *nā*, and assertions with *le* with assertions with *ka*. My impression is that the meanings of all of these final particles are quite subtle and that a native speaker with training in linguistics is required before full illumination will be possible.

Chapter 11
Noun-phrase structure

1. Introduction

The noun phrase is a key constituent in the grammar of any language. It is obvious that noun phrases are crucial for establishing reference and for predicating stable properties in copular constructions. In Dolakha Newar noun phrases also carry the casemarkers that clarify the propositional relationship between the referents and the verb.

Noun phrases may contain a number of elements and have a wide variety of structures. The elements which occur when a noun phrase is headed by a noun are different than those which occur when a noun phrase is headed by a pronoun. Noun phrases can be coordinated, as can elements within the noun phrase. Noun phrases can also be put in apposition to one another and be embedded within one another. This chapter will spell out the details of this range of structures and, where possible, describe the functions that noun phrases of different structures play in discourse.

2. Elements of the noun phrase and their order

Noun phrases may contain a number of different lexical elements, which have been discussed in previous chapters. Table 34 lists the lexical elements of the noun phrase, with examples and cross-references to relevant sections:

Table 34. Lexical elements of the noun phrase

Element	Example	Translation	Section
Demonstrative	ām kehẽ=uri	'that younger sister'	§5.5
Genitive	mica=e sāŋat=pen	'daughter's friends'	§4.4.2.2
Relative	pali depān coŋ-gu kok	'crow staying on the roof'	§17.2.1
Adjectival	megu=ri mi	'other man'	§7
Quantifier	sõ-gur mec	'three chairs'	§8
Noun	ṭwāŋsona	'rhodedendron'	§4
Pronoun	chipen nis-mā=ŋ	'both of you'	§5.2

All of these elements are optional. This is because nominal referents do not have to be overtly mentioned in discourse; noun phrases are often omitted in connected speech. Also, there is not a single category on this list that is obligatorily present in every noun phrase; this includes the category of noun (as noun phrases may be headless).

In addition to the lexical elements of the noun phrase presented above, noun phrases also may contain the grammatical elements listed in Table 35:

Table 35. Grammatical elements of the noun phrase

Element	Morphemes	Section
Plural clitic	=*pen*, =*pista, etc.*	§4.4.1
Case clitic	=*na*, =*ta*, =*e, etc.*	§4.4.2
Clitic of individuation or extension	=*(u)ri* or =*(u)ŋ*	§4.4.3; §10.2
Topic or focus particle	*wā* or *tuŋ*	§10.3

These grammatical morphemes always follow the lexical elements and occur in the order presented. Note that the clitics of extension or individuation do not co-occur with the topic and focus particles (§10.2 and 10.3). The grammatical morphology of the noun phrase will not be further discussed in this chapter.

Turning to the combinatorial possibilities of lexical elements of the noun phrase, it should first be noted that pronouns and nouns behave differently in this regard. Pronouns are quite limited in the lexical categories they may co-occur with and in the ordering of those elements. Pronouns may be modified by quantifiers (especially numerals), which are consistently ordered after the pronoun, e.g. *chipen nis-mā=n* [2p two-CL=ERG] 'you two (ERG)'.

Noun phrases which have nominal heads or are headless are much more complicated structurally. The ordering of noun-phrase elements is relatively fixed. The only element which exhibits flexibility in its ordering is the quantifier, which can occur in three separate positions. Putting the quantifier aside for the moment, noun-phrase elements occur in the order represented in (1):

(1) Ordering of elements within the noun phrase
    (exclusive of quantifiers)
    1. Demonstrative
    2. Genitive
    3. Relative Clause
    4. Adjective
    5. Noun

Examples of noun phrases containing these elements in a variety of combinations are given in examples (2)–(9):

Section 2   Elements of the noun phrase   263

(2) Demonstrative-Noun
    ām   khunu
    that day

    'that day'

(3) Genitive-Noun
    hirā=e   jā
    diamond=GEN   rice

    'diamond rice'

(4) Relative Clause-Noun
    [thamun je   yeŋ-a]_REL ṭhãĩ
    2hERG   work do-NR2   place

    'place where you work'

(5) Adjective-Noun
    bã̄la-ku   onsā-mi
    beautiful-NR1   man-person

    'beautiful man'

(6) Demonstrative-Genitive-Noun
    ām   rājā=e   kae=n
    that king=GEN   son=ERG

    'that king's son'

(7) Demonstrative-Adjective-Noun
    u   anauṭhā   khā
    this strange   talk

    'this strange talk'

(8) Genitive-Adjective-Noun
    caitbar=e   ḍwā-ku   melā
    Caitbar=GEN   big-NR1   festival

    'big festival of Caitbar'

(9) Relative Clause-Adjective-Noun
[chanta bi-e]ᴿᴱᴸ   mā-sā-ku   mā-sā-ku   cijbij
2sDAT give-NR2 NEG-tasty-NR1 NEG-tasty-NR1 things

'untasty things that they give you'

Quantifiers can occur in three separate positions within the structure presented in (1): they can directly follow the demonstrative, and they can either directly precede or directly follow the noun. The latter means that in headless noun phrases the quantifier ends up in final position. It should be noted, however, that although there are three positions that the quantifier may occupy, there may be only one quantifier in any given noun phrase. We can incorporate the quantifier into the noun-phrase schema as in (10).

(10) Positional possibilities of the quantifier with respect to other noun-phrase elements
  1. Demonstrative
  2. Quantifier
  3. Genitive
  4. Relative Clause
  5. Adjective
  6. Quantifier
  7. Noun
  8. Quantifier

Demonstratives followed by quantifiers are exemplified in (11) through (13):

(11) Demonstrative-Quantifier
āpen sō-mā=ŋ
those three-CL=EXT

'all those three'

(12) Demonstrative-Quantifier-Noun
ām   thi-mnā jāki=uri
that one-CL uncooked.rice=IND

'that one grain of rice'

(13) Demonstrative-Quantifier-Relative-(postposed) Noun
u   nis-mā [likhana ha-e]ᴿᴱᴸ=ri]ɴᴘ₋ᴄs [gun]ᴄᴄ [misāmi=pen]ᴴᴱᴬᴰ ?
this two-CL behind   bring-NR2=IND   who   woman=PL

'Who are these two women whom you bring behind you?'

Example (13) is particularly interesting and highly unusual. It is a copular clause, although the copula itself has been omitted (§12.3). The head of the noun phrase which instantiates the copula subject has been postposed to clause-final position.

Although these examples clearly demonstrate that demonstratives precede quantifiers, it is much more common for quantifiers to occur in phrase-initial position without a preceding demonstrative. Phrase-initial quantifiers are especially common in noun phrases which constitute the first mention of a referent in the discourse, or a referent which is non-specific. Most commonly, the numeral one with a classifier occurs in this position, however other numerals and other quantifiers may also occur.[64] Examples are given in (14)–(19):

(14) Numeral-Noun (two times)
   thi-gur des=ku   thi-mā misāmi da-u
   one-CL country=LOC one-CL woman exist-3PA

   'In a country, there lived a woman.'

(15) Numeral-Genitive-Noun
   thi-gur dhan=e   pwāka
   one-CL wealth=GEN packet

   'a packet of wealth'

(16) Numeral-Numeral-Noun
   nis-gur sõ-gur   bākas
   two-CL   three-CL box

   'two or three boxes'

(17) Numeral-Adjective-Adjective-Noun
   thi-gur bãla-ku   hēga-u   sona
   one-CL   beautiful-NR1 red-NR1 flower

   'a beautiful red flower'

(18) Quantifier-Noun
   gatkeŋ mi=pista
   many   person=PL.DAT

   'many people'

(19) Quantifier-Genitive-Noun
dokhu sāŋat=e jā
all friend=GEN rice

'all the friends' rice'

The second position in which the quantifier appears is directly before the noun. I only have seven examples of this ordering, five where the quantifier is positioned between a genitive and a noun, and two where it is positioned between an adjective and a noun. When the quantifier precedes the genitive, there are two possible syntactic structures. First, the quantifier may modify the genitive noun, and the two together form a noun phrase which is then embedded as a modifier of the head. Example (19), *dokhu sāŋat=e jā* 'all the friends' rice', exemplifies this structure. The quantifier *dokhu* 'all' modifies *sāŋat* 'friend' and the two together form a phrasal constituent. This constituent is then embedded by the genitive clitic and modifies the head noun *jā* 'rice'. The structure can be represented as in (20):

(20) [[*dokhu sāŋat =e*]$_{NP}$ *jā*]$_{NP}$

In the second structure underlying a sequence of Quantifier-Genitive-Noun, the genitive forms a phrasal constituent with the head noun and this constituent is modified by the quantifier. This structure is exemplified by example (15), *thi-gur dhan=e pwākā* 'one packet of wealth'. In this example, the embedded genitive phrase consists only of a single word which modifies the head noun. These together form a phrasal constituent which is in turn modified by the numeral. This analysis is motivated by the semantic structure of the noun phrase. The genitive modifier expresses the content and hence the essential quality of the packet; thus the two nouns are closely linked semantically and structurally. This is represented in (21):

(21) [*thi-gur* [[*dhan=e*]$_{NP}$ *pwākā*]$_{NP}$]$_{NP}$

Thus we see that the Quantifier-Genitive-Noun order reflects two distinct structures: [[Quantifier-Genitive] Noun] and [Quantifier [[Genitive] Noun]]. The same is not true of the opposite order of modifiers. The order Genitive-Numeral-Noun has only one possible structure underlying it, that in which the numeral plus the noun together form a constituent which as a whole is modified by the genitive, i.e. [Genitive [Numeral Noun]]. This is true because a genitive cannot modify a numeral independently of the following noun, hence the genitive and the numeral alone cannot form a constituent. Consider the phrase *āme das mās* [3sGEN ten month] 'her ten months', which refers to a woman's term of pregnancy. The combination of the quantifier plus the numeral together specify the standard period of time for gestation, while the genitive makes it clear whose pregnancy is being discussed. The combination of the numeral and the noun together signal the concept of gestation; they are crucially related (and possibly lexicalized), so are not interrupted by the genitive noun phrase. Another example is *jana thi-mā mica* [1sGEN one-CL daughter] 'my one daughter'. The information provided by the numeral applies to the daughter alone; it contains information inherent in the following noun, much like *dhan=e pokā* above. By contrast, the genitive is establishing a relationship between the daughter and an external participant; hence it is positioned outside of the numeral-noun conjunct.

In my data, the most frequent order for adjectives and numerals is Numeral-Adjective-Noun. This follows from the same type of reasoning as above; the adjective is specifying an inherent aspect of the noun and so is positioned closer to it than a numeral (especially as numerals have broader-level discourse functions such as introducing new referents). I do have two examples of the numeral directly preceding the noun; one is given in (22):

(22)　ãku　　ekdam　bãla-ku　　　　ekdam　thi-gur　din　da-u　　hã
　　　there　very　　beautiful-NR1　very　　one-CL　　day　exist-3PA　EVID

'There it was a very beautiful day.'

This example was produced in a single intonation unit. However the adjective *bãla-ku* 'beautiful' is given a significant prosodic accent, with unusual elongation of the initial vowel, the effect of which is to intensify the concept of the beauty. The speaker then repeated the intensifier, which is quite unusual, and then the numeral and noun follow. Although two examples do not constitute sufficient data on which to base a generalization, the marked prosodic structure suggests that these example might involve the left dislocation of the adjectival phrase in order to give it special highlighting. More examples of this structure are needed before a full understanding of this ordering is obtained.

The final position for quantifiers is post-nominal. The quantifier is the only lexical noun-phrase element which may occur after the noun within the noun phrase. Although this ordering occurs with considerable frequency, it is difficult to find a single unifying analysis that explains the post-nominal positioning in every case. However, there are several patterns which emerge from the data. First, the numeral is more likely to follow a noun that denotes a kin term than a noun of another semantic category, e.g. *didā=pen nis-mā=ŋ* [e.brother two-CL=EXT] 'both older brothers', *ām kae mica sõ-mā=ta* [that son daughter three-CL=DAT] 'those three sons and daughters'. Second, the numeral is more likely to come after a noun if it has a genitive modifier, e.g. *lū=e bo thi-pta* [gold=GEN plate one-CL] 'one plate of gold'. As discussed above, the ordering Quantifier-Genitive-Noun reflects two possible syntactic structures; the postposing restricts the number of possible underlying structures to one (that where the quantifier modifies the combination of the genitive and the noun). This syntactic disambiguation may motivate the post-nominal ordering in such cases. Finally, the specification of a noun followed by a quantifier can have a topic-comment structure. The noun phrase up to and including the noun appears to establish a topic, which the quantifier plus the remainder of the clause comments upon:

(23) ām ṭhākkar āmli=ŋ nar-gi
that trouble that.much=EXT eat-1sPST

'Trouble, I experienced that much of it.'

(24) dāl pē-gur ŋa-gur jukun kururura hā-ke
dal four-CL five-CL only EXPR bring-CAUS.PART

'Of the lentils, only four or five he brought *kururura* (sound of lentils in a metal bowl).'

This suggests the possibility that there may be two noun phrases involved, that which establishes the topic, and the resumptive quantifier. It is unclear whether such an analysis can be justified in purely syntactic terms.

It should also be mentioned that numerals are likely to occur as the final element of noun phrases which are headless. In these examples, the numerals appear to function as the head in that they specify the individual who has the properties denoted by the modifiers, e.g. [*tiŋgriŋga*]_ADJ *thi-mā* [skinny one-CL] 'one skinny one', [*rāja=ke oŋ-gu*]_REL *thi-mā=n=ri* [king=ALL go-NR1 one-CL=ERG=IND] 'one who went to the king'.

3. Coordination

In addition to the variety of syntactic structures created by combining the lexical categories above, noun phrases may be further complicated by the process of syntactic coordination, which may occur at the level of the noun phrase or among noun-phrase elements.

Coordination is distinct from compounding (§4.3.1). Whereas compounding simply juxtaposes two nouns that together denote a single referent, coordination links two distinct noun phrases or noun-phrase elements, each with its own independent referent. In addition, coordination entails the use of a conjunction, usually *ho* 'and'. There is no native conjunction 'or' in Dolakha Newar; occasionally one of the Nepali morphemes with this meaning, *ki* or *aṭhewā*, are borrowed for this purpose.

When noun phrases are coordinated, they form one complex noun phrase, which receives only one casemarker.⁶⁵ A simple example, where the conjoined noun phrases each consist of a simple noun, is given in (25). A more complicated example involving the conjunction of headless noun phrases is given in (26). To clarify the structure of the construction, large brackets are used at the level of the coordinated noun phrase.

(25)　⌈[bobu]$_{NP}$　*ho*　[kae]$_{NP}$⌉ =n=ri
　　　⌊father　and　son　⌋ =ERG =IND

　　　'the father and son'

(26)　⌈[hāluwā chu-ku=ke　oŋ-gu]$_{NP}$ *ho* [bhānche=ke oŋ-gu]$_{NP}$⌉ =ta
　　　⌊haluwa cook-NR1=ALL go-NR1 and cook=ALL　go-NR1⌋ =DAT

　　　'the one who went with the haluwa cook and the one who went with the cook'

Note that this structure differs syntactically from apposition, where two coreferential noun phrases, each independently casemarked, are put into a single clause with no conjunction (discussed directly below).

Most of my examples of coordination are simpler than those given above, as the complex noun phrase is absolutive, hence unmarked for case, and the conjoined noun phrase consist of simple nouns. Some examples of coordinated structures within clauses are given in (27)–(29):

(27)　⌈[nās]$_{NP}$ *ho*　[sãpar]$_{NP}$ deŋ-an
　　　⌊nose　and　bun　⌋ cut-PART

　　　'Cutting off their noses and buns...'

(28)　⌈[hi]$_{NP}$ *ho* [dudu]$_{NP}$ yer-a
　　　⌊blood and milk　⌋ come-3sPST

　　　'Blood and milk came out.'

(29)　⌈[chi]$_{NP}$ *ho* [ji]$_{NP}$ wā dampat mil-ai　ju-en
　　　⌊2s　and 1s⌋ TOP spouse suitable-BV be-PART

　　　'You and I are suitable spouses...'

Coordination may also join elements that occur inside the noun phrase, specifically relative clauses, example (30), and genitive noun phrases, example (31).

(30) ⌈[*thamun yeŋ-a*]_{REL} ***ho*** [*jin yeŋ-a*] ⌉_{REL} *jāki*
⌊2hERG do-NR2 and 1sERG do-NR2⌋ uncooked.rice

'the rice which you earned and which I earned'

(31) Elicited
ām jana ⌈[*dāi=e*]_{NP} ***ho*** [*kīja=e*] ⌉_{NP} *chẽ*
that 1sGEN ⌊e.brother=GEN and y.brother=GEN⌋ house

'the house(s) of my elder brother and younger brother'

Example (31) may refer either to one house shared by both brothers or to two houses, one belonging to each.

It is also possible to conjoin just the nouns, and to use a single genitive casemarker at the level of the coordinated noun phrase, i.e. *ām jana* [*dāi ho kīja*]=*e chẽ*. [that 1sGEN e.brother and y.brother=GEN house] 'that house of my brothers'. A narrative example of this structure is given in (32):

(32) ⌈[*āmu parāsar risi*]_{NP} *ho* [*makche ganda*]⌉_{NP} =*e ritidān*
⌊that Parasar Risi and Makche Ganda⌋ =GEN intercourse

'the intercourse of Parasar Risi and Makche Ganda'

Quantifiers are not coordinated in my data. Instead, quantifiers simply follow one another in sequence, e.g. *jāki pē-gar ŋā-gar* [rice five-CL six=CL] 'five or six grains of rice'. Similarly, adjectives may follow one another in sequence and do not require syntactic coordination, e.g. *bãla-ku hēga-u sona* [beautiful-NR1 red-NR1 flower] 'beautiful red flower'. Conjoined demonstratives are not attested in my data.

4. Apposition

Another structure which is not uncommon in my discourse data is apposition. Apposition involves the predication of two noun phrases, each of which refer to the same referent. It differs from coordination in three ways. First, in appositive structures the two noun phrases are coreferential. Second, it does not involve a conjunction. Third, each of the noun phrases carries its own casemarker. Most examples of apposition in my discourse data do not have an intonational boundary between the appositive noun phrases, although some do. The length of the noun phrase could well be one factor in determining this, with longer apposed noun phrases more likely to have an intonational boundary than shorter apposed noun phrases. Apposition appears to be used when the speaker wants to provide additional clarification about the identity of a referent. Examples are given in (33)–(37). Note that in (34) the second appositive noun phrase involves coordination:

(33) [jin phoŋ-a misā]$_{NP}$ [jin khoŋ-a keṭi wā]$_{NP}$
1sERG ask.for-NR2 woman 1sERG see-NR2 girl TOP

khe tuŋ ma-khe
be FOC NEG-be

'This is not the woman I asked for (in marriage), the girl whom I saw.'

(34) [isi]$_{NP}$ [bā ho ji]$_{NP}$ gãū=ku on-ŋasin
1pEXC father and 1s village=LOC go-when

'When we, father and I, went to the village.'

(35) [ota]$_{NP}$ [parāsar risi=ta]$_{NP}$ kho tār yeŋ-an bi-u
3sDAT Parasar Risi=DAT river cross do-PART give-IMP

'Ferry him, Parasar Risi, across the river.'

(36) [āmu keṭi nāpa]$_{NP}$ [āmu si-ku misā nāpa]$_{NP}$
that girl ASSOC that die-NR1 woman ASSOC

ritidān ju ju-en con-a
intercourse happen(NR1) be-PART stay-3sPST

'It happened that he had intercourse with that girl, with that dead woman.'

Appositive noun phrases may also be postposed (§14.4):

(37) [jāri=ta]$_{NP}$ sat-ai mal-a [āmta wā]$_{NP}$
b.in.law=DAT invite-BV must-3sPST 3sDAT TOP

'We must invite my brother in law, him.'

5. Lists

In addition to the structures of coordination and apposition, noun phrases may also be simply juxtaposed in a list. Lists of noun phrases differ from coordinated structures in that they do not form a single noun phrase and do not involve a conjunction. Lists differ from apposition in that the noun phrases are not coreferential. The following example includes a list of six noun phrases followed by *ānagu,* the demonstrative of type, which appears to serve a summary function:[66]

(38) [*kurāmuni*]$_{NP}$ [*ger*]$_{NP}$ [*baji*]$_{NP}$ [*cāku*]$_{NP}$ [*cāklat=pen*]$_{NP}$
condensed.milk ghee beaten.rice sweets chocolate=PL

[*ekdam sā-ku sā-ku phalphul=pen*]$_{NP}$ **ānāgu** *jukun*
very tasty-NR1 tasty-NR1 fruit=PL like.that only

pita kā-en bir-ai
out take-PART give-3sPR

'Dairy products, ghee, beaten rice, sweets, chocolates, very tasty tasty fruits, only things like that (he) takes out and gives (her).'

It is possible for lists to occur independently of the clause, that is, without playing the role of arguments. In example (39) the speaker has just related the birth of three sons. She then uses the list as a summary and a reminder to hearer what the three sons were named. Each name is in its own intonation unit, with rising intonation on the first two, and falling on the last. Thus the prosodic structure provides the list with internal coherence. (The symbol // indicates a marked-rising terminal pitch contour; the symbol \ indicates a falling terminal pitch contour).

(39) *bidur* // *paṇḍuk* // *dirṭarasṭra* \
Bidur Panduk Dirtarastra

'Bidur, Panduk, Dirtarastra.'

6. Noun-phrase embedding

This chapter has already illustrated some examples where noun phrases occur embedded within other noun phrases. The genitive construction involves such embedding as the phrase itself contains a noun phrase which may be elaborated to any size or structure. For example in (40) the genitive noun phrase consists of a demonstrative, a noun and a postposed numeral:

(40) [[āmu sāŋat thi-mā=e]ₙₚ jā]ₙₚ
      that friend one-CL=GEN rice

      'that one friend's rice'

The embedding of a genitive phrase into a noun phrase constitutes a recursive structure, as it is possible to embed a genitive phrase into a noun phrase which is within another genitive phrase repeatedly. I have no examples where this goes beyond two levels of embedding:

(41) [[[syeti tātā=e]ₙₚ mica=e]ₙₚ chẽ]ₙₚ
      Syeti Tata =GEN daughter=GEN house

      'Syeti Tata's daughter's house.'

Noun phrases within genitive phrases may also contain an embedded relative clause:

(42) [[[jin mega miŋe hā-e]ᵣₑₗ jāki=e]ₙₚ jā]ₙₚ
      1sERG yesterday before bring-NR2 rice=GEN rice

      'the cooked rice of the uncooked rice which I brought yesterday and before'

And of course, relative clauses themselves may be highly complex, actually constituting relative "structures" of multiple clauses (see §19.3.2).

I have only one example in which a postpositional phrase is embedded as a modifier of a noun. It is given in (43). The postposition is *bāre* 'about', which is borrowed from Nepali. I would thus consider this to be a marginal structure in Dolakha Newar:

(43) [u tu [nis-gur simā=e bāre]ₚₚ thi-gur bãla-ku bākhan]
      this FOC two-CL tree=GEN about one-CL beautiful-NR1 story

      'this one beautiful story about two trees'

The modification of nouns by postpositional phrases normally requires an intervening verb. For example, one would not say *jana hākhen mi* [1sGEN front person] for 'the person in front of me', instead one would use the verb *con-* 'be at; stay' embedded into a relative clause, e.g. *jana hākhen coŋ-gu mi* [1sGEN front stay-NR1 person] 'the person who is in front of me'.

7. Summary of noun-phrase structures

This chapter has illustrated a wide range of noun-phrase structures in Dolakha Newar. The great range of attested structures can be attributed to three properties of noun phrases: the positional range of the quantifier, the coordination of noun phrases, and the embedding of noun phrases. The latter two mechanisms are the ones which give the greatest range of structures, as they allow for the construction of complex noun phrases from simple noun phrases. Coordination and embedding differ in that coordination involves a conjunction and coordinates two noun phrases at the same level of structure, whereas embedding involves the use of a genitive noun phrase as a modifier of another noun. These two structures can then be differentiated from apposition and lists, both of which put distinct noun phrases in sequence without syntactically combining them to form a complex phrase. Whereas apposition involves two noun phrases which are coreferential, lists involve noun phrases which refer to distinct referents.

Chapter 12
Clause types

1. Introduction

In this chapter, I will discuss the six major clause types in Dolakha Newar: copular clauses, which have two core arguments related by a copular verb; verbless clauses, which have two core arguments but lack a copular verb; intransitive clauses, which have a single core argument; dative-experiencer clauses, which have one or two core arguments, one a semantic experiencer in dative case; transitive clauses, which have two core arguments; and ditransitive clauses, which have three. For each clause type, I will outline the clause structure, the casemarking of elements, the word order, and other issues which arise.

2. Copular clauses

Copular verbs are those verbs which are relational in function, and serve to relate two arguments, a copula subject (CS) and a copula complement (CC), within a single clause (Dixon 2004). Copular verbs are relational by nature, and as such are semantically devoid of specific referential content. Copular clauses are similar to intransitive clauses in that they tend to lack prototypical properties of transitive verbs: they are non-dynamic, do not involve volition or agency of an argument, do not involve affected objects, and are not kinetic (Hopper and Thompson 1980). On the other hand, copular clauses differ from intransitives in allowing two arguments. These arguments are not, however, equivalent to the subjects and objects of transitive verbs in either their grammatical or their semantic properties.

The structure of a copular clause in Dolakha Newar is: [CS] [CC] COPULA. The construction is striking in the regularity of the positioning of the copula complement directly in front of the copular verb. Other clausal elements, such as temporal adverbs, generally precede the copula subject, although they occasionally occur between the copula subject and the copula complement.

There are two copular verbs in Dolakha Newar: the highly irregular *khyaŋ*, and the regular r-stem verb *jur-*. The latter also functions as an intransitive verb as discussed in §12.2.2.1. The functions of these verbs include equation, identity, and attribution. It is common for copular verbs cross-linguistically to also code existence, location, and possession. In Dolakhae these functions are coded with an intransitive verb *dar-*, discussed in §12.4.1 below.

2.1. The copula *khyaŋ*

The copula *khyaŋ* is morphologically irregular, as it does not inflect for tense, person, or number. The forms of the verb which I have recorded are given in (1); see also §6.7.1:

(1) *khyaŋ ~ kheŋ ~ khyaū ~ kheū*   Present Affirmative
     ma-khe   Present Negative
     khya-u ~ khe-u   NR1

It is important to note that this verb only has present-tense forms; copular clauses in any other tense must use the verb *jur-*. This copular verb negates, but does not take any other prefixes or causative inflection. The nominalized form is the only non-finite form attested; to use copular clauses in complex sentences it is necessary to use *jur-*, which has the full range of non-finite forms used in clause linkage.

The following examples illustrate the copula being used with a first-person copula subject (2), and with a third-person-plural copula subject (3). Note that the form of the copula does not change, indicating that there is no agreement for person or number:

(2) [*ji*]$_{cs}$ [*chana kaimu*]$_{cc}$ **khyaŋ**
     1s   2sGEN husband   be

   'I am your husband.'

(3) [*u nis-mā*]$_{cs}$ [*chana dāju*]$_{cc}$ **khyaŋ**
     this two-CL   2sGEN e.brother   be

   'These two are your brothers.'

One function of the copula *khyaŋ* is to state the identity of a referent, as in (2) above, or to predicate that two noun phrases, the copula subject and the copula complement, refer to a single referent, as in (3) and (4)–(5) below. In both types of example, the copula complement contains a noun phrase:

(4) [*jin   phoŋ-a   misā*]$_{cs}$ [*jin   khoŋ-a*
     1sERG ask-NR2 woman   1sERG see-NR2

   keṭi wā]$_{cc}$ **khe tuŋ ma-khe!**[67]
   girl TOP   be FOC NEG-be

   'The woman whom I asked (to marry) is not the girl whom I see!'

(5)   [mucā=pen na-u]$_{cs}$ [u   he]$_{cc}$ **khyaŋ**
        child=PL eat-NR1   this SPEC   be

        'The one who eats children is this very one.'

Note that neither the copula subject nor the copula complement is casemarked.

The verb *khyaŋ* is also used in constructions with predicate adjectives. In these constructions the copula complement is filled by an adjective. In (6) below, the copula complement is a native Dolakhae verbal adjective; in (7) it is an adjective borrowed from Nepali:

(6)   [āmu mandir]$_{cs}$ [bãla-ku]$_{cc}$ **khyaŋ**
        DEM temple   beautiful-NR1   be

        'That temple is beautiful.'

(7)   [būsi ho twãŋsona]$_{cs}$ [nikkai prakhyāt]$_{cc}$ **khyaŋ**
        Bunsi and Rhodedendron   very   popular   be

        'Bunsi and Rhodedendron are very popular.'

Finally, it is also possible for the copula complement to contain a purpose clause. This construction is quite rare in my data:

(8)   [osai   ci   khursāni]$_{cs}$ [chanta na-i-ta]$_{cc}$ **khyaŋ**
        this.here salt chili   2sDAT   eat-INF-PURP   be

        'This here ground salt and chilis are to eat you (with).'

For all three of these functions, stating identity, equating noun phrases, and predicating attribution, it is also possible to use a verbless clause (see below). In general, the use of verbless clauses is the unmarked structure for these functions, and the use of the copular verb is emphatic, emphasizing the speaker's belief in the truth of the statement.

2.1.1. *Additional functions of* khyaŋ

The copula *khyaŋ,* and its negative counterpart *ma-khe,* have an additional function which is to predicate truth or falsehood. These examples have only one argument (S), so these clauses are technically intransitive:

(9)   [u   khā]ₛ khyaŋ   rā   ma-khe   rā?
      this talk   be.true Q   NEG-be.true Q

   'Is this talk true or not true?'

(10) lo   [chana khā]ₛ **khyaŋ**
      EXCL   2sGEN   talk   be.true

   'Oh, your talk is true.'

(11) ām   chẽ=e   dani=n   rāk   yeŋ-an
      that house=GEN   owner=ERG   anger do-PART

      "ma-khe"   hat-ai!
      NEG-be.true   say-3sPR

   'The owner of that house became angry and said: "It isn't true!".'

(12) **ma-khe-u**   ju-en   con-a
      NEG-be.true-NR1   be-PART   stay-3sPST

   'It turned out not to be true.'

Related to this meaning of *khyaŋ* is the use of the verb in forming tag questions. Both the forms *khyaŋ rā* [be.true Q] 'Is it so?' and its negative counterpart *ma-khe rā* [NEG-be.true Q] 'Isn't it so' are found. These are generally set off into separate intonation units. The following two examples are taken from conversational data:

(13) Speaker 1: "āmta   syāŋ-an   ām rājā ju-i"
                 3sDAT   kill-PART 3s king become-FUT

                 ha-ku   ju-en.   con-a
                 say-NR1   be-PART   stay-3sPST

      'They said: "The one who kills her will be king".'

      Speaker 2: mantri,   **ma-khe**   rā?
                 minister   NEG-be   Q

      'Minister, wasn't it?'

(14) depān   con-a   **ma-khe**   rā?
      on.top   stay-3sPST   NEG-be.true   Q

   '(He) stayed on top, isn't that right?'

In narrative, tag questions are often used by the narrator to check to see if the audience has understood:

(15) sor-ŋasin   mica   siŋ-an   con-a   **ma-khe**   rā?
      look-when   daughter die-PART stay-3sPST NEG-be.true Q

'When they looked, their daughter was dead. Isn't that so?'

(16) bimesor thākur nakas utpatti   ju-gu   **khe**   **rā?**[68]
      Bimsen   Lord   first creation be-3PA   be.true   Q

'Lord Bimsen was his (own) first creation. Right?'

Also related to the meaning of *khyaŋ* as 'be true', is the use of the copula in an emphatic construction. This construction emphasizes the speaker's belief in the truth or falsehood of the proposition being expressed. The copula follows a clause nominalized with either NR1 or NR2; this is thus a direct grammaticalization of the intransitive use of *khyaŋ* to predicate truth or falsehood. In this construction the subject noun phrase is replaced by a nominalized clause:

(17) [chana nimtiŋ chuŋ-a]ᴄʟ₋ₛ   **ma-khe!**
      2sGEN   benefit cook-NR2   NEG-be.true

'This is not cooked for your benefit!'

(18) ākheri=ku [mā=n   ho   dāi=n   hātiŋ
      end=LOC   mother=ERG   and   e.brother=ERG   nothing

      pāp yeŋ-a]ᴄʟ₋ₛ   **ma-khya-u**   ju-en   con-a
      sin do-NR2   NEG-be.true-NR1   be-PART   stay-3sPST

'In the end, it turned out that the mother and elder brother were not acting sinfully.'

2.2. The copula *jur-*

Since the copula *khyaŋ* is extremely limited morphologically, it cannot perform all the functions that verbs normally perform in Dolakhae. The verb *jur-* on the other hand, makes up for the deficiency of *khyaŋ* as it is non-defective, so can indicate different tenses, be causativized, and participate in clause linkage through its non-finite morphology.

The copula *jur-*, like *khyaŋ*, predicates identity, equation, and attribution. Also, like the other copula, its copula complement may contain a noun phrase or an adjective. The copula *jur-* is used instead of *khyaŋ* to indicate entrance into a state in the past or the future. Hence it is often best translated as 'become':

(19) āle [kaimu]_{cs} [subbā]_{cc} *jur-a*
      then husband   official   become-3sPST

   'Then my husband became an official.'

(20) [makche ganda=e   nām]_{cs} [sathai woti]_{cc} *jur-a*
      Makche Ganda=GEN name   Sathai Woti   become-3sPST

   'Makche Ganda's name became Sathai Woti.'

(21) [buḍā]_{cs} [besna pachuta]_{cc} *ju-en*
      old.man   very   remoseful   become-3sPART

   [jāŋal]_{cc} *ju-en*   bo-en   on-a
   bird   be-PART fly-PART   go-3sPST

   'The old man became very remorseful, he turned into a bird, and flew away.'

(22) āu   [thika]_{cc} *jur-a*
      now just.right   be-3sPST

   'Now everything is just right.'

(23) āle   [lyāsi   misā]_{cc} *jur-a*
      then young   woman   be-3sPST

   'Then she became a young woman.'

The copula *jur-* is also used instead of *khyaŋ* to indicate past states which do not continue into the present. In such cases the verb is in past-anterior tense:

(24) [optecā]_{cc} *ju*   ām   tākku
      small   be(3PA) that time

   'He was small (i.e. a child) at that time.'

(25) [ām]_{cs} [tuhurā]_{cc} *ju*
      3s   orphan   be(3PA)

   'He was an orphan.'

(26) [dāju=ri]_cs [calākh]_cc **ju** hã
 e.brother=IND clever be(3PA) EVID

 'The elder brother was clever.'

(27) [pharsi=e chē]_cs [suntali=e chē=lān]_OBL [ṭāen]_cc **ju**
 pumpkin=GEN house Suntali=GEN house=ABL far be(3PA)

 'The pumpkin's house was far from Suntali's house.'

Finally, *jur-* is used instead of *khyaŋ* in any case when a non-finite form is called for to produce structures of clause linkage.

(28) [bidur]_cs [ghartini=e kae]_cc ***ju-en***
 Bidur house.servant=GEN son be-PART

 'Bidur being the son of a house servant...'

(29) [āmu]_cs [dwā-ku]_cc ***ju-ene*** pāŋ simā bur-a
 3s big-NR1 become-PART fruit tree grow-3sPST

 'It became big and grew into a fruit tree.'

(30) simā=ku [pharsi]_cs [arai]_cc ***ma-ju-en*** kota jut-a
 tree=LOC pumpkin stable NEG-be-PART down fall-3sPST

 'The pumpkin was not stable on the tree and fell down.'

(31) libi [dosari]_cc ***ju-eni*** "isi tuŋ con-da
 later pregnant become-PART 1pEXC FOC stay-PURP

 ye-i" hat-cu
 come-1FUT say-3sPST

 'Later, she became pregnant and they said: "We will come to stay".'

2.2.1. *Other functions of* jur-

The verb *jur-* has a number of other functions in the language. Most importantly, it functions as an intransitive verb to indicate that something happens or occurs. The structure of this construction is intransitive, i.e. [NP]_s *jur-*. If an affected argument is present, it occurs in dative case as an oblique noun phrase, positioned before the subject:

(32) hāti **ju?**
what happen(3sPA)

'What happened?'

(33) bihā **ju-e** khā lā-u
marriage happen-NR2 talk tell-IMP

'Tell the story of how your wedding happened (occurred).'

(34) thijita dukha **jur-a**
1pINC.DAT trouble happen-3sPST

'Hardship/trouble happened to us.'

(35) e bā thaeta hāti **jur-a?**
hey father 2hDAT what happen-3sPST

'Hey father, what happened to you?'

A related use of *jur-* is to predicate the passage of time. In this case, the subject noun phrase denotes a particular time or a period of time:

(36) balni **jur-a**
evening become-3sPST

'It became evening.'

(37) pā̃ch cha sāl **jur-a**
five six year pass-3sPST

'Five or six years passed.'

I also have two narrative examples where *jur-* has a locational function. These are the only two attested examples in my data, and they both occurred in the same text, so were produced by the same speaker. Generally location is predicated by the existential verb *dar-*.

(38) dāti=ku tāto dāi **jur-a**
middle=LOC Tato e.brother be-3sPST

'In the middle was Tato Dai.'

(39) ji=uri   hākhena **jur-gi**
      1s=IND   front   be-1sPST

  'I was in front.'

Finally, the verb *jur-* is used to incorporate intransitive Nepali verbs into the Dolakhae morphological structure. See §6.3 for more details.

3. Verbless clauses

All of the primary functions of the copular clauses – predicating identity, equation and attribution – are also performed by verbless clauses. Like copular clauses with *khyaŋ*, verbless clauses may only be found in present tense contexts and in environments where non-finite, negative, causative or other verbal morphology is not required. When eliciting simple equational clauses from consultants, such as 'My name is Kalpana', the initial response from the consultant is a verbless clause:

(40) [jana   nām]cs   [kalpanā]cc
      1sGEN   name   Kalpana

  'My name is Kalpana.'

When asked whether *khyaŋ* is also acceptable, consultants readily produce it but state that its use is emphatic.

Verbless clauses may be thought of as a variant of copular clauses. This analysis seems preferable to considering it to be an entirely different structure, since both copular clauses and verbless clauses involve two arguments, and since in both types the second argument can be realized either as a noun phrase or as an adjective. The simplest analysis is to assume that the two are structurally parallel and that verbless clauses consist of copula subjects and copula complements in that order:

(41) [makche ganda]cs [jana   nām]cc
      Makche Ganda   1sGEN   name

  'Makche Ganda is my name.'

(42) [āme   nām]cs [hāti]cc ?
      3sGEN   name   what

  'What is her name?'

(43) [āmu wā]_cs [hābi tuŋ]_cc ka
      3s   TOP   before FOC   ASS

   'She (was the one) before.'

(44) [upen nis-mā]_cs [gusṭule bā̃la-ku]_cc le
      3p   two-CL   how.much beautiful-NR1 PRT

   'They two are so beautiful.'

(45) Elicited
      [ām]_cs [pujāri] _cc
      3s   priest

   'He is a priest.'

4. Intransitive clauses

Intransitive clauses have a single core argument, the S, which is also the grammatical subject of the clause (see §13.2). Intransitive subjects are not case-marked, hence are absolutive. Subjects generally precede the verb in intransitive clauses, although this order is not absolute, see §14.4. Other elements, such as oblique noun phrases and adverbials, commonly occur in these clauses.

The basic structure of the intransitive clause is: [NP]_s V_INTR. All intransitive clauses share this structure. A number of intransitive clauses are illustrated in (46) through (61). These illustrate intransitive verbs of a variety of semantic types:

(46) [māji]_s **sit-a**
      boatman   die-3sPST

   'The boatman died.'

(47) āle [ām nis-mā=ŋ]_s   **mwāt-a**
      then that two-CL=EXT   survive-3sPST

   'Then the two both survived.'

(48) [kok]_s ānthi   **hal-a**   ka
      crow   that.manner call.out-3sPST   ASS

   'The crow called like that.'

(49) [mucā]ₛ hātta **khor-a?**
child   why   cry-3sPST

'Why did the child cry?'

(50) [tilo kāki]ₛ ma-ḍiŋ-gu   ni   ju-en   **con-a**
Tilo aunt   NEG-sleep-NR1 yet   be-PART stay-3sPST

'It turned out that Tilo Auntie was not asleep yet.'

(51) [thamu=ri]ₛ ānthi   **ŋil-agu**   rā?
2h=IND   that.manner   laugh-2hPR   Q

'Why are you laughing like that?'

(52) ḍo   tuŋ   **mo-ḍoŋ-gi**
stand FOC   NEG-stand-1sPST

'(I) didn't stand up at all.'

(53) [dokhu sāŋat=e   jā]ₛ   **but-a**
all   friend=GEN   rice   cook-3sPST

'All the friends' rice was cooked.'

(54) āle   [āpe   naita tŏita]ₛ **gat-a**
then 3pGEN   food drink   enough-3sPST

'Then their food and drink was enough.'

(55) āle   [pharsi]ₛ   **tapjyāt-a**
then pumpkin   break-3sPST

'Then the pumpkin broke.'

(56) āle   ninpatti [āmu cilā]ₛ **jor-a**
then daily   that goat   graze-3sPST

'Then that goat grazed every day.'

(57) [chi] hātta **gyāt-an?**
2s   why   fear-2sPR

'Why do you fear?'

(58) āle [mucā=pen]ₛ din prāti din ḍwākar-hin
then child=PL day by day grow-3pPST

'Then the children grew day by day.'

(59) basanta ritu=ku [twāŋsona]ₛ bā̃laske hor-a
spring season=LOC rhodedendron beautifully bloom-3sPST

'In the spring season, the rhodedendron blooms beautifully.'

(60) lāj cār-agi
shy feel-1sPR

'(I) feel shy.'

(61) āle [āme mikhā]ₛ chor-a
then 3sGEN eye burn-3sPST

'Then his eyes burn.'

There are two subtypes of intransitive clauses which deserve more detailed discussion. The first is the set of existential, possessive and locational clauses which share a common existential verb *dar-*. The second is the set of intransitive clauses denoting motion.

4.1. Existence, location, and possession

The verb *dar-* is the existential predicate of Dolakha Newar. In earlier work (Genetti 1994, 2003a), I referred to this as a copula because it has functions commonly coded by copular verbs in the languages of the world, namely existence, possession, and location, and because it is highly irregular morphologically, like *khyaŋ*, but unlike the other intransitive verbs. After further reflection, however, I now consider *dar-* to be an intransitive verb. The reason for this is that it does not generally occur in a structure which can be analyzed as having both a copula subject and a copula complement. Existential and possessive examples have only one argument. Locational examples do have a second NP, but it is almost always casemarked as locative or followed by a locative postposition, hence is oblique. One can thus analyze the locational examples as intransitive clauses with an oblique locative noun phrase and an S argument, parallel in structure to, for example, a motion verb with a locative noun phrase:

(62) [āmu ŋā=e pyāṭā dupān]₀ʙʟ [hirā=e mālā]ₛ **da-u**
that fish=GEN stomach inside diamond=GEN necklace exist-3PA

'The diamond necklace was in the stomach of that fish.'

(63) [ām]ₛ [hāluwā chu-ku=ke]₀ʙʟ **on-a**
3s haluwa cook-NR1=ALL go-3sPST

'She went to the haluwa cook.'

If one were to consider *dar-* to be a copula, one would need to allow copula complements to contain locational noun phrases. However, as noted in the discussion of copula complements, copular constructions are striking in the regularity of their word order: the copula subject always precedes the copula complement. In locational clauses on the other hand, the locative-marked NP may either precede or follow the copula subject. This flexibility of word order is also found with intransitive clauses, but not with copular clauses. This is thus another reason to consider *dar-* to be an intransitive verb, rather than a copula complement.

It should be noted that there are a couple of cases where *dar-* is used with two non-casemarked NPs. These can be analyzed as copular, as indicated by the square brackets:

(64) Attributive
[sō-mā tuŋ]cs [bācā gyār]cc **da-u**
three-CL FOC a.little fear have-3PA

'The three of us were a little afraid.'

(65) Naming
[ue nām]cs [sāt graha]cc **da-u**
3sGEN name seven planet have-3PA

'His name was "Seven Planets".'

(66) Locational
[chi misāmi]cs [kātākāt mārāmār haŋ-a ṭhāĩ]cc **dam**
2s woman katakat maramar say-NR2 place exist

'You, woman, are at the place where one says "katakat maramar".'

Examples of this type are rare in my data so apparently *dar-* only occasionally functions as a copula.

The verb *dar-* has the following forms; these are further discussed in §6.7.2:

(67) Forms of *dar-*
    dam/damu   present
    dat-a   past
    da-u(ju)   past anterior
    da-eu   future
    ma-da   negative past/present
    ma-dau(ju)   negative past anterior
    ma-da-eu   negative future
    da-i   infinitive
    da-en   participle
    da-e   NR2
    da-u   NR1
    da-ker-   CAUS ('make')

Note that, unlike the copula *khyaŋ*, the verbal inflection of *dar-* does differentiate all four verbal tenses. This verb is defective, however, in not agreeing with the subject in either person or number, as the following examples illustrate:

(68) First-person subject
    [*ji*]$_s$ **damu**
    1s   exist

    'I exist.' (implication in context: 'You have me and are not alone.')

(69) Second-person subject
    [*chi misāmi*]$_{cs}$ [*kātākāt mārāmār haŋ-a*   *thãĩ*]$_{cc}$ **dam**
    2s woman katakat maramar say-NR2 place exist

    'You, woman, are at the place where one says "katakat maramar".'

(70) Plural subject
    [*dāju kīja*]$_s$ **da-u** *hã*
    e.brother y.brother exist-3PA EVID

    'There was once an elder brother and a younger brother.'

The basic meaning of the verb *dar-* is existence. As such it is commonly used at the beginning of narratives to establish the existence of the characters and setting of the story:

(71) [*parāsar risi*]$_s$ **da-u**   *hã*   *thi-mā*
    Parasar Risi exist-3PA EVID one-CL

    'There was once (a man named) Parasar Risi.'

(72) [kaimu kāt]ₛ **da-u**
      husband wife exist-3PA

      'There lived a husband and wife.'

(73) [thi-gur gã̄ū]ₛ **da-u**   hã̄
      one-CL village exist-3PA EVID

      'There once was a village.'

It is also used more generally to predicate the existence or non-existence of entities. One example comes from the following conversational exchange. Note that the first line utilizes a common reduplicative construction used for emphasis (see §15.6):

(74) Speaker 1:
      [dolakhā khã̄=e   me   wā]ₛ **da**   tuŋ **ma-da**
      Dolakha talk=GEN song TOP exist FOC NEG-exist

      'There are no songs at all in the Dolakha language.'

      Speaker 2:
      [ām nini=n   thau tuŋ dak-e   me]ₛ **dam** le
      that aunt=ERG REFL FOC make-NR2 song exist PRT

      'There is the song that Auntie herself made up.'

More examples of the existential use of *dar-* are given in (75)–(77):

(75) [gār]ₛ **dam**
      wound exist

      'There was a wound.'

(76) mebu **ma-da**
      other NEG-exist

      'There is no other.'

(77) āle [ḍwā-ku cār guṭhi yār]ₛ **dam**
      then big-NR1 four guthi member exist

      'Then there are four big guthi members.'

Possessive clauses maintan the same basic syntactic structure as existential clauses: a subject noun phrase followed by the existential verb. The subject noun phrase, however, is generally complex, containing a dependent possessor in genitive or allative case. The literal translation is thus "his/her/its X exists".

(78) [āme   santān]ₛ **ma-da-uju**
     3sGEN heir   NEG-exist-3PA

   'He had no heirs.'

(79) [jana   thi-gur khā]ₛ **dam**
     1sGEN one-CL   talk   exist

   'I have one thing to say.'

(80) [ame   mica   thi-mā]ₛ **dam**
     3sGEN daughter one-CL   exist

   'He has a daughter.'

The existential verb is also used to predicate the location of inanimate objects. Generally the location, marked either by a locative clitic or a postposition, precedes the intransitive subject:

(81) [ām   sona=e   tal=ku=ri]₀ʙʟ   [thi-gur dhan=e
     DEM flower=GEN   under=LOC=IND   one-CL   wealth=GEN

     pwākā]ₛ **dam**
     packet   exist

   'Underneath that flower there is a packet of money.'

Many examples of this construction are better translated as predicating that something exists at a particular place, rather than predicating the location of objects. The previous example falls into this category. It is the first mention about the packet of money and it is the existence of the packet, as much as its location, which is important. Similarly in the following example, it is clear from context that the speaker is emphasizing that there is no television at her house (i.e. lack of existence), not that a television which otherwise exists is not located at her house:

(82) [tibi=uri]_S   [thau chē=ku]_OBL **ma-da**
     television=IND REFL house=LOC NEG-exist

   'There is no television at my house.'

The next example is similar in that the context makes clear that it is the existence of the daughter which is important, not her location at the house:

(83) [thae=uri   chē=ku]_OBL [thi-mā mica]_S **dam**
     2HON.GEN=IND house=LOC one-CL daughter exist

   'In your household there is one daughter.'

These examples all have in common that they constitute the first mention of the referent of the subject noun phrase.

It should be noted that the location of animate referents, including deities, is predicated with the verb *con-* 'sit; stay; reside', not with the existential verb *dar-*:

(84) From a description of the Bhimsen temple
      jau   khenna mā=uri   **con-a**
      right side   mother=IND stay-3sPST

   'On the right side is the mother.'

      khau khenna draupati **con-a**
      left   side   Draupati stay-3sPST.

   'On the left side is Draupati.'

      hākhena ganesa deu **con-a**
      front   Ganesh god stay-3sPST

   'In the front is the god Ganesh.'

(85) kae bö̃=ku   **con-a** (* dam)
      son floor=LOC stay-3sPST

   'The son sat on the floor.'

(86) kobi   **con-a**   ka   luŋā twāpar=ku
      below stay-3sPST ASS rock flat.top=LOC

   '(The tiger) was below, on the top of rock.'

4.2. Intransitive clauses with motion verbs

The two motion verbs *yer-* 'come' and *on-* 'go' are extremely prolific in Dolakha Newar, as in most languages of the world. Each of these verbs has two semantic components, motion and direction, with *yer-* denoting motion toward the deictic center, and *on-* denoting motion away from the deictic center. A number of other intransitive verbs denote manner of motion, rather than direction. Some of these verbs are given in (87):

(87) bor-   'fly'
      bwāt-   'run'
      gar-   'climb; ascend'
      tul-   'roll'
      timmut-   'jump'
      jur-   'swing'
      jwāl-   'swim'
      liŋār-   'walk'

Generally, such verbs are combined with *yer-* 'come' or *on-* 'go' which then provide the directional component of the motion. This is accomplished by putting the motion verb denoting manner in the participial form, and then following it with *yer-* or *on-*:

(88) ām thau mula **liŋā-en**   on-a
     3s REFL road walk-PART go-3sPST

   'He went walking on his own road.' OR 'He walked away on his own road.'

(89) **bwāŋ-an** yer-a
     run-PART come-3sPST

   'She came running.' OR 'She ran towards (the girl).'

(90) **bo-en**   on-a
     fly-PART go-3sPST

   '(The bird) went by flying.' OR '(The bird) flew away.'

As indicated by the multiple translations, there are two possible analyses for this construction. One analysis takes the final motion verbs as grammaticalized auxiliaries indicating direction, and the preceding verbs as the main lexical verb of the clause. By this analysis these examples are monoclausal with auxiliary verbs (e.g. 'flew away'). The other analysis is to assume these are biclausal, and that the final motion verb is being modified by the clause in participial form (e.g. 'went by flying'). While one may construct particular discourse and even syntactic contexts which biases one interpretation over the other, in most examples in natural discourse, either interpretation is equally plausible. Full discussion of the participial construction is provided in Chapter 19.

Another intransitive motion verb *pul-* 'return', also commonly occurs with *yer-* or *on-*. However, unlike the verbs listed in (87), *pul-* does not denote manner of motion, but path. In particular, it denotes a path back toward a previously established location. This verb generally occurs with *yer-* 'come':

(91) mãji=e   mica   makche=ri   chẽ
     boatman=GEN daughter Makche=IND house

pul-en   yer-a
return-PART come-3sPST

'The boatman's daughter Makche returned to the house.'

Another form of this verb, *lipul-*, has lexicalized with the adverbial *li* 'back; backwards' as the first etymon. Interestingly, this verb does not occur in my data with *yer-*, but always occurs independently, e.g. *chẽ lipul-a* 'returned back to the house'. Presumably this is due to the directional component being part of the lexical structure of the verb.

Locational goals are represented by oblique noun phrases inflected with the locative *=ku* or, if animate, the allative *=ke* (§4.4.2.9):

(92) [jana   darbār=ku]$_{OBL}$ **yā**
     1sGEN   palace=LOC   come.IMP

'Come to my palace.'

(93) [bhãnche=ke]$_{OBL}$ **on-a**
     cook=ALL   go-3sPST

'She went to the cook.'

Ablative case (§4.4.2.9) may indicate either source from which the motion emanated or path of motion:

(94) [ãku=lān]$_{OBL}$ [ithi]$_{OBL}$ **on-gi**
     there=ABL   here   come-1sPST

'From there I came here.'

(95) āle [ā̃ku=lān]_OBL [thi-mā hātti]_OBL pita **yer-a**
      then there=ABL   one-CL elephant   out   come-PART

   'Then an elephant came out from there.'

(96) [mebu=ri   lõ=lān]_OBL **ye**-e-lagin
      other=IND road=ABL   come-NR2-because

   'Because he came via a different road...'

(97) [dwālŋā=e   mula=lān] thãta **yer-gi**
      Dwalnga=GEN   road=ABL   up   come-1sPST

   'I came up taking the road from Dwalnga.'

5. Dative-experiencer clauses

Another basic clause type, the dative-experiencer clause, exhibits properties of both intransitive and transitive clauses. With intransitive clauses, this construction shares the use of intransitive verbs, either *jur-* 'be, become, happen', *yer-* 'come', *pyāṭāwāt-* 'be hungry', or *mal-* 'need'. With transitive clauses, it shares the possibility of involving two core arguments. However, the similarity to transitive clauses ends there. As the name suggests, dative-experiencer clauses have a core argument which is a semantic experiencer marked by dative case. There is no agentive argument or affected object. Rather than assuming that dative experiencers are either A, S, or O arguments, thus equating them to other types of predicates, I prefer to analyze dative-experiencer constructions independently with a different argument structure altogether. All dative-experiencer constructions allow an experiencer argument marked with dative case. I will refer to this as EXP. Many dative-experiencer clauses incorporate a second noun phrase which denotes an emotional, physical, or cognitive state. These noun phrases act as part of the lexical structure of the verb (some may be compounds; all appear to be lexicalizations), and not as grammatical arguments. However, in some dative-experiencer constructions there is an additional noun phrase which does have the properties of an argument. It denotes the the stimulus for the state, and so will be referred to as STIM.

The majority of dative-experiencer clauses utilize Nepali vocabulary, either verbs, nouns, or both. There are three distinct syntactic patterns that are formed with Nepali borrowings. In addition, there are several constructions which utilize only native Dolakha Newar vocabulary. However, for each of these patterns, there is a parallel pattern in Nepali, so these could be seen as Nepali calques.

Although there are a number of different patterns with respect to argument structure and the provenance of the vocabulary, the dative-experiencer clauses all share the feature of having a verb with reduced inflectional possibilities. While the verb may take the full range of non-finite suffixes for the purpose of clause combination, and may vary in tense, the finite verb in these constructions does not inflect for person or number, but is consistently third-person singular.

In the following sections, I will discuss each distinct pattern with dative experiencers in turn. Discussion of grammatical relations and dative-experiencer clauses can be found in §13.4.

5.1. Nepali pattern 1: Emotional and cognitive states

In the first pattern, a noun denoting an emotional or cognitive state is combined with a verb. Both are borrowed from Nepali, and the verb is incorporated into Dolakha Newar by the addition of the borrowed-verb suffix *-ai* and the intransitive Dolakhae verb *jur-* (see §6.3). The argument structure of the clause is identical to the argument structure of the same noun-verb combination in Nepali, requiring a semantic experiencer in dative case. The borrowed Nepali verb may be either *lāgnu* or *parnu*, both verbs of very general meaning, but which may be roughly translated as 'feel' and 'happen; fall into' respectively.

In the majority of examples, the borrowed noun denotes an emotional state and directly precedes the verb:

(98)   [janta]$_{EXP}$ wā   ekdam **pir**   **lāg-ai**   **jur-a**
        1sDAT   TOP very   worry   feel-BV   be-3sPST

       'I am very worried.'

(99)   āle   [āpista]$_{EXP}$ ekdam **dāhā**   **lāg-ai**   **jur-a**
       then 3pDAT   very   jealous   feel-BV   be-3sPST

       'Then they felt very jealous.'

(100) [būsi=ta]$_{EXP}$ biŋkeŋ **pir**   **par-ai**   **jur-a**
        Bunsi=DAT   very   worry   happen-BV   be-3sPST

       'Bunsi became very worried.'

In the following example, the noun denotes a concrete object and the construction as a whole indicates desire for that object. Note that in this example it is the dative-marked experiencer which directly precedes the verb:

(101) [amrit ri]_STIM [dānab-pista]_EXP **lāg-ai   jur-a**
elixir TOP   giant=PL.DAT   feel-BV   be-3sPST

'The giants desired the elixir.'

5.2. Nepali pattern 2: Emotional and cognitive states with stimulus noun

In the second pattern, there are technically three NPs: the dative-marked experiencer, a noun denoting a cognitive or emotional state, and a stimulus noun. Again the verb is borrowed from Nepali and incorporated via the borrowed-verb suffix and the Dolakhae verb *jur-*. The most common construction utilizes the Nepali combination *man parnu* 'to like'. While this is technically a noun-verb combination, it is used with high frequency and can be said to have lexicalized:

(102) āle [suntali=ta]_EXP [ām sona]_STIM biŋkeŋ **man   par-ai   jur-a**
then Suntali=DAT   that flower   very   heart happen-BV be-3sPST

'Then Suntali very much liked that flower.'

(103) [chana khā]_STIM [ista]_EXP **man   par-ai   ma-ju**
2sGEN talk   1pEXC.DAT like happen-BV NEG-be

'We don't like your talk.'

One may also find three nouns co-occurring in the following construction, a direct calque on a Nepali structure. Once again, the noun denoting the cognitive state, *thāhā* must directly precede the verb, here the existential verb *dar-*, which corresponds to the Nepali attributive copula *cha* (a form of the complex Nepali existential verb *hunu.*)

(104) [u]_STIM [janta]_EXP **thāhā   ma-da**
this 1sDAT knowledge NEG-have

'I don't know this'

The only other example in my data which has three NPs utilizes the Nepali noun *samjhanā*, which is a derived form of the verb *samjhanu* 'to remember'.

(105) [u khabar]_STIM [chanta]_EXT **samjhanā   ma-da-eu**
this news   2sDAT   memory   NEG-have-3FUT

'This news you will not have a memory of.'

5.3. Nepali pattern 3: Forgetting and remembering

Dolakha Newar has native vocabulary items for the verbs 'remember' and 'forget'. They are *lūwon-* 'remember' and its negated counterpart *lūmowon-* 'forget'. Both are regular transitive verbs taking an ergative-marked subject and an object. Dolakhae speakers also utilize verbs borrowed from Nepali for these concepts: *samjhanu* 'remember' and *birsanu* 'forget'. When these verbs are borrowed, the Nepali argument structure is borrowed as well. These thus require a dative-marked experiencer, and optionally an unmarked stimulus noun:

(106) [chanta]_{EXP} **birs-ai ju-eu**
 2sDAT forget-BV be-3FUT

 'You will forget.'

(107) āle [āmu bisnu bāgabān=ta]_{EXP} [lyās misā]_{STIM} *tuŋ*
 then that Vishnu god=DAT young woman FOC

 samj-ai jur-a.
 remember-BV be-3sPST

 'Then that God Vishnu remembered the young woman.'

5.4. Dolakhae pattern 1: Experience of uncontrollable events

The fourth of the dative-experiencer constructions may either utilize all native Dolakha Newar vocabulary items or may borrow nouns indicating states from Nepali. In either case, the verb *jur-* is used as the primary verb, and means 'to happen'. An unmarked noun indicating a state or event is required, and experiencers, if present, are casemarked dative:

(108) [thijita]_{EXP} **bāmala-ku ju-en**
 1pINC.DAT bad-NR1 happen-PART

 'A bad thing happened to us...'

(109) [janta]_{EXP} hātiŋ **ma-ju**
 1sDAT nothing NEG-happen

 'Nothing happened to me.'

(110) [chanta]_EXP sukha   **ju-eu**
      2sDAT   happiness   happen-3FUT

'You will be happy.'

5.5. Dolakhae pattern 2: 'like to', 'want to' using *yer-* 'come'

The second Dolakhae pattern is found with the verb *yer-* 'come'. When preceded by a clause ending in an infinitive verb, the construction as a whole means either 'like to; want to X'. The infinitive clause is syntactically a complement (§18.2.4). The experiencer of this emotional state may be casemarked with the dative (110)–(112) to reflect the non-volitional matrix verb, or the casemarking may reflect the transitivity of the complement verb (113):

(111) [āmta]_EXP [lokhu tõ-i]_COMP   **yer-a**
      3sDAT   water   drink-INF   come-3sPST

'He wanted to drink some water.'

(112) [janta]_EXP [pāŋ ekdam na-i]_COMP **yer-a**
      1sDAT   fruit very   eat-INF   come-3sPST

'I very much want to eat some fruit.'

(113) [janta]_EXP [ināgu   khã=pen khā lā-i]_COMP **mā-yā**
      1sDAT   this.type talk=PL talk tell-INF   NEG-come

'I don't like to tell stories of this type.'

(114) [ji_s bebahārik=ku   par-ai   ju-i]_COMP **yer-a**
      1s   family.life=LOC touch-BV   be-INF   come-3sPST

'I want to experience family life.'

The optional assignment of case to the complement clause subject is a type of "backward control" of casemarking by the matrix verb over the complement subject.

5.6. Dolakhae pattern 3: *mal(dan)-* 'need'

The Dolakhae verb *mal(dan)-* 'need' also takes a dative-marked experiencer as core argument, but only when the thing needed is an object which can be represented by a noun phrase. If what is needed is an action or event, then *mal-* takes a clausal complement which controls the casemarking of its subject (see §18.2.4). The order of the two noun phrases in a *mal(dan)-* clause is free; the dative experiencer can either precede or follow the noun phrase denoting what is needed:

(115) [u   rāje]_STIM   [janta]_EXP mā=ŋ   māl
       this kingdom   1sDAT   need=EXT   (NEG)need

       'I don't need this kingdom!'

(116) [ista=ŋ]_EXP   nichi   [u]_STIM **maldan-a**
       1pEXC.DAT=EXT   one.day this   need-3sPST

       'We need this one day.'

5.7. Other Dolakhae predicates with dative experiencers

Two other common Dolakha Newar predicates also require dative experiencers. One is the lexicalized expression *rāk yer-* 'become angry' constructed of the emotional state noun *rāk* and the verb *yer-* 'come'. This combination is used to indicate an anger which comes upon one spontaneously:

(117) [sihā=ta]_EXP besna **rāk** **yer-a**
       lion=DAT   very   anger   come-3sPST

       'The lion became very angry.'

This example is used at a point in the story when the lion thinks that another lion has come into his territory. The use of this construction implies that the lion cannot help but become angry at this turn of events. This can be contrasted with the expression *rāk yet-* 'become angry', constructed with the transitive verb *yet-* 'do'. This combination is used when the development of the anger is volitional or otherwise under the control of the experiencer. This construction requires an ergative subject:

(118) [sihā=n]_A besna **rāk** **yeŋ-an**
       lion=ERG   very   anger   do-PART

       'The lion became very angry...'

This clause was found in the same story as the previous example. It is used when the lion becomes angry at a rabbit who showed up late for his appointment to be eaten. The use of the transitive verb implies that the lion has some control over the anger. The same semantic distinction is made by the Nepali verbs *ris uṭhanu*, constructed from *ris* 'anger' and *uṭhanu* 'arise', and *risāunu*, the latter being an overtly causative form which indicates some degree of volition.

Another predicate which requires an experiencer casemarked with the dative is *pyāṭāwāt-* 'to be hungry':

(119) [*janta*]$_{EXP}$ ***pyāṭāwāt-a***
 1sDAT hunger-3sPST

 'I am hungry.'

(120) [*buḍā=ta*]$_{EXP}$ *besna* ***pyāṭāwāŋ-an*** *con-a*
 old.man=DAT very hunger-PART stay-3sPST

 'The old man was getting hungry.'

6. Transitive clauses

Transitive clauses are those which have two core arguments: an A, which carries ergative case, and an O, which either takes dative case or is not casemarked, hence absolutive. (Further discussion of case assignment can be found in §4.4.2.) Grammatically, the A constitutes the grammatical subject and the O constitutes the grammatical object (Chapter 13). Transitive verbs have a number of inflectional suffixes which are distinct from those of intransitive verbs (§6.4). The most common of these is the third-person-singular past, which is *-ju* on transitive verbs and *-a* on intransitive verbs.

Although there are many transitive verbs, transitive clauses have a remarkable degree of syntactic uniformity. A full discussion of transitivity, casemarking, and the small handful of ambitransitive verbs can be found in §4.4.2.4. Here it will only be said that the two arguments, A and O, normally precede the verb and that A normally precedes O (a full discussion of constituent order may be found in Chapter 14). Either or both arguments may be omitted if the reference is unimportant or clear from discourse context.

Transitive clauses of a variety of types are illustrated in (121)–(131):

(121) [*bhut-na*]$_A$ [*janta wā*]$_O$ *guli* ***khyāŋ-an*** *tar-ai*
 ghost-ERG 1sDAT TOP how.much scare-PART put-3sPR

 'Ghosts scare me so much.'

Section 6 Transitive clauses   301

(122) [tātā=n]ᴀ   [u]ₒ **lār-ai**   ka
       e.sister=ERG this tell-3sPR ASS

       'Elder sister tells this.'

(123) [jin wā]ᴀ **mā-tā-gi**
       1s   TOP   NEG-hear-1sPST

       'I didn't hear.'

(124) [bāl bāhādur=e   khā]ₒ   [dhōr=na]ᴀ **bu-en**
       Bal Bahadur=GEN chicken jackal=ERG carry-3sPART

       'The jackal carried (away) Bal Bahadur's chicken...'

(125) [isin   tuŋ]ᴀ **so-i**
       1pEXC.ERG FOC   watch-1FUT

       'We will watch (you).'

(126) [āmta]ₒ   kho=ku   ŋat-a   on-a
       3sDAT   river=LOC   throw-PURP   go-3sPST

       '(She) went to throw him in the river.'

(127) [sõ-mā=ta=ŋ]ₒ   [māji=n]ᴀ   **yeŋ-an**
       three-CL=DAT=EXT boatman=ERG take-PART

       'The boatman took all three of them...'

(128) [thi-mā jogi=ta]ₒ   **nāplat-cu**
       one-CL yogi=DAT   meet-3sPST

       '(He) met a yogi.'

(129) [kāpas]ₒ **hā-sin**   nā
       cotton   bring-HON.IMP   AGR

       'Please bring cotton.'

(130) āle [āmun]ᴀ [hātiŋ   sabda]ₒ **mā-tār-ju**
       then 3sERG   nothing   word   NEG-hear-3sPST

       'Then she didn't hear a word.'

(131) [bobu=ri=n]$_A$ si-en
father=IND=ERG know-PART

'The father knew...'

The only transitive verb which merits particular discussion is probably the most common: *yet-* 'do'. As with most other transitive verbs, this verb is consistently transitive; it always allows an ergative-marked A and it consistently takes the transitive forms of suffixes. This verb differs from other transitive verbs in several respects. First, due to its vague semantic structure, this verb may function as an anaphoric pro-verb, referring to an action or series of actions whose reference is clear from preceding discourse. In this function it generally co-occurs with the distal demonstrative of manner *ānthi*:

(132) litaŋ ānthi   yet-ŋa
again that.manner do-when

'When (they) again acted in that manner...'

(133) [cicā=uri dāi=na]$_A$ ānthi   tuŋ yeŋ-an   on-a
small=IND e.brother=ERG that.manner FOC do-PART go-3sPST

'The younger elder brother, acting in that same manner, went.'

(134) thanu thanu kesi   kesi   yet-ŋa
today today tomorrow tomorrow do-when

'When (he) did (that) over a period of time...'

Related to this is the use of the verb to refer to a manner of action that is being demonstrated through gesture. In this case, the proximal demonstrative of manner is used.

(135) ithi   yeŋ-an   lita   tiŋgriŋga   kota yer-a
this.manner do-PART later tall.skinny down come-3sPST

'Acting in this manner, later a tall and skinny one came down.'

The verb *yet-* 'do' is also used to refer to future action of an unspecified or unknown nature. This is often found in questions, when the speaker is wondering what action to take:

(136) āu   hāti   yer-iuri?
      now what do-NR3
      'Now what do (I) do?'

This verb is also unusual in that it may be used in combination with nouns to form noun-verb compounds. This has allowed for the expansion of verbal experessions. Most of the nouns used in these compounds are Nepali in origin. Some examples are given in Table 36:

Table 36. Some noun-verb compounds with *yet-* 'do'

bihā yet-	marriage do-	'marry'
je yet-	work do-	'work'
ultā yet-	reverse do-	'translate'
jāl yet-	net do-	'trap'
pujā yet-	ceremony do	'worship'
bājā yet-	music do	'play music'
wāsar yet-	medicine do	'practice medicine'
helā yet-	insult do	'insult'
khisi yet-	ridicule do	'ridicule'
kalpanā yet-	imagination do	'imagine'
pās yet-	pass	'pass (test)'
bipi yet-	?	'swallow with difficulty'
dharma yet-	religion do	'undertake actions for religious reasons'
sewā yet-	service do	'be of service to others'
sāhā yet-	care do	'care for someone'
salāhā yet-	conference do	'confer'

The two parts of a noun-verb compound are never separated by anything other than a verbal prefix. The usual case is for the noun to occur in the absence of any other argument that may be construed as the O. Thus the noun of the compound appears to play this role, making the clause as a whole transitive:

(137) [kae=uri=n=uŋ]$_A$ [je]$_O$ **yeŋ-an**
      son=IND=ERG =EXT   work   do-PART
      'The son also doing work...'

However, with a few verbs, referential O arguments are incorporated as grammatical objects and co-occur with the noun of the compound:

(138) pharsi=n   suntali=ta   **bihā**   **yeŋ-an**
       pumpkin=ERG Suntali=DAT marriage do-PART

   'The pumpkin married Suntali...'

(139) thijita   mepsin   **helā**   **yer-eu**
       1pINC.DAT other.ERG insult do-3FUT

   'Others will insult us.'

These examples could be considered ditransitive, taking two objects, however the tight link between the abstract noun and the verb suggest lexicalization. These constructions are thus intermediate in argument structure. They are all morphologically transitive and have a noun that can be construed as an O, but a few compounds additionally allow the incorporation of a referential object.

The verb *yet-* 'do' is also used to refer to actions which produce noises referred to by onomatopoeic expressions. Thus *wããã yet-* refers to the production of a scream 'Waaa!'; *taŋ taŋ yet-* refers to an action that resulted in the production of a sound similar to 'tang tang' (in this case, dropping diamonds onto a gold plate), *swã̄ swã̄ yet-* indicates a person panting, etc.

7. Ditransitive clauses

Ditransitive clauses allow for three core arguments: the agentive A, the "patientive" O, and the recipient R. Of the three, the A is the grammatical subject while the O and R are both grammatical objects (§13.3). The unmarked ordering of consituents in ditransitive clauses appears to be AROV (§14.3). This is the order provided by consultants in elicitation.

Ditransitive verbs can be divided into two classes: verbs of transfer (such as *bir-* 'give') and verbs of speaking (such as *hat-* 'say').[69] The semantic relationships that hold between the arguments and the verb are different in the two types of clauses and these differences are reflected in slightly different morphosyntactic behaivor.

7.1. Ditransitive clauses with transfer verbs

In the argument structure of a ditransitive transfer verb, an A argument in ergative case is the volitional instigator of the transfer, an O argument in either absolutive or dative case is the object of transfer, and an R argument in the dative case is the recipient of the object of transfer, either physically or metaphorically:

(140) [ām thi-mnā jāki=uri]₀   [jin]_A [ām jogi=ta]_R **bir-gi**
      that one-CL uncooked.rice=IND 1sERG that yogi=DAT give-1sPST

'I gave that handful of rice to that yogi.'

(141) [thi-tākā dyābā daṇḍa]₀ **tiret-cu**   [sāŋat=pista]_R
      one-CL money fine   pay-3sPST friend=PL.DAT

'He paid a fine of one rupee to his friends.'

(142) [jin]_A [chanta=ri]_R [thi-gur khā]₀ **syẽ-i**
      1sERG 2sDAT=IND one-CL talk teach-1sFUT

'I will teach you one thing.'

(143) [janta]_R [chemā]₀ **bi-sin**
      1sDAT forgiveness give-IMP

'Please forgive me.' (lit. 'Please give me forgiveness.')

In all of these examples, the O is inanimate and so does not take dative case. However, it is also possible for the O of a ditransitive clause to be animate and given, in which case both the O and the R will take dative case:

(144) āle āmta bhānche=ta **bir-ju**
      then 3sDAT cook=DAT give-3sPST

'Then (the king) gave her to the cook (in marriage).'

7.2. Ditransitive clauses with speaking verbs

Ditransitive clauses with speaking verbs differ have different semantic values for the O and R arguments than do clauses with transfer verbs. The R argument is semantically the addressee; it is consistently in dative case. The O argument refers to the speech itself. Occassionally this is realized as a simple noun, as in the following examples:

(145) [jin]_A [chanta]_R [thi-gur khā]₀ **har-i**
      1sERG 2sDAT   one-CL talk say-1FUT

'I will say one thing to you.'

(146) āu   [u   khā]ₒ [gunta]ᴿ ŋe-i?
      now   this talk   who.DAT   ask-1FUT

'Now to whom will I ask this thing?'

More commonly, the O is realized as an embedded complement containing a direct quote:

(147) [āmun]ₐ ["u   jaŋgal=e   rājā ji tuŋ khyaŋ mebu
      3sERG   this jungle=GEN king 1s FOC be   other

      ma-da"]ₒ   **hat-ai**
      NEG-exist   say-3sPR

'He said: "I am the king of this jungle. There is no other".'

(148) [mā=uri=n]ₐ   ["ji je   yet-a   ū-i"]ₒ   **haŋ-an**
      mother=IND=ERG   1s   work do-PURP go-1FUT   say-PART

      pita yer-a
      out come-3sPST

'The mother said: "I'm going to work", and came out.'

(149) [suntali=n]ₐ   ["sona kha-ita"]ₒ [pharsi=ta]ᴿ   **hat-ai**
      Suntali=ERG   flower 2hFUT   pumpkin=DAT   say-3sPR

'Suntali says to the pumpkin: "You will pick the flower".'

The embedded complement can be syntactically quite simple, containing a single clause or even a single word (such as an exclamation). It can also be syntactically complex, containing more than one syntactic sentence (as in (147) above). Although these direct quotes differ in many ways from prototypical objects, there is still evidence that they do constitute syntactic objects in this language. However, they will never be casemarked, as the referent of the verb is abstract hence inanimate. The object status of complements of speaking verbs is more fully discussed in §18.2.3.

The incorporation of direct speech into narrative discourse is extremely common in my data. The verb *haŋ-an,* the participial form of the verb *hat-* 'say', has particularly interesting behavior; see §19.4.3. A discussion of quoted speech and syntactic complexity may be found in §21.3.

Chapter 13
Grammatical relations

1. Introduction

At various points in this book, core arguments of verbs have been identified by their grammatical roles: S (single core argument of an intransitive clause), CS (primary argument of a copular clause), A (more agentive argument in a transitive or ditransitive clause), O (more patientive argument in a transitive or ditransitive clause), and R (recipient argument in a ditransitive clause). In dative-experiencer constructions (§12.5), we have also distinguished between the EXP (experiencer) and STIM (stimulus) arguments. When we examine the morphosyntactic behavior of the language, however, we notice that it is rarely the case that each core grammatical role is grammatically distinguished in every environment. Instead, we usually find that certain sets of arguments share grammatical properties. For example, S, CS, and A form a set, as the finite verb agrees with these arguments in person and number; O and R do not share this grammatical property. Such sets constitute the "grammatical relations" of a language. The strength of a particular grammatical relation may be determined by the extent to which independent morphosyntactic behavior revolves around that particular set of arguments (keeping in mind that a set may contain only a single member).

In Dolakha Newar, there are two grammatical domains which identify independent sets of core arguments. Putting dative-experiencer constructions aside for the time being, the casemarking facts of the language divide the grammatical roles into three distinct sets: ergative (A); absolute (S, CS, and some O[70]); and dative (remaining O and R). Morphosyntactic evidence from other domains independently identifies a subject (S, CS, and A) and an object (O and R). Thus the core arguments participate in two systems of grammatical organization simultaneously. This is schematized in Figure 18:

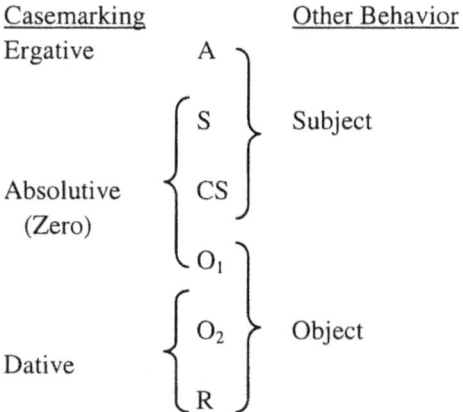

Figure 18. Two systems of grammatical organization

The casemarking facts were fully discussed in §4.4.2. Here I will only say that beyond casemarking there is no other morphosyntactic behavior which identifies ergative, absolutive, or dative as independent grammatical categories.

This chapter will thus focus on the subject and object grammatical relations. It will also demonstrate that dative-experiencer constructions are grammatically independent, and that neither EXP nor STIM participate in the behavior of the other categories.

2. Subject: A, S, and CS

There are four areas of the morphosyntax which revolve around the notion of subject. These are finite verb agreement, the distribution of nominalizers in the formation of relative clauses, backwards control of anaphora in complementation structures, and reflexives. Other morphosyntactic arenas which are used to identify subjects in other languages are not relevant in Dolakhae. These include casemarking (§4.4.2), constituent order (§14), and anaphora and control in participial and adverbial clauses (see §19.5.1 and §20.3.1 respectively).

2.1. Verb agreement

The subject category is robustly attested in the verb-agreement patterns of Dolakha Newar. The verb agrees in person, honorific status, and number with the subject, A or S, of the clause. The agreement patterns are fully discussed in Chapter 4; here I will only give a handful of examples which illustrate the centrality of the subject category in this morphosyntactic environment:

(1) First-person-singular A
*jin   galti   **yet-ki***
1sERG mistake do-1sPST

'I made a mistake.'

(2) First-person-singular S
*mā   āu   ji   **on-gi***
mother now 1s go-1sPST

'Mother, now I went.'

(3) First-person-plural A
*isin   airāk   kā-en   **tar-agu***
1pEXC.ERG liquor take-PART put-1pPR

'We take and keep the liquor.'

(4) First-person-plural S
*isi   kesi   tuŋ   **on-agu***
1pEXC tomorrow FOC go-1pPR

'We go tomorrow.'

(5) Second-person-plural A
*chipsin   **sir-amin**   nā?*
2pERG know-2pPR AGR

'Do you know?'

(6) Second-person-plural S
*hātta   **mā-yār-min**   chipen?*
why NEG-come-2pPST 2p

'Why didn't you come?'

(7) Third-person-plural A
*titā   kehẽ   sõ-mā=n   khã   lā-en   **con-hin**   nā*
e.sister y.sister three-CL=ERG talk talk-PART stay-3pPST AGR

'The three sisters were talking.'

(8) Third-person-plural S
muca̅=pen din prati din **dwākar-hin**
child=PL day by day grow-3pPST

'The children grew day by day.'

These examples show that the verb agrees with the subject argument for person, regardless of whether it is the A argument of a transitive verb (the first example in each pair) or the S argument of an intransitive verb (the second example in each pair). Examples (3)–(8) also illustrate that the verb agrees with the number of the subject. Copula subjects also trigger verb agreement.[71] The following elicited sentences exemplify this last point:

(9) Elicited: second-person-singular CS
chi mucā tākku cicā **ju-un**
2s child time small be-2sPA

'You were small as a child.'

(10) Elicited: third-person-singular CS
ām mucā tākku cicā **ju**
3s child time small be(3PA)

'He was small as a child.'

We can thus say that in Dolakha Newar finite verb agreement is with the grammatical subject.

While it is satisfying to make clear and unequivocal statements such as that of the last sentence, it is often the case that the facts are somewhat more complicated than such fine distillations imply. The verb agreement patterns quickly sketched here and discussed in detail in Chapter 6 are regularly produced by consultants in elicitation with no deviations. However, in connected discourse, a small percentage of examples evidence "disagreement", i.e. failure of the verb to follow the expected pattern of agreement with subject. There are two patterns of such "disagreement". The first and rarer pattern is when a third-person verb form is used with a first-person subject; this emphasizes the subject's lack of control over the events denoted in the clause. The second, somewhat more common, pattern is when a third-person-singular verb occurs with a third-person-plural subject. Both patterns are discussed and exemplified in §6.4.3.4. Here I will simply suggest that the presence of these patterns does not significantly dilute the strength of the category subject. Such examples are few in number, consultants do not produce them in elicitation (although they still consider them to be grammatical when shown the pattern in connected discourse), and at least the first pattern has a strong semantic motivation. Thus, despite this complication, the basic generalization regarding subject agreement holds.

2.2. Complementation structures

As discussed in §18.2.4, when the verbs *bir-* 'give' or *yer-* 'come' are used with an infinitive complement clause, they mean 'let; allow' or 'want to; like to' respectively. Both of these structrures exhibit syntactic behavior that argues for the presence of a grammatical subject. In the permissive construction, the subject of the complement clause receives the dative casemarker typical of direct objects; it can be said to undergo "raising":

(11) Elicited
 [mā=n]$_A$ [janta$_S$ dolkhā=ku   ū-i]$_{COMP}$ ma-bi-u
 mother=ERG 1sDAT Dolakha=LOC go-INF NEG-give-3PA

 'Mother did not let me go to Dolakha.'

(12) [janta$_A$ jā   na-i]$_{COMP}$ bi-eu
 1sDAT rice eat-INF give-3FUT

 '(He) will let me eat.'

The complement-taking predicate *yer-* 'come' invokes a dative-experiencer structure. There are two possible syntactic analyses of this structure. In one, the dative-marked experiencer can be seen as being the regular subject of the complement-taking predicate, in which case, the coreferential subject argument of the complement clause is obligatorily omitted:

(13) [janta]$_{EXP}$ [∅$_A$ ināgu   khā=pen khā lā-i]$_{COMP}$ **mā-yā**
 1sDAT   this.type talk=PL talk tell-INF NEG-come

 'I don't like to tell stories of this type.'

In the other, the dative-marked argument is seen as being the subject of the complement clause, but its casemarking is controlled by the matrix verb:

(14) [janta$_{EXP}$ ināgu   khā=pen khā lā-i]$_{COMP}$ **mā-yā**
 1sDAT   this.type talk=PL talk tell-INF NEG-come

 'I don't like to tell stories of this type.'

In either case, it is the subject argument which is targeted by the construction, either by obligatory omission of the subject of the complement clause, as in the former analysis, or by backwards control, as in the latter. While the complement clause in (13) has an A argument, the same structure can be found with S arguments (e.g. *janta ḍī yer-a* [1sDAT sleep(INF) come-3sPST] 'I want to sleep'), or with CS arguments (e.g. *janta rani ju-i yer-a* [1sDAT queen be-INF come-3sPST] 'I want to be a queen').[72] On the other hand, it should be noted that I do have one example where the subject of the complement clause receives casemarking not from the complement-taking predicate, but from the complement verb:

(15) [*ji*ₛ *bebahārik=ku   par-ai   ju-i*]_COMP **yer-a**
      1s family.life=LOC touch-BV be-INF   come-3sPST

'I want to experience family life.'

The conditions under which this occurs deserves further exploration.

2.3. Relative clauses

The second area of the morphosyntax where the category of subject is pivotal is the relative clause. As discussed extensively in Chapter 17, Dolakha Newar has three nominalizers which are used in a variety of environments, including the formation of relative clauses. The nominalizer glossed NR1 (nominalizer/relativizer 1) is found in realis examples when the head noun is coreferential with the subject of the relative clause, either S, A, or CS:

(16) Head noun coreferential with S
      [*pali depān coŋ-gu*]_REL *kok*
      roof on   stay-NR1   crow

      'The crow that is on the roof...'

(17) Head noun coreferential with A
      [*ām thẽ tuŋ boŋ-gu*]_REL *sāŋat=pen*
      3s like FOC read-NR1   friend=PL

      'Friends who read just like him (i.e. are educated).'

(18) Head noun coreferential with CS
      [*jogi ju*]_REL   *mi*
      yogi be(NR1)   man

      'The man who became a yogi...'

By contrast, the nominalizer NR2 is found in realis contexts when the head noun is coreferential with a non-subject argument, i.e. O, R, or oblique.

(19) Head noun coreferential with O
[jin **phoŋ-a**]_{REL}   misā
1sERG ask.for-NR2 woman

'The woman whom I asked for (in marriage)...'

(20) Head noun coreferential with R
[kathā **haŋ-a**]_{REL} sāŋat=na
story tell-NR2 friend=ERG

'The friend to whom the story was told...'

(21) Head noun coreferential with oblique argument
[thamun je **yeŋ-a**]_{REL} thãĩ
2hERG   work do-NR2   place

'The place where you work...'

Once again, while this pattern is overwhelmingly followed in my data, there is some evidence that the pattern is not absolute. In elicitation, my consultants have demonstrated that while they prefer NR2 with non-subject heads, NR1 is grammatically acceptable *if* the verb is intransitive and the subject of the relative clause is third person, e.g. *bulbul ciḍiyā coŋ-gu thãĩ* [bulbul bird stay-NR1 place] 'The place where the bulbul bird was'. As discussed in §17.3, this deviation from the dominant pattern appears to be a reflection of the historical distribution of the suffixes; NR1 was originally associated with intransitivity and third-person subjects. The fact that these forms are acceptable but not preferred indicates that the reanalysis of the morphology in relative clauses to a pattern based exclusively on grammatical relations is close to complete. This reanalysis both reflects and strengthens the development of the grammatical relation of subject in this language.

2.4. Reflexives

The use of reflexives is somewhat limited in Dolakha Newar. So-called "true reflexives", where a reflexive pronoun is used in a core argument role (e.g. English *he killed himself*), are not attested in this language. Instead, the reflexive pronoun *thau* most commonly functions as a possessive reflexive, e.g. 'my own', etc. The functions of this pronoun are discussed more fully in §15.5. Here it will just be said that the reflexive pronoun may have a subject argument, S, A, or CS, as its antecedent:

(22) Reflexive with antecedent S
āpen **thau** chē oŋ-an
3p REFL house go-PART

'They went to their own house...'

(23) Reflexive with antecedent A
āmun **thau** mica tuŋ chor-ai kesi pāŋ simā=ku
3sERG REFL daughter FOC send-3sPR tomorrow fruit tree=LOC

'She sends her own daughter tomorrow, to the fruit tree.'

(24) Reflexive with antecedent CS
āmu **thau** tuŋ utpatti ju bimesor thākur
3s REFL FOC creation be(3PA) Bimsen lord

'He was his own creation, Lord Bimsen.'

Note that the reflexive may have as its antecedent a subject argument in a matrix clause:

(25) Reflexive with subject antecedent in matrix clause
pharsi=n **thau** mica=ta phoŋ-a khoŋ-an
pumpkin =ERG REFL daughter=DAT ask.for-NR2 see-PART

birbahādur chakka par-ai jur-a
Birbahadur surprise feel-BV be-3sPST

'Seeing that the pumpkin had come to ask for his$_i$ own daughter in marriage, Birbahadur$_i$ felt surprised.'

Crucially, I have no examples of a reflexive having as its antecedent any non-subject argument and speakers reject such examples in elicitation. In discussion of the following elicited example, native speakers consistently interpret the sentence as indicated, with the reflexive pronoun necessarily referring to the subject of the clause and not to the recipient object:

(26) Elicited
āmun misāmi=ta **thau** mucā bir-ju
3sERG woman =DAT REFL daughter give-3sPST
'She$_i$ gave the woman her$_i$ own daughter.'

If one wished to specify that the child belonged to the woman receiving it, the reflexive would be replaced by *āme tuŋ* [3sGEN FOC]. Thus, the category of subject is pivotal in the morphosyntax of reflexives.[73]

3. Objects: O and R

The grammatical category of object is clearly independent of subject in that objects do not control casemarking, do not trigger NR1 when coreferential with the head of a relative clause, and may not serve as antecedents of reflexives. Objects may be differentiated from obliques in that they fill argument slots in the lexical structure of verbs. Objects are also the only arguments that have been found to be antecedents of the emphatic possessive phrase *āme tuŋ* 'his/her own' (discussed below).

In many languages, one can grammatically distinguish between classes of objects. The most common division is between direct objects (O arguments of transitive and ditransitive verbs) and indirect objects (R arguments of ditransitive verbs). This system may be represented as in Figure 19:[74]

Transitive:	A		O	V
Ditransitive:	A	R	O	V
		Indirect	*Direct*	

Figure 19. Categories of indirect and direct objects

Another common division is between primary objects (O arguments of transitive and R arguments of ditransitive) and secondary objects (O arguments of ditransitive) (Dryer 1986). This pattern can be represented in Figure 20:

Transitive:	A	O		V
Ditransitive:	A	R	O	V
		Primary	*Secondary*	

Figure 20. Categories of primary and secondary objects

However, in Dolakha Newar, neither of these patterns is in evidence. Instead, all O and R arguments appear to constitute a single grammatical relation of object, as represented in Figure 21:

Transitive: A   O   V
Ditransitive: A   R   O   V
                        Object

Figure 21. The category of object in Dolakha Newar

3.1. Object casemarking

In some languages, casemarking patterns argue for a division of the object category into two classes. Either the indirect objects with dative case contrast with direct objects with accusative case (e.g. in Latin), or else a single casemarker is used on R and transitive O (primary object) in contrast to the unmarked ditransitive O (secondary object) (Dryer 1986: 816–818). However, in Dolakha Newar, neither of these patterns is in evidence. The basic pattern is that R arguments are obligatorily marked with the dative case and O arguments are marked with the dative case only if human and given (Genetti 1997). Since ditransitive verbs generally have inanimate or non-human patients (the themes of transfer verbs or the quotes of utterance verbs), the O arguments of ditransitives are seldom casemarked. However, they can be. In (27), the O of the ditransitive verb is human and given, so takes dative case:

(27)   āle   [āmta]$_O$ [bhānche=ta]$_R$ bir-ju
        then   3sDAT   cook=DAT   give-3sPST

'Then he gave her (in marriage) to the cook.'[75]

The existence of such examples indicates that casemarking does not group R arguments exclusively with the O of transitive verbs, hence does not distinguish a primary-object pattern. The fact that many Os of transitive verbs are not casemarked (all those that are non-human or new) also argues against a primary-object analysis. (For further discussion, see Genetti 1997: 49–52.)

One might also be tempted to argue that R arguments constitute indirect objects since the dative case is obligatory there, whereas O arguments constitute direct objects since the assignment of dative case on O is dependent on semantic and pragmatic factors. However, the fact that casemarking is obligatory on R arguments certainly results from the fact that the referents of R arguments are overwhelmingly human and given, thus in this environment the casemarking has become grammatical. This distinction, however, would be based on only a small number of highly unusual examples, thus would constitute only weak evidence for a syntactic division of object classes. There is no other morphological or syntactic behavior that distinguishes O from R (see Genetti 1997 for further discussion).

3.2. Relative clauses

As noted above, relative clauses in which the head noun is coreferential with the object (O or R) are formed with the NR2 nominalizer, as in examples (19) and (20). This fact is also generally true of oblique relative clauses. However, oblique arguments are not core arguments, meaning that they are not specified in the lexical structure of the verb. Thus we can make the generalization that objects are the only core arguments that require NR2 in the formation of relative clauses.

3.3. The emphatic possessive āme tuŋ

Only objects, O and R, may function as antecedents of the emphatic possessive construction āme tuŋ (composed of the genitive third-person pronoun followed by the focus particle). Although I have no simple examples of this form in my discourse data, I have many elicited examples which my speakers produced while we explored the syntax of reflexives. While the reflexive pronoun has a subject noun phrase as its antecedent, the antecedent of āme tuŋ may only be an object (O or R):

(28) Elicited: Reflexive pronoun with antecedent A
 rām=na   mucā **thau** mā=ta   bir-ju
 Ram=ERG child REFL mother=DAT give-3sPST

 'Ram$_i$ gave the child to his$_i$ own mother.'

(29) Elicited: Emphatic possessive with antecedent O
 rām=na   mucā **āme**   **tuŋ** mā=ta   bir-ju
 Ram=ERG child 3sGEN FOC mother=DAT give-3sPST

 'Ram gave the child$_i$ to his$_i$ own mother.'

(30) Elicited: Emphatic possessive with antecedent R
 rām=na   krisna=ta   **āme**   **tuŋ** kitāb bir-ju
 Ram=ERG Krisna=DAT 3sGEN FOC book give-3sPST

 'Ram gave Krisna$_i$ his$_i$ own book.'

This construction thus constitutes evidence for the grammatical relation of object, consisting of O and R.

4. Dative-experiencer constructions

There are a number of distinct types of dative-experiencer constructions. These are fully discussed in §12.5. The primary question to ask regarding dative-experiencer constructions and grammatical relations is whether or not the dative-marked argument constitutes a grammatical subject. In other words, does it share grammatical properties with S, CS, and A? The evidence argues that the dative-marked experiencer is unique in only sharing some of the morphosyntactic properties of S, CS, and A.

4.1. Subject behavior and dative experiencers

The most robust of the criteria for subject in this language is the ability of subjects to trigger verb agreement (§6.4). As discussed above, the finite verb agrees with the subject in person and number. However, the verb does not agree with a dative-experiencer argument, but must be in third-person-singular form:

(31) [janta]$_{EXP}$ **pyāṭāwāt-a**
      1sDAT   hungry-3sPST

      'I am hungry.'

(32) [thijita]$_{EXP}$ pāp lāg-ai   **jur-a**
      1pINC.DAT   sin touch-BV   be-3sPST

      'We have sinned.'

This constitutes a substantial difference between dative experiencers and subjects.

The second criterion that distinguishes the grammatical relation of subject is the appearance of the NR1 nominalizer in subject relative clauses. Dative experiencers do act like subjects in this regard. The examples below illustrate relative clauses built off several varieties of the dative-experiencer construction; they all use NR1 in the relative clause. NR2 is unattested in my data and judged ungrammatical by at least some native speakers.

(33) [[bhut]$_{STIM}$ lāg-ai   **ju**]$_{REL}$ misāmi
      ghost   touch-BV   be(NR1)   woman

      'Woman possessed by a ghost...'
      (cp. ām misāmi=ta but lāg-ai jur-a 'That woman is possessed by a ghost.')

(34) [so-i **mā-yā-u=pen**]ᴿᴱᴸ
watch-INF NEG-like-NR1=PL

'(People) who don't like to watch...'
(cp. *mi=pista so-i mā-yā* 'People don't like to watch.')

(35) Elicited
[[*dyābā*]ₛₜᵢₘ **mal-gu**]ᴿᴱᴸ *mi*
money   need-NR1 man

'Man who needs money...'
(cp. *ām mi=ta dyābā mal-a* 'That man needs money.')

(36) Elicited
[*pyāṭāwā-ku*]ᴿᴱᴸ *mucā*
hungry-NR1   child

'Hungry child...'
(cp. *mucā=ta pyāṭāwāt-a* 'The child is hungry.')

The third criterion which syntactically distinguishes subjects is their behavior in infinitive complements. This behavior is not relevant to dative-experiencer constructions. This is for two reasons. First, the complement-taking predicate *bir-* 'give' is permissive in meaning and hence semantically incompatible with the non-volitional and non-control predicates of dative-experiencer constructions. Second, evidence for subject under the complement-taking predicate *yer-* involves "raising" of the subject of the complement clause by marking it with dative case. As dative experiencers already have dative case, there is no way to tell whether or not it has been raised.

The fourth ctriterion which syntactically distinguishes subjects is that only subjects can function as antecedents for reflexives. Dative experiencers do function in this manner, e.g. *janta thau wāsti mal-a* [1sDAT REFL clothes need-3sPST] 'I need my own clothes'. Therefore dative experiencers do share this subject property with A, S, and CS.

In sum, dative experiencers share with grammatical subjects the ability to serve as antecedents of reflexives and NR1 marking on the verb when they head a relative clause. However they differ significantly from subjects in not triggering agreement on the finite verb. They are thus a syntactically unique class.

Chapter 14
Constituent order

1. Introduction

So far this book has examined the sound system of Dolakha Newar, the lexical classes, the structure of noun-phrase constituents, the argument structure of basic clause types, and the grammatical relations which the arguments hold with the verbs. We will now turn to the question of the ordering of those arguments, focusing specifically on noun-phrase constituents which function as core arguments, that is, arguments which fill roles specified in the argument structure of a verb.

While it might seem that tracking the relative order of A, S, O, and R and their positioning with respect to the verb is a relatively straightforward matter, the majority of clauses in connected discourse actually have no overt arguments or only one overt argument. Dolakha Newar speakers make extensive use of "zero anaphora", or the omission of arguments which could in principle be phonologically realized. Arguments are omitted under a number of conditions. For example, arguments whose referents are unimportant to the discourse will usually be omitted, as in (1):

(1) āmu indira gandi=ta syā-ku mi=ta phā̃si bi-e le
    that Indira Gandhi=DAT kill-NR1 man=DAT hanging give-NR2 PRT

    '(They) hung the man who killed Indira Gandhi.'

Here the identity of the executioner is unknown and unimportant.

The opposite condition may also trigger the omission of arguments, as arguments are commonly unexpressed if their referents are recoverable from the discourse context. In example (2), the speaker is addressing someone who has come to the village for a visit and so it is clear that the comment refers to her.

(2) nis-nu sõ-nu cõ-i mal-a ka
    two-day three-day stay-INF must-3sPST ASS

    '(She) must stay two or three days.'

Arguments are also commonly omitted when the referent has been mentioned in the immediately preceding discourse, as in the second line of example (3):

(3) āle ām tākku bobu=ri kānā ju-i doŋ-guju
then that time father =IND blind be-INF finish-3sPA

buḍā ju-en kānā ju-i doŋ-guju
old.man be-PART blind be-INF finish-3sPA

'At that time, the father became blind. (He) grew old and became blind.'

The issue of zero anaphora is further complicated by the syntactic structure of complex sentences. In sentences where clauses have been tightly combined, it is not always possible to uniquely determine which clause a noun phrase is an argument of. Consider example (4).

(4) āle chin githi yeŋ-an hā-en bi-na?
then 2sERG how do-PART bring-PART give-2sFUT

'Then what will you do to bring (it) and give (it) (to me)?'

Here we have one ergative-marked noun phrase followed by a string of three transitive verbs. One could assume that the ergative noun phrase is the argument of only the first clause, as it is contiguous with it, and that the subjects of the clauses instantiated by the final two verbs have been omitted. However, the syntax of clause combining suggests that the inter-clausal structure is tightly integrated and that multiple verbs may share overt arguments. Further discussion of these issues may be found in Chapters 19 and 21. Here I will say only that I consider the ergative-marked noun phrase in (4) to be the subject of all three transitive verbs simultaneously and that there is no zero anaphora of any subject argument in this example. The object noun phrase of the final two verbs has been omitted under zero anaphora, as it is easily recoverable from context (the referent is a sum of money).

Because of such grammatical complexity that arises in the interweaving of clauses, it is difficult to count the number of clauses that occur in a given text and hence to calculate the percentage of overt arguments that occur per clause over a stretch of discourse, i.e. the "referential density" (Durie 2003).[76] A more insightful approach to these issues is one which takes into account the essential nature of the core syntax of the language. The key unit of discourse structuring in this language is not the clause but the sentence (see also Genetti and Crain 2003), which may be composed of a number of clauses with greater or lesser degrees of integration.

Given the issues just discussed, the question remains as to how to study constituent order, which examines ordering between arguments and the verb. We can begin with the following observation: if a verb or a string of verbs has only one overt core argument, with overwhelmingly greater than chance frequency, the overt argument will precede the verb or verb string. This is true regardless of the grammatical role of the argument (A, S, O, R). Thus the orders AV, SV, OV, and RV are all frequently attested in my database. Although I have hundreds of verbs with a single overt argument, I have only six examples which do not conform to the observation above. Three have VO order and three have VS order. (Post-verbal positioning of arguments is further discussed below.) We can thus confidently affirm that Dolakaha Newar is a verb-final language.

With this basic ordering established, the discussion of constituent order may then focus on cases where a verb or a string of verbs has more than one overt core argument. This will necessarily involve transitive or ditransitive verbs, as intransitive verbs have only one core argument, the S. In my discourse database, I have about 200 examples of such cases. The current study thus focuses on the relative order of A, O, R and the verb in these examples. It will show that the basic order of constituents is A(R)OV, but that the pragmatic status of arguments may lead to alternate orders. In particular, arguments which are topics have a tendency to be fronted, while arguments which are focused have a tendency to be positioned directly before the verb.

It should be noted that the ditransitive verb *hat-* 'say' has been given special treatment due to its unique function. This verb is used extensively to incorporate quoted material into narrative discourse. Direct quotes are syntactically embedded as object complements of the quotative verb (§18.2.3), and hence constitute the O in such examples. However, embedded direct quotes have been excluded from the current study of constituent order. This is because direct quotes are not discourse referents and also because their ordering is highly predictable. Direct quotes regularly occur directly before the quotative verb. While embedded direct quotes have been excluded from the current study, the relative ordering of the A (speaker) and the R (addressee) is included.

2. Transitive verbs: AOV and OAV orders

When two core arguments, A and O, precede a transitive verb (or a string of verbs, one of which is transitive), the unmarked order is for the A to precede the O. We may consider AOV to be the unmarked order of the major constituents of a transitive clause for the following reasons. First, AOV occurs more frequently than OAV at a greater than 2:1 ratio. Second, AOV is the order naturally volunteered by consultants in elicitation when they are asked to translate examples which have no established discourse context. Third, AOV is the order found when the A and O referents have similar pragmatic status. The example in (5) illustrates the last point.

Section 2 *Transitive verbs: AOV and OAV orders*   323

(5) bobu   ho   kae=n=ri   thi-gur   anauthā=e   cij
     father and son=ERG=IND   one-CL   strange=GEN thing

     khoŋ-a   ju-en   con-a   [kwākarbeŋ =na]₍ₐ₎ [sā]o na-e
     see-NR2 be-PART stay-3sPST frog=ERG   cow   eat-NR2

     'It turns out the father and son saw a very strange thing: a frog eating a cow.'

The third line of this example contains a nominalized complement clause which has been postposed and put into its own intonation unit to give it special emphasis. This clause introduces two new referents which have equal pragmatic status; they are both new participants so they both lack topicality and they are both equally in focus. Thus there are no pragmatic features which might influence the ordering of arguments. In such cases, the A consistently precedes the O.

In many of the examples of AO ordering, the O argument is unimportant in the story. It may be inanimate, non-specific, non-referential, and/or non-individuated. Examples of such cases are given in (6)–(8):

(6) [chipen nis-mā=n]₍ₐ₎   [jā]ₒ   na-en   yā
     2p   two-CL=ERG   rice   eat-PART   come.IMP

     'You two eat rice and come back'.

(7) [kehẽ=uri=n]₍ₐ₎   [sut-pānt]ₒ   phi-ene
     y.sister=IND=ERG   suit-pant   wear-PART

     'The younger sister wearing a suit with pants...'

(8) [dokhusenuŋ]₍ₐ₎ [baji]ₒ ta-e   ju-en   con-a
     all.ERG   bets   put-NR2   be-PART stay-3sPST

     'It turns out they all placed bets.'

In addition, the A argument, usually the animate instigator of an event, tends to be an important character in the story and hence have the pragmatic status of topic. Topics are referents which have been discussed in the preceding discourse and which the events and states being related in the clause provide information about (§10.3.2). Topical arguments are usually found in clause-initial position. This makes sense as the topic constitutes the "starting point" (Chafe 1994: 82–91) from which the rest of the clause proceeds. In (9) the topical status of A is reinforced by the topic particle; however topics can also occur without the particle, as in (10) and (11):

(9)   [āmun wā]_A hātiŋ   [jawāph]_O bi   ma-pha-ene
      3sERG TOP   nothing answer   give NEG-able-PART

      'He was unable to give any answer.'

(10) [jin]_A [āmu māji=e   mica]_O   hā-i
      1sERG   that boatman=GEN   daughter bring-1FUT

      'I will bring that boatman's daughter.'

(11) [āmun]_A [hirā=e   mālā]_O khoŋ-an   khor-a   ka
      3sERG   diamond=GEN   garland   see-PART   cry-3sPST ASS

      'He saw the diamond necklace and cried.'

In example (10), the speaker has just been asked whom he will marry. Thus he constitutes the referent of the pronoun *ji* and the topic of this clause. The remainder of the clause following the pronoun provides new information about his intended actions. In (11), the speaker has just been asked why a child is crying. The child (the referent of *āmun*) is the topic, the previously mentioned participant about whom the clause relates new information. The remainder of the first clause, including both the O argument and the verb *khoŋ-an*, constitutes the new information (or the "focus") which is set against the backdrop of the presupposition that the child is crying.

It is most common in discourse for the A argument of a transitive clause to be a topic and for the O argument of a transitive clause to either be the focus or to be non-topical, i.e. inanimate, non-specific, and/or non-individuated. When arguments have these prototypical pragmatic values the constituent order is AOV. When the pragmatic status of A and O are reversed, such that the O is the topic and/or the A is the focus, the ordering of the constituents may also be reversed. In example (12), a woman has just been explaining to a prince how her life force is tied up with a diamond necklace:

(12) [āmu hirā=e   mālā]_O   [thamun]_A hā-i
      that diamond=GEN   garland   2hERG   bring-INF

      phar-sa ji   mwāt-agi
      able-if 1s   survive-1sPR

      'If you bring that diamond necklace, I will survive.'

The diamond necklace is clearly the topical referent, that which has been discussed and that needs to be manipulated for the resolution of the story. It is grammatically and semantically the O of the clause but it is placed before the A due to its status as a topical argument. The A argument, together with the verb, constitutes the new information and the focus of the clause. For this reason the A argument and the verb are adjacent and the resulting constituent order is OAV.

A similar example is given in (13):

(13) [u khā=ri]ₒ [āmu mucā=n]ₐ sir-ai
      this talk=IND that child=ERG know-3sPR

'That child knows this talk.'

At the point in the story where this clause occurs, it has just been established that the goat, the girl's magical protector, is to be killed. The noun phrase *u khā=uri* refers to this fact which thus constitutes the topic of the clause. It represents the information which is known and which provides the point of departure for the new information; the girl's knowledge of the coming events. This constitutes the focus, so it follows the topic. The result is OAV order.

The O argument of a transitive clause also precedes the A when the A is realized by a noun phrase containing an indefinite or interrogative pronoun. In both cases, the A is the focus of the clause, so is in preverbal position:

(14) [jin thē]ₒ [thakkar wā]ₒ **[gunān]**ₐ nar-ju?
      1sERG like trouble TOP who.ERG eat-3sPST

'Who has eaten (experienced) trouble like me?'

(15) āpista **gunānuŋ** phon-da mā-yā
      3pDAT nobody.ERG ask.for-IP NEG-come

'No one came to ask for them (in marriage).'

In (14), the presupposed information (what is known) is that someone has been massaging the addressee (a young child) with oil. The only information not known is the identity of A, hence the interrogative pronoun in used. As the requested information, this constitutes the focus of the clause. In (15), a slightly different situation arises. Here the topic argument *āpista* refers to five sisters who have been discussed in the previous discourse. After turning down multiple suitors, they are confronted by the unfortunate situation reported in the clause. The new information and focus is the now empty set of possible suitors. This is conveyed by the indefinite pronoun in the A position, followed by a negated verb. (Indefinite pronouns with negated verbs are further discussed in §15.6.)

In a few examples of OAV order, the O is not particularly topical nor the A in focus. Instead, the O is "heavy", containing significantly more lexical material than the A. This appears to motivate the switch in constituent order, as in (16):

(16)   [*āme*   *dyābā=e*   *dobbar*   *dyābā*]ₒ   [*jin*]ᴀ   *pul-i*   *mal-a*
         3sGEN   money=GEN   double   money   1sERG   pay-INF   must-3sPST

        'I must pay money (equal to) double of his money.'

3. Ditransitive verbs: AROV and other permutations

Ditransitive verbs allow for three arguments, the A, the O and the R, the latter referring to the recipient of transfer verbs or the addressee of utterance verbs. If the R is omitted and the clause has only A and O overtly expressed, the ordering follows the principles outlined in the section above.

The unmarked order for arguments of ditransitive verbs is for A to precede R, and for R to precede O. In my database, I have 18 examples of overt expression of both A and R; in 15 (83%) the A precedes the R. I also have 35 examples with overt R and O; in 26 (74%) the R precedes the O.

In the prototypical ditransitive clause, both the A and the R are animate, definite, and often topical. The O, by contrast, is generally inanimate and is often new and/or non-specific. An example of this type is given in (17):

(17)   [*jin*]ᴀ   [*chanta*]ʀ   [*thi-gur khā*]ₒ   *har-i*
         1sERG   2sDAT   one-CL talk   say-1FUT

        'I will tell you one thing.'

When all three arguments are overt, the speaker may deviate from this unmarked order and place either the O or the R in clause-initial position. As with the transitive clauses discussed above, this occurs when the fronted argument is the topic of the clause:

(18)   [*janta*]ʀ   *chē=ku*   [*cijmā=n*]ᴀ   [*nai*]ₒ   *ma-bi-u*
         1sDAT   house=LOC   stepmother=ERG   food   NEG-give-3PA

        'At the house my stepmother doesn't give me food.'

(19) [ām thi-mnā   jāki =uri]ₒ   [jin]ₐ [ām jogi=ta]ᵣ
      that one-measure uncooked.rice=IND   1s   that yogi=DAT

   bir-gi
   give-1sPST

   'I gave that one measure of rice to that yogi.'

Example (18) occurs in response to a question about why the speaker is unhappy and constantly crying. The referent *janta* thus constitutes the known information and the topic. This contrasts with the rest of the clause, which contains all new information. Example (19) occurs after discussion of a particular portion of rice. The rice is thus the topic and what happened to it (the gift of it to the yogi) is the new information.

When only the R and the O are overt, we find that the unmarked order is ROV. Once again, however, the same pragmatic conditions motivate reversals in ordering. O may be placed in initial position if it is a topic, as in (20); R can be positioned directly before the verb if it is focused, as in (21); and O can precede R if both of these conditions hold, as in (22).

(20) [u   khā]ₒ [daju=ri=ta]ᵣ   hat-ai
      this talk   e.brother=IND=DAT   say-3sPR

   'He says this talk to his brother.'

(21) la   tyasale   [jana thi-mā mica]ₒ   [chanta tuŋ]ᵣ bir-agi
      then therefore 1sGEN one-CL daughter 2sDAT   FOC give-1sPR

   'Then in that case I give my daughter to you.'

(22) [u   khā=ri]ₒ   [guntaŋ]ᵣ   da-hat!
      this talk=IND   nobody.DAT   PROH-say

   'This thing don't tell to anybody!'

4. Post-verbal arguments

Although relatively rare, core (and oblique) arguments may also be positioned at the end of a syntactic sentence, after the finite verb and any post-verbal particles. I have a total of 25 examples of this in my discourse database. This is enough to establish post-verbal positioning as a real pattern, but one that occurs in less than 1% of my data. Given the limited data set, it is difficult to say with certainty what motivates this positioning. However, I am able to make a few observations that may point in useful directions for future study of this phenomenon.

In a few examples, post-verbal arguments are in a separate intonation unit from the clause preceding. These appear to be "afterthoughts" of the speaker, essentially clarification of the identity of a referent that had been omitted and that the speaker judges may be unclear. In the following example, each intonation unit is represented on a separate line and slashes indicate a falling intonation contour (§3.4.1):

(23) [thi-mā=n]$_A$ kho=ku   ṭin-da   on-a
      one-CL=ERG   river=LOC throw-PURP   go-3sPST

      [ām mucā=ta=uri]$_O$
      that child=DAT=IND

      'One went to throw (him) into the river, that child.'

Post-verbal noun phrases also occur when an overt argument before the verb is particularly heavy. The post-verbal positioning allows for a clear separation of the two arguments. In such examples, the post-verbal argument may be intonationally linked, or in a separate intonation unit.

(24) [thi-tākā   dyābā   danḍa]$_O$ ṭiret-cu   [sāŋat=pista]$_R$
      one-rupee   money   fine   pay-3sPST   friend=PL.DAT

      '(He) paid a one rupee fine to his friends.'

About 25% of my examples of post-verbal noun phrases occur in information questions. In most of these examples, the post-verbal argument refers to the addressee:

(25) āu   githi yeŋ-an   mwāt-ke-i   mal-a   [chanta]$_R$?
      now   how   do-PART   survive-CAUS-INF   must-3sPST   2sDAT

      'Now how must I act (i.e. what must I do) to make you come alive?'

I have one example where the post-verbal argument in a question refers to the speaker:

(26) [thi-gur dyābā =e   jāki]$_O$ guli   bi   [jin]$_A$?
      one-CL   money=GEN   uncooked.rice   how.much   give.1FUT 1sERG

      'How much rice do I give for one paisa?'

There still remain about ten examples outside of these categories for which I have no ready explanation. I can say that these examples, like the questions, tend to be very short, consisting either of a single clause or of a single sentence in which two verbs share all arguments. They are all pronounced rapidly and under a single intonation contour. They thus appear to be relatively simple, coherent and bounded units.

Chapter 15
Clause-level syntactic constructions

1. Introduction

Chapter 12 outlined the basic clause types of Dolakha Newar. The purpose of this chapter is to discuss a variety of other clause-level constructions which interact with, add to, and otherwise complicate the basic clause types of the language. These include a causative construction, the affected-participant construction, non-declarative constructions, reflexives and reciprocals, negation, and comparatives.[77]

2. Causative constructions

Dolakha Newar has lexical and morphosyntactic means of expressing causation. Lexically, there are a number of pairs of verbs where the intransitive member begins with a voiced consonant and the transitive member begins with a voiceless aspirated consonant. The transitive verb consistently has a causative meaning, such that an agent causes the event to occur. Examples are given in (1):

(1)
Intransitive		Transitive	
gyāt-	'fear'	khyāt-	'scare'
ḍin-	'sleep'	ṭhin-	'make sleep; put to bed'
ḍon-	'wake up'	ṭhon-	'rouse'
ṭapjyāt-	'break (INTR)'	ṭapchyāt-	'break (TR)'

Verbs in such pairs constitute regular intransitive and transitive verbs and do not exhibit any odd morphological or syntactic behavior. For example, they have the same argument structure as other intransitive and transitive verbs. Subjects of intransitives are unmarked for case, e.g. *ji gyāt-agi* [1s fear-1sPR] 'I am afraid', while transitive clauses have ergative subjects and dative objects (if human and given), e.g. *thaeta dhū=n khyāŋ-a* [2hDAT tiger=ERG be-NR2] '(A story about) a tiger scaring you'.

The morphological causative utilizes the productive causative suffix *-ker*, which attaches to the verb stem. Its full inflection is given in §6.6.2. Here it will only be noted that this suffix derives an r-stem verb with regular r-stem inflection, with one exception. There are two participial forms of the causative suffix. The form *-ke-en* is the expected causative form, and this does occasionally occur. More common, however, is the shortened version, -ke, e.g. āmun mucā=ta na-ke con-a [3sERG child-DAT eat-CAUS.PART stay-3sPST] 'He is feeding the child'.

There are a number of verbs which take the causative suffix with sufficient frequency that they might be considered to be lexicalized. These include the verbs given in (2):

(2) Simplex   Causative
     dat-   'exist'   da-ker-   'make'
     nar-   'eat'   na-ker-   'feed'
     bon-   'read'   bon-ker-   'teach'
     sor-   'see'   so-ker-   'show'

There appears to be a preference for the causative suffix to be used in cases of direct causation, meaning action by an agent to bring about a physical affect on a patient. Indirect causation, such as causation brought about by telling somebody to do something, is signaled by use of a direct quote. For example, the verb na-ker- 'feed', may only be used to denote a situation where one places the food into the mouth of another, as when a mother is feeding a very young child. If a mother were making an older child eat, the appropriate sentence would be: mā=n mucā=ta "na-u" hat-cu [mother=ERG child=DAT eat-IMP say-3sPST] 'The mother said to the child: "Eat!"'. This complementation strategy is further discussed in §18.3.2.

The morphological causative is a valence-increasing device; that is, it syntactically incorporates an additional core argument (the "causee") to the clause. Intransitive verbs are thus rendered transitive and allow for an ergative-marked subject. In most cases, the causee will be human and given, and so will be in dative case:[78]

(3) Elicited
     āmun   janta   **nil-ker-ju**
     3sERG   1sDAT   laugh-CAUS-3sPST

     'He made me laugh.'

(4) āu   githi   yeŋ-an   **mwāt-ke-i**   mal-a   chanta?
     now   how   do-PART   survive-CAUS-INF   must-3sPST   2sDAT

     'Now how must (I) act to make you survive?'

However, if the causee is inanimate, then it does not take dative casemarking. This is perfectly in line with the principles for assignment of dative case, discussed in §4.4.2. An example is āmun jā but-ker-gi [3sERG rice cook-CAUS-

3sPST] 'He made the rice cook/cooked the rice'; under no circumstance that I am aware of can *jā* 'rice' be in dative case.

When the causative suffix is bound to a transitive verb, a ditransitive verb with two objects is derived. One object is the causee and the other is the patientive O of the verb root. Again, dative casemarking follows the normal patterns of assignment. Since the causee of a transitive verb is generally human and given, it will be in dative case. In most causative constructions, the patientive O of the ditransitive verb is either absent or inanimate and hence not casemarked:

(5) Elicited
 *āmun   mucā=ta   jā   **na-ker-ju***
 3sERG child=DAT rice eat-CAUS-3sPST

 'She made the child eat rice; fed the child rice.'

(6) *āle   mucā=ta   bā=uri=n   **bon-ker-ju***
 then   child=DAT   father=IND=ERG   read-CAUS-3sPST

 'Then the father made the child read; taught the child.'

I also have several elicited examples where both the causee and the patientive O of the causativized verb are human and given, so dative-marked. At this point, I suspect that these constructions, while technically possible, are marginal in the language, and that alternative strategies, such as the employment of a direct quote to convey the causation, would be used. One of the elicited examples is given in (7). In the few such examples that I have, the causee consistently precedes the patientive O:

(7) Elicited
? *āmun   janta   mucā=ta   **ḍā-ker-ju***
 3sERG 1sDAT child=DAT beat-CAUS-3sPST

 'He made me beat the child.'

A more natural way to express the meaning of the previous example is to include in the clause the auxiliary verb *lyāt-* 'order; consign'. This follows the infinitive form of a causativized verb and indicates that the causee had no choice but to carry out the action of the verb. The use of this auxiliary necessarily construes the event as realis. Thus, while example (7) was accepted by my consultant when I volunteered it, the original structure which she volunteered is given in (8):

(8) Elicited
āmun janta mucā=ta *ḍa-ke-i*   *lyāt-cu*
3sERG 1sDAT child=DAT beat-CAUS-INF order-3sPST

'He made me beat the child.' (i.e. 'forced')

I have no examples of ditransitive verbs with the causative suffix in my discourse data. An elicited example is given in (9).

(9) Elicited
? āmun janta chanta dyābā *bi-ker-ju*
3sERG 1sDAT 2sDAT money give-CAUS-3sPST

'He made me give you the money.'

Once again, this is an elicited sentence that I think is somewhat unnatural. Since the causative suffix is used primarily when the causee is physically affected, alternative strategies would be more appropriate. For example, one consultant whom I worked with rejected an almost identical sentence meaning 'The thief made me give him all my money', rephrasing it as 'The thief took all my money'. This fact, together with the lack of any ditransitive causative verbs in my discourse data, leads me to believe that such examples are rarely attested.

3. The verb *bir-* 'give' and the marking of affected participants

The verb *bir-* 'give' is a "versatile verb" in Dolakha Newar. That is, it is a verb which has both lexical and grammatical functions. When the verb has a grammatical function, it is syntactically an auxiliary verb; it does not instantiate a new clause but instead contributes meaning to the larger clause of which it is a part. In this environment, the main verb is in participial form and *bir-* indicates that the action of the main verb has a significant effect (positive or negative) on a discourse participant.

The participial construction is discussed in detail in Chapter 19. It instantiates a number of distinct syntactic structures and semantic interpretations. It is often used to place two clauses together which denote events in a sequence, as in (10):

(10) [āme   kuciri=lān   sā-ku   sā-ku   cij   piṭa
     3sGEN   nail=ABL   tasty-NR1 tasty-NR1 thing out

kā-en]_CL   [**bir-ai**]_CL
take-PART   give-3sPR

'(He) took out tasty tasty things from his (magical) fingernails and gave them (to her).'

In this example, there are two events, the removal of the tasty things from the nails, and the transfer of those things to the girl. It is also possible for a participial clause to be interpreted as conveying a manner of action for a following clause, as in (11):

(11) thamun bothā-en   **bi-sin**
      2hERG   divide-PART   give-IMP

'You give it by dividing it up.'

In many examples taken from connected discourse, it is difficult to differentiate these meanings. Example (11) is of this type. It could equally be translated as 'divide it and give it'. This and related issues are discussed in Chapter 19. At this point, I will only note that both types of examples are considered to be biclausal; the clause with the second verb could in principle be expanded by the addition of arguments or adverbials.

These biclausal structures contrast with that in which *bir-* 'give' is an auxiliary. In these constructions, nothing may intervene between the main verb and the auxiliary verb. In addition, *bir-* 'give' does not literally refer to an act of physical transfer (as do the examples above). Instead, the meaning is abstract. The construction essentially indicates that the event denoted by the verb will have a significant effect on a participant in the discourse, most commonly a beneficiary, as in (12)–(14), but also at times a maleficiary, as in (15) and (16):

(12) chana   lās   chop   yeŋ-an   **bi**
      2sGEN   shyness   cover   do-PART   give.1FUT

'(I) will cover your shyness.'

(13) chanta   gunān   tel   lāŋ-an   **bir-ai?**
      2sDAT   who.ERG   oil   rub-PART   give-3sPR

'Who rubs you with oil?'

(14) gakkeŋ mi=pista lā-ke **bi-en** coŋ-guju
many man=PL.DAT heal-CAUS.PART give-PART stay-3sPA

'He used to heal many men.'

(15) ām chandramā=ta catta pwāl-en **bir-ju**
that Chanrama=DAT immeditely strike-PART give-3sPST

'He immediately struck that Chandrama.'

(16) āle mucā=ta besna kucin ti-en **bi-e**
then child=DAT very pinch pinch-PART give-NR2

ju-en con-a
be-PART stay-3sPST

'Then it happened that he pinched the child very hard.'

Note that in (12), the beneficiary is not a grammatical argument of the clause, or is only so obliquely, as the "possessor" of the shyness. Thus this construction indicates a significant effect on some participant, not necessarily an argument, who is identifiable from the broader discourse context. However, usually this participant is a grammatical argument of the main clause verb, as in (13)–(16).

It is also possible for this construction to be applicative, that is, to incorporate an additional argument referring to the affected participant into a clause as an object, as in example (13) above and (17):

(17) janta lukhā khoŋ-an **bi-sin**
1sDAT door open-PART give-IMP

'Open the door for me.'

Here the verb *khon-* 'open' is a transitive verb which takes two arguments, the A and the O, in this case the door. The clause requires the auxiliary verb in order to incorporate the beneficiary *janta* as an object. While this construction allows such an increase in valency, it does not require it. In many cases, such as (15) above, the affected participant already has an argument role in the clause, and an additional slot is not called for.

We can understand the development from a lexical verb meaning 'give' to an auxiliary verb indicating the presence of an affected participant as the result of a common metaphorical process by which events are conceptualized as concrete objects. In many of the examples, a trace of the concrete meaning of 'give' is still discernable. For example, in performing a favor, the action performed can be seen as being a gift to the recipient.

In many instances of this construction, the sense of 'give' as a transfer verb is clearly discernable. For example, in the sentence *jin haŋ-an bi* [1sERG say-PART give(1FUT)] 'I will tell you' the implication is not just that the recipient of the clause will benefit from the information, but also that there is a chunk of information which is "given" from the A to the R.

Many examples taken from connected discourse are ambiguous between whether they constitute one clause with the verb *bir-* 'give' functioning as an auxiliary, or two clauses, with the verb instantiating an independent clause. Consider example (18):

(18) lũ=e   bo   thi-pta   hā-en   **bi-u**
      gold =GEN plate one-CL   bring-PART   give-IMP

'Bring a plate of gold and give it (to him).' OR 'Bring a plate of gold for him.'

Although English, into which I am translating these sentences, requires us to distinguish between these meanings, my impression is that Dolakha Newar does not. If I ask my consultants which of these meanings is the "correct" translation, they wisely inform me that the meanings are the same.[79] If one brings a plate with the explicit purpose of giving it to someone, one also brings it for someone. Although one can produce similar sentences that have unambiguous structures, for example, by inserting a dative-marked argument before *biu*, rendering it unambiguously biclausal, this does not solve the issue of how to analyze this sentence. In later chapters of this book, I will use the term "bistructural" to refer to such cases, which come up quite often in the analysis of complex sentences. Essentially, both structures are equally instantiated and both meanings are equally appropriate. Of course, it is just such structures that allow for grammaticalization to occur, such as the reanalysis of the verb as an auxiliary. The structure occurs with sufficient frequency to allow for a slightly different orientation, a slight relaxing of literality, an adjustment of structural relations. Such a semantic and structural shift, however, does not leave the original structure and meaning behind. Instead, both alternatives coexist and the sentence takes on a chameleon-like quality, one color when viewed in one light, and another color as the light shifts.

4. Non-declarative constructions

The majority of finite verbs in connected discourse are declarative and take the regular inflection of finite morphology presented in §6.4.1. However, there are also a number of non-declarative clause types, some of which have distinct morphosyntactic behaviors. These include imperative, prohibitive, optative, interrogative, and hortative constructions.

4.1. Imperative and prohibitive constructions

The imperative mood is signaled by a distinct set of verbal suffixes, which agree with the subject in number and honorific status, as discussed in §6.5. (As imperatives are obligatorily second-person forms, there is no person agreement.) Imperative clauses do not differ from declarative clauses in their argument structure. Omission of the second-person addressee in imperative clauses is common, as in (19); however it is not required. When the addressee is included, it is necessarily the grammatical subject and is casemarked in accordance with the transitivity of the imperative verb, examples (20) and (21):

(19) dolakhā bhāsā=n **har-sin**
 Dolakha language=INST say-IMP

 'Speak in the Dolakha language.'

(20) chi **cõ**
 2s stay.IMP

 'You stay.'

(21) thamun "khyaŋ" **har-sin**
 2hERG be.true say-IMP

 'You say "It is true".'

Imperatives may have scope beyond the single clause to a sequence of clauses joined by the participial construction:

(22) jā na-en **yā**
 rice eat-PART come.IMP

 'Eat rice and come.'

Such examples, however, where each verb denotes a separate event, are few in connected discourse. Imperatives do not occur with long complex sentences. Rather, imperative constructions tend to be short and succinct. It is common to find imperatives in clauses with the auxiliary bir- 'give' (the construction discussed immediately above). When this construction is combined with the imperative, the command is softened to a request for a favor, generally for the benefit of the speaker:

(23)   ām   tuŋ   lā-en   **bi-sin!**
           that   FOC   tell-PART   give-IMP

           'Please tell that one!'

(24)   simā   thābi   ta-en   **bi-u**
           tree   on   put-PART   give-IMP

           'Put (me) on the tree.'

Imperative verbs do not take the negative prefix *ma-*. Instead, negation of an imperative requires the prohibitive prefix *da-*, which is used in combination with the imperative endings:[80]

(25)   bicaku   pir   **dā-kā-u**   chin
           needlessly   worry   PROH-take-IMP   2sERG

           'Don't you worry needlessly.'

(26)   uku   **dā-yā**   nā!
           here   PROH-come   AGR

           'Don't come here!'

It is also possible to have the prohibitive doubly marked on the verb, with the prefix *da-* on the front of the verb and the prohibitive suffix *-si* on the end. At this point, I do not know the semantic or pragmatic contribution of the second suffix:

(27)   chi   **do-khor-si**
           2s   PROH-cry-IMP

           'Don't you cry.'

The same sentence with prefix only (*do-kho!*) would be appropriate, for example, when one is ordering a child to stop crying.

There is yet an additional prohibitive construction, this one involving a prohibitive auxiliary verb *ma-ṭe*. As far as I am aware, this is the only form of the verb that occurs in Dolakha Newar; the non-negated form is not attested. However, it is clearly a remnant of the Classical Newar verb *ṭeya* 'to permit' (Nepal Bhasa Dictionary Committee 2000: 165). The negated auxiliary follows an infinitive verb form. The meaning is deontic, indicating social prohibitions such as 'one should/must not' or 'it it not permitted/appropriate'.

(28) haḍbaḍ   yer-i   ma-ṭe   ka
      hurriedly do-INF NEG-PROH ASS

'Don't do it hurriedly.' OR '(You/one) should not do it in a hurry.'

(29) Elicited
      kho-i   ma-ṭe
      cry-INF NEG-PROH

'You shouldn't/mustn't cry.'

Example (29) differs from (28) above in being more advisory. It would be appropriate for use when someone is comforting another who is in tears. The form with the prohibitive prefix, by contrast, is more strongly an order. One might use it, for example, when addressing a child who cries because she did not get her way.

I also have one example of the prohibitive auxiliary being used with a third-person subject. The clause constitutes an injunction against a certain type of behavior to which the addressee should adhere. The fact that it has a third-person subject, however, keeps it from being a direct prohibitive:

(30) gunā́n   guntaŋ   helā̃   yer-i   ma-ṭe
      who.ERG nobody.DAT insult do-INF NEG-PROH

'No one should insult anybody.' (i.e. 'Don't insult anybody.')

4.2. Optative construction

Optative constructions are used to convey a wish that something will happen, generally to a third-person participant who is the A or O of the optative verb. The optative construction is especially used in curses, such as the following example, taken from a narrative:

(31) chana   gwāri gulpunuŋ bã́la-ku   ju-en   *tho-cõ*
      2sGEN heel   never   good-NR1 be-PART OPT-stay

yelpanuŋ tapjyāŋ-an **tho-cõ**
always   break-PART   OPT-stay

"'May your heels never be good'; may (they) always break (i.e. crack).'"

Here the optative clauses co-occur with the auxiliary *con-*, normally used to convey continuous aspect, but here more generally indicating durativity.

The optative construction can take on a permissive quality in certain contexts. For example, if someone is requesting to come to the house, it is possible to respond *thā-yā* [OPT-come] 'May he come; He may come; Let him come'.

The optative is generally not possible with either first- or second-person subjects. However, recall that with non-control verbs it is possible for first-person subjects to co-occur with third-person-verb forms. This "disagreement" indicates a lack of volition on the part of the subject and a sense that the event is inevitable (§6.4.3.4). This is possible with the optative construction as well, e.g. *chi tha-si* [2s OPT-die] 'May you die'. On the other hand, the optative cannot be used with a second-person subject when the verb involves a volitional action, e.g. **chin bik tha-na-u* [2sERG poison OPT-eat-IMP] 'May you eat poison'. Here the imperative would be required.

I have in my discourse data one interesting example of the optative construction with a first-person subject. The optative is possible here because it is clear that the event denoted by the optative verb is not volitional and indeed not welcome.

(32)   mucā=pen nis-mā   nāplaŋ-ane jukun **tha-si**
       child =PL two-CL   meet-PART   only   OPT-die

'May I die only after meeting my two children.'

This example is biclausal, with two clauses joined by the participial construction and the first clause limited by the particle *jukun* 'only'. Interestingly, the wish conveyed by the optative prefix extends to the condition expressed in the first clause. It is not that the speaker wishes to die (that she will die is presupposed in this example), but crucially wishes only to die *after* she has again seen her children. Thus the optative has scope over the entire construction, and especially the sequential interpropositional relationship that holds between the two clauses. One interesting aspect of this is that the construction serves as an attempt to exert a certain amount of control over the broader situation (putting a precondition on death and determining its time). This is true despite the fact that *lack* of control is being conveyed by the application of the (normally third-person) optative to a first-person clause. The result is an interesting semantic-grammatical paradox.

4.3. The hortative construction

The hortative construction is used to exhort a group of people, including the speaker, to action. The hortative suffix is *-lau*, which is bound to the infinitive form of the verb, as in (33):

(33)   u=ri   thijin   kā-i-lau!
       this=IND   1pINC.ERG   take-INF-HORT

   'Let's take this one!'

The verb 'go' has a suppletive hortative form *ŋā*, e.g. *āu tu ŋā!* [now FOC go.HORT] 'Let's go right now!' I have one example, however, from a narrative text where the verb 'go' has the hortative suffix:

(34)   isi   chẽ=ku   ũ-i-lau   nā!
       1pEXC.GEN   house=LOC   go-INF-HORT   AGR

   'Let's go to our house!'

Within the narrative, this utterance occurred when two small boys were addressing a king. It is possible that the use of the suppletive *ŋā* was considered too informal for the situation. This requires further investigation.

4.4. Interrogative constructions

Interrogative constructions can be divided into two primary types: those that inquire whether the proposition in the clause is true or false (commonly referred to as "polar" or "yes/no questions"), and those that request specific information about a particular aspect of the event denoted by the clause ("information questions").

Polar questions in Dolakha Newar are quite simple. When one is requesting that the addressee report on the truth or falsehood of the proposition, the clause denoting the proposition is simply followed by the question particle *rā* (§10.4.2.1). In addition, the clause is pronounced with a rising intonation contour (§3.4.3). The morphosyntax of these constructions is the same as in declarative clauses:

(35)   chin   khā   lā-ina   rā?
       2sERG   talk   talk-2sFUT   Q

   'Will you talk?'

(36) thamu=ri ānthi ŋil-agu **rā**?
    2h=IND that.manner laugh-2hPR Q

   'You laugh like that?'

If the clause contains a constituent marked by the focus particle *tuŋ*, then the identity of that constituent is the focus of the question; the information in the remainder of the clause is presupposed:

(37) dolakhā khā tuŋ lā-eu **rā**?
    Dolakha language FOC tell-3FUT Q

   'Will she tell (the story) in the Dolakha language?'

A more elaborate construction repeats the verb of the clause and the question particle, first in the affirmative and then in the negative. My impression is that this is used when the speaker wishes to express that s/he is equally uncertain about whether the proposition is true or false:

(38) u khā khyaŋ **rā** ma-khe **rā**?
    this talk be Q NEG-be Q

   'Is this talk true or not?'

(39) māyā=ku jit-ai ju-i phar-agu **rā** ma-phar-agu **rā**?
    love=LOC win-BV be-INF able-2hPR Q NEG-able-2hPR Q

   'Will you be able to win in love or not?'

Tag questions are used either to solicit the hearer's agreement as to the veracity of the content of the clause or to check that the hearer is following what is being said. In Dolakhae, tag questions are formed by juxtaposing a declarative statement and a tag. There are two tags; the most common is *ma-khe rā?*, formed with the negated copula and the question particle. The other tag is *hārā?* Both tags are produced with rising intonation (§3.4.3):

(40) me tuŋ hal-i mal-a le **ma-khe rā**?
    song FOC sing-INF need-3sPST PRT NEG-be Q

   'It is also necessary to sing a song, isn't that so?'

(41) chatil=ku ḍusi puyā ho turkan tha-en ta-uĩ **hārā**?
    Chatil=LOC millet seed and mustard sow-PART put-1sPA Q

   'I used to sow millet seed and mustard at Chatil, no?'

In information questions, the requested information is indicated by an interrogative word (§5.3). The pronoun generally takes prosodic accent and the final intonation contour is typically falling (§3.4.1) or level (§3.4.2). In some information questions, the sentence-final particle *le* (§10.4.2.6) is also used. Otherwise, the morphosyntax of the clause does not differ from that of a declarative:

(42) bā   ām   **hāti** **le?**
      father that what PRT

   'Father, what is that?'

(43) āpsin **hāti** yer-i   maldan-a   **le?**
      3pERG what   do-INF   need-3sPST   PRT

   'What do they need to do?'

(44) ām   khā **gulpa** har-i?
      that talk when   say-1FUT

   'When will I say that talk?'

(45) chanta **gunān**   tel lāŋ-an   bir-ai?
      2sDAT   who.ERG   oil massage-PART   give-3sPR

   'Who massages you with oil?'

It is interesting to note that in my conversational data, the presupposed information in questions tends not to be expressed. This results in questions which do not constitute entire clauses, but are fragmentary, consisting of interrogative pronouns, noun phrases, or simple verbs followed by a question particle:

(46) gu=ri   **le?**
      which=IND   PRT

   'Which one?'

(47) ām   **rā?**
      that Q

   'That?'

(48) keŋ-gu   **rā?**
      show-NR1 Q

   'Did (they) show (it)?'

5. Reflexives and reciprocals

The reflexive pronoun is *thau*. It is used for all persons and numbers. In limited circumstances (discussed below) it takes the dative casemarker =*ta*, but this represents the full extent of its inflectional possibilities.

The reflexive pronoun is most commonly used within a noun phrase to signal an emphatic or specific possessive relationship between the referent of the pronoun and the immediately following noun. The referent of the reflexive pronoun will either be the subject of the immediate clause, as in (49), the subject of the matrix clause if the pronoun is within a dependent clause (50), or a participant in the broader discourse (almost always the speaker) (51):[81]

(49) ām **thau** mula liŋar-a
      3s REFL road walk-3sPST

  'He_i walked on his_i own road.'

(50) birbāhādur [kānchi mica=n **thau** khā
      Birbahadur youngest daughter=ERG REFL talk

  mān-ai ju-e-lāgin]_ADV.CL khusi jur-a
  obey-BV be-NR2-because happy become-3sPST

  'Birbahadur_i, because his youngest daughter obeyed his_i own talk, became happy.'

(51) tibi=uri **thau** chẽ=ku ma-da
      television=IND REFL house=LOC NEG-exist

  'There is no television at my own house.' (i.e. 'I don't have a television.')

The reflexive pronoun has a specialized use with kin terms, where it denotes that the referent of the kin term is a member of the speaker's immediate family, as opposed to being a member of the extended family or community:

(52) **thau** mica=e lāhā
      REFL daughter=GEN hand

  'her own daughter's hand'

(53) **thau** tuŋ dāju bhai
REFL FOC e.brother y.brother

'my own brothers'

The reflexive pronoun also occurs in an emphatic reflexive construction. Reflexives in such constructions are sometimes referred to as "intensifiers" (e.g. König and Siemund 2005). This construction is used to assert that it was, indeed, the referent of the subject who performed the action of the verb, especially when this is surprising, counter to expectation, or requires clarification. The reflexive pronoun is often followed by the focus particle in this environment:

(54) "rājā=ke ū-i" hak-u=ta **thau** **tuŋ** hār-ju
king=ALL go-INF say-NR1=DAT REFL FOC bring-3sPST

'The king himself brought (married) the one who said: "I will go to a king".'

(55) dāju=ri=n gisā=ri **thau** kā-en
e.brother=IND=ERG cow=IND REFL take-PART

'The elder brother took the cow himself...'

Reflexive pronouns generally do not occur in object position. They are not used in phrases such as 'He killed himself'. In translating this sentence from English, speakers volunteer ām thau tuŋ sit-a [3s REFL FOC die-3SPST] 'He himself died'. A paratactic construction, specifying how the A acted to bring about his own death, would probably be more natural. I do have two examples where the reflexive takes the dative casemarker. In one, the pronoun represents a locational goal of an intransitive verb which has as its antecedent the A of the previous adverbial clause:

(56) pāp yer-sa khene **thau**=ta tuŋ ānāgu
sin do-if PRT REFL=DAT FOC that.type

phal ju ju-en con-a
return be(NR1) be-part stay-3sPST

'It turns out that if one sins, that type (of sin) returns to oneself (the sinner).'

In the other example, the reflexive pronoun refers to the speaker in a dative-experiencer construction. (This is an odd example, as the verb gyāt- 'fear' doesn't normally take a dative experiencer and the verb is inflected for first-person singular, not third person as in other dative-subject constructions. This structure deserves further exploration.)

(57)   **thau=ta**   tuŋ   gibiŋ   ma-gyāt-ki
       REFL=DAT   FOC   nowhere   NEG-fear-1s

'I wasn't afraid anywhere.'

The reflexive pronoun can be reduplicated. When the reduplicated pronoun is casemarked dative, a reciprocal meaning is produced:

(58)   rājā=e   sō-mā   kae   nāpa   ye-en   **thau**
       king=GEN   three-CL   son   together   come-PART   REFL

       thau=ta   ...   sāŋat   nāplaŋ-a   khā   hat-cu
       REFL=DAT   ...   friend   meet-NR2   talk   say-3sPST

'The king's three sons came together and told each other about the ...friends they had met.'

Without the dative casemarker, the reduplicated reflexive pronoun has a distributed meaning:

(59)   chipe   **thau**   **thau**   chē   o-n
       2pGEN   REFL   REFL   house   go-IMP.PL

'You all go to your various houses.'

(60)   sō-gur   janti   **thau**   **thau**   tarikā=n
       three-CL   procession   REFL   REFL   method=INST

       darbār=ku   then-hin
       palace=LOC   arrive-3pPST

'The three processions arrived at the palace, each by its own method.'

(61)   **thau**   **thau**   jamma   ju-en   salāhā   yet-hin
       REFL   REFL   together   be-PART   conference   do-3pPST

'The various ones came together and had a conference.'

6. Negation

Negation in Dolakha Newar is denoted by the negative morpheme *ma-*, which is affixed to the final syllable of the verb stem. Thus it is prefixed to monosyllabic verb stems and infixed between the two syllables of disyllabic verb stems (§6.4.4).[82] The morpheme undergoes vowel harmony as discussed in §2.3.5. The patterns of suffixal inflection on the negated verb differ somewhat from those of the affirmative verb; this is discussed in §6.4.4. The negation denotes that the event denoted by the verb did not, does not, or will not occur:

(62) duta **mā-yā**
 into NEG-come

 '(It) does not come inside.'

(63) āu dār chana kehẽ **mo-cõ**
 now time 2sGEN y.sister NEG-stay

 'At this time, you sister does not stay.'

(64) chū=n hāti khā=ŋ **ma-hat**
 mouse=ERG what talk=EXT NEG-say

 'The mouse didn't say anything.'

(65) cā̃da nijā chu-i **ma-phar-ju**
 quickly lunch cook-INF NEG-able-3sPST

 'She was not able to cook lunch quickly.'

When a clause with an auxiliary is negated, the negative morpheme prefixes to the auxiliary, not to the main verb. This can be seen in (65). In this case, it is the auxiliary which is the focus of negation. Contrast example (66):

(66) ām misā bihā yeŋ-an **ma-bir-ŋasin** tuŋ sit-a
 that woman marriage do-PART NEG-give-when FOC die-3sPST

 'That woman died without having been given in marriage.'

Here the phrase *bihā yeŋ-an bir-* 'to arrange a marriage' is a lexicalization of the construction in which *bir-* 'give' marks an affected patient. The crucial point is that the negative morpheme is positioned on the auxiliary and not on the lexical verb, i.e. **bihā ma-yeŋ-an bir-ŋasin* is not a possible phrase.

The negative affix may co-occur with most non-finite verb forms, the exception being the infinitive (as the following auxiliary will take the negation, as noted above). Examples of negation on nominalized clauses, a participial clause, and several adverbial clauses are given below:

(67) chijna binā nāhak=ku **mo-khoŋ-a**
1pINC.ERG pointlessly uselessness=LOC NEG-see-NR2

khā saŋkā yet-ku
talk suspect do-1pPST

'We pointlessly and uselessly suspected her without seeing (any evidence).'

(68) ināgu yer-i **ma-ji-u** ju-en con-a
this.type do-INF NEG-appropriate-NR1 be-PART stay-3sPST

'It turns out one shouldn't do this type of thing.'

(69) āmun=ri kõsa=ŋ **ma-na-en**
3sERG=IND bone=EXT NEG-eat-PART

'She didn't eat the bones...'

(70) u situgā̃s hātiŋ **ma-jur-sa** ji mwāt-a
this Grass nothing NEG-occur-if 1s survive-3sPST

haŋ-an si-u
say-PART know-IMP

'If nothing happens to this situgrass, know that I survived.'

For discussion of scope of negation in complex sentences, see §19.5.2 and §20.3.1.

Negated verbs often occur with indefinites (§5.4). Not surprisingly, this combination yields a negative indefinite reading. There are usually two ways to translate such sentences into English, either with the negative on the verb or with the negative on the pronoun. This distinction is not made in Dolakhae:

(71) janta **hātiŋ** nai **ma-bi-u**
1sDAT nothing food NEG-give-3sPR

'(She) doesn't give me any food.' OR 'She gives me no food.'

(72) āpe   kae   mica   **gunuŋ**   ma-da-u
      3pGEN   son   daughter nobody   NEG-exist-3PA

   'They didn't have any children.' OR 'They had no children.'

(73) āme   **hātiŋ**   jhar-ai   **ma-ju**
      3sGEN nothing   fall-BV   NEG-happen

   'Nothing fell from her hair.'

If the speaker wishes to give particularly strong emphasis to the fact that an event did not occur, s/he may use an emphatic negation construction. The basic construction places the verb root, minus its final consonant, directly before the negated verb:

(74) ji   wā   **yā**   **mā-yā-gi**
      1s   TOP   come   NEG-come-1sPR

   'I don't come at all.'

It is more common, however, for this to be embellished by either the extensive clitic =(u)ŋ or the focus particle tuŋ. These are positioned between the two repetitions of the verb:

(75) uli-cā   **da**   tuŋ   **ma-da**
      this.much-DIM   exist   FOC   NEG-exist

   'He doesn't even have a little.'

(76) mā=ta   **thi=ŋ**   **ma-thi-en**   thau
      mother=DAT   touch=EXT   NEG-touch-PART REFL

      khopi=ku   on-a
      alcove=LOC   go-3sPST

   'Not touching his mother at all, he went to his own room.'

(77) **ḍo**   tuŋ   **mo-ḍoŋ-gi**
      stand   FOC   NEG-stand-1sPST

   'I didn't stand up at all.'

7. Comparative and superlative constructions

In comparative constructions, two participants are compared with respect to a property. The morphosyntax of most comparative constructions entails an expansion of the simple copular construction. In addition to the copula subject, which contains the comparee (the thing being compared), there is an additional noun phrase called the standard (that which the comparee is compared to). In Dolakha Newar, the standard is directly followed by *soen*, the mark of comparison. This structure is exemplified in (78):

(78) Elicited
[priyesh soen]$_{CP}$ [iŋku]$_{cs}$ [ḍwā-ku]$_{CC}$ khyaŋ
Priyesh MARK Inku big-NR1 be

'Compared to Priyesh, Inku is big.' OR 'Inku is bigger than Priyesh.'

In this example, the basic copular structure is found in *iŋku ḍwā-ku khyaŋ*; the noun phrase containing the standard of comparison and the mark are additional elaborations on this structure. The standard and the mark together can be said to form a "comparative phrase" (CP).

In (79), the copula complement is an adjectival verb. As with other copular constructions, it is also possible for the copula complement to contain a noun phrase:

(79) Elicited
[ām mi soen]$_{CP}$ [chana bā]$_{cs}$ [bãla-ku mi]$_{CC}$ khyaŋ
that man MARK 2sGEN father good-NR1 man be

'Compared to that man, your father is a good man.'

Comparative constructions can be formed from non-copular clauses. Interestingly, the comparee within the comparative phrase is assigned the same casemarking as the standard. This indicates that although it is within the comparative phrase, it nevertheless holds a grammatical relation with the verb. If both the standard and comparee are A arguments, then both will have ergative case:

(80) Elicited
[priyesh=na$_A$ soen]$_{CP}$ [iŋku=n]$_A$ bãlaske [pyākhan]$_O$ ur-ai[83]
Priyesh=ERG MARK Inku=ERG well dance dance-3sPR

'Compared to Priyesh, Inku dances well.' OR 'Inku dances better than Priyesh (dances).'

Section 7 *Comparative and superlative constructions*   351

If the two noun phrases being compared are O arguments, then both receive dative case (assuming the conditions for case assignment are met, see §4.4.2.6):

(81)   Elicited
       [mā=n]_A   [rām=ta_O   soen]_CP [rājendra=ta]_O
       mother=ERG Ram=DAT MARK   Rajendra=DAT

       [gatkeŋ thõsi]_O bir-ju
       much   meat   give-3sPST

       'Mother gave more meat to Rajendra than to Ram.'

It is also possible for both noun phrases to receive dative case in dative-experiencer constructions:

(82)   Elicited
       [rām=ta_O   soen]_CP [rājendra=ta]_O [dyābā]_O mal-a
       Ram=DAT MARK   Rajendra=DAT   money   need-3sPST

       'Rajendra needs money more than Ram.'

It may be noted that all of the examples of comparatives given so far have been elicited. The construction shows up only rarely in connected discourse and the examples which I have are complicated. The simplest example has a time adverbial as the standard and the comparee ('now') is implicit, rather than being overtly specified:

(83)   [chi]_S [pahilā soen]_CP besna gal-ai   jur-a
       2s   before   MARK   very   thin-BV   be-3sPST

       'Compared to before, (now) you are very thin.'

Much more complicated are my other two examples, taken from the same narrative. There are two ways to analyze the example given in (84). The first analysis, represented by the square brackets and labels, views the comparative phrase as modifying the adjective within a larger adjective phrase; essentially, the comparative phrase takes the same position as an intensifier.

(84)   [u   jaŋgal=ku]_OBL [[[thamu soen =uŋ]_CP ḍwā-ku]_AP
       this jungle=LOC   2h   MARK-EXT   big-NR1

mebu rājā]ₙₚ₋ₛ da-u   ju-en   con-a
other king   exist-NR1 be-PART stay-3sPST

'It turns out that in this jungle, there is another king bigger than you.'

The alternative analysis is to view *thamu soen=uŋ ḍwā-ku* as a relative clause modifying the head *mebu rājā*. The two analyses are quite equivalent, the only difference being whether one views the head of the construction as being coreferential with a zero noun phrase within the adjectival phrase/relative clause. Since the use of the comparative mark naturally implies a comparee, this difference becomes simply a matter of theoretical perspective. I prefer to analyze this sentence as bistructural, simultaneously embodying two different structural analyses.

The final example has yet another layer of complication as it occurs within an indirect quote which is in turn within a relative clause:

(85)   [[*ji   soen   ḍwā-ku*]ₒ *ha-ku*]ᵣₑₗ *sihā*ₕₑₐᴅ
         1s MARK big-NR1   say-NR1 lion

'The lion who says he is bigger than me.'

The ditransitive verb *hat-* 'say' takes an object complement containing the quoted material (§18.2.3). In example (85), the quoted material is *ji soen ḍwāku*. (To avoid over-use of square brackets, the internal constituency of this clause is not represented in the example.) One can see the comparative phrase *ji soen* either as directly modifying the adjective or as coming from a relative clause, as discussed for the example above. The subject of the quotative verb is *sihā* 'lion'. Without the relativization, the construction would mean 'The lion said he is bigger than me' with the indirect quote constituting the object complement of 'say'. The relative-clause formation extracts the A as the head noun, leaving a gap within the relative clause. The result is a multilayered construction of considerable complexity.

The mark of comparison, *soen*, has an unusual phonotactic form for a single morpheme. This is due to its etymology. It is transparently derived from *so-en*, the participial form of the verb *sor-* 'look'. Apparently the synchronic comparative construction is the result of a syntactic reanalysis of an originally biclausal structure, e.g. [*priyesh so-en*]_CP [*inku ḍwā-ku khyaŋ*]_CL 'Looking at Priyesh, Inku is big', example (78) above. One problem with this analysis synchronically is that the standard of comparison which is presumably the object of *so-en* does not take object casemarking. In addition, in non-copular examples, such as (80)–(85), the standard is assigned case by the final verb, and not by *so-en*. In addition to this evidence is the fact that my consultant considers *soen* to be a single morpheme, equivalent to *than* in English.

Section 7 Comparative and superlative constructions

Comparative constructions are easily converted into superlative constructions. The standard of comparison is simply replaced by *dokhunuŋ* 'all'. This can either constitute the entire noun phrase, or it may modify another noun:

(86)   *dokhunuŋ janābar soen   kisi   ḍwā-ku khyaŋ*
        all   animal   MARK   elephant big-NR1 be

'The elephant is the biggest of all the animals.' (lit. 'Compared to all the animals, the elephant is big.')

Chapter 16
Tense and aspect

1. Introduction

The grammatical category of tense indicates the time of a state or event relative to a reference point established in the discourse context. This reference point, which I will refer to as the "time axis", is most commonly the time of the speech event ("now"), especially in conversational discourse. However speakers can also use a variety of linguistic devices to shift the time axis to another point in time. For example, in relating a narrative, speakers commonly shift the time axis to the time in which the events took place or are imagined to have taken place. Regardless of how the time axis of temporal deixis is established, tense fixes events on a timeline as being prior to (past), at (present), or after (future) that point. Languages differ in the number of tense categories they have; not all languages distinguish past, present, and future grammatically, and many languages make finer-grained distinctions on the time line, resulting in more than three grammatical tenses (see Comrie 1985: 83–101).

Whereas tense locates states and events on a timeline relative to the time axis, aspect is expression of the temporal structure of a situation. For example, aspect distinguishes between whether an event is viewed from the outside as a unitary whole, as in the English sentence *he read the book*, or from the inside as an ongoing activity, as in *he was reading the book*. Both sentences could refer to the same event and both have past tense, but they differ in how they orient the hearer with respect to the situation.

In Dolakha Newar, tense is a grammatical category realized in the inflectional system of the verb. The language distinguishes four tenses: past anterior, past, present, and future. These categories, and their various uses, are outlined in §16.2. Aspect, on the other hand, is signaled by the use of auxiliary verbs. These are discussed in §16.3.

2. Tense

One of the significant differences between the grammar of Dolakha Newar and the grammar of the dialects of the Kathmandu Valley is the inflectional tense system. The Kathmandu dialect is typically described as having a two-way inflectional tense distinction (past versus non-past) plus an additional stative form (Hale 1973, 1986; Malla 1985). Hargreaves (2005: 8–11) argues for a different interpretation, with a two-way distinction for conjunct forms (past versus non-past), and three-way distinction in tense and aspect for disjunct forms (non-past, past perfective, past imperfective), with the stative morpheme of the earlier analyses reintpreted as past imperfective in disjunct. Both analyses stand in stark contrast to Dolakha Newar. In this language there are four clearly inflectional tenses which, together with the person and number affixes, form the suffixal complex of the verb (§6.4).[84] It is clear that both the present and the past-anterior tenses have been innovated. While the past anterior was clearly constructed by adding inflectional suffixes to nominalized (NR1) verb forms, the historical origin of the present tense is unclear (Genetti 1994: 129–130). Whatever their origin, they have now been fully integrated into the Dolakha Newar verb, resulting in a true four-way inflectional system.

Each of the four tenses has a range of functions. The function of a tense in a particular example can be determined by the inherent aspectual structure (or *aktionsart*) of the verb. Most notably, the tenses have different interpretations on stative verbs than they do on event verbs. Further discussion is provided in §16.2.5. Following Comrie (1985), I will use the term "situation" to refer to any event, action, or state.

2.1. The future tense

The future tense in Dolakha Newar is used most commonly in constructing questions or statements about future situations:

(1)   sugā=n   tuŋ   **har-eu**
      parrot=ERG FOC   say-3FUT

      'The parrot will say (it).'

(2)   āu   jin   hāti   **yer-i**?
      now   1sERG   what   do-1FUT

      'Now what will I do?'

(3)   chanta   **na-eu**
      2sDAT   eat-3FUT

      '(She) will eat you.'

(4)   chin   khā   **lā-ina**   rā?
      2sERG   talk   talk-2sFUT   Q

      'Will you talk?'

(5)   ām   rājā   ju-eu
      3s   king   become-3sFUT

      'He will become king.'

Since the future is inherently irrealis and unknown, statements regarding the future are technically predictions and the speaker may have greater or lesser confidence in the likelihood of their coming to pass. For example, in (1) the speaker is quite sure that the parrot will speak, in (3) the speaker is fairly sure that the ogress is planning to eat the young girl, but in (5) the speaker is not entirely sure that the man will become king. Lack of certainty can be explicitly expressed with the particle *jeu* 'maybe' (§10.4.2.3).

The future tense is generally not used with states. Instead speakers must use eventive verbs which indicate the predicted entrance into a state, as in (5) above and (6):

(6)   u=ri   ekdam   moṭo   ju-eu
      this=IND   very   fat   become-3FUT

      'This one will become very fat.'

I do, however, have one example of the stative verb *sir-* 'know' in future tense. It is in the sentence *u tuŋ si-eu* [this FOC know-3FUT] 'he will know'. This is taken from a narrative where some boys are debating the truth of a fact and ask the father of one boy to tell them who is correct. Presumably the father's already has the knowledge of the truth or falsity of the claim, so the state is ongoing from the present. The future is used to predict that at the future time when he is asked, the knowledge will be present.

The future is also used with first-person subjects to signal the speaker's intention to carry out an event:

(7)   ji   kehi   din=ku   ye-i
      1s   some   day=LOC   come-1FUT

      'I will come in some days.'

(8)   jin=ri   sā-ku   sā-ku   bi
      1sERG=IND   tasty-NR1   tasty-NR1   give.1FUT

      'I will give you tasty things.'

(9)   jin   sona   **kha-i**
        1sERG   flower pick-1FUT

        'I will pick the flower.'

However, not all first-person-future statements are statements of intention. They may also be statements of prediction of events outside the control of the subject, e.g. *ji tul-i* [1s fall-1FUT] 'I will fall'.

Future tense is also used for expressions of incredulity about past events reported to be true. One reason this may be appropriate is that the future tense is inherently irrealis and so use of the future in such contexts emphasizes the speaker's lack of belief in the reality of the event and hence the truth of the statement:

(10)   kwākarbeŋ=na   rā   āpaī   kisi   **na-eu?!**
        frog=ERG   Q   that.size elephant eat-3FUT

        'A frog will eat an elephant that big?!'

(11)   hātti   rā pāthi=e   pwākal=lān pita **ye-eu?!**
        elephant Q   pathi=GEN   hole =ABL   out   come-3FUT

        'An elephant will come out of a hole in a pathi (measuring cup)?!'

2.2. The present tense

The present tense is used primarily for any situation which is specified as occurring at or across the time axis established in the discourse. There are a number of different scenarios, laid out below, in which this occurs. The present tense is also used with performative verbs and as an immediate future. Finally, the present tense is used in narrative as a "historical present" which lends a sense of immediacy to a narrative which otherwise has past-tense orientation.

Present tense is used for habitual events which extend across the time axis:

(12)   gunān   tel **lāŋ-an**   bir-ai?
        who.ERG oil massage-PART give-3sPR

        'Who massages you with oil?'

(13)   jin   yeuli   sona=pen   **pir-agi**
        1sERG   any.amount   flower=PL   plant-1sPR

        'I plant any amount of flowers.'

(14) jaba   jin   u   jāŋal hal-gu   **tār-agi**
      when 1sERG this   bird cry.out-NR1 hear-1sPR

  āle   jin   thi-gur bākhan **lūwonker-agi**
  then 1sERG one-CL   story   remember-1sPR

  'When I hear this bird cry out, I remember a story.'

It is similarly used for repeated events which are not habitual but which extend across the time axis. The question in (15) was addressed to a woman who was repeatedly calling to someone she thought she knew, but who turned out to be a ghost:

(15) bhut   hātta **hākar-an?**
      ghost why   call-2sPR

  'Why do you (repeatedly) call a ghost?'

Another example is (16), which is used to ask for someone's position on a particular question of short-term relevance:

(16) hāti   **hat-ai?**
      what   say-3sPR

  'What does he say?'

The present tense is also used for the expression of ongoing events, presented as a whole without internal structure (i.e. non-continuous), which occur at the time axis. For example, (17) is used to address a man in the middle of a journey.

(17) chi gibi   **on-an?**
      2s   where go-2sPR

  'Where do you go?'

The example in (18) is asked of people who have come to the house and who continue to arrive:

(18) hātta **yer-ahin?**
      why   come-3pPR

  'Why do they come?'

In another example, an angry wife addresses her husband as follows:

(19)   thamu=ri   ānthi   ŋil-agu   rā?
       2h=IND   that.manner   laugh-2hPR   Q

   'You laugh like that?'

All of these examples represent events which occur over a period of time extending over the time axis, but which are still presented as bounded and non-continuous.

Whether an event with present-tense marking is interpreted as habitual, repeated, or ongoing depends on the broader discourse context. For example, (17) in a different context could be used could have a habitual reading. However, since the story makes clear that the addressee is on a particular pilgrimage, the hearer can infer that it is not habitual.

Present tense is also used to predicate current states with the copula *khyaŋ*, and in clauses with the auxiliaries *sir-* 'know', *sar-* 'know how', and *phar-* 'be able':

(20)   ji   chana   kaimu   **khyaŋ**
       1s   2sGEN   husband   be

   'I am your husband.'

(21)   uli=ŋ   satya   **khyaŋ**
       this.much=EXT   truth   be

   'This much is true.'

(22)   āmun   sukha   **sir-ai**
       3sERG   happiness   know-3sPR

   'She knows happiness.'

(23)   jin   khã   lā-i   **sar-agi**
       1sERG   talk   talk-INF   know.how-1sPR

   'I know how to talk.'

(24)   ātmā=ku   jit-ai   ju-i   **phar-agu**   ra?
       soul=LOC   win-BV   be-INF   able-2hPR   Q

   'Are you able to win in your soul?'

Similarly, present tense is commonly used with the existential verb *dar-* to indicate current existence, location, or possession:[85]

(25) ji **damu**
 1s exist

 'I exist.' (i.e. 'I am here (to comfort you).')

(26) jana thi-gur khã **dam**
 1sGEN one-CL talk exist

 'I have one matter (to talk about).'

(27) ām sona=e tal=ku=ri thi-gur dhan=e pwākā **dam**
 that flower=GEN below=LOC IND one-CL wealth=GEN packet exist

 'There is a packet of riches under the flowers.'

With first-person subjects, present tense can be used to indicate the intention of immediate action:

(28) ota jin **syāt-agi!**
 this.DAT 1sERG kill-1sPR

 'I'll kill this one!' (implied: this instant)

(29) thae hākhena jin pariwār niyojan **yet-agi**
 2hGEN front 1sERG family planning do-1sPR

 'I will do family planning in front of you.' (implied: immediately)[86]

(30) isin **ton-agu**
 1pEXC.ERG drink-1pPR

 'We'll drink it.' (implied: right now)

Related to this is the use of the present with performative verbs, verbs whose utterance brings about the action they denote. I have only two examples of this in connected discourse:

(31) jana thi-mā mica chanta tuŋ **bir-agi**
 1sGEN one-CL daughter 2sDAT FOC give-1sPR

 'I give my daughter to you.'

(32)　jin　āmu　māji=e　　　mica　　　hā-i　　　　**hat-agi**
　　　1s　that　boatman=GEN　daughter　bring-1FUT　say-1sPR

　　　'I say I will bring that boatman's daughter.'

The final function of the present tense is what is known as the "historical present". It is the use of present tense when recounting past-tense events in order to make the events seem more vivid and immediate. Different speakers use the historical present with different frequencies. Some speakers seem more inclined to use it only at the climax of the story, whereas others use it more broadly for text structuring. In order to illustrate the interplay of tense in narrative, I will present an abbreviated version of a short narrative in §16.2.6 below.

2.3. Past tense

The past tense is primarily used for the expression of events which occurred prior to the time axis. The following examples are taken from conversation:

(33)　ji　wā　lwāp　　　tuŋ　**mo-ḍoŋ-gi**
　　　1s　TOP　stand.up　FOC　NEG-rise-1sPST

　　　'I didn't stand up.'

(34)　mā　　　mica　　　　kothā　**yer-gu**
　　　mother　daughter　room　come-1pPST

　　　'Mother and daughter, we came from the room.'

(35)　aṭ　　baje　　　**syāt-cu**
　　　eight　o'clock　kill-3sPST

　　　'(They) killed (them) at eight o'clock.'

(36)　chātā　　　thāta　**ŋat-ki**
　　　umbrella　up　　throw-1sPST

　　　'I threw the umbrella up.'

The past tense is also the primary tense use in the presentation of mainline events in narrative (although the present tense can also be used when the speaker wishes to make the events particularly vivid, as discussed directly above).

(37) ā̃ku tuŋ silā **jur-a**
      there FOC stone become-3sPST

   'He turned to stone right there.'

(38) ām   he   rājā=e   kae sikār **on-a**   hā̃
      that SPEC king=GEN son hunt   go-3sPST EVID

   'That very king's son went hunting.'

(39) libi ām chē   **then-ju**
      later that house arrive-3sPST

   '(They) arrived at the house.'

(40) simā=ku pharsi arai   ma-ju-en   kota **jut-a**
      tree=LOC pumpkin stable NEG-be-PART   down fall-3sPST

   'The pumpkin, not being stable on the tree, fell down.'

The past tense is also commonly used with stative verbs to indicate present states. This is because the past-tense morphology indicates the entrance into the state, allowing the hearer to infer that the state is ongoing (states that are no longer ongoing are marked with the past anterior; see below):[87]

(41) janta   pyātāwāt-a
      1sDAT hunger-3sPST

   'I am hungry.'

(42) mātri=ta=ŋ   mal-a
      Matri=DAT=EXT   need-3sPST

   'Matri also needs (some).'

(43) janta pāŋ   ekdam na-i   yer-a
      1sDAT fruit very   eat-INF come-3sPST

   'I like to eat fruit very much.'

(44) ām gibi con-a?
      3s where stay-3sPST

   'Where is he?' (lit. 'Where does he stay?')

(45) Elicited
jana   kāpal syāt-a
1sGEN head hurt-3sPST

'My head hurts.'

The past tense is also used on clauses which denote events upon which other events are contingent. The event with the past-tense marker will be temporally prior to the contingent event. Thus past-tense marking is found even in non-past contexts.

(46) "mā   thaeta hātiŋ āpat   par-ai   **jur-a**" hat-ŋasin
       mother 2hDAT nothing trouble befall-BV be-3sPST say-when

"ji samj-ai   jur-sin nā"
1s remember-BV be-IMP AGR

'"Mother, if any trouble befalls you," he said: "Remember me".'

(47) u   **hat-mun**   harsa=uri   thijita   bāmala-ku ju-en
       this say-2sPST   if=IND   1pINC.DAT   bad-NR1   be-PART

'If you say this, bad things will happen to us...'

(48) gun jana   chẽ   **con-a**   āmun   jin   khā lār-na
       who 1sGEN house stay-3sPST 3sERG 1sERG talk talk-when

dokhunuŋ "khyaŋ" har-i   mal-a
all   be.true say-INF must-3sPST

'Whoever comes to my house, s/he, when I talk, must say: "It is true".'

Finally, the past tense may be used with future events if the speaker holds a strong conviction that they will come to pass. This function of the past tense appears to be rare and reserved for truly extraordinary situations. In one example, a speaker sees a ghost and is certain her death is at hand, so she said: *syāt-cu ka!* [kill-3sPST ASS] 'I'm killed!'

2.4. Past-anterior tense

The past-anterior tense (which I referred to as past habitual in my previous work), has three main functions. The first function of the past anterior is to denote events which were habitual in the past but which are no longer ongoing:

(49) buḍe=na   nijā   dak-e   **yeŋ-guju**
      old.woman=ERG lunch make-PART   take-3sPA

   'The old woman used to make lunch and bring it (to him).'

(50) ŋā-pul   khu-phul   **ha-kuĩ**
      five-time   six-time   say-1sPA

   'I used to say it five or six times.'

(51) uku=lān   moti   jhar-ai   **ju-ju**   sã̄=lān
      here=ABL   pearl   fall-BV   be-3sPA   hair=ABL

   'From here pearls used to fall, from her hair.'

(52) sihā=n   ninpatti=ŋ   nis-mā   sõ-mā   janābar=pen   **na-uju**
      lion=ERG   everyday=EXT   two-CL   three-CL   animal=PL   eat-3sPA

   'The lion used to eat two or three animals everyday.'

The second function of the past anterior is to denote past states, that is, states which ended prior to the time axis:

(53) thamu pahilā jana   chẽ=ku   nokar   **cõ-gupe**
      2h   before 1sGEN   house=LOC   servant   stay-2hPA

   'Before, you used to be a servant in my house.'

(54) āme   mica=ta   jukun   māyā   **ye-kuju**
      3sGEN   daughter=DAT   only   love   do-3sPA

   '(She) used to love only her own daughter.'

(55) mikhā=n   **mo-khoŋ-guju**
      eye=INST   NEG-see-3sPA

   '(He) no longer saw with his eyes.'

(56) kae=uri   opteca   ju
      son=IND   small   be(3sPA)

   'The son was small.'

One can include in this generalization past existence, possession, and location which are signaled by the past-anterior form of the existential verb:

(57) āle   āme   cilā   thi-mā **da-uju**
then 3sGEN goat   one-CL exist-3sPA

'Then she used to have a goat.'

The third function of the past anterior is to denote single events that took place in the remote past. In other words, a single event which is denoted by a verb in the past-anterior tense is explicitly marked as having occurred at a time considerably prior to the time axis:

(58) jin   thaeta pahilā tuŋ   **ha-kuĩ**   le
1sERG 2hDAT   before FOC   say-1sPA   PRT

'I said to you before.'

(59) pusata mahina=e   barta con-ŋasin
Pusata month=GEN   fast   stay-when

tirtha   ū-i-ta   **oŋ-gu**   parāsar risi
pilgrimage go-INF-PURP   go-3sPA   Parasar Risi

'During the fast of the month of Pusata, Parasar Risi went to go on a pilgrimage.'

(60) Elicited
ji   mucā tākku thi-pul   pokhara   **oŋ-guĩ**
1s   child time   one-time   Pokhara   go-1sPA

'When I was a child, I went to Pokhara one time.'

Note that whether an event verb with past-anterior tense is interpreted as past habitual or remote past depends upon the context. Adverbials may play a role in disambiguating these two meanings, as in (60). Broader contextual factors, such as the previous discourse, may also be relevant. Example (58), for example, refers to a single event denoted in the previous discourse. The hearer can clearly establish this as the antecedent, so does not attribute a habitual meaning to this verb.

The past habitual and past stative functions both share the quality of imperfectivity; they are both used to express situations which lasted over a period of time, even though that period of time has now ceased. The use of the past anterior to code the remote past, however, does not fit this characterization. There are numerous examples with the past-anterior tense that clearly refer to single events. The example in (60) was especially elicited to confirm this function; it specifies both that the event occurred in the distant past (the speaker's childhood) and that it only occurred one time.

Although this third function may at first appear disparate, all three functions have in common the explicit marking of a gap in time between the end point of the state or event and the temporal reference point, the time axis. This is illustrated in Figure 22. The time axis in this figure indicates the present moment; the past is represented on the left, and the future on the right. While the simple past tense may be used on any event that takes place in the past (or any state that began in the past and continues through the present), the past anterior is used to indicate that the situation denoted by the verb was concluded prior to the present moment. The past anterior can thus be said to profile the *end-point* of the situation, denoted by the heavy left bracket in Figure 22. The onset of the situation is not explicitly referenced but must be inferred; this is denoted by the dotted line. This tense thus codes events which are both anterior (temporally prior) and past.[88]

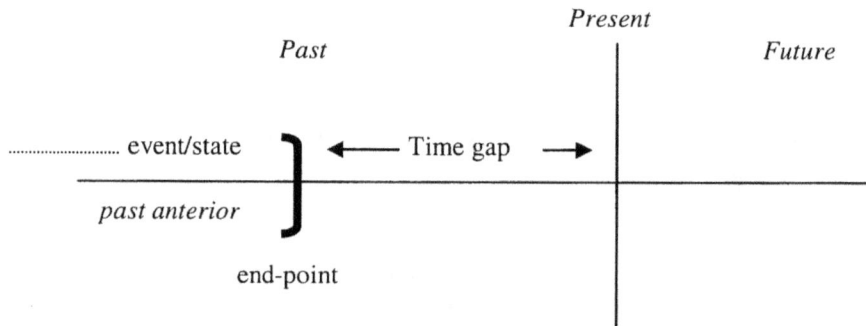

Figure 22. Past-anterior tense for prior situations

2.5. A system of four tenses

This survey of the function of the tenses has demonstrated that all four inflections are indeed used to locate events with respect to the time axis, hence have as their primary function the coding of grammatical tense. It is interesting to note, however, that the four tenses do not occur as four entirely discrete categories. The boundaries of the present are especially porous as present tense can be used to indicate intention of immediate action (hence with future situations), and may also be used for past events in narrative (the historical present).

In addition to this slight overlap between tense marking and our conceptual boundaries between past, present, and future, in some tenses there are interesting differences in the way tense is used and interpreted in imperfective situations (habituals and states) as opposed to perfective situations (self-contained events). (For discussion of continuous aspect, see §16.3.1.) These differences are not found in the future tense. I believe this is due to the irrealis nature of the future, and the fact that the use of the future with verbs of any situation simply predicts its occurrence.[89] This is true whether one is talking about events (habitual or not) or states. Of course, verbs which are inherently stative will be interpreted as such and additional specification of habituality can be conveyed by independent linguistic means, such as by the use of the adverbials. The point is that the tense itself does not get used or interpreted differently depending on the aspectual structural of the situation.

In the past anterior, states, habituals, and events also have the same basic interpretations. Since the past anterior explicitly profiles the end-point of a situation, its use emphasizes a time gap between that end-point and the time axis (Figure 22). It is the end-point of the situation (hence the onset of the time gap) which is profiled by the tense, while the beginning of the situation is left unspecified; the internal temporal structure is again conveyed by the inherent semantics of the verb, adverbials, and broader contextual factors.

Moving to the past tense, past events which are perfective are portrayed as single, bounded units which occurred at some point prior to the time axis. They are not explicitly marked as having internal temporal structure and an onset as distinct from an end-point. In Figure 23 below, these are represented by single points which occur any time to the left of the time axis. When a stative verb, however, has past-tense marking, a *present* state is denoted. This is because present states must have begun in the past, in order to extend across the time axis into the present. In addition, the end-point of the state is not explicitly indicated. Thus the use of past tense with stative verbs explicitly profiles the entrance into the state; this pattern is opposite to that found with past anterior. In Figure 23, the profiling of the entrance into the state is marked with the heavy left bracket.

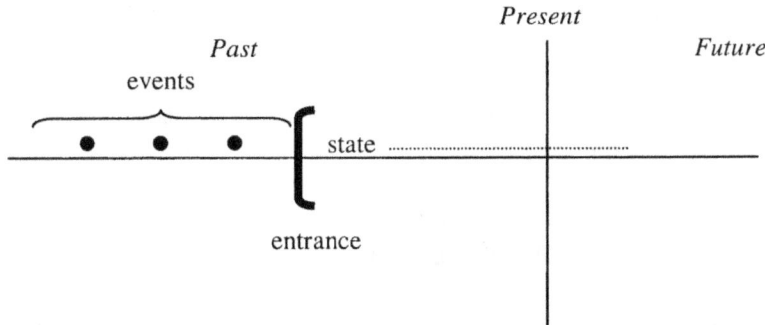

Figure 23. Past tense for past events and present states

Turning to the present tense, whether an event is habitual, repeated, or presented as a bounded whole, it will be inflected with the present tense if it extends over the time axis. It is interesting that neither the onset nor the end-point of such events is explicitly denoted. A few stative verbs – the copula *khyaŋ*, the verb 'know' *sir-*, the verb 'know how' *sar-*, and the verb *phar-* 'able'; see examples (20)–(24) – may also be used in the present tense. These differ from those marked with the past in not explicitly denoting the entrance point; the tense conveys simply that the state is in existence at the time axis. The onset of the state must be inferred and the end-point will exist somewhere in the murky future. What is explicitly profiled by the present tense is the reality of the situation at the time axis. Thus is represented by the heavy line in Figure 24.

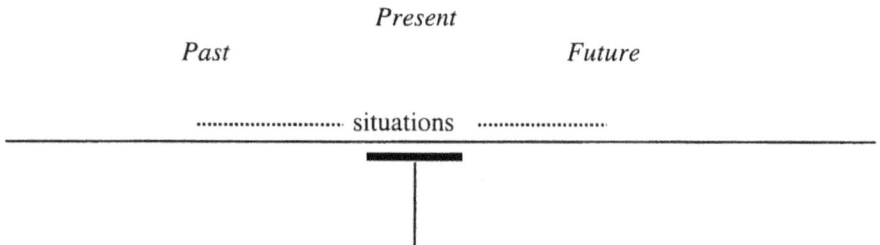

Figure 24. Present tense for present events

We thus see that the four tenses have quite distinct semantic qualities and that they profile different phases of the situations with which they occur. The interpretation of the tense in a particular example is due to a complex interplay of this profiling, the inherent semantic structure of the verb, and independent elements of the clause and the discourse.

2.6. The interplay of tenses in a narrative text

The four tenses are skillfully manipulated by speakers for the purposes of structuring a narrative tense. In order to illustrate this function of the tense system as well as to allow a deeper understanding of the tenses through a contextualized analysis, the use of tenses within an abbreviated spoken narrative will now be presented. Since the focus of this exercise is to allow for an explication of the tense system, the narrative is abridged by removal of all non-finite clauses. Places where material has been omitted are marked with ellipses [...] in the translation. I have also minimally edited the texts by removing repetitions and false starts.

The first three sentences of the story convey the setting. They are all in past-anterior tense which serves to set the temporal deixis of the story in the remote past and to indicate that the states and habitual events denoted no longer exist:

(61) thi-gur des=ku   sugā=pen **da-u**   hā
      one-CL country=LOC parrot=PL exist-3PA EVID

'In a country there lived some parrots.'

āle ām sugā=pen thau pariwār mil-ai ju-en   **coŋ-gu**
then that parrot=PL REFL family join-BV be-PART stay-3PA

'Then those parrots used to stay together in families.'

āle   ninpatti āpen bū=ku   nar-a   **oŋ-gu**
then daily   3p   field=LOC eat-PURP go-3PA

'Then every day they went to the fields to eat.'

Following this, the main narrative begins. The speaker switches to present tense in the first sentence, but then, possibly because she judges that the primary events of the story are still some ways off, she switches to past tense for the next six sentences. The two stative verbs are in the past anterior; this is appropriate as it profiles the end-point of the state, so places the state as exclusively in the past:

(62) bū=e   dani=n   āpista jāl ta-en   **tar-ai**
      field=GEN owner=ERG 3pDAT net put-PART put-3sPR

'... The owner of the field puts a net for them.'

āpsin ām jāl ta-en   ta-e   khā **ma-si-u**
3pERG that net put-PART put-NR2 talk NEG-know-3PA

'They didn't know the net had been put there.'

āle jāl ta-en   ta-e   khā **ma-si-u**
then net put-PART put-NR2 talk NEG-know-3PA

'Then (they) didn't know the net had been put there.'

jāl=ku   **kin-a**
net=LOC trap-3sPST

'... The net trapped them.'

dokhunuŋ jāl=lān   phutk-ai **jur-a**
all   net=ABL escape-BV be-3sPST

'... all of them escaped.'

370   *Chapter 16   Tense and aspect*

> *thi-mā=ri   jāl=ku   tuŋ   coŋ-an   **coŋ-a***
> one-CL=IND net=LOC FOC stay-PART stay-3sPST
>
> 'One of them was staying in the net.'
>
> *āle   āmu   bū=e   dani=n   **yer-a**   āku*
> then that field=GEN owner=ERG come-3sPST there
>
> '... Then the owner of the field came there.'

At this pivotal point, the meeting of the two main characters (the owner of the field and the parrot), the speaker switches to historical-present tense, and maintains it for four sentences. Note that the past-tense inflection of *coŋ-a* is used to indicate continuous aspect. Although the tense marking is past, the interpretation is present, as with stative verbs.[90]

(63)   *āmta   **jon-ai***
       3sDAT catch-3sPR

   '...He catches him.'

   *āmun   **hat-ai**   ki   "janta   chin   da-syāt*
   3sERG   say-3sPR   COMP 1sDAT   2sERG   PROH-kill

   '... He says: "Don't kill me".'

   *āmun   besna   rāk   **yeŋ-an**   coŋ-a*
   3sERG   very   anger   do-PART   stay-3sPST

   'He is getting very angry.'

   *āmun=ri   ām=ri   sugā=ta   syār-i   **mwāl-ai***
   3sERG=IND that=IND   parrot=DAT   kill-INF   try-3sPR

   '...He tries to kill that parrot.'

At this point, the speaker shifts from producing the voice of the narrator to producing the voice of the parrot. Part of this shift involves a resetting of the time axis from a point external to the narrative to a point internal to the narrative, the time within the story being related. The parrot says:

(64)   *chin   janta   **da-syāt***
       2sERG   1sDAT   PROH-kill

   '"Don't you kill me.

*chana guli   isin   pahilā yā   **nar-gu?***
2sGEN how.much 1pEXC.ERG before unhusked.rice eat-1pPST

How much of your rice did we eat?

*ām dokhunuŋ dyābā jin   chanta hā-en   **bi***
that all   money 1sERG 2sDAT bring-PART give.1FUT

I will bring and give you all of that money.

*chanta jin   dyābā dak-e   **bi***
2sDAT 1sERG money make-PART give.1FUT

I will make money and give it to you."

hat-ai
say-3sPR

He said.'

In the first line of (64), the parrot uses an imperative, which is independent of the tense system. The second line is in the past tense, referring to the eating that has taken place prior to the moment of speech at which the time axis is set. It is still conceptualized as a single event, probably because the parrot is requesting a value for all of the rice, so the internal temporal structure is not relevant. The parrot then switches to the future, in order to express his intentions of future action. The final line utilizes both the quotative verb and the present tense to mark the end of the quoted material and switch the time axis back to the time of the narrative. The present tense also links up with the previous use of the present for the main line of the story.

This conversational turn is followed by four others. All four of them are similar in using the future tense and the imperative for the speech of the interlocutors and in marking the end of the conversational turn by *hat-ai*, the present-tense form of 'say'. There is also one use of a stative verb in present tense, when the parrot says *jin khā lā-i sar-agi* [1sERG talk talk-INF know.how-1sPR] 'I know how to talk'. Again this is appropriate as the time axis is set at the time of the character's conversation, a time at which the state is true.

After the conversational exchange, the story continues in present tense:

(65) *mi-ta   **yen-ai***
     sell-PURP bring-3sPR

'... He brings it to sell.'

372   Chapter 16   Tense and aspect

   āle dokhusenuŋ u sugā=e mol guli
   then all.ERG this parrot=GEN price how.much

   ... haŋ-an **hat-ai**
   ... say-PART say-3sPR

   '... Then everyone says: "How much is the price of this parrot".'

This is followed by a conversational exchange of three more turns with similar properties. The speaker continues to use the present tense through the resolution of the story in the following lines:

(66) ām sugā=ta thi-mā sāuji=n   **ŋyāt-ai**
   that parrot=DAT one-CL shopkeeper=ERG buy-3sPR

   'Then a shopkeeper buys the parrot.'

   āme pasal=ku ta-en **tar-ai**
   3sGEN shop=LOC put-PART put-3sPR

   'He puts and keeps him in his shop.'

The speaker then shifts back to past tense for the coda of the story:

(67) āle ām bū=e dani=n=ri dyābā yeŋ-an
   then that field=GEN owner=ERG=IND money take-PART

   oṇ-a
   go-3sPST

   'Then the owner of the field took the money and went.'

   āmu khusi **jur-a**
   3s happy become-3sPST

   'He was happy.'

Interestingly, the speaker then decides to change the overall tense orientation from the remote past, with which she began, to the present, and to depict the owner as someone currently alive and making his living selling parrots. To facilitate this switch, she moves back to the present tense. Now, however, the function of the tense is not the historical present, but rather to express ongoing states and habitual events. The following sentences conclude the story. Note that the final sentence contains a copular clause but that the copula has been omitted; this is only possible in present-tense contexts (§12.3).

(68)   āle   āmu=nasi āmu bū̃=e   dani=n   yelpanuŋ
       then that=since that field=GEN owner=ERG always

   ã̄ku   jāl   ta-en   **tar-ai**
   there net   put-PART   put-3sPR

   'Then since then, that field owner always puts his net there.'

   sugā=pista   **na-ker-ai**   yā
   parrot=PL.DAT   eat-CAUS-3sPR   uncooked.rice

   '... He feeds the parrots rice.'

   ām   thanu ekdam dhani mi
   3s   today very   rich   man

   '... Today he is a very rich man.'

3. Aspect

Interacting with the four inflectional tense categories are six auxiliary verbs which are used to denote various components of aspect, the internal temporal structure of an event. These six verbs fall into two distinct classes. In one class are the auxiliaries *tal-* 'put' and *con-* 'stay'. These are "versatile verbs" which have both lexical and aspectual meanings; these meanings, while distinct, are closely related. These auxiliaries are incorporated into the clause via the participial construction (§19.4.1). The verbs in the second class of auxiliaries are not versatile verbs. Although it is possible for these auxiliaries to occur independently when a lexical verb is omitted, the meanings of the auxiliaries do not change in this environment and the content of the omitted lexical verb is always recoverable from context. Thus verbs in this class have consistent aspectual meanings. These auxiliaries follow the lexical verb in infinitival form in a complementation strategy (§18.3.1).

3.1. The auxiliary *con-* 'stay': continuous aspect

As a lexical verb, *con-* means 'sit', 'stay; reside', or 'be at (of an animate referent)', as illustrated by the following examples:

(69) apsoc thau bicyauna=ku **con-a**
    regret REFL bed=LOC stay-3sPST

    'He sat on his bed, regretful.'

(70) ji hātta kho=e dāti=ku jukun cõ-i mal-a?
    1s why river=GEN middle=LOC only stay-INF must-3sPST

    'Why must I stay in the middle of the river only?'

(71) kobi **con-a** ka
    below stay-3sPST ASS

    '(The tiger) was below.'

When *con-* follows a verb in participial form, a variety of syntactic and semantic relationships may hold between the two verbs. The two verbs may each instantiate separate clauses. When this occurs, one possible semantic interpretation is for the events denoted by verbs to be in a sequential relationship:

(72) kursi hā-en **co-n**
    chair bring-PART sit-pIMP

    'Bring a chair and sit.'

Another possible semantic interpretation is for the first participial verb (and any other clausal elements associated with it) to provide adverbial information about the manner in which the subject sits, stays, or is located:

(73) jana hākhena dhū=n ithi yeŋ-an **coŋ-gu**
    1sGEN front tiger=ERG this.manner do-PART stay-NR1

    ju-en con-a
    be-part stay-3sPST

    'It turns out that the tiger was in front of me, doing like this.'

Whether a given example is interpreted as involving sequencing or adverbial modification depends on contextual factors; see §19.4.5 for full discussion.

It is important to note that in examples like (73), in which the verb *con-* is modified by another verb specifying manner, the activity denoted by the manner verb and the activity denoted by *con-* are cotemporaneous, with roughly the same starting and ending points. Because the meaning of *con-* is inherently durative, its durativity is naturally extended to the action of the manner verb which is thus interpreted as extending over a period of time. This is how *con-* has developed into a marker of continuous aspect. It is used to mark situations that are, will be, or were ongoing.

As a marker of continuous aspect, *con-* does not instantiate an independent clause; rather it is incorporated as an auxiliary into the clause with the preceding lexical verb.

(74) ãku   tuŋ   coŋ-an   con-hin
      there FOC   stay-PART   stay-3pPST
      'They were living right there.'

The primary evidence in support of this claim is that in this construction nothing is allowed to intervene between the lexical verb and the auxiliary. In addition, negation must be on the auxiliary verb; the lexical verb cannot be independently negated. Furthermore, the lexical verb and its auxiliary come under a single intonation contour. These facts are true for all auxiliaries in the language.

In many cases, particular instances of this construction may have more than one syntactic and semantic interpretation. Consider example (73) above. The translation given is based on a biclausal analysis, with *con-* functioning as one lexical verb and the participial clause as its modifier. An equally appropriate analysis, however, treats the sentence as a single clause, with the participial verb functioning lexically and *con-* as the auxiliary marking continuous aspect, i.e. 'It turns out that the tiger was doing this in front of me'. Both translations are equally well suited to the context of the narrative where this sentence occurred. Although English makes a syntactic distinction between biclausal and monoclausal structures for this sentence, note that, in actual fact, there is not a significant semantic difference between them. That is, if a tiger is in front of me acting in a particular manner (biclausal), then it is acting continuously in that manner in front of me (monoclausal). In English the two translations do differ in the degree to which the location of the tiger is independently predicated (i.e. *was in front of me*) but at the semantic level this distinction appears to be minimal. While the word order of the English translations clearly distinguishes between the biclausal structure (*was in front of me, doing this*) and the monoclausal structure (*was doing this in front of me*), in Dolakha Newar both meanings have the same syntactic instantiation: V-PART *con-*. I consider such examples to be "bistructural", that is, they can be analyzed as instantiating both structures equally well, and both semantic interpretations. Of course, it is the presence of "bistructuralism" that allows for grammaticalization and syntactic reanalysis to occur.

It is important to note that, despite the presence of a great number of bistructural examples, there are clear examples where the verb *con-* is functioning as an auxiliary and cannot be interpreted lexically. This is especially clear in examples with two instances of *con-*, as in (74) above and (75):

(75) kehẽ   ho   cicā=uri   dāi   **coŋ-an**   **con-hin**
     y.sister and   small=IND   e.brother stay-PART   stay-3pPST

'The younger sister and the younger elder brother were staying there.'

If this sentence had a single instance of the verb *con-*, the predicate would translate simply as 'stayed there', meaning they didn't move from a particular place. The use of the auxiliary in (75) is continuative, indicating that the two children continued to stay, and hence implies a prolonged period of time. An analysis of the first instance of *con-* as modifying the second does not follow, as in this role the first verb would not provide any new information not already contained in the second. There are other clear examples where *con-* must be semantically interpreted as an auxiliary, as in (76):

(76) āmu   ḍoli   bu   nichi   **dã̄lāŋ-an** cō-i   mal-a
     that doli   carry-NR1   all.day fast-PART   stay-INF   must-3sPST

'That *doli* carrier must fast all day/be fasting all day.'

A *ḍoli* is a type of a litter which is carried through the streets during festivals. The *ḍoli* carrier is clearly not staying somewhere fasting, which would be the necessary semantic interpretation if *con-* were functioning as a lexical verb. Instead, *con-* is used to indicate that the fasting is continuative, occurring over an extended period of time (all day).

Further examples of *con-* with a continuous meaning are given in (76)–(80). In each, the use of the auxiliary indicates that the activity denoted by the verb occurred over an extended period of time:

(77) ā̃ku   tuŋ   cachi   **pi-en**   **con-a**
     there FOC   night   wait-PART   stay-3sPST

'He was waiting right there at night.'

(78) ināgu   cij   pita   **ye-en**   **con-a**
     this.type   thing   out   come-PART   stay-3sPST

'Things of this type were coming out; kept coming out.'

(79) siliŋga   risi=e   sarāp   par-ai   ju-en   coŋ-gu
      Silinga Risi=GEN curse befall-BV be-PART stay-3PA

   'They were feeling the curse of Silinga Risi.'

(80) mica   siŋ-an   con-a
      daughter die-PART stay-3sPST

   'The daughter is dead.'

Example (80) is interesting in that it could also mean 'The daughter is/was dying.' In the context of the narrative that this was taken from, however, it is clear that the daughter was already dead. I believe the auxiliary is being used here to specifically indicate that she is still dead; the daughter later comes back to life. Interestingly, this referent is later referred to with a headless relative clause as *siŋ-an coŋ-gu=ta* [die-PART stay-NR1=DAT] 'the continuously dead one'. This can be contrasted with *si-ku* 'the dead one', the normal way of expressing this concept.

Another interesting example of the continuative meaning of *con-* is given in (81). This was uttered as a curse, using the optative mood.

(81) yelpanuŋ   tapjyāŋ-an   tho-cõ
      always   break-PART   OPT-stay

   'May (your heels) always break.'

The use of the auxiliary and the adverb together clearly indicate that the curse is to last over an extended period of time (always), and hence that the heels of the person cursed will break continually.

In many examples the auxiliary *con-* has a progressive rather than a continuative meaning, indicating that an activity is explicitly ongoing either at the time axis, (82)–(84), or at another point determined in the discourse:

(82) un   dwārā   cul-en   con-a
      3sERG uneven.teeth sharpen-PART stay-3sPST

   'She is sharpening her fangs.'

(83) mucā   kho-en   con-a   hã
      child   cry-PART   stay-3sPST EVID

   'The child is crying.'

(84) mula   then-ŋasin   kwākarbeŋ=na=uri   āpaī   dwā-ku   kisi
     road   arrive-when   frog=ERG=IND   that.size   big-NR1   elephant

   na-en   **bi-en**   **con-a**
   eat-PART   give-PART   stay-3sPST

   'When we arrived on the road, a frog was eating an elephant that big.'

In example (84), the time axis is set by the adverbial clause, and the event of the following clause is specified as ongoing at that point. It is more common for the continuous clause to be specified first and hence to form a backdrop to the action that is to come:

(85) thi-nu=ri   mā=uri   sã   **cheŋ-an**   **con-nasin**
     one-day=IND   mother=IND   hair   comb-PART   stay-when

   'One day, when the mother was combing her hair...'

(86) buḍā=n   nichi   sã   **wā-en**   **coŋ-gu**
     old.man=ERG   one.day   cow   plow-PART   stay-3PA

   'One day, the old man was plowing with the cow.'

(87) nemlā   tikne   thẽ   **to-en**   **con-a**
     moon   blinding   like   rise-PART   stay-3sPST

   'The moon was rising as if to blind.'

It is also possible for the auxiliary *con-* to occur with stative verbs. According to Comrie (1985: 26), this is the feature which differentiates the continuous aspect from progressive aspect; progressive aspect does not occur with stative verbs. Generally this is used with states that are temporary, such as emotions and desires. The use of the continuous aspect indicates that the state was entered into and was extended over a period of time, example (88)–(90), or was in effect at the time axis, (91):

(88) sibaji   sumake   lās   **cā-en**   **con-a**
     Sibaji   silently   embarrassment   feel-PART   stay-3sPST

   'Siba silently felt embarrassed for a long period of time.'

(89) khusi   **ju-en**   **coŋ-gu**   wā
     happy   be-PART   stay-NR1   TOP

   'When they were continuing to feel happy...'

(90) *nispatta tuŋ **ju-en** coŋ-gu*
dark FOC be-PART stay-3PA

'It was dark continuously.'

(91) *janta ŋe-i **ye-en** coŋ-a*
1sDAT listen-INF come-PART stay-3sPST

'I am wanting to listen.'

The continuous aspect may occur in all four tenses. Continuous aspect in the present tense indicates that the state or activity is in process at the present moment:

(92) *khusi din **bityāŋ-an** con-ahin*
happy day spend-PART stay-3pPR

'They are spending happy days.'

(93) *hāti khā=ku **lwāŋ-an** coŋ-agu?*
what talk=LOC fight-PART stay-2hPR

'What are you fighting about?'

In the past tenses, the distinction between the past continuous and past-anterior continuous is harder to pin down. Both indicate that the activity or state was ongoing but has not continued to the present moment. It appears that the past anterior is used when the speaker wishes to indicate that the events took place in the remote past. In narratives it is often found conveying background information as in (94); see also (86) and (90).

(94) *bãla-ku keṭi **mwāl-en** coŋ-guju*
beautiful-NR1 girl search-PART stay-3sPA

'He was searching for a beautiful girl.'

By contrast, the simple past is more likely to be used for the primary events in the narrative:

(95) *titā kehẽ sõ-mā=n khā **lā-en** con-hin*
e.sister y.sister three-CL=ERG talk talk-PART stay-3pPST

'The three sisters were talking.'

However, this distinction does not seem to be absolute. Further investigation of the interaction of tense and the continuous aspect is warranted.

It is important to note that there is a slight inflectional twist in the system. It appears that the predicted third-person-present form of the verb *con-* is not possible; at least the predicted form *con-ai* is unattested in my data and explicitly rejected by my consultants as a possible form of the auxiliary. This inability to occur in the present tense is only restricted to third-person singular; all other person/number combinations may occur freely in the present. The reason for this restriction is uncertain; however I will make the following conjecture. As discussed in Genetti (1994), the four-way system of tenses attested in Dolakha Newar (and at least some other eastern dialects) appears to be an innovation by this branch of the family. In the Kathmandu Valley dialects there are two primary tenses, described as "past" and "non-past". With the verb *con-*, the most common form of the verb as an auxiliary is *con-a*, the "past-disjunct" form. Because it is used as a continuous auxiliary, as well as a common lexical verb indicating residence, location for animate beings, etcetera, this verb is one of the most frequent lexemes in the language, and it occurs most of the time in the third-person-singular form. My hypothesis is that while the modern tense system developed in Dolakha Newar, the diffusion of the present tense did not extend to this very common verb. Instead, in the third-person singular only, the original system of past, non-past, and remote past remains. The other person-number combinations were less frequent, so less entrenched, hence more amenable to the extension of present tense.

Whatever the reason for the historical development, we now have an interesting synchronic situation, whereby the continuous auxiliary occurs with all four tenses in the first-person, second-person, and third-person plural, but only in three tenses in the third-person singular. In the four tense system, present is used for situations which continue at the time axis, and the two pasts appear to differ in remoteness. In third-person singular, the past anterior also indicates a remote past, e.g. (86), but the simple past tense indicates either a past not explicitly marked as remote, e.g. (78) above, or a present, e.g. (83).

I have no examples from connected discourse of *con-* occurring in the future tense. However, I do have elicited examples, as in (96):

(96) Elicited
 ām yer-nasin ji je yeŋ-an cõ-i
 3s come-when 1s work do-PART stay-1FUT

 'When he comes, I will be working.'

Whether or not the future form of the auxiliary *con-* can be used in non-progressive contexts requires further investigation.

3.2. The auxiliary *tar-*: extended state and perfect aspect

As a lexical verb, *tar-* means 'put' and 'keep'. Thus it refers either to the placement of an object – usually concrete, but also abstract, as in (98) – or to extended possession of an object:

(97)   u   wā   thābi **ta-i**   mal-a
       this   TOP   up   put-INF   must-3sPST

   '(You) must put this up.'

(98)   bāji   **ta-u**
       bet   put-IMP

   'Place (your) bets.'

(99)   ām   misā=ta=ri   **tar-ju**
       that woman=DAT=IND   keep-3sPST

   'He kept that woman/wife.'

It is quite common for *tar-* to occur in the participial construction as the second verb in a series. As with *con-*, discussed above, there are several syntactic and semantic relationships that may hold in such a situation. First, the verb *tar-* may instantiate an independent clause. In this case, the event it denotes may be sequentially ordered with respect to the preceding verb:

(100) co-en   tar-agi
       write-PART   keep-1sPR

   'I wrote down and keep (the information).'

(101) isin   airāk   kā-en   tar-agu
       1pEXC.ERG   liquor   take-PART   keep-1pPR

   'We took and keep the liquor.'

Present tense is used in these examples to indicate that the possession of the item still continues. The preceding event is necessarily temporally prior (e.g. one must take the liquor before one can keep it), so these events are technically in the past.

It is also common in biclausal constructions for the participial verb to specify the manner in which something is put:

(102) t̃ãs   yeŋ-an   **tar-ju**
stick do-PART   put-3sPST

'(He) put (it on the door) by sticking.'

(103) kōsa   ŋaŋ-an   **ta-e**   ṭhãĩ
bone   throw-PART   put-NR2   place

'The place where the bones are put by discarding/discarded and put.'

The meaning of *tar-* as an auxiliary is an extension of the first of these constructions, specifically of a biclausal example where *tar-* means 'keep'. As a verb, *tar-* denotes temporally extended possession; as an auxiliary *tar-* denotes a temporal extension of the result of the lexical verb. The interplay of these meanings can be seen in one narrative, where the phrase *bi-en tar-* [give-PART put-] is used on several occasions to denote the giving of diamond rice to be used as a reminder of an invitation. The verb *bir-* 'give' has as its result the transfer of the diamond rice to the recipient. The auxiliary *tar-* indicates that the rice will remain at that location for an extended period of time. In addition, note that the diamond rice will also have a later effect on the possessor. Another example is given in (104):

(104) rājā=ta   lū=e   sihãsan   hā-en   phyākṭuk-e   **tar-ju**
king=DAT gold=GEN throne   bring-PART   sit-CAUS(PART)   put-3sPST

'They brought a throne and made the king sit in it.'

In both cases, the resultant state brought about by the verb (here the positioning of the king on the throne) continues for an extended period of time.

An example with an intransitive verb is given in (105):

(105) āu   bhut=na   janta   wā   guli   khyāŋ-an   **tar-ai**
now   ghost=ERG   1sDAT TOP how.much scare-PART put-3sPR

'Now ghosts have scared me so much.'

In this example it is very clear that *tar-* is not functioning lexically, as there is no object referred to in the clause that could be put or kept. Instead, the auxiliary is denoting a temporal extension of the result of the lexical verb. Since the auxiliary is in the present tense, the implication is that the result of the lexical verb (the speaker's fear) continues up to the present. Since the auxiliary specifies an extended resultant state, one also infers that the event that brought about the state is necessarily in the past, hence anterior. Furthermore, the extension of the state to the present must also be relevant to the present or else it would not be articulated. Thus *tar-* is indicating present relevance of an anterior event, also known as perfect aspect. Some other examples where *tar-*marks an extended state with current relevance (i.e. perfect) are given in (106)–(108):

(106) *mucā=pisin   lukhā ṭi-en   tar-ai*
      child=PL.ERG door lock-PART put-3sPR

  'The children have locked the door.'

(107) *gãjal=na   uŋ-an   tar-ai*
      eyeliner=INST draw-PART put-3sPR

  '(Someone) has applied eyeliner (to the child).'

(108) *jimŋā-phā   yā=ta   dyābā bi-en   ta-uĩ*
      fifteen-pathis uncooked.rice=DAT   money give-PART put-1sPA

  'I had given (her) money for fifteen pathis of rice.'

In every case the resultant state had continued and was relevant at the time axis (the moment of the speech event in the first two examples, the time related in the narrative in the third).

3.3. The auxiliary *d(h)on(-ker)-* 'finish': completive aspect and sequential ordering

The verb *d(h)on(-ker)-* means 'to finish'. Although it can occur independently (e.g. *āu don-a ka* [now finish-3sPST ASS] 'Now (it) is finished'), it usually occurs as an auxiliary following a verb in an infinitive form (see §18.2.4 for syntactic discussion of this complementation strategy). The verb has both causative and non-causative forms. In elicitation, one consultant was consistent in never using the causative form with intransitive verbs. Either the simplex or the causative form could be used with transitive verbs, apparently with no difference in meaning. In my discourse data, the causative form is quite rare, and only occurs with the participial ending *-ke*, producing *don-ke*; two of those examples have intransitive verbs. It is unclear whether the causative form has any particular semantic effect; further investigation of this issue may (or may not) reveal motivated patterns. For the present discussion, both simplex and causative forms will be discussed as a single category.

The primary meaning of *d(h)on(-ker)-* is completion of the event denoted by the lexical verb (this auxiliary does not occur with inherently stative verbs in my data). As this auxiliary overwhelmingly occurs in the past or past-anterior tenses, the event denoted by the lexical verb is marked as having been completed prior to the time axis, hence anterior to the time axis. Thus, like the auxiliary *tar-* 'put', this auxiliary extends into the perfect realm. However, unlike *tar-*, this verb does not emphasize an extended resultant state, but rather the completion of the event. This can be seen in the following examples:

(109) *(phãsi)*   *bi*   ***doŋ-ju***
      (hanging)   give(INF)   finish-3sPST

   'They've given it (to them).' (In context: 'They've executed them; completed the execution.')

(110) *ām belā nikkai khīga-i*   ***doŋ-gu***
      that time very   dark-INF finish-3PA

   'At that time, it had become very dark.' (lit. 'The darkening was finished.')

(111) *pe-mā   mica=ta   ŋe-i*   ***doŋ-ju***
      four-CL dauther=DAT   ask-INF   finish-3sPST

   'He had finished asking (i.e. had already asked) four daughters.'

(112) ***sir-i   doŋ-ju***   *ām   mucā*
      die-INF   finish-3sPST   that   child

   'That child has already died.'

When the auxiliary *don(-ker)-* is in participial form, it indicates completion of the event of the participial clause prior to the event of the following clause.

(113) *janta   syār-i   **don-ke**   chi do-khor-si*
      1sDAT   kill-INF finish-PART   2s   PROH-cry-IMP

   'After I am killed, don't you cry.'

(114) *ritidān   ju-i   **doŋ-ani**   āme   kae   byās*
      intercourse happen-INF   finish-PART   3sGEN   son   Byas

      haŋ-a   janm-ai   jur-a
      say-NR2   born-BV   be-3sPST

   'After they finished having intercourse, their son named Byas was born.'

(115) iri=ŋ   biha   **yer-i**   **doŋ-ani**
       daughter.in.law=EXT marriage   do-INF   finish-PART

       sanatanu rājā sit-a
       Sanatanu king die-3sPST

       'After (they) married the daughters-in-law, King Sanatanu died.'

Again the auxiliary can be seen as marking anteriority, except that in this case the relationship of anteriority holds between events, as opposed to holding between an event and the time axis, as one finds with finite verbs (the difference is in the nature of the time axis, rather than being in the meaning of the auxiliary itself). Thus with the participial construction, a perfect meaning, with its emphasis on resultant state, is not found.

3.4. The auxiliary *ṭen-* and the suffix *-rai:* 'be about to'

Another auxiliary which is found following the infinitive form of the lexical verb is *ṭen-* 'be about to'. This verb has irregular inflection, as one finds it with stem-final /r/ in some forms, e.g. *ji ū-i ter-a* [1s go-INF about.to-3sPST] 'I am about to go' and a stem-final /n/ in others. I only have a handful of examples of this auxiliary, so the full details of the inflectional irregularity are unknown. An example of this auxiliary taken from conversational discourse is given in (116):

(116) dolakhā=e   me   hal-i   **ten-agi**
       Dolakha=GEN song   sing-INF   about.to-1sPR

       'I am about to sing a Dolakha song.'

Semantically, this auxiliary indicates the subjects' intention to immediately perform the event denoted by the lexical verb. It is interesting to note that a similar effect can be produced through what appears to be a verbal suffix *-rai*. This suffix also is found on the infinitival verb and it is likely to have developed from an old auxiliary that has now significantly reduced:

(117) sāŋat=pen   ū-i-rai
       friend=PL   go-INF-about.to

       'My friends are about to go.'

(118) ā dāju! janta dhū=n **na-i-rai!**
 oh e.brother 1sDAT tiger=ERG eat-INF-about.to

 'Oh, brother! A tiger is about to eat me!'

3.5. The auxiliaries *suru yet-* and *twārtar-*; inception and cessation

The remaining two aspectual auxiliaries are *suru yet-* 'start' and *twārtar-* 'stop'. Again I have only a few examples of each, so cannot speak at length about them. Both auxiliaries follow the lexical verb in the infinitive form. These auxiliaries are aspectual in that they profile different temporal phases of an event. Note that *twārtar-* differs from *don(-ker)-* 'finish' in that it does not necessarily imply that the action of the preceding verb was completed, a goal reached, etc. For example, in (119), the speaker was interrupted in her sorting of the mustard by the appearance of a tiger:

(119) āle āmun khā **lā-i** **suru** **yet-ai**
 then 3sERG talk talk-INF begin do-3sPR

 'Then he starts talking.'

(120) jin wā ām **turkan** **wa-i** **twārtār-gi**
 1sERG TOP that mustard sort-INF stop-1sPST

 'I stopped sorting that mustard.'

Chapter 17
Nominalization and related structures

1. Introduction

One of the hallmarks of a Tibeto-Burman language is the extensive use of structures referred to in the Tibeto-Burman literature as "nominalization". Although particular Tibeto-Burman languages may differ in the number of morphemes that are used to nominalize clauses and in whether these morphemes are bound to the verb or are independent particles, the languages appear to be similar in the range of morphosyntactic structures that these clauses enter into. Essentially, nominalization in these languages creates dependent clauses which either (1) modify a noun within a noun phrase, (2) function as a noun phrase within a clause, or (3) occur non-embedded in the position of a typical finite clause. This particular congruence of syntactic functions has been referred to as 'Standard Sino-Tibetan Nominalization' (Bickel 1999: 271) and has been reported on in a number of languages (e.g. Bickel 1995, 1999; DeLancey 1989, 1999; Ebert 1994; Genetti 1992; Kölver 1977; Matisoff 1972; Noonan 1997).

Standard Sino-Tibetan Nominalization differs from the idea of nominalization as a derivational process by which "a predicate becomes nominalized, assuming the form of a verbal noun, and takes over the role of head noun of the noun phrase" (Noonan 1985: 60). Nominalization in Sino-Tibetan languages usually does not create a noun that functions as the head of a noun phrase. Nominalized verbs generally cannot be preceded by demonstratives, and notional arguments of the nominalized verb are not found in genitive case. Instead, Sino-Tibetan languages employ "clausal nominalization" (Comrie and Thompson 1985: 391–393), under which the unit which is nominalized constitutes an entire clause or multiple clauses. Nominalized clauses have most of the properties associated with independent clauses, for example, they assign case to their arguments, although the expression of some verbal categories may be limited (Genetti 1992). Dolakha Newar represents a classic case of Standard Sino-Tibetan Nominalization.

Nominalization in Dolakhae is signaled by one of three verbal suffixes, glossed NR for nominalizer/relativizer. NR1 has allomorphs *-gu*, *-ku*, and *-u*, NR2 has allomorphs *-e* and *-a*, and NR3 has the single allomorph *-iuri*. In §17.2 I outline the syntax of nominalization, demonstrating that nominalized clauses occur in four syntactically distinct constructions: relative clauses, nominal complements, verbal complements, and independent clauses. The distribution of the three nominalizing suffixes varies with the syntactic structure. A detailed discussion and historical analysis of the morphological patterns is presented in §17.3.

2. The syntax of nominalization

Nominalized clauses have three distinct functions: they may modify a noun within a noun phrase, they may function as a noun phrase in relation to a verb (i.e. act as verbal complements), and they may occur non-embedded in a matrix clause. Nominalizations are dependent structures in two senses of the term. First, with the exception of non-embedded nominalizations, nominalized clauses are in a dependent-head relationship with another element, either a noun or a verb. Second, nominal complements are dependent in that they are non-finite; the tense and person/number of a nominalized clause are determined by other elements of the context.

2.1. Modification of nouns within a noun phrase

Nominalized clauses modify nouns in two distinct syntactic constructions: relative clauses and nominal complements. These two constructions differ in the following way: in relative clauses, the head (modified) noun is coreferential with an argument of the relative clause, and that argument is obligatorily absent from the relative clause. In nominal-complement constructions, the head noun is not coreferential with an argument of its complement clause, and all clausal arguments may be specified. These constructions are exemplified in (1) and (2) respectively:

(1) ji   wā   [[Ø ma-pha-u]$_{REL}$ mi]$_{NP}$
     1s   TOP   NEG-able-NR1   person

   'I am a person who is ill/disabled.'

(2) [[kwākarbeŋ=na   kisi   na-e]$_{NOM.COMP}$ khã]$_{NP}$ lār-ai
      frog=ERG   elephant   eat-NR2   matter   tell-3sPR

   '(He) tells the news of the frog eating an elephant.'

In (1), the head noun *mi* is coreferential with the subject of the intransitive verb *phar-* 'be able'. The subject noun phrase is obligatorily absent from the relative clause (a fact represented by the symbol Ø) and there is a strong grammatical relationship between that zero argument and the head noun. In (2), by contrast, the head noun *khã* does not have a semantic role within the complement clause, nor does it have a grammatical relationship with any complement clause argument. Both arguments of the complement clause (*kwākarbeŋ* 'frog' and *kisi* 'elephant') are overt (phonetically instantiated) noun phrases.

Both relative clauses and nominal complements consistently precede the head noun. I have no examples of post-head modification (unless expressed as an afterthought in an independent intonation unit), nor of internally-headed relative clauses.

It should be noted that both relative clauses and nominal complements constitute modifiers of nouns within a single unified noun phrase and do not occur as independent noun phrases in appositional relation with the heads (cf. DeLancey 1999; Noonan 1997). This can be seen from the fact that the plural and case clitics may not occur on relative clauses or on nominal complements when they precede a head noun. These clitics are phrasal elements which may only be marked once at the end of a noun phrase. By contrast, apposition is a relationship which holds between two noun phrases which are independent but coreferential (§11.4). They agree in the marking of number and case, with both noun phrases being marked. The patterns of case and number marking are different when there is a single head noun modified by a relative clause or a nominal complement. Case and number may only be marked once, on the head noun. Thus to pluralize the noun phrase *dolakhā oŋ-gu mi* 'the person who went to Dolakha', one must pluralize only the head noun, *dolakhā oŋ-gu mi=pen* 'the people who went to Dolakha'. Native speakers consider double plural marking to be unacceptable; i.e. **dolakhā oŋ-gu=pen mi=pen* is not a well-formed noun phrase.

2.1.1. Relative clauses

Relative clauses are nominal modifiers that precede the head noun. The head noun is assigned case in accordance with its role in the matrix clause. The position of the argument coreferential to the head noun in the relative clause is obligatorily omitted, in what is commonly known as a "gapping strategy" (Comrie 1981: 144–146). Example (3) illustrates this structure (the relative clause is in square brackets and the head noun is bold):

(3)   [[*jin*   *mega*   *miɲe* Ø *hā-e*]$_{REL}$ ***jāki**=e*]$_{NP}$ ***jā***]$_{NP}$
        1sERG   yesterday   before   bring-NR2   uncooked.rice=GEN   rice

        'Cooked rice (made) of the uncooked rice I brought yesterday and the day before.'

In this example, the head of the relative clause is *jāki*. This noun is coreferential with the object of the relative verb *hā-e* 'bring'. This fact can be determined by the obligatory absence of the NP in the object argument position within the relative clause (the "gap", represented by the symbol Ø), by the use of NR2 as the nominalizer, and by the semantics of the proposition. The head of the relative clause *jāki* is in turn casemarked with the genitive clitic, and the whole NP consisting of the head plus the relative clause modifies yet another head noun, *jā*.

All three of the Dolakha Newar nominalizers may be used to form relative clauses, although the use of NR3 is quite rare. Most relative clauses are realis; they restrict the interpretation of the referent of the head noun by referring to a previous or ongoing event or state involving the head noun. However, irrealis relative clauses are possible, as in (4):

(4)   [Ø *hākhen cō-iuri*]_{REL}]_{NP} *gun?*
        front   stay-NR3   who

'Who will be the one to stay in front?'

The distribution of the other two nominalizers is complex. The dominant pattern, which is overwhelmingly attested in my textual data and which consultants prefer in elicitation, is for NR1 to be used when the head noun is coreferential with the subject of the relative clause and for NR2 to be used elsewhere. However, in elicitation, two consultants have demonstrated that while they prefer NR2 with non-subject heads, NR1 is also possible *if* the verb is intransitive and the subject of the relative clause is third person. This pattern, and its relation to the distribution of the nominalizers in other syntactic environments, will be discussed in §17.3.

The use of NR1 when the head noun is coreferential with the subject of the relative clause is found regardless of whether the subject is the A argument of a transitive verb (5), the S argument of an intransitive verb (6), or a copula subject (7):

(5)   [[Ø *indira gandi =ta   syā-ku*]_{REL} *mi=ta*]_{NP}   *syāt-cu   rā?*
        Indira Gandhi=DAT kill-NR1 man=DAT kill-3sPST Q

'Did (they) kill the man who killed Indira Gandhi?'

(6)   [[Ø *ām pipāna ye-u*]_{REL} *mi=pen*]_{NP-S} *gun?*
        that veranda come-NR1 person=PL who

'Who are the people who came to the verandah?'

(7) [[Ø jogi ju]ᴿᴱᴸ mi]ɴᴘ
   yogi become(NR1) man

   'the man who became a yogi'

The nominalizer NR2 is primarily used when the head noun is coreferential with any argument that is *not* the subject of the relative clause. Thus, it is found with objects in various semantic roles, examples (8)–(10), with locatives (11), and with time expressions (12):

(8) [[thau tuŋ Ø dak-e]ᴿᴱᴸ me]ɴᴘ₋ᴄˢ dam
    REFL TOP   make-NR2   song   exist

   'There is the song that you made yourself.'

(9) [[āmun Ø hā-en   ta-e]ᴿᴱᴸ nis-sar   dyābā]ɴᴘ₋ᴏ
    3sERG bring-PART put-NR2 two-hundred rupees

   āmu chē   dani=n   kār-ai
   that house owner=ERG take-3sPR

   'The house owner takes the two hundred rupees which he had brought.'

(10) [[kathā Ø haŋ-a]ᴿᴱᴸ sāŋat=na]ɴᴘ₋ᴀ [[Ø khā ha-ku]ᴿᴱᴸ
     story   say-NR2   friend =ERG   story say-NR1

   sāŋat=ta   tuŋ]ɴᴘ₋ᴏ besna khisi yeŋ-a
   friend=DAT TOP   very insult do-NR2

   ju-en   con-a
   be-PART stay-3sPST

   'It turns out the friend to whom the story was told very much insulted the friend who had told the story.'

(11) kharāyo nāpa   [[inār Ø da-u]ᴿᴱᴸ thāĩ=ku]ɴᴘ   on-hin
     rabbit ASSOC   well   exist-NR1 place=LOC go-3pPST

   'They went with the rabbit to the place where the well was located.'

(12) [[Ø phār pul-en   ye-e]ᴿᴱᴸ tākku]ɴᴘ
     back return-PART come-NR2 time

   'At the time when they returned.'

Example (10) is especially interesting as the nominalizers are critical in clarifying basic case relations. This example is taken from a story in which one friend tells another friend that he saw a frog eating an elephant. The friend to whom the story was told does not believe it and insults the story teller. The sentence simultaneously refers to two events, the original storytelling, represented in the relative clauses, and the insulting, represented in the matrix clause. The grammatical relations of the two referents are reversed in these two events. Thus the first head noun refers to the subject of the matrix but the object of the relative, whereas the second head noun refers to the object of the matrix but the subject of the relative. While the casemarkers on the head nouns are tracking the case relations in the matrix clause, the two nominalizers are tracking the case relations in the relative clause.

Head nouns are often omitted from noun phrases with relative clauses, especially when the referent of the head noun is recoverable from context, or when it is not referring to a specific referent. When this occurs, the plural and case clitics are bound to the verb of the relative clause:

(13) [[Ø kātākāt mārāmār ha-ku]$_{REL}$Ø=pen]$_{NP}$
katakat maramar say-NR1=PL

'Those who say: "katakat maramar".'

(14) [[Ø gād coŋ-gu]$_{REL}$Ø=n tuŋ]$_o$ syāŋ-an bi-e rā?
guard stay-NR1=ERG FOC kill-PART give-NR2 Q

'Is it the case that the one who stood guard killed her?'

Headless relative clauses may be used to indicate a profession, e.g. *me hal-gu* 'singer', *ḍoli bu* 'litter carrier'. These expressions thus take on a derivational character, such that one might consider these to be actor nominalizations. However, any one of these phrases can be expanded to include additional clausal information, e.g. *āmun syeŋ-a me hāl-gu* [3sERG teach-NR2 song sing-NR1] 'the one who sang the song that he taught', thus the process appears to be truly syntactic.

Adjectival verbs are put into attributive form via relative-clause formation. For example *hẽga-u son-a* 'red flower' could equally be translated 'flower that is red'. However, these forms appear to have lexicalized. See §7.2 for further discussion.

When headless relative clauses are bound by the individuating clitic =*uri* (§10.2.1), they refer to a specific referent:

(15) [[∅ rājā=ke   ye-u]ʀᴇʟ ∅=ri]ɴᴘ
          king=ALL come-NR1=IND

   'the one who came with the king'

(16) [[∅ lũmowoŋ-gu]ʀᴇʟ ∅ =ri]ɴᴘ
          forget-NR1=IND

   'the one who forgets'

When used with adjectival verbs, the combination of the nominalizer plus the individuating morpheme allows the adjective to refer to an individual who has the properties of the adjective, e.g. *cicā-u=ri* 'the small one'. In the absence of the clitic, the nominalized adjective refers to the property itself. In this sense, it appears to be the individuating clitic which actually has the nominalizing function; it creates a nominal that can head a noun phrase, e.g. *ām cicā-u=ri* 'that small one'.

Relative clauses can be coordinated with the conjunction *ho* (§11.3), in which case both relative clauses modify the same head noun:

(17) [[thamun ∅ yeŋ-a]ʀᴇʟ   ho   [jin ∅ yeŋ-a]ʀᴇʟ   jāki]ɴᴘ
       2hERG   bring-NR2 and   1sERG bring-NR2   rice

   'the uncooked rice that you brought and that I brought'

It should also be noted that while the term "relative *clause*" is commonly used in linguistics, relative structures in Dolakha Newar are not actually restricted to single clauses but may also contain combinations of clauses. For example, (18) has a relative structure which contains a participial clause. In example (19), the relative structure contains a purpose clause, whereas the relative in (20) contains an embedded direct quote:

(18) dokhunuŋ kõsa   ŋaŋ-an   ta-e   ṭhã̄ī
      all   bone   discard-PART   put-NR2   place

   'the place where they put the bones by discarding them; discard and keep the bones...'

(19) [[kār-a   oŋ-gu]ʀᴇʟ ∅=pen]ɴᴘ
         take-PURP   go-NR1=PL

   'the ones who went to take it'

(20) [["rājā=ke   ū-i"   ha-ku]$_{REL}$ Ø=ta]$_{NP}$
       king=ALL go-1FUT say-NR1=DAT

'the one who said: "I will go to a king"'

2.1.2. Nominal complements

Nominal complements, like relative clauses, are used to modify nouns within a noun phrase. Unlike relative clauses, however, the noun that is modified is not coreferential with an argument or adjunct of the dependent clause. The nouns being modified are always abstract, and tend to refer to speech events, thoughts, arrangements, etc. An example is given in (21):

(21)   [[bihā   ju-e]$_{NOM.COMP}$ khā]
         marriage happen-NR2   talk

'the talk of how the wedding came about'

Note that the head noun *khā* is not an argument of the complement verb *jur-*; this is the crucial characteristic that shows this is not a relative clause.

The head noun of a nominal-complement construction may be unexpressed if its referent is clear from context, as in (22):

(22)   [[thaeta dū=n   khyāŋ-a]$_{NOM.COMP}$ Ø]$_{NP}$ thamun har-sin
         2hDAT   tiger=ERG scare-NR2   2hERG   say-IMP

'Tell (a story) about a tiger scaring you.'

There is a common naming construction utilizing nominal complements which are headless, e.g. *byās haŋ-a* 'one called Byas'.

Turning to the distribution of the nominalizers, I have only one example of NR1 occurring in a nominal-complement construction, so this appears to be rare. NR2 and NR3 are both attested, NR2 being used in realis environments, and NR3 being used in irrealis environments. Thus it is possible to elicit the following contrast:

(23)   Elicited
       ji   kathmaṇḍu oŋ-a   khā   jana   mā=n   sir-ju
       1s Kathmandu go-NR2 talk   1sGEN mother=ERG know-3sPST

'My mother knew about my going to Kathmandu.'

(24) Elicited
   ji   kathmaṇḍu   ū-iuri   khā   jana   mā=n   sir-ju
   1s   Kathmandu   go-NR3   talk   1sGEN   mother=ERG   know-3sPST

   'My mother knew about my plans to go to Kathmandu.'

Example (24) is appropriate when the nominal complement refers to a trip to Kathmandu that already occurred, whereas (25) is appropriate if the trip is only planned; whether or not the trip will actually be realized is not known.

It is possible to give an alternative analysis to examples, such as (23) and (24), that involve the abstract noun *khā*. Rather than treat the noun as the head of the object noun phrase, one can analyze it as a grammaticalized complementizer. Under this analysis, the dependent clause is no longer NP-internal, modifying a noun. Instead it functions as the object NP itself, constituting an object complement. These two analyses are schematized in (25):

(25) a. [[clause]$_{NOM.COMP}$ N]$_{NP.OBJ}$ V$_{TR}$
   b. [clause]$_{NP.OBJ}$ COMP V$_{TR}$

While both analyses are possible synchronically, there is some evidence that favors the grammaticalized analysis presented in (25b). A full discussion of this point may be found in §18.2.1.1.

2.2. Verbal complements

Nominalized clauses may occur as independent noun phrases which hold argument relations with verbs; in this role they are called verbal complements. Most commonly verbal complements are found in the object relation, although in two constructions nominalized clauses function as copula subjects. A full discussion of verbal complementation may be found in Chapter 18. Here I will simply list and exemplify the complement types that involve nominalization, and present the distribution of the nominalizers.

2.2.1. Simple nominalized (verbal) complements

Simple nominalized complements[91] occur in the object role when they complement verbs of perception. Due to their semantic nature, they are never case-marked. The dative casemarker is found on objects which have human and given referents (§4.4.2.6), but verbal complements are abstract, referring to events. Several examples of verbal complements occurring with perception verbs are given in (26)–(28):

(26) [pharsi=n   thau mica=ta   phoŋ-a]$_{NP-O}$ khoŋ-an
     pumpkin=ERG REFL daughter=DAT ask.for-NR2   see-PART

   'Seeing the pumpkin asking for his own daughter...'

(27) dokhsenuŋ [kharāyo lipul-e]$_{NP-O}$ khoŋ-an
     all.ERG   rabbit   return-NR2   see-PART

   'All of them seeing the rabbit return...'

(28) jaba jin   [u   jāŋal hal-gu]$_{NP-O}$ tār-agi
     when 1sERG this bird cry.out-NR1   hear-1sPR

   'When I hear this bird cry out.'

Discussion of the syntax of this construction can be found in §18.2.1.

Turning to the distribution of the nominalizers, complements of perception verbs do not co-occur with NR3. This is presumably due to semantic incompatibility; one cannot directly perceive an event which has not been realized. The distribution of the other two nominalizers is partially based on the transitivity of the complement verb. Transitive verbs are suffixed by NR2, e.g. (26). Intransitive verbs, however, may be marked by either suffix. In my database half are suffixed by NR1, e.g. (28), and half by NR2, e.g. (27). In elicitation, consultants consistently prefer NR1 with intransitive verbs and NR2 with transitive verbs, although they admit that there may be some variation.

2.2.2. *Nominalized verbal complements plus* khā

Nominalized clauses followed by *khā* may be analyzed as verbal complements of cognition and utterance verbs, or as complements of an abstract noun. An assessment of the syntactic arguments regarding this point is provided in §18.2.1.1.

The distribution of the nominalizers in verbal complements of cognition and utterance verbs follows a different pattern than that found in verbal complements of perception verbs. NR1 is never found with cognition and utterance verbs. Instead NR2 is used in realis contexts and NR3 in irrealis contexts. This distinction was exemplified in (23) and (24) above.

2.2.3. Verbal complement of the stative copula khyaŋ

Nominalized clauses also function as verbal complements in two constructions involving copulas. The first is an emphatic construction, where the nominalized clause occurs before the stative copula *khyaŋ*. Syntactically, the nominalized clause fills the role of copula subject. Semantically, the construction is used to assert the speaker's belief in the truth (or, if the copula is negated, the falsity) of the proposition of the nominalized clause:

(29) [chana nimtiŋ chuŋ-a]$_{NP-CS}$ **ma-khe!**
2sGEN benefit cook-NR2 NEG-be.true

'(This) is not cooked for your benefit!'

(30) [[mā=n ho dāi=n hātiŋ pāp yeŋ-a]$_{CS}$
mother=ERG and e.brother=ERG nothing sin do-NR2

ma-khyā-u]$_{NP-CS}$ ju-en con-a
NEG-be.true-NR1 be-part stay-3sPST

'It turns out that it is not true that mother and elder brother were committing sins.'

(31) [bilacini=n na-e]$_{NP-CS}$ khyaŋ
Bilacini=ERG eat-NR2 be

'Bilacini did eat them; It is true that Bilacini ate them.'

All of my examples of this construction in connected discourse have the NR2 nominalizer. In elicitation, my consultants prefer NR2, but also allow NR1 as a possible alternative if the subject of the nominalized clause is third person.

At this point it is interesting to contrast two sentences which on the surface appear to be very similar, but which actually are structurally quite distinct. They are given in (32) and (33):

(32) mohi pujā ye-ku khyaŋ
farmer ceremony do-NR1 be

'The farmer is one who performed the ceremony.'

(33) mohi=n pujā ye-ku khyaŋ
farmer=ERG ceremony do-NR1 be

'It is true that the farmer performed the ceremony.'

These two sentences differ on the surface only in the absence, example (32), or presence, example (33), of the ergative morpheme. However, two very different structures underlie them. The first sentence is an equational copular clause. The copula subject is *mohi* which is equated with the noun phrase in the copula complement, a headless relative clause *pujā ye-ku* 'the one who performed the ceremony'. In (32), by contrast, the ergative marking on the first noun phrase crucially indicates that it is the subject of the transitive verb. Thus *mohi=n pujā ye-ku* is an entire complement clause, functioning as the copula subject in the emphatic equational construction. The difference between these structures can be further seen under pluralization. To indicate multiple farmers performing multiple ceremonies, the equational structure in (32) requires both NPs to be plural: *mohi=pen pujā ye-ku=pen khyaŋ*; this further emphasizes the independence of the two noun phrases. To pluralize the subject in (33) however, one can only mark the plural on the subject of the clause, not on the nominalizer, e.g. *mohi=pisin pujā ye-ku khyaŋ* 'It is true that the farmers performed the ceremony'. From these examples we can see that the distinction between relative clauses and nominalized clauses may be subtle and must be carefully attended to.

2.2.4. Verbal complement of the grammaticalized phrase ju-en con-a

The other construction that can be analyzed as involving a verbal complement in copula subject position involves the set expression *ju-en con-a*. This expression is transparently constructed from the participial form of the copula *jur-* followed by the continuous auxiliary verb *con-* (lexically 'stay'). The entire expression appears to have originated from a meaning similar to 'was occurring'. Today, this construction is used with a more general meaning usually translatable as 'it happened that' or 'it turned out that'. It marks a turn of events, often counter to expectation. Some examples of this very common construction are given in (34)–(36):

(34)   [āmu si-ku]$_{NP\text{-}CS}$ *ju-en*   *con-a*
          3s   die-NR1   be-PART   stay-3sPST

          'It turns out he died.'

(35)   [yā   khoŋ-an   gyā-ku]$_{NP\text{-}CS}$ *ju-en*   *con-a*
          unhusked.rice see-PART fear-NR1   be-PART stay-3sPST

          'It turns out that they saw the rice and were afraid.'

(36) [ām misā wā mwāŋ-an ye-u]ₙₚ₋cs ***ju-en con-a***
that woman TOP survive-PART come-NR1 be-PART stay-3sPST

'It turns out that woman came alive.'

Note that in (35) *ju-en con-* has scope over two clauses linked by the participial construction. Syntactically, we can see that it is the chain of two clauses which is nominalized and functions as the verbal complement in copula subject role.

In narrative discourse, *juu-en con-a* is used with surprising frequency. For many speakers it shows up at each new turn of events, even at the end of every sentence. In these cases, its mirative meaning is barely discernable, and it becomes a marker of the ends of episodes. In line with this repeated use comes phonological reduction. Although I consistently write this form out in its original morphemic glory, in actuality speakers generally reduce it considerably in rapid speech. The first word is generally pronounced *jin*, and the second either reduces to *con* or *cõ*. Thus this construction appears less like a copula with a nominalized complement – as structurally represented in (34)–(36) – and more like a sentence with a disyllabic particle. In line with this analysis is the observation that *ju-en con-a* never varies its form: it never appears in another tense, the final verb does not occur in any non-finite form, it is never negated, etc. Interestingly, as this construction always occurs in sentence-final position, to analyze *ju-en con-a* as a sentence-final particle results in a dramatic increase in the frequency with which nominalized verb forms occur in a sentence-final matrix clause. This weakens the contrast between the nominalized forms and the finite forms, and opens up the possibility of a reinterpretation of the nominalized clauses as part of the broader finite system. I do not believe that this has fully occurred in Dolakha Newar.

Only the nominalizers NR1 and NR2 precede *ju-en con-a*; the irrealis nominalizer is not attested in this environment. The two nominalizers which are found show an interesting pattern. Nominalized intransitive verbs are found overwhelmingly with NR1, while nominalized transitive verbs are split, with about 80% of examples found in narrative having NR2 and about 20% having NR1. A more detailed analysis of the transitive verbs with NR1 turns up an interesting fact: virtually all of these examples have imperfective aspect. They are either progressive (37), habitual (38), or future indefinite (39).

(37) dhū=n ānthi ānthi balyeŋ-an coŋ-gu
tiger=ERG that.manner that.manner stalk-PART stay-NR1

ju-en con-a
be-PART stay-3sPST

'It turns out a tiger was stalking me in that manner.'

(38) gunān   bi-u   ju-en   con-a?
     who.ERG give-NR1   be-PART   stay-3sPST

'Who does it turn out has been giving these to you?'

(39) lita   ota   ultā   yeŋ-an   keŋ-gu   ju-en   con-a
     later   this.DAT translate   do-PART   show-NR1   be-PART   stay-3sPST

'It turns out that later she will translate this and show it to people.'

Thus the distribution of the suffixes in these examples involves the interaction of transitivity and aspect.[92]

2.3. Non-embedded nominalizations

The use of nominalizations in independent sentences is an interesting aspect of many Tibeto-Burman languages (e.g. Bickel 1999; Hargreaves 1991: 35–40; Matisoff 1972; Noonan 1997). Pinpointing the precise function of non-embedded nominalizations and how they differ from independent finite clauses is rather delicate. Matisoff (1972: 246) provides a particularly insightful starting point when he writes:

> The verbal event is being objectified, reified, viewed as an independent fact, endowed with a reality like that inhering in physical objects – in short, nominalized. It is standing on its own, and is not a constituent of any sentence higher than the one to which it belongs itself.

Bickel (1999: 280–287) analyzes non-embedded nominalizations in several Kiranti languages as focus marking. He reports that the construction is used to put focus on new information as compared with presupposed information in the clause. He provides the following example from the language Belhare, spoken in eastern Nepal. (In his glosses, 3U refers to third-person undergoer, 1sA to first-person-singular agent, N to the nominalizing suffix.)

(40) Belhare example from Bickel (1999: 281)
     hale   mand-u-ŋŋ-ha!
     earlier finish-3U-1sA-N

'It's earlier that I finished!'

In this example, the fact that the task at hand is finished is known or presupposed information while the focus is the adverb *hale* 'earlier'. The focused element, in addition to being an adverb, can also be a noun phrase or an entire proposition.

In Dolakha Newar, I have only nine examples of non-embedded nominalizations in my discourse data. Interestingly, they are all found in conversational discourse or in conversations embedded into narratives. Six of the examples are statements and three are questions. I also have some elicited examples of this construction, especially with questions. While the data at hand is not enough for a confident analysis of the functions of non-embedded nominalization, it appears that most of the examples can be interpreted as focus constructions. Example (41) occurred during a conversation about the execution of the assassins of Indira Gandhi. The fact that she was assassinated was well-known information. The focus of the question is on whether or not the assassins were her bodyguards. In this case, the focus particle *tuŋ* is also found, so focus could be considered to be doubly marked.

(41)   *gāḍ   coŋ-gu   tuŋ   syāŋ-an   bi-e   rā?*
       guard stay-NR1   FOC   kill-PART give-NR2   Q

       'Was it her guard that killed her?'

In the following example, the focus is on the time adverbial:

(42)   *pus=na   phoŋ-a   rā?*
       Pus=ABL   ask.for-NR2 Q

       'Was it in (the month of) Pus that he asked?'

Further evidence that non-embedded nominalizations might constitute focus constructions was provided by my consultants during elicitation. For example, the following sentence is appropriate if it is known that some child threw a rock and one wishes to find out which child it was:

(43)   *guri   mucā=n   luŋā   ŋaŋ-a?*
       which   child=ERG   rock   throw-NR2

       'Which of children was it who threw the rock?'

Another example involved the discussion of a particular blouse. If I was told that my sister had sewn the blouse, I might reply in surprise as follows:

(44)   *jana   tātā=n   laŋgi   su   rā?*
       1sGEN   e.sister=ERG   blouse   sew.NR1   Q

       'Was it really my sister who sewed this blouse?'

I only have six examples of non-embedded nominalizations occurring in statements. Two of these are clearly amenable to a focus analysis:

(45) mansu̱ lal=na syen-gu ka
Mansu Lal=ERG teach-NR1 ASS

'It was Mansu Lal who taught us (that song).'

(46) phãsi bi-e le
hanging give-NR2 PRT

'It was by hanging (that they were executed).'

Note that (45) cannot be analyzed as an equational construction with a headless relative clause (i.e. 'Mansu Lal was the one who taught us') because the ergative marking on the A clearly marks it as internal to the nominalized clause.

In the remaining four examples it is not as clear that there are established presuppositions against which the new information is focused, but perhaps the use of the nominalization itself helps to establish the contrast. For example, in one conversational exchange two women have said they are leaving. Another speaker remarks:

(47) jā ma-na-e ni āle
rice NEG-eat-NR2 yet then

'Then you didn't eat yet.'

In this case, the known information is establilshed by the broader context and is not represented in the clause – the fact that they are leaving and that there would be a reason for this. The use of the nominalization could be seen as explicitly marking the speaker's deduction about the reason why they are leaving as focused, hence related to the fact of their leaving ('It's because you didn't eat yet').

In another example, a woman had related a story in which she had gone to harvest wheat, encountered a jackal upon her return to the village, fallen, and scattered all the wheat of her harvest. She then produced the following sentence:

(48) chatil=e sāīlā dāju=n bi-e
Chatil=GEN third.child e.brother=ERG give-NR2

'My third eldest brother of Chatil gave (me some wheat).'

There was no previous (or following) discussion of anyone assisting her by making up for her loss. Perhaps the use of the nominalized clause helps to instantiate the presupposition that someone helped her out of the unfortunate situation.

Somewhat more puzzling is the following example, produced when the speaker was leaning out the window addressing her father:

(49) bā   tir-i   mal-a   haŋ-a   le
     father put.tika-INF must-3sPST say-NR2 PRT

'Father, (they) say you must put on a tika.' (as part of a ritual)

There was no preceding recorded conversation regarding the requirement that the father put on a tika (a mixture of rice and vermillion powder put onto the forehead as part of a reigious ritual), however, there could have been a private conversation that occurred outside the room where the tape recorder was. One can speculate that the use of *hanga* serves as a way for the speaker to defer responsibility for the statement of what her father must do, thus allowing the utterance to be a point of information as opposed to a command or a prescriptive statement coming from the daughter. Why she chose to use the nominalized form, and how this fits in with focus constructions (if at all) is unclear. It is clear that non-embedded nominalizations, and their interaction with different types of discourse and sentence-final particles, represent a fruitful area for further study.

In the nine textual examples I have of non-embedded nominalizations, eight have NR2 and one has NR1. The use of NR2 occurs with first-, second-, and third-person examples, with transitive and intransitive verbs, and in perfective and imperfective contexts. In elicitation, both consultants require NR2 for clauses with first- and second-person subjects. However, they prefer NR1 for clauses with third-person subjects, although allow that NR2 is also possible. We turn now to a full discussion of the distribution of nominalizers.

3. The distribution of the nominalizers

Of the three nominalizers in the language, NR3 is the least frequent in my discourse data, the most predictable and the most semantically consistent. It appears to be a relatively recent addition, derived from the conjunction of the infinitive plus the individuating clitic =*uri* and it has a quite unvarying semantic meaning of irrealis. It is found only in some of the syntatctic environments that nominalized clauses occur in. The distributional restrictions can be attributed to its semantic content; it is semantically incompatible with perception verbs, the emphatic functions of verbal complements of *khyaŋ*, and the surprise at the turn of events conveyed by complements of *ju-en con-a*.

The other two nominalizers, NR1 and NR2, both appear to be older morphemes that have been in opposition for centuries. This can be seen from their quite idiosyncratic phonological realizations across the four verbal conjugation classes (§6.6.1), their small phonological size, and their relatively unpredictable allomorphy (especially with NR2). As has been demonstrated, their relative distribution varies with the syntactic environment in which they occur. In addition, there is some variation across types of data. In some syntactic environments, patterns of use in discourse differ slightly from the intuitions of my consultants. In addition, for some examples my consultants will prefer one suffix but still accept the other one, whereas in other examples they judge only one suffix to be grammatically correct.[93]

An overview of the distribution of the two nominalizers can be found in Table 37. This table specifies the factors that are involved in determining the distribution of the two suffixes in each of the syntactic environments in which they occur. In cases where the textual data and the intuitions of my consultants agree, a single form is given (e.g. in relative clauses where the head noun is coreferential with the subject, NR1 is found in both data sets). In cases where there are differences, the data are listed separately. Forms in parentheses indicate acceptable alternatives to the preferred (non-parenthesized) forms. Shaded areas indicate that no data is available.

Presented in Table 37, the patterns look rather daunting; however it is possible to find underlying motivations. The system has, at its essence, the concept of transitivity. However, different parameters of transitivity are relevant in different morphosyntactic environments. In addition, frequent patterns of distribution in certain environments have resulted in reanalysis, and this has effectively obscured the original outlines of the system.

The morpheme which occurs in the widest number of environments is NR2. In that sense, this can be considered the unmarked form. This morpheme is most strongly associated with transitivity. It is found in several explicitly transitive contexts: in oblique relative clauses, in transitive nominalized complements, and in transitive perfective complements of *ju-en con-a*. In environments where the person of the subject is relevant, NR2 is associated with first- and second-person subjects.

NR1 occurs less frequently than NR2, both in Table 37, and in overall token frequency in connected discourse in my data. NR1 is associated with intransitive verbs, imperfectivity, third-person subjects, and subject relative clauses.

Although the conditions triggering the distribution of the suffixes appear to be disparate, they are actually interconnected. To understand the patterns, it is useful to bring up the notion of Transitivity in the broad sense (which I will indicate with a capital "T"). Transitivity is a scalar notion. Events may be more or less Transitive, depending on a number of independent "transitivity parameters"

Table 37. Distribution of NR1 and NR2 nominalizers

Syntactic Environment	Distribution in Texts	Distribution in Elicitation
Relative clauses		
Head = subject	NR1	
Head = object		
first-/second-person subject	NR2	
third-person subject	NR2	NR2 (NR1)
Head = oblique		
Transitive	NR2	
Intransitive		
first-/second-person subject		NR2
third-person subject	NR2/NR1	NR2 (NR1)
Nominal complements	NR2 (NR1)	
Simple nominalized complements		
Intransitive	NR1/NR2	NR1
Transitive		
first-/second-person subject	NR2	NR2
third-person subject		NR2 (NR1)
Complements of cognition verbs w/ khã	NR2	
Verbal complements of khyaŋ		
first-/second-person subject	NR2	NR2
third-person subject		NR2 (NR1)
Verbal complements of ju-en con-a		
Intransitive	NR1	
Transitive		
Perfective	NR2	
Imperfective	NR1	
Non-embedded nominalizations		
first-/second-person subject	NR2	
third-person subject	NR2 (NR1)	NR1 (NR2)

(Hopper and Thompson 1980). The prototypical transitive event is one with a volitional agent, a telic or punctual event, and an individuated and totally affected patient. Particular propositions will denote events that are more or less similar to this prototype. As Hopper and Thompson point out, languages differ in which parameters are taken as relevant in determining the degree of Transitivity of a proposition, and hence its morphosyntactic structure. In Dolakha Newar, the parameters which are relevant to the distribution of the nominalizers are perfectivity (perfective events are more Transitive than imperfective events), volition (volitional events are more Transitive), and number of participants (events with two or more participants are more Transitive; the term "transitive" has been used throughout the book in this sense).

Beginning with number of participants and perfectivity, we can see that in verbal complements of *ju-en con-a* only two-participant perfective verbs are marked with NR2, the Transitive nominalizer. Imperfective clauses are marked like intransitive complements, with the NR1 nominalizer. Thus perfectivity overrides the number of participants in determining whether the complement clause is to be marked as Transitive (NR2) or Intransitive (NR1).

In a number of syntactic environments, the person of the subject is relevant to the distribution of the nominalizers. This is especially true in the elicited data reflecting the intuitions of the consultants. The general pattern is to use NR2. However, consultants also accept NR1 in clauses with third-person subjects. Thus NR2 is associated with first and second person, while NR1 is associated with third. In order to understand this pattern of distribution and its relation to Transitivity, we must consider the role of volition. In this language, first-person events may be marked with third-person morphology if the event is non-volitional (§6.4.3.4). Thus it is natural for someone to say *ji tul-eu* 'I will fall', using the third-person-singular suffix, when falling would be a non-volitional event (as in most instances). To use the first-person suffix in the clause *ji tul-i* 'I will fall' would be to indicate an intentional fall. Thus third person in this language is roughly associated with non-volitional events and hence Intransitivity. First person, on the other hand, is more strongly associated with volition and hence Transitivity. The optional marking of various examples with third-person subjects by NR1 appears to be an old reflex of this correlation.

Recall, however, that in the cases where person is being marked, the NR1 form represents an acceptable, but not a preferred, pattern. The dominant pattern is for all three persons to be marked the same way, with NR2. This seems to indicate that the role of person as a relevant parameter in the distribution of suffixes may be dying out. The fact that we find different patterns in the discourse data than we find in the elicited data appears to be indicative of an incomplete historical change.

This discussion still leaves open the distribution of the suffixes in relative clauses. We see that non-subject relative clauses tend to be marked with NR2, except that consultants agree that NR1 is possible with third-person subjects. NR1 is also the only form found with subject relatives. The key to this puzzle is again person. If NR1 was originally a third-person nominalizer, we can explain its reanalysis as a marker of subject relatives. Note that first- and second-person pronouns do not generally occur as heads of subject relative clauses. This is because the identity of first and second person is always recoverable from the discourse context, so restrictive relative clauses have no function. In addition, non-restrictive relative clauses with first- and second-person subjects tend to take the form of apposition with a third-person relative clause. An example of this type is given in (50):

(50) ginā̆gu   ṭhā̆kkar na-en   coŋ-gu   mi   ji
      how.much trouble eat-PART stay-NR1 person 1s

'I, a person who is experiencing (eating) so much trouble.'

Due to this fact, subject relative clauses with first- or second-person subjects are either vanishingly rare or unattested. This allows for the reanalysis of NR1 as a marker of third-person clauses to a marker of subject relative clauses. A necessary correlation of this change is that NR2 must come to be used as marker of non-subject relatives. This is the pattern which occurs overwhelmingly in the textual data and which both consultants prefer. Thus this change appears to be close to completion.

Chapter 18
Complementation

1. Introduction

In the languages of the world, it is often found that there is a set of verbs which may or must take clauses as noun-phrase arguments. Noun phrases functioning as arguments of such verbs are referred to as "(verbal) complements". The phenomenon as a whole is referred to as "complementation". Verbs which take complements may be referred to as "complement-taking predicates" or CTPs (Noonan 1985). The CTPs in a language generally fall into discrete semantic classes and CTPs of different classes take different types of complements (Givón 1980, 1990: 515–561). For example, we will see that the morphosyntax of complements of perception verbs differs from that of complements of utterance verbs.

There are four syntactically distinct complementation structures in Dolakha Newar, and a fifth which constitutes a combination of two others. These are discussed in §18.2. In addition, there are a number of verbs which may require complements in other languages, but which in this language are verbal auxiliaries. This verb-auxiliary construction constitutes a "complementation *strategy*" (Dixon 1995, 2006) in that, while it has a similar function to complementation in other languages, it doesn't involve the embedding of a clause as a noun phrase. Another complementation strategy, based on the participial construction, is also found. Complmentation strategies are outlined in §18.3. The description of complementation given here is largely based on Genetti (2006).

2. Complementation structures

Since complementation refers to the phenomenon of clauses functioning as noun-phrase arguments, it is not surprising that the majority of complementation structures in this language involve nominalization. Chapter 17 provided an outline of nominalization in the language – including a survey of the syntactic structures nominalized clauses appear in – and detailed discussion of the distribution of the nominalizers. In this chapter, the focus will be on the syntax of complementation.

2.1. Simple nominalized complements

Simple nominalized complements are clauses with verbs affixed by NR1 or NR2 and which are then embedded as object arguments of CTPs, specifically perception verbs. This structure is exemplified in (1–3), examples (26)–(28) in Chapter 17:

(1) [pharsi=n   thau mica=ta   phoŋ-a]$_{NP\text{-}O}$ khoŋ-an
    pumpkin=ERG REFL daughter=DAT ask.for-NR2 see-PART

'Seeing the pumpkin asking for his own daughter...'

(2) dokhsenuŋ [kharāyo lipul-e]$_{NP\text{-}O}$ khoŋ-an
    all.ERG   rabbit   return-NR2 see-PART

'All of them seeing the rabbit return...'

(3) jaba jin   [u jāŋal hal-gu]$_{NP\text{-}O}$ tār-agi
    when 1sERG this bird cry.out-NR1 hear-1sPR

'When I hear this bird cry out.'

In all of these examples, the arguments of the complement clause are case-marked for their grammatical relations with the complement clause verb. The complement clause in (1) has a transitive verb, so the subject has the ergative clitic. The given and human object has dative case. In (2) and (3), the verbs of the complement clauses are intransitive; their subjects are therefore not case-marked.

It is also possible for the subject of the complement clause to be grammatically treated as the object of the matrix clause. This is referred to as "raising". Consider example (4):

(4) cilā=n   ninpatti [āmta kho-en coŋ-gu]$_{NP\text{-}O}$ khon-ai
    goat=ERG daily   3sDAT cry-PART stay-NR1 see-3sPR

'The goat sees her crying every day.'

In this example the complement clause is referring to an ongoing activity; the goat sees the girl as she cries. The referent of the girl plays a double role in this construction: she is what the goat sees, and she is the one who cries. This doubling of the semantic roles allows for the variability in casemarking. The referent is referred to by a single argument, which can be treated grammatically either as an argument of the CTP, or as an argument of the complement clause. Example (4), with raising, can be contrasted with examples such as (1). In this example, raising is not possible. Note that the complement in (1) refers not to an ongoing activity, but to a situation as a whole. The verb *khon-* 'see' in this example indicates a cognitive state rather than direct perception; the father realizes or comes to understand that a pumpkin has come to ask for his daughter in marriage. There is no argument which plays a double role, and hence no raising of the subject. However, it is important to note that not all activity-type complements exhibit raising. Example (2) is of this type. Consider also (5) below which, like (4), explicitly codes an ongoing activity with the continuous auxiliary *con-* 'stay'. Here, however, the subject of the complement clause is not raised:

(5) [*jogi tikreŋ-an coŋ-a*]_{NP-O} *khoŋ-an*
yogi stand-PART stay-NR2 see-PART

'Seeing the yogi standing there.'

In elicitation, my consultants are happy to accept examples of perception verbs with activity complements both with and without dative casemarking on the complement subject. They have not been able to identify a meaning difference that correlates with the presence or absence of the dative casemarker which indicates raising. It should be noted, however, that not all activity predicates allow raising; the independent structure of the complement clause plays a role in determining whether or not raising is grammatically possible. Raising is restricted from occurring in complements which may take their own dative-marked object. For example, in (6) the ergative pronoun unambiguously marks the subject of the complement clause:

(6) Elicited
jin [*āmun pujā yeŋ-a*]_{NP-O} *sor-agi*
1sERG 3sERG ceremony do-NR2 watch-1sPR

'I watched him worship (someone or something).'

In this example, if the third-person pronoun had dative casemarking, it would necessarily refer to the object of the complement clause and could not refer to the subject of the CTP. Thus, the only translation of *jin āmta pujā yeŋ-a sor-agi* is [1sERG 3sDAT ceremony do-NR2 watch-1sPR] 'I watched (someone) worship him/her'. Consultants also do not like examples that put two dative-marked arguments in the same complement clause. They feel that constructed sentences such as *jin mohi=ta āmta pujā yeŋ-a sor-agi* [1sERG farmer=DAT 3sDAT worship do-NR2 watch-1sPR] 'I watched the farmer worship him' sound awkward and they prefer such sentences to have the complement subject in ergative case.

As mentioned above, complementation involves clauses functioning as arguments of complement-taking predicates. In order to argue for complementation, one must present data which establish that complement clauses are indeed grammatical arguments. In the case of simple nominalized complements, two facts can be used to establish that they are grammatical objects. First, the perception verbs are grammatically transitive, with ergative-marked subjects and morphological markers of transitivity. In this language, transitive verbs require that there be at least a notional object; the nominalized clause naturally fills this role. The second fact has to do with constituent order. In all the examples presented so far, the complement clause follows the subject of the CTP. However, it is possible for the complement clause to precede the subject, so that the subject intervenes between the complement and the CTP. This is illustrated in (7):

(7) Elicited
     [jin   wāsti   hi-e]$_{NP-O}$ āmun   sor-ai
     1sERG   clothes wash-NR2   3sERG   watch-3sPR

     'He watches me wash the clothes.'

This flexibility in ordering is commonly found with subject and object noun phrases (see Chapter 14), a fact which argues for the analysis of nominalized complements as objects. This ordering also shows that the complement and the CTP are not inextricably linked, but that the complement has a degree of syntactic independence. This may be contrasted with the behavior of verbs and auxiliaries in the complementation strategy discussed in §18.3.

Simple nominalized complements may express most of the categories of independent clauses. Because the suffixal complex of the verb is necessarily taken up by nominalizers, the inflectional categories of the finite suffixes are not expressed (tense, person/number/honorific status of subject). Aspectual categories, coded by auxiliary verbs, may be marked, as in example (5). Complements of perception verbs are not negated; this may be attributed to the semantic fact that one cannot directly perceive an event that does not occur. Otherwise, simple nominalized clauses may express all the richness of independent clauses.

Although I have been referring to complement *clauses* throughout this discussion, it is more accurate to refer to complement *structures*, as the units which are nominalized and function as objects of perception verbs may themselves be multiclausal structures. Example (8) illustrates this point quite nicely:

(8) [sācā   cumṭu   ṭikre-ke   bwāŋ-an   bwāŋ-an
      calf   tail   straight-CAUS.PART   run-PART   run-PART

```
kho     dupān   swaṭṭa  morlu-en    ye-ene      dudu
river   inside  EXPR    bathe-PART  come-PART   milk
```

```
toŋ-a]_NP-O    khon-ju
drink-NR2      see-3sPST
```

'(They) saw the calf run and run with its tail sticking out, bathe inside the river, come out, and drink milk.'

In this example, the object complement of *khon-ju* 'saw' comprises the first word of the example through *toŋ-a,* the nominalized form of 'drink'. This includes four (or five) clauses linked by the participial construction. The first participial clause *cumṭu ṭikre-ke* 'making his tail straight' modifies the following repeated participial clause *bwāŋ-an bwāŋ-an.* Thus the noun *cumṭu* 'tail' is a nominal object of a participial clause which modifies another participial clause which is embedded into a complement clause. This degree of beautiful syntactic complexity is not unusual in this language.

2.1.1. Nominalized complement plus khā

The next type of verbal complement to be discussed is a subtype of the first. It again involves a nominalized complement but in this construction the complement is followed by a complementizer, *khā*. This type of complement is found with CTPs which are cognition and utterance verbs. Semantically, these complements refer to general facts or situations, rather than to activities. Consider the contrasting examples in (9) and (10):

(9)   Elicited
```
āmun    [rām  ye-u]_NP-O    tār-ju
3sERG   Ram   come-NR1      hear-3sPST
```

'S/he heard Ram come.'

(10)   Elicited
```
āmun    [rām  ye-u]_NP-O    khā     tār-ju
3sERG   Ram   come-NR1      COMP    hear-3sPST
```

'S/he heard that Ram came.'

In example (9), the complement is of the activity-type; the clause denotes the direct hearing of the noise that Ram made upon coming in. By contrast in (10), the complement is of the fact-type. The subject hears *about* Ram's coming, probably by hearsay, but does not in fact hear Ram. Example (10), with its NR1 nominalizer indicating a realis event, can additionally be contrasted with example (11), which uses the irrealis NR3 nominalizer. The complement in this example does not denote a fact, but only a potential event. It may be referred to as a potential-type complement. (See Dixon (2006) for a discussion of activity-, fact-, and potential-type complements.)

(11) Elicited
 āmun [rām yer-iuri]$_{NP-O}$ khã tār-ju
 3sERG Ram come-NR3 COMP hear-3sPST
 'S/he heard that Ram might come.'

For more on the distribution of the nominalizers, see §17.3.

The primary syntactic question with this type of complement is whether it should, indeed, be analyzed as a nominalized complement plus an abstract complementizer *khã*. *Khã* is transparently related to a noun of the same form, which refers to a topic that has been orally discussed or to a fact that has been transmitted through speech. It may be translated as 'talk', 'matter', or 'news'. Thus, an alternative syntactic analysis takes *khã* not as a grammaticalized complementizer but as the nominal head of a complex-object noun phrase. The clause preceding the noun would then be analyzed as complementing the noun (a "nominal complement" as opposed to a "nominalized complement"; see §17.2 for discussion). These two analyses are represented in (12) and (13):

(12) [(NP) (NP) V-NR]$_{NP-O}$ khã V$_{TR}$
 complement clause COMP CTP

(13) [[(NP) (NP) V-NR]$_{NOM.COMP}$ khã]$_{NP-O}$ V$_{TR}$
 complement clause talk

In (12), the complement clause is interpreted as the object, with the complementizer effectively linking the two clauses together. In (13), *khã* is the head of the noun phrase, and is modified by a nominal-complement clause. In accordance with this analysis, sentence (11) could be more literally translated as 'S/he heard the talk of Ram's coming'. This structure would then be considered to be a complementation *strategy* (see below) as opposed to a complementation structure.

While the construction can be analyzed in either way, I believe that two arguments favor the analysis represented in (12), where *khã* is analyzed as a complementizer. The first argument is semantic. It is possible for a complement of this type to refer to an event or state generally and not to something spoken *per se*. Consider example (14):

(14) āpsin [ām jāl ta-en ta-e]_{NP-O} khā ma-si-u
      3pERG that net put-PART put-NR2 COMP NEG-know-3PA

'They didn't know that the net had been put there.'

In the story that this sentence was taken from, there is no explicit discussion of the putting of the net; the complement refers to the fact of the net's presence only. Thus the specific meaning of *khā* is gone. This semantic bleaching is expected under grammaticalization.

The second argument in favor of viewing *khā* as a complementizer is that in this construction it does not have nominal properties. It cannot pluralize or co-occur with demonstratives, behavior that is normally characteristics of nominal heads of noun phrases.

Nominalized complements plus *khā* have almost all of the same internal properties as simple nominalized complements. However, there are no semantic restrictions that prohibit expression of negation. In addition, these complements do not allow raising; this may be attributed both to the semantic character of the complements (they do not code activities) and to the presence of the complementizer.

The latter point allows for an interesting observation. In contrasting these two types of complements, we can see that the CTP and the simple nominalized complement have a tighter, more integrated structure than do the CTP and the nominalized complement plus *khā*. There are three ways in which simple nominalized complements have a tighter syntactic bond with the CTP: (1) the absence of the complementizer, which physically and functionally separates the complement and the CTP; (2) the ability for arguments which have semantic roles in both predicates to be raised; (3) the inability for independent negation of the complement. This tighter syntactic bond is paralleled by a tighter conceptual bond: the activity and its perception occur simultaneously, and the act of perception could not occur in the absence of the activity; thus the perception verb entails its complement. Cognition and utterance verbs, on the other hand, have a looser semantic bond with their complements. Events coded by complements of cognition verbs may be removed in time from the cognition verb itself, e.g. a person may have arrived a month ago, but I may only hear about it today. In addition, there is no semantic entailment between the CTP and the complement; one can learn about an event that has not occurred, as in (11). Thus we see a nice parallelism between tightness of semantic bond and tightness of syntactic structure. This phenomenon is referred to as iconicity (Givón 1985; Haiman 1983, 1985).[94]

2.1.2. *Indirect quotation*

In Dolakha Newar narrative discourse, speakers use quotation both to advance the story-line and to express the ideas, thoughts, and reactions of the characters. The majority of quoted speech in the narratives constitutes direct quotation; it represents the speech that the characters would use if they were actually living out the story. The use of direct quotation gives an immediacy to the narrative which enlivens it and draws in the audience. In embedding direct quotation into a narrative, the speaker produces a shift in his or her role. Instead of producing the voice of the narrator, the speaker produces the voice of the speaker. This move is accomplished by shifts in temporal, locational, and personal deixis.

While direct quotation is the most common way to embed a character's speech in Dolakha Newar narrative, indirect quotation is also attested. Indirect quotation reports on the speech of the characters without including the deictic shifts that characterize direct quotation. One way of incorporating indirect quotation is to use the nominalized complement plus *khã*, as in example (15):

(15)   āmu pharsi=n   birbahādur=ta   āme   mica
       that pumpkin=ERG   Birbahadur=DAT   3sGEN   daughter

       phon-da   ye-e   khã   hat-cu
       ask.for-PURP   come-NR2   COMP   say-3sPST

   'That pumpkin said to Birbahadur that he had come to ask for his daughter.'

If the speaker had chosen to produce direct quotation instead of indirect quotation in this sentence, the embedded sentence would be something like *thape mica phon-da yer-gi* 'I came to ask for your daughter', with a second-person pronoun to register that the addressee was a speech-act participant, and a first-person finite verb. The use of the nominalized construction in (15) results in third-person reference being maintained throughout.

2.2. Direct quote followed by *haŋ-a khã*

A third complementation structure, which is related to the nominalized complement plus *khã* and the issue of indirect quotation, involves the sequence *haŋ-a khã*. The verb *haŋ-a* is the nominalized (NR2) form of the verb *hat-* 'say'. It may be followed by the complementizer *khã* to produce complements of cognition verbs. The complements of these predicates constitute indirect quotes, as in (16):

(16)   Elicited

[āme   mā=ta]_NP-EXP   [bārmun   nāpa   bihā   yer-eu]_NP-STIM
3sGEN mother=DAT   Brahmin   ASSOC   marriage   do-3sPR

haŋ-a   khā   thāhā   ma-da
say-NR2 COMP   knowledge   NEG-exist

'Her mother didn't know about her talking of marrying a Brahmin.'

The indirect quality of the predicate can be determined by the third-person form of the verb *yer-eu*. The construction doesn't refer to a specific act of speaking, but refers more generally to something that has been discussed.

There are two possible analyses of this construction. One analysis takes this structure simply as an example of the nominalized complement followed by *khā*. By this analysis, the complement of the CTP *ṭhāhā ma-da* 'don't know' is the verb *hat-* 'say', which in turn has its own complement, the indirect quote. The second analysis takes *haŋ-a khā* as a unified whole, functioning as a morphologically complex complementizer. The indirect quote is then analyzed as the complement of the cognition verb. Although I have only a handful of examples of this construction, I am inclined towards the latter view. The primary reason for this is that semantically it is the embedded quote which functions as the complement of the cognition verb, not the verb *hat-* 'say'. In most examples, the verb is not predicating an act of speaking, and the expression of the speech act does not fit into the sentence. This is true of example (17):

(17)   [gunān   guntaŋ   helā   yer-i   ma-ṭe]_NP-STIM
        nobody.ERG   nobody.DAT   insult   do-INF   NEG-PROH

haŋ-a   khā   ṭhāhā   jur-a
say-NR1 COMP   knowledge   become-3sPST

'One comes to know that nobody should insult anybody else.'

Here the speaker is conveying the moral of a story. The matrix verb is *ṭhāhā jur-* 'come to know' or 'learn'. What one learns is the moral, represented as the indirect quote, and not that people say the moral. Thus, while this construction is clearly an extension of the nominalized complement plus *khā*, it appears to have independent semantic properties, to be restricted to a small set of cognition verbs, and to be used only with indirect-quote complements.

Because the complements in these constructions are indirect quotes and not nominalized clauses, they are able to express the full range of verbal categories, such as tense, as in (16), and mood, as in (17). The complements clearly have the internal structure of clauses, as the casemarking of arguments indicates.

Again the complements have the status of arguments, appearing either as O arguments of transitive verbs, or as unmarked stimulus arguments in dative-subject constructions.

2.3. Quotative complements

The fourth type of verbal complement to be discussed does not involve nominalization, but the simple embedding of direct quotes as objects of quotative verbs. Quotative verbs are ditransitive, with ergative-marked subjects and two objects. One object is the R, the dative-marked addressee, and the other is the O, which represents the speech itself. The latter may be realized as a simple NP headed by a nominal. Example (18) illustrates this structure with the most common quotative verb, *hat-* 'say':

(18)   *jin*   [*chanta*]_{NP-R} [*thi-gur khā*]_{NP-O} *har-i*
       1sERG   2sDAT   one-CL matter   say-1FUT

   'I will tell you one thing.'

However, it is more common for the object in this construction to be a direct quote. Direct quotes may be units of any size which are appropriate to the conversational discourse represented in the narrative. Since directly quoted speech embodies the deictic orientation of the reputed speaker, direct quotes may also contain vocatives, imperatives, exclamations, or other elements that give the speech a lively and natural character. Example (19) illustrates a direct quote consisting of two syntactic sentences:

(19)   *āmun*   ["*u   jaŋgal=e   rājā ji tuŋ khyaŋ*
       3sERG   this jungle=GEN king 1s TOP be

   mebu ma-da"]_{NP-O} *hat-ai*
   other NEG-exist say-3sPR

   'He said: "The king of this jungle is me. There is no other".'

The analytical question which arises is whether or not embedded direct quotes of this type really constitute grammatical objects, hence whether the quoted material constitutes a complement of the utterance verbs. The primary argument in favor of this position is the highly integrated nature of quotative sentences. Quotative verbs are ditransitive with ergative-marked noun phrases. They license an NP in object position which refers to the speech itself. This can be filled by a nominal, as in (18) or by a direct quote, as in (19). The usual position for the quoted material is, as with other objects, between the subject and the quotative verb. However, the quotative verb may precede the subject; as we have seen, this word-order flexibility is typical of arguments. Consider also the fact that if direct quotes were syntactically independent of the quotative verb, it becomes difficult to explain the ergative morphology on the subject, which becomes a syntactic fragment (Genetti and Slater 2004; see also the discussion in §21.3.1).

This analysis is further strengthened when one considers prosodic structure. Example (20) is transcribed prosodically, with each intonation unit on a separate line (prosodic categorization and transcription are discussed in Chapter 3).

(20) (1.9)   mā́ji=n   ^"lau! ō ! /\
              boatman=ERG   lo   go(IMP)

      ... ota   ^parāsar risi=ta , /
          3sDAT   Parasar Risi=DAT

      ... kho tār   yeŋ-an   ^bi-u"   hat-cu   hã . \
          river cross do-PART   give-IMP say-3sPST   EVID

'The boatman said: "Lo! Go! Ferry Parasar Risi across the river".'

Note that both the subject of the sentence and the quotative verb are not put in separate prosodic units from portions of the quoted material. This implies that the direct quote and the quotative clause are tightly integrated elements. Examples such as this, which combine elements from the quotative clause and the embedded quote in a single prosodic unit, are not unusual.

The embedding of direct quotation is a commonly used narrative device. It is not unusual for entire conversations to be embedded within a single grammatical sentence; each conversational turn constitutes an embedded object of a quotative verbs, and the quotative verbs are put into sequence via the participial construction or other means of clause combining. However, even in such extensive examples of embedding, there is syntactic integration and each direct quote constitutes the object of a quotative verb. For full discussion and exemplification of these points, see Genetti and Slater (2004).

2.4. Infinitive complements

There are four verbs in this language which take infinitive complement clauses: *jir-* 'to be appropriate; should', *mal-* 'to be necessary; must', *bir-* 'to give', and *yer-* 'to want to, like to, be skilled at'. The first two are modal verbs with similar syntactic behavior. They are both intransitive and they both take a complement clause with an infinitive verb as their subject argument:

(21) [ḍoli bu nichi dã̀lāŋ-an cõ-i]_{NP-S} mal-a
 doli carry(NR1) all.day fast-PART stay-INF must-3sPST

 'The doli carrier must be fasting all day.'
 (lit. 'It is necessary for the doli carrier to be fasting all day.')

(22) Elicited
 [chin mucā=ta lokhu ton-ke-i]_{NP-S} jir-a
 2sERG child=DAT water drink-CAUS-INF appropriate-3sPST

 'You should make the child drink water.'
 (lit. 'It is appropriate for you to make the child drink water.')

The primary argument that these examples contain complements in the subject role is that the finite verb always takes third-person agreement. It does not agree with the subject of the complement clause, as can be seen in (22). The complement subject, in this example, is second person, but the suffix on the finite verb is third person. (This may be contrasted with the complementation *strategy* discussed in §18.3, where verbs denoting secondary concepts agree with the subject of the lexical verb.) Semantically, the situation as a whole is construed as being either necessary or appropriate. Syntactically, the embedded clause acts an abstract argument that triggers third-person agreement on the verb.

Different syntactic structures are found with the other two verbs that take infinitive complements. When *bir-* 'to give' occurs with an infinitive complement, it has a permissive meaning of 'let' or 'allow'. Syntactically, the matrix verb has its own referential subject to which it assigns ergative case, and the subject argument of the complement clause is raised to the object role of the matrix clause, hence receives dative casemarking typical of transitive objects:

(23) Elicited
 [āme mā=n]_{NP-A} [āmta_A bārmun nāpa
 3sGEN mother=ERG 3sDAT Brahmin ASSOC

 bihā yer-i]_{COMP} ma-bi-u
 marriage do-INF NEG-give-3PA

 'Her mother did not allow her to marry a Brahmin.'

The verb *yer-* instantiates yet another structure, although with some syntactic similarities. As a complement-taking predicate, *yer-* means 'want to; like to; be skilled at'. The experiential nature of this predicate thus gives it a dative-subject argument structure. As discussed in §13.2.2, repeated here for the reader's convenience, there are two possible syntactic analyses of this structure. In one, the dative-marked experiencer can be seen as the regular subject of the complement-taking predicate, in which case, the coreferential subject argument of the complement clause is obligatorily omitted:

(24) [janta]$_{EXP}$ [∅$_A$ inãgu khã=pen khã lã-i]$_{COMP}$ **mã-yã**
1sDAT this.type talk=PL talk tell-INF NEG-come

'I don't like to tell stories of this type.'

In the other, the dative-marked argument is seen as the subject of the complement clause, but its casemarking is controlled by the matrix verb, resulting in raising:

(25) [janta$_{EXP}$ inãgu khã=pen khã lã-i]$_{COMP}$ **mã-yã**
1sDAT this.type talk=PL talk tell-INF NEG-come

'I don't like to tell stories of this type.'

On the other hand, it should be noted that I do have one example where the subject of the complement clause receives casemarking not from the complement-taking predicate, but from the complement verb:

(26) [ji$_S$ bebahãrik=ku par-ai ju-i]$_{COMP}$ **yer-a**
1s family.life=LOC touch-BV be-INF come-3sPST

'I want to experience family life.'

Thus, as in simple nominalized complements, raising appears to be optional.

It should be noted that this structure, like most dative-subject constructions in this language (see §12.5), appears to be a calque on a similar Nepali structure. The Nepali verb with this meaning is *man parnu*, transparently constructed of *man* 'mind, opinion, feeling' and *parnu* 'be concerned with, happen, occur'. The parallelism between the two languages can be seen in (27):

(27) Nepali: malãi pokhara jã-na man par-cha
1sDAT Pokhara go-INF feeling happen-3sPR

Dol.: janta pokhara ũ-i manpar-ai jur-a
1sDAT Pokhara go-INF like-BV happen-3sPST

'I like to/want to go to Pokhara.'

3. Complementation strategies

In addition to true complementation, under which a clause takes on the role of an argument of another verb, many languages have what can be called "complementation strategies" by which a verb from a restricted set is linked to another verb or clause (Dixon 1995, 2006). In Dolakha Newar, there are two complementation strategies.

3.1. Infinitive verb plus grammatical auxiliary

The first complementation strategy to be discussed involves a clause ending with an infinitive verb which is then followed by an auxiliary verb. This strategy differs from the infinitive complementation *structure* in that the primary lexical verb plus the auxiliary form a single verbal complex. This strategy is exemplified in (28)–(31):

(28) *upsin* [*kā-i mwāl-ai*]_{V.COMPLEX}
    3pERG take-INF try-3sPR

   'They try to take it.'

(29) *jin* [*khā lā-i sar-agi*]_{V.COMPLEX}
    1sERG talk talk-INF know-1sPR

   'I know how to talk.'

(30) *didā nis-mā=ŋ jaŋgal* [*ū-i don-gu*]_{V.COMPLEX}
    e.brother two-CL=both jungle go-INF finish-3PA

   'Your two brothers finished going to the jungle.'

(31) *āpisna ām tākku gunuŋ keṭā* [*nāplar-i ma-phar-ju*]_{V.COMPLEX}
    3pERG that time nobody boy meet-INF NEG-able-3sPST

   'At that time they were unable to meet any boys.'

(32) *thamu māyā=ku* [*jit-ai ju-i pha-ita*]_{V.COMPLEX} *ra?*
    2h love=LOC win-BV happen-INF able-2hFUT Q

   'Will you be able to win in love?'

As with most cases of complementation, the casemarking of arguments of such examples is determined by the lexical (infinitive) verb. Thus we can compare the ergative-marked subject of the transitive verb in (31) with the unmarked, hence absolutive, subject of the intransitive verb in (32).

The primary clue that tells us that these constructions have a significantly different structure than the infinitive complements, is that the final verb reflects the person and number of the subject of the lexical verb. Thus (28), (30), and (31) have third-person verb forms, (29) has a first-person verb form, and (32) has a second-person form. This agreement pattern is what is expected with monoclausal structures; subject agreement is realized on the final verb of the clause, regardless of whether that verb is the main verb or the auxiliary. On the other hand, if the examples in (28) through (32) were analyzed as biclausal, one cannot explain the conflict in subject properties, with case being assigned by the verb of one clause, but agreement being realized on the verb of another.

In addition to this morphological argument, one can also find justification for the analysis from constituent ordering. As noted in §18.2.1, subject noun phrases may intervene between object complements and the CTP. This flexibility of ordering is typical of noun phrases. However, it is not possible to move a subject NP between an infinitive and a following auxiliary verb, as illustrated in (33):

(33)　　Elicited and judged ungrammatical
　　　　*khēja　ŋyār-i　jin　lūmonker-gi
　　　　egg　　buy-INF　1sERG　forget-1sPST

　　　　'I forgot to buy eggs.'

This restriction is not found with nominal arguments. For example, ām khā jin lūmonker-gi [that talk 1sERG forget-1sPST] 'I forgot that talk' which has two nominal arguments does exhibit flexibility in constituent order. This argues that the clause ending in an infinitive verb is not a noun phrase, and hence is not a true complement.

3.2. Embedded quotation with haŋ-an

In §18.2.3, it was shown that embedded quotations constitute object complements of utterance verbs. It is possible to combine the embedding of quotations as objects of hat- 'say' with the participial construction (§19.4.3), to create a complementation strategy for relating other cognition and utterance verbs to the embedded quote. Consider example (34):

(34)   *"ji gyāt-a"*   *haŋ-an*   *sir-ai*   *jeu*
        1s fear-3sPST say-PART   know-3sPR maybe

'Maybe he knows I am afraid.'

In this example, the direct quote *ji gyāt-a* 'I am afraid' is embedded as the complement of *haŋ-an*, the participial form of the verb *hat-* 'say'. Semantically, however, the embedded quotation is related to the cognition verb *sir-* 'know'. Since *sir-* is not an utterance verb, the only type of true object complement it may take is the nominalized complement plus *khā* (§18.2.1.1). If that complement structure were substituted in (34), however, the meaning would change to 'He knows about my being afraid', which is more general in its meaning, does not imply direct knowledge, and may include more than just the fact of the fear, for example, the reason for the fear as well. The complementation strategy with *haŋ-an* allows for the immediacy of direct-quote complements in the absence of direct embedding of the quote as the object of *sir-*.

There is another possible analysis of constructions such as (34). This is to analyze the participial verb *haŋ-an* as a grammaticalized complementizer, and to analyze the direct quote as a true object complement of *sir-*. Evidence in favor of this position is that *haŋ-an* occurs frequently before cognition and utterance verbs and seems to serve a similar function to a complementizer in that it links the cognition or utterance verb with the direct quote. Examples like (35) seem particularly suggestive of this analysis:

(35)   [*"chi do-õ"*]$_{NP-O}$ *haŋ-an*   *hat-cu*
        2s PROH-go   say-PART   say-3sPST

'She said: "Don't you go".'

Here we have *haŋ-an*, the participial form of the verb *hat-* 'say', occurring before *hat-cu*, the inflected form of the verb 'say'. In this "double-say" construction, *haŋ-an* appears to be lexically superfluous, suggesting that it may have a grammatical role as a complementizer.[95]

On the other hand, given that one of the primary functions of the participial construction is to allow one clause to specify the manner of another, it is also possible to see *haŋ-an* clauses as being independent. For example (34) may be translated as 'Maybe he knows, saying I am afraid', with the 'saying' clause describing the manner of his knowing. Similarly, (35) may be translated as 'She spoke, saying: "Don't you go"'. Thus, an analysis of *haŋ-an* as a grammaticalized complementizer is not required by the semantics. See §19.4.3 for further discussion of *haŋ-an* serving a role similar to a complementizer with direct quotes.

4. Complement-taking predicates and their complements

Table 38 presents the complement-taking predicates I have found in Dolakha Newar, together with the complement structures and complementation strategies I have found occurring with each one. It will be noted that many of the cognition verbs involve borrowed Nepali vocabulary (designated by (N) in the translation column). In some cases, native Dolakha Newar terms and Nepali terms are used interchangably (e.g. the forms for 'try').

Group 1 in the table comprises the set of verbs which occur with simple nominalized complements. The direct perception verbs form a coherent semantic class. The verb *sukar-* 'pretend' also fits into this class, although it does not fit semantically. This verb is somewhat idiosyncratic and doesn't fit with any of the other semantic classes of verbs. The verb *khā lār-* 'to talk' fits into this category because it is a compound verb which already involves the noun *khā*. This prohibits it from occurring with the other utterance verbs in Group 2, the nominalized complements with the complementizer *khā*, as it would sound redundant. The only verb in Group 1 to be able to occur with two complement types is *tār-* 'hear'. This is because the verb can be used not only to hear sounds, but also to hear speech. When this verb occurs with a nominalized complement plus *khā* it means 'hear about', thus occurs with a fact-type or potential-type complement. This was exemplified in §18.2.1.1 above.

Group 2 consists of a set of cognition verbs utilizing vocabulary borrowed from Nepali. These apparently are much more limited in their range of complements than other cognition verbs.

Group 3 primarily contains utterance verbs, although *ṭhāhā dat-* 'to have knowledge; know' also falls into this class as I have one example where it follows a direct quote. When these verbs are used with nominalized complements plus *khā* they refer more generally to a topic, e.g. 'ask about', 'talk about', 'know about'. When they occur with a direct quote X they mean 'ask X', 'say X', 'know X'. When they occur with the complementation strategy with *haŋ-an*, they mean 'ask by saying', 'say by saying' (see discussion in §18.3.2).

A similar semantic distinction is found with the cognition verbs in Group 4. These differ from the verbs in Group 3 in not allowing the direct embedding of quoted material as objects.

The Group 5 verbs are even more limited, allowing only the complementation strategy. This is presumably because one imagines, suspects, hopes, and fears specific things rather than topics.

Group 6 has different behavior. The verbs for remembering and forgetting are used as auxiliaries when what is forgotten or remembered is an activity that is to be performed, as in example (36):

(36) jin   khẽja ŋyār-i   lumonker-gi
     1sERG   egg   buy-INF   forget-1sPST

   'I forgot to buy eggs.'

On the other hand, the verbs are used as complement-taking predicates with nominalized complements plus *khā* when they refer to facts or prior discussion:

(37) jin   khẽja ŋyār-iuri khā   lumonker-gi
     1sERG   egg   buy-NR3   COMP   forget-1sPST

   'I forgot about buying eggs.'

Group 7 consists of the deontic modal verbs and one verb of liking. These have in common that they all take infinitive complements. Infinitive complements are never in object position. They either occur as intransitive subject arguments (with the deontic modals), or as stimulus arguments (with the verb of liking).

Group 8 is the largest group, consisting of the verbs that occur as auxiliaries. These include a number of verbs with aspectual meanings, as well as modals, the Nepali verb for 'want', and two verbs of 'trying'. All of these meanings are commonly found cross-linguistically as grammatical morphology, so to see them treated here as auxiliary verbs is not surprising.

426 Chapter 18 Complementation

Table 38. Complement-taking predicates, complement types, and complement strategies

Group	Verb	Translation	Semantic Type	Complement structures				Complementation Strategies	
				Simple Nominal.	Nominal. + khā	Dir. Quote	INF	INF + AUX	Quote + haŋ-an
1	khon-	'see'	Perception	X					
	tār-	'hear'	Perception	X	X				
	sor-	'watch'	Perception	X					
	sukar-	'pretend'	Acting	X					
	khā lār-	'talk'	Utterance	X					
2	thāhā jur-	'came to know' (N)	Cognition		X				
	prasta jur-	'became clear' (N)	Cognition		X				
	patālyā yet-	'discover' (N)	Cognition		X				
3	hat-	'say'	Utterance		X	X			X
	ŋen-	'ask'	Utterance		X	X			X
	thāhā dat-	'have knowledge' (N)	Cognition		X	X			
4	sir-	'know'	Cognition		X				X
	bicār yet-	'think' (N)	Cognition		X				X
	cin yet-	'decide' (N)	Cognition		X				X
	pir yet-	'worry' (N)	Cognition		X				X
5	kalpanā yet-	'imagine' (N)	Cognition						X
	sankā yet-	'suspect' (N)	Cognition						X
	āsā yet-	'hope' (N)	Cognition						X
	gyāt-	'fear'	Cognition						X
6	līwonker-	'remember'	Cognition		X			X	
	lūmonker-	'forget'	Cognition		X			X	

Section 4 Complement-taking predicates   427

7	jir-	'should; be appropriate'	Modal		X	
	mal-	'must; be necessary'	Modal		X	
	yer-	'like; want; be skilled at'	Modal		X	
	man par-ai jur-	'like' (N)	Liking		X	
8	twãrtar-	'stop'	Aspect			X
	suru yet-	'begin' (N)	Aspect			X
	d(h)un-	'finish'	Aspect			X
	ten-	'about to'	Aspect			X
	phar-	'able'	Modal			X
	sar-	'know how'	Modal			X
	mwãl-	'try' (< 'search')	Trying			X
	kosis yet-	'try' (N)	Trying			X
	cahai yet-	'want' (N)	Cognition			X
	bir-	'let' (< 'give')	Giving			X

Chapter 19
The participial construction

1. Introduction

One of the most important and widely used constructions in Dolakha Newar discourse is the one I refer to as "the participial construction". The term "participial" has been chosen as the label for this construction for two reasons. First, similar constructions are found in many languages of South Asia and the verb forms on which they are based have come to be known as "conjunctive participles" in the South Asian linguistic literature (e.g. Davison 1981; Kachru 1981; Masica 1991). Second, because of this tradition, in the literature on other Newar dialects, verb forms with similar functions are glossed PART for participle. Thus the terminology follows established linguistic tradition for the language and for the area. The fact that the chosen label for the construction is based on linguistic tradition leaves open the issue of the syntactic analysis and its typological interpretation. In Genetti (2005), I argue that in our current view of the typology of clause linkage, the Dolakha participial construction should be analyzed as an "Asian converb" construction. However, choosing the label is not nearly as important as understanding the nature of the construction and how it is used by speakers. The goal of this chapter is to provide a full description and analysis of the syntax of the participial construction and its diverse functions. Much of the description and analysis is based on Genetti (2005); the current chapter represents an expansion of the descriptive portion of that paper.

Every language has at its heart one or more features which, from the perspective of a linguist, are fundamental to the very nature of the language. They give the language its beauty, its unique personality, and its genius. In my view, the Dolakha Newar participial construction is this. At once complex and subtle, flexible and full of variation, it is the brightest thread which intricately weaves together the varying strands of argument structure, casemarking, reference, and meaning to create the complex fabric of Dolakha Newar discourse.

2. Morphology of the participial construction

The Dolakha Newar participial construction inflects across the four verb classes as shown in (1):

(1) n-stem   *toŋ-an*   drink-PART
     t-stem   *syāŋ-an*   kill-PART
     r-stem   *bi-en*   give-PART
     l-stem   *pwāl-en*   strike-PART

The only unpredictable form is found with the causative suffix *-ker*. This generally inflects like a regular r-stem verb, so one would expect the participial form to be *-ke-en*. This form does occur, but it is more common to find a shorter form ending in *-ke*, e.g. *na-ke-en* and *na-ke* are both participial forms of the verb 'feed' (< 'eat' + CAUS). There appears to be no difference in meaning between the *-ke* and *-ke-en* forms.

In addition to the simple participial forms listed in (1), it is also possible to add an additional vowel. This is pronounced either as *-i* or *-e*, depending on the speaker, so it serves to create trisyllabic forms, *toŋ-an-i*, etc. The functional difference between the two forms is subtle and varies across speakers. A full discussion of these points will be deferred until §19.6. At this point, both the simple participial form and the participial plus the extra vowel will be treated the same way and glossed as PART.

Participial verb forms may be further suffixed by *-li*. Elsewhere in the language, this morpheme means 'back' or 'backwards'. When suffixed to the participial form of the verb it explicitly designates that the event of the clause to which it is suffixed was completed prior to the event of the following clause; it is thus translated as 'after'.

3. Defining characteristics of the construction

Genetti (2005: 40) lays out the defining characteristics of the construction as follows:

> (i) Two or more verbs or clauses occur in a sequence. Non-final verbs are inflected with the participle; final verbs may inflect with the full range of verb morphology.
>
> (ii) The construction forms a chain of verbs or clauses whose status with respect to the surrounding text is determined by the morphology on the final verb.
>
> (iii) The participle is vague in meaning; it has no particular semantic entailment, instead the semantic relation between the participial clause and the surrounding clauses is determined from the context.
>
> (iv) A participial clause is neither a nominal argument, a nominal modifier, nor a complement of the following verb or clause.

3.1. Point (i)

Point (i) involves both syntactic and morphological criteria. The structures which the participial construction joins may be either separate verbs or separate clauses. When the construction is used to link two verbs into a single clause, the second verb is a grammaticalized auxiliary, as in (2):

(2)   kehē   ho   cicā=uri   dāi   **coŋ-an**   con-hin
        y.sister and small=IND e.brother stay-PART stay-3pPST

       'The younger sister and the elder brother continued to stay.'

Here the verb *con-* 'stay' is used twice; the first time as a lexical verb, and the second time as a grammaticalized auxiliary indicating continuous aspect. The construction is one clause with a complex predicate. Nothing can intervene between the two verbs. The use of the participial construction to incorporate a grammaticalized auxiliary is very common. This structure will be discussed in more detail in §19.4.1.

It is also common to find the participial construction being used to link separate clauses. When it does, the two clauses may share arguments or each retain its own. Thus the example given in (3), taken from a conversation, has two clauses which share a subject, given once at the beginning of the chain:

(3)   āmun   jā   **na-en**   ye-eu   ka
        3sERG rice eat-PART come-3FUT ASS

       'He will eat his meal and come back.'

In example (4), the shared subject referent receives two overt lexical mentions. Note also that the transitive clauses have separate objects:

(4)   ām   kehē=uri   sut-pānt   **phi-ene**   tap   **phi-en**
        that y.sister=IND suit-pant wear-PART hat wear-PART

        sara   **ga-en**   ām   kehē   tuŋ   on-a
        horse climb-PART that y.sister FOC go-3sPST

       'That younger sister, putting on a pants suit, putting on a hat, and riding a horse, that younger sister went.'

The participial construction is also used to join clauses which have different subjects. Example (5) illustrates this pattern, and also gives a taste of the complexity that multiple uses of this construction in a single sentence entails:

(5) bihā **yeŋ-an hā-en ta-ene** āme chitrāŋga
marriage do-PART bring put-PART 3sGEN Chitrangga

bicitrāŋga haŋ-a nis-mā kae janm-ai jur-a
Bicitrangga say-NR2 two-CL son born-BV be-3sPST

'(The king) having married and brought (her to the house), their two sons named Chitrangga and Bicitrangga were born.'

The collocation *bihā yeŋ-an hār-* is a lexicalized phrase meaning to marry a woman and bring her into the household; *hār-* is in the participial form since the following verb *tar-* 'put' is being used grammatically to signal perfect aspect. That verb is also in participial form since it links the whole clause to the following. The two independent clauses denote events that are in sequence.

The morphological property described in (i) is an essential characteristic of construction. In sequences of clauses or verbs connected by this construction, only the non-final verbs are suffixed with the participle. The final verb may take the full range of inflection. This creates a morphological asymmetry between the linked clauses or verbs; participial clauses are in a dependency relationship with the final clause in a chain.

3.2. Point (ii)

The second characteristic of the construction, given as point (ii) above, is that the clauses or verbs linked by the construction form a chain which becomes a single syntactic unit, whose syntactic status with respect to the surrounding text is determined by the morphology of the final verb. If the verb is finite, as in the examples above, then the unit is sentence-final and independent. If, however, the final verb carries non-finite morphology, then the whole chain assumes the structural relationship indicated by it. For example, in (6), the entire chain forms the simple nominalized complement of the verb *khon-ai* (see §18.2.1):

(6) [thõsi=e kawāph dak-e **hā-en** ta-e]$_{NP-O}$ khon-ai
meat=GEN ball make-PART bring-PART put-NR2 see-3sPR

'He sees that she made, brought, and put meatballs.'

Another example is given in (7), where the linked verbs are marked as adverberial clauses by the conditional suffix (§20.2.1):

(7) uku bulbul ciḍiyā thi-mā **hā-en**   ta-i   darsa
    here Bulbul bird   one-CL bring-PART put-INF if

'If you bring and put the Bulbul bird here...'

Finally, in (8), the entire chain is relativized and modifies the head noun ṭhãī 'place':

(8) [dokhunuŋ kōsa ŋaŋ-an   ta-e]ᵣₑₗ   ṭhãī
    all   bone discard-PART put-NR2   place

'The place where the bones were put by discarding.'

3.3. Point (iii)

The characteristic given in point (iii) above pertains to the semantic relationship that exists between clauses linked with this construction. As can be seen from the examples above, there is no one semantic entailment of the participle. Instead, the meaning of the construction is vague. The semantics of the verbs, real-world knowledge about how events and states interact, and prosody are the primary elements that determine the semantics of the interpropositional relationships. The most common relationships found are manner, e.g. example (8), and sequence, e.g. examples (5) and (6). It is often the case that more than one semantic interpretation is possible, as in (4), the last two lines of which can be interpreted as either sequential (e.g. 'mount and go') or as modifying ('go riding').

3.4. Point (iv)

The final point in the characterization of the participial construction is a negative one, put in to show what the construction is not. The construction is morphosyntactically distinct from nominalization and relativization (Chapter 17) and complementation (Chapter 18). This construction is not as distinct from adverbial clauses. This issue is discussed in §20.3.2.

4. Structures and functions of the participial construction

The Dolakha Newar participial construction is used to incorporate grammaticalized auxiliaries into a clause, to create standard collocations, to produce recapitulations in narrative, in constructions with direct-quote complements, and to join clauses which relate events or states. In the latter function, the nature of the interpropositional relationship varies from simple sequences to overlapping states and events, to manner, causal, and temporal modification. Which of these functions pertains in a given example of the construction depends upon a combination of lexical and propositional semantics, real-world knowledge about how events and states affect each other, discourse context, and prosodic cues.

The structure of the participial construction varies depending upon whether or not each verb in the string constitutes an independent predicate, or whether one functions as a grammaticalized auxiliary, in which case it does not instantiate an independent clause. The following description exemplifies and discusses each function of the construction, its corresponding structural realizations, and the variety of contextual factors which influence its interpretation.

4.1. Incorporating a grammaticalized auxiliary into a clause

There are three "versatile verbs" (Matisoff 1969) which become auxiliaries when linked to another verb by the participial construction. When functioning as an auxiliary, the verb *con-* 'sit; stay' indicates continuous aspect (see §16.3.1), the verb *tar-* 'put; keep' denotes maintenance of a state or lasting effect (§16.3.2), and the verb *bir-* 'give' marks clauses with affected participants, including recipients of favors (§15.3). Clear examples of these three verbs functioning as auxiliaries are given in (9)–(11):

(9)   *ināgu   cij   pita **ye-en**   con-a*
       this.type thing out come-PART stay-3sPST

       'Things of this type were coming out.' (Not 'came and stayed')

(10)   *āu   bhut=na   janta wā   guli   **khyāŋ-an**   tar-ai*
       now ghost=ERG 1sDAT TOP how.much scare-PART put-3sPR

       'Now ghosts have scared me so much.' (Not 'scared and put')

(11)   *"janta kho   pār   tār   **yeŋ-an**   bi-u"   hat-cu   hã*
       1sDAT river across cross do-PART give-IMP say-3sPST EVID

       'He said: "Ferry me across the river".' (Not 'cross and give')

When verbs are incorporated as auxiliaries, the resulting structure is monoclausal. No arguments or adjuncts may intervene between the main verb and its auxiliary. If the clause is to be negated, the negative morpheme must be prefixed to the auxiliary as the final verb in the chain. As the structure is that of a single clause with a single complex predicate, there must always be a single subject referent.

Since the three verbs in question are versatile verbs, it is also possible to find nearly identical examples, but where the verbs function lexically, and there is more than one clause. Examples include (12), which indicates events in sequence, and (13), in which *tās yeŋ-an* 'to stick' indicates the manner of the final verb *tar-* 'put'.

(12)   āpen=ri   jaŋgal=ku   **oŋ-an**   coŋ-gu   hā
       3p=IND   jungle=LOC   go-PART   stay-3PA EVID

       'They went and lived in the jungle.'

(13)   sakhi hā-ene   tā̃s   **yeŋ-an**   tar-ju
       dung bring-PART   stick   do-PART   put-3sPST

       'Bringing dung, he put (the grass on the door) by sticking it.'

Whether one of these three verbs is functioning as a grammatical auxiliary, as in (9)–(11) or as a lexical verb, as in (12) and (13), is entirely determined by the discourse context and cannot be predicted by the morphosyntax alone. For example, in a different discourse context, (12) could easily mean 'They were going to the jungle'. In the current narrative, it is clear that the three sisters who are experiencing hardship have been forced to reside in the jungle.

It is also not unusual to find examples which, even in context, could be interpreted either as a main verb plus auxiliary verb or as a string of two clauses. Example (14) is of this type:

(14)   hirā=e   jā   **hā-en**   bi-u
       diamond=GEN   rice   bring-PART   give-IMP

       'Bring and give him the diamond rice.' OR 'Bring the diamond rice for him.'

In this example, both interpretations are equally plausible. In the first interpretation, which takes the sentence as consisting of two distinct clauses, one with the verb *hār-* 'bring' and one with the verb *bir-* 'give', the addressee of the command is told to perform two separate, sequential actions, first to bring the diamond rice, and then to give it to the king. In the second interpretation, the structure constitutes a single clause. The verb *bir-* functions as a grammaticalized auxiliary and serves to instantiate a benefactive argument of the main verb. Thus the addressee is told to bring the diamond rice for the king. The interesting thing about this conundrum is that, although we can propose two distinct syntactic analyses for the sentence, the two meanings are not distinct in the context the sentence occurs in. If one brings diamond rice and gives it to the king, then clearly one brings the diamond rice *for* the king. Of course it is exactly this type of closeness in meaning and structure that allows for the grammaticalization of auxiliary verbs and the syntactic reinterpretation of a biclausal structure as monoclausal. Although in a language like English, the morphosyntax requires us to distinguish between monoclausal and biclausal structures and meanings, this is not the case in Dolakha Newar. Particular instances of the participial construction are hauntingly bistructural. We will see this aspect of the construction again later in the chapter.

4.2. Lexicalized expressions

The Dolakha Newar participial construction is used in certain conventionalized collocations. These collocations are lexicalized in the sense that speakers seem to always treat them as a unit, and they often have specialized meanings which aren't necessarily derivable from the lexical meanings of each independent verb. Some collocations, such as *mwaŋ-an yer-a*, 'came alive' from 'survive' plus 'come', are relatively rare. Two very common collocations involve the verb *bihā yet-* 'to marry'. When combined with *bir-* 'give', the phrase becomes *bihā yeŋ-an bir-*, which means 'to give (one's daughter) in marriage' or 'to arrange a marriage'. The combination *bihā yeŋ-an hār-*, using *hār-* 'bring', means to marry a woman and bring her into a household as wife.

It is an interesting question whether these collocations constitute one or two clauses. The fact that they are lexicalized and seem to function as a unit would favor a monoclausal interpretation. On the other hand, the participial construction commonly instantiates a biclausal structure. Thus, one can also analyze the clause boundary as one part of the collocation that has become frozen. Once again, the construction takes on a bistructural quality.

Another collocation, which occurs with great frequency in my narrative data, is *ju-en con-a*, formed from the verbs *jur-* 'to be; become; happen' and *con-* 'stay', which, as noted above, may also indicate continuous aspect. As a collocation, *ju-en con-a* means 'it turns out that' or 'it came about that', with a mild mirative force (expression of surprise). This collocation takes a verbal complement; a fuller discussion and exemplification of this construction may be found in §17.2.2.4.

4.3. With direct-quote complements

As is common in South Asian languages (Hock 1982; Masica 1976, 1991; Noonan 1999; Saxena 1988), quotative constructions in Dolakhae often involve the participial construction. In particular, direct-quote complements are commonly followed by the verb *hat-* 'say' in its participial form, *haŋ-an*, and this often co-occurs with another quotative verb:

(15)   *"chi do-ō"*   ***haŋ-an***   *hat-cu*
       2s   PROH-go   say-PART   say-3sPST

      'She said: "Don't you go".'

(16)   *jogi=ta*   *"bulbul ciḍiyā*   *kār-a*   *ū-i*   *mula gibi"*
       yogi=DAT   Bulbul bird   take-PURP   go-1FUT   road   where

       haŋ-an   *hat-cu*
       say-part   say-3sPST

      'She said to the yogi: "I will go to take the Bulbul bird. Where is the road?"'

This "double-say" construction is discussed at some length in Genetti (2005: 46–49). There I argue that *haŋ-an* is not a grammaticalized complementizer. One reason for this is that, given that one of the primary functions of the participial construction is to allow one clause to specify the manner of another, it is always possible to analyze *haŋ-an* clauses as syntactically independent. For example, (15) may be accurately translated as 'She spoke, saying: "Don't you go"'. Thus there is no semantic requirement that *haŋ-an* be analyzed as a grammaticalized and semantically empty complementizer.

Another argument against analyzing *haŋ-an* as a complementizer is that it does not exhibit the expected properties of a gramamtical morpheme. Its use is not obligatory, as quotative clauses may occur with out it, as in (17):

(17)   *āmun*   *"wāsti pha-u"*   *hat-ai*
       3sERG   clothes   carry-IMP   say-3sPR

      'He said: "Carry it in your clothes".'

Neither is this morpheme particularly reduced phonologically. Although speakers may reduce the form to a single syllable, this is not uncomon for lexical items, and in many instances both syllables are clearly audible. One can also ask whether there are cases where *haŋ-an* in this construction has necessarily lost its lexical interpretation and appears to be strictly grammatical. Clearly not, as the 'spoke, saying' analysis can always be recovered from the lexical verb plus the participial construction. Finally, there is no evidence that *haŋ-an* has taken on any status in the grammar independent of this construction or has been extended to other grammatical contexts. Thus the evidence in favor of *haŋ-an* being a truly grammatical element is weak.

One might wonder whether the half-lexical, half-grammatical nature of *haŋ-an* might not indicate that it is in the process of gramamaticalizing, but that it has not yet reached the point of full completion – as Noonan (1999) suggests has happened to a similar form in Chantyal. However, there is no reason to think that this construction is historically recent, as the analogous construciton is found in Classical Newar texts going back at least a couple of hundred years (Jørgensen 1931, 1939, 1941), and it is possible that this was a feature of Proto-Newar. We cannot simply assume that the construction is transitional (although neither can we assume that it is not).

I prefer to analyze the sequence *haŋ-an hat-cu* as a conventionalized syntactic pattern or collocation that speakers may make use of in natural discourse. Children hear it as they acquire language (both in their native language and in the languages around them) and they adopt the pattern themselves. This leaves open the question of the syntactic analysis of this collocation. Should it be analyzed as comprising two clauses, the main quotative clause, and a modifying participial clause? There are clearly times, such as when the quotative verb is something other than 'say', when a biclausal analysis seems appropriate. Consider example (18):

(18)　"ām hāti hal-a?"　　　　**haŋ-an**　ŋyen-ju
　　　　that what cry.out-3sPST say-PART ask-3sPST

　　　'He asked, saying: "What cried out?"'

Here the participial clause can be interpreted as specifying the manner of the final clause, stating specifically how the question was asked. A biclausal analysis is thus appropriate. (Actually "triclausal" if one counts the embedded complement-clause object referring to the reported speech as well; I'll be ignoring complement clauses in the ensuing discussion.) However in the many cases where *haŋ-an* is followed directly by another instance of *hat-* 'say', e.g. examples (15) and (16), the case for a modifying function of the participial clause is considerably weakened. In these instances, the conventionalization of the construction has blurred the internal syntactic structure. While the modifying interpretation of *haŋ-an hat-cu* is always accessible, the lexical redundancy of the two verbs, together with the high token frequency of the collocation, appear to allow the modification entailment to be dropped. Thus the conventionalization of the construction allows for a competing syntactic analysis of the structure as a unified whole, without an internal clause boundary. Once again the participial construction appears to have a bistructural analysis. This can be represented as in Figure 25. Here the outside box represents the construction as a whole. The dotted line separating the two verbs represents a clause boundary that is always available as one interpretation, but that can also recede, allowing for the analysis as a unified whole. My current belief is that such structural malleability may be stable, and may persist through succeeding generations.

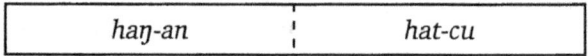

Figure 25. Bistructural analysis

4.4. Recapitulations

The term "recapitulation" refers to a process common in South Asian narrative, where one begins a syntactic sentence by repeating, often in abbreviated form, the substance of the preceding finite clause or sentence. This has also been referred to as "tail-head linking"; see Longacre (1968: 8–9) and Thompson and Longacre (1985: 208–211). The recapitulated material ends with a verb in participial form. An example of this strategy is given in (19):

(19)   ām   māji=e   mica   makche=ri
       3sERG   boatman=GEN   daughter   Makche=IND

       chē   pul-en   yer-a
       house   return-PART   come-3sPST

       chē   pul-en   ye-en   ām kanyā kanyā tuŋ jur-a
       house   return-PART   come-PART   3s   virgin virgin TOP be-3sPST

   'That boatman's daughter Makche returned to the house. Having returned to the house, she lived as if she were a virgin.'

In recapitulation, the participial construction is being used for narrative purposes; it serves as a transition between preceding and following events across a major syntactic (sentence) boundary. There is typically temporal succession between the recapitulated events and those of the new sentence, and there is no requirement that the recapitulations modify what follows. Syntactically, the participial form in recapitulations always creates a clause boundary between the recapitulated material and the new material of the sentence. Prosodically, recapitulations are generally contained in a single intonation unit with the verb at the end and marked rising intonation. This is appropriate as one then anticipates the next episode of the story to be related.

4.5. Joining clauses which denote actions, events, and states

One of the most common functions of the participial construction is to join distinct clauses which denote actions, events or states. As the structure can be used iteratively, this often leads to long chains of clauses joined with the participle, but often additionally integrated with other clause-combining constructions (such as complementation), hence the characterization of this (and surrounding) languages as "clause chaining" (Crain 1992; DeLancey 1991; Genetti 1994: 144–149; Hale and K. P. Shrestha 1999; Hargreaves 1991).

As well as joining clauses which denote events in temporal sequence, the construction also joins clauses where events and states overlap, and where actions, events, or states conveyed by a participial clause modify the action of the following clause. Whether the clauses in a participial construction are interpreted as being sequential, have temporal overlap, or involve modification depends upon a combination of contextual factors. In many cases there is no single obvious interpretation, rather, the same example could be translated as having either a sequential or a modifying relationship between linked clauses. An example of this is given in (20):

(20) āmu oho=pen dokhunuŋ **bu-en** on-a
      3s   silver=PL all   carry-PART go-3sPST

This example can be translated with either a sequential reading, 'She picked up the silver and left', or with a modificational reading 'She went carrying the silver'. When translating into English, we are required to choose one of these two translations. However, speakers of the language do not see these as distinct, indeed, as they rightly point out, if the girl in the story picked up the silver and left, then she obviously left carrying the silver. This example illustrates the fact that the structure itself is not limited to either a sequential or a modificational reading, and that a distinction between sequence and modification cannot always be made.

4.5.1. Sequences of events

The participial construction is the primary means to indicate a sequence of events in Dolakhae. There is no structure of syntactic coordination in the language that may be used to join independent finite clauses into one sentence. The participial construction is used as the functional equivalent of coordination in languages like English. The ordering of participial clauses with respect to other participial clauses and finite clauses reflects the natural ordering of events being expressed. In my data, participial clauses never express events that are subsequent to events expressed in a following participial or finite clause,[96] and speakers do not accept constructed sentences of this type in elicitation settings.

The participial construction may be used to link two clauses denoting events with a sequential relationship, as in (21), or it may be used to link multiple clauses denoting events in a sequential chain, as in (22). To aid the reader in interpreting the examples, participial verbs are bolded:

(21) āmu jurukka **ḍoŋ-an** khā lār-ju hā āle
 3s EXPR stand-PART talk talk-3sPST EVID then

 'She stood right up and talked.'

(22) āle **haŋ-an** **bi-eni**
 then say-PART give-PART

 sāŋat=e bā wā sarāsar **oŋ-an**
 friend=GEN father TOP directly go-PART

 nāg=pen **hātyeŋ-an** pukhur dupān **oŋ-an**
 serpent=PL expel-PART lake inside go-PART

 ŋā syāŋ-an **hā-en**
 fish kill-PART bring-PART

 ŋā=e pyāṭā=ku coŋ-gu hirā=e mālā
 fish=GEN stomach=LOC stay-NR1 diamond=GEN garland

 jana sāŋat=na nichi phir-ai
 1sGEN friend=ERG one.day wear-3sPR

 'Then having said that (to my friend), my friend's father immediately went, expelled the serpents, went into the lake, killed and brought the fish, and one day my friend put on the diamond necklace that was in the fish's stomach.'

Complex examples such as (22) are not unusual in the construction of Dolakha Newar narrative, and often involve other types of clause combinations. (In (22), the only other type of clause combining is the relative clause ŋā=e pyāṭā=ku coŋ-gu 'That was in the fish's stomach'.)

Example (22) also illustrates the fact that subject referents may be the same or different across clauses linked by the participle. In the first line, the subject is the speaker. It then shifts to the friend's father, who is the subject of the next five participial verbs, and then it finally shifts to the friend.

4.5.2. Overlapping events and states

Clauses linked with the participial construction may also predicate events and states which overlap temporally, as in (23) and (24):

(23) mā   khāt=ku   ḍiŋ-an   *coŋ-an*   kae   bō=ku   con-a
     mother bed=LOC   sleep-PART stay-PART son   floor=LOC stay-3sPST

'The mother was sleeping on the bed; the son sat on the floor.'

(24) nis-mā siba pārbati atāli=ku   *coŋ-an*
     two-CL Siva Parbati balcony=LOC stay-PART

   musukka ŋil-en   coŋ-gu
   EXPR   smile-PART stay-3PA

'The two of them, Siba and Parbati, were sitting on the balcony, and were smiling prettily.'

In all of my narrative examples where this construction is used to relate a state which overlaps temporally with another event or state, the state denotes location or position of a referent. Overlapping actions may be predicated in two clauses joined by this construction, in which case, they can be interpreted as modifying (see below).

4.5.3. Modifying relationships

An equally important function of the participial construction is to link two clauses where the first clause modifies the second. Three primary types of modification have been found: manner, causal, and temporal. These are contrasted with cases of linear sequencing, and so can be thought of as "non-sequential".

Modifying clauses specify the manner in which the action of the following clause is performed. Manner modification is especially common with motion verbs, but it is certainly not limited to them. The following list gives predicates used with the participial construction to modify motion verbs:

(25) pwāl-en yer-   return-PART come-   'come returning'
      bwāŋ-an yer-   run-PART come-   'come running'
      bu-en yer-   carry-PART come-   'come carrying'
      jol-en on-   swim-PART go-   'go by swimmng'
      nuɲ ma-hā-en on-   sound NEG-bring-PART go- 'go silently'
      liŋā-en on-   walk-PART go-   'go by walking'
      nāpa hā-en yer-   together bring-PART come- 'come with someone'

Another common pattern is to use the verb *yet-* 'do' preceded by an adverbial, interrogative, or demonstrative to provide additional specification about the manner in which the action of the following verb was carried out. Representative examples are given in (26)–(30):

(26) haṭanapaṭa **yeŋ-an** thi-mā=n   kho=ku   ṭin-da   on-a
      hurriedly   do-PART   one-CL=ERG river=LOC throw-PURP   go-3sPST

'Acting in a hurried manner, one went to throw (the baby) in the river.'

(27) githi **yeŋ-an** mwāt-ke-i   mal-a   chanta?
      how   do-PART   survive-CAUS-INF   must-3sPST 2sDAT

'How must I act to make you come alive?'

(28) cicā=uri   dāi=na   ānthi   tuŋ **yeŋ-an** on-a
      small=IND   e.brother=ERG   that.manner TOP do-PART   go-3sPST

'The younger of the elder brothers went doing exactly the same thing.'

(29) tāŋtāŋ **yet-k-e**   hirā=e   jā   ta-en   bir-ju
      EXPR   do-CAUS-PART   diamond=GEN   rice   put-PART   give-3sPST

'She gave him the diamond rice, making it go "tangtang".'

(30) ām   jal=na   dokseta   **chir**   **yeŋ-an**   bi-u
      that liquid=INST   all.DAT   sprinkle   do-PART   give-IMP

'Give the liquid to all of them by sprinkling it.'

One can also find other examples of manner modification with two predicates, neither one being a motion verb or *yet-* 'do', but where a manner interpretation is natural from the context, as in (31) and (32):

(31) āle   thapaka   chata   sirak=na   **phā-ke**   ta-en
     then   slowly   carefully quilt=INST cover-CAUS.PART   put-PART

'Then he slowly and carefully placed the quilt causing it to cover (her)...'

(32) āle   ekdam   khwāl   **khīga-ke**   daṇḍa   tiret-cu
     then   very   face   dark-CAUS.PART   fine   pay-3sPST

'Then he paid his fine, making his face dark (i.e. scowling).'

Note that in (32) one can also interpret the clauses as being in a sequential relationship. Thus an equally felicitous translation would be "He made his face dark (scowled) and paid the fine"; both translations are appropriate for the context, so in this case the context does not differentiate them. In truth, the difference between these translations is minimal, and the native speakers I have worked with are not interested in imposing a difference. Again, the distinction is one made systematically in the grammar of languages such as English, but not in the grammar of Dolakha Newar. The important point is that the participial construction itself does not impose either a sequential or a modifying reading, and contexts can often allow for multiple interpretations.

It is also possible for one clause to modify another by specifying its cause. The causal relationship is inferable from general knowledge about how states and events interact.

(33) ghartini=e   kae   **ju-en**   rāje   bi
     house.servant=GEN   son   be-PART   kingdom   give(INF)

     ma-jir-a
     NEG-appropriate-3sPST

'Because he was the son of a house servant, it was inappropriate to give him the kingdom.'

(34) simā=ku   pharsi   ar-ai   **ma-ju-en**   kota   jut-a
     tree=LOC   pumpkin   stable-BV   NEG-be-PART   down   fall-3sPST

'Because the pumpkin was unstable on the tree, it fell down.'

In neither of these examples is the causal relationship explicitly marked; there is nothing about the morphology or the construction which requires a causal reading.

It is also possible to interpret some participial clauses as involving temporal modification, such as the following:

(35) janta **syāŋ-ane** chi do-khor-si
 1sDAT kill-PART 2s PROH-cry-IMP

 'When/after they kill me, don't you cry.'

In the immediately preceding sentence in this narrative, the narrator has made clear that both interlocutors have learned that one of them is to be killed. The interpretation of the interpropositional relationship as temporal in this example is based on the fact that the event predicated in the first clause constitutes shared knowledge. The point of this sentence is to tell the girl what to do *after* this event will take place.

If the participial clause contains new information, then both events indicated by the construction are asserted equally, and they are in a simple sequential relationship. Example (36) illustrates this; both the verb *ŋeŋ-an* 'ask' and the verb *yā* 'come' are under the scope of the imperative and both are new information:

(36) thi-gur khā **ŋeŋ-an** yā
 one-CL matter ask-PART come.IMP

 'Ask him one thing and come back.'

Thus we can see that the information status of the predication, whether it is new to the discourse and moves the plot forward, or whether it is given information between the speaker and the hearer, also plays an important role in determining the semantic nature of the interpropositional relationship.

In addition to the semantic and pragmatic context, prosody can also be an important cue for the hearer as to how to interpret the interpropositional relationship between clauses linked by the participial construction. A brief study of 200 examples of the participial construction which unambiguously had either a modifying or a sequential function revealed different prosodic patterns for the two groups. In particular, those which modified the following clause were much more likely to be put into the same intonation unit with the following verb than were participial clauses indicating sequences. The results are summarized in Table 39:

Table 39. Intonation boundaries across modifying and sequential participial clauses

Participial and following verb are:	Modifying		Sequential	
	#	%	#	%
In th same intonation unit	66	73.0	32	29.7
In different intonation units	24	27.0	78	70.3
Total	90	100.0	110	100.0

We can see that while 73% of the modifying clauses are in the same intonation unit as the following clause, only about 30% of the sequential clauses are. The converse is also true, as clauses with sequential relationships are much more likely to be in separate intonation units. These results are not surprising. The conceptual bond is tighter between a modifying clause and a modified clause than between clauses in a sequential relationship. Speakers are more likely to put an intonation boundary between elements with a looser conceptual bond, and treat that which is tight conceptually as a single unit prosodically. This is another example of iconicity in language (Givón 1984, 1985, 1991; Haiman 1983, 1985).

4.5.4. Multiple participial verbs

The examples of the participial construction given so far have been carefully chosen for the purpose of clarity, and are actually simpler than many of the examples in the database. It is not uncommon to have two, three, or even four participial verbs in a sentence, and the various structures and functions the construction allows may be combined. Consider first example (37):

(37) suikucca **ju-en** **bwāŋ-an** yer-a   hã
      quickly be-PART   run-PART   come-3sPST EVID

   'Being quick, he came running.'

The two participial verbs in this example are both adverbial. The first predicate, *suikucca ju-en*, has scope over the combination of the last two, *bwāŋ-an yer-a*.

It is also possible for a single auxiliary to have scope over two participial verbs, as in (38) and (39):

(38) āpen indra prasat=ku   ām   he   ŋā-mā=ta
      3p   Indra Prasat=LOC that SPEC five-CL=DAT

      lahi-en   **coŋ-an**   con-hin
      raise-PART   stay-PART   stay-3pPST

   'They were living at Indra Prasat, raising those five children.'

(39) mucā cākalcukul=na **metha-en** **kho-en** con-a   hã
      child EXPR=INST   play-PART   cry-PART   stay-3sPST EVID

   'The child was playing and crying (intermittently).'

Whether or not a final auxiliary has scope over more than one participial clause is determined by context. Example (38) could equally mean 'Having raised the five children, they were living at Indra Prasat', however it is clear from the story that the raising of the children took place at Indra Prasat.

Examples of this sort, where the different functions and structures of the participial construction combine, are not uncommon. As this overview has shown, the construction is very flexible, instantiating a wide variety of structures and functions. It is this flexibility that allows seemingly limitless combinations of predicates and arguments with a remarkably diverse array of syntactic structures.

5. Issues in syntactic analysis

The preceding discussion has emphasized the diversity and flexibility of the participial construction. The only constraints imposed by the construction have to do with ordering: participial verbs must be clause-final; auxiliary verbs follow lexical verbs; modifying clauses precede modified clauses; and clauses in sequential relationship must be ordered so as to reflect the sequencing of events.

Other restrictions, of the type commonly found on related constructions in other languages (see e.g. Haspelmath and König 1995), are not in evidence in this language. Genetti (2005) presents detailed argumentation to show that the participial construction does not impose constraints on anaphora, control, the scope of interrogative or imperative mood, or the scope of negation. The interpretation of these categories is based entirely on broader contextual factors and is not determined by the construction itself. The argumentation of the points made in Genetti (2005) will be summarized briefly here.

5.1. Anaphora and control

There is no evidence that there are any purely syntactic restrictions on the control of pronominal or unexpressed arguments in this language (outside of complement structures). For example, in biclausal examples of the participial construction where each clause has a different subject, the two subjects may both be expressed – as in (23) above, repeated here as (40) – only the first clause subject may be expressed (41), only the second clause subject may be expressed (42), or neither may be expressed (43):

(40) mā   khāt=ku   ḍiŋ-an   **coŋ-an**   kae   bõ=ku   con-a
     mother bed=LOC sleep-PART stay-PART   son   floor=LOC stay-3sPST

   'The mother was sleeping on the bed; the son sat on the floor.'

(41) sõ-mā   ju-ene   āmta=uri   ekdam dukha   bi-en
     three-CL happen-PART   3sDAT=IND   much trouble give-PART

   'There were three of them, and (the king) gave them lots of trouble.'

(42) kucin ṭi-en   bi-en   mucā besna khor-a
     pinch pinch-PART   give-PART   child very cry-3sPST

   '(He) pinched (the child), and the child cried very much.'

(43) dosari   ju-ene   "isɪ   tuŋ con-da
     pregnant become-PART   1pEXCL   FOC stay-PURP

   ye-i"   hat-cu
   come-1FUT   say-3sPST

   '(She) became pregnant, and (her sisters) said "We are the ones who will come".'

These examples illustrate the lack of restriction on the interpretation of unexpressed arguments in the participial construction; there is no evidence of obligatory control across clauses. Similar examples could be given to show that the same alternatives are available across adverbial clause boundaries, and even across sentence boundaries. The referential interpretation of pronouns and unexpressed arguments is dependent on discourse, as opposed to syntactic, factors.

5.2. Scope of illocutionary force and negation

If two chained clauses are put into a yes/no question, under most circumstances both clauses are under the scope of interrogation, as in the following elicited example:

(44) Elicited
     āmun   biskut   ŋyāŋ-an   chē   yer-a   rā?
     3sERG biscuit buy-PART   house come-3sPST   Q

   'Did he buy biscuits and come home?'

It is possible for interrogation to apply only to the second clause in the participial construction. This can only happen if the event coded by the first clause is presupposed:

(45) Elicited
āmun biskut ŋyār-i doŋ-an chẽ yer-a rā?
3sERG biscuit buy-INF finish-PART house come-3sPST Q

'Having bought biscuits did he come home?'

Here the verb *d(h)on-* 'finish' indicates the successful completion of the first event as information shared by the participants in the conversation. Scope of interrogation is thus dependent on the presuppositions of the speaker, and the aspectual marking of the clause.

Pragmatics, and especially presuppositions, also play a role in the interpretation of the scope of imperative mood. When a participial chain is closed by an imperative verb, normally the scope of the imperative will extend to the participial clause. This was shown in (36) above, repeated here as (46):

(46) thi-gur khā **ŋeŋ-an** yā
one-CL matter ask-PART come.IMP

'Ask him one thing and come back.'

However, in the following example, the information in the first clause is presupposed and the imperative applies only to the second clause:

(47) janta **syār-i don-ke** chi do-khor-si
1sDAT kill-INF finish-PART 2s PROH-cry-IMP

'After I am killed, don't you cry.'

In this example, it is already clear from the discourse context that the speaker is going to be killed. The first clause thus constitutes shared information and so disallows an imperative reading. There is also a prosodic boundary, with the first participial clause being in a separate intonation unit with anticipatory rising intonation. It is interesting to note that in a different discourse (and probably prosodic) context, this same sentence could be interpreted with the imperative having scope over the whole sentence, i.e. 'Kill me and don't cry'. As with interrogation, one cannot predict scope of illocutionary force simply on the basis of syntax; non-structural factors must be taken into account.

The same conclusion is found when we consider the scope of negation. Participial verbs are independently negated. When the events denoted by the joined clauses are sequential, there is often a causal implicature:

(48) āmun wā hātiŋ jawaph bi **ma-pha-ene**
3sERG TOP nothing answer give(INF) NEG-able-PART

pulis chor-ju
police send-3sPST

'He was unable to answer anything and sent the police (to arrest the suspects).'

In other cases, negated participial verbs are best translated as 'without doing X'. In the examples which I have of this, the participial clause does not modify the following clause, for example, by expressing the manner. Instead, it predicates the non-occurrence of the first event, often counter to expectation:

(49) mā=ta **thi=ŋ** **ma-thi-en** thau
mother=DAT touch=EXT NEG-touch-PART REFL

khopi=ku on-a
alcove=LOC go-3sPST

'Not touching his mother at all, he went to his own room.'

When the final verb of the participial construction is negated, the negation generally has scope only over the final clause:

(50) bidur ghartini=e kae **ju-en**
Bidur house.servant=GEN son be-PART

raje bi ma-jir-a
kingdom give(IMP) NEG-be.appropriate-3sPST

'Bidur being the son of a house servant, it was not appropriate to give him the kingdom.'

I do have one elicited example, however, where negation of the final verb is interpreted as applying to the participial clause. As far as I can determine, this interpretation is only possible because the verb has habitual aspect; my consultant insisted that this sentence was best with the adverb that reinforces the habitual interpretation:

(51) Elicited
āmun nitheŋ nijā **yeŋ-an** bū mo-õ
3sERG daily lunch take-PART field NEG-go
'He goes to the field everyday without taking his lunch.'

In this example, it is the habitual aspect which allows the shift in the scope of negation, as opposed to anything particular about the syntactic structure or interpropositional semantics. Here the finite verb is expressing a culturally expected and predictable daily routine ('going to the field'; note that one does not habitually 'not go to the field'). The negation thus can only apply to the first clause of the sequence. Since this is the only example I was able to elicit with backward scope of negation, and since it is itself dependent on the independent feature of habitual aspect, it is clear that scope of negation is contextually, not syntactically, determined.

In sum, this section has illustrated that scope negation and illocutionary force in the participial construction depends crucially on factors external to the syntax. The same was seen to be true of the interpretation of anaphora. We now turn to phenomenon of case prolepsis and its syntactic implications.

5.3. Case prolepsis

In the description of the structures instantiated by the participial clause, one significant syntactic point was the presence or absence of clause boundaries. Specifically, it was shown that some instances of the participial construction result in monoclausal structures, others in biclausal structures, and others which could be interpreted either way; the latter were called "bistructural". Another interesting syntactic issue is the status of arguments that have semantic roles in multiple predicates joined by the participial construction. Consider the example in (52):

(52) āle āmun lita khunu khasi=ta **ḍu-en** yen-ai
then 3sERG next day goat=DAT pull-PART bring-3sPR

'Then the next day he pulled the goat and brought him.' (OR 'brought by pulling')

Here we have a single noun phrase with ergative casemarking and a single noun phrase with dative casemarking but two transitive verbs. The referents of the two noun phrases have the same semantic roles with respect to the two verbs. The interesting question which comes up is whether the noun phrases constitute grammatical arguments of the first verb only, the second verb only, or both verbs simultaneously. Although it is a somewhat radical view in current approaches to syntax, I favor the latter view. I analyze this example as involving two clauses which share the same arguments. To demonstrate why I favor this approach (beyond the advantage of its surface transparency and functional clarity), it is important to look in more detail at the casemarking facts of this construction.

When two participial clauses occur in a sequence, and one is transitive and the other is intransitive, if the subjects are coreferential, an overt subject NP at the beginning of the sequence may be in either the ergative or the unmarked absolutive case. In (53) and (54) below, the subject NPs each agree with the transitivity of the first verb in the sequence: *yeŋ-an* 'take' in (53) co-occurs with an ergative-marked subject, while *oŋ-an* 'go' in (54) co-occurs with an unmarked (hence absolutive) subject NP:

(53)   Clause 1 is transitive, clause 2 is intransitive, subject is ergative
       bū=e   dani=n   dyābā   **yeŋ-an**   on-a
       field=ERG   owner=ERG   money   take-PART   go-3sPST

       'The ownder of the field took the money and left.'

(54)   Clause 1 is intransitive, clause 2 is transitive, subject is absolutive
       sāŋat=e   bā   wā   sarāsar   **oŋ-an**
       friend=GEN   father   TOP   directly   go-PART

       nāg-pen   hātyeŋ-an
       serpent=PL   expel-PART

       'My friends father immediately went, expelled the serpents...'

In these two examples, the two verbs in the construction differ in transitivity, and the casemarking reflects the transitivity of the verb of the *first* clause. Contrast now examples (55) and (56). Once again, the two verbs in the participial construction differ in transitivity, however in both of these examples, the casemarking of the subject NPs reflects the transitivity of the *second* verb in the sequence:

(55)   Clause 1 is intransitive, clause 2 is transitive, subject is ergative
       bū=e   dani=n   **ye-ene**   āmta   jon-ai
       field =GEN   owner=ERG   come-PART   3sDAT   catch-3sPR

       'The owner of the field came and caught him.'

(56) Clause 1 is transitive, clause 2 is intransitive, subject is absolutive
chi   misāmi   hātta   ithi   **yeŋ-an**   yer-an?
2s   woman   why   this.manner   do-PART   come-3sPR

'Why do you, woman, come here doing this (in this manner)?'

In (55), the subject noun phrase is marked ergative in accordance with the final verb *jon-ai* 'catch', while in (56) the subject is unmarked (absolutive) to reflect the transitivity of the final verb *yer-an* 'come'. I refer to this phenomenon, where the casemarking of a subject NP reflects the transitivity of a non-adjacent verb, as "case prolepsis" (Balthasar Bickel, personal communication).

Case prolepsis is very flexible. In example (57), an ergative subject is separated from the transitive verb by two intransitive participial clauses:

(57) Elicited
rām=na   pipāna   **morlu-en**   duta   **ye-en**   nar-ju
Ram=ERG   outside   bathe-PART   into   come-PART   eat-3sPST

'Ram bathed outside, came inside, and ate.'

It is possible to have three or even more clauses intervene between a verb and its proleptic subject. In addition, arguments may appear at any position within the chain, however, they may only hold grammatical relations with predicates which follow them. There are no cases of "rightward case assignment" with a verb in a participial clause assigning casemarking to an argument which follows it.

5.4. A syntactic analysis of the participial construction

The discussion so far has shown that the participial construction is malleable and speakers mold it into a wide variety of syntactic structures. An ideal syntactic analysis would be one that would inherently reflect the malleability of the construction.

The development of syntactic theory in modern linguistics has been based substantially on the analysis of Indo-European languages. Due to this fact, a fundamental concept in modern syntax is that of the "matrix" or "main" clause. This clause is considered to be the core of the sentence and other clauses are analyzed as "subordinate" to it. In my opinion, however, this distinction is not relevant to the Dolakha Newar participial construction. Although the final verb in the construction is suffixed with finite or other verbal morphology that links the chain of clauses to the surrounding discourse, this is the result of its final positioning only. The finite morphology has scope over the whole chain in much the same way as a clitic casemarker can have scope over a complex NP. The final clause has no particularly privileged behavior which gives it greater syntactic or semantic importance when compared to the other clauses in the chain.[97] Thus we begin our syntactic sketch of the construction as in (58). "X" indicates clausal arguments or adjuncts and MORPH indicates either finite or clause-linkage morphology.

(58) [[X V-PART] [X V-PART] [X V]]$_{chain}$ - MORPH

The structure in (58) represents a string of clauses, each with its own adjuncts and arguments, together forming a larger unit (for the moment called "chain"). The final morphology affixes to this chain, so has the whole sequence of clauses under its scope.

Case prolepsis is a phenomenon that applies to chains of verbs which have the same subject. It can be defined as the ability of subject nominals to be casemarked for any of the verbs in a same-subject chain. We can then analyze the subject nominal as the instantiation of a single subject shared by the entire chain of clauses and holding grammatical relations with each verb. This can be illustrated in (59), an analysis of the example given in (57) above. Three separate syntactic units are conjoined into a larger unit which takes *rām* as the subject. It is the third, transitive verb which assigns case to the subject here.

(59)   Elicited
       [rām=na   [[pipāna morlu-en]   [duta ye-en]   [nar-]]$_{CHAIN}$-ju]$_S$
       Ram=ERG outside bathe-PART   into   come-PART   eat-3sPST

       'Ram bathed outside, came inside, and ate.'

Note that the subject noun phrase is represented as the subject of the entire chain, not the subject of any one clause. Which of the verbs in the chain actually does assign casemarking is a complex problem. In Genetti (1988), I studied this phenomenon in the Kathmandu dialect of Newar, and found that overall clausal importance determined which clause in a chain assigned case to a shared subject. I assume similar principles are at work here.

My own conception of the structure of the participial construction has been largely inspired by the insights of Role and Reference Grammar,[98] but differs from that model in the conception of clause structure. In my view, the syntactic structures instantiated by the participial construction can be fully accounted for by linkage at two levels of clause structure. One level is the full clause which includes all arguments and adjuncts. The second level is the clause without its subject. For want of a better term, I refer to this level as the verb phrase, although I do not wish to claim that this unit is equivalent to verb phrases in languages of other typologies. An example of two full clauses which are joined by the participial construction is (23), repeated here as (60):

(60) [[mā khāt=ku ḍiŋ-an coŋ-an]$_{CL}$ [kae bō =ku con]$_{CL}$ -a]$_S$
mother bed=LOC sleep-PART stay-PART son floor=LOC stay-3sPST

'The mother was sleeping on the bed; the son sat on the floor.'

Here each of the two clauses has its own subject and the two combine to form a single sentence.

I define the "verb phrase" in this language as a syntactic constituent containing all clausal elements except the subject. The joining of two verb phrases by the participial construction creates a complex verb phrase which takes a single subject. Thus we can clarify the structure in (59) by providing labels for the syntactic constituents as follows:

(61) [rām=na [[pipāna morlu-en]$_{VP}$ [duta ye-en]$_{VP}$ [nar-ju]$_{VP}$]$_{VP}$]$_S$
Ram=ERG outside bathe-PART into come-PART eat-3sPST

'Ram bathed outside, came inside, and ate.'

The three verb phrases are linked by the participial construction to form a larger complex verb phrase. This verb phrase then takes the single noun phrase as its subject. Any of the three verbs could assign case to this noun phrase; in this example it is the final verb which does.

The model sketched so briefly here nicely reflects the syntactic malleability of the participial construction, as it allows for the creation of a wide array of structures. This is because arguments and adjuncts can be constituents either at the level of the simplex verb phrase or at the level of the complex verb phrase. The level of the constituent will then determine its scope. This is true not only of subjects, but also of objects and adverbials, which also can be grammatically related to multiple predicates. Thus we can contrast example (62), where an object noun phrase is within the simplex verb phrase and so is grammatically related only to one verb, with (63), where the object (*siru=ta* 'siru') is positioned in the complex verb phrase and holds grammatical relations with both verbs in the chain:

(62) [ji [[yā **bu-en**]$_{VP}$ [dwālŋā=e mula=lān thãta
1s unhusked.rice carry-PART Dwalnga=GEN road=ABL up

yer-gi]$_{VP}$]$_{VP}$]$_S$
come-1sPST

'I came up by the Dwalnga road carrying rice.'

(63)   [āmun [siru=ta   tuŋ   [[**bu-ene**]$_{VP}$ [bwāt-ker-ai]$_{VP}$]$_{VP}$]$_S$]
       3sERG Siru=DAT TOP carry-PART run-CAUS-3sPR

'She picked up Siru and made her run.'

In (52), repeated here as (64), the object and the adjunct are constituents of the complex verb phrase and relate equally to both verbs:

(64)   āle   [āmun [lita khunu khasi=ta   [[**du-en**]$_{VP}$ [yen-ai]$_{VP}$]$_{VP}$]$_S$]
       then 3sERG next day   goat=DAT pull-PART   bring-3sPR

'Then the next day he pulled the goat and brought him.' (OR 'brought by pulling')

In sum, this section has briefly sketched an account of the syntax of the participial construction which allows for a reflection of the great variety of structures as well as the facts of casemarking. Case prolepsis is seen as being the natural result of a clause-combining construction which allows for the joining of both clauses and verb phrases, resulting in conjuncts at the clause and verb-phrase level. Since arguments and adverbials can be constituents either at the lower level of the individual conjuncts or at the higher level of the complex conjunct, one finds a wide variety of relationships between arguments, adjuncts, and predicates. The syntax is remarkably flexible, directly paralleling the semantic and pragmatic flexibility of the construction.

6. The participle followed by -*li* and -*i*

As was mentioned in §19.2, in addition to the short participial form constructed with the suffix -*en*/-*an*, there are two other suffixes which may be added to it. One is -*li*. This morpheme is obviously related to *li* 'back', *likhana* 'behind', and *lichilen* 'backwards'. When the suffix is added to a participial verb, it indicates that the event of the clause to which it is suffixed was fully completed prior to the onset of the event of the following clause; I thus gloss it as 'after'. Examples are given in (65) and (66):

(65) ban=ku   yeŋ-an   **ta-en-li**
     forest=LOC   bring-PART   put-PART-after

   āle   āmu   twāsmica=ta   jikāet-cu
   than that best.friend=DAT   exchange-3sPST

   'Then after bringing her to the forest and putting her there, they exchanged her best friend.'

(66) amrit   toŋ-an   bi   **doŋ-an-li**
     elixir   drink-PART   give.INF   finish-PART-after

   āmta   chandramā=n   khon-ju
   3sDAT   Chandrama=ERG   see-3sPST

   'After he had finished drinking the elixir, Chandrama saw him.'

More often than not, the suffix -li co-occurs with the auxiliary verb d(h)on- 'finish', as in (66). The two together strongly signal the anteriority of the event of the first clause with respect to the event of the second.

Forms ending in -i appear to have a similar basic meaning, although it is not as regular or as easily identified. My consultants think -i is derived from -li, which seems likely given the general similarity in meaning. The final vowel is pronounced either as -i or as -e, with different speakers apparently preferring one or the other.

Not all speakers have evidence of -i in their speech. In the narrative data, the two oldest speakers and one slightly younger showed no evidence of it at all. Younger speakers varied in their frequency of use, with some speakers using it sparingly and others with considerable frequency. For some, it appears to be simply a trisyllabic allomorph of the regular participial suffix.

The strongest generalization that one can make about the distribution of forms with -i is that they occur most commonly on clauses that denote completed events. This occurs about 85% of the time, with about 40% of those examples being recapitulations (§19.4.4). However, although the majority of examples with the added vowel have a sense of completion to them, my consultants are reluctant to translate them as 'after'. They are more inclined to say that the participles with and without the extra vowel mean the same thing. In addition, there are many examples of completed clauses that have the short form of the participle. Finally, in a minority of examples (about 15%), the long form of the participle occurs on clauses which do not denote completed events.

It is possible that longer participial forms, rather than having a specific meaning, are used in a semantically general way to indicate greater conceptual independence between clauses. Cases where the two clauses are more integrated conceptually would be less likely to have *-i*. Although the notion of conceptual integration is difficult to pin down, the data appear to suggest that more detailed research along these lines may be fruitful. The tendency for *-i* to occur on clauses where the event has been completed aligns with this analysis, as sequences of discrete events are generally less semantically integrated than events with temporal overlap. Also, there is a strong tendency to use *-i* when there is a switch in subject, as in (67):

(67) māji   **si-eni**   āle   mucā=pen   din   prati din   dwākar-hin
      boatman   die-PART   then   child=PL   day   by   day   grow-3sPST

'The boatman having died, then the children grew day by day.'

Speakers who use *-i* do so overwhelmingly in such cases. However, *-i* is clearly not a marker of switch reference, as it occurs in many examples of same-subject chains as well.

In elicitation, speakers have intuitions which seem to provide additional support for the idea that *-i* marks semantic independence. In contrasting the sentences in (68) and (69), my two primary consultants agree that the form with *-i* indicates that event of the first clause is entirely completed prior to that of the second:

(68) Elicited
      āmun   wāsti   **hi-en**   pār-ju
      3sERG   clothes wash-PART   put.to.dry-3sPST

'She washed the clothes and put them out to dry.'

(69) Elicited
      āmun   wāsti   **hi-eni**   pār-ju
      3sERG   clothes wash-PART   put.to.dry-3sPST

'She washed the clothes, and then put them out to dry.'

Example (68) is appropriate for someone who washes some clothing, hangs it to dry, then washes some more, thus repeatedly doing both actions in turn. In (69) on the other hand, the completive sense of the *-i* makes it specifically appropriate for someone who first washes all the clothes, then takes them all to hang out. Thus in (69) the two actions have greater independence, while in (68) they are more tightly integrated.

Clauses with the final *-i* are not interpreted as being under the scope of a final continuous auxiliary, as shown in (70):

(70) Elicited
　　　āmun　wāsti　**hi-eni**　　　pā-en　　　　　con-a
　　　3sERG　clothes　wash-PART　put.to.dry-PART　stay-3sPST

　　　'She washed the clothes and is hanging them out to dry.'

This prohibition can be seen as stemming from the semantic conflict between the completive meaning of the -i suffix and the continuous meaning of the auxiliary. In the absence of the suffix, the auxiliary does have scope over the chain, i.e. *āmun wāsti hi-en pā-en con-a* means 'She is washing and putting out the clothes'. Again we see evidence of a tighter semantic structure in the absence of the -i and greater clausal independence with its presence.

A final pair of sentences which gives further support to the analysis is given in (71) and (72), which illustrate differences in the interpretation of the scope of the interrogative mood:

(71) Elicited
　　　āmu　**ye-en**　　　　con-a　　　　rā?
　　　3s　　come-PART　sit-3sPST　Q

　　　'Did he come and sit down?' OR 'Having come, did he sit down?'

(72) Elicited
　　　āmu　**ye-eni**　　　con-a　　　　ra?
　　　3s　　come-PART　sit-3sPST　Q

　　　'Having come in, did he sit down?'

In (71), the suffix is absent from the participial verb and the interrogative either has scope over the entire chain or only over the second clause; both interpretations are possible. Example (72), by contrast, only has one interpretation: the participial clause does have the suffix and the scope of interrogation does not extend to that clause. In this case, the semantic independence conveyed by -i and its subsequent exclusion from the scope of the interrogative mood results in an interpretation of the first clause as conveying presupposed information outside the scope of the question.

Although this analysis is conceptually satisfying, as there is an iconic correlation between greater phonological separation and greater semantic separation, the system is actually not this clean. While it is clear that there is generally a degree of greater semantic independence in participial chains additionally marked by -i, there are many examples in texts with similar degrees of independence where the verb is marked with the shorter participial form. There are also what seem to be chains with tight semantic integration that have -i.

As an example of this, we will return one last time to the use of *haŋ-an,* the participial form of the verb *hat-* 'say'. In §19.4.3 above, the "double-say" construction with the sequence *haŋ-an hat-cu* was analyzed as a conventionalized collocation. However, it turns out that the *-i* has made inroads even into this collocation:

(73) *"jir-a   ka" **haŋ-ani**   hat-cu*
      be.appropriate-3sPST ASS say-PART say-3sPST

'He said: "It is okay".'

In this example there is only a single event being predicated, yet the *-i* is found on the participial form of the verb. Thus the notions of completion and semantic independence are absent. My overall impression is that such uses of the suffix give the examples a rhythmic quality that is otherwise lacking; however this is purely speculation at this point.

As I have shown, the semantic distinction between the participle with *-i* and the participle without are difficult to confidently pinpoint synchronically. The extra vowel is primarily used on clauses which denote events which are completed prior to the beginning of the next clause, however its use in such cases is far from obligatory and there are a number of counter-examples. This meaning may be broadening out to mark sequences of events which have greater semantic independence in contrast to sequences of events which are semantically integrated. However, even this, more general meaning, does not fully explain the presence and absence of *-i*.

Chapter 20
Adverbial clauses

1. Introduction

I will use the term "adverbial clause" to refer to any clause which includes a morpheme that marks a specific interpropositional relationship between that clause and the one which follows. Note that this definition excludes participial clauses, as the participial suffix is vague in its meaning and does not have a specific semantic entailment (see §19.3.3). Because of this, the participial construction is used in a wide range of structures, a feature not found with adverbial clauses. Despite these differences, there are many similarities between non-finite adverbial clauses and participial clauses; explicit comparison is made in §20.3.2.

The majority of adverbial clauses are formed by adding a suffix to a non-finite verb form. Thus, overwhelmingly, adverbial clauses are non-finite. The syntactic and semantic properties of non-finite adverbial clauses are fully outlined below. However, I also have a small number of examples where the marker of the interpropositional relationship occurs clause-initially. These examples involve adverbial markers borrowed from Nepali (specifically *jaba* 'when, since' and *yedi* 'if') and are clearly calques on the Nepali structure. Such adverbial clauses involve finite verb morphology, as the following example illustrates:

(1) ***jaba*** jin u jāŋal hal-gu ***tār-agi***
when 1sERG this bird cry.out-NR1 hear-1sPR

āle jin thi-gur bākhan lūwonker-agi
then 1sERG one-CL story remember-1sPR

'When I hear this bird cry out, then I remember one story.'

Such examples will not be further discussed in this chapter.

2. Types of adverbial clauses

Non-finite adverbial clauses are constructed by the addition of an adverbial suffix, either to a verb stem directly or to another non-finite suffix. There are nine adverbial suffixes attested in my data. Interestingly, they do not all affix to the same non-finite stem; hence they appear to have independent histories. The nine suffixes, their meanings, and the forms of the verb to which they suffix are given in Table 40

Table 40. Adverbial suffixes

Form	Gloss	Meaning	Verb form
-sa	'if'	conditional	stem
-saŋ	'although'	concessive	stem
-na(sin)/ -ŋa(sin)	'when'	temporal: general	stem
-ho	'when'	temporal: sequential	infinitive
-sāt	'as soon as'	temporal: immediate	infinitive
-li	'after'	temporal: after	participle
-ta	PURP	purposive	infinitive
-a/-da	PURP	purposive	stem
-thẽ	'as if'	simulative	infinitive
-lāgin	'because'	causal	NR2

Although I am treating all of these as suffixes, in some cases their morphological status is unclear. While the morphemes which attach directly to the verb stem are unambiguously suffixes, creating a single word, those that follow non-finite verb forms could be considered to be clitics or particles. The evidence does not strongly favor one analysis over the other. All of these morphemes directly follow the verb; nothing else can intervene. This suggests that they might be suffixes, but does not unambiguously require them to be suffixes. The phonological evidence on this point is also not clear. There are no phonological rules that could apply between these forms and the preceding stem and hence argue for an analysis as separate words. The prosodic evidence is also equivocal. Determining whether or not they are independently stressed is not really possible, as these forms almost always occur at the ends of intonation units, and hence the final syllable is prosodically prominent. However, this can be attributed to the intonation and does not mean that the morpheme has independent lexical stress. The purposive -*ta* is transparently the dative clitic. This morpheme is bound when it occurs in the noun phrase so it seems likely that it is also bound here. Within a noun phrase it functions as a clitic, attaching to the final word of the phrase regardless of its lexical class. Here, it always follows a verb, so analyzing it as a suffix seems appropriate. Of the others, *thẽ* and *lāgin* occur independently as postpositions, however that does not necessarily mean that they are not bound when they function as markers of adverbial clauses. After considering the evidence, it appears to me the best course of action is to treat all of these forms as being in the same morphological class. This is because they are in paradigmatic alternation, and there is no persuasive evidence against this analysis. Since at least some of these forms are unambiguously bound, I will treat all the forms as bound suffixes.

A few comments can be made about the historical provenience of these suffixes. In Tibeto-Burman (and many other verb-final) languages, a very common pattern is for postpositional or clitic casemarkers to grammaticalize into markers of adverbial clauses. Genetti (1991) outlines the historical relationship of case postpositions and adverbial subordinators in Kathmandu Newar, showing that the process of grammaticalization has occurred repeatedly in that language over at least several centuries.

In Dolakha Newar, it is possible to clearly establish historical links between synchronic adverbial suffixes and at least three casemarkers. The suffix -thẽ 'as if' is clearly recognizable as the postposition thẽ(nāgu) 'like' (§4.4.2.11). The conditional -sa, which is an etymon in the concessive -saŋ, can be traced to the locative casemarker -sa in Classical Newar. Finally, the purpose marker -ta is transparently the dative clitic. It is also possible that the general temporal marker, which is pronounced -na(sin) by some speakers and -ŋa(sin) by others, may be etymologically traced to the ergative/instrumental -na found in the modern language plus the Classical Newar ergative -sen. On the other hand, while the development from an initial /ŋ/ to /n/ may be attributed to the common process of assimilation in place of articulation to a preceding coronal consonant, there are no phonological processes that would motivate the change from a coronal to a velar place of articulation (except for dissimilation, which is a comparatively rare process, and which I have seen no evidence for in this language).

It should be noted that all four suggested developments are semantically regular. The development of locative markers into conditionals, datives into purposives, and ergative/instrumentals into temporals, are well attested cross-linguistically (Genetti 1986, 1991). It is also obvious that 'as if' and 'like' have the same semantic content, both indicate that one thing (an object or an event) has the appearance of another.

The suffix -li 'after' is a common etymon in the language. It is found in the adverbs li and lichilen 'backwards' and in the postposition likhana 'behind'. Its original lexical class is unknown. As a marker of adverbial clauses, its meaning has been extended from the spatial realm to the temporal realm, a common semantic process in the development of adverbial suffixes (Genetti 1986).

The concessive -saŋ apparently has a bimorphemic etymology. The -sa appears to derive from the old locative casemarker which developed into the conditional, as mentioned above. Although it is difficult to ascertain this with certainty, it seems likely that the final *-ŋ* is etymologically the clitic of extension discussed in §10.2.2. Semantically, the combination of the conditional with the clitic would result in a meaning similar to English 'even if'. While in English 'even if' is a "concessive conditional" coding "frustrated implication" (Thompson and Longacre 1985: 198), the Dolakhae concessive has this meaning only in some environments. It is a definite concessive elsewhere.

The causal adverbial suffix *-lāgin* appears to be composed of the Nepali postposition *lāgi* 'for the sake of' combined with native Newar ergative/instrumental *-n*. Although it occurs rarely, *lāgin* does occur as a postposition following a genitive noun, e.g. *santān=e lāgin* [*heir*=GEN sake.of] 'for the sake of heirs'. This postpositional use is related semantically to its use as an adverbial suffix in that both denote the motivation for an event to occur. It is interesting to note that in Nepali, the postposition *lāgi* is used as a marker of purpose adverbial clauses. Purpose clauses also indicate the motivation for an event, but, as Thompson and Longacre (1985: 185) point out, they differ from causal (or "reason") clauses in that the event of the purpose clause is not realized at the time of the main clause event. Since the postposition is neutral with respect to whether the referents of the noun phrase are realized or not realized, it is interesting to see that this morpheme has developed differently in this regard in the two languages. The causative clauses in Dolakhae must be realized in order for the event of the main clause to take place, whereas the purpose clauses in Nepali must be unrealized at the time of the main-clause event.

2.1. Conditional adverbial clauses

The conditional suffix is *-sa*. It is bound directly to the verb stem. The pattern of stem inflection across the four conjugation classes is exemplified in (2):

(2) n-stem   *on-sa*   go-if
     t-stem   *har-sa*   say-if
     r-stem   *bir-sa*   give-if
     l-stem   *pwāl-sa* strike-if

While n-stem, r-stem, and l-stem verbs retain their stem-final consonants when inflected with the conditional, the final consonant of t-stem verbs changes to /r/. This is a unique pattern of stem inflection across classes. While stem-final /t/ is realized as /r/ in future and infinitive inflections, n-stem and r-stem verbs lose their stem finals in these environments.

The majority of conditional adverbial clauses in my database are irrealis. The speaker predicts or asserts what will happen if the unrealized event of the conditional clause should come to pass.

464   *Chapter 20   Adverbial clauses*

(3)   āmu   hirā=e   mālā   thamun   hā-i
      that   diamond=GEN   necklace 2hERG   bring-INF

   phar-sa ji mwāt-agi
   able-if 1s   survive-1sPR

   'If you bring that diamond necklace, I will survive.'

(4)   thi-pā   māri   **bir-sā**   thi-gur   khā   har-i
      one-CL   bread   give-if   one-CL   talk   say-1FUT

   'If you give me one bread, I will tell you one thing.'

(5)   āu   gatkeŋ   **pwāl-sa**   gatkeŋ   mi   ju-eu
      now   many   strike-if   many   man   become-3sFUT

   'Now if I strike it many times, (the pieces) will become many men.'

If the matrix clause contains an imperative, then the construction is used to enjoin the hearer to follow a course of action should the events of the conditional clause be realized:

(6)   hātiŋ   āpat   par-ai   **jur-sa**   ji   samj-ai
      nothing   trouble   befall-BV   be-if   1s   remember-BV

   jur-sin   nā   mā
   be-IMP   AGR   mother

   'If any trouble befalls you mother, remember me.'

The conditional clause can also be counterfactual, that is, it can refer to events which circumstances will never allow to be realized. The conditional clause of the following example refers to a girl's mother who had already passed away:

(7)   mā   **dar-sa**   guli   khusi   ju
      mother   exist-if   how.much   happy   be(NR1)

   'If her mother were alive, how happy (she, i.e. the mother) would be.'

Conditional clauses are often followed by the particle *khene*. Most of the time, this particle occurs with the verb 'say', creating the expression *har-sa khene* 'if (one) says'. This expression often follows a question using *hāti* 'what' and a finite verb, thus producing expressions such as 'if (you) say: "What happened'". Rhetorically, this construction is used to topicalize the events of the following clause, highlighting them as new information.

(8)   hāti   yeŋ-a   ju-en   con-a   **har-sa**   **khene**
      what do-NR2 be-PART stay-3sPST say-if PRT

       sitha-ku daker-nasin ... libi   deu   caḍ-ai   jur-a
       sap-LOC make-when ... later god enter-BV be-3sPST

       'If (you) say: "What did (you) do?", when it was made out of sap ... later the god entered.'

Some speakers, however, use this construction frequently, so that it loses some of its rhetorical force. In these cases, the construction appears to be a formulaic linker between events in a narrative.

It is also possible for *khene* to occur with conditional clauses containing verbs other than *hat-* 'say'. These clauses differ from other conditional clauses in coding realis, habitual events:

(9)   jana   hātta   yeuli   sona=pen   **pi-en**
      1sGEN why any.amount flower=PL plant-PART

       tar-sa khene dokhunuŋ wail-ai   jur-a?
       put-if PRT   all   wilt-BV be-3sPST

       'Why, if I plant any amount of flowers, do they all wilt?'

(10)   pāp **yer-sa** **khene**
       sin do-if   PRT

       thau=ta   tuŋ   ānāgu   phal   ju   ju-en   con-a
       REFL=DAT FOC that.type return be(NR1) be-PART stay-3sPST

       'If (one) sins, that type (of thing) returns to oneself.'

2.2. Concessive adverbial clauses

As mentioned above, the concessive adverbial suffix appears to be derived from the conditional suffix plus the clitic of extension *-ŋ*. This analysis is strengthened by the fact the pattern of stem alternation found with the concessive is the same as that found with the conditional.

Concessive clauses can have a "concessive conditional" meaning (Thompson and Longacre 1985: 196), translatable as 'even if' in English. This meaning is found in cases where the event of the conditional clause codes an event which is not ideal, but which circumstances may require one to resort to:

(11) dak-e   **har-saŋ**   jir-a
      make-PART   say-although   be.appropriate-3sPST

'Even if you make up (a story) and tell it, it is okay.'

More commonly concessive clauses are found in classic concessive environments. In such cases, the concessive and matrix clauses relate two events that have a particular semantic relationship. While pragmatic factors would lead one to normally expect that if the event of the first clause is true, the event of the second clause should be false, this expectation is negated in concessive constructions. That is, even though the event of the first clause is true, that of the second clause is also true contrary to expectation. Consider example (12):

(12) chiji   mica=ta   yeku sā-ku   **nake-saŋ**
      1pINC.GEN daughter=DAT   much tasty-NR1 feed-although

      āu   gal-ai   ju
      now thin-BV be(NR1)

'Although we feed our daughter many tasty things, she is now thin.'

The normal expectation is that if one feeds a child large quantities of good food, the child will not be thin. The use of the concessive emphasizes the fact that this expectation was not met. A similar example is given in (13):

(13) pharsi=ta   **jur-saŋ**   mica   bi
      pumpkin=DAT   be-although   daughter   give.1FUT

'Although he is a pumpkin, I will give (him) my daughter (in marriage).'

In some cases, the difference between the conditional and the concessive is very subtle. Recall that when the conditional is used with the particle *khene*, it can indicate habitual (realis) actions. Example (9) above is taken from a story (given in the appendix) about a man who plants many flowers but they all wilt. The use of the conditional plus *khene* is appropriate because the planting of the flowers is habitual and hence the problem is ongoing. The following sentence, taken from the same story just a few clauses later, uses the concessive rather than the conditional:

(14)   ām   sona   yeuli   sāhā **yer-saŋ**   wail-ai
       that flower any.amount care do-although   wilt-BV

       ju-en   on-a
       be-PART go-3sPST

   'Although he cares for the flowers any amount, they wilt.'

Note that this example differs subtly from (9) in that the verb being used is *sāhā yer-* 'to care for'. One expects that if one cares for flowers (and does not simply plant them), they will survive. That expectation is not met in this case, hence the concessive marking in the first clause. My impression is that the conditional plus *khene* would work here as well, but would simply not explicitly mark the reversal in expectation.

2.3. Temporal adverbial clauses

There are four markers of temporal adverbial clauses: *-na(sin)/-ŋa(sin)*, *-ho*, *-sāt*, and *-li*. The four have different morphological realizations and different semantic entailments.

The most common of the temporal adverbial suffixes has four allmorphs: *-na*, *-nasin*, *-ŋa*, and *-ŋasin*. The distinction in place of articulation for the initial consonant appears to be idiolectal. I have heard both the coronal and the velar forms produced by more than one speaker, but in my observations, speakers appear to be consistent about regularly using one or the other. For ease of exposition, I will use the coronal initial as the citation form of the suffix in the following discussion.

The suffix *-na(sin)* is bound directly to the verb stem. Its inflection across stem classes is given in (15). Stems retain the stem-final consonants in all four classes:

(15)   n-stem   *on-na(sin)*   go-when
       t-stem   *hat-na(sin)*   say-when
       r-stem   *bir-na(sin)*   give-when
       l-stem   *pwāl-na(sin)*   strike-when

An interesting question is whether the long form of the suffix *-nasin* and the short form *-na* are simply alternants of the same suffix or whether they are, in fact, two distinct adverbial suffixes. My consultants consider them to be simply long and short alternates, and for this reason I will gloss them the same. However, there environments do differ slightly, as described below.

The short suffix *-na* often occurs with repeated verbs to indicate a repeated, habitual, or ongoing (i.e. imperfect) situation which is still in effect when the situation denoted by the following clause occurs. The long suffix *-nasin* generally does not occur in repeated sequences; although I do have some examples where the very last verb in such a sequence has *-nasin*, e.g. (19) below.

(16) ānthi **yet-ŋa yet-ŋa** āle āpe naita tõita
 that.manner do-when do-when then 3pGEN food drink

 gat-a
 enough-3sPST

 'Doing that again and again, their food and drink was enough.'

(17) ām=ri **on-ŋa on-ŋa on-ŋa** thi-mā jogi=ta
 that=IND go-when go-when go-when one-CL yogi=DAT

 nāplat-cu
 meet-3sPST

 'As he was going along, he met a yogi.'

(18) man=ku saŋkā ju-en **con-ŋa con-ŋa con-ŋa**
 heart=LOC suspect be-PART stay-when stay-when stay-when

 ... rājā=e kae sikār on-a hā
 king=GEN son hunt go-3sPST EVID

 'Feeling suspicious in his heart, when he was living continually like that...the king's son went hunting.'

(19) lita **on-ŋa on-ŋa on-ŋasin**
 later go-when go-when go-when

 thi-mā mi=ta nāplat-cu
 one-CL man=DAT meet-3sPST

 'Later, when (he) was going along, (he) met a man.'

In the following extended example, the short suffix *-na* is used repeatedly to indicate ongoing states and repetition of events. Note, however, that in the last three clauses the verbs are not directly repeated (as in the examples above), nevertheless the effect is the same. This is due partly to the use of the contrastive adverbials and to the contrastive meanings of the verbs:

(20) **mwāt-ŋa** **mwāt-ŋa** ānthi **con-ŋa** **con-ŋa**
survive-when survive-when that.manner stay-when stay-when

libi ām misā ānthi nichi **sit-ŋa**
later that woman that.manner day die-when

cachi **mwāt-ŋa** nichi **sit-ŋa**
night survive-when day die-when

'Then continuing to survive, living on and on like that, then that woman dying during the day, living at night, dying during the day...'

It is also possible to find the short suffix on non-repeated verbs when they occur with repeated temporal adverbials which denote the passages of time:

(21) thanu thanu kesi kesi **yet-ŋa** āmun
today today tomorrow tomorrow do-when 3sERG

jāki hār-ju
uncooked.rice bring-3sPST

'Doing this every day, he brought (home) rice.'

While the majority of examples of the short form of the suffix explicitly denote ongoing situations via the repetition of verbs and adverbials, there are still some examples that do not fit this characterization. In these cases, the long form of the suffix could be used as well with no clear difference in meaning:

(22) **ŋen-ŋa** mā=uri =n hat-cu
ask-when mother=IND =ERG say-3sPST

'When (he) asked, his mother said...'

(23) ithi **jur-na** ām janābar=pen biŋkeŋ dukhi ju-en
like.this be-when that animal=PL much trouble be-PART

'When it was like this, the animals experienced a lot of trouble...'

(24) āle   "ji" **hat-na**   rāk   yet-ai
      then   1s   say-when   anger   do-3sPR

   'Then when (she) says: "I", they become angry.'

The long form of the suffix *-nasin* is used to provide a more general temporal setting for the following clause. In the following examples, the situation denoted by the *-nasin* clause is completed prior to the onset of the situation of the following clause; the two clauses thus denote events in sequence:

(25) dā̃kare=pen   mil-ai   ju-en   **sor-nasin**
      traveller=PL join-BV   be-PART   look-when

      bulbulbul=na dudu yer-a
      ONOM=INST   milk come-3sPST

   'The travellers came together and when they looked, milk came bubbling out.'

(26) **bwāklur-ŋasin**   thi-gur   kuṭhā   khār-a   hā̃
      pour-when   one-CL   room   full-3sPST   EVID

   'When he poured it out, one room filled.' (i.e. 'it filled one room')

(27) thābi   simā=lān   tuŋ   ŋaŋ-an   **bir-nasin**
      above   tree=ABL   FOC   throw-PART   give-when

      āle   "chana pāŋ   khi=ku   jut-a"   hat-ai
      then   2sGEN   fruit feces=LOC   fall-3sPST   say-3sPR

   'When she threw (it) down from above in the tree, then (the ogress) said: "Your fruit fell in shit".'

However, not all examples are of this type. It is also common for the situations of the *-nasin* clause to be ongoing with respect to those of the following clause, resulting in an interpretation of temporal overlap:

(28) ḍulet-a   **on-ŋasin**   sāŋat=pista   nāplaŋ-ane
      stroll-PURP   go-when   friend=PL.DAT   meet-PART

   'When he went for a stroll, he met his friends...'

(29) janchi **phen-ŋasin** ām swālhār-a
sash untie-when that fall-3sPST

'When he untied his sash, that (diamond rice) fell.'

(30) tirtha **on-ŋasin** āle kho pār tār-ai
pilgrimage go-when then river across ferry-BV

ju-i maldan-a hā gaŋgā
be-INF must-3sPST EVID Ganges

'When he went on a pilgrimage, then he needed to cross the river Ganges.'

It is also possible for the when clause to denote a relatively punctual event, when the following clause is imperfective:

(31) **sor-ŋasin** mica siŋ-an con-a
look-when daughter die-PART stay-3sPST

'When (they) looked, the daughter was dead.'

Whether or not the relationship between the situations expressed in the two clauses is sequential or overlapping depends upon the semantics of the predicates and the pragmatics of the general context.

The adverbial suffix *-ho*, which is bound to the infinitive form of the verb, is also a general marker of temporal relations and is also translatable as 'when'. However, there is one striking difference in behavior between *-na(sin)* and *-ho*. Over 85% of the examples of *-ho* in my database occur in very brief clauses which function as recapitulations of the directly preceding events. Recapitulation is a common narrative device used by Dolakhae speakers, allowing continuity across sentence boundaries. Most recapitulations involve the participial construction (§19.4.4), however *-ho* clauses is also found in this environment. An example is given in (32):

(32) a. āmu hirā=e mālā tapakka kumālni-na
that diamond=GEN necklace carefully Kumalni=ERG

hā-en phi-e ju-en con-a
bring-PART put.on-NR2 be-PART stay-3sPST

'It turns out Kumalni carefully brought and put on that diamond necklace.'

b. hirā=e   mālā   **phi-ho**   āmu misā
    diamond=GEN   necklace put.on(INF)-when   that woman

   si-ku   ju-en   con-a
   die-NR1   be-PART   stay-3sPST

   'When she put on the diamond necklace, that woman died.'

While -*na(sin)* can also be used in this environment, it is relatively rare. We may thus say that -*ho* plays a greater role in discourse structuring than -*na(sin)*.

Of the remaining 15% of examples of -*ho* (nine total in my database), six are used in environments where -*na(sin)* could also be used and three are used with clauses which denote the passage of time:

(33) nichi **ju-i-ho**   isi   mā   sit-a
      day   be-INF-when   1pEXC.GEN   mother   die-3sPST

      'When it became day, our mother died.'

The adverbial suffix -*sāt*, which like -*ho* is bound to the infinitive form of the verb, is also a marker of temporal relations. However it is distinct semantically, as it signals that the situation expressed by the second clause occurred immediately after the event of the first clause. I thus gloss it 'as soon as'.

(34) sibaji=n   **khō-i-sāt**   puklukka atāli=lān   kothā
      Sibaji=ERG   see-INF-as.soon.as   EXPR   balcony=ABL room

      bõ=ku   jhar-ai   ju   ju-en   con-a
      floor=LOC   fall-BV   be(NR1)   be-PART   stay-3sPST

      'It turns out that as soon as Sibji saw (the woman), he fell – puklukka! – off the balcony and onto the floor of the room.'

The adverbial suffix -*li* is similarly endowed with greater semantic specificity. When it follows a verb in participial form, it indicates that the situation expressed in the following clause temporally follows the event of the first clause. The meaning, however, seems to be a bit stronger than simple temporal sequencing, as this morpheme additionally emphasizes the completion of the situation denoted by the adverbial clause. Indeed, it often co-occurs with the auxiliary *d(h)on-* 'finish'. I thus gloss this morpheme as 'after':

(35) ban=ku   yeŋ-an   **ta-en-li**   āle   āmu
      forest =LOC bring-PART   put-PART-after   then that

   twāsmica=ta   jikā   yet-cu
   best.friend=DAT   substitute   do-3sPST

   'After they brought and kept her in the forest, they substituted her best friend.'

(36) amrit   toŋ-an   bi   **dhoŋ-an-li**   āmta
      elixir   drink-PART   give(INF)   finish-PART-after   3sDAT

   chandramā=n   khon-ju
   Chandrama=ERG   see-3sPST

   'After he had finished drinking the elixir, Chandrama saw him.'

Given that the semantics of this suffix indicate the completion of one event prior to the onset of another, it is not surprising that it also occurs in recapitulations. Further discussion of recapitulations can be found in §19.4.4.

2.4. Purposive adverbial clauses

There are two types of purposive adverbial clauses. In one, the adverbial suffix is bound directly to the verb stem. Its inflection across conjugation classes is shown in (37):

(37) n-stem   con-da   'to stay'
      t-stem   yet-a   'to do'
      r-stem   kār-a   'to take'
      l-stem   pul-da   'to pay'

From this, we can see that the suffix follows the stem-final consonant. It appears as -da after /n/ and /l/ and -a elsewhere. I will refer to these as -da purpose clauses. The other type of purposive adverbial clause is constructed morphologically by the suffixation of the dative casemarker -ta to the infinitive form of the verb. I will refer to these as -ta purpose clauses. Of course, one cannot help but be struck by the phonological similarity between these two affixes. It appears to me likely that they both have the same historical source, the dative casemarker, but that the two represent independent developments at distinct historical periods. The fact that the -da clauses are suffixed directly to the stems suggests that the affixation may have occurred at a very early period, prior to the development of the modern system of non-finite inflection. The voicing of the initial consonant of the suffix following the voiced finals of the stems represents a regular morphophonological process. The loss of the consonant in t-stem verbs is also explainable as degemination. The loss of the consonant in r-stem verbs is not readily explainable, other than simply noting that of the four conjugation classes, the inflection of r-stem verbs is the most irregular.

The two types of purpose clauses occur in distinct, if overlapping, environments. The -da clauses are much more restricted. They tend to be very short without many overt arguments or adjuncts (although these are not prohibited), and, most interestingly, they can only be followed by a motion verb, or a verb with a significant motion component, such as *yen-* 'take (somewhere)', *chusar-* 'send', etcetera. In addition, nothing may intervene between the verb of the -da clause and the following verb. Thus the two clauses are knit into a tight construction.

(38) thi-mā=n   kho=ku   *ṭin-da*   on-a
      one-CL=ERG river=LOC throw-PURP   go-3sPST

'One went to throw (the baby) in the river.'

(39) mucā ithi   lwāp   *ṭhon-da*   on-gi
      child like.this   up   pick.up   go-1sPST

'I went to pick up the child like this.'

(40) misā   sõ-mā   *kā-ker-a*   chor-ju
      woman three-CL   take-CAUS-PURP   send-3sPST

'(He) sent (someone) to make (them) take the three women.'

The -ta purpose clauses are more loosely integrated. While they may be followed by a single motion verb in the following clause, example (41), it is also common for the following clause to be significantly elaborated, with its own arguments and adjuncts, (42)–(43). In addition, the semantic relationship may be less direct. While the -da purpose clause denotes motion directed to allow the instigation of an event, the -ta purpose clause may denote a situation which simply facilitates the second event in some way, (43).

(41) sanatanu rājā gaŋgā   asnān   *yer-i-ta*   on-a
      Sanatanu king Ganges bath   do-INF-PURP   go-3sPST

'King Sanatanu went to bathe in the Ganges.'

(42)   ṭwāŋsona=ta   bihā   **yer-i-ta**   keṭā mwāl-hin   hã
        Rhododendron=DAT marriage do-INF-PURP boy search-3pPST EVID

'In order to marry (off) Rhododendron, they searched for a boy.'

(43)   isin=uri   chaba=ku   tãho   **tha-i-ta**
        1pEXC.ERG=IND Chaba=LOC barley sow-INF-PURP

        likhana gwār   ta-upe   ka
        behind shelter put-1pPH ASS

'In order to sow barley at Chaba, we used to put up a shelter in the back.'

2.5. Causal adverbial clauses

The causal adverbial suffix is *-lāgin*. This suffix is bound to the NR2 (nominalized) form of the verb.

The causal adverbial suffix specifically denotes a relationship of causation between the adverbial clause (the cause) and the following clause (the effect).

(44)   āme   hatār **ju-e-lāgin**   bimesor thākur=ta
        3sGEN haste be-NR2-because Bimsen lord=DAT

        caṭan=na   pwāl-ju
        spoon=INST strike-3sPST

'Because of his haste, he struck Lord Bimsen with a spoon.'

(45)   chuccā **ju-e-lāgin**   āle   ānthi   chū   yer-nasin
        greedy be-NR2-because then that.manner mouse come-when

        wā   ām   cimtām kak-e   chor-ai
        TOP that poker   throw-PART send-3sPR

'Because (she) was greedy, then when the mouse came like that, (she) threw the poker at it.'

(46)   mula=ku   tuŋ   **khīga-e-lāgin**   ām thi-gur chē=ku
        road=LOC FOC dark-NR2-because 3s one-CL house=LOC

bās   con-da   on-a
shelter stay-PURP   go-3sPSG

'Because it was dark on the road, he went to shelter in one house.'

2.6. Simulative adverbial clauses

The morpheme *-thẽ* is suffixed to the infinitive verb form. It is used to indicate that something occurred which was similar in appearance to the situation denoted by the clause, but that was not, in fact, actually that situation. Hence this morpheme is glossed 'as if'. In the following example, the speaker describes seeing something that she thought was someone coming carrying shiny straw, but which was actually a ghost:

(47) libi   lilililin kota yer-a   sū   ho
     later   EXPR   down come-3sPST   rice.straw and

     ḍusili   bu-en   ye-i-thẽ
     millet.straw carry-PART   come-INF-as.if

'Later twinkling (it) came down, as if it came carrying rice and millet straw.'

I have four examples where the verb suffixed by *-thẽ* is repeated several times, then followed by the verb *jur-* 'be, become, happen'. This construction is used to show a frustrated attempt to carry out a particular action:

(48) ãku   jō-i-thẽ   jō-i-thẽ   jō-i-thẽ
     there catch-INF-as.if catch-INF-as.if   catch-INF-as.if

     jur-a   cilā-cā=ta
     be-3sPST   goat-DIM=DAT

'It happened as if I would catch as if I would catch as if I would catch the little goat.'

3. Syntax of adverbial clauses

3.1. Dependency and subordination

As with many other terms in linguistics, the terms "dependency" and "subordination" are defined differently by different linguists. I will thus clarify my own use of these terms.

I will use the term "dependent clause" to refer to a clause which does not normally occur independently (distributional dependency), and which relies on another clause for the specification of particular morphological categories (morphological dependency), specifically (for this language) tense. It is clear that non-finite adverbial clauses are dependent in both senses. Regarding the first point, the vast majority of adverbial clauses occur preceding another clause which they modify. While it is possible in conversation to find utterances that consist only of adverbial clauses, these are only found when the discourse context supplies an understood event or state which is not articulated. For example, at one point in a conversation my consultant and her aunt were discussing a particular song that her aunt had composed. My consultant uttered the sentence in (49):

(49)   ām nini=n thau tuŋ dak-e   me   dam le
         that aunt=ERG REFL FOC make-NR2 song exist PRT

'There is the song that auntie herself made.'

The aunt then produced the following adverbial clause:

(50)   chana pāju **sit-ŋasin**
         2sGEN uncle die-when

'When your uncle died.'

It is understood from the discourse that this clause modifies the sentence which her niece just produced. Such examples could be seen as "co-constructions" of sentences, with the adverbial clause being a syntactic "appendage" onto the sentence produced by the previous speaker. It should be noted that such examples are extremely rare in my corpus and are certainly not sufficient in number to negate the distributional dependency of this clause type.

In addition to the distributional dependency of adverbial clauses, these clauses also exhibit morphological dependency. Adverbial clauses are not marked for tense and so depend on the matrix clause for tense specification. Although the temporal relations between the two clauses are generally determined by the adverbial morphology, the overall tense of the sequence of events is determined by the final verb. In the following example, the adverbial clause is interpreted as future, as the finite clause on which it depends is future:

(51)   jā   **nar-ŋasin**   ... chipista samjhanā ye-eu
        rice eat-when ... 2pDAT memory come-3sFUT

'When you eat rice, you will remember.'

When the finite verb has past inflection, the adverbial clause is also interpreted in the past:

(52)   jaŋgal=ku **on-ŋa**   ām rājā nāplat-cu
        jungle=LOC go-when that king meet-3sPST

'When (he) went to the jungle, (he) met that king.'

Thus, adverbial clauses have morphological dependency.

I will use the term "subordinate" to indicate a dependent clause which, in addition to being morphologically and distributionally dependent, also exhibits syntactic behaviors distinct from those found with non-dependent (i.e. finite) clauses. Potentially relevant criteria for languages of this typology include the interpretation of pronominal arguments and zero anaphora, scope of negation, scope of illocutionary force, focusability, and positioning of the adverbial clause.

Beginning with the interpretation of pronominal arguments and zero anaphora, adverbial clauses do not exhibit any restrictions in this area. The anaphoric referents for pronouns and unexpressed arguments are not required to be in the same syntactic sentence as the adverbial clause, but simply must be inferable from the discourse. Thus in example (53) the S of the adverbial clause is unexpressed; it clearly refers to the three children who are the protagonists of the story. This is clear from the discourse context. Note that the children are not referents in the following clause, thus the resolution of zero anaphora cannot be said to be syntactically determined.

(53)   sukhā=n   **con-ŋasin** nichi=uri   thi-mā   budyā
        happiness=INST stay-when one.day=IND one-CL old.woman

        ye-ene   con-da   yer-a
        come-PART stay-PURP come-3sPST

'When (they) were living like that, one day an old woman coming, came to stay.'

The same argument can be made for the following example, which has a pronominal argument. The referent of the pronominal argument is clearly identifiable from the context as the story's protagonist. As in the previous example, this character is not referenced in the following clause. Again, the determination of anaphoric relations is determined by discourse, not syntactic, factors.

(54) āmu rāches=na **āmta na-i-ta** ... thau
that ogress=ERG 3sDAT eat-INF-PURP ... REFL

dwārā cul-da oŋ-gu ju-en con-a
fang sharpen-PURP go-NR1 be-PART stay-3sPST

'In order for that ogress to eat her, (she) went to sharpen her fangs.'

Turning to scope of negation, we can note that adverbial clauses are independently negated; they do not take their value for negation from the matrix clause, nor are they prohibited from being negated. Thus their syntactic behavior in this regard is the same as in non-dependent clauses. The following example illustrates a negated adverbial clause:

(55) māyā **ma-yeŋ-a-lāgin** ... jana kehē=ta
love NEG-do-NR2-because ... 1sGEN sister=DAT

jukun sā-ku sā-ku nai bir-ai
only tasty-NR1 tasty-NR1 food give-3sPR

'Because they did not love her, they give my sister only tasty tasty food.'

Turning to illocutionary force, as most adverbial clauses contain presupposed information, it is natural that most of these clauses will not be under the scope of questions or imperatives. An example of this is given below:

(56) **lār-na** bistār-na la-u
speak-when slowly-INST speak-IMP

'When (you) speak, speak slowly.'

Here it is presupposed that the addressee will speak, so the imperative, instructing the addressee how to speak, only has scope over the final clause. However, an imperative can have scope over an adverbial purpose clause, as in the following example:

(57) pasal=ku **yeŋ-ane** mir-a ō
store=LOC take-PART sell-PURP go(IMP)

'Go to take me to a store and sell me.'

In this example, the adverbial purpose relation holds not only between the verb *mir-* 'sell' and the final verb, but holds over the participial chain 'take to a store and sell' (see §19.3.2). The imperative illocutionary force extends to the entire construction, including within its scope the whole participial chain. In the text where this line occurred, the action of taking and selling the speaker (a parrot) constitutes new information, a new suggestion of future action, and is not presupposed. Hence the extension of illocutionary force is possible. From this discussion, we can conclude that, as with participial clauses, whether or not illocutionary force extends to adverbial clauses depends upon pragmatic variables, not syntactic variables.

Adverbial clauses do differ from non-dependent clauses in that some types are able to co-occur with the focus particle *tuŋ* (§10.3.3). However, I have only a handful of examples of this in my corpus, and they all occur in clauses with temporal interpropositional relationships. Two occur with negated verbs and the suffix *-nasin* 'when'. The semantic effect of this is to emphasize that the event of the matrix clause occurred in the absence of the expected event of the adverbial clause. This construction thus translates well into English with 'without':

(58) rāches **ma-yer-nasin** tuŋ dokhunuŋ bu-en on-a
ogress NEG-come-when FOC all carry-PART go-3sPST

'Without the ogress coming, she took it all and left.'

(59) ām misā bihā yeŋ-an **ma-bir-ŋasin** tuŋ
that woman marriage do-PART NEG-give-when FOC

ām sit-a
3s die-3sPST

'That woman died without having been given in marriage.'

I also have the following examples with non-negated 'when' clauses:

(60) jana kae thi-pul **ŋen-ŋasin** tuŋ jhark-ai jur-a
1sGEN son one-CL ask-when FOC abuse-BV happen-3sPST

'Even when I asked my son one time, he abused me.'

(61)   dhū=n   kobi   **khon-ŋasin**   **tuŋ** tul-gu
       tiger=ERG down   look-when   FOC   fall-NR1

   ju-en   con-a
   be-PART   stay-3sPST

   'It turns out that right when the tiger looked down, I fell.'

Note that the scope of the focus particle differs with the context. In (60), the scope can be interpreted either as involving both the verb and the quantifier, e.g. 'even asking one time', or just the quantifier itself, e.g. 'asking even one time'. Both interpretations are possible in the narrative context. In (61) there is no quantifier and the scope of the focus particle is on the suffix -*ŋasin*, creating the meaning 'right when'. Thus, although it is possible for adverbial clauses to co-occur with the focus particle, and in this regard they exhibit morphosyntactic behavior which is unlike that of non-dependent clauses, this construction does not appear to be robust and hence to constitute strong evidence for a significant syntactic distinction between adverbial and non-dependent clauses.

Another criterion that might establish that adverbial clauses are subordinate is freedom of positioning. In the vast majority of cases, adverbial clauses entirely precede the following clause. With only two exceptions, all of the examples cited in this chapter to this point are of this type. In both of the exceptions, the adverbial clause is positioned entirely after the finite verb. Examples (49) and (50) illustrated a co-construction where the adverbial clause was added by a second speaker providing additional information about the event of the finite clause. Example (47), though produced by a single speaker, similarly had the adverbial clause positioned entirely after the finite clause. Thus we can see that right extraposition of adverbial clauses, though rare, is possible in this language. Note, however, that in these cases the adverbial clauses entirely follow the finite clause; there is no syntactic integration of the two.

In addition to adverbial clauses entirely preceding or entirely following the matrix clause, it is also possible, though again rare, for adverbial clauses to be positioned *within* the matrix clause. I have three examples of this structure. In all three, the adverbial clause is positioned between the argument and the verb of the matrix clause. In (62) and (63), the adverbial clause is positioned between the subject and the intransitive verb. In both examples, the subject of the adverbial is not coreferential with the subject of the other clause. In (64), the adverbial clause is positioned after both subject and object arguments, and the adverbial clause subject is coreferential with the object of the other clause:

(62) āle birbahādur **kānchi** mica=n thau khā
then Birbahadur youngest daugther=ERG REFL talk

mān-ai ju-e-lāgin khusi jur-a
obey-BV be-NR2-because happy become-3sPST

'Then Birbahadur, because his youngest daughter was obeying his own words, became happy.'

(63) libi ām situgā̃s wā **pe-nu da-i-ho** sit-a
later that situ.grass TOP four-day exist-INF-when die-3sPST

'Later that situ grass, when four days had passed, died.'

(64) ām mucā=ta bobu=ri=n **mucā ju-e-lāgin**
that child=DAT father=IND=ERG child be-NR2-because

muryā=ku ta-ene
lap=LOC put-PART

'Then the father, because he was a child, put the child on his lap...'

It is interesting to note that in all three examples the adverbial clauses are prosodically separated and constitute independent intonation units. The degree of prosodic separation is least in (63), which the speaker produces very quickly without pauses, but one can still hear distinct terminal contours preceding the adverbial clause and at the end of it.

Returning, then, to the question of whether adverbial clauses are subordinate in addition to being dependent, it appears that the evidence for subordination is weak. The examples of adverbial clauses co-occurring with the focus particle turn out to be rare and limited to one type of adverbial clause (*-nasin* clauses), and to have variable interpretations. Similarly, there are only three examples in my corpus of adverbial clauses being positioned between the arguments and verb of another clause. Thus these also are rare as well as being prosodically marked. One could say that these examples are still embedded; however, that does not necessarily imply that all adverbial clauses are therefore embedded, hence subordinate. If the goal of the analysis is to syntactically characterize the vast majority of examples of adverbial clauses, we must say that adverbial clauses are not subordinate in this language. If, instead, one takes as a goal a syntactic characterization based on the limits of the construction, one could say that adverbial clauses are weakly subordinate. I prefer the former approach.

3.2. Adverbial and participial clauses and the notion of converb

In this grammar, I have described adverbial and participial clauses in separate chapters, suggesting that they constitute independent structures. However, the two clause types are more similar than different in their morphological and syntactic properties. Both adverbial and participial clauses are marked by suffixes. Both are non-finite. Both types of clauses are dependent, exhibiting both distributional dependency and morphological dependency, but neither presents strong evidence for subordination. Both types exhibit independence with regards to criteria such as interpretation of zero anaphora and pronominal arguments, and scope of negation. Both types are overwhelmingly positioned before the matrix clause; however, both types can be postposed or produced as an independent utterance by the speaker.

Despite these similarities, there are also a few differences between adverbial and participial clauses. For example, the focus particle can follow participial clauses but occurs only rarely with adverbial clauses and then only when the marker of the adverbial clause is *-nasin*. The two dependent clause types also differ in terms of positioning. While adverbial clauses may be positioned within the matrix clause, this appears to be a rare and prosodically marked structure. Participial clauses appear to allow this sort of ordering, as seen by the phenomenon of case prolepsis (§19.5:3). However, by my analysis, this is not due to "insertion" of a participial clause inside of another clause, but is due to the flexible structuring of the participial construction which allows the linking of clauses as the level of the verb phrase (§19.5.4). I have only minimal evidence of case prolepsis with adverbial clauses. I think this is due to the fact that the majority of adverbial clauses in narrative are sentence initial and are highly anaphoric, thus their arguments, especially subjects, are commonly unexpressed. In addition, the indication of the specific propositional relationship provided by the adverbial suffix sets up a stronger semantic barrier between the clauses which seems to prohibit the same degree of clausal integration as one finds with the participial construction. Overall, however, the similarities between adverbial and participial clauses appear to be greater than their differences, hence to instantiate the same syntactic category. Within current syntactic typology, both types can be considered to be "Asian converbs" (Bickel 1998; Genetti 2005).

It is important to note that although participial and subordinate clauses in Dolakhae share syntactic behavior and instantiate the same syntactic category, they are different in some interesting respects. The participial construction is highly flexible and multifunctional (being used in quotative constructions, verb-auxiliary constructions, modification, and sequencing, etc.), and this allows for its repeated use even within a single sentence. Adverbial clauses, by contrast, are quite limited in the structural configurations in which they can appear and they do not generally occur in a sequence or chain. They occur overwhelmingly in sentence-initial position, although they are not syntactically restricted to this position. These differences in behavior of participial and adverbial clauses can be accounted for by their difference in "syndesis" (Lehmann 1988), or explicit marking of the interpropositional relationship. In the case of adverbial clauses, this explicit marking both restricts their freedom of occurrence, and makes them suitable for their discourse function of expressing rhetorical relations. It is because of this marking that adverbial clauses do not take on the functional range of participial clauses, and because of their discourse function that they do not easily combine into long chains. Participial clauses, by contrast, are asyndetic, and the semantic relation between clauses or verbs joined by the construction must be interpreted from context. This vagueness in meaning allows for both the functional range and the frequency of the construction, and sets the stage for the grammaticalization of verbs into auxiliaries, the lexicalization of frequent collocations, and the freezing of syntactic patterns such as *haŋ-an hat-* 'saying said'.

Chapter 21
The sentence: Prosodic and syntactic structuring

1. Introduction

The past four chapters have examined the morphosyntactic properties of nominalization, complementation, the participial construction, and adverbial clauses. All of these mechanisms allow for the combination of clauses to create multiclausal units. These multiclausal units may be further combined with other clauses or combinations of clauses resulting in increasingly complex syntactic structures. However, these complex structures are internally coherent within the highest unit of syntax: the syntactic sentence.

The sentence in Dolakha Newar is the central unit of syntactic and discourse structuring. The division of a narrative discourse into sentences is relatively straightforward, as sentence boundaries are almost always marked by the presence of a non-embedded finite verb, which may be followed by sentence-final particles (§10.4.2) and occasionally by a postposed noun phrase (§14.4). Within these well-defined boundaries, however, the syntax may in principle instantiate an infinite number of internal structures. It is at the sentence level that one can witness the interaction of the clause-combining strategies described in previous chapters and the genius of the design principles that form the basis of the grammar.

It is important to remember, however, that the syntactic structuring of discourse only gives a partial view of how speakers are segmenting the speech stream into units and relating those units to each other. Simultaneous to the syntactic structuring of speech is the prosodic structuring of speech. Just as clauses can combine by regular principles into higher-level units that are syntactic sentences, so intonation units can be combined into higher-level units which I call "prosodic sentences". Although our knowledge of prosody generally, and my knowledge of Dolakha Newar prosody in particular, is not as detailed and extensive as our knowledge of syntax, examining the interaction of the syntactic and prosodic levels allows us greater insight into how speakers simultaneously utilize these distinct domains in the formation of sentences and the construction of narrative.

The goal of this chapter is to elucidate a number of features of sentences in Dolakha narrative discourse. This includes an examination of the the pervasive phenomenon of embedded quotation (§21.3), the syntactic structures that arise when different clause-combining strategies are intertwined (§21.4), and the interaction of syntax and prosody (§21.6). Before launching on this exploration, however, it is important to propose a clear definition of the term syntactic sentence (§21.2). The prosodic sentence will be defined in §21.5.

2. Defining the syntactic sentence

The syntactic sentence in Dolakha Newar may be defined as in (1):

(1)　　The syntactic sentence is a syntactically coherent unit of one or more clauses that contain exactly one non-embedded finite verb.

By "syntactically coherent" I mean that all noun phrases are either verbal arguments or oblique elements, that there are no "stray" elements unrelated semantically and syntactically to other material (as one might find in periods of speaker disfluency), and that each non-finite clause is integrated with the subsequent unit following the principles described in the previous chapters.

By "finite", I mean a verb form that bears suffixes indicating either the tense/person/number complex, or the imperative, prohibitive, or optative moods. It is important that the modifier "non-embedded" be part of the definition, as many sentences contain direct speech which is embedded into larger quotative frames. Consider example (2):

(2)　　āle　"bā　ām　hāti　**hal-a**"　　haŋ-an　ŋen-ju?
　　　 then　father　that　what　cry.out-3sPST　say-PART　ask-3sPST

　　　 'Then he said: "Father, what cried out?"'

This sentence contains a direct-quote complement which includes the verb *hal-a*, which is finite due to its third-person-singular past-tense suffix. This finite verb is sentence-final only at the level of the embedded direct quote. It is sentence-internal with respect to the higher syntactic level, as the direct quote constitutes the grammatical object complement of the transitive verb *haŋ-an* (§18.2.3). It is the non-embedded finite verb *ŋen-ju* which marks the end of the integrated set of three clauses (the embedded clause, the participial clause, and the matrix clause) which together form a complete syntactic sentence.

By the definition given above, non-finite verbs cannot end complete syntactic sentences. Instead, non-finite verbs indicate that a syntactic relationship holds between the non-finite clause and a following element, either a noun (in the case of relative clauses), a verb (in the case of nominalizations and complement clauses), or a clause (in the case of participial clauses).

There are two quite limited constructions which constitute exceptions to this. The first is the construction I refer to as "non-embedded nominalization", which appears to function as a focus construction (§17.2.3). This construction is an exception to the generalization that sentences end in a non-embedded finite verb, as nominalizations are non-finite. One can identify non-embedded nominalizations by the absence of a following head noun or complement-taking predicate, and by the production of intonation contours typical of sentence ends. In my narrative data, this construction is rare; when it does occur, it is usually in quoted speech.

The second construction which constitutes an exception to the definition of sentence is the correlative construction, which combines two finite clauses in a tightly integrated fashion. This is exceptional in that it involves two finite verbs but only one syntactic sentence. Although the two clauses in this construction are finite, they do not show the syntactic independence characteristic of separate sentences, but are syntactically and semantically integrated. As this construction does not involve nominalization, complementation, or the participial construction, it has not been previously described. A brief overview is thus given here.

2.1. The correlative construction: Two finite clauses in one syntactic sentence

The correlative construction involves the combination of two clauses, both with finite verbs. The first, "correlative", clause contains an interrogative pronoun which is necessarily coreferential with an argument of the second clause. This argument is usually instantiated by a deictic pronoun, as in examples (3)–(5):

(3) jana   nasputi=ku   **guli**   nyen-a   **āmli**   bi-sin
     1sGEN   ear=LOC   how.much   fit-3sPST   that.much   give-IMP

  'However much (rice) fits into my ear, give me that much (rice).'

(4) āmta   **hāti**   phon-ai   thanu   ṭule=ŋ   **āmu**   bir-ai
     3sDAT   what   ask.for-3sPR   today   until=EXT   that   give-3sPR

  'Whatever (one) asks him for, even until today he gives it.'

(5) **gunān**   bāmā=e   khã   ŋen-ai   **āmun**   sukha   sir-ai
     who.ERG   parent=GEN   talk   listen-3sPR   3sERG   happiness   know-3sPR

  'Whoever listens to his/her parent's advice, s/he knows happiness.'

Functionally, the interrogative pronoun defines an indefinite set of possible referents (e.g. various amounts (3), various things (4), various people (5)). The correlative clause identifies a subset of those referents (respectively in the examples: the particular amount that fits in the ear, the subset of things that one asks him for, the subset of people who listen to their parents). The second clause then predicates something about that subset, which is generally referred to by a deictic pronoun. Correlative clauses have a similar function to relative clauses in that they define a set of possible referents by associating that set with a predication in which it is an argument. However, with correlative clauses, the referents of the set are generally unknown, non-specific, and indefinite.

Examples (6) and (7) illustrate that the coreferential argument in a correlative structure need not be realized by a deictic pronoun in the second clause, but may be elided. It is interesting that these are my only two examples of this structure, and both have a copula as the verb in the first clause:

(6)   mucā=e   mā=ri   **gun**   khyaŋ   dudu   mut-ke   bi-u
         child=GEN   mother=IND   who   be   milk   squirt-CAUS.PART   give-IMP

         'Whoever is the child's mother, squirt breast milk (into the child's mouth).'

(7)   **hāti**   khā   khyaŋ   janta   har-sin
         what   talk   be   1sDAT   say-IMP

         'Whatever the talk is, tell it to me.'

Note also that example (6) illustrates that the coreferential argument may have different grammatical *roles* in the two clauses; in the first clause, the argument *gun* is the copula subject, whereas in the second clause, it is the A. Example (8) illustrates that the argument need not hold the same grammatical *relation* either, as the coreferential argument is the grammatical object of the first clause and is grammatically oblique (in a postpositional phrase) in the second:

(8)   bā=n   **gunta**   bir-agu   āme   nāpa   ū-i
         father=ERG   who.DAT   give-2hPR   3sGEN   with   go-1FUT

         'Father whomever you give me to, I will go with him.'

Although the correlative construction contains two finite clauses, I am strongly inclined to analyze the construction as comprising a single syntactic sentence. This is primarily due to its constructional nature. Syntactic sentences in this language are strongly delineated and constitute significant and independent units of a discourse. The correlative construction does not instantiate two sentences in this sense; it is highly limited, and the two clauses are not each expandable by the various types of clause combining found in the language. Instead, the construction is both specialized and limited in its functional and structural properties. It requires the use of an interrogative pronoun in the first clause and either a pronoun or an elided noun phrase in the second. It is also required that the arguments be coreferential. Such constraints on functional and syntactic cross-referencing are not found across the boundaries of ordinary sentences.

The correlative construction appears to be a calque on similar patterns in Indo-Aryan languages. I make this presumption based on the fact that the majority of Tibeto-Burman languages do not utilize correlative constructions, but that they are common in Indo-Aryan languages (Masica 1991: 410–411) and in at least some other Tibeto-Burman languages in the Indian subcontinent (Subbarao and Kevichusa 1999). One significant difference is that Indo-Aryan languages tend to have a distinct set of relative pronouns which occur in the correlative clause; Dolakhae, which lacks relative pronouns, uses interrogative pronouns.

3. Quoted speech

The incorporation of reported speech into narrative is a pervasive phenomenon in Dolakha Newar. The majority of reported speech is incorporated as direct quotation. It allows for the direct expression of the words, thoughts, and feelings of the narrative's characters, and thus enriches and enlivens the story. Indirect quotation is also attested within complements of *haŋ-a khā* [say-NR2 talk]; this is discussed in §18.2.2.

One way to conceptualize the incorporation of direct speech into a narrative is to consider the different roles or "voices" that the speaker takes on in narrative production.[99] These are listed in (9):

(9)   Voice of self
      Voice of narrator
      Voice of character
      Voice of character producing the voice of another character

The voice of the self is grounded in the physical and temporal setting in which the narrative is told. This voice is often produced before and after the narrative, when the speaker may ask questions about the microphone, relate that s/he is about to begin, or indicate that s/he is finished. Sometimes the voice of self is temporarily produced in the middle of the narrative as an aside, either providing clarification about something in the immediate physical environment, evaluative commentary, or metalinguistic comments.

The beginning of a narrative, and hence the shift from voice of the speaker to voice of the narrator, is indicated a number of ways, depending largely on the genre of the narrative and whether it is embedded into a broader discourse or produced independently, as for a linguist with a tape recorder. Since most of my narratives are folk stories, the most common device to mark the beginning of a narrative is the use of a conventionalized sentence, generally a variation on *thi-gur des=ku thi-mā XX da-u* [one-CL country=LOC XX exist-3PA] 'In a country there lived a XX', where XX is one or more of the major characters in the story. In addition, speakers often pause substantially before beginning the narrative, and they generally start with a relatively slow rate of speech which speeds up as the story moves past the initial phases.

More complex than shifting from the voice of the speaker to the voice of the narrator is the shift from the voice of the narrator to the voice of one of the characters. This is the process involved in the incorporation of reported speech. A simple example is given in (10); quoted material is given in bold:

(10)   kehẽ=uri=n   "āu ṭhika   jur-a   ka"   haŋ-an   hat-cu
        y.sister=IND=ERG   now just.right be-3sPST ASS   say-PART   say-3sPST

'The younger sister said: "Now everything is just right".'

The quotative frame in this example is *kehẽ=uri=n ... haŋ-an hat-cu*. For these words the speaker maintains the voice of the narrator. In the production of the direct quote, *āu ṭhika jur-a ka*, the speaker produces the voice of the character, here the younger sister who is one of three protagonists in the story. The quotative frame, while not always used, serves to aid in marking the transition between these voices. This is especially true of the quotative verbs, which generally follow the quoted text, and overtly mark the shift back to the mainline narrative.

Most quotative constructions have the structure shown in (10). The element that precedes the direct quote is an ergative-marked noun phrase (sometimes there is also a dative-marked noun phrase that refers to the addressee), and this could in principle be followed by any transitive predication. There is thus no overt marker in the quotative clause which signals the speaker's shift from the voice of the narrator to the voice of character prior to the production of the quoted material. Instead, the shift must be inferred from the changes in deixis that occur when the speaker shifts into the direct quote. In (10), the use of the temporal adverb *āu* 'now' marks a shift in temporal deixis; it clearly does not refer to a "now" at the narrative level (as the narrative denotes events in the past), so it signals a shift to the quotative level and the perspective of the character. In addition to shifts in temporal deixis, it is also common to find shifts in personal deixis (e.g. production of first-person pronouns), or spatial deixis (e.g. 'here').

In addition to the deictic shifts that are marked through the speaker's use of personal pronouns, adverbials, tense makers, and demonstratives, speakers may also mark the shift to a character's voice by prosodic means. For example, it is quite common for there to be an intonation break between the beginning of the quotative frame and the direct quote. In addition, speakers often mark the voice of the character by changes in amplitude, pitch, or degree of accentuation, and by the production of particular terminal intonation contours. The direct quote in the following example occurs without any quotative frame. Instead, there are a number of prosodic and lexical cues which together indicate the status of the material as a direct quote. Example (11) is transcribed prosodically. Prosodic transcription conventions are given in Table 41; full discussion of prosodic categories is provided in Chapter 3.

(11)   .. ∧ *daŋga*   *par-ai*   *ju-*   *ju-eni*   "*lo*   *bāˈbu.*   /\
         astonishment feel-BV be-FS be-PART EXCL baby

       .. ∧ *thijin*   *u*   *anauṭhā khā*   *khoŋ-gu.*   __
         1pINC.ERG this strange matter see-1pPST

       . *ām kāran=na,*   /
         that reason=INST

       .. *ināgu*   *khā=ri*   *gunˈta=ŋ*   *da-hat.*"   \\
         this.type matter=IND who.DAT=EXT PROH-say

'He felt astonished: "Lo, Baby! We saw a strange thing. For that reason, don't tell this type of thing to anyone!"'

The prosodic cues that indicate the shift to the voice of the character begin with the emphatic accent on the vocative noun in the first intonation unit, together with the rise-fall terminal intonation contour, which is primarily used for exclamatory utterances. The speaker is clearly producing an intonation pattern that might reflect the real intonation of a person producing this utterance in the circumstances of the story. The second intonation unit has the high-level intonation contour which is most typically found with quoted speech, so serves to mark this as a continuation of the character's voice. The third intonation unit has a rising contour to mark non-finality and anticipation of an additional unit. The final unit contains an emphatic accent of truly dramatic proportions followed by an equally dramatic fall accompanied by creaky voice. Thus the prosody allows for the dramatization of the direct quote and circumvents the need for an overt quotative frame.

Table 41. Prosodic transcription conventions

Prosodic Transcription Conventions		
Terminal contours		
High-falling terminal contour	\\	
Mid-falling terminal contour	\	
Level terminal contour	—	
Rising terminal contour	/	
Marked-rising terminal contour	//	
Rise-fall terminal contour	∧	
Transitional continuity		
Final transitional continuity	.	
Continuing transitional continuity	,	
Accents		
Phrasal accent	^	
Emphatic accent	!	
Pause (written at the beginning of the line)		
Short pause (100-200 milliseconds)	.	
Medium pause (300-600 milliseconds)	..	
Long pause (over 700 milliseconds)	( )	duration specified

While the majority of quotative frames are of the type shown in (10), with elements of the frame both preceding and following the direct quote, there is also another, less common, structure which, in my data, is used primarily by younger speakers. In this structure, the quotative verb is followed by the morpheme *ki*, a complementizer borrowed from Nepali, with the direct quote postposed. This appears to be a direct calque on the Nepali quotative construction. An example is given in (12):

(12) āmun hat-ai ki *"janta chin da-syāt"!*
3sERG say-3sPR COMP 1sDAT 2sERG PROH-kill

'He said: "Don't you kill me!"'

When speakers use this structure, the shift to the character's voice is overtly marked. The shift back to the voice of the narrator is most commonly accomplished by a recapitulation, such as *ānthi hat-ŋasin* [that.manner say-when] 'When (s/he) said that'.

3.1. Quoted speech and syntactic complexity

The pervasive incorporation of quoted speech in narrative discourse often leads to syntactic sentences of considerable complexity. As argued in §18.2.3, direct quotes are grammatically object complements, functioning as grammatical objects of utterance verbs. In addition, direct quotes may themselves be complex, containing dependent clauses, examples (13)–(15), or multiple sentences, examples (16)–(17).

(13)   thi-mā=n   "bhānche=ke   ū-i   darsa
         one-CL=ERG   cook=ALL   go-INF   if

         janta   jā   uli   uli   khene   na-ita   bi-eu"   hat-ai   hā
         1sDAT   rice   little   little   PRT   eat-PURP   give-3FUT   say-3sPR   EVID

         'One said: "If I go to a cook, he will give me a little bit of rice to eat".'

(14)   āle   "hirā=e   jā   hirā=e   jā
         then   diamond=GEN   rice   diamond=GEN   rice

         hā-en   bi-u"   hat-cu
         bring-PART   give-IMP   say-3sPST

         '(The bird) said: "Bring and give (him) diamond rice".'

(15)   āle   "oho   uṣṭule   jāl   yeŋ-an
         then   oho   this.much   net   do-PART

         jana   kae   mica   tukā   ju-en   con-a"   haŋ-an
         1sGEN   son   daughter   actually   be-PART   stay-3sPST   say-PART

         bobu=ri=n   si-en
         father=IND=ERG   know-PART

         'Then, saying: "Oho, doing this much of a net (i.e. there has been this much deception), it turns out these are actually my sons and daughter", the father knew.'

494   Chapter 21   The sentence

(16)   āle   pharsi=n   "janta   bu-en   simā   thābi
       then pumpkin=ERG 1sDAT carry-PART tree   top

       ta-en   **bi-u**   **jin**   **sona**   **kha-i"**   hat-cu
       put-PART give-IMP 1sERG flower pick-1FUT say-3sPST

       'Then the pumpkin said: "Carry me and put me on the top of the tree. I will pick the flower".'

(17)   āmun   "**u**   **jaŋgal=e**   **rājā** **ji** **tuŋ** **khyaŋ**
      3sERG this jungle=GEN king 1s FOC be

      mebu ma-da"   hat-ai
      other NEG-exist say-3sPR

      'He said: "The king of this jungle is me. There is no other".'

The incorporation of direct speech containing multiple independent finite clauses is common. In many examples, the direct quotations contain extended conversational turns, as in (18):

(18)   thē-i-ho   "**chi** **hātta** **yer-an?** **chana** **mega**
      arrive-when 2s   why   come-2sPR 2sGEN yesterday

      miɲe   **oŋ-gu** **nis-mā=ŋ** **chana** **didā=pen** **khyaŋ.**
      before.yesterday go-NR1 two-CL=EXT 2sGEN e.brother=PL be

      chi misāmi hātta ithi   yeŋ-an   yer-an?
      2s woman why like.this do-PART come-2sPR

      chi misāmi kātākāt mārāmār haŋ-a   ṭhāĩ dam.
      2s woman katakat maramar say-NR2 place exist

      chi do-ō."   haŋ-an   hat-cu.
      2s PROH-go say-PART say-3sPST

      'When she arrived, (the yogi) said: "Why do you come? The two who went yesterday and the day before are your older brothers. Why do you, woman, come doing this? You are at the place called Katakat Maramar. Don't go".'

Despite the fact that the embedded quotations are complex, even containing multiple independent sentences, matrix clauses in such sentences are still syntactically coherent. Example (18) is a typical OV sentence, containing only one non-embedded finite verb, *hat-cu* 'said', in the last line. This construction allows for the expansion of the object into, in principle, an infinite number of syntactic sentences of any level of complexity. Of course, speakers and hearers are constrained by processing considerations. In the preceding example, the grammatical object is about as long and complex as any in my data. It is interesting to note that most of the sentences in embedded quotations are short and to the point; perhaps the overall syntactic complexity of the construction is balanced by reduced syntactic complexity in the embedded sentences.

The combination of the embedding of direct quotes as syntactic objects with the use of the participial construction on quotative verbs allows for a single syntactic sentence to contain an entire dialogic conversation, as exemplified in (19) (also discussed in Genetti and Slater 2004: 18–21). The finite verbs of the embedded quotations are underlined; the fourth line is a verbless equational clause so has no finite verb.

(19) dokhuseŋ sabhā jur-ŋasin bisma=ta tu
all meeting happen-when Bhisma=DAT FOC

"*chin tu yer-i mal-a u rāje.*
2sERG FOC do-INF must-3sPST this kingdom

chin tu yer-i mal-a u rāje."
2sERG FOC do-INF must-3sPST this kingdom

haŋ-an hat-nasin
say-PART say-when

"*ji yā pariwār niyojan ju-i doŋ-gu mi.*
1s TOP family planning happen-INF finish-NR1 man

tyāgi barta =n jin ma-yet-ki.
denial fast=INST 1sERG NEG-do-1sPST

u rāje janta mā=ŋ māl.
this kingdom 1sDAT need=EXT (NEG)need

gāddi=ku co=ŋ mo-con-gi." *haŋ-a-lāgin*
throne=LOC stay=EXT NEG-stay-1sPR say-NR2-because

496   Chapter 21   The sentence

"āu   hāti   yer-iui   le."   hat-ŋasin
now   what   do-NR3   PRT   say-when

"e   hātiŋ   āpat   par-ai   jur-sa
EXCL anything trouble befall-BV happen-if

ji   samj-ai   jur-sin   nā   mā."   haŋ-an
1s   remember-BV   happen-IMP   AGR   mother say-PART

byāsji   haŋ-an   ta-u
Byasji   say-PART   put-3sPA

'When they all had a meeting, (someone) said to Bhisma: "You are the one who must rule this kingdom. You are the one who must rule this kingdom." When (someone) said that, (he) said: "As for me, I am a man who has had family planning (vasectomy). Because of (my commitment to) self-denial and fasting, I will not do it. I do not need this kingdom. I won't sit on the throne at all." Because (he) said that, (they) said: "Now what to do?", and when (they) said that, [Satyawati remembered that] (Byas) had said: "Hey, if any trouble befalls you, remember me mother".'

I consider this to be a single syntactic sentence, since it has only one finite verb which is not embedded within a direct quote. All the quotative verbs prior to the last line are in non-finite forms. This sentence begins with an adverbial clause, then contains four direct quotes, three of which are internally complex. First, the people of the country address Bhisma, then Bhisma replies, then the people wonder what to do. Finally, Byas' earlier speech to his mother is recalled. This extended conversation strikes a native English speaker as being rather long and unwieldy as a single sentence, hence the more natural-sounding English translation given, with the information parsed into multiple English sentences. However, in Dolakha Newar this is clearly a single well-formed syntactic sentence, which follows all the regular principles of clause combining for the language.

It is important to note that imposing any syntactic sentence boundaries internal to this sentence results in problematic fragmented structures. For example, if one wished to analyze this section of the narrative as a series of shorter syntactic sentences, one could try imposing syntactic boundaries at the completion of each embedded syntactic sentence. For example, the middle lines could be syntactically parsed as follows:

(20) u   rāje   janta   mā=ŋ   mā̲l̲
      this kingdom 1sDAT   need=EXT NEG.need

      'I don't need this kingdom.'

(21) gāddi=ku   co=ŋ   mo-coŋ-gi
      throne =LOC stay=EXT   NEG-stay-1sPR

      'I won't sit on the throne.'

(22) haŋ-a-lāgin   āu   hāti yer-iui   le?
      say-NR2-because   now what do-NR3   PRT

      'Because he said this: "Now what to do?"'

(23) hat-ŋasin
      say-when

      'When they said this...'

When this analysis is applied to the entire exchange in (19), a number of problems arise. For example, the dative-marked argument in the first line of the example is an argument of the quotative verb *hat-nasin* 'when said' in the fourth line. An analysis which puts a sentence boundary after each finite embedded clause would necessarily parse these into separate syntactic units, leaving the dative-marked noun phrase "stranded" and its dative casemarking unexplained. Another problem would be the status of the now sentence-initial quotative verbs such as *haŋ-a-lāgin* in (22). Such examples do not occur with any nominal or deictic reference to the quoted material, a gap which has no explanation if these really constitute separate sentence-initial clauses. Also, in this analysis, such verbs appear to have the character of recapitulation (§19.4.4), but rather than repeating the previous predicate (which in this analysis lacks a verb), they produce the verb that the previous predicate was missing.

All of these problems are avoided if one identifies the syntactic sentence as a coherent syntactic unit ending in a non-embedded finite verb and understands the long-distance grammatical relationships between elements with intervening quoted material. An interesting question that such complexity brings up is the issue of preplanning. Although there is no direct psycholinguistic evidence, it appears to me that such sentences, though complex, do not require that the speaker have the entire sentence planned ahead of time. Instead, the syntax of the language is structured in such a way as to allow the speaker a considerable degree of "online" flexibility in deciding when to close the sentence off; indeed, the speaker has that option at every non-embedded verb. This, in turn, results in flexibility in the amount of content to be packaged into a single syntactic sentence. In the example given, a solution to a conflict is proposed in the first quotation, but is dashed in the second. The third quotation repeats the hopelessness of the situation, while the fourth points the way to the actual solution. Since the syntax of the language is able to incorporate through embedding the entire array of syntactic structures, the speaker can in this way use the sentence as a significant unit in structuring the discourse (Genetti and Slater 2004).

4. Other types of syntactic complexity

Chapters 17 through 20 described the major strategies by which clauses are combined into sentences: nominalization, complementation, the participial construction, and adverbial clauses. The goal of each chapter was to outline the syntactic properties of each type of clause combining and to comment on how each is used in Dolakhae discourse. This was most easily accomplished by selecting examples that were relatively straightforward, and not complicated by the interaction of distinct syntactic structures. While a necessary approach for expository reasons, this has perhaps led to an oversimplified view of Dolakha Newar syntax. Interaction of distinct types of clause combining is common, and the resulting syntactic structures are notably complex. The complexity, however, is easily analyzable once the basic design principles of *linear sequencing* and *hierarchical organization via embedding* are understood.

Clauses are put into *linear sequences* by one of two construction types, the participial construction and the adverbial-clause construction. At the end of each clause, a speaker has the choice either to close off the syntactic sentence by the production of a finite verb or to continue the sentence. If continuation is chosen, the speaker then can choose to specify the nature of the interpropositional relation between the joined clauses with an adverbial suffix, or can choose not to specify interpropositional relations by adding the participial suffix. Both of these construction types result in a linear sequence of clauses. Within each clause, any argument position can in turn be *embedded* in one of two ways, creating a hierarchical structure. It can be realized as a clause, hence constitute a complement, or it can contain a clause internal to the noun phrase, i.e. a relative clause. Speakers mark these two types of embedding by the morphology on the verb of the embedded clause, the presence or absence of a head noun, or by the various means for marking embedded direct quotation outlined in §19.4.3. The syntactic complexity of Dolakha discourse is largely due to the *recursion* of these structures. Thus, any embedded constituent can be syntactically expanded by linear sequencing, and any clause in a linear sequence can be syntactically expanded by embedding. While the discussion in Chapters 17 and 18 primarily focused on nominalized and complement *clauses*, in actual fact, embedded constituents often consist of multiclausal structures which themselves have varying degrees of complexity.

We can represent linear sequencing and embedding in a simple graphic format. Horizontal arrows can represent linear sequencing, with clause boundaries marked by a "pipe" (short vertical line). Vertical arrows can represent embedding; the point of intersection between the vertical and horizontal lines represents the NP which is either embedded itself or contains a relative clause. Thus Figure 26 illustrates a structure where two clauses are in linear sequence and the first contains a single embedded clause.

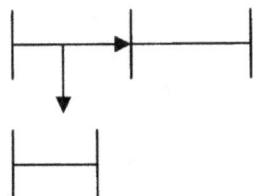

Figure 26. Structural representation of two clauses in sequence, the first of which contains an embedded clause

We will begin our discussion of complexity with a relatively simple example, given in (24):

(24)   āmun   hā-en   ta-e   ni-sar   dyābā
       3sERG bring-PART   keep-NR2   two-hundred   money

       āmu chẽ   dani=n   kār-ai
       that house owner=ERG   take-3sPR

   'The householder took the two-hundred rupees that he had brought and had with him.'

In this example, the O of the transitive verb *kār-* 'take' is given in the first line. The head noun *dyābā* 'money' is modified by a numeral and by a relative construction, *āmun hā-en ta-e* [3sERG bring-PART keep-NR2] 'that which he brought and kept (i.e. had with him)'. This relative construction contains two verbs joined by the participial construction. Together they form a complex verb phrase which share a single subject *āmun* 'he' and a single object. The object is obligatorily not realized within the relative clause, as it is coreferential with the head noun. This example illustrates a linear structure (the participial construction) within an embedded structure (the relative clause), as illustrated in Figure 27:

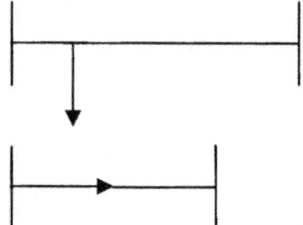

Figure 27. The participial construction within an embedded clause

The next example is taken from the same narrative. The relative clause has the same structure as in (24), but in this example, the noun phrase that contains the relative clause functions as the object of an infinitive clause which is the syntactic complement of the verb *mal-a* 'must':

(25) āmun   hā-en   ta-e   dyābā   pul-i   mal-a
      3sERG   bring-PART   put-NR2   money   pay-INF must-3sPST

'(He) must pay the money he has brought and has with him.'

Thus this is an example of a linear structure within an embedded structure which is itself embedded, as illustrated in Figure 28:

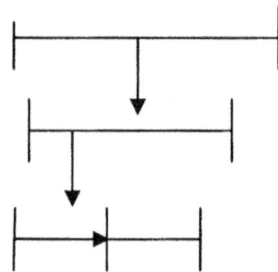

Figure 28. A participial clause within an embedded clause which is itself embedded

Example (26) illustrates a syntactic sentence in which a relative clause is embedded in a noun phrase which is an argument of a complement clause. This complement clause is embedded within a participial clause, which is in linear sequence with two other clauses:

(26) [chẽ=ku=ri=na   chanta   bi-e   mā-sā-ku
      house=LOC=IND=ABL   2sDAT   give-NR2   NEG-tasty-NR1

mā-sā-ku   cijbij]~NP~
NEG-tasty-NR1 things

sumake na-e   sukā-en   janta   hā-en   bi-u
silently   eat-NR2 pretend-PART 1sDAT   bring-PART give-IMP

'Silently pretend to eat the not-tasty not-tasty food that they give you from in the house and bring and give it to me.'

This structure is represented in Figure 29:

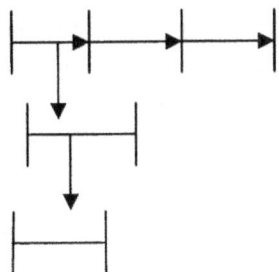

Figure 29. An embedded clause within an embedded clause within the first clause of a participial chain

The final example to be discussed is complicated not only because of the combination of hierarchical and linear structures, but also because of the ability of the participial and adverbial structures to conjoin verb phrases as well as entire clauses (see §19.5.2). The example is given in (27).

(27) *āle   buḍā   jā   na-i-ta   on-nasin*
      then old.man rice   eat-INF-PURP go-when

   thõsi=e   kawāph   dak-e   hā-en   ta-e   khon-ai
   meat=GEN   ball   make-PART   bring-PART   put-NR2   see-3sPR

   'Then when the old man went to eat rice, he saw that (she) had made, brought, and put meatballs.'

Beginning with the basic syntactic structure, we can see that this example consists of two adverbial clauses followed by a finite clause. The finite clause contains a complement structure, which consists of three clauses in linear order, linked by the participial construction, as represented in Figure 30:

502   Chapter 21   The sentence

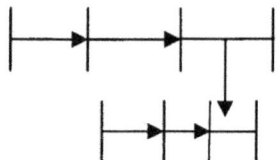

Figure 30. A three-clause participial chain embedded into a finite clause preceded by two adverbial clauses

While Figure 30 represents the basic overall structure of the sentence in linear and hierarchical terms, it does not do justice to its complexity. Note that the argument *buḍā* 'old man' does not have a casemarker. This means that it is necessarily the subject of the intransitive verb *on-nasin* 'go-when' rather than the transitive verb *na-i-ta* 'to eat'. While this type of case prolepsis is common with the participial construction, it is rare with adverbial clauses. Its existence here implies a tight integration of the two clauses. Following the analysis of case prolepsis with participial clauses (§19.5.1), I will assume that it indicates that this example involves the combination of two verb phrases into a complex verb phrase, and that they thus share a single subject. This analysis is represented with square brackets in (28):

(28)   āle   [buḍā]$_{SUBJ}$ [[jā   na-i-ta]$_{VP}$ [on-nasin]$_{VP}$]$_{VP}$
       then   old.man   rice eat-INF-PURP   go-when

'When the old man went to eat rice...'

Moving to the next line, we see that the transitive verbs combined by the participial construction all share the same object, which is mentioned once, before the first verb. Following the analysis of such constructions given in Chapter 20, this single noun phrase is analyzed as the object of a complex verb phrase containing all three verbs. The noun phrase and complex verb phrase together are embedded as the complement object of *khon-ai*, as shown in (29):

(29)   [[thōsi=e   kawāph]$_O$ [[dak-e]$_{VP}$ [hā-en]$_{VP}$ [ta-e]$_{VP}$]$_{VP}$]$_{NP-O}$ khon-ai
       meat=GEN   ball   make-PART   bring-PART   put-NR2   see-3sPR

'He saw that she had made, brought, and put meatballs.'

There are a number of repercussions of this type of syntactic analysis, the details of which are beyond the scope of the present book. One point which I will discuss briefly is that the analysis given here, which allows verbs and verb phrases to be combined linearly into complex VPs, implies that there is considerably less zero anaphora in the syntax of this language than one might otherwise assume. For example, under this type of analysis, the complex verb phrase in (29) has only one unexpressed argument, the A, referentially the woman who made the meatballs. The expressed O holds grammatical relations with all three verbs. A more traditional analysis that did not allow for the combination of verbs into complex verb phrases would necessarily analyze this example as having five unexpressed arguments. Each of the three clauses would have an unexpressed A, and two of the clauses would have an unexpressed O. The analysis given seems preferable to one which ignores the tight integration of the structure.[100]

Another interesting theoretical issue that this analysis raises is the nature of the syntactic unit "clause". Throughout this book, I have been using the term as it is commonly used in linguistics, to refer to a verb with its associated arguments and adjuncts. However, when one begins to examine the syntax of complex sentences in more detail, the notion of clause shifts subtly. Consider again the final line of example (30). How many clauses are involved? The analysis given here, which combines verb phrases into complex VPs, suggests that the embedded portion is a single "clause" with multiple predicates. By the more traditional analysis, in which every verb instantiates a clause, the embedded portion constitutes three clauses. However, the combination of three clauses would not constitute a syntactic sentence, as it doesn't end in a non-embedded finite verb. Instead, it represents a syntactic level intermediate to the clause and the sentence.

As is often the case, the complex syntax of the language allows for multiple analyses and interpretations, each based upon different theoretical assumptions and with distinct theoretical implications. The approach taken briefly here and in Chapter 19 is both innovative and non-conformist. In my opinion, it best represents the organizational principles of this language. While I am aware that many will take issue with some of the analysis, I hope that it will provide a brief shift in perspective that may prove insightful.

5. Defining the prosodic sentence

Chapter 3 described various aspects of the prosody of Dolakha Newar, including the division of speech into intonation units, types of phrasal accents, four phonological terminal intonation contours (fall, level, rise, rise-fall), and the two-way functional distinction of transitional continuity (final, continuing). In this chapter, we will examine the combination of intonation units into higher-level prosodic units. I call these units "prosodic sentences", due to their fascinating parallels with syntactic sentences in this language. These parallels exist not only at the level of structure (discussed below), but also at the functional level: prosodic and syntactic sentences are both used to exhaustively divide the narrative into internally coherent units which serve to organize the discourse. Syntactic and prosodic sentences largely overlap, but speakers may choose to offset the boundaries for interesting functional effects (§21.6.2).

The prosodic sentence in Dolakha Newar is defined by Genetti and Slater (2004) as in (31):

(31) The prosodic sentence is a prosodic macro-unit optionally containing any number of prosodic units with continuing intonation and necessarily ending in a prosodic unit with final intonation.

Thus prosodic sentences usually comprise multiple intonation units. The prosodic cohesion is produced by the interplay between the continuing transitional continuity of the non-final intonation units and the final transitional continuity of the final intonation unit. Consider examples (32) and (33) (note that the last IU in (32) is too long to fit on one line so is wrapped over two lines):

(32) .. *pusata ^mahinā=e, //*
       Pusata month=GEN

       .. ***barta ^con-ŋasin, //***
       Barta stay-when

       ... (2.12) *ith-- ^tirtha   ū-i-ta   oŋ-gu*
                 FS   pilgrimage go-INF-PURP go-3PA

       *parāsar risi. *
       Parasar Risi

       'When he was observing the fast of the month of Pusata, Parasar Risi went to go on a pilgrimage.'

(33) ... (1.2) *kwākarbeŋ=na ā'pāī   sā   nar-ŋasin,   //*
                 frog=ERG   that.big cow   eat-when

       ... *libi   bobu   ^daŋgai   par-ai   jur-a.*   \
       later   father astonishment feel-BV   be-3sPST

       'When he saw a frog eating a cow that big, then the father was astonished.'

Both of these are typical examples of prosodic sentences, where the continuing units have rising intonation and the final units have falls. However, not all prosodic sentences are of this type. For example, falling intonation can be used in continuing contexts, usually when it marks a contrastive noun phrase (§3.4.1), thus can indicate continuing transitional continuity, as in the following example (note that the second intonation unit in (34) is too long to fit on one line, so it has been wrapped and further indented):

(34)　．^thi-mā=n,　　＼
　　　　one-CL=ERG

　　　．．^bhānche=ke　ū-i　　darsa　janta　jā
　　　　cook=DAT　　go-INF　if　　1sDAT　rice

　　　　　　uli-uli　　　na-i-ta　　　　　　^bi-eu　　　　hat-ai　　hã.　　＼＼
　　　　　　little-little　eat-INF-PURP　give-3FUT　say-3sPR　EVID

'One (of the three) said: "If I go to a cook, he will give me a little rice to eat".'

It is important to note that there appears to be substantial inter-speaker variation in the frequency and function of particular contours. The following example was produced by a speaker who never used a marked rise in the data examined, but instead made extensive use of rise-fall contours in the environment where others used marked rise. He also frequently used level contours on intonation units which consisted of a single noun phrase. However, it is clear from the morphosyntax and discourse structure that each of these units has continuing transitional continuity. The speaker doesn't reach a possible completion point, syntactic or prosodic, until the production of the last intonation unit in the example, which has a falling intonation contour:

(35)　　．．．(.09)　āle　　ām　　^tākku,　　／＼
　　　　　　　　　then　that　time

　　　．^bau=ri,　　　—
　　　　father=IND

　　　^kānā　ju-i　　　　　doŋ-guju.　　＼
　　　blind　become-INF　finish-3pPA

'Then at that time, the father had become blind.'

It should be noted that prosodic sentences do not necessarily contain syntactic sentences, but may co-occur with lists or other types of structures, as in the following example, which summarizes the order of birth of three sons:

(36)   ... bi^dur,   //
       Bidur

       ... pan^ḍuk,   //
       Panduk

       ... ^ḍirtarāstra.   \
       Dhirtarastra

       'Bidur, Panduk, Dhirtarastra.'

In the absence of morphosyntax or other lexical material, it is the prosodic structure which provides cohesion to these otherwise independent morphosyntactic units, and thus creates the list.

6. Syntax-prosody interactions

6.1. Parallels in syntactic and prosodic structure

One of the reasons why prosodic sentences are of particular interest in Dolakha Newar is that the verb-final syntactic typology of the language allows a number of interesting parallels between the syntactic and the prosodic structures of the language (Genetti 2003b). One way in which the prosodic and syntactic levels are parallel is in the positioning of the morphosyntactic and prosodic structural cues. At the morphosyntactic level, the cues consist primarily of the verbal suffixes that occur clause-finally. Finite suffixes indicate completion at the syntactic level, while non-finite suffixes mark various types of dependent clauses, hence non-completion. At the prosodic level, the cues of continuation and finality are the terminal intonation contours, with the locus of the significant intonational movement occurring at the end of the intonation unit. Since many prosodic units end in a clause-final verb, this means that the markers of prosodic and syntactic continuity are usually produced simultaneously in this language. This situation is unlikely to be found in languages, such as English, which mark clausal relationships with clause-initial adverbial conjunctions. Consider example (37):

(37) .. ^khu-mā mucā janm-ai ju-ene,   /
     six-CL child born-BV be-PART

ām mucā=pen thau thau ^ṭhã̄ī on-a.   \
that child=PL REFL REFL place go-3sPST

'The six children were born and those children went to their own homes.'

In this prosodic sentence, the terminal rising contour of the first intonation unit is entirely realized on the participial suffix *-ene*. In the second unit, the falling contour is realized over the last two words, with about of a third of the contour occurring on the finite suffix. Thus, the markers of continuation and finality at both levels are cotemporaneous.

Another parallelism between the morphosyntactic and prosodic levels comes from the positioning of dependent, non-finite clauses prior to the finite clause. This pervasive syntactic pattern is directly paralleled by the prosodic structure in which a sequence of units with continuing transitional continuity is followed by a unit with final transitional continuity. This parallelism is represented in (38):

(38) *Morphosyntax*   *Prosody*
      non-finite   continuing
      non-finite   continuing
      finite   final

Thus, in this language, non-finite clauses overwhelmingly occur with continuing transitional continuity, while finite clauses overwhelmingly occur with final transitional continuity. In contrast, languages which allow the positioning of dependent clauses after the finite clause may have weaker correlations between clause type and intonation contours.

Finally, the third and most intriguing parallel between the syntactic sentence and the prosodic sentence is that both types allow for embedding. Prosodic embedding occurs when one prosodic sentence is completely contained within another prosodic sentence (Genetti and Slater 2004). This phenomenon is robust in Dolakha Newar, and occurs primarily in the incorporation of direct quotation into the narrative. Often the embedded quotation extends over multiple intonation units, which together form an independent prosodic sentence. This prosodic sentence is then embedded into a higher-level prosodic sentence at the level of the mainline narrative. Example (39) illustrates this pattern. The example contains six intonation units, one on each line; for ease of reference, the lines have been lettered and the quoted material is given in bold:

(39) a. ... bisma=ta   ŋen-ŋasin,   //
        Bhisma=DAT ask-when

  b. "^e.   ∧
     EXCL

  c. ... ^kāsi oŋ-an,   /
         Kasi go-PART

  d. ^jal-ai   jur-sa jukun,   /
     burn-BV be-if   only

  e. u   ^pāp kaṭaun-ai jur-^a."   ∧
     this sin   cut-BV   be-3sPST

  f. ... hat-cu.   \\
         say-3sPST

'When they asked Bhisma, (he) said: "E! Only if (you) go to Kasi and [die by] burning will this sin be cut from you".'

This example contains a complete syntactic sentence, with the sentence boundary indicated by the non-embedded finite verb found in prosodic unit (f). The sentence contains embedded quoted material, beginning in line (b) and ending in line (e). This embedded material is prosodically and syntactically complete. At the prosodic level it contains two prosodic sentences, one in line (b) and one in lines (c)–(e), each ending with a final intonation contour. At the syntactic level it contains an exclamatory particle, followed by a participial clause, an adverbial clause, and then a finite clause. The embedded material is set within a larger sentence, containing a participial clause in (a) and ending in the finite verb in (f). Hearers in Dolakha Newar have no problem in understanding that the participial construction begun in line (a) is suspended during the switch to the quoted material. The lexical cue of the exclamatory particle and the prosodic cue of exclamatory intonation both indicate the switch from the mainline to the quotative level. The same cues which instruct the hearer to suspend the converbal construction begun in line (a) until the production of the final finite verb are also used to suspend the prosodic sentence begun in the same line. Hearers know that the final intonation in line (b) is not linked with that in line (a). Instead, the prosodic sentence is suspended until line (f), when the switch back to the mainline narrative is accomplished with the production of the quotative verb. We can represent this embedding as follows:

a. non-final intonation
    b.   final   (end of first embedded pros. sent.)
    c.   non-final
    d.   non-final
    e.   final   (end of second embedded pros. sent.)
f. final (end of non-embedded prosodic sentence)

Thus we can clearly see that the embedding occurs at the prosodic level in parallel to the embedding which occurs at the syntactic level.

We have seen that there are three clear parallels between the syntactic and prosodic structuring of narrative. First, at both the syntactic and prosodic levels, the marking of continuation and finality occur at the end of the relevant unit; such marking commonly overlaps temporally. Second, at both the syntactic and prosodic level, the non-final units (non-finite clauses, continuing intonation units) precede the final units. This is in keeping with the overwhelmingly head-final structuring of the language. Third, embedding is attested at both the syntactic and prosodic levels, and again these tend to co-occur temporally. These parallels allow speakers to orchestrate their production of syntactic and prosodic units, coordinating the two levels such that comparable structures are produced simultaneously, providing mutual reinforcement. However, it is also possible for speakers to skew the two levels, such that either boundary locations or marking of continuation/finality do not co-occur. I refer to such units as "syntax/prosody mismatches" (Genetti 2003b, in press), discussed in the following section.

6.2. Syntax/prosody mismatches

As mentioned in the preceding section, the syntactic and prosodic boundaries in the language are usually correlated in the production of narrative. Genetti and Slater (2004), found that in one Dolakhae narrative, 86% of prosodic-unit boundaries followed either a noun-phrase or a clause boundary, hence that the boundaries between syntactic and prosodic units overwhelmingly co-occur. Similar striking results were found for the co-occurrence of the marking of continuation and finality: 81% of the finite clauses in the narrative occurred with final intonation, while 99% of the non-finite clauses occurred with continuing intonation. However, these two dimensions are not obligatorily correlated, and speakers may choose to skew the two levels for interesting rhetorical effects. The fact that the relationships between syntax and prosody are non-obligatory renders the attested correlations even more interesting; speakers are choosing to produce parallel structures the majority of the time. When speakers make the opposite choice, so that the two modalities do not run in tandem, they provide evidence for their independence. The study of such syntax/prosody "mismatches" – cases that go against common patterns of correlation between syntax and prosody – is particularly interesting when they are examined in the larger discourse context; speakers produce mismatches in order to achieve particular communicative aims.

One type of syntax/prosody "mismatch" is a mismatch in the positioning of syntactic and prosodic boundaries. An example is given in (40):

(40)   *pusata   ^main=e,   //*
       Pusata   month=GEN

       barta   ^con-ŋasin,   //
       fast   stay-when

       'When it was the fast of the month of Pusata...'

Syntactically, this example consists of a simple intransitive clause with a subject and an intransitive verb. The subject noun phrase contains a genitive modifier *pusata main=e* 'of the month of Pusata' preceding the head noun *barta* 'fast'. The result is a well-formed and integrated clause. Although this is one integrated syntactic unit, the speaker made a decision to distribute the clause over two prosodic units. While one might expect a break between the subject noun phrase and the verb as the major constituents of the clause, the speaker does not produce this. Instead, she breaks the noun phrase itself apart, putting the genitive modifier into one prosodic unit, and the head in another. In order to understand this seemingly odd decision, one must look more broadly at the narrative context. This sentence was produced in the first line of a long and involved narrative. The genitive modifier is set off prosodically in order to establish the temporal reference of the following episode. At the same time that the speaker separates *pusata main* prosodically, she also smoothly produces the genitive clitic, marking it as dependent on the following head, and constructing a well-formed and integrated syntactic sentence.

Another type of syntax/prosody mismatch is found in the marking of finality and continuation. That is, a unit can be marked as final in one modality and simultaneously marked as continuing in another. An example of this is given in (41):

(41) sampati ^ma-da,   /
      wealth   NEG-have

   jin   ^ma-bi-gi   chana   bā=ta.   \\
   1sERG   NEG-give-1sPST   2sGEN   father=DAT

   'She will not have wealth; I won't give her to your father.'

This example consists of two finite clauses in sequence, each containing a finite verb, and each constituting an independent syntactic sentence. By contrast, the example contains only one integrated *prosodic* sentence; it has one line with continuing intonation and one with final intonation. The locus of the mismatch is the first line, *sampati ma-da*, 'She will not have wealth', which is marked as final at the syntactic level and continuing at the prosodic level. To understand why the speaker produced this mismatch, one again needs to consider the wider context of the narrative. This example is an embedded direct quote in a conversation regarding marriage negotiations. It is spoken by the father of the prospective bride, who is concerned for her financial future and therefore (at this stage of the negotiations) refuses to give the girl in marriage. The continuing intonation functions here to mark a significant relationship between the proposition of the first line and that of the second. The context allows the speaker to infer that the interpropositional relationship is causal; it is because of his conviction that she will be destitute that he is refusing the marriage. This raises the question of why the speaker did not then mark this causal relationship explicitly by using the causal converb adverbial form *ma-da-e-lāgin* [NEG-exist-NR2-because] 'because she will not have'. I believe the answer is that the production of the finite verb form allows the material of this clause to be presented as an assertion, clarifying and strengthening the father's position in the negotiation. Since the speaker can indicate the interpropositional relationship with prosody, the verb form is free to be used for independent rhetorical purposes.

It is clear from these examples that a full understanding of how speakers weave syntax and prosody together can only be arrived at through a detailed qualitative analysis of a particular discourse at a particular point in time. While quantitative studies are clearly important in showing overall patterns and trends in the data, they must be balanced by detailed examination of the use of particular forms in context.

6.3. Narrative sentences

Despite the interesting presence of syntax/prosody mismatches, the most common pattern is for speakers to simultaneously produce markers of continuation or finality at both the syntactic and prosodic levels. When speakers produce markers of finality at both levels, the result is a significant boundary in the narrative. These boundaries are marked not only by the production of markers of syntactic and prosodic finality, but also by other prosodic cues (such as significant pause and pitch reset), and sentence-final particles (§10.4.2). In addition, they are very commonly followed by recapitulations at the beginning of the next sentence (§19.4.4). These well-marked boundaries delineate significant units in the narrative which are cohesive at both the syntactic and prosodic levels. Genetti and Slater (2004) label these units "narrative sentences", as they are the primary units into which narratives are divided. Speakers thus use these units to organize and present the material of the discourse.

It is not possible to say that narrative sentences are equivalent to a particular unit of discourse production, such as an episode or larger unit equivalent to a paragraph. The reason for this is that narrative sentences vary greatly in length. They may contain a single clause, as in (42):

(42)   ^bhānche=ke   on-a.   \
       cook-ALL   go-3sPST

       'She went to the cook.'

Or, they may have extensive internal syntactic and prosodic complexity, as in (43). (Finite verbs are in underlined. Note that the second intonation unit is quite long and wraps onto two lines, with the second line indented.)

(43)   .. hat-na   hat-na   hat-na   hat-na   hat-^na,   /
          say-when   say-when   say-when   say-when   say-when

          ... (.08) libi   ām   chē   <u>then-ju</u>   chē   <u>then-ju</u>
                   later that house   arrive-3sPST house   arrive-3sPST

                   nik ∧ kai bobu   kae   chē   theŋ-ane,   //
                   very   father son   house   arrive-PART

          . kae=uri   ^ḍulet-a   <u>on-a</u>   ḍulet-a   on-nasin,   //
            son=IND   stroll-PURP   go-3sPST   stroll-PURP   go-when

          thau   ^sāŋat   ^sāŋat=pista=uri,   //
          REFL   friend   friend=PL.DAT=IND

             .. ^nāplaŋ-ane   āmta,   //
                meet-PART   3sDAT

Section 6   Syntax-prosody interactions   513

"^*gulpa* <u>*har-i,*</u>   //
when   say-1FUT

^*gulpa* <u>*har-i,*</u>   //
when   say-1FUT

^*gulpa* <u>*har-i"*</u>   *haŋ-an   āmta,*   //
when   say-1FUT say-PART 3sDAT

u   ekdam, _
3s very

.. *ut^tsuk   lāg-ai   <u>jur:-a</u>.*   //
   impatient feel-BV become-3sPST

'They talked and talked and talked and talked, and then they arrived at the house and when they arrived at the house, the son went for a stroll and when he went for a stroll, he met his friends, saying: "When will I tell, when will I tell, when will I tell?", he felt very impatient.'

This example contains as many as 17 clauses (depending on whether you count repeated verbs as separate clauses). It contains four syntactic sentences, as one can see from the two non-embedded finite verbs in the second intonation unit (*then-ju*, repeated twice), the non-embedded finite verb in the third intonation unit (*on-a*), and the non-embedded finite verb in the final intonation unit (*jur-a*). With the exception of the reiteration of *chē then-ju* in the second line, each of these syntactic sentences is complex, containing one or more adverbial, participial, or complement clause. However, there is only one prosodic sentence, as the first nine intonation units have clearly continuing intonation (usually a strong rise), and only the final line has the fall marking final transitional continuity. It is the double marking of finality at both the syntactic and prosodic levels that marks an end to this narrative sentence.

The prosodic structuring of example (43) serves to background information that is contained in the first three syntactic sentences. Note that the very long second intonation unit consists of three clauses which contain repetitions of the same predicate. The first two contain the finite verb, while the latter recapitulates (and expands upon) the material in the first two. The verb itself is in the participial form, the most common form of the verb in recapitulations. The placement of all of this in one intonation unit serves to de-emphasize the events of the finite verb, and the use of the recapitulation clearly marks the material as background with respect to what follows (as recapitulations are always back-grounding devices). A similar phenomenon is found in the third intonation unit, although there the recapitulated verb is in an adverbial form.

Overall, the first intonation unit is anaphoric, referring back to the quoted speech in the immediately preceding discourse. The repetition of the verb allows the implication that the conversation went on for a while, but the rising intonation together with the adverbial form marks it as backgrounded with respect to what follows. The returning home and the going out for a stroll by the son are also backgrounded, as discussed above, and then the speaker produces the foreground of the sentence, the fact that the son was impatient to tell his friends of the remarkable experience he had. This is conveyed by first expressing the meeting of the friends in a participial clause, and then, more importantly, by the rapid repetition of *gulpa har-i*, which itself conveys the boy's impatience, by lexical content, repetition, and rate of speech. The impatience is then explicitly expressed and denoted by a finite verb. Thus the prosodic structuring guides the hearer's attention not to the homecoming or the boy's decision to go out, but to his impatience and clear intention to tell his friends his news. As telling the news goes against his father's explicit injunction against this, we can see why this is an important element of the story, and prosodically and syntactically foregrounded.

This somewhat lengthy discussion has served to emphasize four points. First, as mentioned above, syntactic and prosodic structures do not always run in tandem, but can be offset to allow the speaker to structure the discourse in creative ways or for other functional purposes. Second, narrative sentences can be quite lengthy and complex. Note that while this narrative sentence contained one prosodic sentence and multiple syntactic sentences, it is also possible to find narrative sentences which contain multiple *prosodic* sentences; this is especially true in the case of prosodic embedding, e.g. examples (39)–(40). Third, when we compare examples (42) and (43), we can see that narrative sentences vary greatly in their length and complexity. This makes it difficult to equate them to a single discourse unit. Speakers have great latitude in the structuring of these sentences, which they exploit for rhetorical and other reasons. Fourth, this example serves to illustrate the richness of analysis and depth of understanding which one can obtain about connected speech when one simultaneously examines the prosodic and syntactic structuring. This leads to deeper insight into the speaker's intentions in the use of specific forms and a fuller appreciation of the skill with which speaker's deftly coordinate these two independent levels of structure.

7. Closing words

It is my hope that this volume has presented a portrait of Dolakha Newar which is accurate and at times insightful. Looking over these pages which I have finally completed, it is clear that I have said a great deal (perhaps more than I should have), yet still I am left with the sense that I have only scratched the surface. This final chapter, in particular, seems just to hint at the dizzying complexity of the syntactic structure. I do hope, however, that these notes will encourage someone to follow me in the study of this language, someone who can take this volume as a starting point, surely prove me wrong on some aspects of my analysis, and take our understanding to a greater depth. My dearest hope is that this person will be a speaker of Dolakha Newar or the descendent of one, a true inheritor of this rich language, the gift of the countless generations who have shaped it.

Appendix A
List of verbal affixes

The following table lists every allomorph of every verbal affix in Dolakha Newar, together with its function, gloss, and distributional pattern. It is hoped this will provide a useful key for users of the grammar, as well as a summary of the morphology for those interested in conducting comparative work. Note that each *allomorph* constitutes a separate entry, so that a number of morphemes have several entries. This allows for the clear specification of the environment that each allomorph occurs in.

Form	Function	Gloss	Occurs with
TENSE			
-gu	Past Anterior	PA	N-stems, L-stems
-ku	Past Anterior	PA	T-stems
-u	Past Anterior	PA	R-stems
∅	Past	PST	All stems
-a	Present	PR	All stems
-e	Future	FUT	third person in T-stems, R-stems, L-stems; third-person singular in N-stems
-i	Future	FUT	All other forms
PERSON AND NUMBER			
-ĩ	First-person singular	1s	Past anterior
-gi	First-person singular	1s	Past and present
∅	First person	1	Future
-pe	First-person plural Second-person honorific	1p/2h	Past anterior
-gu	First-person plural Second-person honorific	1p/2h	Past and present
-n	Second-person singular	2s	Past anterior and present
-mun	Second-person singular	2s	Past
-na	Second-person singular	2s	Future
-min	Second-person plural	2p	Past anterior, past, present
-nan	Second-person plural	2p	Future
-ta	Second-person honorific	2h	Future
(-ju)	Third-person singular (optional)	3s	Past anterior
-ju	Third-person singular	3s	Past; transitive verbs
-a	Third-person singular	3s	Past; intransitive verbs
-i	Third-person singular	3s	Present

-ŋ	Third-person singular	3s	Future of N-stems
-u	Third person	3	Future of non-N-stems
-ŋ	Third-person singular of negative transitive verb in past or present	3s	N-stems
-u	Third-person singular of negative transitive verb in present	3s	R-stem
∅	Third-person singular of negative verb in past or present	(none)	All stems for intransitive verbs; also with L-stems and T-stems for transitive verbs
-tan	Third-person plural	3p	Past anterior of all stems and future of N-stems
-hin	Third-person plural	3p	Past and present
-ju	Past anterior (optional)	PA	All person/number suffixes
MOOD			
-ŋ	Imperative/Prohibitive singular non-honorific	IMP	N-stem
-u	Imperative/Prohibitive singular non-honorific	IMP	R-stem
∅	Imperative/Prohibitive singular non-honorific	IMP	T-stem, L-stem
-sin	Imperative honorific	IMP	All stems
-n	Imperative plural non-honorific	pIMP	N-stem, R-stem
-un	Imperative plural non-honorific	pIMP	T-stem
-dun	Imperative plural non-honorific	pIMP	L-stem
da-	Prohibitive	PROH	All stems
-gu	Prohibitive honorific	2h	N-stems, R-stems, L-stems
-ku	Prohibitive honorific	2h	T-stems
-min	Prohibitive plural non-honorific	2p	All stems
tha-	Optative	OPT	All stems
∅	Third-person-singular optative	(none)	All stems
-hin	Third-person-plural optative	3p	All stems
NON-FINITE FORMS			
-i	Infinitive	INF	All stems
-an	Participle	PART	N-stems, T-stems
-en	Participle	PART	R-stems, L-stems
-gu	Nominalizer/relativizer 1	NR1	N-stems, L-stems
-ku	Nominalizer/relativizer 1	NR1	T-stems

-u	Nominalizer/relativizer 1	NR1		R-stems
-a	Nominalizer/relativizer 2	NR2		N-stems, T-stems
-e	Nominalizer/relativizer 2	NR2		R-stems, L-stems
-sa	Conditional		if	All stems
-nasin -ŋasin	Temporal		when	All stems
-saŋ	Concessive		although	All stems
-da	Purposive	PURP		N-stems, L-stems
-a	Purposive	PURP		R-stems, T-stems

Appendix B
Phonological and grammatical words

The concept of "word", though intuitively clear to laymen as well as to linguists, has been notoriously difficult to define. Dixon and Aikhenvald (2002a), in editing the seminal volume *Word: A cross-linguistic typology*, have proposed independently identifying "phonological words" and "grammatical words", and then assessing the degree to which they overlap. To this purpose, phonological words are defined as units minimally one syllable in length which have at least one phonological defining property (segmental features, prosodic features, or phonological rules) (Dixon and Aikhenvald 2002b: 13). Grammatical words, by contrast, consist of a number of grammatical (and presumably lexical) elements which always occur together creating cohesiveness, occur in a fixed order, and have a conventionalized coherence and meaning (Dixon and Aikhenvald 2002b: 19). The purpose of this appendix is to summarize the evidence for phonological and grammatical word in Dolakha Newar.

Phonological words in Dolakha Newar have the following features:

(1) They are minimally one syllable in length, and adhere to the syllable-structure patterns of the language (§2.4.1)

(2) They form the domain for the following phonological rules as specified:

Vowel harmony (domain: prefix and root) (§2.3.5)

Vowel accommodation by various phonological rules (domain: root and affix or clitic) (§2.3.4)

Regressive gemination (domain: root)(§2.5.2)

Labialization (domain: entire word) (§2.5.1)

Syllable reduction (domain: entire word) (§2.5.3)

(3) When pronounced in isolation, the first syllable will receive stress

Throughout this grammar, I have transcribed phonological words with spaces preceding and following; affixes and clitics are defined as such in part because they form a single phonological word with their hosts.

One must assess the status of grammatical words in Dolakha Newar on a class-by-class basis. The majority of word classes in Dolakha Newar do not exhibit affixation (demonstratives, pronouns, quantifiers with the exception of numerals, adverbs, adjectives). Words in these classes have significant freedom of positioning with respect to other word classes, hence they constitute independent grammatical words.

Inflected verbs constitute single grammatical words because they co-occur with affixes in a set order, and never have more than one affix of a given type (e.g. tense). Verbal affixes never appear on any word other than a verb root, hence they are clearly not independent elements. Verbal affixes are obligatory under the conditions specified in this grammar, and root and affix combinations have coherent and conventionalized meanings.

A combination of a numeral plus its classifier also constitutes a single grammatical word. This is because you cannot have one without the other and the two occur in a fixed order.

Much more complex is the morphology related to nouns and noun phrases. The single nominal suffix (the diminutive) is a derivational morpheme and clearly forms a grammatical word with its host. The clitics, however, are much more complicated. There are three clitic positions: one for the plural (§4.4.1), one for the set of clitic casemarkers (§4.4.2) and one for the clitics of individuation and extension (§10.2). Of the three, it appears that the plural is not an independent grammatical word, but forms a grammatical word with its host. The reason for this is that the plural and its host have a conventionalized coherence and meaning that speakers readily identify. It also is more closely bound to the lexical noun than the other clitics: if there is a noun, the plural will be bound to it. The primary reason that I have analyzed the plural as a clitic as opposed to a suffix is that the plural morpheme still appears in the absence of a nominal head, for example, on a headless relative clause or a headless genitive phrase. This implies that the plural has a slight degree of morphological freedom not typically found with affixes. On the other hand, the degree of independence is not great; this is why I have described the plural as being intermediate between a clitic and an affix (§4.4.1).

The casemarkers and clitics of individuation and extension, by contrast, appear to be independent grammatical words and do not form a single grammatical word with their morphological host. This is largely due to their phrasal nature; they can be bound to any element of a noun phrase, as long as it is NP-final, hence they are found bound to numerals, demonstratives, adjectives, nouns, etc. Because of this morphological freedom, these clitics do not come in a fixed order with respect to what precedes them and hence they have a greater degree of freedom. The difference between the distributional pattern of the casemarker and that of the plural can be seen in the noun phrase $d\bar{a}i$=pen $s\bar{o}$-$m\bar{a}$=n [e.brother=PL three-CL=ERG] 'three brothers (ergative)'. The plural is on the nominal head, as there is one, but the casemarker is on the NP-final numeral. Hence the casemarker has much more grammatical independence and can be considered a distinct grammatical word.

The clitics of individuation and extension have the same distributional patterns of the casemarkers, i.e. NP-final. Hence the same argument of grammatical independence with respect to the preceding word will hold. An interesting question is whether the casemarker and the clitics of individuation and extension together form a single grammatical word. In other words, would a noun phrase like $k\bar{\imath}ja$=n=$uŋ$ [younger.brother=ERG=EXT] constitute a two grammatical words (with the two clitics combining to form a single grammatical word) or three? The answer is clearly three. While the casemarker and the clitics of individuation and extension do come in a strict order, they also occur independently of each other. In addition, the clitics of individuation and extension have greater distributional freedom and are not restricted to NP-final position (e.g. they can occur on adverbials), hence can appear in clausal positions not open to the casemarkers. Thus, these clitics constitute grammatical words in their own right.

Looking now to the congruence of phonological and grammatical words, we see that most of the time single phonological words are single grammatical words. The combination of a clitic casemarker or a clitic of individuation or extension with a host will create a single phonological word that contains two grammatical words, while a host that takes both a clitic casemarker and a clitic of individuation or extension will constitute a single phonological word but three grammatical words. There are no examples of single grammatical words that constitute more than one phonological word.

Appendix C
Dolakha Newar word list

This wordlist presents the basic vocabulary of Dolakha Newar, collected in texts and elicitation. Pronouns and proper names have been excluded. Complete information on pronouns and their forms can be found in Chapter 5.

Words of Indo-Aryan origin have been included in this list, as they form an important component of the Dolakhae lexicon. These words have been labeled with "(Nep)" following the gloss; it is likely that there are others in the list that I have not recognized as being Indo-Aryan so have not marked. I also have not attempted to differentiate loans from Sanskrit or other Indo-Aryan tongues from loans from Nepali. A few loans whose sources are originally English (although possibly borrowed through Nepali) are also marked. Borrowed Nepali verbs have been given in their Dolakhae forms: intransitive verbs are listed with the "borrowed-verb" suffix -*ai*; transitive verbs with the /*yet*/ ending. See §6.3 for full discussion.

Native Dolakhae verbs are presented in stem form (§6.4.2). The class of the verb can be determined from the stem-final consonant. Verbs where the addition of the causative suffix has created a new lexical item have been included, but the causative suffix is separated with a hyphen, e.g. *na-ker* 'feed'. The transitivity of verbs is labeled in cases of potential ambiguity or where transitive and intransitive alternants are both found.

The lexical class of a word is indicated only in cases of potential ambiguity; otherwise the class can be easily determined from the English translation. Expressive vocabulary has been glossed EXPR. Where possible, the nature of the thing expressed has been given in parentheses, e.g. *gargar* EXPR (roaring fire). Compounds have been hyphenated when known.

The alphabetical order used in this word list is given below:

a, ã, ā, ā̃ b, c, ch, d, ḍ, e, ẽ, g, h, I, ĩ, j, k, l,
m, n, ŋ, o, õ, p, ph, r, s, t, ṭ, u, ū, w, y

a

acār	acar (Nep)
airāk	liquor (Nep)
ajaŋ	still (adv) (Nep)
amrit	elixir (Nep)
anauṭhā	strange (Nep)
ani	then (Nep)
antim	end (Nep)
apsoc	regret (Nep)
arai	stable (adj.)
asnān	bath (Nep)
atāli	balcony (Nep)
aṭ	eight (Nep)

ā

ākheri	end (Nep)
āle	then; and then
ālu	potato (Nep)
ām, āmu	that
āmli	that much
ānāgu	that type; like that
ānthi	that manner
āpaĩ	that size; that big
āpat	trouble
ārā	saw (n.)
ātmā	soul (Nep)
āu	now

ã

ãku	there
ãti	intestines

b

baeŋkar	huge
bahar	young, fertile (of female animals)
bajai	grandmother (Nep)
bajaŋ	hookah
baje	o'clock (Nep)
baji	rice, beaten
balla	finally
balni	evening
balyet-	stalk
ban	forest (Nep)
ban-bati	lynx
bandagobi	cabbage (Nep)
ban-khā	pheasant
ban-phā	wild pig
barkhi	period of mourning (of mother's death)
barkhun	pigeon
barsa	year (Nep)
barta	fast (n.) (Nep)
baru	in that case
basanta	spring (Nep)
batijā/batiji	nephew/niece (Nep)
batthar	dilapidated
bā	father
bābu	term of endearment
bācā	a little
bācā	oath, bet (< Nep bāchā)
bācā	classifier for oaths
bāgabān	god
bājā	drum
bājā thyāt-	play music
bāje	grandfather (Nep)
bāji	bet (Nep?)
bākas	box (Eng)
bākhācākhā	partly completed
bākhan	story
bāmā	parents
bāmala-ku	<bā-ma-lāt ugly, bad
bāmalaske	badly
bāpi; bā̃pi	rib
bārcā	bowl
bāre	about (Nep)
bārmun	Brahmin
bārpāŋ	tomato
bās	shelter
bātho	clever (Nep)
bāti	a little
bã̄ḍā	pot (Nep)

bã̄la-ku		bujiŋ	housefly
<bã̄lat-	beautiful; good	bulbul	Bulbul (bird species)
bã̄laske	beautifully; nicely	bulbulbul	expr (bubbling)
belā	time (Nep)	bur-	carry
belcā	rolling pin	bur-	give birth
besna	very	bur-	sprout; grow
bhai	younger brother (Nep)	bur-	rub; massage
bhā̄nche	cook (Nep)	but-	cook (INTR)
bhāsā	language (Nep)	buthur	stove
bhut	ghost (Nep)	butni, bunni	sack
bicaku	needlessly	bū̃	field (irrigated)
bicara	late (passed on)	bwāklur-	pour
bicyauna	bed (Nep?)	bwār	worry
bihā	marriage; wedding (Nep)	bwārā	barn; shed
bikara	snake	bwāt-	run
bikh	poison (Nep)	bwāṭṭa	EXPR
binā	pointlessly		
binā	niece	c	
bini	nephew	cachi	night; one night
biŋkeŋ	very; many; much	caḍ-ai	enter (Nep)
bir-	give	cakku	knife
birāt-	err; make mistake	cal-ai	be in use (Nep)
birs-ai	forget (Nep)	calākh	clever (Nep)
biruwā	plant	calan	custom (Nep)
bisār-	send something via intermediary	calti	sweat
		casmut-	scratch (TR)
bittā	wall (outer surface)	caṭan	cooking spoon
bityāt-	spend time (Nep)	caṭṭa	imməditely (EXPR)
bo, bho	plate	caukos	door frame
bõ, bhõ	ground; floor	cākalcukul	expressive (babbling of baby)
bochu	squirrel		
bobu	father (reference, endearing)	cākar-	sweet, be (v.)
		cāklat	chocolate (Eng)
bohar-	bloom	cāku	sweets (n.)
bon-	read	cānas	midnight; late night
bon-ker-	teach (lit. cause to read)	cār	four (Nep)
bor-	fly	cār-	feel
borā	green beans	cã̄di	silver (Nep)
bõr	paper	cã̄ḍa	quickly (Nep)
boṭhār-	distribute; divide	ci	salt
buḍā	old; old man (Nep)	cicā	small
buḍe, buḍi; buḍyā old woman (Nep)		cicā-kocu	chickenpox

cicār-	small, be (v.)	chen-	comb
cic-bā	step-father	cher	head
cic-mā	step-mother	cherā	mat, woolen
ci-chū	house shrew	cheuri	skin; bark
ciḍiyā	bird	chē	house
cij, cijbij	thing, things (Nep)	chir-	sprinkle
cikan	oil	chit-	pull
cikār-	cold, be (v.)	chobu	caterpillar
ciku	ant	cho-ker-	burn (in a fire) (TR)
cilā	goat	chop	cover (Nep)
cimtām	poker	chor-	burn (of fire) (INTR)
ciplebhẽde	eggplant	chor-	send (e.g. letter)
cir-	tie	chu	cook (n.)
co	urine	chur-	cook (rice, porridge)
con-	stay; sit; reside	chuccā	greedy
cor-	write	chusār-	send (someone)
cumbar-	sharp, pointed, be (v.)	chut-	cook (bread) (TR)
cukā	side, top	chū	mouse; rat
cul-	sharpen	chwi	great grandchild
culā	finger, toe		
cumṭu	tail	**d**	
cuphi	machete (khukri)	da-chi	one year
cur-	put on shoes, socks	dai	elder brother (Nep)
cwãcwã	expr (crying)	daker-	make
cyā	eight	dampat	spouse (Nep)
cyā	tea	daṇḍa	fine (Nep)
cyāt-	burn (of small flame, e.g. candle) (INTR)	daŋga	astonishment (Nep)
		dar-	existential verb
		darbār	palace (Nep)
ch		dari	yogurt
cha	six (Nep)	dāi	elder brother (Nep)
chae	grandchild	dāju	elder brother
chakka	surprise (Nep)	dāker-	boil (TR)
charbut-	snap (of rope)	dāku	fat (n.)
chasar-	itch	dāl	dal; lentil
chata	carefully	dānab	giant (Nep)
chāi	makeup	dār-	boil (of liquid in a pot) (INTR)
chākkal	noon		
chār-	pare	dār	time
chāta	umbrella (Nep)	dāti	middle
chāuri	animal young	dãkare	traveller
chemā	forgiveness	dãlāt-	fast (v.)

debgan	god		ḍ	
deor	brother-in-law		ḍaḍelo	log
depān	on; on top; above		ḍāhā	jealous (Nep)
des	country (Nep)		ḍāktar	doctor (Eng)
deu	god (Nep)		ḍār-	beat (TR)
dhan	wealth (Nep)		ḍār-	fall over (INTR)
dhani	rich (Nep)		ḍās	bedbug
didā	elder brother		ḍen-	cut
dila	resting spot		ḍin-	sleep
din	day (Nep)		ḍoli	litter
disā	directions (Nep)		ḍon-	stand, wake up; get up
dobā	uncle		ḍon-	build
dobar	double (Nep)		ḍōr, ḍhōr	jackal
dokhu, dokhunuŋ	all		ḍulet-	stroll (Nep)
dol	thousand		ḍur-	pull; drag
			ḍusi	millet
don-, dhon-	finish		ḍusi-li	millet straw
dosari	pregnant		ḍwākar-	big, be (v.); grow
dū, dhū	tiger		ḍwāku-kocu	smallpox
dub-ai	sink (v.) (Nep)		ḍwāku-mulā	thumb
dudu	milk			
dudubari	butterfly; moth		e	
dudu-kãkar	fresh corn		ekdam	very (Nep)
duk-coi	mourning perios (13 days)		g	
dukha	trouble (Nep)		gakkeŋ; gatkeŋ	many; much
dukhi	sad (Nep)		gal-	thin, emaciated, be (v.)
duku	goat (male)		gala	neck
dulā	palm of hand		galaĩcā	carpet
dulbi	earthworm		gal-ai	thin; skinny, be (v.) (Nep?)
dupān	inside			
dupās	wick (for puja)		galti	mistake (Nep)
duta	into		gan	hammer
dwāŋnir-	push		ganthan	conversation
dwārā	fangs; pointed, uneven teeth		gar-	climb; ascend; ride (an animal)
dyābā	money; rupee		gara	deep (adj.); pit (in ground)
dyāmma	thick (of clouds)			
dyāt-	measure (length or volume)		gargar	EXPR (roaring fire)
			gat-	enough, be (v.)

gatke, gakke	extremely	*gyāt-*	fear (v.)
gāddi	throne (Nep)		
gāḍ	guard (Eng)	**h**	
gān-	dry (INTR)	*hajār*	thousand (Nep)
gāntāŋ	thin; emaciated	*hakar-*	call
gār	wound	*hal-*	call; call out; cry out
gãjal	eyeliner (Nep)	*halli*	turmeric
gãũ	village (Nep)	*hat-*	say
ger	ghee	*hatār*	haste (Nep)
geri	ankle	*hati*	there
ghartini	house servant (Nep)	*haṭanapaṭa*	hurriedly
gibi	where	*hā*	root
gilās	glass (Eng)	*hābi*	before, earlier
ginãgu	what type	*hākar-*	black, be (v.)
ginlā	insult	*hākon-*	crawl
gisā	cow	*hākupāku*	black raspberry
githi	how	*hākhen, hākhena*	front, in front of; before
gīja	gums (Nep)		
goi	nut	*hār-*	bring
gõgar	rooster	*hār-*	fall (of ripe fruit falling from a tree)
gõs	mustache		
graha	planet (Nep)	*hār-ai*	lose-bv (Nep)
gu	which	*hāti*	what
gu	nine	*hātiŋ*	nothing; anything (what=EXT)
gubāju	priest (Buddhist)		
gukhi	rope	*hātta*	why
guli	how many; how much	*hātti*	elephant (Nep)
gulpa	when	*hātyāt-*	push aside; expel (a spirit) (Nep)
gulpanuŋ	never (when=EXT)		
gun	who; which (animate)	*hãsā*	winnowing basket
gunuŋ	nobody (who=EXT)	*he*	specific identity particle
guri	which (inanimate)		
guṣṭule	so much	*hẽgar-*	red, be (v.)
gut	group	*helā*	insult
gut-	to be damaged (INTR)	*hi*	blood
gutker-	to damage (TR)	*hil-*	exchange; trade
gutni, bunni	sack	*himāl*	himalaya
guthi	civic group	*hir-*	wash (clothes)
gwār	barn; shelter	*hirā*	diamond (Nep)
gwāri	heel	*ho*	and
gwārtāk	round	*hor-*	bloom
gyār	fear (n.)	*huhujāna*	owl

hukuna	over there	*jā-sin*	come (syncretic honorific imperative)
hur-	peel or scrape off		
hut-	bark (of dog) (TR)	*jāudir-*	rest a load
		je	work
i		*jeu*	maybe
ijār	drawstring on pants	*jhar-ai*	fall-BV (Nep)
il-	spread (clay, mortar, dung)	*jhark-ai*	abuse-BV (Nep)
		jhyālā	window
imā	eagle	*ji, jhi*	ten
ināgu	this type; like this	*jikāet-*	exchange; substitute (Nep)
inār	well (n.) (Nep)		
iri	daughter-in-law	*jimŋā*	fifteen
iskul	school (Eng)	*jir-*	be appropriate
itār	lamp	*jit-ai*	win (Nep)
ithi	here	*jogi*	yogi (Nep)
ithi	this manner; like this	*jon-*	catch; grab; hold
ittaŋ	again (variant of *littaŋ*)	*jor-*	graze (INTR)
		jor-	leak
		joret-	earn
j		*jukun*	only
jaba	when	*juju bāje*	grandfather < king (Ktm) + grandfather (Nep)
jaga	field		
jagā	flood		
jal	liquid (Skt)	*jur-*	be; become; happen
jal-ai	burn (Nep)	*jurukka*	EXPR (quickly) (Nep)
jamma	together; all (Nep)	*jut-*	fall
janābar	animal (Nep)	*jwāl-*	swim
janchi	sash	*jyālā*	cost
janm-ai	be born (Nep)	*jyātar-*	heavy
janti	procession (Nep)		
jaŋgal	jungle	***k***	
jar-	sharp		
jati	possessions; things	*ka*	assertion particle
jau	right (i.e. not left)	*kabul*	bet
jawāni	youthful (Nep)	*kae*	son
jawāph	answer (Nep)	*kaimu*	husband
jā ~ jõ	waist	*kaĩci*	scissors
jā	rice	*kajit*	civic group
jāŋal	bird	*kakana*	bracelet
jāki	uncooked rice	*kakucā*	adam's apple
jāl	net (Nep)	*kaker-*	throw
jāri	brother-in-law	*kalpanā*	imagination (Nep)
		kampalimpa	rainbow

kansa	after tomorrow	*kisi*	elephant
kanyā	virgin (Nep)	*kisim*	type (Nep)
kaparā	chamber pot	*kitāb*	book (Nep)
karbul	pea	*kitke tar-*	put against
karchē	boiled soybeans	*kīja*	younger brother
kastimā	bee	*kobi*	down; below
kathā	story (Nep)	*kok*	crow
kaṭaun-ai	cut (Nep)	*kota*	down
kaṭhi	stick	*koṭhā, kuṭhā*	room
kawāph	ball	*kōisa*	knife held with foot
kāki	aunt (younger brother's wife)	*kōsa*	bone
kālat	wife	*kucin ṭir-*	pinch (verb)
kālsi	next year	*kuciri*	claws, fingernails
kām	work (Nep)	*kukhurikā*	EXPR (rooster crow; Nep)
kānā	blind (Nep)	*kulā*	peel; shell
kānchi	youngest (Nep)	*kulsi*	stair
kāpal	head	*kumlo*	bundle
kāpas	cotton	*kunā*	corner
kār-	take	*kurāmuni*	condensed milk (Nep)
kāran	reason (Nep)	*kursi*	chair
kā-sukā	sacred thread	*kururura*	EXPR (pouring of hard small things, e.g. dal)
kāt	wife		
kāwli	cauliflower (Nep)	*kusā*	raincoat (traditional, of leaves or bamboo)
kãcā	branch		
kãkar	corn; corn kernel	*kusi*	flea
kãkar-li	corn husk	*kuṭhā*	room
kãkar-sã	corn silk	*kū*	smoke
kãrā	arrow	*kwāitāk*	curved; bent; hunchbacked
kehē	younger sister		
kehi	some (Nep)	*kwākar-beŋ*	frog
ken-	show	*kwāker-*	heat (verb)
ken-	celebrate	*kwāluŋmā*	pestle
kerā	banana (Nep)	*kwāt-*	hot, be (v.)
kesi	tomorrow	*kyātar-*	soft
keṭā	boy (Nep)		
keṭi	girl (Nep)	**kh**	
kē	lentils		
ki	complementizer (Nep)	*khabar*	news (Nep)
kin-	trap	*khacin*	later same day
kipā	shade; shadow	*khali*	thigh
		khapa	feather

khaptu	back (body part; in reference to carrying things)	*khwārā*	hoof
		khwāl	face
		khyaŋ	be, be rue (copula)
khar-	pick (flower)	*khyāt-*	scare
kharāyo	rabbit (Nep)		
khasi	goat	**l**	
khau	left (as opposed to right)	*lachi*	one month
		laḍanta	fight (Nep)
khā	talk; matter; language	*laglaglag*	expr (shivering)
khā	chicken; fowl	*lahar*	queue
khār-	full, be (v.)	*lahir-*	raise children
khār-	pick	*laŋgi*	blouse (Nep)
khāṭ	bed (Nep)	*lapti*	leaf
khāyar-	bitter	*lar-*	cut grass
khe	suppletive negative form of stative copula	*lā*	month
		lābā	garlic
khene	conditional particle	*lāg-ai*	feel, be touched by, experience (Nep)
khenna	side		
khēja	egg	*lāhā*	hand, arm
khi	feces	*lāj, lās*	embarrassment, shyness (Nep)
khicā	dog		
khicā-wā	canine tooth	*lā-ker-*	heal (TR)
khisi	insult	*lākmā*	shoe
khīgar-, khiŋar-	dark, be (v.)	*lāŋ-an*	massage; rub (PART)
		lāŋtā, laiŋtāŋ	naked
kho	river	*lār-*	talk; tell
khobi	tears	*lār-*	heal; recover from illness (INTR)
khon-	open		
khon-	see		
khopi	alcove	*lāsā*	bed
khoptu	lower back	*lāṭa*	dumb
khor-	cry; weep	*le*	particle
khosu	cloud; fog	*len-*	be left over (of food)
khu	six	*ler-*	choose
khu	thief	*li*	back, backwards, after
khunu	day	*libāt-*	be late
khur-	steal	*libi*	later
khursāni	chili (Nep)	*lichilen*	backward
khusi	happy (Nep)	*likhana*	after; behind
khwāgar-	cold (of liquids), be (v.)	*lilililin*	EXPR (twinkling)
khwātar-	thick (of clothes, bankets, books)	*liŋar-*	walk
		lipul-	return (INTR)
khwārsi	walnut	*lita*	later; next

litaŋ	again	*mālā*	garland; necklace (Nep)
lokhu	water		
lokhu-bati	otter	*mān-ai*	obey; celebrate (Nep)
lon	womb	*māŋas*	dream
lon-	weigh	*māri*	bread
lor-	well suited	*māyā*	love (Nep)
lor-	vomit	*me*	other
lõ	road	*me*	song
lubar-	warm	*me*	tongue
lukhā	door	*me hal-*	(song) sing
luŋā	rock; stone	*mebu*	other
luŋmā	mortar, flat	*mega*	yesterday
lusi	pestle, for suba	*melā*	fair; festival (Nep)
lū	gold	*mes*	water buffalo, female
lūmon(ker)-	forget	*methar-*	play
lūwon(ker)-	remember	*mi*	fire
lwāp	up (e.g. stand up)	*mi*	person; man
lwāt-	fight	*mica*	daugher
lyās, lyāsi	young	*mikhā*	eye
lyāt-	order; commission	*mikhā-sã*	eyebrow; eyelash
lyuri	bronze	*mil-ai*	join; be well-suited (Nep)
m		*miŋe*	before yesterday
mahina, main	month (Nep)	*mir-*	sell
mahal	palace (Nep)	*mirga*	deer
makar	monkey	*misā, misa-mi*	woman
mal-	need (v.)	*mo*	chaff
mal-, maldan-	must; need	*mogara*	upper back
man	feeling; heart (Nep)	*mohi*	farmer
mandir	temple (Nep)	*mokā*	occasion
maŋpar-ai	like (v.) (Nep)	*mol*	price (Nep)
mantri	minister (Nep)	*mon-*	swell
masti	forehead	*mon-*	boil (TR)
matlab	care (Nep)	*mor-*	be finished; gone
mā	mother	*morlur-*	bathe
mā-bā	mother-father, parents	*moti*	pearl (Nep)
mā-cilā	goat, female	*moṭo*	fat
mā-khe	hen	*mucā*	child
māji	boatman	*mukan*	mushroom
māl	irregular negative of *mal-* need	*mula*	road
		mur-	dig
maila	second eldest (Nep)	*murki*	fist

muru	needle	*ne*	iron
muryā	lap	*nemlā*	moon
musukka	EXPR (smiling)	*ni*	two
mut-	squirt; spray (INTR)	*ni*	yet
muthu	mouth	*ni*	snot; pus
mwāl-	search	*ni, nii*	twenty
mwāl-	try	*nibār*	sun
mwār	soybeans, dried	*nichi*	day; one day
mwāsar-	yellow, be (v.)	*nienin*	day by day
mwāt-	live; survive	*nijā*	lunch; snack
mwātker-	save (<live-CAUS)	*nikkai*	very
		nimtiŋ	benefit
n		*ninas*	afternoon
nagarā	drum (round)	*nini*	aunt
nai, naita	food	*ninmā*	mother-in-law
nakas	first	*ninpatti*	daily; everyday
na-ker-	feed (<eat-caus)	*nir-*	grind
nakka	just now	*nis*	two
nakti	star	*nispatta*	dark
naku	cheek	*nitheŋ*	daily
naŋsir	cuticle	*nokar*	servant (Nep)
nar-	eat	*nugar*	heart
nas	seven	*nulu*	new
nasa	vein	*nur-*	step on
naskan	mirror	*nyāmnyām*	temples (body part)
nasputi	ear	*nyen-*	fit (INTR)
natra	or else (Nep)	*nyāt-*	express (milk from cow)
nā	agreement particle		
nā	odor		
nāg	serpent (Nep)	**ŋ**	
nāga	last year	*ŋat-*	throw; discard
nāhak	uselessness (Nep)	*ŋā*	fish
nāi	butcher caste	*ŋā*	five
nāl-	tired	*ŋār-*	bite
nām	name (Nep)	*ŋen-*	ask
nānicā	pupil of eye	*ŋen-*	listen; hear
nāpa	together; assoc. postposition	*ŋil-*	laugh; smile
		ŋilā	spit
nāplat-	meet	*ŋyāt-*	buy
nār-	knead		
nās	nose	**o**	
nāscā	late night	*oho*	silver

oli	garden	*pālo*	ginger
on-	go	*pāŋ, paiŋgu*	fruit
onsā-mi	man	*pāp*	sin (Nep)
onsir-	be acquainted with; know (someone)	*pār*	across (Nep)
		pār-	dry (clothes; food)
oŋti	run-off (water coming in sheets off roof)	*pāthi*	pathi (unit of measure) (Nep)
opaĩ	that big	*pãch*	five (Nep)
opte, optecā	tiny; small (adj.)	*pãti*	mosquito
optecār-	tiny, be (v.)	*pe, pẽ*	four
or-	bring in clothes from drying	*peŋker-*	kick
		pẽ	leech
osai	this here	*pẽgar-*	sour
õgar-	green, be (v.)	*pi*	forty
		pilākā	calf of leg
p		*pilipili*	dim (of light)
pachuta	remoseful (Nep)	*pipāna*	outside; verandah
pahilā	before (Nep)	*pir*	worry (Nep)
paksin	witch	*pir-*	plant (seedlings)
palaŋ	bed (Nep)	*pir-*	wait
pali	roof	*pir-*	demolish (e.g. an old house)
pamṭu	wing		
par-ai	befall; feel; happen (Nep)	*piri*	sister-in-law (elder brothers wife)
pārbati	Parbati	*pita*	out
pariwār	family (Nep)	*pokā*	packet
parsi	sari	*pomṭu*	wing
pasal	shop (Nep)	*põ*	hail
paschim	west (Nep)	*põṭa*	bamboo, large sp.
pat	leaf (< Nep)	*prakhyāt*	popular (Nep)
paṭi	side (<Nep)	*prāti*	by (Nep) in *din prāti din* 'day by day'
paṭhyauri	young, virile (of male animals)		
		pujā	ceremony; worship (Nep)
pā	ax		
pāchār-	carry against the shoulder (e.g. a baby)	*pujāri*	priest (Nep)
		puklukka	expr (tumbling)
pāhā-beŋ	toad	*pukhur*	lake; pond
pāju	uncle	*pul-*	pay
pāk-ai	ripen (Nep)	*pul-*	return
pākhā	incline; hill	*pulcā*	terrace wall
pālkā	mustard species, broad leaf	*pumi*	wasp
		pur-	pull up from ground

pura	bead	*phir-*	lick
purba	east (Nep)	*pho*	phlegm
put-	burn (of body parts) (INTR)	*phoŋa*	pillow
		phon-	ask for; beg
puyā	seed	*phuphucā*	fontanelle
pwākal	hole; pit (in ground)	*phur-*	blow
pwāl-	peel (e.g. fruit)	*phutar-*	brown, be (v.)
pwāl-	strike; behead	*phutk-ai*	escape (Nep)
pwāl-	till	*phutta*	EXPR
pwārcir-	wrap	*phyāktar-*	seat (someone)
pwāstur-	twist; wring		
pwāṭṭa	EXPR	**r**	
pyāj	onion (Nep)	*rā*	question particle
pyākhan	dance	*rāches*	ogress (Nep)
pyāt-	become wet	*rādi*	rug (Nep)
pyāṭā	belly; stomach	*rājā*	king (Nep)
pyāṭāmāri	pregnant	*rāje*	kingdom (Nep)
pyāṭāwāt-	hungry, be (v.)	*rājkumār*	prince (Nep)
		rāk	anger
ph		*rāk-mura*	angry
phakar-	astringent, acerbic (as unripe persimmon)	*ritidān*	sexual intercourse (Nep)
phal	return	*ritu*	season (Nep)
phalāk	plank		
phalphul	fruit (Nep)	**s**	
phar-	be able; become well	*sabda*	word (Nep)
phār-	chop (wood)	*sabhā*	meeting (Nep)
phark-ai	return (Nep)	*sadāŋ*	always
pharsi	pumpkin (Nep)	*sakhi*	dung
phasa	wind	*salāhā*	conference (Nep)
phasi	sheep	*salŋā*	fishes, small, dried
phāsi	jackfruit	*samet*	accompanying (Nep)
phā	pig	*samj-ai*	remember (Nep)
phāŋā	blanket	*samjhanā*	memory (Nep)
phāŋā-kocu	measles	*sampati*	wealth (Nep)
phār-	cover oneself (TR)	*santān*	heir; offspring (Nep)
phār-	chop (wood)	*sanyāl*	evening
phãsi	hanging (means of exceution)	*saŋkā*	suspect (Nep)
		saŋsi	nit
phen-	untie	*sar-*	know how
phir-	put on clothes; wear clothes	*sar*	hundred
		sara	horse

saram	modest (Nep)	sirak	quilt
sarāp	curse (Nep)	sit-	die
sarāsar	directly (Nep)	situgā̃s	grass species
sar-chi	one-hundred	sitha	sap
sarir	body (Nep)	siṭhu	plough
sat-ai	invite (Nep)	sī	wood
satar-	call	soen	mark of comparison
satya	truth (Nep)	sojjā	porridge
sā	cow	sona	flower
sābun	soap (French)	sor-	look; watch
sācā	calf (bovine)	sotu	flour
sāŋat	friend	sõ	three
sāhā	care (Nep)	suba	mortar for beating rice
sāl	year (Nep)	subbā	official (Nep)
sālar-	thin	subi	EXPR (call of bird)
sānahi	horn (muscial)	sugā	parrot (Nep)
sār-	tasty, be (v.)	suikucca	quickly
sāt	seven (Nep)	sukār-	pretend
sāwār-	plough	sukul	mat of straw
sāuji	shopkeeper (Nep)	sukha	happiness (Nep)
sã	hair	sul-	hide
sã̄par	bun (hair)	sumake	silently; silent
sã̄rpuli	ribbons	suni	morning, early to mid
sã̄wā	molars	sur-	sew
sel	marrow	suru	begin (Nep)
sēlā	liver	sut-	dry (INTR)
sen-	teach	sut-	shrink
sı	louse	sut-pānt	suit-pant
sier-	grey, be (v.)	suṭho, suṭhi	dried ginger
sigri	necklace	sū	straw (rice); thatch
sihā	lion		
sihā̃san	throne (Nep)	swābāu, sobāu	habit
sijal	copper	swālāhā	nest
sikār	hunt (Nep)	swālhār-	fall, drop
sil-	wash	swāṭṭa	EXPR (splashing?)
silā	stone	swã	breath, panting
simā	tree	swã̄hārā	field or garden, non-irrigated
sindar	red powder (Nep)		
sipā̃ī	soldier	swi	thirty
sir-	know	syāt-	hurt (of body parts) (INTR)
sir-	die		
sir-	fruit (of tree)	syāt-	kill

syāudār-	bow to touch head to feet of respected person	ṭul-	roll on ground
syen-	teach	ṭuleŋ	until
		ṭulke	until, up to
t		ṭulle	during
tal	below; under	tuni	until
tannā	bedcover	tuphi	broom
tap	hat	tupri	topi (hat)
tapakka	carefully; suddenly	turi, turkan	mustard
tapchyāt-	break (TR)	tut-	shiver
tapjyāt-	break (INTR)	twāer-	white, be (v.)
tar-	put; keep	twākar-	lighter (e.g. of dawn), be (v.)
tara	but (Nep)	twāle	neighbor
tarawāra	sword	twārtar-	stop (doing something); leave behind
tara on-	go with (someone)		
tarikā	method (Nep)		
tāŋtāŋ	EXPR (clanking)	twāsmica	girl's best friend
tākku	time	tyāgi	denial (Nep)
tār	lock (n.)	tyasale	therefore (Nep)
tār-	hear		
tār-ai	cross; ferry (Nep)	**th**	
tārcā	key	thanu	today
tātā, titā	elder sister	thāŋrā	ledge of house to dry corn
tā̃cho	barley		
tā̃s	stick (Nep)	thari	variety
ti	broth; liquid	tharthar	EXPR (shivering)
tibi	television (Eng)	thau	reflexive pronoun
tiŋgriŋga	tall skinny	thābi	up, above
tika	tika (Nep)	thākar-	difficult
tikne	blinding (of light)	thām	pillar
tinmut-, timmut-	jump	thār-	weave
tir	bank (of river)	thāta/thā̃ta	up
tir-	light; ignite	thekhi	dowry
tir-	pinch	then-	arrive
tir-	thread needle	thenāgu	like
tiret-	pay (Nep)	thẽ	like
tirtha	pilgrimage (Nep)	thi	one
tisā	jewelry	thikar-	full, be (v.)
tu	dandruff	thin-	touch
tu, tuŋ	focus particle	thon-	block
tukā	actually	thon-	stuff
tul-	fall (from a height)	thote	gap of missing tooth

thōsi	meat	*ṭhon-*	pick up; wake up; cause to rise
thuprā	many		
thur-	understand	*ṭhor-*	break down; take apart
thur-	find	*ṭhor-*	lay (egg)
		ṭhoṭa	stairway
ṭ		*ṭhun-*	bury
ṭakacā	whitewash (made with white clay)	*ṭhun-*	braid
ṭāen	far	**u**	
ṭāhāgar-	tall; long, be (v.)	*un-*	apply eyeliner
ṭap	earrings, post	*uku*	here
ṭār-	fix	*ukuna*	over here
ṭen-	be about to	*uli*	this much; this little
ṭēburi	navel	*ulisṭule*	this much
ṭikret-	stand; be straight	*uli-uli*	a little
ṭikhi	bamboo, small sp	*ultā*	translate (Nep)
ṭin-	throw away; discard	*upaĩ*	this size; this big
ṭir-	close; lock (e.g. door or window)	*upādre*	tyrannical (Nep)
		ur-	circle; dance
ṭit-	dip food	*usṭule*	this much
ṭon-	drink; smoke	*uta*	here
ṭor-	rise (of sun, moon)	*utpatti*	creation (Nep)
ṭōita	drink (n.)	*utsuk*	impatient
ṭuhurā	orphan (Nep)		
ṭun-	ripe, be (v.)	**w**	
ṭusi	cucumber	*wā*	rain
ṭuṭi	leg, foot	*wā*	topic particle
ṭuṭidāri	shin	*wāl-*	mix; knead
ṭū	sugarcane	*wāl-*	paint
ṭū	maggot	*wail-ai*	wilt (Nep)
ṭwāle	neighbor	*wār-*	plow
ṭwāŋsona	rhododendron	*wāsar*	medicine
ṭwāpar	flat top of a rock	*wāsā*	bull
		wāsta	care (Nep)
ṭh		*wāsti*	clothes
ṭhar-	sow	*wē*	crazy (of male)
ṭhāhā	knowledge (Nep)	*wini*	crazy (of female)
ṭhākkar	trouble		
ṭhāĩ	place	**y**	
ṭhika	just right (Nep)	*yau*	somebody; anybody
ṭhin-	cause to sleep	*yā*	come (irregular imperative)

yā rice, unhusked
yākar mica only child
yāl- chew
yālāguri gland
yārgar- be hanging (INTR)
yārkhār- hang (TR)
yārling earrings, large, round
yeku, yekku many
yelpanuŋ always
yen- take with one
yer- come
yet- do
yeuli however much; any amount
yẽgar- light (in weight)
yẽsa sickle

Appendix D
Text: A boy makes his fortune

The following is the transcription of a story told by Miss Bisnu Laxmi Shrestha, a native of Dolakha. The story was told in the spring of 1989, shortly after Miss Shrestha moved to Kathmandu. The story was related to other members of her family; I was not present.

This text is both phonemically and prosodically transcribed. It is divided into sentences; each sentence is numbered. The prosodic transcription follows the conventions laid out in Chapter 3, with the exception that separate intonation units are not represented on separate lines but run continuously within a syntactic sentence. Boundaries between intonation units can be identified by the transcription marks which indicate intonation contours. For example, in sentence (1), the boundary between the two intonation contours is marked by //**, which indicates a high-rising intonation contour (//) followed by a medium-length pause. The transcription conventions can be found in the following table:

Phrasal Accent (transcribed before accented syllable)	
Normal phrasal accent	^
Emphatic accent	!
Terminal Pitch Contours (transcribed after intonation unit)	
High fall	\\
Mid fall	\
Level	–
Rise	/
Marked rise	//
Rise-fall	∧
Transitional Continuity	
Final transitional continuity	.
Continuing transitional continuity	,
Pause (transcribed after intonation unit)	
Short pause (100-200 milliseconds)	*
Medium pause (300-700 milliseconds)	**
Long pause (more than 700 milliseconds)	(length)
Lengthening (transcribed after lengthened sound)	:

For other published texts see Genetti (1994, 2003) and Genetti and Slater (2004).

(1)
thi-gur maŋgal=e rājā=e des=ku=^ri , //** nis-mā ^mā
one-CL Mongol=GEN king=GEN country=LOC=IND two-CL mother

kae da-uju . /**
son exist-3sPA
In the country of a Mongol king, there lived a mother and son.

(2)
ām ^mā kae ek'da::m naita tōita , / ek'da:m dukha ju . **
that mother son extremely food drink extremely trouble be.3PA
That mother and son had a lot of trouble (having enough) food and drink.

(3)
āle āpen=ri , // dukha haŋ-an māuri=n khāli='e: twāle
then 3p=IND trouble say-PART mother=ERG only=GEN neighbor

mi=pe ^je yet-a oŋ-guju . /
person=PL(GEN) work do-PURP go-3sPST
Then they, saying there is trouble, the mother only went to work for the neighbors.

(4)
^je yet-a oŋ-ŋa oŋ-ŋa , / māuri=n=ri ãku ^tu
work do-PURP go-when go-when mother=ERG=IND there FOC

Na-en ye-u , //* ^kaeuri=ta=uri , //** āpsina bi-en , //**
eat-PART come-3PA son=DAT=IND 3pERG give-NR2

je yeŋ-a jyālā , //* jāki thi-mnā nis-mnā
work do-NR2 cost uncooked.rice one-measure two-measure

yeŋ-an hā-en , //** ^chē=ku chu-en ^nake-uju . *
take-PART bring-PART house=LOC cook-PART feed-3sPA
When (she) went to work, the mother used to eat there. The son – they gave her (her pay), with the money from working, she took and brought one or two measures of rice, cooked it at home, and fed (her son).

(5)
jur-na   jur-na: , /   thanu thanu kesi   kesi
happen-when happen-when today today tomorrow tomorrow

*yet-ŋa   yet-ŋa , //** kae   ḍwā--^kuː   jur-aː . **
do-when do-when   son   big-NR2   become-3sPST
This happening, time passed, and the son became big.

(6)
*lyās-^mā jur-a . *
young-CL become-3sPST
He became a young man.

(7)
āle   ju-eni , //   kae=n   hat-^cu   māuri=ta . ***
then become-PART   son=ERG say-3sPST mother=DAT
Then becoming (a young man), the son spoke to his mother.

(8)
*^māː . /\\   ^ji=ŋ   je   yet-a   ū-i . /***
mother   1s=EXT work do-PURP go-1FUT
"Mother, I also will go to work."

(9)
*kaeuri=n   ^wā , // māuri=ta   hat-cu . *
son=ERG TOP   mother=DAT say-3sPST
The son spoke to the mother.

(10)
*^māː . /\\   ^ji=ŋ -- **   ^thamun je   yeŋ-a   ṭhāī*
mother   1s=EXT   2hERG   work do-NR2   place

^tuŋ , *   ^ji=ŋ   je   yet-a   ^ū-i . /**   haŋ-a^ne   hat-cu   āleː . *
FOC   1s=EXT work do-PURP go-1FUT   say-PART   say-3sPST then
"Mother, the place where you work, I also will work," he said.

(11)
*haŋ-an=uri , //** ^māː   kaeu^ri   on-a   je   yet-a . ***
say-PART=IND   mother son   go-3sPST   work do-PURP
Saying this, the mother and son went to work.

(12)
oɲ-ŋa   oɲ-ŋa , /   kaeuri=^n=uŋ , //   je   yeŋ-an , //**
go-when   go-when   son=ERG=EXT   work   do-PART

thanu   thanu   kesi   kesi   yet-ŋa , //   ā^mun
today   today   tomorrow   tomorrow   do-when   3sERG

**ja^ki   hār-ju . **
uncooked.rice   bring-3sPST
Going repeatedly, the son working, as time passed, he brought (home) rice.

(13)
jā^ki   hā-ene , //   ^māuri=^ta   hat-cu . **
uncooked.rice   bring-PART   mother=DAT   say-3sPST
Bringing the rice, he spoke to his mother.

(14)
^ mā . /**   ji^n=uŋ   je   yeŋ-an   ^jāki
mother   1sERG=EXT   work   do-PART   uncooked.rice

hār-gi . /**   thamun   yeŋ-a   ^ho   jin   yeŋ-a , /**
bring-1sPST   2hERG   bring-NR2   and   1sERG   bring-NR2

jāki   ^wā: , /\\   dokhu'nuŋ   jamma   yeŋ-an , //
uncooked.rice   TOP   all   together   do-PART

jā   chu-^sin: . **   ji   je   ye^t-a   on-gi . /**   haŋ-a^ne   hat-^cu: . **
rice   cook-IMP   1s   work   do-PURP   go-1sPST   say-PART   say-3sPST
"Mother! I also worked and brought rice. The rice which you brought and which I brought, put it all together and cook it. I am going to work," so saying, (he) spoke.

(15)
haŋ-ane , //   kaeuri=n , //*   je   ye^t-a   o^n-a: . **
say-PART   son=ERG   work   do-PURP   go-3sPST
So saying, the son went to work.

(16)
haŋ-ane , // (1.2) māuri=n , //*   ^jā   chu-i , //*   haŋ-ane , //*   ^jā
say-PART   mother=ERG   rice   cook-1FUT   say-PART   rice

^kẽ   but-ke , //   jāki   ^thi-mnā   len-ke , //*
lentil cook-CAUS.PART uncooked.rice one-CL   save-CAUS.PART

^thi-mnā=uri , //** len-^ke   tar-^juː . **
one-CL=IND   save-CAUS.PART keep-3sPST

That being said, the mother said "I will cook rice," cooked rice and lentils, and saving one mana of uncooked rice aside (for another time), she saved and kept one mana.

(17)
ta-ene , // ^jā   but-^ke   māuri=n , //* ^je   yet-a
put-PART   rice cook-CAUS.PART   mother=ERG   work do-PURP

^ũ-i . /\ haŋ-ane , / pita yer-aː . /**
go-1FUT   say-PART   out come-3sPST

Putting it aside, the mother cooked rice and saying "I will go to work," she came out.

(18)
yer-nasain   waa , /* thi-^mā   jo^gi lukhā=ku   thikre^ŋ-an
come-when   TOP   one-CL   yogi   door=LOC   stand-PART

coŋ-an   coŋ-a . **
stay-PART stay-3sPST

When she came, one yogi was staying, standing at the door.

(19)
jo^gi thikreŋ-an   coŋ-a   khoŋ-an , //* ^khacinta   haŋ-an
yogi   stand-PART   stay-NR2   see-PART   saved.food   say-PART

ta-e   thi-^mnāː   jāki=uri , //**   māuri=ta , //** māuri=n , //
put-NR2   one-CL   uncooked.rice=IND   mother=DAT   mother=ERG

hā-en , /   ām   jogi=^ta   bir-juː . **
bring-PART   that yogi=DAT   give-3sPST

Seeing the yogi standing there, the mother brought the one mana of food saved for later and gave it to the yogi.

(20)
bi-eni , //   māuri , /*   je:=^ku   on-a: . \\
give-PART mother   work=LOC go-3sPST
Having given (it), the mother went to work.

(21)
je   yet-a   oŋ-ane , //   balni   jur-a , //**   je
work do-PURP go-PART   evening become-3sPST   work

^yeŋ-ane=uri , //** balni   mā: kae=ŋ , /*   nis-^mā=ŋ
do-PART=IND   evening mother son=EXT   two-CL=EXT

phark-ai   ju^r-a   chē=^ku: . **
return-BV be-3sPST   house=LOC
Going to work and it became evening. Working, in the evening, the two returned home.

(22)
chē=ku   ye-en=uri , //**   kaeuri=n   hat-cu . \\ (.87)
house=LOC   come-PART=IND   son=ERG   say-3sPST
Coming to the house, the son spoke.

(23)
jin   mega   miŋe   hā-e   jāki=e   jā
1sERG   yesterday day.before   bring-NR2   uncooked.rice=GEN   rice

^chur-mun   nā   mā . //**   haŋ-a^ne   māuri=ta   ŋen-ju . **
cook-2hPST   AGR   mother   say-PART   mother=DAT   ask-3sPST
"Did you cook the rice from the rice brought yesterday and before?" the son asked his mother.

(24)
haŋ-ane   māuri=n=ri , //*   hat-cu . **
say-PART   mother=ERG=IND   say-3sPST
He having said this, the mother spoke.

(25)
thi-mā   ^jogi: , *   ye-en   coŋ-gu , //   ^ām   thi-mnā
one-CL   yogi   come-PART   stay-3PA   that   one-CL

jāki=uri , //**   ām   ^jogi=ta   bir-gi . /
uncooked.rice=IND   that yogi=DAT   give-1sPST

haŋ-ane   hat-^cu.\\ **
say-PART say-3sPST
"A yogi came and stayed; that one measure of rice I gave to the yogi," she said.

(26)
haŋ-ane=uri, //**   ^la. /*   āu   ^thanu   hā=e   jāki=e
say-PART=IND   EXCL   now   today   bring=NR2 rice=GEN

jā   chu._   haŋ-ane, //*   kaeuri=n=^ri hat-^cu. *
rice cook(IMP) say-PART   son=ERG=IND say-3sPST
(She) having spoken, the son said: "La! Cook rice from the uncooked rice brought today," the son spoke.

(27)
āle   u   mā=uri=ta   hat-cu   kae=uri=n, //**   ^mā. /*
then :his mother=IND=DAT say-3sPST son=IND=ERG   mother

ji   āu   on-gi, //   darma   yet-a. /**   haŋ-ane   hat-cu.**
1s now go-1sPST dharma do-PURP   say-PART say-3sPST
Then the son spoke to his mother: "Mother! Now I am going, to do dharma," so saying, (he) spoke.

(28)
āle   ān^thi   haŋ-an, //   thau   mu^la   lingār-a. /*
then like.that say-PART   REFL   road   walk-3sPST
Saying like that, he walked on his own road.

(29)
āle   kae=u^ri   on-ŋa   on-ŋa   on-ŋa, //   ^thi-mā   mi=n, //*
then son=IND go-when go-when go-when   one-CL   man=ERG

nāplat^-cu   mula=^ku.**
meet-3sPST road=LOC
Then as the son went along, a man met (him) on the road.

(30)
mula=ku nāplat-ŋa, //   ām   mi=n   hat^-cu.
road=LOC meet-when   that man=ERG say-3sPST
When (he) met (him) on the road, that man spoke.

(31)
*bābu . // ^chi gibi on-an . _** haŋ-ane ŋen-^ju . **
young.one 2S where go-2sPR say-PART ask-3sPST
"Young one, where do you go?" he asked.

(32)
*ām kae=u^ri=n hat-^cu . /** ji: , /\ deu=e , \ se^wa yet-a*
that son=IND=ERG say-3sPST 1s god=GEN service do-PURP

*liŋ^gār-agi . / haŋ-ane , //** ām mi=^ta ja^wāph bir-ju .**
walk-1sPR say-PART that man=DAT answer give-3sPST
That son said: "I am walking to do the service of God," so saying, he answered that man.

(33)
jawāph bi-ene , // ām mi=n , // ām^ta hat-cu . **
answer give-PART that man=ERG 3sDAT say-3sPST
Giving the answer, that man spoke to him.

(34)
*^chin , /** deu=e ^sewā yet-a on-sa , * thi-gur khã*
2sERG god=ERG service do-PURP go-if one-CL matter

*ŋeŋ-an ^yā haŋ-ane ām^ta hat-^cu . ***
ask-PART come(IMP) say-PART 3sDAT say-3sPST
"If you are going in the service of God, ask him one thing and come back," so saying, he spoke to him.

(35)
^hāti khã ^khyaŋ janta har-^sin haŋ-an hat-^cu . *
what matter be 1sDAT say-IMP say-PART say-3sPST
"Tell me what is (that) matter," he said.

(36)
haŋ-ane , // jin yeu'ling sona=pen pir-agi , /\ tara
say-PART 1sERG however.many flower=PL plant-1sPR but

pi-en , / on-ngasin , / ām sona ^ma-mwā , / dokhu'nuŋ
plant-PART go-when that flower NEG-survive all

*wail-ai   ju-en   si^t-a . \\   hātta   ju-eu . _   **haŋ-an   hat-cu .** **
wilt-BV be-PART die-3sPST   why   happen-3FUT say-PART say-3sPST

That being said, "However many flowers I plant, but I plant them and when I go, those flowers do not survive. All of them wilted and died. Why will that happen?" he said.

(37)
āle   ^jir-a: , //**   jin   ŋeŋ-an   ^ye-i
then be.appropriate-3sPST 1sERG ask-PART come-1FUT

haŋ-ane , //**   ām   thau   mu^la   liŋā-en   o^n-a . **
say-PART   3s   REFL   road   walk-PART   go-3sPST

Then "Okay. I will ask and come (back)," so saying, he went walking on his own road.

(38)
^lita   on-ŋa   on-ŋasin , //   on-a , /   thi-mā   mi=n   nāplat-cu . *
later go-when go-when   go-3sPST   one-CL   man=ERG meet-3sPST

When he went, he went, a man met him.

(39)
thi-mā   mi=^ta   nāplat^-cu . *
one-CL man=DAT meet-3sPST

He met a man.

(40)
ām   ^mi: , //**   kho=e   ^dāti=ku   coŋ-an   coŋ-gu   hā . /**
that man   river=GEN middle=LOC stay-PART stay-3PA EVID

That man was staying in the middle of a river.

(41)
^coŋ-ŋa   coŋ-ŋa , //   āle   ām   ṭuhura   keṭā=^ri   on-a . /
stay-when stay-when   then that   orphan   boy=IND   go-3sPST

When he was there, then that orphan boy went.

(42)
*liŋār-ŋa   kho=e   ^dāti=ku   coŋ-gu   ^mi=n   ^nāplat-cu . *
walk-when river=GEN middle=LOC stay-NR1 man=ERG meet-3sPST

When he was walking along, a man in the middle of a river met (him).

(43)
nāplat-ŋasin , //** ^chi , \\ uku   ^yā   le , / **haŋ-an**
meet-when   2s   here come(IMP) PRT say-PART

satar-ju , / āle   ām   ^mi=e   na^pa   oṇ-a . /
call-3sPST then that man=GEN ASSOC go-3sPST
When they met, (he) called, saying: "You come here!", then (he) went to where that man was.

(44)
chi   gibi   ū-i^ta   yer-an . _ **haŋ-an**   **hat-cu** . \
2s   where go-PURP come-2sPR say-PART say-3sPST
He said: "You come to go where?"

(45)
ji   ^darma   yet-a   ū-i . /** oṇ-agi , // **haŋ-ane**   ām:
1s dharma do-PURP go-1FUT go-1sPR   say-PART that

^ṭuhura   keṭā=n   **hat-^cu** . /
orphan   boy=ERG say-3sPST
"I go to go do dharma," that orphan boy said.

(46)
haŋ-ane , //** āmun , //** jana   thi-gur ^khā   dam . /**
say-PART   3sERG   1sGEN one-CL matter exist

chin   ^janta , ** āmta: , \ ŋeŋ-an   ^yā   **haŋ-an**   ^**hat-cu** .\\
2sERG 1sDAT   3sDAT   ask-PART come(IMP) say-PART say-3sPST
Saying that, he said: "I have one matter. You (ask me) ask him and come (back)," he said.

(47)
haŋ-ane , / ^jir-a   hāti   khā   har-^sin . \\
say-PART   be.appropriate-3sPST what matter say-IMP

haŋ-ane   āmun   hat-cu , /** hat-ngasin=ri , /** āmun , \
say-PART 3sERG say-3sPST say-when=IND   3sERG

^ji   hātta   ^kho=e   dāti=ku   jukun cō-i   mal-a . **
1s   why   river=GEN middle=LOC only stay-INF must-3sPST

ji   gulpa^nuŋ pita   ye-i   ma-da . \\ haŋ-ane , /**
1s   never   out   come-INF NEG-have   say-PART

haŋ-an   ^hat-^cu . **
say-PART   say-3sPST

So saying, (he) said: "Okay, tell me that matter," and he said: "Why must I always stay in the middle of the river? I can never come out," so saying, he spoke.

(48)
jir-a: . /\   jin   u   khā=ŋ   ŋeŋ-an   ^ye-i
be.appropriate-3sPST   1sERG this matter=EXT   ask-PART come-1FUT

haŋ-an   ām   thau   mula   liŋar-a . /**
say-PART   3s   REFL   road   walk-3sPST

"Okay. I will ask that matter and come (back)," so saying, he walked on his own road.

(49)
on-ŋa   on-ŋa=ri , //   liŋar-ŋa   liŋar-ŋa , //   liŋar-ŋa , /*
go-when   go-when=IND   walk-when   walk-when   walk-when

thau   ^deu=e   ṭhāī   then-ju . _
REFL   god=GEN   place   arrive-3sPST

When he went on, when he was walking along, he arrived at the place of his god.

(50)
āle   āmun=^ri   hat^-cu . **
then   3sERG=IND   say-3sPST
Then he spoke.

(51)
pahila=e   mi=n , /   ^jana   hātta   yeu^li   sona=pen
before=GEN   man=ERG   1sGEN   why   however.much   flower=PL

pi-en   tar-sa   khene , /   dokhunuŋ   wail-ai   jur-a . /
plant-PART   put-if   if   all   wilt-BV   be-3sPST

haŋ-ane , /** ŋen-ju . \\
say-PART   ask-3sPST

The first man: "Why is it that however much I plant flowers, they all wilt?" so saying he asked.

(52)
ŋen-ŋasin , //* āmun   hat-cu . \
ask-when   3sERG say-3sPST

When he asked, he spoke.

(53)
deu=na   ja^wāph   bir-^ju . /**
god=ERG   answer   give-3sPST

The god answered.

(54)
jawāph bi-ŋa , /   ^ām: sona-e   tal=ku=ri , *   thi-gur
answer give-when   that   flower-GEN   under=LOC=IND   one-CL

dhan=^e: pwākā dam . /\   ām   da-e-lāgin , //   ām
wealth=GEN   packet exist   that exist-NR2-because   that

sona   yeu'li: sāhā   yer-^saŋ   wail-ai   ju-en
flower   any.amount   care   do-although   wilt-BV   be-PART

on-a . // (.97)   ^ām   dhan   pita   ma-kā   tulle , //   yeu^li
go-3sPST   that   wealth   out   NEG-take   until   any.amount

bir-sa   khe^ne   ma-ji   haŋ-ane   hat-cu . //
give-if   if   NEG-appropriate   say-PART   say-3sPST

When (he) gave his answer (he) said: "Under the flowers there is a packet of wealth. No matter what amount of care he gives those flowers, they wilted. Until that wealth is taken out, if he gives any amount of care, it won't be successful."

(55)
ām thi-gur ānthi   hat-cu . \\
3s one-CL that   say-3sPST

He said that one.

(56)
āle   ^lita me-gu=ri   mi=e   ŋen-ju , //** hāt^ta
then next other-CL=IND man=GEN ask-3sPST   why

ānthi   kho=e   dāti=ku   ju^kun   co-i   mal-a
that.manner river=GEN   middle=LOC   only   stay-INF must-3sPST
ām=ri . _** haŋ-ane   ŋen-ŋa , // (.96) āmun , //** hat-cu , //**
3s=IND   say-PART   ask-when   3sERG   say-3sPST

ām   mi=n   hat-cu , //* aame   mi∧ca: . ** thi -mā
that man=ERG say-3sPST   3sGEN   daughter   one-CL

dam . /** mi^ca: misā   thi-mā   dam , // ām   mica
exist   daughter   woman   one-CL   exist   that daughter

bihā   yeŋ-an   ma-bi   ^tulle=uri   ām   ānthi=^ku
marriage do-PART   NEG-give   until=IND   3s   that.manner=LOC

co-i   mal-a . ** āmun   haŋ-ane   hat-cu . _
stay-INF must-3sPST   3sERG say-PART say-3sPST

Then (he) asked the next man's: "Why must he only stay in the middle of the river in that manner?" When he asked, he said: "He has a daughter. There is one daughter. Until that daughter is married he must stay like that," he said.

(57)
haŋ-ane=ri , //   phark-ai   ju-ene , //   yer-a: . *
say-PART=IND   return-BV   be-PART   come-3sPST
So saying, returning he came.

(58)
phark-ai   yer-ŋa   yer-ŋa , //* ^thau   mula   yer-ŋa
return-BV come-when   come-when   REFL   road   come-when

yer-ŋa , //* pahi^lā=e   mi=ta   tu , // ām   ṭhāĩ=^ku   nāplat-cu . //
come-when   first=GEN   man=DAT   FOC   that place=LOC   meet-3sPST
When he returned, when he came along his own road, he met the first man at that place.

(59)
nāplaŋ-ane=uri, //** hāti hat-^cu. /*
meet-PART=TOP what say-3sPST
Having met (him), (he) said: "What?"

(60)
^thae ^khā:, * ŋeŋ-an yer-gi, //** hāti ha^t-ai. *
2h matter ask-PART come-1sPST what say-3sPR

haŋ-a^ne hat-^cu. \\
say-PART say-3sPST
"I asked your matter and came back." "What does (he) say," he said.

(61)
hāti hat-ʲai **haŋ-an** ām mi=n hat-^cu. *
what say-3sPR say-PART that man=ERG say-3sPST
"What does he say," the man said.

(62)
hat-nasin, //** thae sona pi-e ṭhāī=ri, /\ dhan=e, /**
say-when 2hGEN flower plant-NR2 place=IND wealth=GEN

pwāka gaḍeŋ-an tar-ai hā, // ām dhan mā-kā
packet bury-PART put-3sPR EVID that wealth NEG-take

thae sona yeu^li sāhā yer-saŋ, // wail-ai ju-en
2hGEN flower any.amount care do-although wilt-BV be-PART

on-a. \ **haŋ-a^ne:** hat-cu. \\
go-3sPST say-PART say-3sPST
When (he) said (this), "It is said that (someone) buries and keeps a packet of wealth in the place where your flowers are planted. Don't take that wealth, although you give your flowers any amount of care, they wilted and died," (he) said.

(63)
haŋ-ane, //** la ām dhan phyāŋ-ane, // pita yer-sa
say-PART EXCL that wealth dig.up-PART out come-if

khene, // ^chanta tu, // kā-u._** **haŋ-an** ām mi=n
if 2sDAT FOC take-IMP say-PART that man=ERG

haŋ-cu. **
say-3sPST

(The boy) having spoken, that man said: "La! Dig up that wealth. If it comes out, you take it."

(64)
haŋ-a^ne, /** *satna^nuŋg*, /\ *ām tal=ku dhan=e pwā^kā*
say-PART   immediately   that under=LOC wealth=GEN packet

coŋ-gu ju-en co^n-a. \\
stay-NR1 be-PART stay-3sPST

Saying this, immediately, it turns out the packet of wealth was under (there).

(65)
ām mi=n tuŋ kār-^ju. //**
that man=ERG FOC take-3sPST

That man took (it).

(66)
lita ãku=lān on-ŋa on-ŋa, //** *kho=e dāti=ku*
next there=ABL go-when go-when   river=GEN middle=LOC

mi-ta nãplat-^cu. \\
man=DAT meet-3sPST

Next when he was going from there, he met the man in the middle of the river.

(67)
nāplaŋ-an amu^n=uŋ ŋen-ju. **
meet-PART 3sERG=EXT ask-3sPST

(They) having met, he also asked.

(68)
hāti ha^t-ai haŋ-an hat-cu. **
what say-3sPR say-PART say-3sPST

"What does (he) say?" he said.

(69)
^thae=ri: ^chē=ku:, \ *thi-mā mica dam hāt-ai*. /**
2hGEN=IND house=LOC   one-CL daughter exist say-3sPR

ām misā bihā ma-yet tulle=uri , / thamu , \\
that woman marriage NEG-do until=IND 2h

u^ta cō-i mal-a hat-ai . /\ uku=lān pita
right.there stay-INF must-3sPST say-3sPR here=ABL out

ye-i ma-da hat-ai . ** haŋ-a^ne hat-cu . **
come-INF NEG-have say-3sPR say-PART say-3sPST

"He says in your house there is one daughter. He says until that woman is married, you must stay right there. You cannot come out," he said.

(70)
la . /\ tyasale , \\ jana thi-mā mica chanta ^tu
EXCL therefore 1sGEN one-CL daughter 2sDAT FOC

bir-agi . ** chanta ^tu yaŋ \\ . haŋ-ane , // ām mi=n=uŋ
give-1sPR 2sDAT FOC take(IMP) say-PART that man=ERG=EXT

hat-cu . \\
say-3sPST

"La, in that case, I give you my one daughter. You take (her)," so saying, that man spoke.

(71)
haŋ-ane , //** ām mi=n , //** ām^ta mi^ca bir-ju . \\
say-PART that man=ERG 3sDAT daughter give-3sPST

Saying this, that man gave him his daughter.

(72)
bi-ene , //** hā^ti hat-cu , \ har-sa=uri khene , //** ām mi=n
give-PART what say-3sPST say-if=IND if that man=ERG

hat-cu . **
say-3sPST

(He) gave (her), and if (you) ask what he said, that man spoke.

(73)
jana mi^ca ya-ŋ chan^ta . // la . ** dhan sampati
1sGEN daughter take-IMP 2sDAT EXCL wealth riches

dokhu^nuŋ ya-ŋ . \\   jin   dokhu^nuŋ bu-ke   chanta
all   take-IMP   1sERG   all   carry-CAUS.PART   2sDAT

chor-agi . /\   haŋ-ane , // je   mi=pen   mwāl-en , // dokhu^nuŋ: , /\
send-1sPR   say-PART   work   man=PL   search-PART   all

dhan   sampati   āmta   bu-ke   bi-en , //** mica=ŋ
wealth   riches   3sDAT   carry-CAUS.PART   give-PART   daugher=EXT

āmta   bi   chor-ju . /**
3sDAT   give.INF   send-3sPST

"I give my daughter to you. La. Take all wealth and riches. I will send you away, making you carry all of it," so saying, he looked for workers, made him carry the wealth and riches, he also gave his daughter to him.

(74)
āle   bāu^ri=n   hat-cu . \\ (1.11)
then   father=ERG   say-3sPST
Then the father spoke.

(75)
^chẽ   then-ju , /\   āle   on-nga   on-a   ^chẽ   then-ju . /**
house   arrive-3sPST   then   go-when   go-3sPST   house   arrive-3sPST
(He) arrived at the house. Then when he went, he went. He arrived at the house.

(76)
āle   māuri=n   bāuri=n   ŋen-ju . **
then   mother=ERG   father=ERG   ask-3sPST
Then his mother and father asked.

(77)
^u: nis-mā   likhana   ha-e=uri   gun . /**   misāmi=pen _
this   two-CL   behind   bring-NR2=IND   who   women=PL

haŋ-ane   hat-cu . \
say-PART   say-3sPST
"These two who you bring behind you are who," she said.

(78)
haŋ-ane=uri   u   nis-mā   thape   iri   tuŋ   khyaŋ
say-PART=IND   this   two-CL   2hGEN   d.in.law FOC   be

haŋ-aˆne hat-∧cu. \\
say-PART say-3sPST
(She) saying this, (he) said: "These two are your daughters-in-law."

(79)
haŋ-aˆne ām iri=pisna, //** ṭuṭi=ku syāudār-ju. ∧**
say-PART that d.in.law=PL.ERG foot=LOC bow-3sPST
So saying, those daughters-in-law bowed down to her feet.

(80)
ṭuṭi=ku syāudā-eˆne āle, // maˆjān ninmā iri, //** ām
foot=LOC bow-PART then perfectly m.in.law d.in.law that

ˆṭuhurā ju, //** majān coŋ-an, //** sukhā=n bityāt-hin. \\
orphan be(NR1) perfectly stay-PART happiness=ERG spend-3pPST
They having bowed down, then perfectly the mother and daughters-in-law, the one who was an orphan, lived perfectly, and spent time in happiness.

Notes

1. Matisoff (1986) provides a thorough discussion of the reasons for this state of affairs, as well as a catalog of all TB languages known to him at that time, together with their assorted names.
2. With such typological divergence attested in the daughter languages, the question of the typological nature of Proto-Tibeto-Burman (PTB) is difficult to answer. It is clear that the languages of this family are split between two linguistic areas or *Sprachbund;* hence both sides have been amenable to typological change resulting from language contact. Not surprisingly, proposals as to the structure of PTB are split along the same typological lines. One view is that PTB was morphologically simple, with no pronominal verb morphology and a minimal case system (for representative work see LaPolla 1992). Another view reconstructs extensive verb morphology and a full system of case elements (for representative work see DeLancey 1987). At this point of our scholarship, the field is split over these issues which are subjects of intensive debate.
3. Slusser (1982: 27) states, however, that there were Abhiras in northern India as well as southern. She also notes that there are not records to document a relationship between the Abhiras of India and those of Nepal, but calls such a relationship "probable".
4. Levy (1984), which focuses on the cycles of ritual in Bhaktapur, and Lewis (1984), which examines Buddhist tradition among the Tuladhar merchants of Kathmandu, provide extensive discussion of this aspect of Newar society.
5. On the other hand, as the term "Nepal" now designates the entire country and not just the Kathmandu Valley, some non-Newars feel that use of Nepal Bhasa just for the Newar language is inappropriate.
6. From the official translation published in 1992 by His Majesty's Government, Ministry of Law, Justice and Parliamentary Affairs, as reproduced in the *Himalayan Research Bulletin XI*, 1991.
7. From the official translation published in 1992 by His Majesty's Government, Ministry of Law, Justice and Parliamentary Affairs, as reproduced in the *Himalayan Research Bulletin XI*, 1991.
8. Actually, the Newar spoken in Kathmandu does not represent a single homogenous variety, but a set of sub-dialects. These are likely to reflect the many geographic and social divisions of the Newar community; however, there have been no detailed studies of the clearly attested variation in this city.
9. Interestingly, preliminary reports in the same publication listed a total population of approximately 10,000. This discrepancy with the actual survey results may be due to the recent trend of many Dolakha residents to move to other parts of the country, particularly the Kathmandu Valley, in order to find employment and increased socioeconomic success. It is possible that the original number of 10,000 may refer to

an estimate of the total number of Dolakha Newars, while 5,645 may refer to the actual number of people residing in Dolakha at the time.
10. However, they also state that the area was heavily settled by Tamangs, Thangmis, and Sherpas, ethnic groups that have clearly in this locality for many centuries.
11. According to K. Pradhan (1991: 209, note 10) there is some disagreement among historians as to the actual dates of Amsuvarma's reign. Slusser (1982: 25) states his rule "lasted from about A. D. 605–621, but his assumption of power at the courts of Sivadeva I preceded this by a decade".
12. Some evidence indicates that Dolakha had a closer relationship with Patan and Lalitpur than with Kathmandu (Vajrācārya and T. B. Shrestha 1974: 18).
13. It is also possible that there are lexical borrowings from other languages, e.g. Tibetan, Tamang, and Thangmi. Determining which lexical items are borrowings and which are cognate will be quite difficult.
14. In cases where the syllable-final consonant was nasal, the lengthened vowel was nasalized.
15. Note that [ḍ] and [r] never constrast, even following prefixes. This is because the only prefixes in the language are verbal, and there are no native r-initial verbs.
16. The verb *yer-* 'come' has irregular stem variation, with the vowel /e/ becoming /ā/ in certain circumstances (§6.8.3).
17. Phonetically, this verb and the following one have a glide [w] between the two [o] vowels (§2.3.2)
18. The two exceptions to this generalizations are *lyuri* 'bronze' and *wē* 'crazy man'. It is possible that the former is derived from *li=uri* with the clitic used for individuation. The latter exception is unusual in having a gender distinction: 'crazy woman' is *wini*. As words differentiated by gender are not generally found in the Newar lexicon, it is possible that these words are borrowings.
19. As it is difficult to incorporate special characters into Praat diagrams, I am using the following orthographic conventions in these figures: /ā/ is represented as <aa>; /ŋ/ is represented as <ng>; nasalized vowels have the tilde typed after the vowel rather than above it; retroflex consonants are represented by capitals.
20. This token and that of Figure 2–5 were produced by a female speaker with a high-pitched voice. The figures have been adjusted to display a maximum pitch of 375 (as opposed to 300) hertz.
21. Note that this transcription practice will only be used in this chapter and in Chapter 21.
22. The transcription system is based on Du Bois et al. (1993).
23. It is important to note that not all contrastive noun phrases have falling intonation. Of the 19 contrastive noun phrases in the narratives, 12 were pronounced with falling intonation, four had rising intonation, one level, and three co-occurred with the rise-fall contour. Not all contrast is marked intonationally, especially as there are other means of marking contrast in the language and other discourse factors which shape intonation curves.
24. One may note that in both cases it is the NR1 suffix which is used in the lexicalization. This is in keeping with the predominant use of NR1 in relative clauses in which

the referent of the head noun holds the role of subject. For more on the distribution of the nominalizing suffixes, see Chapter 17.
25. This terminological division is not ideal, as in some languages some morphemes traditionally labeled as adpositions actually cliticize. Here I am specifically employing this terminology to differentiate the two morphological classes of casemarkers in this language.
26. Note that these lexical items are not nouns, as they never can occur as arguments of verbs, they do not inflect like nouns, and they may not appear as the head of a complex noun phrase.
27. For discussion of grammatical relations (subject and object), see Chapter 13.
28. The aspirated initial consonant is the reflex of an old causative prefix *s- in Proto-Tibeto-Burman (Benedict 1972: 97).
29. One can wonder whether the transitive variant may have had the causative prefix *s- at some point in the history of the language, but that due to the laryngeal nature of the consonant, the reflex could not be preserved as a distinction in aspiration, as with other verbs.
30. The Nepali facts are considerably more complicated than this, but perfectivity is undoubtedly one relevant factor.
31. See Hopper and Thompson (1980) for a full discussion of these and other "transitivity parameters".
32. See Masica (1976) for work on linguistic area. See Verma and Mohanan (1990) for a range of papers on dative-experiencer constructions. Ichihashi-Nakayama (1994) contains a discussion of the dative-experiencer constructions in Nepali.
33. For an extensive study of objects, including a quantitative study on the use of dative case and a qualitative study on the syntactic status of objects, see Genetti (1997).
34. One consultant says that *jana likhana* [1sGEN behind] 'behind me', with the pronoun in genitive case, is the correct form, but that *ji likhana* [1s behind], with the pronoun in absolutive case, is acceptable as "a shortcut".
35. An alternative analysis of inflectional verb classes is provided by R. L. Shrestha (2000b). One significant difference in that analysis is that she analyzes the class of verbs which I refer to as r-stem as vowel-final stems, inserting the /r/ by phonological rule. Her primary argument for the analysis is that there are numerically more forms in this paradigm which lack the /r/ than have it. In my opinion, there is insufficient phonological motivation to justify insertion of an /r/. In addition, analyzing the /r/ as underlying also allows one to present the underlying similarities of the four inflectional classes. As is often the case, there are multiple ways to analyze a linguistic system, each with its own advantages and disadvantages.
36. One could equally say that the past-tense morpheme is zero.
37. Interestingly, the same pattern of deletion is found with the nominalized NR1 form, suggesting that this nominalizer is a likely historical source for the past-anterior-tense paradigm. This paradigm is not found in the Newar dialects of the Kathmandu Valley and I have argued that it is a Dolakhae innovation (Genetti 1994: 130).
38. When the past anterior is used with third-person subjects, it is common to omit the person/number complex, and to form the verb simply with the stem plus tense suffix. Verbs constructed in this manner are thus always identical to the nominalized forms

with NR1, and there is no obvious way to differentiate the two. My own practice has been to assume that these are past-anterior forms if they occur in sentence-final contexts, and are nominalized forms in contexts that would normally require a nominalizer (e.g. before the concatenation *ju-en con-a*). The problem is that the nominalized forms are found in sentence-final contexts when they occur in focus constructions (§17.2.3). My practice has been to assume that they are nominalizers in focus constructions if they occur with first- or second-person subjects, if the past-anterior tense is inappropriate in the context, or if it appears that a focus reading is contextually favored. However, there still remain cases where it is unclear to me which form the speaker intended.

39. During elicitation of verbal paradigms and sentences out of context, some speakers prefer to follow all verbs inflected with the future tense with the particle *jeu* 'maybe'. In naturally occuring discourse, the use of *jeu* is clearly optional, occurring roughly 10% of the time. Thus this morpheme still functions as a particle and is not a regular suffix of the future paradigm.

40. The original study on this system is Hale (1980). Hargreaves (1991, 2005) is the most extensive study of the discourse-interactional and semantic aspects of the system. Genetti (1994: 103–107) sketches the system briefly.

41. Given the variation in patterns of verbal inflection across the Newar family, one naturally wonders what the system of the proto-language was like, and how the dialects could have diverged to such an extent in this core area of their morphosyntax. This question is of particular importance, as the answer may have implications for larger historical questions, such as the positioning of Newar within the Bodic branch of Tibeto-Burman, and whether or not verbal agreement should be reconstructed at various levels of the family. Discussion of these issues is beyond the scope of the current work. The interested reader is referred to Genetti (1994: 128–136), van Driem (1992, 1993, 2001, 2003, 2004) and Kansakar (1999b).

42. "Subject" for this language is defined as the agentive argument of a transitive or ditranstive verb (the "A" argument), and the single core argument of the intransitive verb (the "S" argument). See Chapter 13 for a more detailed discussion of grammatical relations.

43. I also have elicited examples of this phenomenon with second-person subjects, although I do not have any examples in naturally-occurring discourse.

44. In Genetti (1994: 109), I analyzed the disagreement in example (8), as being the result of embedding of the clause as an indirect quote. This analysis was based in part upon some elicited examples in which an alternation of first- and third-person morphology with a first-person subject occurred with a control verb (*nāplat-* 'meet'). Since I have never found examples of this type in my body of naturally-occurring data, I am reluctant to base an analysis upon it at this time. It could be that more extensive research in this area will turn up more evidence in support of this other analysis.

45. The only exception to this is the verb *mal-* 'need', which has an irregular negative form *māl*. This verb does not inflect for separate persons, as it occurs only in dative-experiencer constructions, so is necessarily in the third-person singular.

46. It is interesting that these are the same two classes that lost their stem finals in the alternate second-plural inflection of the past anterior. It thus appears that these past-anterior forms are formed off the present/past with the addition of the suffix -ju.
47. The presence of separate inflections in these somewhat peripheral grammatical areas is interesting historically, as the Kathmandu dialect does not inflect verbs in these moods but simply uses the uninflected stem.
48. The verb yer- 'come' has irregular vowel alternations; it surfaces with the stem vowel /ā/ in the negative and imperative forms, and with /e/ elsewhere. It also has an irregular honorific form: jāsin (§6.8.3).
49. This parallelism is odd given that the imperative forms have second-person subjects, while the negative forms have third-person subjects. It could be that this paradigm predates the development of person agreement.
50. Another possible derivational affix is -(s)ke which forms an adverb from an adjectival verb, e.g. bālat- 'good; beautiful' and its negative counterpart bāmalat- 'bad; ugly', are used to derive bālaske 'well' and bāmalaske 'badly' respectively.
51. In Genetti (1994), I also list ma-khu as a possible negative form. However, this form does not occur in my textual data, and in my elicited data it occurs rarely and in the speech of one speaker only. Since ma-khu is the negative form of the cognate copula in the Kathmandu dialect, and since the speaker in question also speaks Kathmandu Newar, I assume at this point that this form is borrowed from that dialect, and is not a true Dolakhae form.
52. This example makes use of an emphatic construction in which the verb is preceded by the CV of the verb stem, followed by the emphatic parrticle he.
53. This example utilizes an emphatic negative construction.
54. Loss of the stem-final /r/ is regular for negated intransitive verbs of this class; see §6.4.
55. See Genetti and Hildebrandt (2004) for a discussion of the two adjective classes of Manange. In that language, the evidence for shared syntactic behavior between the two classes is considerably stronger.
56. In eliciting the numerals, I found speakers were particularly unclear about the form for 'seventy', probably due to the additional /s/ in 'seven'. I had to check with many people before I found one who could confidently give me this form.
57. I have also found a vigesimal system in the very closely related dialect spoken in Tauthali. However, that system is not cognate, but is based on the morpheme -bāgal 'group', e.g. nis-bāgal [two-group] 'forty', etc.
58. The Dolakha dialect differs from the Kathmandu dialect in this regard. See Bhaskararao and Joshi (1985).
59. These forms are intermediate between sortal and mensural classifiers. One can see them as either differentiating "sorts" of times (e.g. days versus months) or of being measures of mass nouns.
60. An anonymous reviewer asked whether =uri occurs on predicate nominals. I have no examples in my data but did not explicitly attempt to elicit this structure.
61. This is different from also in English where only the second noun phrase in a series will be marked, e.g. *John went; George also went.*

62. I also have three examples of this particle following a finite clause, all of which have first-person subjects. I currently do not understand why it is used in this environment.
63. The particle also occurs as *tu* although this is relatively rare. As far as I can determine, *tu* and *tuŋ* never contrast, so I will not discuss them separately. The final =*ŋ* suspiciously has the same form as the clitic of extension; however, I cannot be certain that this is its source.
64. In some languages, e.g. Mandarin Chinese (Li and Thompson 1981: 130) and Hebrew (Givón 1981), the numeral one plus a classifier (if the language allows one) is used to mark indefinite reference. While noun phrases which are new to the discourse are generally indefinite in Dolakhae, there are many indefinite noun phrases which are not preceded by the numeral one plus a classifier. Thus this construction does not seem to have grammaticalized to coding indefiniteness in this language.
65. I do have one example from discourse where both conjuncts receive the ergative casemarker. However, there is a significant intonation boundary between them and a long pause, which suggests the speaker may not have fully planned to produce a co-ordinated structure at the time the first casemarker was produced. I also have some elicited data from one consultant which suggests such structures are also possible, e.g. *jana mā=n ho dāi=na* [1sGEN and e.brother=ERG] 'my mother and elder brother'.
66. One piece of evidence that this is a list of distinct noun phrases, as opposed to a single noun phrase, is the presence of the plural clitic on two separate elements in the list. The plural clitic only has scope over the immediate noun phrase, and not to every element in the list.
67. This example has emphatic negation marked by the affirmative verb, followed by the focus particle, followed by the negated verb.
68. This is the only example I have found of the form *khe* without the negative prefix. It was produced by one of the oldest speakers I worked with.
69. Causativized transitive verbs can also produce a ditransitive structure, see §15.2. Caused motion verbs, like 'move' or 'put' have an optional locative element. The verb *chor-* 'send' technically can be ditransitive with an inanimate O and an animate and dative-marked recipient, but speakers prefer to use the verb *bir-* 'give' in such constructions (i.e. *bi chor-*). The verb *chor-* 'send' is more commonly used to send someone or something to a place or to send someone away.
70. O arguments which receive dative case are generally human and given; all others are absolutive. See §4.2.6.
71. This is true for the eventive copula *jur-* 'be, happen, become'; the stative copula *khyaŋ* is defective and does not have an agreement paradigm (see §6.7.1).
72. One could also consider the complementation strategy involving auxiliaries following infinitive verbs as exhibiting a similar type of backwards control. I prefer to analyze such examples as monoclausal, due to the fact that the final verb agrees in person and number with the subject. See §18.3.1 for discussion.
73. It is possible for a reflexive to have its referent contextually determined, rather than being determined through antecedence in the discourse, in which case it refers to the speaker, e.g. *tibi=uri thau chē=ku ma-da* [television=IND REFL house=LOC NEG-have] 'I don't have a television at my own house'. However, this does not negate the gen-

eralization that if a reflexive has an antecedent in the discourse, it will be a subject argument. See §15.5.
74. These figures are based on Dryer (1986: 814).
75. This could equally mean 'Then he gave the cook to her'. As far as I know, there is no way to differentiate the O and R roles in this example. Culturally, however, it is more common for the bride to be conceptualized as the one given and received.
76. The concept of referential density (e.g. Bickel 2003) depends strongly on the the assumption that each overt noun phrase can only serve as a core argument of only one verb. I do not hold to this assumption. The syntactic patterns of Dolakha Newar strongly suggest that a single overt noun phrase can serve as an argument of more than one verb. These issues are discussed in Chapter 19, §5.2 and in Chapter 21.
77. For information on emphatic constructions with the copula *khyaŋ* and with the collocation *ju-en con-a*, see §17.2.2.
78. I have close to 100 examples of causatives in connected discourse, but none have all arguments expressed. For that reason, I will primarily use elicited data to illustrate the casemarking patterns.
79. Note that in the past tense there is an implicature that the transfer of the object did indeed take place. Otherwise, one would say something such as 'bring in order to give'.
80. This prefix, like the negative and optative, undergoes vowel harmony as discussed in §2.3.5.
81. Section 13.2.4 discusses reflexives with respect to grammatical relations. Crucially in a sentence with two logically possible antecedents, the reflexive obligatorily refers to the subject. To have the grammatical object be the antecedent, the reflexive must be replaced by the possessive pronoun followed by the focus particle, *āme tuŋ*.
82. When verbs are borrowed, the borrowed verb is necessarily followed by a native verb (*jur-* for intransitives and *yet-* for transitives) which takes all the inflections, including the negative prefix. See §6.3.
83. The verb *ur-* 'dance' is a cognate-object verb, requiring the noun *pyākhan* 'dance' as its object. The two together form a compound.
84. In recent fieldwork, I found that the Tauthali Newar dialect also has four inflectional tenses along with a similar parardigm for person and number. This system of verbal inflection appears to establish an eastern branch of dialects in the Newar family.
85. This verb has irregular inflection, with two present forms *dam*, *damu* (§6.7.2). For information on clause structure, see §12.4.1.
86. This example was produced in a retelling of a portion of the great Hindu epic, the Mahābhārata. In one part of the story, a prince is arranging a second marriage for his father, and the father of the proposed bride worries that the prince himself will marry and that the power of the prince's wife and children will eclipse the prospects of his own daughter. In the traditional story, the prince addresses the father's fears by taking a vow of celibacy. In the version I recorded, the speaker has the prince resolve the situation as shown in the example. In current parlance, when a man "does family planning", he has a vasectomy. This is an interesting modern take on the story which effectively disqualifies the prince as a progenitor, yet to my mind it leaves one without the sense of self-control and moral rectitude implied by the original version.

87. Despite the past-tense morphology, the salient meaning is not that the state has been entered into (inception) but that it is ongoing. There are a number of other means to indicate entrance into a state. With adjectival verbs, one would nominalize the adjectival verb and use the *jur-a* 'became' as the main predicate. Other verbs would require the use of distinct auxiliaries, see §16.3.3.5.
88. It should be noted that I am not using the term 'anterior' in the sense of Bybee et al. (1994: 54) who collapse "anterior" with "perfect". I see perfect as differing from anterior in additionally having a sense of current relevance. Current relevance is not an inherent component of the past-anterior tense in Dolakhae. Perfects are discussed in §16.3.2.
89. Technically speaking, the future tense may be considered not to be a tense at all, but to be a modal category (prediction). However, since it occurs in a four-way paradigmatic relationship with the other three tenses, I will continue to call it a tense.
90. The verb *rāk yet-* using the volitional verb *yet-* 'do', indicates that getting angry is a volitional choice of the actor. The past tense would be *rāk yet-cu*. The auxiliary is clearly indicating continuous aspect.
91. I will use the term "simple nominalized complements" to refer to nominalized complements of verbs. This contrasts with the term "nominal complement" which refers to nominalized complements of nouns.
92. In other languages, one can also find nominalized clauses functioning as NPs in a construction known as "action nominalization". An example in English is the nominalization *smoking cigarettes* in the sentence *Smoking cigarettes is bad for one's health*. Although I have elicited such constructions in Dolakha Newar, I have never come across them in connected discourse. Speakers prefer other means of presenting information that might be packaged as an action nominalization in English. For example, the English sentence *Her dancing was beautiful*, might be rendered in Dolakhae with an adverbial clause, e.g. *pyākhan ur-nasin ām bãla-ku jur-a* [dance dance-when that beautiful-NR1 happen-3sPST] 'when she danced, she was beautiful'. On the other hand, speakers accepted as possible my constructed examples which used nominalization, e.g. [*āmun pyākhan u-e*] *bãla-ku* [3sERG dance dance-NR2 beautiful-NR1]. Given the marginal nature of this construction, it will not be further commented upon.
93. To further complicate matters, there are slight differences in the intuitions of my two consultants. At this point, I see these differences as being due to one consultant having a stronger preference for the normative pattern, so I have not highlighted them here. Details may be found in Genetti (1994: 154–171).
94. See Givón (1980, 1990: 515–561) for a discussion of iconicity in the complementation of English.
95. Double-say constructions, such as this one, are not unique to Dolakha Newar, nor to Newar as a family. Rather, they are widely attested in South Asia, occurring in Nepali and Hindi, as well as in other regional languages (see e.g. Hock 1982; Masica 1991: 403; Noonan 1999; Saxena 1988).
96. I do have some examples of postposed participial clauses, but they all express events or states which overlap temporally with the event or state of the matrix, and not sequences, e.g.:

nas-nu	ṭulle	na-i	tuŋ	mal-a	pyāṭā	dar-ai	ju-en
nine-day	until	eat-INF	FOC	need-3sPST	stomach	bloat-BV	happen-PART

'For nine days, I needed to eat, my stomach bloating.'

97. This fact has allowed for the grammaticalization of versatile verbs in final position into auxiliaries. If final verbs were always of primary syntactic and semantic importance, they would be unlikely to bleach semantically and lose their argument structure.
98. This analysis of clause linkage is similar but not identical to "core juncture" of Role and Reference Grammar (Foley and Van Valin 1984; Van Valin and LaPolla 1997). Genetti (2005) compares the two approaches and notes problems encountered in applying Role and Reference Grammar to the current construction.
99. This conceptualization of different "voices" of the speaker in the production of narrative originated with Jim Reed, a former graduate student at the University of California, Santa Barbara.
100. Note that this analysis has repercussions for the notion of *referential density*, a calculation of the ratio of overt NPs as to argument slots in a stretch of discourse (e.g. Bickel 2003). My analysis, which allows a single overt argument to function as an argument of multiple verbs, would result in a much higher calculation of referential density than one which assumes that each overt noun phrase can only be a grammatical argument of one verb.

References

Aikhenvald, Alexandra Y.
    2003   *Classifiers: A Typology of Noun Categorization Devices.* New York: Oxford University Press.

Basham, Arthur L.
    1963   *The Wonder That Was India: A Study of the History and Culture of the Indian Sub-continent Before the Coming of the Muslims.* New York: Hawthorne Books.

Bendall, Cecil
    1903   The history of Nepal and surrounding kingdoms. *Journal of the Asiatic Society of Bengal* 1: 1–33.

Benedict, Paul K.
    1972   *Sino-Tibetan: A Conspectus.* Cambridge: Cambridge University Press.

Bhaskararao, Peri, and Sunder Krishna Joshi
    1985   A study of Newari classifiers. *Bulletin of the Deccan College Research Institute* 44: 17–31.

Bickel, Balthasar
    1995   Relatives à antécédent interne, nominalisation et focalisation: Entre syntaxe et morphologie en Bélharien. *Bulletin de La Société de Linguistique de Paris* XC (1): 391–427.
    1998   Converbs in cross-linguistic perspective. *Linguistic Typology* 2: 381–397.
    1999   Nominalization and focus in some Kiranti languages. In *Topics in Nepalese Linguistics*, Yogendra P. Yadava and Warren W. Glover (eds.), 271–296. Kamaladi, Kathmandu: Royal Nepal Academy.
    2000   Space, territory, and a stupa in Eastern Nepal: Exploring Himalayan themes and traces of Bon. In *New Horizons in Bon Studies*, Samten G. Karmay and Yasuhiko Nagano (eds.), 685–702. Osaka: National Museum of Ethnology.
    2003   Referential density in discourse and syntactic typology. *Language* 79: 708–736.

Bradley, David
    1979   *Proto-Loloish.* London: Curzon Press Ltd.
    1997   Tibeto-Burman languages and classification. In *Papers in Southeast Asian Linguistics No. 14: Tibeto-Burman Languages of the Himalayas*, David Bradley (ed.), 1–72. Canberra: Pacific Linguistics Research School of Pacific and Asian Studies, Australian National University.

Bybee, Joan L., Revere Perkins, and William Pagliuca
    1994   *The Evolution of Grammar: Tense, Aspect, and Modality in the Languages of the World.* Chicago: University of Chicago Press.

Chafe, Wallace
- 1987 Cognitive constraints on information flow. In *Coherence and Grounding in Discourse*, Russel S. Tomlin (ed.), 21–51 Amsterdam: John Benjamins.
- 1994 *Discourse, Consciousness, and Time: The Flow and Displacement of Conscious Experience in Speaking and Writing*. Chicago/London: University of Chicago Press.

Comrie, Bernard
- 1981 *Language Universals and Linguistics Typology: Syntax and Morphology*. Chicago: University of Chicago Press.
- 1985 *Aspect: An Introduction to the Study of Verbal Aspect and Related Problems*. Cambridge: Cambridge University Press.

Comrie, Bernard, and Sandra A. Thompson
- 1985 Lexical nominalization. In *Language Typology and Syntactic Description Volume III: Grammatical Categories and the Lexicon*, Timothy Shopen (ed.), 349–398. Cambridge: Cambridge University Press.

Crain, Laura Diane
- 1992 Clause chaining in Nepali discourse. Unpublished Archival Material, University of California, Los Angeles.

Davison, Alice
- 1981 Syntactic and semantic indeterminacy resolved: A mostly pragmatic analysis for the Hindi conjunctive participle. In *Radical Pragmatics*, Peter Cole (ed.), 101–128. New York: Academic Press.

DeLancey, Scott
- 1987 Sino-Tibetan languages. In *The World's Major Languages*, Bernard Comrie (ed.), 797–810. New York: Oxford University Press.
- 1989 Verb agreement in Proto-Tibeto-Burman. *Bulletin of the School of Oriental and African Studies* 52 (2): 315–333.
- 1991 The origins of verb serialization in Modern Tibetan. *Studies in Language* 15 (1): 1–23.
- 1999 Relativization in Tibetan. In *Topics in Nepalese Linguistics*, Yogendra P. Yadava and Warren W. Glover (eds.), 231–249. Kamaladi, Kathmandu: Royal Nepal Academy.

Dixon, Robert M. W.
- 1995 Complement clauses and complementation strategies. In *Grammar and Meaning: Essays in Honour of Sir John Lyons*, Frank R. Palmer (ed.), 175–220. Cambridge: Cambridge University Press.
- 2004 Adjective classes in typological perspective. In *Adjective Classes: A Cross-Linguistic Typology*, Robert M. W. Dixon and Alexandra Y. Aikhenvald (eds.), 1–49. New York: Oxford University Press.
- 2006 Complement clauses and complementation strategies in typological perspective. In *Complementation: A Cross-Linguistic Typology*, Robert M. W. Dixon and Alexandra Y. Aikhenvald (eds.), 1–48. (Explorations in Linguistic Typology 3.) Oxford: Oxford University Press.

Dixon, Robert M. W., and Alexandra Aikhenvald
- 2002a *Word: A Cross-Linguistic Typology*. Cambridge: Cambridge University Press.
- 2002b Word: A typological framework. In *Word: A Cross-Linguistic Typology*, Robert M. W. Dixon and Alexandra Aikhenvald (eds.), 1–41. Cambridge: Cambridge Univesity Press.

Doherty, Victor S.
- 1978 Notes on the origins of the Newars of the Kathmandu valley. In *Himalayan Anthropology: The Indo-Tibetan Interface*, James F. Fisher (ed.), 433–445. Paris/Gravenhage: Mouton Publishers.

Doke, C. M.
- 1935 *Bantu Linguistic Terminology*. London: Longmans.

Dorian, Nancy C.
- 1994 Varieties of variation in a very small place: Social homogeneity, prestige norms, and linguistic variation. *Language* 70: 631–696.
- 2001 Surprises in Sutherland: Linguistic variability amidst social uniformity. In *Linguistic Fieldwork*, Paul Newman and Marthat Ratliff (eds.), 133–151. Cambridge: Cambridge University Press.

Dryer, Matthew S.
- 1986 Primary objects, secondary objects, and antidative. *Language* 62 (4): 808–845.

Du Bois, John W., Stephan Schuetze-Coburn, Susanna Cumming, and Danae Paolino
- 1993 Outline of discourse transcription. In *Talking Data: Transcription and Coding in Discourse Research*, Jane A. Edwards and Martin D. Lampert (eds.), 45–89. Hillsdale: Lawrence Erlbaum Associates Publishers.

Durie, Mark
- 2003 New light on information pressure: Information conduits, "escape valves", and role alignment stretching. In *Preferred Argument Structure: Grammar as Architecture for Function*, John W. Du Bois, Lorrain E. Kumpf, and William J. Ashby (eds.), 159–196. Amsterdam: John Benjamins.

Ebert, Karen H.
- 1994 *The Structure of Kiranti Languages*. Zürich: ASAS-Verlag.

Foley, William A., and Robert D. Van Valin, Jr.
- 1984 *Functional Syntax and Universal Grammar*. Cambridge: Cambridge University Press.

Gellner, David N.
- 1992 *Monk, Householder, and Tantric Priest*. Cambridge: Cambridge University Press.

Genetti, Carol
- 1986 The grammatical development of postpositions to subordinators in Bodic languages. *Proceedings of the Twelfth Annual Meeting of the Berkeley Linguistics Society* 12: 387–400.
- 1988 A syntactic correlate of topicality in Newari narrative. In *Clause Combining in Grammar and Discourse*, John Haiman and Sandra A. Thompson (eds.), 29–48. Amsterdam: John Benjamins.

1990   A descriptive and historical account of the Dolakha Newari dialect. Ph.d. diss., Department of Linguistics, University of Oregon.
1991   From postposition to subordinator in Newari. In *Approaches to Grammaticalization*, Elizabeth Traugott and Bernd Heine (eds.), 227–256. Philadelphia: John Benjamins.
1992   Semantic and grammatical categories of relative-clause morphology in the languages of Nepal. *Studies in Language* 16 (2): 405–427.
1994   *A Descriptive and Historical Account of the Dolakha Newari Dialect* (Vol. 24). Tokyo, Japan: Institute for the Study of Languages and Cultures of Asia and Africa.
1997   Object relations and dative case in Dolakha Newari. *Studies in Language* 21 (1): 33–62.
1999   Variation in agreement in the Nepali finite verb. In *Topics in Nepalese Linguistics*, Yogendra P. Yadava and Warren W. Glover (eds.), 542–555. Kamaladi, Kathmandu: Royal Nepal Academy.
2003a   Dolakhā Newār. In *The Sino-Tibetan Languages*, Graham Thurgood and Randy J. LaPolla (eds.), 353–370. London: Routledge.
2003b   Syntax, prosody, and typology: Evidence from prosodic embedding in Dolakha Newar. In *Proceedings of IP 2003, Interfaces Prosodiques/Prosodic Interfaces*, Amina Mettouchi and Gaëlle Ferré (eds.), 111–116. Nantes, France: Acoustique, Acquisition, Interpretation.
2005   The participial construction in Dolakha Newar: Syntactic implications of an Asian converb. *Studies in Language* 29 (1): 35–87.
in press   Complementation in Dolakha Newar. In *Complementation: A Cross-Linguistic Typology*, Robert M. W. Dixon and Alexandra Y. Aikhenvald (eds.), 137–158. (Explorations in Linguistic Typology 3.) Oxford: Oxford University Press.

Genetti, Carol, and Laura Diane Crain
2003   Beyond preferred argument structure: Sentences, pronouns, and given referents in Nepali. In *Preferred Argument Structure: Grammar as Architecture for Function*, John W. Du Bois, Lorrain E. Kumpf, and William J. Ashby (eds.), 197–223. Amsterdam: John Benjamins.

Genetti, Carol, and Kristine Hildebrandt
2004   The two adjective classes in Manange. In *Adjective Classes: A Cross-Linguistic Typology*, Robert M. W. Dixon and Alexandra Aikhenvald (eds.), 74–97. Oxford: Oxford University Press.

Genetti, Carol, and Keith Slater
2004   An analysis of syntax/prosody interactions in a Dolakhā Newār rendition of the Mahābhārata. *Himalayan Linguistics* 3: 1–91.

Givón, Talmy
1980   The binding hierarchy and the typology of complements. *Studies in Language* 4 (3): 33–77.
1981   On the development of the numeral 'one' as an indefinite marker. *Folia Linguistics Historica* 2 (1): 35–53.
1984   *Syntax: A Functional-Typological Introduction, Volume I*. Amsterdam: John Benjamins.

1985 Iconicity, isomorphism, and non-arbitrary coding in syntax. In *Iconicity in Syntax*, John Haiman (ed.), 187.219. Amsterdam: John Benjamins.
1990 *Syntax: A Functional-Typological Introduction, Volume II.* Amsterdam/Philadelphia: John Benjamins.
1991 Serial verbs and the mental reality of 'event': Grammatical vs. cognitive packaging. In *Approaches to Grammaticalization*, Elizabeth Traugott and Bernd Heine (eds.), 81–128. Amsterdam: John Benjamins.

Glover, Warren W.
1970 Cognate counts via the Swadesh list in some Tibeto-Burman languages of Nepal. In *The Tone Systems of Tibeto-Burman Languages of Nepal*, F. K. Lehman (ed.), 23–36. (Occasional Papers of the Wolfenden Society 3.) Urbana: Department of Linguistics, Univeristy of Illinois.

Grierson, G. A.
1927 *Linguistic Survey of India, Volume 1.* Delhi/Varanasi/Patna: Motilal Banarsidass.

Haiman, John
1983 Iconic and economic motivation. *Language* 59: 781–819.
1985 *Iconicity in Syntax.* Amsterdam: John Benjamins.

Hale, Austin
1973 On the form of verbal bases in Newari. In *Issues in Linguistics: Papers in Honor of Henry and Rene Kahanee*, Braj B. Kachru, Robert B. Lees, Yakov Malkiel, Angelina Pietrangeli, and Sol Saporta (eds.), 279–299. Urbana: University of Illinois Press.
1980 Person markers: Finite conjunct and disjunct verb forms in Newari. In *Papers in South-East Asian Linguistics 7,* Ronald L. Trail (ed.), 95–106. Canberra: Pacific Linguistics [Series A, No. 53].
1986 User's guide to the Newari dictionary. In *Newari-English Dictionary: Modern Language of the Kathmandu Valley*, Thakur Lal Manandhar (author) and Anne Vergati (ed.), xxii–xlvi. Delhi: Agam Kala Prakashan.

Hale, Austin, and Thakur Lal Manandhar
1980 Case and role in Newari. In *Papers in South-East Asian Linguistics 7*, Ronald L. Trail (ed.), 79–93. Canberra: Pacific Linguistics [Series A, No. 53].

Hale, Austin, and Kedar P. Shrestha
1999 On the senses of the Newar conjunctive participle *-a:*. In *Topics in Nepalese Linguistics*, Yogendra P. Yadava and Warren W. Glover (eds.), 287–336. Kathmandu: Royal Nepal Academy.
2006 *Newār (Nepāl Bhāṣā).* (Languages of the World/Materials 256.) Muenchen: Lincom Europa.

Hale, Austin, and David Watters
1973 A survey of clause patterns. In *Clause, Sentence, and Discourse Patterns in Selected Languages of Nepal, Volume II: Clause*, Austin Hale

and David Watters (eds.), 175–249. Norman: Summer Institute of Linguistics.

Hansson, Gerd
1991 *The Rai of Eastern Nepal: Ethnic and Lingusitic Grouping Findings of the Linguistic Survey of Nepal.* Kirtipur, Kathmandu: Linguistic Society of Nepal and Centre for Nepal and Asian Studies, Tribhuvan University.

Hargreaves, David
1991 The concept of intentional action in the grammar of Kathmandu Newari (Nepal). Ph. D. diss., Linguistics, University of Oregon.
2003 Kathmandu Newar (Nepāl Bhās'ā). In *The Sino-Tibetan Languages*, Graham Thurgood and Randy J. LaPolla (eds.), 371–384. London: Routledge.
2005 Agency and intentional action in Kathmandu Newar. *Himalayan Linguistics* 5: 1–48.

Hashimoto, Mantaro J.
1977 *The Newari Language: A Classified Lexicon of its Bhadgaon Dialect* (Vol. 2). Tokyo: Institute for the Study of Languages and Cultures of Asia and Africa.

Haspelmath, Martin, and Ekkehard König (eds.)
1995 *Converbs in Cross-Linguistics Perspective: Structure and Meaning of Adverbial Verb Forms.* Berlin: Mouton de Gruyter.

His Majesty's Government
1993 *Nepal and Figures 1993.* Kathmandu: Central Bureau of Statistics.

Hock, Hans Henrich
1982 The Sanskrit quotative: A historical and comparative study. *Studies in the Linguistic Sciences* 12 (2): 39–85.

Hodgson, Brian Houghton
1847 On the aborigines of the sub-Himalayas. *Journal of the Asiatic Society of Bengal* 16: 1235–1244.

Hopper, Paul J., and Sandra A. Thompson
1980 Transitivity in grammar and discourse. *Language* 56 (2): 251–299.

Ichihashi-Nakayama, Kumiko
1994 On dative 'subject' constructions in Nepali. In *Aspects of Nepali Grammar*, Carol Genetti (ed.), 41–76. (Santa Barbara Papers in Linguistics 6.) Santa Barbara: Department of Linguistics, University of California, Santa Barbara.

Joshi, Sunder Krishna
1984 A descriptive study of the Bhaktapur dialect of Newari. Ph. D. diss., University of Poona.
1992 *Nepalbhashaya Bhashavaijñanik Vyakaran.* Kathmandu: Lacoul Publications.

Jørgensen, Hans
1931 *Vicitrakarṇikavadanoddhrtha.* London: The Royal Asiatic Society.
1936 *A Dictionary of the Classical Newari.* (Historisk-filologiske Meddelelser XXIII/1) Copenhagen: Levin & Munksgaard.

1939   *Batisputrikhakatha: A Tale of Thirty-Two Statuettes.* Copenhagen: Munksgaard.
1941   *A Grammar of the Classical Newari.* (Historisk-filologiske Meddelelser XXVII/3) Copenhagen: Levin & Munksgaard.

Kachru, Yamuna
1981   On the syntax, semantics, and pragmatics of the conjunctive participle in Hindi-Urdu. *Studies in the Linguistic Sciences* 11 (2): 35–50.

Kalinchowk Youth Club
1988   *Comprehensive Baseline Survey of Dolakha Village Panchayat.* Kathmandu: Lasata Press.

Kansakar, Tej R.
1999a   The syntactic typology of Newar and Tamang languages. *Gipan* 1 (1): 1–42.
1999b   Verb agreement in Classical Newar and Modern Newar dialects. In *Topics in Nepalese Linguistics*, Yogendra P. Yadava and Warren W. Glover (eds.), 297–336. Kamaladi, Kathmandu: Royal Nepal Academy.

Kölver, Ulrike
1977   *Nominalization and Lexicalization in Modern Newari* (Vol. 30). Köln: Arbeiten des Kölner Universalien-Projekts.

Kölver, Ulrike, and Iswaranand Shresthacarya
1994   *A Dictionary of Contemporary Newari (Newari-English).* Bonn: VGH Wissenschaftsverlag.

König, Ekkehard, and Siemund, Peter
2005   Intensifiers and reflexives. In *The World Atlas of Language Structures*, Bernard Comrie, Matthew Dryer, Martin Haspelmath, and David Gil (eds.), 194–197. Oxford: Oxford University Press.

Ladefoged, Peter
1993   *A Course in Phonetics.* 3d ed. Fort Worth: Harcourt Brace College Publishers.

LaPolla, Randy J.
1992   On the dating and nature of verb agreeement in Tibeto-Burman. *Bulletin of the School of Oriental and African Studies* 55 (2): 298–315.
2001   The role of migration and language contact in the development of the Sino-Tibetan language family. In *Areal Diffusion and Genetic Inheritance*, Alexandra Y. Aikhenvald and Robert M. W. Dixon (eds.), 225–254. Oxford: Oxford University Press.

Laver, John
1994   *Principles of Phonetics.* Cambridge: Cambridge University Press.

Lehmann, Christian
1988   Towards a typology of clause linkage. In *Clause Combining in Grammar and Discourse*, John Haiman and Sandra A. Thompson (eds.), 181–226. Amsterdam/Philadelphia: John Benjamins.

Levy, Robert I.
1984   *Mesocosm: Hinduism and the Organization of A Traditional Newar City in Nepal.* Berkeley: University of California Press.

Lewis, Todd Thornton
    1984   The Tuladhars of Kathmandu: A study of Buddhist tradition in a Newar merchant community. Ph. D. diss., Graduate School of Arts and Sciences, Columbia University.

Li, Charles, and Sandra A. Thompson
    1981   *Mandarin Chinese: A Functional Reference Grammar.* Berkeley/Los Angeles/London: University of California Press.

Longacre, Robert
    1968   *Philippine Languages: Discourse, Paragraph, and Sentence Structure.* Santa Ana, California: Summer Institute of Linguistics.

Maddieson, Ian
    2005   Tone. In *The World Atlas of Language Structures*, Bernard Comrie, Martin Haspelmath, Matthew S. Dryer, and David Gil (eds.), 58–61. Oxford: Oxford University Press.

Mali, Indra
    1979   *Dolakha Bhashika Va Chum* [The Dolakha dialect and other topics]. Kathmandu: Cibhaa Prakasan.
    1982   *Paharī Bhās.Ikā Chagū Adhyayan* [A Study of the Pahari Dialect]. Kathmandu: Thapu Puca.

Malla, Kamal P.
    1982   *Classical Newari Literature: A Sketch.* Kathmandu: Educational Enterprise.
    1985   *The Newari Language: A Working Outline.* Tokyo: Institute for the Study of Languages and Cultures of Asia and Africa.
    1990   The earliest dated document in Newari: The palmleaf from Uku Bahah NS 235/AD 1114. *Kailash* XVI (1): 15–25.

Masica, Colin
    1976   *Defining A Linguistic Area: South Asia.* Chicago: University of Chicago Press.
    1991   *The Indo-Aryan Languages.* Cambridge: Cambridge University Press.

Matisoff, James A.
    1969   Verb concatenation in Lahu: The syntax and semantics of "simple juxtaposition". *Acta Linguistica Hafniensia* 12: 69–120.
    1972   Lahu nominalization, relativization, and genetivization. In *Syntax and Semantics*, John P. Kimball (ed.), 237–257. New York: Academic Press.
    1986   The languages and dialects of Tibeto-Burman: An alphabetic/genetic listing, with some prefatory remarks on ethnonymic and glossonymic complications. In *Contributions to Sino-Tibetan Studies*, John McCoy and Timothy Light (eds.), 3–75. Leiden: E. J. Brill.
    1990   On megalocomparison. *Language* 66: 106–120.
    1994   Regularity and variation in Sino-Tibetan. In *Current Issues in Sino-Tibetan Linguistics*, Hajime Kitamura, Tatsuo Nishida, and Yasuhiko Nagano (eds.), 36–58. Osaka: National Museum of Ethnology.
    1997   *Sino-Tibetan Numeral Systems: Prefixes, Proforms, and Problems.* (Vol. 114). Canberra, A.C.T., Australia: Pacific Linguistics Research School of Pacific and Asian Studies, Australian National University.

Nepal Bhasa Dictionary Committee
 2000 *A Dictionary of Classical Newari.* Kathmandu: Cwasā Pāsā.

Nepali, Gopal Singh
 1965 *The Newars, and Ethno-Sociological Study of a Himalayan Community.* Bombay: United Asia Publication.

Newami, Darasha.
 1984 Bandipur ya Newa: wa Nepal Bhasa [Bandipur Newar and the Newar language]. *Nhasala* 9.9: 25–27.
 1993 Bandipur ya Nepal Bhasa [*The Bandipur Dialect of the Newar Language*]. Kathmandu: Ram Bhakta Bhomi.

Noonan, Michael
 1985 Complementation. In *Language Typology and Syntactic Description*, Timothy Shopen (ed.), 42–140. Cambridge: Cambridge University Press.
 1997 Versatile nominalization. In *Essays on Language Function and Language Type*, Joan Bybee, John Haiman, and Sandra A. Thompson (eds.), 373–394. Amsterdam: John Benjamins.
 1999 Converbal constructions in Chantyal. In *Topics in Nepalese Linguistics*, Yogendra P. Yadava and Warren W. Glover (eds.), 401–420. Kathmandu: Royal Nepal Academy.

Payne, Thomas
 1997 *Describing Morphosyntax: A Guide for Field Linguists.* Cambridge: Cambridge University Press.

Poffenberger, Mark
 1980 *Patterns of Change in the Nepal Himalaya.* Delhi: The Macmillan Co. of India.

Pradhan, Indu
 2001 Dolakhali Lokgitko Sangkalak, Vagikaran ra Vislesan [Musical classification and analysis of folk songs of Dolakha]. M. A. thesis, Nepali Department, Tribhuvan University.

Pradhan, Kumar
 1991 *The Gorhka Conquests: The Process and Consequences of the Unification of Nepal, With Particular Reference to Eastern Nepal.* Calcutta: Oxford University Press.

Pradhan, Uma
 2003 Dolakha Newarbhasa Vidhyarthiharule Vakya Lekhanma Garne Trutiharuko Adhyayan [A study of errors of Dolakha Newar students while writing sentences]. M.A. thesis, Nepali Department, Tribhuvan University.

Saxena, Anju
 1988 On syntactic convergence: The case of the verb *say* in Tibeto-Burman. *Proceedings of the Fourteenth Annual Meeting of the Berkeley Lingusitics Society* 14: 355–388.

Sayami, Prem
 1986 *Dolakhaya Nepalbhasa Khanpumuna* [Collection of Dolakha Newar]. Kirtipur: Nepal and Asian Research Center.

Shafer, Robert
    1952   Newari and Sino-Tibetan. *Studia Linguistica* 6: 92–109.

Shakya, Daya R.
    1992   Nominal and verbal morphology in six dialects of Newari. M. A. thesis, Department of Linguistics, University of Oregon.
    2000   One language, two systems: Nepāl Bhāsā verb morphology (data from ten dialects). Paper presented at the 6th Himalayan Language Symposium (June 15–17), University of Wisconsin, Milwaukee.

Shrestha, Bal Gopal
    1999   The Newars: The indigenous population of the Kathmandu Valley in the modern state of Nepal. *Contributions to Nepalese Studies* 26 (1): 83–117.

Shrestha, Omkareshwor
    2000   Verb morphology in the Tansen dialect of Nepal Bhasha. M.A. Thesis, Central Department of English, Tribhuvan University.
    2001   *Tansen Neva: Bhasikay Rupayana Paddhati* [Inflection system in the Tansen dialect of Nepalbhasa]. Yala: Nepalmandala Gha:ca: dhuku.

Shrestha, Rudra Laxmi
    1989   Verb inflection in the Dolakha dialect of Nepal Bhasa. *Rolamba* 9 (2): 40–50.
    1993   *Dolkha Newa: Bhasaya Varnanatmak Adhyan* [A Descriptive Study of Verb Morphology of Dolkha Dialect]. Yala: Nepalmandala Gha:ca: dhuku.
    2000a   *Dolakha Bhasakaya Khāgwa:puca:* [Collection of Dolakha Newar vocabulary]. Yala: Nepalmandala Gha:ca: dhuku.
    2000b   *Dolakhā Newa: Bhayyā Kriya: Chagu Adhyayan* [Verb Morphology of Dolakha Newar: A Study]. Yala: Nepalmandala Gha:ca: dhuku.
    2003   Verbal morphology of the Badikhel Pahari dialect of Newar. In *Themes in Himalayan Languages and Linguistics*, Tej R. Kansakar and Mark Turin (eds.), 145–162. Heidelberg/Kathmandu: South Asia Institute and Tribhuvan University.

Shrestha, Uma
    1990   Social networks and code-switching in the Newar community of Kathmandu City. Ph.D. diss, Department of Linguistics, Ball State Univeristy.

Shrestha, Yaclav Kumari
    2002   Dolakhako Newari ra Nepāli Bhasaka Vakyaraccanako Vyatireki Adhyayan[Contrastive study of Nepali and Newari languages of Dolakha]. M. A. thesis, Nepali Department, Tribhuvan University.

Shresthacarya, Iswaranand
    1981   *Newari Root Verbs*. Kathmandu: Ratna Pustak Bhandar.

Slusser, Mary S.
    1982   *Nepal Mandala: A Cultural Study of the Kathmandu Valley*. Princeton: Princeton University Press.

Subbarao, K.V., and Mimi Kevichusa
    1999   Relative clauses in Tibeto-Burman. Manuscript. Department of Linguistics, Delhi University.

Tamot, Kashinath
- 1985 Bhāsā kālakrama vijñānakatham. khvapayā Nepāla bhāsā [Lexicostatics of Bhaktapur Newari]. *Gan* 5.5: 143–157.
- 1987 Presence of Tibeto-Burman prohibitve prefix in Dolakha Newari. Paper presented at the 18th Annual Conference of the Linguistic Society of Nepal, Tribhuvan University, Kathmandu.
- 1989 Etymological notes on two words of ritual seeds of an ancient inscription. Paper presented at the 20th Annual Conference of the Linguistic Society of Nepal, Tribhuvan University, Kathmandu.

Tautscher, Gabriele
- 1998 Kalingchok and Silung: A 'female' and 'male' mountain in Tamang tradition. In *Tibetan Mountain Deities, their Cults and Representations (Proceedings of the 7th Seminar of the International Association For Tibetan Studies, Graz 1995)*, Anne-Marie Blondeau (ed.), 169–180. Vienna: Verlag der Österreichischen Akademie der Wissenschaften.

Thomason, Sarah Grey, and Terrence Kaufman
- 1988 *Language Contact, Creolization, and Genetic Linguistics*. Berkeley: University of California Press.

Thompson, Sandra A., and Robert Longacre
- 1985 Adverbial clauses. In *Language Typology and Syntactic Description*, Timothy Shopen (ed.), 171–234. Cambridge: Cambridge University Press.

Tuladhar, Jyoti
- 1985 Constituency and negation in Newari. Ph. D. diss., Linguistics, Georgetown University.

Turin, Mark
- 1999 Shared words, shared history? A case of Thangmi and Late Classical Newar. *Newah Vijñana: The Journal of Newar Studies* 3: 9–17.

Turner, Ralph Lilley
- 1980 Reprint. *A Comparative and Etymological Dictionary of the Nepali Language*. Indian reprint ed. New Delhi: Allied Publishers Private Limited. Original edition, London: Routledge and Kegan Paul Limited, 1931.

Vajrācārya, Dhanavajra, and Kamal P. Malla
- 1985 *The Gopalarajavamsavali*. Wiesbaden: Franz Steiner Verlag Weisbaden GMBH.

Vajrācārya, Dhanavajra, and Tek Bahadur Shrestha
- 1974 *Dolakhako Aitihasik Ruprekha* [Perspectives on Dolakha History]. Kathmandu: Nepal and Asian Research Center.

van Driem, George
- 1987 *A Grammar of Limbu*. Berlin: Mouton de Gruyter.
- 1992 In quest of Mahākirāantī. *Contributions to Nepalese Studies, Journal of the Centre of Nepal and Asian Studies of Tribhuvan University* 19 (2): 241–247.
- 1993 The Newar verb in Tibeto-Burman perspective. *Acta Linguistica Hafniensia* 26: 23–43.

1997	Sino-Bodic. *Bulletin of the School of Oriental and African Studies*, 60 (3): 455–488.
2001	*Languages of the Himalayas: An Ethnolinguistic Handbook of the Greater Himalayan Region* (Vol. 2). Leiden: E. J. Brill.
2003	Mahakiranti revisited: Mahakiranti or Newaric. In *Themes in Himalayan Languages and Linguistics*, Tej R. Kansakar and Mark Turin (eds.), 21–26. Heidelberg and Kathmandu: South Asia Institute and Tribhuvan University.
2004	Newaric and Mahakiranti. In *Himalayan Languages: Past and Present*, Anju Saxena (ed.), 412–418. Berlin: Mouton de Gruyter.

Van Valin, Robert D. Jr., and Randy J. LaPolla
  1997 *Syntax: Stucture, Meaning and Function. (Cambridge Textbooks in Linguistics)*. Cambridge, Cambridge University Press.

Verma, Manindra K., and Tara Mohanan (eds.)
  1990 *Experiencer Subjects in South Asian Languages*. Stanford: CSLI Publications.

Yadava, Yogendra P.
  2003 *Population Monograph of Nepal*. Kathmandu: Central Bureau of Statistics.

Index

Abhiras, 7
ablative, 118, 120-121, 293
absolutive
    in ditransitive clauses, 304; and locational postpositions, 123; objects, 113-115, 300; and pronouns, 129-132; and postposition *thē(nāgu)* 'like', 125; subjects, 106-110, 284
accent. *See* phrasal accent
accommodation, 44, 519
acoustic phonetics, 33, 34
actor nominalizations, 392
addressee, 305
adjectival phrases, 235
adjectivals
    as compared with nouns, 212-213; **description of, 195-213**; lexical classes of, 195, 212-213; simple, 207-212; as verbs, 195-207
adjectival verbs
    agreement of, 201; attributive borrowed, 206; compounds, 206; as copula complements, 350; **description of, 195-207**; as differentiated from adjectives, 207; and headless relative clauses, 94; inflection of, 202-204; irregular, 204-205; as a lexical class, 202, 206; negation of, 202; predicative uses of, 199-202, 206; referential uses of, 198-199; uses of, 197-198, 393;
adjectives
    with comparative phrases, 353; as copula complements, 279-280; as differentiated from nouns, 90; as differentiated from adjectival verbs, 207; historical reconstruction of, 196; and intensifiers, 235; nominalized, 393; ordering within the noun phrase, 262-264, 266-267; in sequence, 270. *See also* adjectival verbs; simple adjectives; predicate adjectives.
adverbials
    and the clitic =*na*, 116-117; and deixis and anaphoric reference, 129, 146; **description of, 228-236**; focused, 251; and interrogatives, 136; and intonation, 83; in intransitive clauses, 284; as a lexical class, 228; and manner, 442; shared by multiple clauses, 454; temporal, 244, 246, 367
adverbial clauses
    and adverbial suffixes, 461; causal, 475-476; clause-initial markers, 460; clause chains within 431; and the clitic of individuation, 242; comparison with participial clauses, 483-484; concessive, 465-467; conditional, 463-465; definition of, 460; **description of, 460-484**; and focus, 480-481; historical development of, 462-463, 473; negation of, 348; positioning of, 481-482; purposive, 473-475; simulative, 476; syntax of, 477-484, 501-502; structure of, 378; temporal, 188, 467-473; tense in, 479; and the topic particle, 248; verb forms in, 187-188
adverbs
    directional, 231; and focus particle, 248; as a lexical class, 228; locational; 230-232; manner, 232-235; positioning of, 228; and postpositions, 123-124; temporal, 228-230
affected arguments, 281
affectedness, 109
affirmative verb forms, 167
affricates, 33-39
"afterthoughts", 328

agreement particle, 258-259
agreement, *See under* verb agreement
allative, 101-102, 121-122, 290
'all/every', 215-216
allophones, 48, 50-51, 61
"ambitransitive", 107
amplitude, 71, 79-80, 85
anaphora, 147, 446-447. *See also* zero anaphora.
animate referents, 291
appeals, 84-85, 87
applicatives, 335
apposition
    description of, 270-272; differentiated from coordination, 269-271; distinguished from relativization, 389; and first- and second-person modification, 406-407
approximants, 36, 41-42, 48-50, 55-56, 59-62
argument structure, 110. *See also* grammatical relations, valence, and transitive and intransitive verbs.
arguments
    affected, 281; post-verbal, 327-329; shared, 453-455. *See also* constituent order, and grammatical relations.
aspect
    completive, 383-385; continuous, 370, 373-380, 430, 433; **description of, 373-386**; imperfective, 399, 468, 471; perfect, 381-385, 431; perfective, 367
aspiration, 33-35
assertions, 259
assertive particle, 255-257
assimilation, 43, 167, 193
associative plural, 98
associative postposition, 124-125, 135
auxiliaries
    bir- 'give', 333-337; *con-* 'stay', 340, 373-380; and complementation strategies, 421-422; continuous, 410; *d(h)on(-ker)-* 'finish', 383-385; and grammaticalization, 292, 435; negation of, 347, 375; and the participial construction, 333-336, 374, 381-382, 430, 433-435, 445, 457-458; prohibitive, 338; *suru yet-* 'start', 386; *tar-* 'put'/'keep', 381-383; *ten-* 'be about to', 385-386; *twartar-* 'stop', 386; and "versatile verbs", 373

background information, 379
"backward control", 298
Badikhel Pahari dialect, 14
Balami dialect, 14
Bandipur dialect, 14
Belhare, 400
benefactive, 334
Bhaktapur dialect, 14
bilabials, 35, 42
bilingualism, 22, 95
"bistructural" analysis
    definition of, 375; and grammaticalization, 336, 435; and the participial construction, 434-435, 438, 450; and relative clauses, 352
borrowing
    of adjectival verbs, 206; of adverbial markers, 460, 463; calques, 117, 294-297, 422; of complementizers, 492; of conjunctions, 269; definition of, 21-22; of manner adverbs, 232-234; of nouns, 90-91, 95-96; and problems of phonemic distinction, 37; from Nepali in dative-experiencer clauses, 294, 296, 300; of numerals, 219-220; of postpositions, 273; of quantifiers, 215; of question words, 136; of simple adjectives, 208; of verbs, 156-157
breathy voice, 25, 32-36, 38, 40

calques, 117, 294-297, 422
case
    clitics, 389, 392; in complex sentences, 409-420, 450-455; and demonstratives, 142; **description of, 100-127**; relevance to nouns, 96-97; postpositions, 103-106

casemarkers
　ablative, 118, 120-121, 293; allative, 101-102, 121-122, 290; clitics, 101; combination of, 102; concatenation, 132; dative, 113-116, 124, 134, 331-332, 395; ergative/instrumental, 103, 106-110, 116, 133-134, 126; genitive, 101-102, 105, 135; and grammatical wordhood, 520-521; and interrogative words, 133; locative, 102, 117-120, 123, 151; "mediative", 121; morphological status of, 103-106; and pronouns, 132. *See also individual cases.*
case prolepsis, 450-455, 483, 502
causal adverbial clauses, 475-476
causation, 331
causative
　and transitivity, 108-109; verb forms, 190, 383
causative constructions
　lexical, 330; morphological, 330-333
cessation of events, 386
"Classical Newar"
　description of, 15-16; historical manuscripts in, 10; historical reconstruction and, 196, 338, 437, 462
clause chains, 439-446
clause combining, 496. *See also* participial construction; dependent clauses; clauses.
clause-initial particles, 252-254, 460
clauses
　adverbial, 460-484; copular, 78, 265, 275-283, 287, 398; dative-experiencer, 294-300; ditransitive, 304-306; finite clauses, 70; headless relative, 90-91, 94-95, 97, 241, 398; and intonation units, 70; intransitive, 281, 284-294; non-finite, 246, 248, 251; participial, 70, 242, 246, 348, 393, 483-484, 500; possessive, 290; purpose, 277; relative, 129, 270, 273; as syntactic units, 503; transitive, 300-304; verbless, 199, 277, 283-284
characteristics, 149
classifiers
　consistency, 221-224; general, 224-225; interaction with clitics, 97, 104; mensural, 220-221, 225-227; numeral, 218-227; other, 226; plus numeral as a single grammatical word, 520; shape, 221-224; sortal, 220-225
clitic of extension
　allomorphy of, 238; as a derivative of the concessive adverbial suffix, 465; **description of, 242-245**; and grammatical wordhood, 520-521; and indefinite pronouns, 138-140; and negation, 244, 349; and non-finite verb forms, 187; as phonologically bound, 237-239; and plural referents, 243; relevance to nouns, 96, 127
clitic of individuation
　and adjectival verbs, 94, 198; and adverbial clauses, 242; allomorphy of, 238; **description of, 239-242**; and grammatical wordhood, 520-521; and headless relative clauses, 392-393; in irrealis nominalizer, 403; and non-finite suffixes, 189; as phonologically bound, 237-239; positioning of, 241; relevance to nouns, 96, 127; and simple adjectives, 209
clitics
　of case, 100-127, 389, 392; definition of, 237; as distinguished from postpositions, 106, 123; ergative/instrumental, 103; and grammatical wordhood, 520-521; of individuation and extension, 237-245; of number, 97, 132; ordering of, 262. *See also individual clitics.*
"co-constructions", 477
collocations, 435, 437
comparative and superlative constructions, 350-353

complementary distribution, 36-37, 49
complementation,
—complement types: activity-type, 410, 412-413, 424; copular, 199, 201-203, 206, 210, 235, 275, 277, 279-280, 287; fact-type, 412-413; infinitive, 112, 298, 311, 418-420, 425; nominalized plus *khã*, 396, 412-414, 423-425; potential-type, 413; quotative, 417; simple nominalized, 409-412, 424, 431
—description of, 408-427
—and grammatical relations: complement clauses as grammatical arguments, 306, 411; as a criterion for subject, 311-312, and copular subjects, 398
—and quotation: direct followed by *haŋ-a khã*, 415-417; direct, 415-418, 424, 436-438, 493; embedded with *haŋ-an*, 422-423; indirect, 415
—semantics of: 424
—strategies: 331, 373, 408, 411, 413, 419, 421-424
—syntax of: complementizers, 395, 412-414, 423, 436-438; complexity, 411-412; constituent order, 411; degree of integration, 414; raising, 409-410, 414, 419-420; structural analysis 501-502
—and verbs: auxiliaries, 425; cognition and utterance, 396, 412, 415-417, 422-424; complement-taking predicates 408, 426-427; and complement types, 424-427; expression of verbal categories, 411, 416-417; infinitive plus grammatical auxiliary, 421-423; modal, 418-419, 425; perception, 395-396, 409-412, 424
complementizers
borrowed, 492; *haŋ-an* 'say', 395, 423. 436-437; *khã* 'talk; matter', 412-414
completion of events, 383, 455-459
completive aspect, 383-385

complex sentences
and argument sharing, 321; as intonation units, 70; and non-finite verb forms, 186
compounds
of adjectival verbs, 206; contrasted with coordination, 268; in dative-experiencer clauses, 294; involving the negative affix, 176; nominal, 90-93; and phonotactics, 63; pronominal, 132; verbal, 155, 235, 303, 424
concessive
adverbial clauses, 465-467; verb forms, 187
conditional
adverbial clauses, 463-465; verb forms, 187
conjunct/disjunct, 25, 169, 174, 355
conjunctions, 220, 268-269, 393
"conjunctive participle", 428
connected speech, 66, 69
consonants
description of, 32-44; devoicing of, 167-168, 187; phonological processes, 42-43. *See also individual places and manners of articulation.*
constituency, 266
constituent order
basic order, 322; and complementation strategies, 422; **description of, 320-329**; of direct quotes, 322, 417-418; of ditransitive clauses, 326-327; and focus, 324-327; and heavy noun phrases, 325-326, 328; one overt argument, 321-322; postverbal arguments, 327-329; and pragmatic status of arguments, 323-327; and topics, 323-327; in transitive clauses, 322-326; verb-final, 322
constructions
causative, 330-333; comparative and superlative, 350-353; clause-level, 330-353; copular, 350; dative-subject, 417, 420; emphatic,

279; emphatic reflexive 345; emphatic negation, 349; equational, 402; hortative, 341; imperative and prohibitive, 337-339; interrogative, 341-343; optative, 339-340; reflexives and reciprocals, 344-346
consultants, 29-30
contact. *See* language contact.
continuation, 84-85
continuous aspect, 370, 373-380, 430, 433
continuous auxiliary, 410
control, 173-174, 446-447, 479
converbs, 428-459, 483-484. *See also* participial construction.
conversation
   and the assertive particle, 255; data, 31; and the particle *āle*, 252-254; and questions, 343; and tag questions, 278; and tense, 354
coordination
   and casemarking, 269; differentiated from apposition, 270-271; of noun phrase elements, 268-270; and the participial construction, 439-441
copula complements
   adjectival verbs as, 199, 201-203, 206, 350; adjectives as, 279-280; and casemarking, 277; and the existential verb, 287; function in copular clauses, 275; and intensifiers, 235; simple adjectives as, 210
copulas
   description of, 275-284; *jur*, 279-283; *khyaŋ*, 199-200, 276-279; verb forms, 190-191
copular clauses
   copula complements, 275, 277, 287; copula subject, 275-277, 287, 350, 397-398; **description of, 275-283**; function of, 276-277, 279; as a marker of finality, 78; with predicate adjectives, 277; as a variant of verbless clauses, 283
copular construction, *See* copular clauses.

correlative constructions, 487-489
counterfactuals, 464
count nouns, 214
curses, 339

data, 29-31
dative
   and the associative postposition, 124; casemarking of, 113-116, 331-332, 395; in comparative constructions, 351; in ditransitive clauses, 304; objects, 300, 316; interrogative pronoun, 134; on two arguments in a clause, 332
dative-experiencer clauses
   and adjectival verbs, 201; borrowing from Nepali in, 294, 296, 300; and casemarking in comparative constructions, 351; and complementation, 417, 420; **description of, 294-300**; and grammatical relations, 318-319; and the reflexive pronoun, 345-346; structure of, 294
decimal numerals, 217-219
declaratives, 337
deictic pronouns, 142-145, 147-148, 151-152, 487
deixis, 129, 147, 490
deletion, 44, 168
demonstratives
   description of, 141-153; distal, 141, 146; dual function of, 131; etymological similarities with interrogatives, 133; and the focus particle, 248; of location, 151-153; of manner, 146-148, 245, 302, 442; and nominalized verbs, 387; ordering within the noun phrase, 262-264; plural, 144; proximal, 141, 144, 146-147, 151-152; of quantity, 149-150, 245; relationship to pronouns, 129; of size, 151; of type and characteristic, 148-149
dentals, 36
deontic, 339
dependency, 101, 388, 431

dependent clauses
  definition of, 477; **description of, 477-482**; and intonation, 83; positioning of, 507. See also adverbial clauses; complementation; participial construction; relative clauses.
derivation
  nominal, 93, 392
detransitivization, 108
devoicing, 167-168, 187
Dhulikhel dialect, 14
dialects of Newar
  Badikhel Pahari, 14; Balami, 14; Bandipur, 14; Bhaktapur, 14; Dhulikhel, 14; Gamal, 14; Gopali, 14; Kathmandu, 13-14, 34, 132, 172, 174, 193, 196, 218, 354, 380, 453; Newar, 24-25; Pahari, 14; Pyangāõ, 14; Tasen, 14; Tauthali, 15, 169
diminutive, 205, 214
diphthongization, 57
diphthongs, 44, 57, 169
direct causation, 331
direction, 292-294
directionals, 230-231
direct quotes
  and demonstratives, 146; and complementation structures, 415-418, 422-423; and intonation, 79, 87; and the participial construction, 436-438; syntactic analysis of 486 See also complementation, participial construction, reported speech.
"disagreement", 340
discourse
  and constituent order, 322-329; data, 30-31; and intonation, 69, 88; introduction of referents, 267; particles with discourse function, 245-252; referential density, 321; and tense-aspect, 485, 504-505, 512 (see also narrative: structuring of); syntactic complexity of, 498; zero anaphora, 320-322.
disfluencies, 78
dissimilation, 169, 219
distals, 141, 146

distributives, 198, 346
ditransitive clauses
  casemarking in, 316; and the causative suffix, 332; constituent order of, 326-327; structure of, 304-306; with speaking verbs, 305-306; with transfer verbs, 304-305
Dolakha
  Bhimsen temple, 18-19; history of, 1, 19-21; location of, 17; population of, 17; size of, 17
Dolakha Newar
  previous work on, 22-23; typological characterization of, 23-24
Dolakha language
  overview, 17-25; endangerment of, 17-18; names for, 10-11; number of speakers of, 17
duals, 7, 100
dubitative particle, 257-258
durativity, 374-375

emphatic accent, 491
emphatic constructions, 279, 345, 349, 397
end-point, 366
English, 95, 136, 157, 375
epenthesis, 180
equational constructions, 402
ergative/instrumental
  in comparative constructions, 350; in ditransitive clauses, 304; evidence for phonological boundedness, 103; interrogative pronoun, 133-134; as an oblique, 116; and the postposition 'like', 126; as a subject, 106-110, 300,
ergativity, 106-110
events
  cessation of, 386; completion of, 383; future tense and, 356, 367; inception of, 368; mainline, 361; ongoing, 358; and perfectivity, 366; repeated, 358; in sequence, 470
evidentials, 169, 258
exclamatory utterances, 86-87
exclusive, 129, 170

584 *Index*

existence, 286-292, 360, 364-365
existential
    dar-, 286, 360, 364-365; verb forms, 191-192, 288
experiencers, 110-113, 294-300
expressive vocabulary, 232-233
extended states, 381-383
extension. *See* clitic of extension.

favors, requesting, 338
finite clauses, 70
first mention, 265, 291
focus
    and adverbial clauses, 480-481; and adverbials, 251; and constituent order, 324-327; constructions, 401, 487; marking, 248-252, 257, 400-403
focus of negation, 347
focus particle
    and adverbs, 248; and clitics of individuation and extension, 237, 240; and demonstratives, 147, 152; **description of, 248-252**; and interrogative constructions, 342; and negation, 349; with participial and adverbial clauses, 483; and the reflexive pronoun, 345
free variation, 48-49
fricatives, 35, 38-40
functional load, 61, 68
fundamental frequency, 66, 80-81, 83, 85
future tense, 355-357, 366-367, 371, 380, 399
future verb forms
    immediate, 189; morphophonology of, 169; nasalization in, 167, 171; negative paradigm, 178; reconstruction of, 168

Gamal dialect, 14
"gapping strategy", 389
gemination
    in ideophones, 234; intensifying, 214; regressive, 519
gender, 96, 208-210

general classifier, 224-225
genitive
    in complex postpositions, 105; coordination of, 270; function of the allative, 121; and the interrogative pronoun, 135; and locational postpositions, 123; and nominalized verbs, 387; ordering within the noun phrase, 262-264, 266-267; and the plural clitic, 97; in possessive clauses, 290; syntactic positioning of, 101-102
"given", 113-114
glides, 41-42, 48-50, 55-56, 59-62
glottal stop, 50
goal, 102, 118, 122, 293
Gopali dialect, 14
grammaticalization
    and bistructural analyses, 336, 435; of the complementizer *khā*, 414; and continuous aspect, 374-375, 380; and embedded quotation with *haŋ-an*, 422-423, 437; of mark of comparison, 352; of motion verbs, 292
grammatical relations
    in comparative constructions, 350; in complement clauses, 409-420; and correlative clauses, 488; dative-experiencer constructions, 318-319; **description of, 307-319**; direct quotes as syntactic objects, 417-418; objects, 315-317; subjects, 308-315
grammatical roles, 488

habitual
    and adverbial clauses, 465, 468; and nominalization, 399; and the participial construction, 449-450; and the past-anterior tense, 363-364; and the present tense, 357; and the tense system, 366
head, 101
headless relative clauses, 90-91, 94-95, 97, 241, 398
hearsay particle, 258

hiatus, 50, 53-55
"historical present", 361, 370
historical reconstruction
    of adjectives, 196; of verb forms, 167, 170-172, 180
history. *See under* Dolakha.
honorifics
    imperative, 179, 181-182, 193; personal pronouns, 130, 170, 172; prohibitive, 184
hortative, 189, 193
hortative constructions, 341
human/non-human, 134

iconicity, 414, 445, 458-459
ideophones, 233-234
illocutionary force, 447-450, 479-480
imperative
    and the agreement particle, 258-259; and conditional adverbial clauses, 464;constructions, 337-339; honorific, 179, 181-182, 193; inflection of adjectival verbs, 203; and intonation, 86; and the particle *le*, 259; plural, 179-180; scope of, 448; verb forms, 179-182, 184
imperative constructions, 337-339
imperfective, 399, 468, 471
imperfectivity, *See* past anterior tense, continuous, progressive.
inanimate objects, 290
inception of events, 386
inclusive, 129, 132, 170
indefinite pronouns, 245, 325
indefinites, 129, 138-141, 348
indirect causation, 331
indirect objects, *See* objects.
indirect quotes, 352, 415-417
individuation 109. *See also* clitic of individuation.
Indo-Aryan, 8, 91, 95, 489
"Indosphere", 3
infinitive
    complements, 418-420; verb forms, 187
infixation, 155, 175-176

inflection. *See individual lexical classes.*
information questions, 250, 343
innovations, 168
instrumental. *See* ergative/instrumental.
intensification, 214
intensifiers
    and adjectives, 235; as compared with the positioning of comparative phrases, 351-352; and the demonstrative *gusṭule*, 150; **description of, 235-236**; dual function as a quantifier, 215; lack of co-occurrence with adverbs, 228; modification of attributive adjectival verbs, 198; modification of nouns, 213; positioning of, 235; the pronoun *guli* as an, 136; reflexives as, 345
intensity, 64, 66
intention, 356, 360, 385
interactional particles, 255-260
interference. *See* substratum interference.
interpropositional relationship, 340
interrogative constructions, 341-343
interrogative pronouns, 325, 487
interrogatives
    and adverbials, 136; as a component of indefinite pronouns, 138; and demonstratives, 141, 150; **description of, 133-138**; and manner, 442; and numeral classifiers, 220; relationship to pronouns, 129
intonation
    and adverbial clauses, 482; and adverbials, 83; and auxiliaries, 375; and hesitation, 153; of information questions, 343; marked rising, 258; and the participial construction, 444-445; and post-verbal arguments, 328, 329; and quoted speech, 418, 491-492; and recapitulations, 438; of tag questions, 278, 342; transcription conventions, 69-70. *See also* prosody.

intonation units, 69-70, 75, 81, 85, 503-514
intransitive clauses
and adverbials, 284; **description of, 284-294**; formation with the verb *jur-*, 281; with motion verbs, 292-294; structure of, 284
intransitive verbs
borrowing of, 157; casemarking of, 107-110; classification of, 154; imperative forms, 181; nasalization in, 167
irrealis
and adverbial clauses, 463-464; suffix, 189; and the future tense, 356-357, 367; relative clauses, 390; and the distribution of nominalizers, 394, 396, 399, 403, 413
irregular verb forms, 190-194, 385. *See also under* adjectival verbs, verb forms.

Kathmandu dialect
adjectives, 196; breathy voice in, 34; cognates, 172; conjunct/disjunct system, 174; numerals, 218; and the participial construction, 453; personal pronouns in, 132; as the standard dialect, 13-14; and tense, 354, 380; and the verb *yer-* 193;
kin terms, 127, 198, 239, 267, 344-345
Kiranti, 171, 400
Kirata, 6, 19

labialization, 42, 519
labio-dentals, 35
language contact, 3, 21-22
language policy, 11
laterals, 41
left dislocation, 267
lexical classes
adjectivals, 195, 212-213; adjectival verbs, 202, 206; adverbials, 228; adverbs, 228; intensifiers, 228, 235-236; nouns, 213; particles and clitics, 237; quantifiers, 214-227; verbs, 154

lexicalization
of causative verbs, 331; in dative-experiencer clauses, 294, 296, 299; of headless relative clauses, 94-95; involving the ablative, 121; involving the negative affix, 176, 347; of kin terms, 127, 239; of motion verbs, 293; of nouns, 90-91, 93; of noun-verb compounds, 304; of nominalized adjectival verbs, 199, 392; and the participial construction, 435; of pronoiminal stems and casemarkers, 132, 133
lexical stress, 44
Licchavis
defeat of the Kirata, 6; migration of, 7; period of, 6, 20
linguistic theory
data, 27; functionalist framework of, 25-28; "panchronic" approach to, 27-28
liquids, 41-42
location
demonstratives of, 151; and the existential verb, 290-291, 360, 364-365; immediate, 145; as an intransitive clause type, 286-292; *jur-* with a function of, 282
locational adverbs, 230-232
locational postpositions, 123-124, 230-231
locatives, 102, 117-120, 123, 125, 391

mainline events, 361
Maithili, 8
Malla period, 8, 20
malefactive, 334
manner
and adverbials, 442; adverbs, 232-235; and case clitics, 116; and demonstratives, 141, 147-148, 245, 302; and interrogatives, 137; and the participial verb, 381-382
manner of articulation
affricates, 33-39; approximants, 36, 41-42, 48-50, 55-56, 59-62;

fricatives, 35, 38-40; stops: nasal, 40-41, oral, 33-39, 50
marked-rising terminal contours, 258
mark of comparison, 352
mass nouns, 214, 225
"mediative", 121
mensural classifiers, 220-221, 225-227
metaphor, 223
metaphorical processes, 335
mirative, 399, 435
modal verbs, 418-419, 425
morphology
    nominal, 96-128; verbal, 154-194.
    See also finite morphology
motion verbs, 230, 292-294
Munda, 7

naming constructions, 394
narrated conversations, *See under* reported speech.
narratives
    background information, 375; beginning of stories, 258, 284; data, 30-31; and focus particle, 249-352; and hearsay particle, 258; and intonation, 75-88; and mirative, 395; and particle *āle*, 253; and quoted speech, 415-418, 489-492; and recapitulation, 438; narrative sentences, 511-514; structuring of, 368-373, 485, 506-509; tense and, 354, 357, 361, 366, 368-373; and topic particle, 248; use of tag questions in, 275
narrative sentences, 511-514
nasals, 40-41, 62, 81
nasalization, 56, 167, 169, 171
negation
    of adjectival verbs, 202; of adverbial clauses, 348; of attributive adjectival verbs, 198; of auxiliary verbs, 347, 375; and the clitic of extension, 244; and complements of perception verbs, 411; **description of, 347-349**; and nominalized complements plus *khā*, 414; and non-specific indefinite meaning,

138-139; position of affix, 175-176; prohibitive, 182, 338; scope of, 447-450, 479; verb forms, 175-178; vowel harmony, 175;
negative morpheme, 58, 155, 347
negative verb forms, 167
Nepali
    adjectival verbs, 206; adverbial markers from, 460, 463; adverbs from, 232-234; bilingualism and language contact, 22; calques 117, 422; complementizers, 492; conjunctions from, 269; dative-experiencer constructions, 111-113, 294, 296; dropping of verb agreement, 175; ideophones, 233; intensifiers from, 236; lexical quantifiers, 215; nouns, 91, 95-96; in noun-verb compounds, 303; numerals 219-220; as an official language of Nepal, 11; phonemic distinction between /r/ and /ḍ/, 37; postpositions from, 273; pronunciation by Dolakhae speakers, 34-35; question words 136-137; simple adjectives 208; split ergativity, 109; verbs, 110, 156-157, 235, 424
Newar
    definition of, 1; position within Tibeto-Burman, 3-5. *See also under individual dialects.*
Newar dialect
    difference between Dolakhae and Kathmandu, 24-25
Newar language
    description of, 10-16; dialects of, 13-15; "Eastern Newar", 15; endangerment of, 12; names for, 10-11; as a national language, 11-12
Newars
    caste system of, 9; culture of, 8-10; **description of, 5-10**; distribution throughout Nepal, 12-13; literary tradition of, 9-10; origins of, 5-8; social organization of, 8-9
new information, 248, 250, 252, 465
new referents, 221, 267

nominal complements
> **description of, 394-395**; modification of nouns in, 388; and omission of head noun, 394; positioning of, 389

nominalization
> actor, 392; and lexicalized adjectival verbs 199; of clause combinations, 393, 399; **description of, 387-406**; functions of, 388; and modification of nouns, 388; morphology of, 387; non-embedded, 399-403, 486-487; and relative clauses, 389-394; syntax of simple nominalized complements, 388, 409-412, 431; in verbal complements, 395-400, 408-414

nominalized adjectives, 393
nominalized clauses, 348
nominalized verbal complements plus *khã*, 396
nominalized verb forms, 167, 187
nominalizers
> distribution of, 390, 394, 396, 399, 403-407; historical discussion of, 404-407; and non-subject relative clauses, 313; and subject relative clauses, 312

non-embedded nominalizations, 399-403, 486-487
non-finite clauses
> and the focus particle, 248, 251; and the topic particle, 246; *See also* adverbial clause, complementation, nominalization, relative clause, participial construction.

non-finite verb forms
> **description of, 186-190**; negation of, 348

non-specific, 138, 141
noun phrases
> adjectival verbs as heads of, 198; and casemarkers, 100-127; classifiers as independent, 224; as complements 408-427; contrastive, 87, 239; and coordination, 268-270; within a copula complement, 276, 269, 350; and deixis and anaphoric reference, 146; demonstratives as heads of, 131, 142; **description of, 261-274**; embedding, 272-273; and the focus particle, 248; headless, 214-215, 264, 268-269; internal structures of, 266 and interrogative pronouns, 134-135; and intonation, 78, 83; and lists, 272; and nominalization, 387-407; with nominal complements, 388-389; oblique, 115, 121-122, 284, 293; omission of, 261, 320-321; ordering, 320-329; order of elements in, 241, 261-268; overt, 389; postposed, 271; pronouns as, 129; and the question particle, 255; with relative clauses, 388-389; referential, 209; stimulus, 294-300; structuring, 268, 268-273; and the topic particle, 246; zero anaphora, 320-321

nouns
> and appositions, 389; borrowed, 90-91, 95-96; as compared with adjectivals, 212-213; count, 214; **description of, 90-128**; as differentiated from adjectives, 90; as differentiated from pronouns, 129; as grammatical words, 520-521; as a lexical class, 212-213; mass, 214, 225; morphology, 96-128; ordering within the noun phrase, 262-264; postposed, 265

number, 96-100, 142, 170
numeral classifiers, 218-227
numerals
> decimal-based, 217-219; **description of, 217-220**; plus classifier as a single grammatical word, 520; sortal, 220-225; vigesimal-based, 219-220

object complements, 352
objects
> absolutive, 113-115, 300; and casemarking, 107, 316; criteria for, 315; dative, 113-116, 300; embed-

ded complements as, 306, 409; embedded direct quotes as, 417-418; and the emphatic possessive *āme tuŋ*, 317; person/number suffixes, 170; in lexicalized relative clauses, 95; and nominalization, 391-392; referential arguments as, 303; and relative clauses, 317; shared by multiple clauses, 454-455
obliques, 115-127, 284, 293
omission of arguments, 300
ongoing events, 358
ongoing states, 200-201, 210-211
onomatopoeia, 234, 304
operators, 446-450, 478-482
optative
　plural, 185-186; prefix, 58, 203; verb forms, 185-186
optative constructions, 339-340
overt arguments, 321, 389

Pahari dialect, 14
palatals, 42
palatalization, 39, 41, 48, 224
palato-alveolars, 33, 34
"panchronic" approach, 27
participial construction
　—and particles: and the clitic of individuation, 242; and the focus particle, 251; and the particle of restriction, 246; and the topic particle, 248

　—primary characteristics:
and auxiliary verbs, 333-336, 373, 374, 381-382, 430, 433-435, 445, 457-458; defining characteristics, 429-432; **description of, 428-459**; bistructural analysis of, 434, 438, 450; casemarking of shared arguments, 451-452; case prolepsis, 450-455; comparison of participial and adverbial clauses, 483-484; control, 446-447; dependency relationship, 431; with direct-quote complements, 422-423, 436; and grammatical arguments, 450-451; and illocutionary force, 447-450; and imperatives, 337, 444; and joining clauses which denote actions, events, and states, 430, 439-446; lexicalized expressions, 435; and multiple participial verbs, 445; recapitulations, 438; syntactic analysis of, 446-455, 498; as a syntactic unit, 431-432; verb inflection, 167, 187, 190, 428-429

　—semantics of: conceptual independence between clauses, 456-457; completed events, 456-459; and information status, 444; manner modification in, 232, 293, 437, 441-443, 449; with overlapping events and states, 441; and prosody 444-445; semantic ambiguity, 439, 443; semantic relationship between clauses, 432; scope of the interrogative, 458; sequences of events, 434, 439-441, 444, 449; temporal modification, 443-444

　—syntax of: ambiguity in number of clauses in, 336; and anaphora, 446-447; comparison with adverbial clauses, 483-484; interaction with other types of clause combining, 393, 399, 431-432; and negation, 348, 447-450; participle followed by *-li* and *-i*, 429, 455-459; same versus different subject, 430, 441, 457; scope of auxiliary, 445; and the sentence, 499; subordination, 452-453
participial verb forms, 167, 187, 190, 428-429
past-anterior tense, 280, 355, 363-369, 379, 383
past-anterior verb forms, 167-168, 171-172, 177
past tense
　and the assertive particle, 256, and completive aspect, 383; and continuous aspect, 379; **description of, 361-363**; in narratives, 371-372; and the tense system, 366-367
past verb forms, 167-169, 172, 178

patients, 114
paucal, 100
pause, 69, 70
perception verbs, 409-412
perfect aspect, 381-385, 431
perfective, 367
perfectivity, 405
performative verbs, 360
permissives, 340, 419
persons, 170
personal pronouns
    description of, 129-133; exclusive, 7, 132, 170; first-person, 129, 130 table 8, 170; forms of, 132-133; honorific, 130, 170, 172; inclusive, 7, 132, 170; second-person, 130 table 9, 170; third-person, 130, 170
person of the subject, 406-407
phonation
    aspiration, 33-35; breathy voice, 25, 32-36, 38, 40; voicing, 33-34
phonemes
    consonants, 32-44; vowel, 44-46
phonetic accommodation, 44
phonological processes
    consonants, 42-43; vowel processes summarized, 57-58; vowels, 54-61. *See also individual names of processes.*
phonological rules, 519
phonotactics
    description of, 61-63; and the mark of comparison, 352; nominal, 90; and phrasal accent, 71; of simple adjectives, 207; verbal, 154-156
phrasal accent
    description of, 70-74; emphatic, 71, 73, 86, 491; on final syllable, 80, 85; normal, 71, 73; and pitch, 83; and level terminal contours, 79
pitch
    and emphatic phrasal accent, 73; and intonation units, 69, 83; and stress, 64; and terminal contours, 79-80; on vowels, 54

place of articulation
    bilabial, 35, 42; dental, 36; glottal, 50; labio-dental, 35; palatal, 42; palato-alveolar, 33, 34; retroflex, 36-38; velar, 38-39
plural
    associative, 98; clitic, 97, 101, 127-128, 389, 392; in dependent clauses, 398; and grammatical wordhood, 520-521; personal pronouns, 129
plural referents, 243
polar questions, 254, 341-342, 447-450
possession, 286-292, 360, 364-365
possessive, 102
possessive clauses, 290
postpositional phrases
    embedded, 273; modifying nouns, 273
postpositions
    and adverbs, 123-124; associative, 124-125, 135; of case, 103-106; 'during', 126-127; *thē(nāgu)* 'like', 125-126; locational, 123-124, 230-231; 'up to', 126-127; 'until', 126-127
postposing
    of nouns, 265; of noun phrases, 271
predicate adjectives, 199-202, 206, 210-212, 277
present relevance, 382-383
present tense, 283, 357-361, 366-369, 371-372, 379-382
present verb forms, 167-169, 171, 178
presuppositions, 343, 402-403, 448, 458
previous mentions, 115
primary objects, 315
Prithvi Narayan Shah, 20-21
progressive, 377, 399 *See also* continuous.
prohibitives
    auxiliary, 338; **description of, 182-185**; honorific, 182, 184; as the negative of an imperative, 338; paratactic, 185; plural, 183-184; prefix, 58, 181

prohibitive constructions, 337-339
pronouns
    definitional limitation of, 129; deictic, 142-145, 147-148, 151-152, 487; as differentiated from nouns, 90; distal, 131; exclusive, 7, 132, 170; first-person, 129, 130 table 8, 170; forms of personal, 132-133; honorific, 130, 170, 172; inclusive, 7, 132, 170; indefinite, 245, 325; interrogative, 325, 487; and noun-phrase elements, 262; proximal, 131; proximity, 130; second-person, 130 table 9, 170; third-person, 130, 131 table 10, 132, 170. *See also* personal pronouns.
"prosodic sentences", 89, 485, 503-506
prosody
    description of, 69-89; and hesitation particles, 145; interaction with syntax, 88, 432, 503-514; prosodic embedding, 507-513; and quoted speech, 490-492
Proto-Newar, 168, 218, 437
Proto-Tibeto-Burman
    agreement systems of, 7; causative prefix *s-, 4; evidence for, 3
pro-verbs, 302
proximals, 131, 141, 146-147, 151-152
punctuals, 471
purpose clauses
    in a copula complement, 277; relativized, 393
purposive adverbial clauses, 473-475
purposive
    verb forms, 188
Pyangāõ dialect, 14

quantifiers
    'all/every', 215-216; borrowed, 215; criteria for a lexical class, 214; **description of, 214-227**; dual function as an intensifier, 215; lexical, 214-217; numerals, 217-220; ordering within the noun phrase, 135-136, 264-268; in sequence, 270

quantity
    degree, 150; markers of, 141, 149-150, 245
questions
    and the agreement particle, 259; information, 250, 343; and non-embedded nominalizations, 401; polar, 254, 341-342, 447-450; and post-verbal arguments, 328; tag, 255, 278-279, 342; and the verb *yet-* 'do', 302; yes/no, 254, 341-342. *See also* interrogatives.
question particle, 254-255, 341-342
quoted speech, *See* reported speech.

raising, 409-410, 414, 419-420
rapid speech, 44, 56
rate of speech, 69
realis
    and adverbial clauses, 465; and auxiliary verbs, 332; and nominalization, 394, 413; and the present tense, 368; and relative clauses, 390
recapitulations, 438, 471, 473, 492, 513
recipients, 113
reciprocals, 346
recursion, 273, 498
reduplication
    for emphasis, 289; of ideophones, 234; and lexical quantifiers, 214; and numerals, 220; of the reflexive pronoun, 346 of the verb stem, 48; and word structure, 63
reference
    and noun phrases, 209; and personal pronouns, 129; and simple adjectives, 209; and adjectival verbs, 198-199
referential arguments, 303
"referential density", 321
reflexives
    as a construction, 344-346; as a criterion for subject, 313-315; emphatic reflexive construction, 345
regressive gemination, 519

relative clauses
  and apposition, 406-407; bistructural analyses involving, 352; and combination of clauses, 393; comparison to correlative clauses, 488; coordination of, 270, 393; as a criterion for object, 317; as a criterion for subject, 312-313; and distribution of nominalizers, 390, 406; embedded, 273; headless, 90-91, 94-95, 97, 241, 398; modification of nouns in, 388-394; and omission of the head noun, 392; ordering within the noun phrase, 262-264; and the participial construction, 432; personal pronouns as heads of, 129; in the syntactic sentence, 498-500
remote past, 365
repeated events, 358
reported speech
  direct quotation, 415-418, 422-423, 436-438; indirect quotation, 415-417; pronominal reference in, 147; prosodic embedding, 508-509; sentence, 489-498; and syntactic complexity, 493-498.
restrictive particle, 237, 246
retroflexes, 36-38
Role and Reference Grammar, 453
roots, 63
rounded vowels, 47, 52, 59
rhyme, 80

Sanskrit, 9, 91
scope, 340
scope of negation, 348
secondary objects, 315
semantics, 140-141, 220
sentence-final particles, 254-260, 512
sentence quoted speech, 489-498
sentences
  complex, 186; **description of, 485-514**; hierarchical organization, 498-503; linear sequencing of clauses in, 498-503; "narrative", 511-514; preplanning of, 497; "prosodic", 89, 485, 503-506, 511-514; syntactic, 486, 511-514; syntax-prosody interaction, 506-514
sequential ordering, 383-385; 434, 439-441, 444, 449
Shah dynasty, 8
simple adjectives
  attributive, 209-210; borrowed, 208; **description of, 207-212**; inflection of, 211; predicative, 210-212; referential, 209-210
simulative adverbial clauses, 476
singular, 129
"Sinosphere", 3
Sino-Tibetan, 2-5, 387
size, 151
'some; any', 140
sonority, 70
sortal classifiers, 220-225
sources, 120
South Asia,
  as a linguistic area, 111, 428
specificity, 241, 249, 265
standard of comparison, 350
"starting point", 323
states
  cognitive, 295-296; and demonstratives of type and characteristic, 149; emotional, 295-296; entrance into, 280; and future tense, 356, 367; gradual entrance into, 212; extended, 382-383; and imperfectivity, 366; ongoing, 200-201, 210-211; and the past-anterior tense, 364, 369; and the past tense, 362; and the present tense, 359, 371; in the participial construction, 441; temporary, 378
stative verbs, 230, 368
stimulus noun phrases, 294-300
stops
  bilabial, 35; dental, 36; glottal, 50; oral, 33-39; phonemic contrasts, 39; retroflex, 36-38; velar, 38-39; voiceless unaspirated, 62
stress
  on clitics, 104; **description of, 64-68**; interaction with intonation, 66-

68; lexical, 44; phrasal (*see* phrasal accent); on phonological words, 519; on postpositions, 105
subjects
  absolutive, 106-110, 284; and complementation, 311-312, 319, 419; criteria for, 308; and dative experiencers, 318; in ditransitive clauses, 304-306, 418; ergative, 106-110; the grammatical, 284, 300, 337; grammatical relations, 308-315; of the imperative, 179; and nominalization, 392; person/number suffixes, 170; of possessive clauses, 290; proleptic, 452; and reflexives, 313-315, 319, 344; and relative clauses, 312-313, 318, 390, 398; and topics, 246; and verb agreement, 308-311, 318
subordinate, 452-453, 478-482
substratum interference, 22
suffixation, 90-91, 97-98, 104
superlative constructions. *See* comparative and superlative constructions.
switch reference, 457
syllables
  and allophones, 51; codas, 61-62; non-initial, 50; nucleuses, 61-62; onsets, 59; open, 52; and phrasal accent, 71, 85; and pitch, 54; in rapid speech, 56; reduction, 44, 519; rhymes, 61-62, 80; and stress, 64; structure in vowel sequences, 53; and terminal pitch contours, 75, 80
syllable structure, 61-63
syndesis, 484
syntactic complexity, 493-506
syntactic constructions
  affected participants, 333-336; negation, 347-349
syntactic finality, 87
syntactic reanalysis, 352, 375, 404
syntax-prosody interactions, 506-514
"syntax/prosody mismatches", 88, 509-511

tag questions, 255, 278-279, 342
"tail-head linking", 438
Tansen dialect, 14
Tauthali dialect, 15, 169
temporal adverbial clauses
  description of, 467-473; verb forms in, 188
temporal adverbials, 244, 246, 367
temporal adverbs, 228-230
temporal overlap, 470
tense and aspect, 354-386
tenses
  and adverbial clauses, 479; anteriority 382-385; **description of, 354-373**; future, 168-169, 171, 178, 187, 189, 355-357, 366-367, 371, 380, 399; historical present, 361, 370; interaction of, 366-368; interplay in narratives, 368-373; and negation, 176-177; past, 168-169, 171-172, 176-178, 256, 361-363, 366-367, 371-372, 379, 383; past-anterior, 168, 172, 177, 280, 355, 363-369, 379, 383; present, 168-169, 171, 176-178, 283, 357-361, 366-369, 371-372, 379-382; remote past, 365; verb forms, 168-169, 176-177
tense and lax vowels, 47, 55
terminal pitch contours
  description of, 75-87; fall, 75-79; high fall, 75-76; level, 79-80; mid fall, 75-76; marked rise, 81, 83; "narrative final", 79; rise-fall, 85-87, 491; rise, 80-85
terminal intonation contours, 69, 73, 491
Tibeto-Burman
  and correlative constructions, 489 **description of, 2-5**; markers of adverbial clauses, 462; number of languages, 2; typological characteristics, 2-3, 489; unusual behavior of 'one', 218; verb morphology 171
time expressions, 391
topicalization, 465

topics
    and constituent order, 323-327; marking of, 246
topic particle, 237, 246-248, 252, 323
transitional continuity, 87-89, 504-505, 509-511
transitive clauses
    constituent order within, 322-326; **description of, 300-304**; and the morphological causative, 331-332; structure of, 300
transitive verbs
    borrowed, 156; casemarking of, 107-110; causative, 330; classification of, 154; nasalization in, 167; *yet-*, 299, 302
transitivity
    casemarking of subjects, 106-110; and nominalization, 108, 396, 404-407; parameters of, 404-405; verb forms, 154
types, 137, 148-149

valence, 331-332, 335
variation
    inflectional, 158; phonetic, 41-42, 49, 51, 129, 191, 238, 456, 467; as a "problem", 28-29; prosodic, 76, 85, 505; of vowel harmony, 58
velars, 38-39
verb agreement
    as a criterion for subject, 308-311; "disagreement", 172-175, 310; and the existential verb, 192, 288; historical evidence for, 7; of person and number, 169-175, 288; in Tibeto-Burman. *See also* verb forms.
verbal complements
    description of, 395-400; distribution of nominalizers, 396; of *ju-en con-a*, 398-400, 406; nominalized plus *kha*, 396
    of the stative copula, 397. *See also* complementation.
verb forms
    in adverbial clauses, 187-188; affirmative, 167; affirmative finite, 168; affirmative and negative compared, 176-178; causative, 190, 383; concessive, 187; conditional, 187; copula, 190-191; **description of, 157-190**; existential, 191-192; historical reconstruction of, 167, 180; hortative, 189, 193; imperative, 179-184, 193; infinitive, 187; irregular, 190-194, 385; **list of verbal affixes, 516-518**; negative, 193; nominalized, 187; non-finite, 186-190; optative, 185-186, 203; participial, 167, 187, 190; person and number, 169-175; **primary tables, 159-166**; prohibitive, 182-185; purposive, 188; in temporal adverbial clauses, 188
verbless clauses, 199, 277, 283-284
verb phrases, 453-455, 499, 501-503
verbs
    adjectival, 94, 195-207, 350, 393; "ambitransitive", 107; borrowed, 156-157; classification of, 154; of cognition and utterance, 412, 415-417, 422-424; **description of, 154-194**; as differentiated from nouns, 90; ditransitive, 304; finite, 154-155, 486; as grammatical words, 520; historical reconstruction, 170-172; motion, 230, 292-294; inflectional morphology of, 157-190; intransitive, 107-110, 154, 157, 167, 180; as a lexical class, 154; modal, 418-419, 425; non-finite, 154-155; **paradigms of, 157-190**; phonotactics, 154-156; of perception, 409-412; performative, 360; stative, 230, 368; stem alternation of, 167-168; stem classes of, 155-158, 167-168, 176-177, 179-181, 183-185, 187-188, 190, 192; tense, 168-169; transitive, 107-110, 154, 156, 167, 299, 302. *See also* verb agreement, verb forms.
"versatile verbs", 333, 373, 433
vigesimal numerals, 219-220
vocatives, 86

voicing, 33-34
voice onset time, 33-34
voice quality, 79
volition, 109, 172-174, 340, 405-406
vowel harmony, 58-61, 182, 185, 193, 519
vowel length, 54, 218
vowels
    and the co-occurrence of glides, 61; **description of, 44-61**; deletion of, 103, 158; devoicing of, 103; fronting, 51; hiatus, 50, 53-55; high, 47, 54-56, 62; in sequence, 53; low, 51-54; mid, 47-51, 54, 61; nasal, 46; phonological processes, 218, 237-238; rounded, 47, 52, 59; shortening, 54-55; tense and lax, 47

wh-questions. *See* information questions.
words
    phonological and grammatical, 519-521, *See also* particular lexical classes.
word formation, 142
word order, 198
    constituent order, 320-329; in intransitive clauses, 287
word structure, 63

yes/no questions. *See* polar questions.

zero anaphora, 478, 503

www.ingramcontent.com/pod-product-compliance
Lightning Source LLC
Chambersburg PA
CBHW081943230426
43669CB00019B/2904